# Readings and Cases in Basic Marketing

**The Irwin Series in Marketing**

Consulting Editor **Gilbert A. Churchill, Jr.**
University of Wisconsin

# Readings and Cases in Basic Marketing

Edited by

## E. Jerome McCarthy
Michigan State University

## John F. Grashof
Kennesaw College

## Andrew A. Brogowicz
Western Michigan University

**Fifth Edition    1987**

Homewood, Illinois  60430

ISBN 0-256-05795-8

Library of Congress Catalog Card No. 86–83136

*Printed in the United States of America*

1 2 3 4 5 6 7 8 9 0 ML 4 3 2 1 0 9 8 7

# Preface

This collection of readings and cases is intended to deepen the beginning student's understanding of marketing—and to help make the study of marketing an interesting and meaningful experience.

While selected especially to complement *Basic Marketing, Ninth Edition,* by E. Jerome McCarthy and William D. Perreault, Jr., the readings and cases in this collection will blend well with most introductory marketing texts. They can also be used effectively in upper-level undergraduate and introductory MBA courses in marketing, as well as in independent study courses.

The collection has been divided into five parts. The first four parts contain 35 readings, which have been grouped as follows:

I. Introduction to Marketing
II. Analyzing Opportunities and Segmenting Markets
III. Developing the Marketing Mix
IV. Planning, Implementing, and Controlling Marketing Strategies

Part V contains 10 problem-solving cases—covering various aspects of marketing strategy planning, implementation, and control.

## READINGS

The 35 readings consist of 43 articles—some of which have been "bundled" together to illustrate changes in strategy over time or to present opposing viewpoints. Each of the articles was carefully selected with the following criteria in mind:

1. The article should expand upon or illustrate concepts typically covered in an introductory marketing course—rather than introducing new concepts.
2. The article should be reasonably concise, readable, and within the scope of a beginning marketing student's understanding.
3. The article should provide a basis for class discussion.
4. The article should make a synergistic contribution to the collection.

In applying these criteria, we relied heavily on comments and feedback from students and colleagues who have used the previous editions of *Readings and Cases in Basic Marketing.* Their valuable suggestions helped us identify articles that make important contributions to student understanding, as well as topics in need of improved coverage.

About two thirds of the 43 articles are new to this edition. Almost half the articles are from professional journals such as the *Journal of Marketing* and *Business Horizons,* while the others are from trade publications such as *Business Week* and *Fortune.* The readings offer the student a balanced selection of timeless classics—such as Theodore Levitt's "Marketing Myopia"—and more recent articles that explain and illustrate key concepts and techniques—such as psychographic segmentation, product positioning, scanner-TV panels, and the retailing of services. Several of the readings give the student an in-depth look at the marketing strategies and tactics of leading firms—such as General Mills, Coca-Cola, Procter & Gamble, General Electric, and American Express.

To help the student focus on the important aspects of the readings, each reading is preceded by a brief introduction and followed by a set of questions. The questions check the student's understanding of the reading's key points—and provide a framework for class discussion. Some of the discussion questions—those indicated by an asterisk (*)—require students to relate concepts discussed in that particular reading to concepts covered in other readings, helping them synthesize what they are learning about marketing.

## CASES

The problem-solving cases complement the readings by further illustrating the scope and complexity of marketing management—and, of course, by giving students a valuable opportunity to try their hand at marketing decision making. The cases can be assigned strictly for discussion purposes, or a detailed written analysis can be required.

The 10 cases contained in this collection tend to be longer and more comprehensive than the cases typically found in introductory marketing texts—but still within the reach of a beginning student. Thirty percent of the cases are new to this edition. Three cases were written especially for this collection and have not been published elsewhere. The other seven cases were highly recommended by our colleagues as cases that students enjoy solving—while learning a lot about marketing in the process.

Although the cases focus on various aspects of marketing strategy planning, implementation, and control, we have purposely refrained from classifying the cases in terms of the primary problem to be solved. This helps to prevent students from approaching a case with a preconceived notion of what the problem is and how to solve it. It also encourages them to examine all the interrelationships among marketing variables—rather than focusing narrowly on a single marketing variable.

## ACKNOWLEDGMENTS

We deeply appreciate the cooperation of the authors, publishers, and journals that graciously allowed us to reprint their material, as well as those organizations that consented to let us write cases based on their experiences. We are also grateful for the many helpful comments and suggestions that we have received from our students and colleagues. Of course, responsibility for any editorial errors or shortcomings is ours alone.

We hope this edition of *Readings and Cases in Basic Marketing* proves interesting and useful to both students and faculty. As always, we welcome your comments and suggestions.

**E. J. McCarthy**
**J. F. Grashof**
**A. A. Brogowicz**

# Contents

**Part V: Cases in Basic Marketing**

□ 1

# Marketing: The new priority

*During the 1970s, finance appeared to be the central element of American business strategy. To increase their profits, firms relied heavily on financial tools such as cost-cutting, cash-flow management, and acquisitions. Corporate hierarchies were said to be dominated by risk-aversive "bean counters" who discouraged innovation and entrepreneurship. Today, however, experienced marketing executives and managers with successful track records are in great demand as more and more firms are making marketing the key element in their long-run strategies. The following article discusses the environmental trends that have caused marketing to become "the new priority" for the 1980s, and explains the many implications this has for the way firms conduct business.*

Question: What do John Sculley and James J. Morgan have in common? Answer: Each is an experienced, highly regarded consumer goods marketer who has recently moved to a top job at a large corporation. Sculley, an alumnus of PepsiCo Inc., is now president of Apple Computer Inc. Morgan, who came from Philip Morris Inc., is chairman of Atari Inc. In the past, Apple and Atari had concentrated more on developing new technologies than on understanding the dynamics of the marketplace—and suffered because of it. The recruitment of Sculley and Morgan is one of the more visible signs that marketing has become the new corporate priority.

Vast economic and social changes have made better marketing an imperative. Realization of that fact has set off a near free-for-all in recruiting circles for successful marketers, now hotter prospects for high-level jobs than executives with financial experience. Companies of every stripe are looking for managers, presidents, or chief executive officers who can not only develop long-term product strategies but also instill an entrepreneurial spirit into corporations that, more often than not, practice risk-avoidance.

## NO BEAN COUNTERS

Says Gerard R. Roche, chairman of Heidrick & Struggles, a top recruiting firm: "Nobody wants

bean counters now. Everybody wants a president with marketing experience—someone who knows about product life cycles and developing product strategies." James R. McManus, chairman of Marketing Corp. of America, a consulting firm, agrees: "Today, companies realize that their raw material, labor, and physical-resource costs are all screwed down and that the only option for dramatic improvement will come from doing a better marketing job."

As companies define marketing more clearly, they no longer confuse it with advertising, which uses media to let consumers know that a certain product or service is available. In essence, marketing means moving goods from the producer to the consumer. It starts with finding out what consumers want or need, and then assessing whether the product can be made and sold at a profit. Such decisions require conducting preliminary research, market identification, and product development; testing consumer reaction to both product and price; working out production capacities and costs; determining distribution; and then deciding on advertising and promotion strategies.

Simple as those steps may sound, many of them were all but forgotten in the 1970s, when inflation kept sales pacing upward and marketing was of secondary importance. Corporate strate-

Source: Reprinted from the November 21, 1983, issue of *Business Week* by special permission, © 1983 by McGraw-Hill, Inc.

gies emphasized acquisitions, cash management, or the pursuit of overseas markets. Then came the recession, with its stranglehold on consumer spending, and companies were forced into trying to understand what made the domestic marketplace tick. They soon discovered that demographic and lifestyle changes had delivered a death blow to mass marketing and brand loyalty. A nation that once shared homogeneous buying tastes had splintered into many different consumer groups—each with special needs and interests.

The emergence of this fragmented consumer population, together with an array of economic factors—intense international competition, the impact of rapid technological change, the maturing or stagnation of certain markets, and deregulation—has altered the shape of competition. "If you have to change how to compete, then all of a sudden marketing is a very important function," says Robert D. Buzzell, a Harvard University School of Business Administration professor who specializes in strategic market planning.

## RALLYING CRY

Robert L. Barney, chairman and CEO of Wendy's International Inc., understands this all too well. "The main thrust today is taking business away from the competition, and that fact, more than any other, is modifying our business," he explains. To pick up market share, the fast-food and hamburger chain is trying to build up its breakfast and dinner business, to achieve greater store efficiencies, and to introduce a slew of new products that will attract a broader spectrum of consumers. Wendy's has not only raised its ad budget by 45 percent but also increased its marketing staff to 70, from 10 five years ago. "You have to out-execute the competition, and that's why marketing is more important than ever before," asserts Barney.

The realization that marketing will provide the cutting edge in the 1980s not only has hit well-known packaged goods marketers—such as Procter & Gamble, Coca-Cola, and General Foods—but is affecting industries that used to be protected from the vagaries of consumer selling by regulatory statutes. Airlines, banks, and financial-services groups are looking for ways to grow and prosper in an environment of product proliferation, advertising clutter, escalating marketing costs, and—despite advances in research and testing—a dauntingly high rate of new-product failures.

With marketing the new priority, market research is the rallying cry. Companies are trying frantically to get their hands on information that identifies and explains the needs of the powerful new consumer segments now being formed. Kroger Co., for example, holds more than 250,000 consumer interviews a year to define consumer wants more precisely. Some companies are pinning their futures to product innovations, others are rejuvenating timeworn but proven brands, and still others are doing both.

Unquestionably, the companies that emerge successfully from this marketing morass will be those that understand the new consumer environment. In years past, the typical American family consisted of a working dad, a homemaker mom, and two kids. But the 1980 census revealed that only 7 percent of the 82 million households then surveyed fit that description. Of those families that reported children under the age of 17, 54 percent of the mothers worked full- or part-time outside their homes. Smaller households now predominate: More than 50 percent of all households comprise only one or two persons.

## MEN ALONE

Even more startling, and most overlooked, is the fact that 24 percent of all households are now headed by singles. This fastest-growing segment of all—up some 80 percent over the previous decade—expanded mainly because the number of men living alone increased. Some 20 percent of households include persons 65 or older, a group that will grow rapidly. Already, almost one out of six Americans is over age 55.

These statistics are significant to marketers. "It means that the mass market has splintered and that companies can't sell their products the way they used to," says Laurel Cutler, executive vice president for market planning at Leber Katz Partners, an advertising agency that specializes in new products. "The largest number of households may fall into the two-wage-earner grouping, but that includes everyone from a manicurist to a Wall

Street type—and that's really too diverse in life-style and income to qualify as a mass market." Cutler foresees "every market breaking into smaller and smaller units, with unique products aimed at defined segments."

Even the auto makers agree. "We've treated the car market as a mass one, but now I'm convinced that concept is dead," says Lloyd E. Reuss, general manager of General Motors Corp.'s Buick Motor Division. Reuss now believes in target marketing: specific products and ads aimed at selected groups.

## CANNED HEALTH

Despite this segmentation, there is enormous common interest in convenience, service, health, cost, and quality. Some companies have already translated these desires into successful products. Makers of soft drinks sell caffeine- and sugar-free products to health- and calorie-conscious consumers. Diet and low-salt foods have found a small but growing number of takers, and so too

have high-quality frozen entrées. Robert A. Fox, the first marketing-oriented CEO in Del Monte Corp.'s 65-year history, has wasted little time getting the company into fancy frozen-food products. And he has repositioned its existing line of canned vegetables and fruits as low-salt and low-sugar items.

Philadelphia's ARA Services Inc. offers the patrons of its workplace cafeterias the option of picking up full dinners for consumption at home. It has also acquired a day-care operation and expanded the number of centers from 40, in 1980, to more than 150. "Changing demographics have a tremendous influence on the services we provide," affirms Joseph Neubauer, ARA's CEO. He says the changes have given marketing "one of the key roles—if not the key one—in corporate strategy."

As families and dwellings grow smaller, the need for more compact products and packages grows more pressing. General Electric Co. downsized its microwave oven and then modeled it to hang beneath kitchen cabinets, thereby freeing valuable counter space. The result: GE went from an also-ran in this category to a strong No. 2.

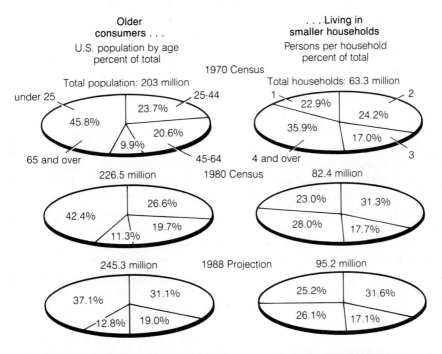

THE CHANGING MARKET

Older consumers . . .
U.S. population by age
percent of total

. . . Living in smaller households
Persons per household
percent of total

1970 Census

Total population: 203 million

under 25 — 45.8%; 25-44 — 23.7%; 45-64 — 20.6%; 65 and over — 9.9%

Total households: 63.3 million

1 — 22.9%; 2 — 24.2%; 3 — 17.0%; 4 and over — 35.9%

1980 Census

226.5 million

42.4%; 26.6%; 19.7%; 11.3%

82.4 million

23.0%; 31.3%; 17.7%; 28.0%

1988 Projection

245.3 million

37.1%; 31.1%; 19.0%; 12.8%

95.2 million

25.2%; 31.6%; 17.1%; 26.1%

Data: U.S. Census. Donnelley Marketing
Information Services American Profile

Data: U.S. Census
Data Resources Inc.'s U.S. Economic Service

## HOW-TO DATA

Yet many new consumer segments are not being mined. Men, for instance, are probably the most ignored of all buying groups—especially for household items. A recent study by Langer Associates Inc. found that men living alone were indeed interested in furniture, cooking, and cleaning and resented their "domestic dummy" stereotype. What they wanted, and what they were not getting, was straightforward how-to information from peer figures.

Teenagers, too, have become a much larger shopping force. A Yankelovich, Skelly & White Inc. poll, undertaken with *Seventeen* magazine, found that nearly 75 percent of teenage girls with working mothers now regularly shop for groceries. Yet few companies try to reach this group to sell anything but games, records, and clothes.

Many companies still gear their products and ads to 18- to 34-year-olds, who dominated the marketplace of the 1970s but have been supplanted in power and size by the 25- to 45-year-olds. "Youth reflected everything we did as a culture for a long time, but that's not where the bulge is today," says Paula Drillman, executive vice president and director of research at McCann-Erickson Inc.

This means that companies must sell to an older, better-educated consumer who regards the marketplace with a jaundiced eye. Drillman, for one, believes that this skepticism accounts for the slow growth of brands in such industries as liquor. "The shopper is saying, 'Why should I pay so much more for Smirnoff when all I do is put it in a glass and mix it with something? Vodka is vodka is vodka.' "

This indifference to brands is partly the result of the massive proliferation of consumer goods. In an attempt to fire up sales, companies have been swamping the market with new products and line extensions backed by ads, coupons, giveaways, and sweepstakes. For instance, of the 261 varieties of cigarettes for sale today, about half are 10 years old or less.

## ME, TOO

This huge influx of products has shifted the balance of power from manufacturers to retailers.

Lawrence C. Burns, a partner with the Cambridge Group, a Chicago firm of marketing consultants, finds that "stores are eliminating slow movers and won't take on any new products unless they are assured of good inventory turns and margins. They want proof that a product really is a success, and the only way companies can provide that is through more regional roll-outs and more test marketing."

But achieving those affirmative results is more difficult because so many of the offerings are basically parity items. Says Robert E. Jacoby, chairman and CEO of Ted Bates Worldwide Inc.: "We seem to be experiencing a never-ending flow of me-too products or line extensions, which makes it difficult to make a unique claim about the product." Roy Grace, chairman and executive creative director of Doyle Dane Bernbach Inc., seconds that view. He comments, "If a new technology appears, most companies can quickly copy it or acquire it. So it's really hard to gain a competitive advantage."

Examples of this difficulty abound. Aseptic packaging, a technology for putting food and drinks in specially prepared foil or cardboard pouches that require no refrigeration, has been embraced by nearly all juice makers during the past 18 months. And after the Food and Drug Administration ruled last summer that aspartame, a natural sweetener, could be used in soft drinks, all the major manufacturers raced to reformulate their diet brands to include it. Even Procter & Gamble Co. is easing up on its age-old philosophy of testing a product for years and bringing it to market only when convinced that some claim of superiority can be made. P&G has rushed its Citrus Hill brand into the spurting orange-juice category, even though it admits it cannot make any unique claims for the juice.

The result is a vicious cycle. With the plethora of new choices, products have much shorter life spans, so a steady flow of new items is needed to keep sales curving upward. "The number of entrants in a given category has increased, and the implication is that there is greater market segmentation and shorter product life cycles," points out Derwyn F. Phillips, executive vice president at Gillette North America. "And we find ourselves really working hard at projecting a given brand's life cycle—when the bell curve is likely to peak and the point at which it is no longer intelligent to support a given brand."

Phillips says that Gillette is now trying to speed up new-product development to prevent its combined market share in a category from shrinking. Half of the company's $2.2 billion revenues last year came from products that did not exist five years ago.

Despite advances in the technology of testing, the level of new-product casualties remains astonishingly high. Two out of three new entries still fail—the same proportion as in the 1960s—while the cost of introducing a new item has skyrocketed. An outlay of some $50 million is needed to launch a national brand in a major category. P&G is said to be spending almost $100 million to roll out Citrus Hill orange juice.

## ANALYSIS PARALYSIS

At those odds and prices, companies are understandably wary about committing themselves to high-risk endeavors. They are demanding more research, more strategic planning, and more "review" committees to weed out problems. More often than not, however, the result of all these checks is total confusion and inactivity. Ellen I. Metcalf, a senior consultant with Arthur D. Little Inc., reports: "In some companies, you can spend six weeks going through psychographics, trendline analysis, quarterly consumer reports, scanner data from grocery products—rooms just full of data. Then you ask, 'How do you use this information?' And they say they don't know what to do with it."

Ad agencies, in particular, resent the analysis-paralysis climate. "There are more and more people [at a company] who can say no and very few who can say yes," laments Barry Loughrane, president and CEO of Doyle Dane. This risk-avoidance atmosphere worries Allen G. Rosenshine, chairman and CEO of ad agency Batten Barton Durstine & Osborn Inc. "Everyone has developed a corporate timidity." That, along with the B-school mentality—quantify everything, take few chances—is threatening the entrepreneurialism that companies need if they are to grow, he feels.

But the outlook may not be altogether bleak. Enlightened companies have recognized the challenge and are radically overhauling their operations to put more emphasis on marketing, seeking top marketing executives, and changing the nature and scope of their jobs. Lester B. Korn, chairman of Korn/Ferry International, says he recently filled the top marketing slot at a major consumer goods company—a $350,000-a-year post that typifies the trend to give marketing more clout. "Companies want marketing executives to be responsible for total business results—they're putting the profit-and-loss in with the job—and that's a big step forward from the past, when they had only been responsible for volume and share growth," he says. Companies hope to create a culture that encourages more risk-taking, accepts some failures, and rewards success.

The hottest companies to recruit from are P&G, Johnson & Johnson, Philip Morris, General Foods, and Thomas J. Lipton—large, disciplined consumer product marketers with broad product lines. "These companies teach their people how to create profitable product lines in brutally competitive industries, and their consistency is what makes them so attractive," says J. Gerald Simmons, president of Handy Associates Inc.

## SUPPORT SYSTEMS

Some executive-search specialists express reservations, however, about placing a P&Ger. "Their support system is just so strong that they end up working for the system rather than being creative," says David S. Joys, executive vice president of Russell Reynolds Associates Inc. "Many clients prefer that a P&G executive go to another company first, and then they'll go after him."

Today, most companies believe that their brightest chances for success in coming years will hinge on the development of innovative products aimed at specific consumer niches. But because of the risks, they are trying to direct development efforts toward producing related items in order to achieve economies of scale and a greater overall market share. "You have to go into areas where you have some right to be in that category," says McManus of Marketing Corp. "Companies that go with a product in search of a market or one that has no fit with their existing businesses are doomed to a bloody nose."

Hershey Foods Corp. learned that very lesson when it tried to get into the canned-frosting business. Hershey's problem: It did not have a cake mix to support its frosting, unlike its chief competitors, General Mills, P&G, and Pillsbury. These rivals discounted the frosting and made up the difference on the cake batter. Hershey, with no companion product to fall back on, had to discount its product to stay in the market. "The competition was suicidal, and while we could have stayed in the market, it wouldn't have been prudent," says Jack Dowd, Hershey Chocolate Co.'s vice president for new-product development. "But you've got to have the right to fail."

The company has recouped with its new Hershey's chocolate milk, packaged in a rich brown container that makes chocoholics drool in anticipation. Hershey had planned to have the chocolate milk in four markets by the end of the year, but strong demand has already put it in 12 cities, and the figure is growing.

**HANG WITH IT**

To minimize the risk of failure with new products, experts make several recommendations. "Companies need to have a high-level executive who will champion the new creation—hang with it—and move fast," says Cutler of Leber Katz, which since 1969 has helped clients develop 10 major brands, including Vantage brand cigarettes, with no failures. "It's vital to get a pilot product up quickly, test consumers' reactions to it, refine it, and get it going."

Speed, however, is not the hallmark of many companies. Up to seven years can elapse between the time a new product is proposed and its nationwide distribution. A product developed in 1976 may meet with wholly different market conditions when it finally makes its debut in 1983. "Developing a new product is like shooting a duck," observes Gary W. McQuaid, marketing vice president at Hershey's. "You can't shoot it where it is; you've got to shoot it where it's going to be."

Aiming too far ahead of the market is just as risky, of course. But for some companies, such as auto makers, the lengthy time it takes to develop a new product leaves no choice. "When we commit to a car, we're four years away from production," says F. James McDonald, GM's president.

"How many people today know what they want four years from now? We really have to roll some dice."

The task of understanding and predicting consumer behavior has led to a nearly insatiable hunger for market research. But experts in the field caution companies about switching from one new technique to another, and they suggest that keeping a steady information base will allow for more accurate projections and comparisons with previous years. Cutler believes that new products often misfire because they "are assigned to junior people at either the company or agency level, since the most experienced people do not want to take their eyes off the main brands. But it is imperative that the team have broad knowledge and have clout—in order to see the new product through review committees and then to get it on the shelf."

Given the slim odds for scoring a new-product hit, many executives are trying to breathe new life into dying brands. "There are dozens of older brands lying around that have been neglected over the years," says Chester Kane, president of Kane, Bortree & Associates, a new-product consulting group. "Companies must discover ways to make them viable for today's consumer."

**RIGHT GUARD REBORN**

Gillette is trying for just such a comeback with its Right Guard deodorant, which dropped from a huge 25 percent share of the deodorant market in the mid-1960s to 8 percent today. The company was loath to let the bronze-canned brand die, since it had produced $500 million in profits during its 23-year life span. For the past two years, all departments—research, marketing, research and development, manufacturing, sales, and finance—as well as the product's ad agency, Young & Rubicam Inc., have been getting together monthly to coordinate plans for rejuvenating Right Guard. Last June, Gillette put the deodorant into new, bold-stripe containers and began a $28.2 million ad campaign—the most expensive in the company's 82 years. Gillette says the deodorant's sales are running 14 percent higher than planned.

Whether a product is new, old, or rejuvenated, the task facing all marketers is to differentiate it from competitors' offerings. The consumer must

be made aware of its usefulness and given a reason to choose it over all other brands. "The finan-
cial-sevices companies are having trouble with
this," remarks Russell Reynolds' Joys. "They all
want a product portfolio that matches the competitors' offerings, but they also must come up with
unique products—carrying higher gross margins—
for the salesmen to really focus on."

Federated Department Stores Inc. is grappling
with these issues. Fearful that its core department
stores were losing their identity with consumers
because of the rapid growth of designer labels
and discounters, it has set up a buying office for
the purpose of creating private-label goods that
would be sold only in its better stores. As a first
step, the company has brought out a line of
sheets and towels under the "Home Concept"
name. The idea is to develop unique, high-quality
merchandise that carries a higher profit margin
and is different from anything a consumer could
buy at a rival department store or discounter—
even a Federated-owned one, such as Gold Circle
Stores.

Advertising plays a major role in carving out
distinct identities for consumer products. The push
is on for harder-hitting, product-selling ads and the
increased use of sales-promotion devices, such
as direct mail and rebates. Broadcast television is
still the preferred medium, because cable is not
yet in enough homes, and viewership data are still
too sketchy to make it efficient as an audience-
targeting device. However, specialty publications
are getting more play from companies that wish to
reach a particular market group—usually a working population that may not have the time to read
more general media or watch TV.

## NUKES AND BAGELS

Furthermore, companies are consolidating their
accounts at a few full-service agencies, rather
than letting a number of agencies handle various
brands. They are doing this on the theory that the
more important an account is to an agency, the
higher the quality of attention the client is likely to
receive. Then, too, that policy promotes efficiency
and more unified marketing, especially for companies that sell overseas. To capitalize on the con-
solidation trend, Bates has centralized in New
York its operations for key multinational clients, in-

cluding Colgate-Palmolive Co. and Mars Inc. The
strategy is to develop "benchmark ads" that can
be launched in the United States and then
adapted for use all over the world.

The need to reorganize corporate priorities to
meet the changing marketplace has caused several companies—quietly and almost surrepti-
tiously—to start their own in-house venture-
capital operations. Companies such as Seagrams, R. J. Reynolds, and Gillette have begun
either funding or acquiring small, diverse businesses in market segments that hold promise. By
experimenting in areas as disparate as nuclear
medicine (Seagrams) and bagel chains (Reynolds), these companies can explore the intrica-
cies of the medical or fast-food businesses—
categories that are likely to become increasingly
important—with little risk.

Gillette North America's just-begun ventures
council—composed of its domestic divisional presidents and three corporate executives—has been
charged with ferreting out opportunities, not necessarily in the consumer packaged-goods area.
"The level of maturity of some of our businesses
says to us that it is very important that we invest
dollars today to grow higher-yield businesses for
tomorrow," says Gillette's Phillips. "We are trying
to motivate people inside and outside the company to help us develop new opportunities for the
future."

## QUESTIONS

1. *What is marketing? How does it differ from
   advertising?*

2. *What environmental trends have made marketing "the new priority" for the 1980s? Explain how and why each trend has made
   marketing a key element of corporate
   strategy.*

3. *According to the article, why are mass marketing and brand loyalty all but dead in the
   marketplace? Explain.*

4. *For what kinds of firms in what kinds of industries has marketing become so important?
   Why?*

5. *Explain how placing greater priority on marketing is changing the way that firms organize
   and operate.*

☐ 2

# The Pampers story: A P&G success

*The following article describes the careful planning—and deliberate series of steps—that went into Procter & Gamble's development, testing, and initial marketing of Pampers disposable diapers. Although P&G started developing disposable diapers in the 1950s, it wasn't until 1970 that Pampers finally achieved national distribution. P&G's pioneering efforts in this market were so successful that by the early 1980s supermarket sales of disposable diapers exceeded $1 billion—and consumers could choose from more than 20 brands and sizes of disposable diapers.*

*As you will see later in Reading 32, P&G has had its hands full trying to cope with all the competition that the initial success of Pampers has attracted. But for now, this article provides a great example of successful marketing strategy planning and implementation. It also demonstrates—especially with regard to pricing—the important role that consumer freedom of choice plays in our economy.*

No one thought up Pampers, the disposable diaper, overnight. The process began when a loving grandfather was baby-sitting for his first grandchild, a job which, of course, included changing diapers. He decided that there had to be something better than cloth diapers, and that the disposable diapers then on the market weren't the answer.

While both the cloth diapers and the disposable diapers available met the need, neither did it very well. Cloth diapers meant laundering, folding, and the general nuisance of storing soiled diapers. The disposable diapers were not as absorbent as cloth and were not strong enough.

The grandfather, a consumer, was also a Procter & Gamble engineer. He knew his company was in business to solve consumer problems like this, so he brought his problem to his associates. He was persuasive enough to make the company want to verify his instincts. At this point, the company had to decide whether or not to try to develop a better way of diapering babies. Since Procter & Gamble, like every business and every individual, has limited resources and unlimited ways of using them, the company had to decide if diapering babies was a consumer need it could satisfy better than others.

Before embarking on a project that would cost millions of dollars, the men and women making decisions for Procter & Gamble had to be able to answer three basic questions:

1. Was there a *real consumer need* for an alternative method of diapering?
2. Did Procter & Gamble have the scientific and technological ability to develop the product?
3. Was the potential market for such a product large enough to offer some promise of making a profit?

To confirm that other consumers shared the engineer's need for an alternative diapering method, Procter & Gamble used consumer market research. Such research can take many forms: interviews with consumers in their homes, telephone interviews, questionnaires, discussion groups. The objectives, however, are always the same: to discover what the consumers want by finding out how they use existing products, what they think of these products, and what their daily habits are. Procter & Gamble, for example, looks

Source: Reprinted with permission from *Consumer Choice*, an educational booklet published in 1977 and prepared by the Educational Services Department, Procter & Gamble, Cincinnati, Ohio 45201.

for clues in the interviews it annually conducts with more than a million consumers. These clues can help the company recognize a need that the consumers have not been able to verbalize.

In the case of Pampers, thousands of mothers were asked how they diapered their babies and how they felt about their current diapering methods and products. The consumer market research showed that mothers found the cloth diapers were uncomfortable for their babies. The cloth diapers bunched up, did not keep the babies dry enough, and required plastic pants which could irritate the baby's tender skin. Obviously, there was a real need for a better way of diapering, since this consumer problem involved more than just the messy task of storing and laundering soiled diapers.

## QUESTION: CAN WE SELL IT AT A PROFIT?

The company had the expertise to develop the product since it had a good deal of experience inventing and manufacturing absorbent paper products like paper towels and facial and toilet tissue.

Now, P&G specialists in product research, engineering, marketing, and advertising all began to examine the basic idea of a single-use disposable diaper. Could it be made? How? Would it satisfy the consumer need? Could it be sold at a profit?

## 15 BILLION DIAPER CHANGES AREN'T HAY

All these questions were critical ones, but the final question—profit—was the most critical of all. In business, this is known as "the bottom line," because the last line of an accountant's column of figures shows the final results of a company's efforts—profit or loss. If a company cannot make a profit, there is no incentive to develop a new product. Profits enable a company to stay in business.

Market opportunity—the potential size of a new market—is crucial in forecasting profit. A company has to have some promise of return on the millions of dollars required to develop a product from the idea stage through production. Procter & Gamble calculated that there were more than 15 billion diaper changes a year in the United States. This was certainly an impressive market, if an effective and efficient alternative method of diapering could be invented.

Such a market would lend itself to a mass-produced product, one that could be produced in high volume but at a relatively low cost per unit. This was important because the company knew the new product would have to be sold at a price that could compete with cloth diapers but at the same time provide some return (profit) on its investment.

Although each diaper sold would return only a tiny amount of the investment required, the return from millions of sales could make the effort worthwhile. Spreading huge research and investment costs over millions or billions of units of a product is an example of what economists call *economy of scale.*

In effect, Procter & Gamble had preliminary answers to the three basic questions mentioned earlier: (1) It found a *real consumer desire or problem*; (2) determined that it had the *technical capacity* to satisfy that desire or solve that problem and (3) estimated there was a large enough *potential market* for such a product to justify the investment required to get the product from idea to mass-produced reality. In deciding that Pampers was a promising investment, Procter & Gamble had made its economic choice to go ahead.

## STARTING PRODUCT DEVELOPMENT

The chain of action and reaction that began with the consumer was developing rapidly. The idea of a disposable diaper had reached the *product development* phase. Chemists and engineers were now assigned the task of inventing a product that would solve the problems consumers were encountering with their current diapering method.

The objective was to develop a product that would be comfortable for the baby to wear (better fit, keep baby drier than cloth), easy to store, disposable, and competitively priced with cloth diapers. The raw materials would have to be safe for babies and the environment in which these diapers would be disposed. After nine months of research, the product development team came up with a diaper pad for insertion in plastic pants. The pad, which used a special pleat for better fit, was absorbent and flushable.

The new disposable diaper was now ready for a pilot test, another form of market research. So a small supply of these unnamed diaper pads and plastic pants was made by hand and given free to parents in Dallas, Texas. Result? Dallas parents turned thumbs down on the product by an overwhelming majority!

What went wrong? The diaper was OK as far as comfort and absorbency were concerned, but the specialists forgot one thing: It gets very hot in Dallas. And while 80 to 90 percent of the babies up North were wearing elasticized plastic pants, Dallas parents weren't about to subject *their* babies to a Turkish bath.

So it was back to the drawing board.

Dallas consumers having spoken, it took another six months to develop a radically new diaper design. Scientists studied new materials and checked them thoroughly for human and environmental safety. Finally, six months later, a new diaper—changed to correct the Dallas problem—emerged. The company retained the things that Dallas parents liked about the diaper pad product—the special pleat for comfort and the absorbent materials for dryness. The new product also retained the disposability feature.

This time, however, plastic pants were replaced by a newly invented, thin sheet of plastic across the back that kept the moisture in but allowed some circulation to alleviate the hothouse effect of plastic pants. Another invention—a porous sheet between the baby and the absorbent material—allowed fluid to pass through to the absorbent material but prevented most of it from coming back through. This kept babies drier and more comfortable.

## ONGOING RESEARCH AND DEVELOPMENT

When the new product was ready for another tryout, 37,000 diapers were made by hand. This time, consumer reaction was overwhelmingly favorable. Parents liked the new diaper and said they would keep on buying it.

All the work needed to bring a product from idea to reality comes under the general category of research and development. This is a common activity in enterprises competing in the consumer marketplace. While work was going on to develop the disposable diaper, scores of other new products were going through similar research and development at Procter & Gamble, and at hundreds of other companies throughout the world. Only a small percentage of these new products would survive the rigorous tests.

At the same time, experiments were being conducted to find ways to improve existing products. This research and development was made possible because Procter & Gamble, and other companies, were able to earn a profit from other products that were already on the market.

## TEST MARKETING A NEW PRODUCT

A product had been designed which appeared to meet consumers' needs for an alternative to cloth diapers. The next step was to introduce the product into the market to see if consumers really agreed that the product solved their problem effectively and efficiently. Despite the checks and rechecks that had already been made with consumers, the only way to determine if the product really solved the problem was to put it on sale under actual market conditions.

Pampers was a totally new product. All manufacturing up to this point had either been done by hand or on a small-scale manufacturing line, and raw materials had been purchased only in small quantities as needed. A decision to make the product available to consumers across the country would require constructing manufacturing facilities, purchasing equipment, hiring additional people, and contracting for huge quantities of raw materials. This would mean the expenditure of millions of dollars.

If, despite the research and testing, not enough customers bought the product, the company would lose money, and its capital investment in machinery would be lost.

To avoid gambling on such an investment, many companies first introduce a new product into a limited area called a *test market*. In a test market, a product that has already been proven safe and effective is put on sale in one or more selected cities with populations that correspond to the composition of the country as a whole. The product is sold exactly as though it were on sale nationally, with advertising, cents-off-coupons, store displays, all of the modern mass-marketing activities that could be used on a national scale to make consumers aware of the product.

The idea is to see if what looked good to the company, and to those consumers who tried the product for free in the preliminary research, still looks good to consumers under actual buying conditions. After the product has been in a test market for a while, sales can be analyzed and projections made about the number of consumers who would buy the product if it were available nationally. Further market research can discover more about consumers' likes and dislikes, and perhaps lead to further product improvement.

P&G's completely redesigned diaper seemed to solve all the problems consumers had with cloth diapers. But before the company could move ahead with test marketing, a lot of work still had to be done.

Engineers had to translate their thoughts and drawings into machines that could mass-produce the new product in quantities sufficient to supply the test market, and with the same quality as the handmade versions. To do this, they had to invent a totally new manufacturing process. It took a year for P&G engineers to design and build a small-scale production line. The machinery, a complex array of metal, wires, and pulleys, had to be adjusted and readjusted before the line began running smoothly enough to produce sufficient diapers for the test market. One hundred cases of the product were first given to consumers to try in their homes, to make sure that the machine-made ones were as satisfactory to consumers as the handmade ones had been.

## PAMPERS, YES—DRI-WEES, NO

While engineering specialists were developing a way to make the product in quantity, with quality, and at high speed, the company's marketing groups were also busy in support of the new product.

Market researchers went back to the consumers for help in giving the new product a name. They tried all kinds of names—Tenders, Dri-Wees, Winks, Tads, Solos, Zephyrs—and, of course, the winner, Pampers. Those parents who were interviewed felt that Pampers best conveyed the feeling of tender, loving care that they gave their babies. The company agreed and thought it was a name that would be easily recognized and remembered.

P&G's newly named product also needed a package—so packaging experts worked toward a solution that would be the right size, protect the contents, and attract the eye. Today's consumer products compete not only in meeting consumer needs but also in visibility.

Other marketing specialists coordinated by an "advertising brand group"—a team set up to manage the total marketing of each product—began comparing what consumers had said they wanted with what the new product had to offer. Their job was to create advertising messages that would communicate these benefits effectively to potential consumers. At the same time, distribution experts were determining how to ship the product from the point of manufacture to the point of sale.

Still other technical experts and buying experts were searching for the best sources of supply, at the lowest prices, for the raw materials that they hoped would be needed in vast quantities. This points out another important economic fact—as the Pampers wheels began to turn, more jobs and more income were created not only for the company and its employees, but also for its suppliers and their employees, and *their* suppliers and *their* employees.

## THE PRICING PROBLEM GETS STICKY

Accountants kept track of the costs that were being calculated by all the other groups: the cost of the raw materials and the cost of manufacturing and distributing the product. Each group had to estimate not only the cost of getting Pampers ready for the test market but also the cost of mass-producing Pampers if they were sold nationally. The accountants and the advertising brand group developed a price based on estimates of how many Pampers they could sell in terms of the total potential market (15 billion diaper changes every year) and how many people would use this new diapering method.

In its first test market (Peoria, Illinois, in 1961), Pampers was offered for sale at a price of about 10 cents per diaper. This figure was based on the costs to produce about 400 million diapers annually, which is the number of Pampers the company estimated could be sold nationally at the 10-cent price mass production would permit. However, a company always loses money in a test market because the product costs much more to produce in the small quantity needed than it does when it is finally in mass production.

The Peoria test was a major disappointment. Instead of the projected national sales level of 400 million diapers, the Peoria test indicated that the most P&G could hope to sell was less than half this amount.

The company could not afford to invest any more capital in the equipment and machinery needed to mass-produce Pampers if this was the best they could expect. But that's what test markets are for—to recheck what the consumer wants and alert the company to changes that need to be made in packaging, marketing, price, or even the product. The company could have moved ahead without the test market, but that could have meant the possible loss of the total investment made for national production and introduction of the product. As it was, P&G had already spent millions of dollars on a product that looked like a failure.

Market research soon found the trouble: price. Consumers liked the disposable diaper idea, but they decided that 10 cents a diaper was too much to pay.

## HOW TO CUT COSTS OF A NEW PRODUCT

The trade-off of 10 cents of their resources for one disposable diaper wasn't worth it. Why hadn't P&G discovered this before? One reason was that consumers sometimes say they'll do one thing but actually do another. Also, consumer habits, needs, wants, and priorities can change from day to day. At this point, test market research confirmed that parents who tried Pampers liked them, but not at the 10-cent price. Encouraged by consumer acceptance of the new product but worried about the pricing problem, P&G turned to the challenge of bringing down that price.

Although Procter & Gamble found some additional ways to reduce the long-range costs of raw materials, production, and delivery, the savings were nowhere near enough to enable the company to lower the price of Pampers. There was only one way to achieve the necessary savings while maintaining quality. That was to increase volume. If, instead of 400 million diapers a year,

Pampers could sell a billion diapers, they could be sold at 6 cents each.

The reasons are fundamental and apply to any mass-produced product. Certain costs, including administrative expenses and other indirect costs, would remain relatively fixed regardless of the number of diapers produced. If more than twice as many diapers were produced and sold, these fixed costs could be spread over the higher diaper volume, thereby reducing the *unit* cost. And with the increased volume, the company could exchange a higher profit per unit for a lower profit per unit but make about the same *total profit.*

In terms of *price, supply,* and *demand,* P&G's management was convinced that *demand* for Pampers at the lower price would be about double what it was at the higher price. The company revised its thinking about the quantity it would be willing to produce (*supply*). P&G was now convinced that the increase in the number of units sold would make up for the lower income per unit at the lower selling price. After the Peoria experience, the risk appeared great, but the company's managers decided to take it.

The product was introduced in Sacramento, California, at the new price. Consumer response was immediate. At the new price, consumers began using Pampers regularly and not just for trips or under special circumstances. And they began making *repeat purchases* of Pampers.

Additional test markets were opened, and Pampers continued to satisfy an increasing number of consumers. Production moved from the prototype line to eight lines in an existing company plant.

As consumer demand grew in each test market, the company made the decision to move Pampers into national distribution.

Soon, additional production facilities had to be built to keep the supply up with the demand. A plant was built in Pennsylvania, then in Missouri, California, and Georgia. Each plant was a large investment for the company, but one it could afford to make because of expected return on the investment. More importantly, in terms of the total market system, each new plant represented more money being channeled into the local communities as payment for land, construction, and wages. New jobs were created, and purchase orders went to hundreds of suppliers for goods and services.

## WHY PRICE WAS HELD, DESPITE DEMAND

It took from 1966 to 1970, though, for all of this to happen. The demand was there, but it took a long time to build each manufacturing plant. Expansion into new geographical areas often had to wait until a new manufacturing facility was completed. For a time, the company was forced to allocate product to its customers, the supermarkets, to ensure fair distribution of the scarce commodity.

Despite the high demand and limited supply—a combination that generally pushes prices up—the company kept the price of Pampers relatively constant. Based on the Peoria test market experience, P&G knew that there would be a radical drop in sales of Pampers at a higher price—consumers had told the company what value they placed on the product, and the company had to live with that value.

By mid-1970—almost 20 years after one grandfather began to grumble—Pampers was available in enough quantity to satisfy demand throughout the United States. The enormous investment of time, talent, and personnel had earned success. By 1976, almost half the babies in the United States were wearing Pampers.

## COMPETITION KEEPS US HOPPING

Pampers was a totally new product. It was the first to satisfy an unfilled consumer need. The company's response to that need and consumer reaction created a market for an entirely new product. Whenever this happens in a market economy, it is not long before other producers channel their resources, from products that are no longer satisfying a consumer need, into the new market. Such was the case with Pampers as other companies entered the market with related products. These companies asked themselves: Can we meet the consumer need that Pampers did, but more efficiently and effectively? Or is there a need or problem Pampers failed to see—on which we can capitalize?

Competition is generally regarded as the keystone of our market economy. Without competition, economies tend to stagnate. Through competition between producers for markets, retailers for customers, employees for jobs and promo-

tions, most needs of people and society can be served. Fair competition in a free market benefits consumers by forcing manufacturers to organize and produce more efficiently in order to keep quality and value up and prices down. Competition forces companies to listen to consumers and follow through with product improvements that will put, or keep, their product out in front in satisfying consumers' needs. P&G's ongoing efforts and investments in response to changing consumer concerns, and competition, are all part of the continuing chain of product design, development, marketing, and improvement.

The 9,000 products sold in supermarkets make up the most competitive marketplace ever seen. Will Pampers survive against its new competitors?

The answer lies in a popular saying not formally considered one of the "laws" of economics—"build a bettter mousetrap, and the world will beat a path to your door." Pampers was successful because it was "a better mousetrap," the best one that could be made at the time. Since then, there have been several important improvements in Pampers to ensure that the product continues to respond to the interests of consumers. New diaper sizes have been added, tape fasteners have replaced pins, new materials have been developed for even greater absorbency. Only by such continuing research and development can P&G hope to hold the major part of a market which it developed by filling a consumer need first effectively articulated by a new grandfather. Remember, its new competitors will be trying to improve their products, too.

## BETTER MOUSETRAP WON'T ASSURE SUCCESS

The production of Pampers is growing more efficient and economical. As the engineers and manufacturing personnel gain experience with the new manufacturing process, they keep getting better at it, so that efficiency goes up while costs remain under control. So they hope, and expect, to keep ahead of the competition. Obviously, the competition hopes to go them one better.

Designing and producing a "better mousetrap" is only a part of the problem of product survival against competition. Nowadays, if one plans and builds a "better mousetrap" and doesn't tell any-one about it, it will only trap one's own mice. In the mass consumer market, there is only one ef-fective way to tell people about your product, and that's *advertising*.

## QUESTIONS

1.  Why was P&G so successful with Pampers when so many new products fail?

2.  In marketing Pampers, P&G introduced a product that previously did not exist. Did P&G create a need for the product? Explain.

3.  What marketing activities and/or processes are illustrated by the Pampers story?

4.  Explain why P&G was able to market Pampers at 6 cents each instead of 10 cents each by planning to more than double its sales volume.

---

## ☐ 3

# Towards a socialist marketing concept— the case of Romania

## *Jacob Naor*

---

*A common misconception is the idea that marketing only takes place under capitalism. However, all political economies need an effective macro-marketing system to direct the flow of goods and services from producers to consumers. While many socialist countries have ignored and even frowned on marketing in the past, several socialist countries have shown an increasing interest in marketing during the past decade.*

*The following article explains how the marketing concept has evolved and been applied in Romania. It then compares Romanian marketing developments with those of Bulgaria and Hungary, two other socialist countries with less central planning. As you read the article, note the similarities and the differences between the way marketing is practiced in the United States and the way it is practiced in the East bloc socialist countries.*

---

The treatment of marketing under socialism has long intrigued Western observers. The tradi-tional Marxist disdain for trade and commerce, based on the notion that the creation of economic utilities was largely confined to the production sector, is well-known. Marketing has thus in the past largely been ignored in Eastern bloc coun-tries. Within the last decade, however, thinking re-garding marketing has undergone a radical transformation. Marketing now appears to have achieved official recognition, and interest in devel-oping marketing approaches suitable for a social-ist environment has greatly increased. This development is not confined to East European bloc members, however. Starting in 1979, reforms in the People's Republic of China permit a return to some form of individual enterprise in com-

Source: Reprinted with permission from the *Journal of Mar-keting*, published by the American Marketing Association, Janu-ary 1986, pp. 28–39. At the time of writing, Jacob Naor was professor of business administration at the University of Maine at Orano.

merce. Private enterprises are now permitted in retailing, production and selling of handicrafts, and provision of services (employing up to seven apprentices and assistants) "to better serve the needs of consumers" and help alleviate unemployment (Reeder 1984, p. 45).

The purpose of this article is twofold: to establish the context within which marketing activities currently take place in Romania, and to offer a socialist Romanian version of the marketing concept, including an assessment of its application in practice. Some recent developments, both in concept and practice, will be analyzed within this context, and implications for marketing practitioners, theoreticians, and policymakers presented.

Since Romania is considered by most Western observers as an ideologically orthodox and conservative member of the East bloc, similar developments may be expected to have occurred elsewhere in the bloc. Examples of such developments in two East bloc countries, one similarly administered (Bulgaria) and one administratively decentralized (Hungary), will be presented. The version of the marketing concept presented and its application in practice in Romania will be based on available published sources as well as on information collected by the author firsthand in Romania.[1]

In the Romanian context "trade" is now officially recognized as an essential and indispensable continuation of material production (Ceausescu 1978, p. 11), an activity that materially affects living standards (Fazekas 1978, p. 32). It is no surprise, therefore, that marketing activities in the domestic sphere, let alone in international trade, have attracted official attention. The economy, it will be seen, appeared in need of basic reforms, and these tended to carry over into the marketing area as well.

## SOME CONTEXTUAL CHARACTERISTICS

Interest in marketing is of recent origin in Romania. Prior to World War II, Romania was one of the least developed countries in Eastern Europe. While some small-scale industrial development did take place prior to the War, large scale industrialization efforts were initiated, and indeed institutionalized, through the introduction in 1951 of a highly centralized five-year planning system. Since that time Romania has achieved some of the highest industrial growth rates in the world (Tsantis and Pepper 1979, p. 5). The essential focus of Romanian development strategy centered on industrial development, particularly the development of heavy industry. Marketing, particularly that involving consumer goods, did not appear to Romanian planners to be of great importance in this context.

The main instrument relied on in Romania's industrialization drive in lieu of a freely functioning market system was a comprehensive and highly centralized national planning system. Fundamental here was the belief that rapid economic development, indeed, social transformation, could not take place under a decentralized Western-style market system. This notion is still central to Romanian thinking. Marketing in Romania must be seen as taking place entirely within the framework of a centrally managed economy in which major and critical resources are allocated according to priorities established at the highest level of the planning hierarchy. It is only recently that market-based demand considerations have been officially recognized as important in determining specific output assortments made available to the population.

## RECENT ECONOMIC REFORMS AND CONSTRAINTS TO REFORM MAKING

Since the late 1960s, Romanian planners have become increasingly aware of the need to adapt the original planning and management system to the evolving complexities of an expanding economy. Starting in 1967, a series of economic reforms was undertaken, a process which is still underway (Naor 1982). Fundamentally, the reforms were intended to shift operational decision-making power from economic ministries to operational levels (enterprises) in order to increase microeconomic efficiency. Thus, since 1978, enterprises and trade organizations were to be self-managed financially (within central plan

[1]Research on a wide range of topics was conducted by the author in Romania from late 1982 through early 1983 under a Fulbright grant. Interviews were conducted with government officials, enterprise executives, and academicians, and covered recent economic reforms in Romania as well as marketing developments.

guidelines) and essentially required to become profit centers.

While the ability and responsibility of enterprises to provide appropriate inputs as to the implementation of central planning guidelines were increased, the "plan" remained the central instrument for the coordination of economic activity and for resource allocation. Marketing activities continued to be carried out within parameters set by centralized plans and within guidelines emanating from above. This essential feature has been retained in Romania to a much larger degree than in other East bloc countries.

An understanding of the constraints within which Romanian economic activities take place is essential for a proper understanding of the role and position occupied by marketing in present day Romania. The constraints are presented in Table 1. As seen from the outline presented, basic political, ideological, and economic constraints appear to delineate the domain available for production and trade activities. For example, sellers' market conditions have traditionally appeared to Romanian planners as a requirement and precondition for rapid, centrally directed growth, and are

**Table 1** □ **Constraints on Romanian economic activities**

| Category | Manifestation |
|---|---|
| *Primary* | |
| Political | East-West nondependence |
| Economic | Continuous rapid growth policy |
| | Continuation of sellers' markets |
| Ideological | Orthodoxy |
| *Secondary*[a] | |
| Political-economic | Little integration within the COMECON system |
| Economic: | |
| Internal | Shrinking resource base |
| External | Growing dependence on imports, accompanied by a world recession and ensuing hard currency crisis[b] |
| Organizational | Maintenance of a highly centralized planning bureaucracy and a highly monopolistic production and distribution structure |
| Ideological | Maintenance of socialist principle of to each according to his/her contribution |

[a]These constraints are either more temporary, time or technology dependent, or are derivable from the primary constraints.
[b]This constraint applies mainly to the post–1980 period.

not likely to change soon. The secondary constraints listed appear to be binding as well, although in some cases, on a more temporary basis. The highly monopolistic production and distribution structure must be singled out as being of crucial importance to the character and role of marketing in Romania. Here, too, little change can be expected in the foreseeable future. The evolution of marketing has taken place within these constraints. Future developments may in all likelihood be expected to be similarly constrained.

## THE SOCIAL ROLE AND FUNCTION OF MARKETING

Having established the environmental constraints of marketing in Romania, one is now in position to examine the official role assigned to it. Various public pronouncements as well as the basic law regulating home trade activities (*Law No. 3,* 1972) will be relied on for this. While no single officially sanctioned version of a Romanian marketing concept is available, the construction of such a concept appears possible on the basis of these sources. The following formulation is proposed:

> The goal of marketing is to meet the needs of the population, which are to be scientifically determined, in an efficient and equitable manner, in order to bring about continuous improvements in the living standard and the quality of life of the population.

Marketing, in a macro-normative sense, is seen here as contributing in a major way to national economic development goals. Scientifically determined need satisfaction, rather than traditionally stressed material production, is emphasized here as central in attempts to raise living standards. This appears to herald a shift from production orientation towards some newly emerging form of marketing orientation. Need satisfaction, which would differ in a crucial way from that promulgated in the West, would, in addition, see some significant constraints. It would have to take account of ideological and centrally determined equity and efficiency considerations as well.

The equity notion must be singled out at this point, since it provides a central ingredient of the ideological constraints underlying Romanian economic activities. Socialist equity, in a broad sense, rests on the basic premise that remuneration or benefits from society should reflect individuals' work efforts, thus their contributions to society (Ceausescu 1978, p. 10). Official pronouncements thus subscribe to the basic socialist notion of "to each according to his/her contribution." Under this formulation, unequal "contributions" would clearly permit unequal rewards and, thus, unequal resource allocations. As will be seen, ideologically permissible differentiation will find appropriate expression in Romanian marketing practices.

While extremely broad in scope, the proposed marketing concept formulation appears to embody and capsulize the official philosophy underlying centralized regulation of marketing activities in Romania. Its operative components—scientific determination of needs, efficiency, and equity—will be focused on throughout the remainder of the article to indicate both the meaning imparted to these concepts and their practical impact on marketing activities in Romania.

## NORMATIVE IMPLICATIONS FOR MARKETING MIX ELEMENTS

### Product

Central to the proposed marketing concept, just as for its Western counterpart, is need satisfaction. However, the Romanian formulation appears to differ in a seemingly crucial way; the scientific determination of needs appears to be at the heart of the concept. Therefore, it is very important to attempt to ascertain the meaning assigned by the authorities to this notion, since clearly this would have a crucial impact on the products that should be made available to the population.

Unfortunately, only a few, rather vaguely worded official pronouncements are as yet available on this crucial issue. One of these, made on the authority of President Ceausescu, reads as follows: "We must develop rational and scientifically determined consumption requirements of the population, both for agricultural as well as industrial goods . . . such requirements to be related to specific work efforts involved . . . while resolutely avoiding consumption for consumption's sake"

(Ceausescu 1978, p. 10). And again, "wasteful, irrational consumption, which characterizes capitalist consumption-based society, must be avoided" (ibid., p. 11). Furthermore, "scientific criteria regarding the structure of consumption must meet the physiological and psychological needs of man". . . and take account of tradition and other relevant domestic characteristics (of consumers), as well as the capabilities of Romanian production (ibid., pp. 10, 32).

All we have here then are normative statements calling for comprehensive rational consumption norms or requirements, which should be scientifically determined and should meet both physiological and psychological consumer needs within their environmental context. Research to scientifically determine rational consumption norms would presumably be undertaken by appropriate centralized research organizations. From another source we learn that it is foreseen that such norms should be available for the entire economy by the year 1990 (Flucsa 1978). Unfortunately, however, no indication is provided in these pronouncements as to how such norms could or should be developed in practice. As to rational consumption, all we are told is that it should not be "wasteful" or "irrational."

However, a second notion appears to be ascribed to scientific need determination as well. "At the level of actual exigencies, socialist commerce has to use, on a large scale, scientific methods in researching the demand for goods, to exert an active role on output . . . (thus) supplying the needs of the population" (*Law No. 3,* 1972, p. 1). Trading organizations and production units should be involved in this scientific effort. They are admonished to "achieve a thorough knowledge of consumer needs" which should guide the operative adaptation of production in order to satisfy goods demand (ibid., p. 12). And the constant growth in output of material goods should lead to systematically and continuously rising living standards (ibid., p. 1).

Scientific need determination is seen in these pronouncements to include normative as well as positive aspects. Existing needs (possibly including "irrational" needs) are to be ascertained through appropriate market research by trade and production units, while the scientific determination of rational consumption requirements would be concurrently pursued. While not ignoring existing market demand, the scientific determination of rational demand accompanied by appropriate consumer education should apparently progressively underlie future consumption. Since such consumption would in turn determine output, output would ultimately be scientifically determined as well. The authorities were apparently hoping that consumption would eventually be based entirely on scientifically determined rational needs. References to existing market demand may thus be in the nature of a concession to the need to usher in that condition gradually.

## Distribution

Cost-efficient need provision is widely stressed in official pronouncements. Just as consumers should avoid wasteful consumption, so should trade organizations avoid wasteful practices. Commercial bodies and organizations "must enhance the economic efficiency of their entire activity," while meeting in an "optimal" way the population's requirements (*Law No. 3,* 1972, pp. 14–15).

A typical admonition regarding efficiency involves the design of channels of distribution. Direct distribution from producers to retailers is advocated to the extent possible (Ceausescu 1978, p. 16). It was stated that this would reduce inventory value losses as well as transportation costs. Demand, at all levels, should be studied carefully to allow production and distribution to be closely geared to requirements, not to exceed them (Ceausescu 1978, p. 17).

The following enumeration of some specific and detailed regulations involving wholesale and retail distribution should serve to underscore the authorities' concern for efficiency:

1. At the wholesale level, disruption in the supply of retailers should be avoided through optimization of transport and supply flows. Transport distances should be reduced by concentrating warehousing of consumer nondurables in major consumption zones.
2. Production should be synchronized with consumption and direct delivery from producers to retail outlets increased; or, in the case of consumer durables, direct delivery from

wholesale warehouses to final consumers should be increased.
3. Production and supply of seasonal goods to retailers, which should account for 70–80 percent of the total retail assortment, should take place within three months preceding the start of the season. The quantity of goods left unsold after the season should be reduced to 10–12 percent of all goods available for sale.
4. Average stockturn ratios at retail to be aimed for should be as follows: 4.3 for 98 percent of total goods turnover, i.e., for normally salable goods; .5 for 2 percent of total goods turnover, i.e., for less salable goods (Fazekas 1978, pp. 57–58).

The above represent an attempt to institutionalize and standardize efficiency levels at both macro and micro levels. The planning system and planners' prerogatives are relied upon here to set standards of efficiency which in market system economies would be determined by market forces. The need for wide ranging bureaucratic controls to enforce such regulations becomes apparent. While material incentives were often tied to the achievement of efficiency standards, such incentives were rarely sufficient in the Romanian context to bring about the results desired (Naor 1982).

## Promotion

The role of promotion in bringing about or facilitating rational consumption must be mentioned at this point. It should have an active role in socialist trade in order to systematically inform and advise consumers regarding functional aspects of new as well as old products, help orient consumers throughout their decision-making processes towards rational and scientifically balanced food consumption, informing them of the availability of stylish goods, and thus, in the process, educating the consumer (Fazekas 1978, p. 61). The social character of promotion is also stressed. It should not contribute actively towards the satisfaction of socially undesirable needs. The promotion (i.e., stimulation of demand) of such goods as cigarettes and alcohol was never permitted beyond meeting existing demand (Fazekas 1978, p. 61). Rational consumption appears to refer here to the use of functional choice criteria by consumers in their decision-making processes.

**Pricing**

Meeting the population's requirements in an equitable manner appears to be the third principle involved in the Romanian approach to marketing. Equity notions clearly affect pricing policies, in addition to product assortments offered to the population. As will be recalled, equity in this context refers to the basic socialist notion of to each according to his/her contribution. Traditionally, wage and salary differentials had been strictly constrained in the ratio of 1:6 between lowest and highest incomes (Ceausescu 1981, p. 508). The provision of goods and services to the population, as well as pricing policies, had to be firmly tied to the contribution of individuals to society through the "quantity and quality" ,of their work (Fazekas 1978, p. 64), which would reflect their ability to pay.

Pricing policy appeared, therefore, to be designed to achieve equity objectives, while attempting at the same time to achieve efficient resource allocation. Prices should reflect socially necessary production and distribution costs, to be centrally determined, which would include appropriate mark-on rates for producers and intermediaries. Lower prices would thus, for example, be assigned to goods on such grounds as lower material and fabrication costs as well as lower margins to producers reflecting ability to pay considerations. Since everyone would be presumed to contribute according to their abilities, pricing should fulfill a social role in making needed goods accessible to lower income strata. Efficiency would be served too, since prices would cover only socially necessary costs, requiring production at some predetermined level of technology. This would apply to distribution as well, since distributional margins would have to compensate wholesalers and retailers only to the extent of technologically and organizationally justifiable expenditures. Centrally set prices were not intended to produce wasteful expenditures, either in production or in distribution.

It appears open to question, however, whether apparent conflicts between the twin objectives of efficiency and equity could readily be resolved.

The authorities were clearly reluctant to permit excessive income differentiation, which would have acted in the direction of more efficient resource utilization, since higher returns would have stimulated higher contributions, and prices were clearly not permitted to reflect the state of consumer or industrial demand. By constraining income differentiation and adhering to the socially necessary cost principle for administrative price setting purposes, the attainment of efficient resource utilization would clearly have to depend on the degree to which administrative regulations could be implemented successfully. Thus, restrictions on the operation of the pricing mechanism and on incentives appear to be major obstacles to the attainment of efficiency objectives.

**IMPLEMENTATION OF THE MARKETING CONCEPT IN PRACTICE**

It is clearly important to attempt to assess the degree to which the principles embodied in the socialist marketing concept are implemented in practice. Their significance would surely be considerably reduced were they solely expressions of good intentions. This section will attempt such an assessment within the limitations of the data available. Not surprisingly, these limitations are particularly severe concerning the details of plan implementations, regarding which often little is found in published sources.

**Product**

Little is known as yet concerning the practical aspects of scientific demand determination and the development of scientific consumption norms. Some scientific norm setting appears, however, to have taken place by 1978. Rational consumption norms were apparently developed for textile and shoe products and had "affected production and trade" in the 1976–1980 five-year plan as well as planning for the 1981–1985 period (Flucsa 1978, p. 223). According to a report by the Home Trade Minister, experts from industry, research organizations, academia, and trade participated in the development of scientific consumption norms. Such norms, the report continues, have already been developed, in addition to those mentioned, for household durable goods (to reduce household work) and for cultural and leisure goods "befitting a civilized way of life" (Fazekas 1978, p. 52). The stated aim with regard to consumer durables was to gradually approach the standards prevailing in economically developed countries (ibid., p. 40). Whether this conflicted with aims of achieving rational consumption was not revealed.

Secondly, in the area of food requirements, by 1978 "scientific" caloric intake norms had been established for various work categories, differentiated by age and climatic conditions (ibid., p. 33). It may be presumed, nevertheless, that beyond these efforts little research has as yet been done, particularly in the intriguing area of psychological need determination.

Scientific norm setting would thus appear at this early stage to influence such decisions as what and how much should be produced in future plan years and what distribution networks would be needed to make the goods available at the retail level. However, some criticism concerning the slow pace of developing such norms has been voiced (ibid., p. 52). Beyond that, no information is available as to how decisions regarding the development of norms are arrived at in practice, or to what degree they are affected by such extrascientific considerations as a desire to institute import substitution measures, or the desire to utilize locally available resources, production capacities, and technologies.

Neither does an examination of reported Romanian consumption trends add much to our ability to explain the norms-related planning process involving consumer goods. As an illustration, Table 2 presents changes in the ownership of some (domestically produced) consumer durables between 1975 and 1980.

The reported percentage increases in the ownership of radio and television appliances exceeded those of the other durables reported, when comparing the 1977–80 increases to those of 1975–77. This is puzzling in light of the widespread participation of women in the labor force and in distribution,[2] since scientifically determined consumption would appear to call for large and rapid increases in the number of labor-saving appliances. But based on these figures, this did not seem to have occurred.

Somewhat more is known regarding the positive aspect of demand determination. By the late 1970s, increasing attention was being paid to the needs of channels of distribution units and central organs for obtaining demand-related information on a current and ongoing basis. Such informational feedback would, it was hoped, increase the market sensitivity and responsiveness of channel members while providing essential inputs for improving the efficiency of macro channel operations. It appeared desirable, therefore, to decentralize much of the demand-related collection and analysis process to the level of operational units. The distribution system was now expected to increasingly match supply and demand more effectively. In addition to the work done by central research organizations, since 1977 demand determination has been entrusted to special managerial councils formed for this purpose at large economic units, assisted by consumer representatives (Bozdog 1978, p. 305). As an additional measure, directors of all trade units were required to keep daily logs to track demand

---

[2]Of the 400,000 people (18.5% of the population) employed in trade and distribution, more than two-thirds were women (Fazekas 1978, p. 32).

**Table 2** ☐ **Ownership of selected consumer durables (units per 100 households)[a]**

| | 1977 (actual) | 1980 (planned) | Percent Increase | |
| --- | --- | --- | --- | --- |
| | | | 1975/1977 | 1977/1980 |
| Radios | 70.4 | 82.7 | 6.5 | 17.5 |
| Televisions | 55.2 | 63.3 | − 1.3 | 14.7 |
| Refrigerators | 38.6 | 49.0 | 31.9 | 26.9 |
| Washing machines | 25.7 | 28.4 | 27.5 | 10.5 |
| Automobiles | 6.1 | 8.4 | 42.0 | 37.7 |

[a]Data provided in Fazekas 1978, p. 39. 1975/1977 ratios are based on actual sales data (in units). 1977/1980 ratios present increases between planned and actually owned units per 100 households.

and supply on a current basis. Daily managers were required to:

- Indicate goods for which there was strong demand, less demand, or no demand.
- Specify inability to meet demand with regard to assortment, color, and sizes.
- Specify demanded goods not available.
- Specify volume, assortment, contracted dates, and quality of supplies, as well as qualitative aspects of deliveries.
- Indicate other relevant aspects of trade activity that day (Fazekas 1978, p. 53).

Managers were expected to deal with supply problems (with recourse to higher authorities, if necessary) within a span of five to seven days, and results were to be noted in the log (ibid., p. 54).

While such logs were undoubtedly kept, by 1978 results were still far from satisfactory. Official reasons then given included lack of interest in ascertaining demand by managers and staff of retail units, lack of interest in using the information collected, insufficient attention paid to expressed consumer opinions and requirements, and poor

utilization of the (research) data made available (by central organs) (Bozdog 1978, p. 306). No information is available as to whether the situation has improved since.

The provided assessment should not come as a surprise, keeping in mind prevailing sellers' market conditions in Romania. Introducing regulations without changing the overly monopolistic structure of industry and trade clearly proved inadequate. It may similarly be presumed that the consumer councils that were activated to aid demand determination could not have materially affected the assortment and quality of goods supplied, despite official hopes to that effect.

## Distribution

Table 3 presents an overview of some organizational aspects of Romanian distribution. The highly centralized structure of distribution and the significance of the cooperative distribution network are noteworthy.[3] Less apparent is the similarly

---

[3]Cooperative organizations in the East bloc are similar in concept to Western cooperatives. Both are based on the cooperative ownership and administration of productive property.

---

**Table 3 □ Some organizational aspects of distribution in Romania[a]**

| General | Percent of trade turnover | |
|---|---|---|
| Romania is divided into 40 administrative regions (judets). Primarily, trade is handled in rural areas by cooperatives,[b] and in urban areas, by State organizations. All wholesalers are organized as State enterprises and are under the Ministry of Home Trade. | Cooperatives: | 23 |
| | State organizations: | 77 |

| Selected wholesalers | | Percent of volume handled through warehouse distribution[c] |
|---|---|---|
| Food: | 1/judet, handles State enterprises and cooperatives | 40 |
| Textile: | 18 total, 1 per 2–3 judets | 80–90 |
| Hardware: | 17 total, 1 per 2–3 judets | 60–70 |

| Retail (state-administered only) | | Percent of total State-administered trade |
|---|---|---|
| General merchandise—under Home Trade Ministry: | | 80 |
| Selected ministry outlets: | Ministry: | |
| Pharmacies | Health | |
| Gasoline distribution | Chemical industry | |
| Fruits and vegetables | Ministry of Agriculture | |
| Other | | 20 |

[a]Information provided to author in personal interviews by a former deputy minister of the Home Trade Ministry.
[b]Produce more than 60 percent of total agricultural output.
[c]Until 1982; current percentages are lower. Remaining volume physically bypasses wholesalers.

highly centralized structure of retailing. In the case of textiles and footwear, for example, retail distribution for Bucharest and surrounding counties (a 4 million population base) is organized through 20 State "chain" organizations (administrative units), covering 7,000 units.[4] A highly centralized network indeed! Nevertheless, the network in general does not appear to be sufficiently developed as yet to meet distribution density criteria desired by planners (Ceausescu 1978, p. 9).

As indicated, the authorities aimed at achieving efficiently functioning networks at all levels of distribution. Thus, efficiency considerations appeared to be behind announced intentions to utilize a systems approach in the planning of selected products from development to final consumption, to include "consumer evaluations" and implementation by cooperating "production and trade organs" (Fazekas 1978, p. 71). No information is available, however, concerning whether this approach has been implemented.

From personal interviews it emerged that in wholesaling, direct distribution was rapidly being implemented, particularly since the economic reforms of 1978. Thus, at the largest textile and footwear wholesaling firm in Romania (handling 20 percent of the turnover of that industry), direct distribution (for which the firm continued to act as a broker) increased from 6 percent in 1978 to over 40 percent by late 1982 and was expected to continue to grow. Direct distribution was expected to bring about reductions in transportation and warehousing costs. Again, no data are available as to whether cost savings were indeed realized.

For the retail level there are indications that some cost reductions were achieved. It appears that the authorities were able to increase considerably the retail turnover per employee by tying employees' compensation to goods turnover (wage increases were presumably tied to increases in average turnover) (Fazekas 1978, p. 64). This was in line with the equity principle as well, since compensation was tied to amount and quality of work performed, as evidenced in sales (turnover) results. For the year 1978, for example, it was expected that 82 percent of the anticipated (unspecified) increase in retail turnover would result from increases in productivity per worker, the rest through increases in personnel employed (ibid., p. 64).

The growth in self-service retailing undoubtedly contributed to these results. By mid-1978, 32 percent of all nonfood retail outlets were of the self-service variety, and self-service food retailing was increasing as well (ibid., p. 64). The use of standard designs for specified retail outlets continued to increase, and updated retail store profiles for textiles, clothing, furniture, automobile spare parts, and electrical appliances were introduced. In major cities, 37 stores modeled after West European hyper-stores had been introduced by mid-1978 (ibid., p. 43), providing presumably considerable economies of scale.[5] Buying on credit of higher priced (Romanian made) consumer durables and cars became widely available in order to achieve "predetermined circulation targets and the raising of living standards" (ibid., p. 45). The authorities clearly recognized that an expansion of the means of payment and some provision of purchase incentives for durables were needed in conjunction with attempts to increase the efficiency of distribution. Yet, despite the incentives provided retail employees, the character of retail activities continued on the whole to be passive. Strong sellers' market conditions apparently sufficed in most cases to move the desired retail volume.

## Promotion

Few changes may be noted regarding either the role or the use of promotion in practice. The role of advertising continued to be confined to that of educating and informing the public, particularly as to products newly introduced to the market. Given sellers' market conditions, this indeed may have been a wholly appropriate role. The authorities relied almost exclusively on television (which by 1980 was expected to be in 63.3 percent of all households—Fazekas 1978, p. 39), presumably for its suitability for demonstrating new products. The announced intentions of the authorities to in-

---

[4]Based on information provided to the author in personal interviews with executives of a major textile products plant in Bucharest.

[5]One of the largest stores of this kind in the capital city received 70 percent of its total purchases directly from the manufacturers.

creasingly popularize rational consumption would have appeared to foreshadow a much larger role for promotion in all its forms. The social and distributional roles of promotion could have clearly been expanded to cover such functions as demarketing, synchromarketing, or countermarketing. To date this does not appear to be the case.

## Pricing

As stated, the principle of from each according to his/her contribution meant in practice income-related inequality, based on the quantity and quality of work performed. As applied to marketing, provision of goods and services as well as pricing could thus take account of growing income differentials, since such were sanctioned on theoretical (as well as presumably practical) grounds. Income differentials and the related differentiation of prices were indeed reflected in the overall categorization of goods. Four general categories of goods were recognized: mass (cheapest), superior, extra, and luxury (most expensive).[6] While no information is available on how category differences are established, it is known that in practice pricing is based on average costs (which presumably are considered to approximate socially necessary cost), both at the manufacturer's level and at all subsequent distribution levels.

While goods with similar cost structures would tend to be priced similarly, final prices by category, even in the absence of cost differentials, would nevertheless differ, as profit (regarded as a cost item by producers and channel members) differed according to category. For textiles, for example, profit mark-ons for mass products in 1982 at the manufacturer's level ranged from 5 to 15 percent of average production costs in that category, while for the luxury category (which generally involved higher production costs as well), profit rates were set at 30 percent. Equity considerations appeared to influence the setting of such rates. Profit rates as well as relevant cost calculations were generally settled through negotiations between the producing enterprise and higher administrative bodies. Thus, enterprises appeared able to influ-

ence the cost and pricing process.[7] In distribution, mark-ons (based on acquisition costs) were set at 13 percent, to include both wholesalers (4.3 percent) and retailers (8.7 percent). Production costs appeared to influence distribution costs, covering any extra costs that might be attached to the distribution of extra or luxury goods.

Beyond considerations regarding the production and pricing of goods, equity considerations affected legislation regarding the distribution of goods as well. To counter the understandable tendency to produce and sell higher priced goods at the expense of cheaper goods, enterprise plans "should provide distinctly the quantities of the main products or goods assortments with cheap prices as well as children's articles" (*Law No. 3, 1972*, p. 11). Trading and production organizations have the obligation to ensure the permanent supply of low-priced goods in adequate quantities, based on concluded contracts between the units. The nonsupply of low-priced products and children's articles (according to plan and/or contract) is considered a trespass against the law (ibid.). While income differentials are thus accepted and provided for, both for goods assortments as well as pricing practices, constraints are provided for too. Such constraints had to be legislated, since under sellers' market and production monopoly conditions, the unrestrained operation of markets could have meant the entire disappearance of such socially important goods from the market. Equity considerations will most likely continue to constrain the catering to income differentials in the future as well.

It would appear that the principles expressed in the socialist marketing concept were being implemented in practice in Romania, albeit with varying degrees of consistency and success. Considerable progress seems to have been made, particularly as to efficiency and equity components. Implementation of scientifically determined consumption appears to be lagging, due presumably to inherent difficulties in establishing consumer goods related consumption norms. Nevertheless, the authorities appear determined to proceed along the lines indicated. Their further progress in

---

[6]From conversations with executives of a major textile products plant, Bucharest.

[7]I was assured by the executives of the textile plant that in "90 percent of the cases," their price proposals are approved "as is."

applying the socialist marketing concept to marketing reality in Romania clearly bears watching.

## SOME DEVELOPMENTS ELSEWHERE IN THE EAST BLOC

What is the extent to which the Romanian concept and practice of marketing differ from those of other East bloc countries? Space and data limitations allow only a brief, limited examination of this issue. In particular two examples were chosen: Bulgaria, which has a somewhat less centrally planned system than that of Romania,[8] and Hungary, which enjoys a highly decentralized administrative system.

Authorities in both countries appear to subscribe to notions of efficiency and equity similar to their Romanian counterparts. However, based on the information available, neither attempted to emulate the Romanian experience regarding rational consumption.

A major equity-related policy aim of Bulgaria as well as Romania and Hungary is to equalize consumption per capita levels between urban and nonurban areas. Unlike conditions prevailing in Romania, this appears to a considerable extent to have been accomplished in Bulgaria (Metotiev 1984, p. 2). However, while the declared aim of the cooperative movement in Bulgaria is to "satisfy the population's needs for consumer goods as fully as possible," nothing is available as to how and by whom such needs should be determined. As in Romania, however, the socialist principle of remuneration appears to provide theoretical backing for equity considerations.

Efficiency considerations appear to dominate the division of tasks between State trading concerns and the cooperative organizations in Bulgaria. The two systems parallel each other to some extent and are in what is claimed to be a state of nonantagonistic competition (Buchett 1984, p. 7). Through mutual discussions agreement is reached as to "who can render the best

service to the people," with cooperatives engaged in smaller scale operations (both in production and distribution) "filling the gaps in the economy," and performing operations not remunerative enough for the large-scale operations of State trading and production organizations (ibid.). Note here that profitability, and presumably cost efficiency as well, are important criteria in determining the allocation of distributional tasks.

Just as in Romania, self-service retailing appears to be increasing in Bulgaria. As indicated, nowhere in the available sources is there a mention of rational consumption, however. The same holds true for available Hungarian sources. On this basis it appears that Romania is at present the only country conducting such research on the basis of policy decisions made at the highest levels of authority. This could possibly be due to Romania's isolated position in the East bloc, which could impel it to attempt to assume a leadership role within the bloc. Whatever the explanation, it appears important to continue to watch the Romanian experiment closely.

As stated, the Hungarian concept of marketing appears to be largely in line with those outlined in this article, despite considerable differences regarding the role of centralized planning in an economy that may be characterized as "market socialism" (Granick 1975, p. 241). Based on available evidence, the Hungarian authorities appear at this stage to be quite content to let the marketplace determine consumer needs in an environment that is still dominated by a relatively small number of extremely large enterprises.[9]

In line with the considerable increase in decision-making authority granted individual enterprises in Hungary since the basic reforms of 1968, enterprises, rather than higher administrative bodies, as in Romania and Bulgaria, engage in the planning and implementation of marketing activities and are continuously urged to do more in this respect. By East bloc standards, considerable market research, advertising, and new product planning is carried out, particularly by large enterprises, primarily for their extensive foreign trade

---

[8]Information regarding Bulgaria is based on publications issued by the Bulgarian cooperative movement which administers consumer goods distribution parallel to State trading companies in "all towns and villages." Membership in cooperatives exceeded 2.5 million in 1984, or about 28 percent of Bulgaria's total population (Burchett 1984, p. 7).

[9]According to one Hungarian source, the ratio of Hungarian enterprises employing over 1,000 employees is still "unjustifiably" high (73 percent) and is exceeded only by that of Romania (80 percent) and Czechoslovakia (90 percent) (Tompe 1982).

involvement but increasingly for the domestic market as well.[10] Indeed, one major marketing journal just celebrating its 17th year of publication, stated that the economic success of the entire economy will depend on the successful application of marketing by enterprises, both on internal and external markets ("Editorial" 1983, p. 195).

Paralleling the strong emphasis on micro marketing (not in evidence in the other systems examined), macro considerations in Hungary appear to revolve around the twin concerns of efficiency and equity as well. Official sources emphasize that the "best and most simple routes" should be used in distribution, and that organizational systems, modernization, and development of competition are "not goals but means in improvement of supplies and increased economic efficiency" (in distribution) (Andriko 1982a, p. 44). In contrast to Bulgaria and Romania where plan reliance is paramount, competitive pressures (presumably from competing large firms) as well as individual initiative are relied on increasingly at all levels of production and distribution to bring about economic efficiency. One example at the retail level is the increasing use of contracting or leasing of state outlets to enterprising individuals, to be run at the risk of the entrepreneur (who through efficiency measures can augment his or her profits beyond those negotiated with the leasing authorities). Retail trends further exemplifying this include the introduction recently of discount stores plus a continuing growth in large department stores and supermarkets (Pinter 1982, p. 59).

The basic tenet of Hungarian "commercial" policy is that "every population strata find the necessary products in our shops" (Andriko 1982b, p. 13). The incomes of such strata would presumably again be based on the socialist principle of remuneration, and remuneration appears to follow egalitarian principles.[11] As in Romania, the authorities were concerned that the needs of low-income population groups and of large families be satisfied by expanding the availability of low-priced articles, resolving to "check to a greater extent the stores' selection in this respect" (ibid.). To this effect it was planned to increase the availability of "so-called generic products" which comprised "excellent quality articles . . . where the simple packaging makes the relative low prices possible" (ibid.).

It appears, then, that, excluding the scientific consumption component, common marketing principles are encountered in socialist East bloc countries despite variations in the degree to which the economies are managed centrally. In practice implementation of such principles tends to vary, of course, depending on the peculiarities of the managerial-organizational arrangements in question. While Romania and Bulgaria, to a lesser extent, continue to attempt to implement most activities through rigorous centrally controlled planning, Hungary, attempting to bring about similar results, relies much more extensively on the interplay of market forces and the display of individual initiative.

As mentioned briefly in the introduction, this appears to be the direction followed by the People's Republic of China as well. Individual enterprise and entrepreneurship is now officially promoted and even accorded political and social status equal to that enjoyed by workers in State-run and collective enterprises (Reeder 1984, p. 46). As recent decrees indicate, centrally controlled and administered planning is being relaxed in the PRC as well, providing power and authority to factory managers to make "all" business decisions (ibid., p. 47). Considerable implications for marketing must clearly be involved here.

## CONCLUSION

Romanian planners and their counterparts in other socialist countries have shown increasing interest in marketing within the last decade. The need to focus on distribution and consumption rather than merely on increasing output has gained official recognition. A socialist (Romanian) marketing concept has been proposed and illustrations provided as to its applicability to Romanian marketing practices as well as those prevailing in the two countries chosen for comparison, Bul-

---

[10]Hungarian foreign trade involvement is extensive. In 1981 the value of exports, of which 30.3 percent went to developed capitalist countries, amounted to 47.3 percent of the national income (*Statistical Pocket Book of Hungary* 1981, pp. 109, 193).

[11]According to a 1980 survey, the average income of managerial personnel ("leaders") in Hungarian industry amounted only to 170–230 percent of that of "subordinate" personnel (Tompe 1982).

garia and Hungary. It was pointed out that portions of the concept are just now being gradually introduced, while much of the central scientific need determination portion is still in the nature of an outline or objective for future research. The basic philosophy appears to be in place, however.

Implications on several levels can be drawn from the materials presented. For marketing practitioners, they offer some insights into basic concepts guiding East bloc policymakers and managers. This could provide general guidance to Western executives charged with commercial negotiations in the East bloc and could also provide guidance concerning the kinds of Western goods and services most likely to meet the needs of such markets (which, as indicated, may often be bureaucratically or, on occasion, scientifically determined).

In the area of comparative marketing systems, several implications present themselves. The Romanian example must be singled out as an ambitious if still somewhat tentative attempt to construct scientifically researched plan-based and plan-coordinated production, distribution, and consumption macro systems. The socialist marketing concept proposed here underlies this effort and maps out the principles involved. As such, it deserves close scrutiny by students of marketing systems of developed and developing economies alike. Depending on the results encountered in implementation, it appears to present an alternative model to predominantly market determined macro systems. In an age of increasing resource constraints and growing potential for governmental intervention, such an approach may be particularly attractive to policymakers of resource-poor economies, since it permits the orderly planning and implementation of major structural changes.

Under pressure to rapidly construct infrastructures and distribution networks, developing countries would be attracted to a model that permits the introduction of such changes rapidly and in a planned way. Indeed, in Romania the 10-year period preceding 1978 saw the addition of close to 52 percent of total retail space then in use (Fazekas 1978, p. 42). The educational role assigned to promotion may appeal to developing countries as well, since educational advances are a basic precondition for accelerated economic growth. And scientific consumption, emphasizing physiological (basic) need satisfaction, would appear to

be of great concern to economic planners attempting to meet basic population needs.

Other socialist countries may well be influenced by the Romanian experience in their ongoing move towards greater decentralization of economic activity. The degree of success of Romanian planners in rapidly implementing marketing-related reforms (such as those involving efficiency and equity) may well enhance the attractiveness of plan-based options over those involving market operations. This may be particularly relevant to the ability to realize important economic objectives, such as the rapid development of high technology sectors which is currently at the forefront of concerns of socialist planners. In addition, the Romanian experience regarding scientific consumption will be carefully watched as well, since socialist planners may hardly be expected to embrace Western notions of an unconstrained consumer society.

For more richly endowed economies, the approach holds fewer attractions. It does not appear to provide much guidance toward the development of flexibility and adaptability to subtle changes in demand which appear crucial for more advanced systems. Despite such drawbacks, rapid systemwide adaptations to technological changes are often crucial for economically developed systems, and some variant of centralized planning may provide the edge in the race to gain technological leadership in international trade.

Implications for policymakers in the West, particularly in the United States, thus could be seen to center on the growing importance of macromarketing planning for market economies. Growing resource shortages and intensified worldwide competitive pressures combine to stress the need for some form of guidance for market forces. National policy planners may do well to look at alternative models (in both East and West) for possible clues as to what form such guidance could take. In addition, notions of equity and efficiency are clearly relevant for all systems, regardless of ideological differences, in an age where social issues and ecological concerns are increasingly gaining attention. If nothing else, the Romanian experience may focus renewed attention on alternative approaches to the issues involved. Lastly, for students of convergence of economic systems, the evolution of Hungarian thought and practice with regard to competition and individual initiative under socialism may be highly instructive.

The notions embodied in the proposed marketing concept could well influence Western thinking and stimulate interest in East bloc marketing developments. Clearly much depends on the success East bloc planners will have in implementing the principles expressed in the concept. Some successes may be noted, but much remains to be done. It remains to be seen whether centrally managed (or, in the Hungarian case, guided) planning will be able to achieve as dramatic results in marketing as it appears to have achieved in production.

## REFERENCES

Andriko, Miklos (1982a). "The Level of Consumer Goods Supply." *Partelet* (November 11), 3–7. (Translated from Hungarian, in *East-European Reports: Economic and Industrial Affairs.* No. 2357, Joint Publication Research Services (JPRS) No. 82505, p. 44.)

———— (1982b). "State Secretary Discusses Trade, Consumer Goods Supply." *Nepszabadsag* (December 11), 5. (In *East-European Reports: Economic and Industrial Affairs.* No. 2365, JPRS No. 82532, p. 13.)

Bozdog, Nicolac (1978). *Proceedings of the National Conference of Employees in Trade and Tourism.* Bucharest: Economic Institute for Trade and Tourism (June 27–28).

Burchett, Wilfred (1984), "Bulgaria—Past, Present, and Future." *Bulgarian Cooperative Review* (No. 1), 7.

Ceausescu, Nicolae (1978). *Proceedings of the National Conference of Employees in Trade and Tourism.* Bucharest: Economic Institute for Trade and Tourism (June 27–28).

———— (1981). *Romania on the Way of Building Up the Multilaterally Developed Socialist Society.* Bucharest: Meridiane Publishing.

"Editorial" (1983). *Marketing-Piackutatas* (No. 3), 195.

Fazekas, Janos (1978). *Proceedings of the National Conference of Employees in Trade and Tourism.* Bucharest: Economic Institute for Trade and Tourism (June 27–28).

Flucsa, Maria (1978). *Proceedings of the National Conference of Employees in Trade and Tourism.* Bucharest: Economic Institute for Trade and Tourism (June 27–28).

Granick, David (1975). *Enterprise Guidance in Eastern Europe.* Princeton. N.J.: Princeton University Press.

*Law No. 3/1972 Home-Trade Law* (1972). Bucharest: Council of State, Editorial Board of the Official Bulletin of the Socialist Republic of Romania, 1–35.

Metotiev, K. (1984). "A Historic Gain." *Bulgarian Cooperative Review* (No. 2), 2.

Naor, Jacob (1982). "Economic Reform Making in Romania—The 1978 New Economic Mechanism." Equipe de Recherche sur la firme et l'Industrie. Universite de Montpellier, France, unpublished research paper.

Pinter, Tibor (1982). "Old and New Tendencies." *Figyelo* (July), 2. (In *East-European Reports: Economic and Industrial Affairs.* No. 2304, JPRS No. 81539.)

Reeder, John A. (1984). "Entrepreneurship in the People's Republic of China." *Columbia Journal of World Business,* 19 (No. 3), 43–51.

*Statistical Pocket Book of Hungary* (1981). Budapest: Statistical Publishing House.

Tompe, Zoltan (1982). "The Leader's Interest." *Valosag* (October), 25–39. (In *East-European Reports: Economic and Industrial Affairs.* No. 2353, JPRS No. 82456.)

Tsantis, Andreas C., and Roy Pepper (1979). *Romania—The Industrialization of an Agrarian Economy under Socialist Planning.* Washington, D.C.: World Bank.

## QUESTIONS

1. How does the "social role" of marketing in Romania differ from that of the United States?

2. Explain how marketing's "four Ps"—product, place, promotion, and price—are implemented in Romania. How does this compare with the way marketing is performed in the United States?

3. Based on the discussion in the article, do you think that the macro-marketing system in Romania works better than or not as well as the U.S. macro-marketing system? Why? On what factors or considerations is your answer based?

*4. Will the same environmental trends that have made marketing "the new priority" in the United States (Reading 1) also force socialist countries to place a higher priority on marketing? Why or why not?

---

*Question relates concepts in this and other readings.

☐ 4

# Nonprofits: Check your attention to customers

*Alan R. Andreasen*

*Many nonprofit organizations have started using marketing techniques as a means of achieving their objectives. But as Andreasen points out in this article, simply using marketing techniques does not mean that an organization is marketing-oriented. After explaining the difference between selling and marketing, he presents seven key indicators for deciding whether a nonprofit organization has a product (or selling) orientation—or a marketing orientation. As you read the article, keep in mind that most of what Andreasen says about nonprofit organizations applies just as well to for-profit organizations.*

The director of an urban art museum describes her marketing strategy as "an educational task." She says: "I assemble the best works available and then display them grouped by period and style so that the museum-goer can readily see the similarities and differences between, say, a Braque and a Picasso or between a Brancusi and an Arp. Our catalogs and lecture programs are carefully coordinated with this approach to complete our marketing mix."

The public relations manager of a social service agency claims: "We are very marketing oriented. We research our target markets extensively and hire topflight creative people with strong marketing backgrounds to prepare brochures. They tell our story with a sense of style and graphic innovation that has won us several awards."

A marketing vice president for a charitable foundation ascribes his success to careful, marketing-oriented planning: "Once a year we plan the entire year's series of messages, events, and door-to-door solicitation. We emphasize the fine humanitarian work we do, showing and telling potential donors about the real people who have benefited from donations to us. Hardly a week goes by without some warm human interest story appearing in the local press about our work. The donors just love it!"

These are the kinds of statements one hears from officials of successful nonprofit organizations that are highly respected for their supposedly innovative marketing approaches. The executives have attended courses and seminars on marketing, and their planning documents and speeches are laced with marketing jargon like "benefit segmentation," "product positioning," and "message strategies."

While they believe they are marketing oriented, these organizations actually have a product-oriented or, at best, a selling-oriented marketing approach. They start with their own organizations and services, determine how they want to market them, and *then* turn to customer analysis to achieve their goals. Despite their protestations to the contrary, they do not begin the process with consumers. The distinction is subtle but important. Managers need to adopt a new view of marketing and its role in their organizations. The first step in this learning process is self-awareness—recognizing the underlying product or selling orientation in the approaches they and their institutions use.

Marketing has certainly achieved wide respectability in the nonprofit world. Hospital administrators, college presidents, and theater directors are

Source: Reprinted with permission of the *Harvard Business Review.* "Nonprofits: Check Your Attention to Customers," by Alan R. Andreasen (May/June 1982). Copyright © 1982 by the President and Fellows of Harvard College; all rights reserved. At the time of writing, Alan Andreasen was professor of marketing at the University of Illinois.

often as familiar with the writings and speeches of marketing experts as they are with those of the traditional management sages. Yet all too many of these managers have adopted the trappings of marketing without grasping its essence. For this reason, marketing among nonprofit heads may go the way of such fads as motivation research and sensitivity training.

## SELLING VERSUS MARKETING

While most readers probably well understand the distinction between a selling or product orientation and a marketing orientation, reconsideration of the terms ensures a common starting point for this article. A *product orientation* involves focusing on an organization's basic offering and a belief that the best marketing strategy for increasing sales is to improve this offering's quality. A *selling orientation* equates the marketing task with persuading target audiences that they ought to accept the offering—that it is superior to any alternatives.

The art museum director described at the outset of the article believes she knows what her audience should learn about art; she sees her principal marketing task as "educational." The public relations manager concentrates not just on what she has to say but on how to say it; effective persuasion is the key element in her marketing strategy. And the charitable foundation's director believes his story is one that donors will just love to hear (of course, he also loves to tell it).

These marketers start with what they wish others to know about their organizations and only later think about customers' needs and wants. This is very different from a modern marketing orientation, which espouses the opposite approach. Institutions shouldn't ignore their own goals, preferences, strengths, and weaknesses; nevertheless, these concerns should not outweigh consumers' interests.

To illustrate, let's consider the typical art museum. As indicated in the opening quotation, most art museum directors see their marketing problem as one of assembling the best collections, displaying them well, and notifying the press and public of their availability. This product orientation manifests itself in the labels museums concoct for works of art, which museum directors see as a key marketing tool to get mass audiences to appreciate the artworks.

What information does a label usually include? First, facts about the artist: name, nationality, dates of birth and death. For whom is this information most important? Certainly for the museum director and his or her peers, since it ensures location of the artwork with others created by artists of the same nationality and period. Often labels also relate information about bequests, including donors' names. Of course, this information helps the director secure more donations (admittedly an important marketing task). On the other hand, given limited space, a donor's name is hardly a key piece of data for most museum-goers. Finally, there is usually a catalog (or inventory) number on the bottom of the label that helps the director keep track of the collection, prevent theft, and schedule repairs.

But what information would consumers like to see posted next to each work? If museum directors talked to consumers, as I have, they would discover that there is not one consumer market but three—each with different needs and wants but united against the typical labels. The three groups and their information needs can be defined as follows:

**The aesthetes.**   Some viewers are most interested in the aesthetic-artistic properties of each work. They want to know about design, use of materials, color, and techniques. They want to know about anything unusual in the artist's style and about good or bad features of the work. The artwork itself is of key importance to this group.

**The biographers.**   These people are fascinated by artists, their lives, their choices of subject matter, and their models. They would like to know how a work fits into the artist's career and what special meaning it has for his or her growth and development. For this group, the key feature is not so much the work but the artist behind it.

**The cultural historians.**   This group usually has had some formal or informal exposure to art of social history. Its members are interested in the work as an element in the sweep of cultural and artistic history. They want to know, for example, why this technique or this subject matter was chosen at this particular time and what the piece tells about the age, the country, and the broader artistic framework. Did the work influence other artists then or later? Does it reflect any of its predecessors? What was the society like that produced this artwork and this artist?

Clearly, three systems—not one—are needed. To some museum directors' surprise, such customer-oriented messages may not only broaden people's appreciation of the arts but also spur museum attendance or even donations. Directors might experience a leap in old-fashioned customer satisfaction, especially among those just beginning to explore museums and the arts.

## KEY INDICATORS

How can nonprofit organizations determine whether they have a selling or product orientation rather than a marketing focus? Among the symptoms that I have found to suggest a product or selling mind set are the following:

**1. Seeing the offering as inherently desirable.**  Nonprofit heads seldom entertain the possibility that potential consumers may not share their enthusiasm about their offerings. They cannot see why, given a clear description of their institution and what it provides, consumers would not want to respond enthusiastically.

Committed theater managers may find it hard to believe that right-thinking people wouldn't wish to attend a well-acted play; charitable organizations' directors sometimes cannot fathom an unwillingness to give; and those who head up nonprofit special-interest groups often can't see why people won't vote for, say, cleaner air or the ERA. Other nonprofits, including organizations designed to push such health-enhancing notions as wearing seat belts and quitting smoking, also are surprised that they have difficulty generating a positive response.

One organization that overcame the notion that its offerings are inherently desirable is the National Cancer Institute. Most women, NCI discovered, agreed that practicing breast self-examination was a good thing to do, and many knew how to do it. Yet the majority were not practicing such examination or, at best, did so only rarely. What was the problem? If the examination yielded nothing, the woman would feel a sense of relief the first few times, but eventually she would become bored at finding nothing and would stop the procedure. But the prospect of "success" was so frightening that most women never even tried the self-examination or, at any rate, didn't check themselves regularly. It was only when NCI understood these barriers—as perceived by the target audience—to an obviously good practice that it began to develop more user-oriented marketing programs. NCI's new stance, based on assurances that progress is being made against breast cancer (and thus one shouldn't fear discovering lumps), has resulted in increased self-detection.

**2. The notion of consumer ignorance.** Nonprofit managers tend to ascribe any lack of interest to the fact that consumers don't fully appreciate the nature of the offer. Or, if customers do understand, managers just haven't found the right incentives to motivate them.

Again the National Cancer Institute provides a good example of what a change to a marketing orientation can accomplish. For many years, the conventional wisdom among those charged with reducing cigarette consumption was that either smokers didn't believe smoking was bad for them or that they were not motivated enough to quit. But consumer surveys revealed that seven out of eight smokers did believe that smoking was a very bad habit and that many of them had in fact tried to stop. NCI concluded that what smokers needed as part of the marketing mix was a set of clear-cut techniques for quitting and a sense of hope that they might succeed. Because of this new consumer perspective, NCI reoriented its program toward action rather than information.

**3. Overemphasis on promotion.**  Many nonprofit organizations place too much stock in advertising and public relations. They are convinced that the director should concentrate on the message and its packaging. (Of course, the message directors usually have in mind is the story they want to tell.)

Many blood-collection agency heads believe that the best way to encourage donations is to tell consumers about the good things donors' blood can do or to stress that giving blood is a civic duty. They believe that people hold back from giving because they don't appreciate the gift's virtues or because they are afraid. Thus, agency heads

reason, consumers need to be told about the benefits and assured that the costs are trivial—indeed, that giving can be fun.

While these messages work for some people,
important segments respond to far different messages. For example, many men, especially blue-
collar workers, can be motivated by challenges to
their masculinity. The macho man who can tell his
co-workers that he is a 20-gallon donor may feel
well rewarded. (Indeed, some pain-and-suffering
in the process might enhance the reward.) Thus,
campaigns in factories focusing on individual giving records (bar charts or 10- and 20-gallon lapel
pins) can be highly effective.

Many social, fraternal, and church group members can be motivated by the let's-all-participate
aspects of a bloodmobile visit. They will respond
to messages about camaraderie, about feeling left
out if you don't join in, or about letting the group
down if you don't go. All these messages have little to say about the occasion for the get-together
or its value to society.

One blood bank director even uses sexual at-
traction as a marketing strategy. This director
found that a small segment of middle-aged men
considered the attentions of the pretty nurses well
worth the inconvenience of regular blood donations. This donor center has built a highly loyal
following. The innovative marketer who listens to
potential customers can gain surprising insights
about what the target audience wants and what
will get it to act.

**4. The secondary role of consumer re-
search.** If one "knows" that the problem lies
with the consumer and that better promotion is the
key to marketing success, the principal role for research is merely to confirm beliefs. Yet, as most
profit-sector marketers will attest, research can
challenge some managers' most fundamental assumptions about their customers. Take as an example officials of a small midwestern hospital who
worried that patients were dissatisfied with some
of its recently hired foreign-born doctors. Staff
nurses reported frequent patient complaints about
the doctors, sometimes because they "couldn't
understand" what the doctors were saying. Moreover, different cultural backgrounds appeared to
be seriously affecting doctor-patient rapport. The
hospital turned to field research to find out how to
cope with the problem.

The research indicated, however, that the
foreign-doctor problem was not really serious in
the eyes of patients or prospective patients. Few
interviewees mentioned the issue voluntarily in the
field study or scored it as a significant blot on the
hospital's image. Doctors instead were rated just
as easy to understand as doctors at rival institutions. Indeed, many patients, far from complain-
ing, perceived the foreign doctors as more serious
and conscientious than their breezy, golf-loving
U.S. counterparts. Needless to say, this research
saved the hospital from spending many promotional dollars to correct a problem that didn't exist.
What was really needed was a marketing program
directed toward the hospital staff, especially the
nurses and foreign doctors.

**5. One best marketing strategy.** Since the
nonprofit administrator is not often in close touch
with the market, he or she may view it as monolithic or at least as having only a few crudely defined market segments. Subtle distinctions are
played down. As a consequence, most nonprofits
tend to develop only one or two marketing strategies, aim them at the most obvious market segments, and then run with them. This climate of
managerial certainty precludes experimentation
either with alternative strategies or with variations
for market subsegments.

Also encouraging this approach is the fact that
nonprofit managers often come from nonbusiness
backgrounds and may fear taking risks. Personal
job survival and slow aggrandizement of the budget and staff are often their paramount objectives.
And since such administrators are typically responsible only to a volunteer board—which meets
irregularly and sometimes prefers to know little
about day-to-day operations—they do their best to
keep a low profile and avoid shaking up the
board. Finally, since most nonprofits are in fact
deficit organizations that make up their losses with
fund raising, aggressive marketing strategies are
unnecessary. These forces, then, support the typical nonprofit manager's natural inclination to be
conventional, not adventuresome.

Yet the opportunities for careful experimentation abound. A case in point is Carleton College.[1]
Since 1978, the Northfield, Minnesota, school has

---

[1]"College Learns to Use Fine Art of Marketing," *The Wall
Street Journal,* February 23, 1981.

systematically explored alternatives to the traditional single-brochure approach. A survey had shown that target high school students saw Minnesota as cold and isolated, Carleton itself as too "cerebral," and the library as too small. The standard brochure was updated to play down the cold weather, point out how easy it is to get to the attractive Twin Cities, and feature a new picture of the library that shows it is really quite large.

More recently, Carleton discovered that regional differences affect perceptions of the college. So the school sends letters to western students emphasizing outdoor activities and Carleton's informality and to Easterners stressing the school's academic prestige. And, finally, the school now informs those from Minnesota about its financial aid and the fact that Carleton enjoys a significant national, not just regional, reputation.

Since 1978, Carleton has seen its yearly applications increase from 1,470 to 1,875, while the response rate from mailings has jumped from 5.9 percent to more than 14 percent. It remains financially solvent and is protecting its reputation as academically selective.

**6. Ignoring generic competition.** While many nonprofit organizations consciously compete—the Heart Fund with the American Cancer Society, the Metropolitan Museum of Art with the Whitney or the Museum of Modern Art—many institutions don't have clear competitors because their services or so-called products are intangible or stress behavior changes. The competitors of those marketing, say, blood donations or forest-fire prevention are not immediately apparent. So it's not surprising that marketers ignore competition at either the product or generic level. But at the product level, blood banks, for example, compete with other charities for donors (who seek dollars, not blood). Even institutions with easily identifiable organizational competitors often face product competition from unlikely quarters. Thus, art museums compete with aquariums for family outings, with books and educational TV for art lovers, and with movies and restaurants as places to socialize.

Nonprofit organizations rarely plan strategies to compete at the product level because they lack a customer perspective. And this failure is even more serious at the nonproduct level. Before people will write their congressman in support of

ERA, for instance, they must give up their long-held ideas and divert their energies to the new cause. Inertia can be a powerful force, but enthusiastic nonprofit marketers tend to ignore it. When they peddle changes in behavior or new ideas, most nonprofits de-emphasize competition from the status quo.

**7. A marketing staff selected for its product knowledge.** In a modern marketing organization, staff members are selected on the basis of their knowledge of customer markets and of marketing research and management techniques. One can learn the key characteristics of a product in a few weeks, but market awareness and marketing expertise take years to master. Once gained, this expertise can be applied to many product or market contexts.

In many nonprofit organizations, knowledge of the product or service counts most. A preference for marketers with a product orientation prevails in nonprofit organizations because of three factors:

First, since marketing is unfamiliar to many nonprofit heads, they don't know how to evaluate marketing skills (while they can evaluate product know-how).

Second, many top nonprofit administrators accumulated most of their experience using product marketing and so are more comfortable working with people who have that orientation. Many business managers of arts organizations were once active performers or were formally trained in music, theater design, or museum curatorship. Most hospital administrators have either medical or public health backgrounds, and college presidents usually have Ph.D.'s in academic disciplines. Seldom are these administrators selected purely for their management skills.

Finally, the world of nonprofits is a fairly clubby one where key people know other big names around the country; thus, a certain amount of favoritism prevails. A prospective staff member with the proper connections and the right vocabulary stands a much better chance of making it than a total outsider. The marketing professional, who probably doesn't know what "needs assessment" or "audience development" means, is at a disadvantage. This self-reinforcement means that the customer-oriented marketer who wants to come in and turn the organization around will be seen (whether consciously or not) as a threat.

## A NEW WAY TO PASS THE HAT

How, then, can the marketing approaches in such organizations be changed? As noted previously, many nonprofit organizations' leaders are convinced they have already adopted the best marketing approaches. So the first step for concerned administrators is to assess the organization's managerial orientation.

It is also a good idea to start a customer research program. Customer research need not be expensive, and (as corporate marketers know) it is an essential precursor of each year's planning.

Furthermore, managers should rub shoulders with experienced marketers. Staff members can go outside regular channels for exposure to customer-oriented marketing. They might attend seminars, conferences, and courses by for-profit professionals or by academics who espouse customer-centered approaches. The institution can also bring a marketing consultant into the organization to evaluate problems and demonstrate how a modern marketer tries to solve them. And it can seek out one or more marketing professionals for the board of directors and observe how such professionals react to marketing problems.

Remember, the organizational atmosphere must change. Changing it is a straightforward process once nonprofit managers and staff become aware of what is at stake. And, since many not-for-profits are still exploring marketing's potential for helping them, the opportunities for adopting a constructive orientation are much greater than in fields where marketing has a longer history.

## QUESTIONS

1. Explain the central thesis of Andreasen's article.

2. If you were the director of a not-for-profit organization—such as a museum—how could you determine whether your organization was marketing oriented?

3. (Following from Question 2) If you discovered that your organization was not marketing oriented, what could you do to bring about a shift to a marketing orientation?

*4. Why has marketing become a "new priority" for nonprofit organizations in recent years (Reading 1)?

---

*Question relates concepts in this and other readings.

# Marketing myopia

## *Theodore Levitt*

*Although Levitt wrote "Marketing Myopia" over 20 years ago, the message contained in this "marketing classic" is as relevant today as it was then. Failure to recognize and respond to changes in lifestyle, social norms, and technology can have a devastating impact on a firm. To best deal with such environmental changes, a firm needs to clearly understand the nature of its business—what it does for its customers—not from the firm's perspective, but rather from the perspective of its customers.*

*Using several illustrations, Levitt shows that some business leaders have not demonstrated a clear understanding of the nature of their firm's business—and have not recognized and dealt with change very well. Even the petroleum industry—despite recent profitability—failed to really understand its business and develop profitable opportunities. Many firms and industries are probably similarly "myopic" right now—but which ones?*

Every major industry was once a growth industry. But some that are now riding a wave of growth enthusiasm are very much in the shadow of decline. Others which are thought of as seasoned growth industries have actually stopped growing. In every case the reason growth is threatened, slowed, or stopped is *not* because the market is saturated. It is because there has been a failure of management.

### FATEFUL PURPOSES

The failure is at the top. The executives responsible for it, in the last analysis, are those who deal with broad aims and policies. Thus:

The *railroads* did not stop growing because the need for passenger and freight transportation declined. That grew. The railroads are in trouble today, not because the need was filled by others (cars, trucks, airplanes, even telephones), but because it was *not* filled by the railroads themselves. They let others take customers away from them because they assumed themselves to be in the railroad business rather than in the transportation business. The reason they defined their industry wrong was because they were railroad oriented instead of transportation oriented; they were product oriented instead of customer oriented.

*Hollywood* barely escaped being totally ravished by television. Actually, all the established film companies went through drastic reorganizations. Some simply disappeared. All of them got into trouble, not because of TV's inroads, but because of their own myopia. As with the railroads, Hollywood defined its business incorrectly. It thought it was in the movie business when it was actually in the entertainment business. "Movies" implied a specific, limited product. This produced a fatuous contentment which from the beginning led producers to view TV as a threat. Hollywood scorned and rejected TV when it should have welcomed it as an opportunity—an opportunity to expand the entertainment business.

Today TV is a bigger business than the old narrowly defined movie business ever was. Had

Source: Reprinted (with deletions) by permission of the publishers from Edward C. Bursk and John F. Chapman, eds. *Modern Marketing Strategy* (Cambridge, Mass.: Harvard University Press, 1964), pp. 24–48. Copyright © 1964 by the President and Fellows of Harvard College. At the time of writing, Theodore Levitt was professor of business administration at the Harvard Business School.

Hollywood been customer oriented (providing entertainment) rather than product oriented (making movies), would it have gone through the fiscal purgatory that it did? I doubt it. What ultimately saved Hollywood and accounted for its recent resurgence was the wave of new young writers, producers, and directors whose previous success in television had decimated the old movie companies and toppled the big movie moguls.

There are other less obvious examples of industries that have been and are now endangering their futures by improperly defining their purposes. I shall discuss some in detail later and analyze the kind of policies that lead to trouble. Right now it may help to show what a thoroughly customer-oriented management can do to keep a growth industry growing, even after the obvious opportunities have been exhausted; and here there are two examples that have been around for a long time. They are nylon and glass—specifically, E. I. du Pont de Nemours & Co. and Corning Glass Works.

*Both companies* have great technical competence. Their product orientation is unquestioned. But this alone does not explain their success. After all, who was more pridefully product oriented and product conscious than the erst-while New England textile companies that have been so thoroughly massacred? The Du Ponts and the Cornings have succeeded, not primarily because of their product or research orientation, but because they have been thoroughly customer oriented also. It is constant watchfulness for opportunities to apply their technical know-how to the creation of customer-satisfying uses which accounts for their prodigious output of successful new products. Without a very sophisticated eye on the customer, most of their new products might have been wrong, their sales methods useless.

Aluminum has also continued to be a growth industry, thanks to the efforts of two wartime-created companies which deliberately set about creating new customer-satisfying uses. Without Kaiser Aluminum & Chemical Corporation and Reynolds Metals Company, the total demand for aluminum today would be vastly less than it is.

### ERROR OF ANALYSIS

Some may argue that it is foolish to set the railroads off against aluminum or the movies off

against glass. Are not aluminum and glass naturally so versatile that the industries are bound to have more growth opportunities than the railroads and movies? This view commits precisely the error I have been talking about. It defines an industry, or a product, or a cluster of know-how so narrowly as to guarantee its premature senescence. When we mention "railroads," we should make sure we mean "transportation." As transporters, the railroads still have a good chance for very considerable growth. They are not limited to the railroad business as such (though in my opinion rail transportation is potentially a much stronger transportation medium than is generally believed).

What the railroads lack is not opportunity but some of the same managerial imaginativeness and audacity that made them great. Even an amateur like Jacques Barzun can see what is lacking when he says: "I grieve to see the most advanced physical and social organization of the last century go down in shabby disgrace for lack of the same comprehensive imagination that built it up. [What is lacking is] the will of the companies to survive and to satisfy the public by inventiveness and skill."[1]

### SHADOW OF OBSOLESCENCE

It is impossible to mention a single major industry that did not at one time qualify for the magic appellation of "growth industry." In each case its assumed strength lay in the apparently unchallenged superiority of its product. There appeared to be no effective substitute for it. It was itself a runaway substitute for the product it so triumphantly replaced. Yet one after another of these celebrated industries has come under a shadow. Let us look briefly at a few more of them, this time taking examples that have so far received a little less attention.

#### Dry cleaning

This was once a growth industry with lavish prospects. In an age of wool garments, imagine

---

[1]Jacques Barzun, "Trains and the Mind of Man," *Holiday*, February 1960, p. 21.

being finally able to get them safely and easily clean. The boom was on.

Yet here we are 30 years after the boom started and the industry is in trouble. Where has the competition come from? From a better way of cleaning? No. It has come from synthetic fibers and chemical additives that have cut the need for dry cleaning. But this is only the beginning. Lurking in the wings and ready to make chemical dry cleaning totally obsolescent is that powerful magician, ultrasonics.

### Electric utilities

This is another one of those supposedly "no-substitute" products that has been enthroned on a pedestal of invincible growth. When the incandescent lamp came along, kerosene lights were finished. Later the water wheel and the steam engine were cut to ribbons by the flexibility, reliability, simplicity, and just plain easy availability of electric motors. The prosperity of electric utilities continues to wax extravagant as the home is converted into a museum of electric gadgetry. How can anybody miss by investing in utilities, with no competition, nothing but growth ahead?

But a second look is not quite so comforting. A score of nonutility companies are well advanced toward developing a powerful chemical fuel cell which could sit in some hidden closet of every home silently ticking off electric power. The electric lines that vulgarize so many neighborhoods will be eliminated. So will the endless demolition of streets and service interruptions during storms. Also on the horizon is solar energy, again pioneered by nonutility companies.

Who says that the utilities have no competition? They may be natural monopolies now, but tomorrow they may be natural deaths. To avoid this prospect, they too will have to develop fuel cells, solar energy, and other power sources. To survive, they themselves will have to plot the obsolescence of what now produces their livelihood.

### Grocery stores

Many people find it hard to realize that there ever was a thriving establishment known as the "corner grocery store." The supermarket has taken over with a powerful effectiveness. Yet the big food chains of the 1930s narrowly escaped being completely wiped out by the aggressive expansion of independent supermarkets. The first genuine supermarket was opened in 1930, in Jamaica, Long Island. By 1933 supermarkets were thriving in California, Ohio, Pennsylvania, and elsewhere. Yet the established chains pompously ignored them. When they chose to notice them, it was with such derisive descriptions as "cheapie," "horse-and-buggy," "cracker-barrel storekeeping," and "unethical opportunists."

The executive of one big chain announced at the time that he found it "hard to believe that people will drive for miles to shop for foods and sacrifice the personal service chains have perfected and to which Mrs. Consumer is accustomed."[2] As late as 1936, the National Wholesale Grocers convention and the New Jersey Retail Grocers Association said there was nothing to fear. They said that the supers' narrow appeal to the price buyer limited the size of their market. They had to draw from miles around. When imitators came, there would be wholesale liquidations as volume fell. The current high sales of the supers were said to be partly due to their novelty. Basically people wanted convenient neighborhood grocers. If the neighborhood stores "cooperate with their suppliers, pay attention to their costs, and improve their service," they would be able to weather the competition until it blew over.[3]

It never blew over. The chains discovered that survival required going into the supermarket business. This meant the wholesale destruction of their huge investments in corner store sites and in established distribution and merchandising methods. The companies with "the courage of their convictions" resolutely stuck to the corner store philosophy. They kept their pride but lost their shirts.

### Self-deceiving cycle

But memories are short. For example, it is hard for people who today confidently hail the twin

---

[2]For more details see M. M. Zimmerman, *The Super Market: A Revolution in Distribution* (New York: McGraw-Hill, 1955), p. 48.

[3]Ibid., pp. 45–47.

messiahs of electronics and chemicals to see how things could possibly go wrong with these galloping industries. They probably also cannot see how a reasonably sensible businessman could have been as myopic as the famous Boston millionaire who 50 years ago unintentionally sentenced his heirs to poverty by stipulating that his entire estate be forever invested exclusively in electric streetcar securities. His posthumous declaration "There will always be a big demand for efficient urban transportation," is no consolation to his heirs who sustain life by pumping gasoline at automobile filling stations.

Yet, in a casual survey I recently took among a group of intelligent business executives, nearly half agreed that it would be hard to hurt their heirs by tying their estates forever to the electronics industry. When I then confronted them with the Boston streetcar example, they chorused unanimously, "That's different!" But is it? Is not the basic situation identical?

In truth, *there* is *no such thing* as a growth industry, I believe. There are only companies organized and operated to create and capitalize on growth opportunities. Industries that assume themselves to be riding some automatic growth escalator invariably descend into stagnation. The history of every dead and dying "growth" industry shows a self-deceiving cycle of bountiful expansion and undetected decay. There are four conditions which usually guarantee this cycle:

1.  The belief that growth is assured by an expanding and more affluent population.
2.  The belief that there is no competitive substitute for the industry's major product.
3.  Too much faith in mass production and in the advantages of rapidly declining unit costs as output rises.
4.  Preoccupation with a product that lends itself to carefully controlled scientific experimentation, improvement, and manufacturing cost reduction.

I should like now to begin examining each of these conditions in some detail. To build my case as boldly as possible, I shall illustrate the points with reference to three industries—petroleum, automobiles, and electronics—particularly petroleum, because it spans more years and more vicissi-

tudes. Not only do these three have excellent reputations with the general public and also enjoy the confidence of sophisticated investors, but their managements have become known for progressive thinking in areas like financial control, product research, and management training. If obsolescence can cripple even these industries, it can happen anywhere.

## POPULATION MYTH

The belief that profits are assured by an expanding and more affluent population is dear to the heart of every industry. It takes the edge off the apprehensions everybody understandably feels about the future. If consumers are multiplying and also buying more of your product or service, you can face the future with considerably more comfort than if the market is shrinking. An expanding market keeps the manufacturer from having to think very hard or imaginatively. If thinking is an intellectual response to a problem, then the absence of a problem leads to the absence of thinking. If your product has an automatically expanding market, then you will not give much thought to how to expand it.

One of the most interesting examples of this is provided by the petroleum industry. Probably our oldest growth industry, it has an enviable record. While there are some current apprehensions about its growth rate, the industry itself tends to be optimistic. But I believe it can be demonstrated that it is undergoing a fundamental yet typical change. It is not only ceasing to be a growth industry but may actually be a declining one, relative to other business. Although there is widespread unawareness of it, I believe that within 25 years the oil industry may find itself in much the same position of retrospective glory that the railroads are now in. Despite its pioneering work in developing and applying the present value method of investment evaluation, in employee relations, and in working with backward countries, the petroleum business is a distressing example of how complacency and wrongheadedness can stubbornly convert opportunity into near disaster.

One of the characteristics of this and other industries that have believed very strongly in the

beneficial consequences of an expanding population, while at the same time being industries with
a generic product for which there has appeared to
be no competitive substitute, is that the individual
companies have sought to outdo their competitors
by improving on what they are already doing. This
makes sense, of course, if one assumes that
sales are tied to the country's population strings,
because the customer can compare products only
on a feature-by-feature basis. I believe it is significant, for example, that not since John D. Rocke-
feller sent free kerosene lamps to China has the
oil industry done anything really outstanding to
create a demand for its product. Not even in product improvement has it showered itself with eminence. The greatest single improvement, namely,
the development of tetraethyl lead, came from
outside the industry, specifically from General Motors and Du Point. The big contributions made by
the industry itself are confined to the technology
of oil exploration, production, and refining.

\* \* \* \* \*

### Idea of indispensability

The petroleum industry is pretty much persuaded that there is no competitive substitute for
its major product, gasoline—or if there is, that it
will continue to be a derivative of crude oil, such
as diesel fuel or kerosene jet fuel.

There is a lot of automatic wishful thinking in
this assumption. The trouble is that most refining
companies own huge amounts of crude oil reserves. These have value only if there is a market
for products into which oil can be converted—
hence the tenacious belief in the continuing competitive superiority of automobile fuels made from
crude oil.

This idea persists despite all historic evidence
against it. The evidence not only shows that oil
has never been a superior product for any purpose for very long, but it also shows that the oil
industry has never really been a growth industry.
It has been a succession of different businesses
that have gone through the usual historic cycles of
growth, maturity, and decay. Its overall survival is
owed to a series of miraculous escapes from total
obsolescence, of last-minute and unexpected re-
prieves from total disaster reminiscent of the Per-
ils of Pauline.

### Perils of petroleum

I shall sketch in only the main episodes:
*First,* crude oil was largely a patent medicine.
But even before that fad ran out, demand was
greatly expanded by the use of oil in kerosene
lamps. The prospect of lighting the world's lamps
gave rise to an extravagant promise of growth.
The prospects were similar to those the industry
now holds for gasoline in other parts of the world.
It can hardly wait for the underdeveloped nations
to get a car in every garage.

In the days of the kerosene lamp, the oil companies competed with each other and against
gaslight by trying to improve the illuminating characteristics of kerosene. Then suddenly the impossible happened. Edison invented a light which was
totally nondependent on crude oil. Had it not been
for the growing use of kerosene in space heaters,
the incandescent lamp would have completely finished oil as a growth industry at that time. Oil
would have been good for little else than axle
grease.

*Then* disaster and reprieve struck again. Two
great innovations occurred, neither originating in
the oil industry. The successful development of
coal-burning domestic central heating systems
made the space heater obsolescent. While the industry reeled, along came its most magnificent
boost yet—the internal-combustion engine, also
invented by outsiders. Then when the prodigious
expansion for gasoline finally began to level off in
the 1920s, along came the miraculous escape of
a central oil heater. Once again the escape was
provided by an outsider's invention and development. And when that market weakened, wartime
demand for aviation fuel came to the rescue. After
the war the expansion of civilian aviation, the die-
selization of railroads, and the explosive demand
for cars and trucks kept the industry's growth in
high gear.

*Meanwhile* centralized oil heating—whose
boom potential had only recently been pro-
claimed—ran into severe competition from natural
gas. While the oil companies themselves owned
the gas that now competed with their oil, the industry did not originate the natural gas revolution,
nor has it to this day greatly profited from its gas
ownership. The gas revolution was made by

newly formed transmission companies that marketed the product with an aggressive ardor. They started a magnificent new industry, first against the advice and then against the resistance of the oil companies.

By all the logic of the situation, the oil companies themselves should have made the gas revolution. They not only owned the gas; they also were the only people experienced in handling, scrubbing, and using it, the only people experienced in pipeline technology and transmission, and they understood heating problems. But, partly because they knew that natural gas would compete with their own sale of heating oil, the oil companies pooh-poohed the potentials of gas.

The revolution was finally started by oil pipeline executives who, unable to persuade their own companies to go into gas, quit and organized the spectacularly successful gas transmission companies. Even after their success became painfully evident to the oil companies, the latter did not go into gas transmission. The multibillion-dollar business which should have been theirs went to others. As in the past, the industry was blinded by its narrow preoccupation with a specific product and the value of its reserves. It paid little or no attention to its customers' basic needs and preferences.

*     *     *     *     *

### Uncertain future

Management cannot find much consolation today in the rapidly expanding petrochemical industry, another oil-using idea that did not originate in the leading firms. The total U.S. production of petrochemicals is equivalent to about 2 percent (by volume) of the demand for all petroleum products. Although the petrochemical industry is now expected to grow by about 10 percent per year, this will not offset other drains on the growth of crude oil consumption. Furthermore, while petrochemical products are many and growing, it is well to remember that there are nonpetroleum sources of the basic raw material, such as coal. Besides, a lot of plastics can be produced with relatively little oil. A 50,000-barrel-per-day oil refinery is now considered the absolute minimum size for efficiency. But a 5,000-barrel-per day chemical plant is a giant operation.

Oil has never been a co... growth industry. It has grov... ways miraculously saved b... velopments not of its own n... has not grown in a smooth ... each time it thought it had a ... ... product safe from the possibility of competitive substitutes, the product turned out to be inferior and notoriously subject to obsolescence. Until now, gasoline (for motor fuel, anyhow) has escaped this fate, but, as we shall see later, it too may be on its last legs.

The point of all this is that there is no guarantee against product obsolescence. If a company's own research does not make it obsolete, another's will. Unless an industry is especially lucky, as oil has been until now, it can easily go down in a sea of red figures—just as the railroads have, as the buggy whip manufacturers have, as the corner grocery chains have, as most of the big movie companies have, and indeed as many other industries have.

The best way for a firm to be lucky is to make its own luck. That requires knowing what makes a business successful. One of the greatest enemies of this knowledge is mass production.

## PRODUCTION PRESSURES

Mass-production industries are impelled by a great drive to produce all they can. The prospect of steeply declining unit costs as output rises is more than most companies can usually resist. The profit possibilities look spectacular. All effort focuses on production. The result is that marketing gets neglected.

John Kenneth Galbraith contends that just the opposite occurs.[4] Output is so prodigious that all effort concentrates on trying to get rid of it. He says this accounts for singing commercials, desecration of the countryside with advertising signs, and other wasteful and vulgar practices. Galbraith has a finger on something real, but he misses the strategic point. Mass production does indeed generate great pressure to "move" the product. But what usually gets emphasized is selling, not mar-

---

[4]The Affluent Society (Boston: Houghton Mifflin, 1958), pp. 152–60.

Marketing, being a more sophisticated and complex process, gets ignored.

The difference between marketing and selling is more than semantic. Selling focuses on the needs of the seller, marketing on the needs of the buyer. Selling is preoccupied with the seller's need to convert his product into cash; marketing with the idea of satisfying the needs of the customer by means of the product and the whole cluster of things associated with creating, delivering, and finally consuming it.

In some industries the enticements of full mass production have been so powerful that for many years top management in effect has told the sales departments, "You get rid of it; we'll worry about profits." By contrast, a truly marketing-minded firm tries to create value-satisfying goods and services that consumers will want to buy. What it offers for sale includes not only the generic product or service but also how it is made available to the customer, in what form, when, under what conditions, and at what terms of trade. Most important, what it offers for sale is determined not by the seller but by the buyer. The seller takes his cues from the buyer in such a way that the product becomes a consequence of the marketing effort, not vice versa.

## Lag in Detroit

This may sound like an elementary rule of business, but that does not keep it from being violated wholesale. It is certainly more violated than honored. Take the automobile industry:

*Here* mass production is most famous, most honored, and has the greatest impact on the entire society. The industry has hitched its fortune to the relentless requirements of the annual model change, a policy that makes customer orientation an especially urgent necessity. Consequently the auto companies annually spend millions of dollars on consumer research. But the fact that the new compact cars are selling so well in their first year indicates that Detroit's vast researches have for a long time failed to reveal what the customer really wanted. Detroit was not persuaded that he wanted anything different from what he had been getting until it lost millions of customers to other small car manufacturers.

How could this unbelievable lag behind con-

sumer wants have been perpetuated so long? Why did not research reveal consumer preferences before consumers' buying decisions themselves revealed the facts? Is that not what consumer research is for—to find out before the fact what is going to happen? The answer is that Detroit never really researched the customer's wants. It only researched his preferences between the kinds of things which it had already decided to offer him. For Detroit is mainly product oriented, not customer oriented. To the extent that the customer is recognized as having needs that the manufacturer should try to satisfy, Detroit usually acts as if the job can be done entirely by product changes. Occasionally attention gets paid to financing, too, but that is done more in order to sell than to enable the customer to buy.

As for taking care of other customer needs, there is not enough being done to write about. The areas of the greatest unsatisfied needs are ignored, or at best get stepchild attention. These are at the point of sale and on the matter of automotive repair and maintenance. Detroit views these problem areas as being of secondary importance. That is underscored by the fact that the retailing and servicing ends of this industry are neither owned and operated nor controlled by the manufacturers. Once the car is produced, things are pretty much in the dealer's inadequate hands. Illustrative of Detroit's arm's-length attitude is the fact that, while servicing holds enormous sales-stimulating, profit-building opportunities, only 57 of Chevrolet's 7,000 dealers provide night maintenance service.

Motorists repeatedly express their dissatisfaction with servicing and their apprehensions about buying cars under the present selling setup. The anxieties and problems they encounter during the auto buying and maintenance processes are probably more intense and widespread today than 30 years ago. Yet the automobile companies do not *seem* to listen to or take their cues from the anguished consumer. If they do listen, it must be through the filter of their own preoccupation with production. The marketing effort is still viewed as a necessary consequence of the product, not vice versa, as it should be. That is the legacy of mass production, with its parochial view that profit resides essentially in low-cost full production.

\* \* \* \* \*

## Product provincialism

The tantalizing profit possibilities of low unit production costs may be the most seriously self-deceiving attitude that can afflict a company, particularly a "growth" company where an apparently assured expansion of demand already tends to undermine a proper concern for the importance of marketing and the customer.

The usual result of this narrow preoccupation with so-called concrete matters is that instead of growing, the industry declines. It usually means that the product fails to adapt to the constantly changing patterns of consumer needs and tastes, to new and modified marketing institutions and practices, or to product developments in competing or complementary industries. The industry has its eyes so firmly on its own specific product that it does not see how it is being made obsolete.

The classical example of this is the buggy whip industry. No amount of product improvement could stave off its death sentence. But had the industry defined itself as being in the transportation business rather than the buggy whip business, it might have survived. It would have done what survival always entails, that is, changing. Even if it had only defined its business as providing a stimulant or catalyst to an energy source, it might have survived by becoming a manufacturer of, say, fan belts or air cleaners.

What may someday be a still more classical example is, again, the oil industry. Having let others steal marvelous opportunities from it (e.g., natural gas, as already mentioned, missile fuels, and jet engine lubricants), one would expect it to have taken steps never to let that happen again. But this is not the case. We are now getting extraordinary new developments in fuel systems specifically designed to power automobiles. Not only are these developments concentrated in firms outside the petroleum industry, but petroleum is almost systematically ignoring them, securely content in its wedded bliss to oil. It is the story of the kerosene lamp versus the incandescent lamp all over again. Oil is trying to improve hydrocarbon fuels rather than to develop *any* fuels best suited to the needs of their users, whether or not made in different ways and with different raw materials from oil.

\* \* \* \* \*

Management might be more likely to do what is needed for its own preservation if it thought of itself as being in the energy business. But even that would not be enough if it persists in imprisoning itself in the narrow grip of its tight product orientation. It has to think of itself as taking care of customer needs, not finding, refining, or even selling oil. Once it genuinely thinks of its business as taking care of people's transportation needs, nothing can stop it from creating its own extravagantly profitable growth.

\* \* \* \* \*

## DANGERS OF R&D

Another big danger to a firm's continued growth arises when top management is wholly transfixed by the profit possibilities of technical research and development. To illustrate I shall turn first to a new industry—electronics—and then return once more to the oil companies. By comparing a fresh example with a familiar one, I hope to emphasize the prevalence and insidiousness of a hazardous way of thinking.

### Marketing shortchanged

In the case of electronics, the greatest danger which faces the glamorous new companies in this field is not that they do not pay enough attention to research and development, but that they pay *too much* attention to it. And the fact that the fastest-growing electronics firms owe their eminence to their heavy emphasis on technical research is completely beside the point. They have vaulted to affluence on a sudden crest of unusually strong general receptiveness to new technical ideas. Also, their success has been shaped in the virtually guaranteed market of military subsidies and by military orders that in many cases actually preceded the existence of facilities to make the products. Their expansion has, in other words, been almost totally devoid of marketing effort.

Thus, they are growing up under conditions that come dangerously close to creating the illusion that a superior product will sell itself. Having created a successful company by making a superior product, it is not surprising that management continues to be oriented toward the product rather than the people who consume it. It develops the philosophy that continued growth is a matter of continued product innovation and improvement.

A number of other factors tend to strengthen and sustain this belief:

1. Because electronic products are highly complex and sophisticated, managements become top-heavy with engineers and scientists. This creates a selective bias in favor of research and production at the expense of marketing. The organization tends to view itself as making things rather than satisfying customer needs. Marketing gets treated as a residual activity, "something else" that must be done once the vital job of product creation and production is completed.

2. To this bias in favor of product research, development, and production is added the bias in favor of dealing with controllable variables. Engineers and scientists are at home in the world of concrete things like machines, test tubes, production lines, and even balance sheets. The abstractions to which they feel kindly are those which are testable or manipulatable in the laboratory, or, if not testable, then functional, such as Euclid's axioms. In short, the managements of the new glamour-growth companies tend to favor those business activities which lend themselves to careful study, experimentation, and control—the hard, practical, realities of the lab, the shop, the books.

What gets shortchanged are the realities of the *market*. Consumers are unpredictable, varied, fickle, stupid, shortsighted, stubborn, and generally bothersome. This is not what the engineer-managers say, but deep down in their consciousness it is what they believe. And this accounts for their concentrating on what they know and what they can control, namely, product research, engineering, and production. The emphasis on production becomes particularly attractive when the product can be made at declining unit costs. There is no more inviting way of making money than by running the plant full blast.

Today the top-heavy science-engineering-production orientation of so many electronics companies works reasonably well because they are pushing into new frontiers in which the armed services have pioneered virtually assured markets. The companies are in the felicitous position of having to fill, not find, markets; of not having to

discover what the customer needs and wants, but of having the customer voluntarily come forward with specific new product demands. If a team of consultants had been assigned specifically to design a business situation calculated to prevent the emergence and development of a customer-oriented marketing viewpoint, it could not have produced anything better than the conditions just described.

\* \* \* \* \*

**Beginning and end**

The view that an industry is a customer-satisfying process, not a goods-producing process, is vital for all businessmen to understand. An industry begins with the customer and his needs, not with a patent, a raw material, or a selling skill. Given the customer's needs, the industry develops backward, first concerning itself with the physical *delivery* of customer satisfactions. Then it moves back further to *creating* the things by which these satisfactions are in part achieved. How these materials are created is a matter of indifference to the customer; hence the particular form of manufacturing, processing, or what-have-you cannot be considered as a vital aspect of the industry. Finally, the industry moves back still further to *finding* the raw materials necessary for making its products.

The irony of some industries oriented toward technical research and development is that the scientists who occupy the high executive positions are totally unscientific when it comes to defining their companies' overall needs and purposes. They violate the first two rules of the scientific method—being aware of and defining their companies' problems, and then developing testable hypotheses about solving them. They are scientific only about the convenient things, such as laboratory and product experiments. The reason that the customer (and the satisfaction of his deepest needs) is not considered as being "the problem" is not because there is any certain belief that no such problem exists but because an organizational lifetime has conditioned management to look in the opposite direction. Marketing is a stepchild.

I do not mean that selling is ignored. Far from it. But selling, again, is not marketing. As already pointed out, selling concerns itself with the tricks and techniques of getting people to exchange their cash for your product. It is not concerned with the values that the exchange is all about. And it does not, as marketing invariably does, view the entire business process as consisting of a tightly integrated effort to discover, create, arouse, and satisfy customer needs. The customer is somebody "out there" who, with proper cunning, can be separated from his loose change.

Actually, not even selling gets much attention in some technologically minded firms. Because there is a virtually guaranteed market for the abundant flow of their new products, they do not actually know what a real market is. It is as if they lived in a planned economy, moving their products routinely from factory to retail outlet. Their successful concentration on products tends to convince them of the soundness of what they have been doing, and they fail to see the gathering clouds over the market.

## CONCLUSION

Less than 75 years ago American railroads enjoyed a fierce loyalty among astute Wall Streeters. European monarchs invested in them heavily. Eternal wealth was thought to be the benediction for anybody who could scrape a few thousand dollars together to put into rail stocks. No other form of transportation could compete with the railroads in speed, flexibility, durability, economy, and growth potentials. As Jacques Barzun put it, "By the turn of the century it was an institution, an image of man, a tradition, a code of honor, a source of poetry, a nursery of boyhood desires, a sublimest of toys, and the most solemn machine—next to the funeral hearse—that marks the epochs in man's life."[5]

Even after the advent of automobiles, trucks, and airplanes, the railroad tycoons remained imperturbably self-confident. If you had told them 60 years ago that in 30 years they would be flat on their backs, broke, and pleading for government subsidies, they would have thought you totally demented. Such a future was simply not considered possible. It was not even a discussable subject, or

an askable question, or a matter which any sane person would consider worth speculating about. The very thought was insane. Yet a lot of insane notions now have matter-of-fact acceptance—for example, the idea of 100-ton tubes of metal moving smoothly through the air 20,000 feet above the earth, loaded with 100 sane and solid citizens casually drinking martinis—and they have dealt cruel blows to the railroads.

What specifically must other companies do to avoid this fate? What does customer orientation involve? These questions have in part been answered by the preceding examples and analysis. It would take another article to show in detail what is required for specific industries. In any case, it should be obvious that building an effective customer-oriented company involves more than good intentions or promotional tricks; it involves profound matters of human organization and leadership. For the present, let me merely suggest what appear to be some general requirements.

### Visceral feel of greatness

Obviously the company has to do what survival demands. It has to adapt to the requirements of the market, and it has to do it sooner rather than later. But mere survival is a so-so aspiration. Anybody can survive in some way or other, even the skid-row bum. The trick is to survive gallantly, to feel the surging impulse of commercial mastery; not just to experience the sweet smell of success, but to have the visceral feel of entrepreneurial greatness.

No organization can achieve greatness without a vigorous leader who is driven onward by his own pulsating *will to succeed.* He has to have a vision of grandeur, a vision that can produce eager followers in vast numbers. In business, the followers are the customers. To produce these customers, the entire corporation must be viewed as a customer-creating and customer-satisfying organism. Management must think of itself not as producing products but as providing customer-creating value satisfactions. It must push this idea (and everything it means and requires) into every nook and cranny of the organization. It has to do this continuously and with the kind of flair that excites and stimulates the people in it. Otherwise, the company will be merely a series of pigeon-

---

[5]Barzun, "Trains and the Mind of Man," p. 20.

holed parts, with no consolidating sense of purpose or direction.

In short, the organization must learn to think of itself not as producing goods or services but as *buying customers,* as doing the things that will make people *want* to do business with it. And the chief executive himself has the inescapable responsibility for creating this environment, this viewpoint, this attitude, this aspiration. He himself must set the company's style, its direction, and its goals. This means he has to know precisely where he himself wants to go, and to make sure the whole organization is enthusiastically aware of where that is. This is a first requisite of leadership, for *unless he knows where he is going, any road will take him there.*

If any road is OK, the chief executive might as well pack his attaché case and go fishing. If an organization does not know or care where it is going, it does not need to advertise that fact with a ceremonial figurehead. Everybody will notice it soon enough.

**QUESTIONS**

1. *What, exactly, does Levitt feel business leaders are myopic about? How could you, as a senior manager, avoid falling into this trap?*

2. *Why does Levitt believe that there is no such thing as a "growth industry"? Do you agree? Why or why not?*

3. *What does Levitt mean by having a "visceral feel of greatness"? Who, in an organization, should have this feel? Is this relevant for someone looking for a permanent job?*

4. *What organizations, if any, do you think Levitt would add to the list if he were writing the article today? That is, are there any organizations or industries that have experienced difficulty in the last 20 years because they were myopic?*

*5. *Compare the concepts discussed by Levitt and Andreasen (Reading 4).*

*6. *Is "marketing myopia" less likely to be a problem in organizations that have made marketing "the new priority" (Reading 1)? Explain.*

---

*Question relates concepts in this and other readings.

# □ 6

# Strategic windows

## *Derek F. Abell*

*Earlier readings (1 and 5) have emphasized that firms must be sensitive to changes in the market. Building on this concept, Abell suggests that the time to invest in a product or market is when a "strategic window" is open—that is, when there is a "match" between the resources and capabilities of a firm and the requirements of a market. Abell suggests that one responsibility of a marketing manager is to follow trends in markets and identify when the "particular competencies" of a firm provide a unique opportunity for growth in a specific market. Similarly, the marketing manager should help a firm see when a window is "shut"— and it will be best for the firm to withdraw from a market since the market will no longer be able to serve the firm profitably.*

Strategic market planning involves the management of any business unit in the dual tasks of *anticipating* and *responding* to changes which affect the marketplace for their products. This article discusses both of these tasks. Anticipation of change and its impact can be substantially improved if an organizing framework can be used to identify sources and directions of change in a systematic fashion. Appropriate responses to change require a clear understanding of the alternative strategic options available to management as a market evolves and change takes place.

## DYNAMIC ANALYSIS

When changes in the market are only incremental, firms may successfully adapt themselves to the new situation by modifying current marketing or other functional programs. Frequently, however, market changes are so far-reaching that the competence of the firm to continue to compete effectively is called into question. And it is in such situations that the concept of "strategic windows" is applicable.

The term *strategic window* is used here to focus attention on the fact that there are only limited periods during which the "fit" between the key re-

quirements of a market and the particular competencies of a firm competing in that market is at an optimum. Investment in a product line or market area should be timed to coincide with periods in which such a strategic window is open. Conversely, disinvestment should be contemplated if what was once a good fit has been eroded—i.e., if changes in market requirements outstrip the firm's capability to adapt itself to them.

Among the most frequent questions which management has to deal with in this respect are:

Should funds be committed to a proposed new market entry? Now? Later? Or not at all? If a commitment is to be made, how large should it be?

Should expenditure of funds on plant and equipment or marketing to support existing product lines be expanded, continued at historical levels, or diminished?

When should a decision be made to quit and throw in the towel for an unprofitable product line or business area?

Source: Reprinted with permission from the *Journal of Marketing*, published by the American Marketing Association, July 1978, pp. 21–26. At the time of writing, Derek F. Abell was associate professor of business administration at the Harvard University Graduate School of Business Administration.

Resource allocation decisions of this nature all require a careful assessment of the future evolution of the market involved and an accurate appraisal of the firm's capability to successfully meet key market requirements. The strategic window concept encourages the analysis of these questions in a dynamic rather than a static framework and forces marketing planners to be as specific as they can about these future patterns of market evolution and the firm's capability to adapt to them.

It is unfortunate that the heightened interest in product portfolio analysis evident in the last decade has failed to adequately encompass these issues. Many managers routinely classify their various activities as cows, dogs, stars, or question marks based on a *static* analysis of the *current* position of the firm and its market environment.

Of key interest, however, is the question not only of where the firm is today but of how well equipped it is to deal with *tomorrow.* Such a *dynamic* analysis may foretell nonincremental changes in the market which work to disqualify market leaders, provide opportunities for currently low-share competitors, and sometimes even usher a completely new cast of competitors into the marketplace. Familiar contemporary examples of this latter phenomenon include such products as digital watches, women's panty hose, calculators, charter air travel, office copiers, and scientific instrumentation.

In all these cases existing competitors have been displaced by new contenders as these markets have evolved. In each case changing market requirements have resulted in a *closing* strategic window for incumbent competitors and an *opening* window for new entrants.

## MARKET EVOLUTION

The evolution of a market usually embodies more far-reaching changes than the relatively systematic changes in customer behavior and marketing mix due to individual product life cycles. Four major categories of change stand out:

1. The development of new primary demand opportunities whose marketing requirements differ radically from those of existing market segments.

2. The advent of new competing technologies which cannibalize the existing ones.

3. Market redefinition caused by changes in the definition of the product itself and/or changes in the product market strategies of competing firms.

4. Channel changes.

There may be other categories of change or variants in particular industries. That doesn't matter; understanding of how such changes may qualify or disqualify different types of competitors can still be derived from a closer look at examples within each of the four categories above.

### New primary demand

In a primary demand growth phase, decisions have to be reached by existing competitors about whether to spend the majority of the resources fighting to protect and fortify market positions that have already been established or whether to seek new development opportunities.

In some cases it is an original entrant who ploughs new territory—adjusting his approach to the emergent needs of the marketplace; in other cases it is a new entrant who, maybe basing his entry on expertise developed elsewhere, sees a strategic window and leapfrogs over the original market leader to take advantage of the new growth opportunity. Paradoxically, pioneering competitors who narrowly focus their activities in the early stages of growth may have the most difficulty in making the transition to new primary demand growth opportunities later. Emery Air Freight provides an example of a company that did face up to a challenge in such a situation.

**Emery Air Freight.**  This pioneer in the airfreight forwarding business developed many of the early applications of airfreight in the United States. In particular, Emery's efforts were focused on servicing the "emergency" segment of the market, which initially accounted for a substantial portion of all airfreight business. Emery served this market via an extensive organization of regional and district offices. Among Emery's major assets in this market were a unique nationwide, and later worldwide, communications network and the special competence of personnel located in the district offices in using scheduled carriers in the most efficient possible way to expedite deliveries.

As the market evolved, however, many new applications for airfreight emerged. These included regular planned shipments of high-value–low-weight merchandise, shipments of perishables, "off-line" service to hard-to-reach locations, and what became known as the TCC (total cost concept) market. Each of these new applications required a somewhat different approach than that demanded by the original emergency business.

TCC applications, for example, required detailed logistics planning to assess the savings and benefits to be obtained via lower inventories, quicker deliveries, and fewer lost sales through the use of airfreight. Customer decisions about whether or not to use airfreight required substantially more analysis than had been the case for emergency use; furthermore, decisions which had originally been made by traffic managers now involved marketing personnel and often top management.

A decision to seek this kind of business thus implied a radical change in Emery's organization—the addition of capability to analyze complex logistics systems and to deal with upper echelons of management.

## New competing technologies

When a fundamental change takes place in the basic technology of an industry, it again raises questions of the adaptability to new circumstances of existing firms using obsolete technology.

In many cases established competitors in an industry are challenged, not by another member of the same industry, but by a company which bases its approach on a technology developed outside that industry. Sometimes this results from forward integration of a firm that is eager to develop applications for a new component or raw material. Texas Instrument's entry into a wide variety of consumer electronic products from a base of semiconductor manufacture is a case in point. Sometimes it results from the application by firms of a technology developed in one market to opportunities in another. Or sometimes a breakthrough in either product or process technology may remove traditional barriers to entry in an industry and attract a completely new set of competitors. Consider the following examples:

Watchmakers have recently found that a new class of competitor is challenging their industry leadership—namely, electronic firms who are seeking end market applications for their semiconductors, as well as a new breed of assemblers manufacturing digital watches.

Manufacturers of mechanical adjustable speed drive equipment found their markets eroded by electrical speed drives in the early 1900s. Electrical drives were based on rotating motor-generator sets and electronic controls. In the late 1950s, the advent of solid-state electronics, in turn, virtually obsoleted rotating equipment. New independent competitors, basing their approach on the assembly of electronic components, joined the large electrical equipment manufacturers in the speed drive market. Today, yet another change is taking place, namely the advent of large computer-controlled drive systems. This is ushering yet another class of competitors into the market—namely, companies whose basic competence is in computers.

In each of these cases, recurrent waves of new technology fundamentally changed the nature of the market and usually ushered in an entirely new class of competitors. Many firms in most markets have a limited capability to master all the technologies which might ultimately cannibalize their business. The nature of technological innovation and diffusion is such that most *major* innovations will originate outside a particular industry and not within it.

In many cases the upheaval is not only technological; indeed, the nature of competition may also change dramatically as technology changes. The advent of solid-state electronics in the speed drive industry, for example, ushered in a number of small, low-overhead, independent assemblers who based their approach primarily on low price. Prior to that, the market had been dominated by the large electrical equipment manufacturers basing their approach largely on applications engineering coupled with high prices and high margins.

The strategic window concept does not preclude adaptation when it appears feasible, but rather suggests that certain firms may be better suited to compete in certain technological waves than in others. Often the cost and the difficulty of acquiring the new technology, as well as the sunk-cost commitment to the old, argue against adaptation.

## MARKET REDEFINITION

Frequently, as markets evolve, the fundamental definition of the market changes in ways which increasingly disqualify some competitors while providing opportunities for others. The trend toward marketing "systems" of products as opposed to individual pieces of equipment provides many examples of this phenomenon. The situation of Docutel illustrates this point.

**Docutel.** This manufacturer of automatic teller machines (ATMs) supplied virtually all the ATMs in use up to late 1974. In early 1975, Docutel found itself losing market share to large computer companies such as Burroughs, Honeywell, and IBM as these manufacturers began to look at the banks' total EFTS (electronic funds transfer system) needs. They offered the bank a package of equipment representing a complete system, of which the ATM was only one component. In essence, their success may be attributed to the fact that they redefined the market in a way which increasingly appeared to disqualify Docutel as a potential supplier.

Market redefinition is not limited to the banking industry; similar trends are under way in scientific instrumentation, process control equipment, the machine tool industry, office equipment, and electric control gear, to name but a few. In each case, manufacturers basing their approach on the marketing of individual hardware items are seeing their strategic window closing as computer systems producers move in to take advantage of emerging opportunities.

## CHANNEL CHANGES

Changes in the channels of distribution for both consumer and industrial goods can have far-reaching consequences for existing competitors and would-be entrants.

Changes take place in part because of product life cycle phenomena—the shift as the market matures to more intensive distribution, increasing convenience, and often lower levels of channel

service. Changes also frequently take place as a result of new institutional development in the channels themselves. Few sectors of American industry have changed as fast as retail and wholesale distribution, with the result that completely new types of outlets may be employed by suppliers seeking to develop competitive advantage.

Whatever the origin of the change, the effect may be to provide an opportunity for a new entrant and to raise questions about the viability of existing competitors. Gillette's contemplated entry into the blank cassette tape market is a case in point.

**Gillette.** As the market for cassettes evolved due to increased penetration and new uses of equipment for automotive, study, business, letter writing, and home entertainment, so did distribution channels broaden into an increasing number of drug chains, variety stores, and large discount stores.

Presumably it was recognition of a possible strategic window for Gillette that encouraged executives in the Safety Razor Division to look carefully at ways in which Gillette might exploit the cassette market at this particular stage in its evolution. The question was whether Gillette's skill in marketing low-priced, frequently purchased package goods, along with its distribution channel resources, could be applied to marketing blank cassettes. Was there a place for a competitor in this market to offer a quality, branded product, broadly distributed and supported by heavy media advertising in much the same way that Gillette marketed razor blades?

Actually, Gillette decided against entry, apparently not because a strategic window did not exist but because profit prospects were not favorable. They did, however, enter the cigarette lighter business based on similar analysis and reportedly have had considerable success with their Cricket brand.

## PROBLEMS AND OPPORTUNITIES

What do all these examples indicate? *First,* they suggest that the "resource requirements" for success in a business—whether these be financial requirements, marketing requirements, engineering requirements, or whatever—may change radically with market evolution. *Second,* they appear to suggest that, by contrast, the firm's resources and key competencies often cannot be so easily adjusted. The result is a *predictable* change in the fit of the firm to its market—leading to defined periods during which a strategic window exists and can be exploited.

The strategic window concept can be useful to incumbent competitors as well as to would-be entrants into a market. For the former, it provides a way of relating future strategic moves to market evolution and of assessing how resources should be allocated to existing activities. For the latter, it provides a framework for diversification and growth.

**Existing businesses**

Confronted with changes in the marketplace which potentially disqualify the firm from continued successful participation, several strategic options are available:

1. An attempt can be made to assemble the resources needed to close the gap between the new critical marketing requirements and the firm's competences.
2. The firm may shift its efforts to selected segments, where the "fit" between requirements and resources is still acceptable.
3. The firm may shift to a "low profile" approach—cutting back severely on all further allocation of capital and deliberately "milking" the business for short-run profit.
4. A decision may be taken to exit from that particular market either through liquidation or through sale.

All too frequently, however, because the strategic window phenomenon is not clearly recognized, these strategic choices are not clearly articulated. Instead, "old" approaches are continued long after the market has changed, with the result that market position is lost and financial losses pile up. Or often only halfhearted attempts are made to assemble the new resources required to compete effectively; or management is simply deluded into believing that it can adapt itself to the new situation even where this is actually out of the question.

The four basic strategic choices outlined above may be viewed hierarchically in terms of *resource commitment,* with No. 1 representing the highest level of commitment. Only the company itself can decide which position on the hierarchy it should adopt in particular situations, but the following guideline questions may be helpful:

To what extent do the changes call for skills and resources completely outside the traditional competence of the firm? A careful analysis has to be made of the gap which may emerge between the evolving requirements of the market and the firm's profile.

To what extent can the changes be anticipated? Often it is easier to adapt through a series of minor adjustments—a stepping-stone approach to change—than it is to be confronted with a major and unexpected discontinuity in approach.

How rapid are the changes which are taking place? Is there enough time to adjust without forfeiting a major share of the market which later may be difficult to regain?

How long will realignment of the functional activities of the firm take? Is the need limited to only some functions, or are all the basic resources of the firm affected—e.g., technology, engineering, manufacturing, marketing, sales, and organization policies?

What existing commitments—e.g., technical skills, distribution channels, manufacturing approaches—constrain adaptation?

Can the new resources and new approaches be developed internally, or must they be acquired?

Will the changes completely obsolete existing ways of doing business, or will there be a chance for coexistence? In the case of new technologies intruding from outside industry, the decision often has to be made to "join-em rather than fight-em." Not to do so is to risk complete obsolescence. In other cases, coexistence may be possible.

Are there segments of the market where the firm's existing resources can be effectively concentrated?

How large is the firm's stake in the business? To the extent that the business represents a major source of revenues and profit, a greater commitment will probably need to be made to adapt to the changing circumstances.

Will corporate management, in the event that this is a business unit within a multibusiness corporation, be willing to accept different goals for the business in the future than it has in the past? A decision not to adapt to changes may result in high short-run returns from that particular business. Looking at the problem from the position of corporate planners interested in the welfare of the total corporation, a periodic market-by-market analysis in the terms described above would appear to be imperative prior to setting goals, agreeing on strategies, and allocating resources.

### New entrants

The strategic window concept has been used implicitly by many new entrants to judge the direction, timing, and scale of new entry activities. Gillette's entry into cigarette lighters, major computer manufacturers' entry into ATMs, and Procter & Gamble's entry into many consumer markets *after* pioneers have laid the groundwork for a large-scale, mass-market approach to the specific product areas, all are familiar examples.

Such approaches to strategic market planning require two distinctly different types of analysis:

1. Careful assessment has to be made of the firm's strengths and weaknesses. This should include audits of all the key resources of the company as well as its various existing programs of activity.
2. Attention should be directed away from the narrow focus of familiar products and markets to a search for opportunities to put unique competencies to work. This requires a broader appreciation of overall environmental, technical, and market forces, and knowledge of many more markets than is encountered in many firms today. It puts a particular burden on marketing managers, general managers, and business planners used to thinking in terms of existing activities.

Analysis of patterns of market evolution and diagnosis of critical market requirements in the future can also be of use to incumbent competitors as a forewarning of potential new entry. In such cases, adjustments in strategy can sometimes be made in advance, which will ultimately deter would-be new competitors. Even where this is not the case, resource commitments may be adjusted to reflect the future changes in structure of industrial supply.

### CONCLUSION

The strategic window concept suggests that fundamental changes are needed in marketing management practice, and in particular in strategic market planning activities. At the heart of these changes is the need to base marketing planning around predictions of future patterns of market evolution and to make assessments of the firm's capabilities to deal with change. Such analyses require considerably greater strategic orientation than the sales forecasting activities which underpin much marketing planning today. Users of product portfolio chart analysis, in particular, should consider the dynamic as opposed to the static implications in designating a particular business.

Entry and exit from markets is likely to occur with greater rapidity than is often the case today, as firms search for opportunities where their resources can be deployed with maximum effectiveness. Short of entry and exit, the allocation of funds to markets should be timed to coincide with the period when the fit between the firm and the market is at its optimum. Entering a market in its early stages and evolving with it until maturity may, on closer analysis, turn out to be a serious management error.

It has been said that while the life of the product is limited, a market has greater longevity and as such can provide a business with a steady and growing stream of revenue and profit if management can avoid being myopic about change. This article suggests that as far as any one firm is concerned, a market also is a temporary vehicle for growth, a vehicle which should be used and abandoned as circumstances dictate—the reason being that the firm is often slower to evolve and change than is the market in which it competes.

## BIBLIOGRAPHY

1. Ben M. Enis, Raymond La Garce, and Arthur E. Prell, "Extending the Product Life Cycle," *Business Horizons,* June 1977, p. 46.

2. Nelson N. Foote, "Market Segmentation as a Competitive Strategy," presented at the Consumer Market Segmentation Conference, American Marketing Association, Chicago, February 1967.

3. The Product Portfolio, Boston Consulting Group Perspective; see also "A Note on the Boston Consulting Group Concept of Competitive Analysis and Corporate Strategy," Intercollegiate Case Clearing House no. 9–175–175; and George S. Day, "Diagnosing the Product Portfolio," *Journal of Marketing* 41, no. 2 (April 1977), p. 29.

4. See the following cases: Emery Air Freight Corporation (B), Gillette Safety Razor Division: The Blank Cassette Project, and Docutel Corporation, Intercollegiate Case Clearing House nos. 9–511–044, 9–574–058, and 9–578–073, respectively.

5. A. C. Cooper, E. DeMuzzio, K. Hatten, E. J. Hicks, and D. Tock, "Strategic Responses to Technological Threats," *Proceedings of the Business Policy and Planning Division of the Academy of Management* (Boston: Academy of Management, 1974).

6. Derek F. Abell, "Competitive Market Strategies: Some Generalizations and Hypotheses," Marketing Science Institute, report no. 75–107, April 1975.

7. Derek F. Abell, "Business Definition as an Element of the Strategic Decision," presented at the American Marketing Association/Marketing Science Institute Conference on Product and Market Planning, Pittsburgh, November 1977.

8. William E. Rothschild, *Putting It All Together: A Guide to Strategic Thinking* (New York: AMACOM, 1976), pp. 103–21.

9. Theodore Levitt, "Marketing Myopia," *Harvard Business Review,* September–October 1975, p. 26.

## QUESTIONS

1. *Explain what is meant by the term "strategic window." Does it have any real value to a marketing manager? Explain.*

2. *How can a firm protect itself against problems in current markets—and at the same time not miss opportunities in new markets?*

3. *Discuss four strategic options available to existing businesses that are being "closed out" by changes in the marketplace.*

*4. *What are the differences between Abell's ideas and Levitt's (Reading 5)? What are the similarities?*

*Question relates concepts in this and other readings.

☐ 7

# Sustainable competitive advantage—what it is, what it isn't

*Kevin P. Coyne*

*To achieve a competitive advantage in the marketplace is a goal of every firm. But as Coyne points out, not every competitive advantage is strategically significant or sustainable over time. Nor does having a competitive advantage guarantee a successful business strategy. This article explains how to recognize and achieve a sustainable competitive advantage. It also discusses the strategic implications of having such an advantage—or of having to compete with another firm that has an advantage over your firm.*

I shall not today attempt to define the kinds of material to be embraced within that shorthand description; and perhaps I could never succeed in intelligibly doing so. But I know it when I see it.

Supreme Court Justice Potter Stewart
*(Jacobellis v. State of Ohio)*

Although it was pornography, not sustainable competitive advantage, that the late Justice Stewart doubted his ability to define, his remark neatly characterizes the current state of thinking about the latter subject as well. Explicitly or implicitly, sustainable competitive advantage (SCA) has long occupied a central place in strategic thinking. Witness the widely accepted definition of competitive strategy as "an integrated set of actions that produce a sustainable advantage over competitors."[1] But exactly what constitutes sustainable competitive advantage is a question rarely asked. Most corporate strategists are content to apply Justice Stewart's test; they know an SCA when they see it—or so they assume.

But perhaps an SCA is not always so easy to identify. In developing its liquid hand soap, Minnetonka, Inc., focused its efforts on building an advantage that was easily copied later. In the wristwatch market, Texas Instruments attempted to exploit an advantage over its competitors that turned out to be unimportant to target consumers. RCA built barriers to competition in the vacuum tube market in the 1950s only to find these barriers irrelevant when transistors and semiconductors were born. CB radio producers built capacity to fill a demand that later evaporated. In each case, the companies failed to see in advance that, for one reason or another, they lacked a sustainable competitive advantage.

Perhaps it is because the meaning of "sustainable competitive advantage" is superficially self-evident that virtually no effort has been made to define it explicitly. After all, it can be argued that the dictionary's definitions of the three words bring forth the heart of the concept. But every strategist needs to discover whether an SCA is actually or potentially present, and if so, what its implications are for competitive and business strategy.

---

[1] "Competitive strategy," as the term is used in this article, is exclusively concerned with defeating competitors and achieving dominance in a product/market segment. It is thus—in concept, and usually in practice—a subset of business strategy, which addresses the broader goal of maximizing the wealth of shareholders.

Source: Reprinted from *Business Horizons,* January–February 1986, pp. 54–61. Copyright © 1986 by the Foundation for the School of Business at Indiana University. Reprinted by permission. At the time of writing, Kevin P. Coyne was an associate in McKinsey & Company's Washington, D.C., office.

Therefore, this article will describe a number of established strategic concepts and build on them to develop a clear and explicit concept of SCA.

Specifically, we will examine:

**The conditions for SCA.** When does a producer have a competitive advantage? How can the strategist test whether such an advantage is sustainable?

**Some implications of SCA for strategy.** Does having SCA guarantee success? Can a producer succeed without an SCA? Should a producer always pursue an SCA?

## CONDITIONS FOR SCA

Any producer who sells his goods or services at a profit undeniably enjoys a competitive advantage with those customers who choose to buy from him instead of his competitors, though these competitors may be superior in size, strength, product quality, or distribution power. Some advantages, however, are obviously worth more than others. A competitive advantage is meaningful in strategy only when three distinct conditions are met:

1. Customers perceive a consistent difference in important attributes between the producer's product or service and those of his competitors.
2. That difference is the direct consequence of a capability gap between the producer and his competitors.
3. Both the difference in important attributes and the capability gap can be expected to endure over time.

In earlier strategy work, these conditions have been jointly embedded in the concepts of "key factors for success" (KFS), "degrees of freedom," and "lower costs or higher value to the customer." In the interest of clarity, however, they deserve separate consideration.

## DIFFERENTIATION IN IMPORTANT ATTRIBUTES

Obviously, competitive advantage results from differentiation among competitors—but not just any differentiation. For a producer to enjoy a competitive advantage in a product/market segment, the difference or differences between him and his competitors must be felt in the marketplace: that is, they must be reflected in some *product/delivery attribute* that is a *key buying criterion* for the market. And the product must be differentiated enough to win the loyalty of a significant set of buyers; it must have a *footprint in the market*.

### Product/delivery attribute

Customers rarely base their choice of a product or service on internal characteristics of the producer that are not reflected in a perceived product or delivery difference. Indeed, they usually neither know nor care about those characteristics. Almost invariably, the most important contact between the customer and the producer is the marketplace—the "strategic triangle" where the producer meets his customers and competitors. It is here that the competitive contest for the scarce resource, the sales dollar, is directly engaged.

Just as differences among animal species that are unrelated to scarce resources do not contribute to the survival of the fittest, so producer differences that do not affect the market do not influence the competitive process. Differences among competitors in plant locations, raw material choices, labor policies, and the like matter only when and if those differences translate into product/delivery attributes that influence the customers' choice of where to spend their sales dollars.

"Product/delivery attributes" include not only such familiar elements as price, quality, aesthetics, and functionality, but also broader attributes such as availability, consumer awareness, visibility, and after-sales service. Anything that affects customers' perceptions of the product or service, its usefulness to them, and their access to it is a product/delivery attribute. Anything that does not affect these perceptions is not.

Having lower costs, for example, may well result in significantly higher margins. But this *business* advantage will become a *competitive* advantage only if and when the producer directly or indirectly recycles the additional profits into product/delivery attributes such as price, product quality, advertising, or additional capacity that increases availability. Only then is the producer's competitive position enhanced. Two examples illustrate this point.

For years, the "excess" profits of a major packaged goods company—the low-cost producer in its industry—have been siphoned off by its corporate parent for reinvestment in other subsidiaries. The packaged goods subsidiary has therefore been no more able to take initiatives or respond to competitive threats than if it did not produce those excess profits. Thus, business advantage may exist, but competitive advantage is lacking. If risk-adjusted returns available from investments in other business exceed those of additional investment in the packaged goods subsidiary, the corporate parent may be making the best business decisions. However, the packaged goods subsidiary has gained no competitive advantage from its superior position.

The corporate parent of a newly acquired, relatively high-cost producer in an industrial products market has decided to aggressively expand its subsidiary. This expansion is potentially at the expense of the current market leader, an independent company occupying the low-cost position in the industry. The resources that the new parent is willing to invest are far larger than the incremental profits generated by the market leader's lower costs. Because the new subsidiary can invest more than the market leader in product design, product quality, distribution, and so forth, it is the subsidiary that has, or soon will have, the competitive advantage.

In short, it is the application, not just the generation, of greater resources that is required for *competitive* advantage.

## Key buying criterion

Every product has numerous attributes that competitors can use to differentiate themselves to gain some degree of advantage. To be strategically significant, however, an advantage must be based on positive differentiation of an attribute that is a *key buying criterion* for a particular market segment and is not offset by a negative differentiation in any other key buying criterion. In the end, competitive advantage is the result of all net differences in important product/delivery attributes, not just one factor such as price or quality. Differ-

ences in other, less important attributes may be helpful at the margin, but they are not strategically significant.

Key buying criteria vary, of course, by industry and even by market segment. In fact, because market segments differ in their choice of key buying criteria, a particular product may have a competitive advantage in some segments while being at a disadvantage in others. Price aside, the elaborate technical features that professional photographers prize in Hasselblad cameras would baffle and discourage most of the casual users who make up the mass market.

In any one product/market segment, however, only a very few criteria are likely to be important enough to serve as the basis for a meaningful competitive advantage. These criteria are likely to be basic—that is, central to the concept of the product or service itself, as opposed to "add-ons" or "features." For example, in the tubular steel industry, there are just two key product/delivery attributes: a single measure of quality (third-party testing reject rate), and local availability on the day required by the customer's drilling schedule.

Texas Instruments (TI) apparently did not fully understand the importance of differentiation along key buying criteria when it entered the wristwatch market. Its strategy was to build upon its ability to drive down costs—and therefore prices (the product attribute)—beyond the point where competitors could respond. But this competitive strategy, which had worked in electronic components, failed in wristwatches because price, past a certain point, was no longer a key buying criterion: customers cared more about aesthetics. TI had surpassed all of its competitors in an attribute that did not matter in the marketplace.

## "Footprint in the market"

To contribute to an SCA, the differences in product/delivery attributes must command the attention and loyalty of a substantial customer base; in other words, they must produce a "footprint in the market" of significant breadth and depth.

**Breadth.**   How many customers are attracted to the product above all others by the difference in product attributes? What volume do these customers purchase?

**Depth.** How strong a preference has this difference generated? Would minor changes in the balance of attributes cause the customers to switch?

Breadth and depth are usually associated in marketing circles with the concept of "branding." Branding can indeed be a source of competitive advantage, as shown by Perrier's spectacular advantage in a commodity as prosaic as bottled mineral water.

But the importance of breadth and depth are not limited to branding strategies. Even a producer who is pursuing a low-price strategy must ensure that his lower price will cause customers to choose his product and that changes in non-price attributes by competitors would be unlikely to lure them away.

## DURABLE DIFFERENTIATION

Positive differentiation in key product/delivery attributes is essential to competitive advantage. However, a differentiation that can be readily erased does not by itself confer a meaningful advantage. Competitive advantages described in such terms as "faster delivery" or "superior product quality" are illusory if competitors can erase the differentiation at will.

For example, Minnetonka, Inc., created a new market niche with "Softsoap." As a result, its stock price more than doubled. Before long, however, 50 different brands of liquid soap, some selling for a fifth of Softsoap's price, appeared on the market. As a result, Minnetonka saw its earnings fall to zero and its stock price decline by 75 percent.

An advantage is durable only if competitors cannot readily imitate the producer's superior product/delivery attributes. In other words, a gap in the *capability* underlying the differentiation must separate the producer from his competitors; otherwise no meaningful competitive advantage exists. (Conversely, of course, no meaningful advantage can arise from a capability gap that does not produce an important difference in produce/delivery attributes.)

Understanding the capability gap, then, is basic to determining whether a competitive advantage actually exists. For example, an attribute such as faster delivery does not constitute a real competitive advantage unless it is based on a capability gap such as may exist if the company has a much bigger truck fleet than its competitors can afford to maintain. Higher product quality does not in itself constitute a competitive advantage. But unique access to intrinsically superior raw materials that enable the producer to deliver a better-quality product may well do so.

A capability gap exists when the function responsible for the differentiated product/delivery attribute is one that only the producer in question can perform, or one that competitors (given their particular limitations) could do only with maximum effort. So defined, capability gaps fall into four categories.

**Business system gaps** result from the ability to perform individual functions more effectively than competitors and from the inability of competitors to easily follow suit. For example, differences in labor-union work rules can constitute a capability gap resulting in superior production capability. Superior engineering or technical skills may create a capability gap leading to greater precision or reliability in the finished product.

**Position gaps** result from prior decisions, actions, and circumstances. Reputation, consumer awareness and trust, and order backlogs, which can represent important capability gaps, are often the legacy of an earlier management generation. Thus, current competitive advantage may be the consequence of a past facilities location decision. BHP, the large Australian steel maker, enjoys important production efficiencies because it is the only producer to have located its smelter adjacent to its iron ore source, eliminating expensive iron ore transportation costs.

**Regulatory/legal gaps** result from government's limiting the competitors who can perform certain activities, or the degree to which they can perform those activities. Patents, operating licenses, import quotas, and consumer safety laws can all open important capability gaps among competitors. For example, Ciba-Giegy's patent on a low-cost herbicide allowed it to dominate certain segments of the agricultural chemical market for years.

**Organization or managerial quality gaps** result from an organization's ability consistently to innovate and adapt more quickly and effectively than its competitors. For example, in industries like computers or financial services, where the competitive environment is shifting rapidly, this flexibility may be the single most important capability gap. In other industries, the key capability gap may be an ability to out-innovate competitors, keeping them always on the defensive.

Note that only the first category, business system gaps, covers actions that are currently under the control of the producer. Frustrating as it may be to the strategist, competitive advantage or disadvantage is often the result of factors he or she is in no position to alter in the short term.

The broad concept of a capability gap becomes useful only when we succeed in closely specifying a producer's *actual* capability gap over competitors in a *particular* situation. Analysts can detect the existence of a capability gap by examining broad functions in the business system, but they must then go further and determine the root cause of superior performance in that function.

Individual capability gaps between competitors are very specific. There must be a precise reason why one producer can outperform another, or there is no competitive advantage. The capability gap consists of specific, often physical, differences. It is likely to be prosaic and measurable, not intangible. Abstract terms, such as "higher labor productivity" or "technological leadership," often serve as useful shorthand, but they are too general for precise analysis. Moreover, they implicitly equate capability gaps with marginal performance superiority, rather than with discrete differences—such as specific work rule differences or technical resources capacity—that are not easily imitated.

For example, if marginal performance superiority constituted competitive advantage, one would expect "focus" competitors—those who have no capability advantage but excel in serving a particular niche through sheer concentration of effort—to win out over more general competitors who decide to invade that niche. But as American Motors learned when Detroit's "Big Three" began producing small cars, and as some regional banks are learning as money center banks enter their markets, "trying harder" is no substitute for the possession of unique capabilities.

Only by understanding specific differences in capability can the strategist accurately determine

and measure the actions that competitors must take to eliminate the gap and the obstacles and costs to them of doing so.

## LASTING ADVANTAGE (SUSTAINABILITY)

If a meaningful advantage is a function of a positive difference in important attributes based on an underlying capability gap, then the sustainability of the competitive advantage is simply a function of the durability of both the attributes and the gap.

There is not much value in an advantage in product/delivery attributes that do not retain their importance over time. Manufacturers of CB radios, video games, and designer jeans saw their revenues decline and their financial losses mount not because their competitors did anything to erode their capability advantages, but because most of their customers simply no longer valued those products enough to pay the price. In each case, industry participants believed that they had benefited from a permanent shift in consumer preferences and began to invest accordingly. In each case they were wrong.

Whether consumers will continue to demand a product over time, and how they can be influenced to prefer certain product attributes over time, are essentially marketing issues, subject to normal marketing analytical techniques. How basic is the customer need that the product meets? How central to its function or availability is the attribute in each question? These may be the key questions to ask in this connection.

The sustainability of competitive advantage is also a function of the durability of the capability gap that created the attractive attribute. In fact, the most important condition for sustainability is that existing and potential competitors either cannot or will not take the actions required to close the gap. It competitors can and will fill the gap, the advantage is by definition not sustainable.

Obviously, a capability gap that competitors are unable to close is preferable to one that relies on some restraint. Unfortunately, a producer cannot choose whether a particular capability gap meets the former or the latter condition.

Consider the two cases more closely.

## Case 1: Competitors cannot fill the gap

This situation occurs when the capability itself is protected by specific entry and mobility barriers such as an important product patent or unique access to a key raw material (for example, DeBeer's Consolidated Mines). In a Case 1 situation, sustainability is assured at least until the barrier is eroded or eliminated (converting the situation to Case 2). Barriers can erode or be eliminated over time, unless they are inherent in the nature of the business.[2]

A more significant danger to Case 1 advantages, however, probably lies not in the gradual erosion of barriers, but in the possibility that competitors may leapfrog the barriers by a new game strategy.

For example, the introduction of the transistor in 1955 did nothing to erode the barriers that RCA had created in vacuum tubes; it simply made RCA's leadership irrelevant. Therefore, although sustainability can be estimated by (1) considering all the changes (environmental forces or competitor actions) that could erode the barriers, and (2) assessing the probabilities of their occurrence over a specified time horizon, there will, of course, always be uncertainty in the estimate.

## Case 2: Competitors could close the capability gap but refrain from doing so

This situation might occur for any one of four reasons.

**1. Inadequate potential.** A simple calculation may show competitors that the costs of closing the gap would exceed the benefits, even if the possessor of the advantage did not retaliate.

For example, the danger of cannibalizing existing products may preclude effective response. MCI, Sprint, and others were able to create the low-price segment of the U.S. long-distance telephone market largely because AT&T did not choose to respond directly for some time. Most

likely it considered that the cost of cutting prices for 100 percent of its customers in order to retain the 1 to 2 percent in the low-price segment was simply too high, and that only when the segment grew to sufficient size would a response become worthwhile.

Other examples of situations where a payoff is not worth the required investment include investing in capacity to achieve "economies of scale" when the capacity required to achieve the required economy exceeds the likely additional demand in the industry; and labor work rules, where the additional compensation demanded by the union in return for such changes would more than offset the potential savings.

The inadequate-potential situation represents a sustainable advantage because the "end game" has already been reached: there are no rational strategic countermoves for competitors to take until conditions change.

**2. Corresponding disadvantage.** Competitors may believe that acting to close the capability gap will open gaps elsewhere (in this or other market segments) that will more than offset the value of closing this one.

For example, a "niche" competitor often relies on this factor to protect him against larger competitors, who (or so he hopes) will reckon that an effective attack on his niche advantage would divert resources (including management time) needed elsewhere, destroy the integrity of their own broader product lines (opening gaps in other segments), or create some other gap.

A "corresponding disadvantage" situation constitutes at least a temporarily sustainable advantage, because for the moment an "end game" has been reached. However, as the attractiveness of competitors' other markets changes, so does their estimate of whether a corresponding disadvantage is present in the niche (as American Motors learned to its cost). In addition, competitors will always be searching for ways to fill the capability gap without creating offsetting gaps. Only if the creation of offsetting gaps is an automatic and inevitable consequence of any such action will the producer's advantage be assured of sustainability in the long run.

**3. Fear of reprisal.** Even though it initially would appear worth doing so, competitors may re-

---

[2] For example, if the business is a "natural monopoly." A natural monopoly exists where either (1) economies of scale cause marginal costs to decline past the point where production volume equals market demand (that is, where the most efficient economic system is to have only one producer); or (2) the social costs of installing duplicate production/distribution systems outweigh the benefits, a situation usually leading to the establishment of a legal monopoly by government fiat.

frain from filling the capability gap for fear of retaliatory action by the producer. The sustainability of the producer's existing advantage depends, in this case, on the competitors' continuing to exercise voluntary restraint, accepting in effect the producer's position in this market segment.

For example, Japanese steel makers voluntarily refrain from increasing their U.S. market share for fear that American producers can and will persuade the U.S. government to take harsh protectionist measures.

"Fear of reprisal" is probably among the most common strategic situations in business, but it must be considered unstable over time, as competitors' situations and managements shift.

**4. Management inertia.**  Finally, there are cases where competitors would benefit from closing the capability gap but fail to do so, either because management has incorrectly assessed the situation or because it lacks the will, the ability, or the energy to take the required action.

For example, Honda's success in dominating the British motorcycle industry is generally attributed to Norton Villiers Triumph's failure to respond to a clear competitive threat until too late.

Psychologists tell us that managers will implement real change only when their discomfort with the status quo exceeds the perceived personal cost of taking the indicated action. This may well explain why competitors often tolerate a performance gap that they could profitably act to close. But it is risky for a producer to rely for long on the weakness or inertia of competitors' management to protect a competitive advantage; by definition the end game has not been reached.

In all four cases, how long competitors will tolerate capability gaps they are capable of closing depends largely on the relationship between the value of the advantage created by the gap and the cost (to each competitor) of closing it. The worse the cost-to-benefit ratio, the longer the advantage is likely to be sustainable, because greater changes in the environment are required before value would exceed cost. Coupled with an informed view of the rate of environmental change in the industry, this ratio thus allows the analyst to estimate sustainability.

## SCA AND STRATEGY

The classic definition of competitive strategy as "an integrated set of actions designed to create a sustainable advantage over competitors" might suggest that possessing an SCA is synonymous with business success—that those producers who have an SCA are guaranteed winners, and that those competitors who lack one should simply exit the business to avoid financial disaster.

This apparently reasonable conclusion is, however, incorrect. Although an SCA is a powerful tool in creating a successful business strategy, it is not the only key ingredient. In fact:

- Possessing an SCA does not guarantee financial success.
- Producers can succeed even when competitors possess an SCA.
- Pursuing an SCA can sometimes conflict with sound business strategy.

### Losing with an SCA

Although an SCA will help a producer to achieve, over time, higher returns than his competitors, there are at least three circumstances where its possessor can fail financially:

**1. If the market sector is not viable.**  In many cases (including most new-product introductions), the minimum achievable cost of producing and selling a particular product or service exceeds its value to the customer. In this situation, an SCA will not guarantee the survival of its possessor; it will tend merely to ensure that his competitors will fare even worse.

**2. If the producer has severe operational problems.**  An SCA can allow management the luxury of focusing more fully on achieving operational excellence, but thousands of companies have failed for operational, rather than strategic, reasons.

**3. If competitors inflict tactical damage.**  An SCA rarely puts a producer completely beyond the reach of competitor actions such as price cuts and "buying" market share, which may be unrelated to the SCA itself. A producer will be particularly vulnerable to such competitive tactics if the SCA is not very important, either because the depth of the "footprint" described earlier is shallow or because the gap in capability is minor.

In these cases, producers must select their actions very carefully. Actions that can and will be imitated may result only in intensified competitive rivalry. And, where the producer's advantage is unimportant, he will have little cushion against the competitive repercussions. For example, recent airline pricing policies and "frequent flyer" programs have done nothing to contribute to the long-term profitability or competitive positions of their originators. Unimaginative direct cost-reduction efforts (cutting overhead or staffs, for example) may improve profitability in the short term. But if competitors can and will imitate these efforts, the only long-run effect may be to raise the general level of misery throughout the industry.

## Competing against an SCA

By definition, not all producers can possess an SCA in a given product/market segment. Other competitors face the prospects of competing (at least for some time) from a handicapped position. Under certain circumstances, however, it is still possible for some to succeed.

Rapidly growing markets constitute one such situation. As long as real market growth over a given period exceeds the additional capacity advantaged competitors can bring on line during that time (due to organizational constraints, risk aversion, and so forth), even weak competitors can thrive. For example, the booming market for microcomputer software over the past five years has enabled many weak competitors to grow rich. Only when market growth slows or the advantaged competitors increase the rate at which they can grow will true competition begin and the impact of an SCA make itself felt.

In markets where true competition for scarce sales dollars is taking place, the number of disadvantaged competitors who can succeed, the degree to which they can prosper, and the conditions under which they can prosper will vary, depending on the value of the advantage held by the "number-one" competitor.

*If the number-one competitor has only a shallow or unimportant advantage,* many disadvantaged competitors can prosper for long periods. As noted earlier, each competitor is unique. When all attributes are considered, each will have a competitive advantage in serving some customers. The disadvantaged competitors are more likely to receive lower returns than the number-one producer, but they certainly may be viable.

*If the number-one competitor has an important advantage* in a given product/market segment, some theorists assert that over the long run there will be only one viable competitor. Others may remain in the segment, but they will be plagued by losses and/or very inadequate returns. If there are six different ways to achieve a major advantage, this reasoning runs, then the market will split into six segments, each ruled by a different competitor, who uniquely excels in the attribute most valued by the customers in that segment.

Be that as it may, in practice other strong competitors may also profitably exist alongside Number One under two conditions:

1. *If the number-one producer's advantage is limited by a finite capacity* that is significantly less than the size of the market; that is, he may expand further, but will not retain his advantage on the incremental capacity. Obstacles to continued advantaged expansion are common: limited access to superior raw materials, finite capacity in low-cost plants, prohibitive transportation costs beyond certain distances. Antitrust laws also tend to act as barriers to expansion beyond a certain level by number-one competitors.

2. *If the size of the individual competitors is small* relative to the size of the market. In this case, a number of strong competitors can expand for many years without directly competing with each other, by taking share from weak competitors rather than each other.

Weak competitors, of course, are likely to fare badly when competition is intense and the depth of the advantage enjoyed by others is great. Their choices are:

1.  To leave the business;
2.  To endure the situation until the advantage is eroded; or
3.  To seek to create a new advantage.

If a weak competitor chooses to pursue a new advantage, then he must ensure that it will be preemptive, or that competitors will not notice his move and will fail to respond until he has consolidated his position. Otherwise, his action is virtually certain to be copied and the intended advantage erased.

### Pursuing the wrong SCA

Although its attainment is the goal of *competitive* strategy, sustainable competitive advantage is not an end in itself but a means to an end. The corporation is not in business to beat its competitors, but to create wealth for its shareholders. Thus, actions that contribute to SCA but detract from creating shareholder wealth may be good strategy in the competitive sense but bad strategy for the corporation. Consider two examples.

**Low-cost capacity additions in the absence of increased industry demand.** Adding low-cost capacity and recycling the additional profits into product/delivery attributes that attract enough customers to fill that capacity is usually a sound business strategy. However, as industry cost curve analysis has demonstrated, if the capacity addition is not accompanied by increases in industry demand, the effect may well be to displace the high-cost, but previously viable, marginal producer. When this happens, prices in the industry will fall to the level of the costs of the new marginal producer, costs which by definition are lower than the costs of the former marginal producer. Thus, the profit per unit sold of all participants will be reduced.

Depending on the cost structure of the industry, the declines in the profit per unit sold can be dramatic (for example, if all the remaining producers have similar costs). In this case, even the producer who added the new capacity will face declining profitability on his pre-existing capacity; in extreme cases his total profit on new and old capacity may fall below the profit he had previously earned on the old capacity alone. While gaining share and eliminating a competitor (good competitive strategy), he has invested *more* to profit *less* (bad business strategy).

**Aggressive learning-curve pricing strategies that sacrifice too much current profit.** Under these strategies, prices are reduced at least as fast as costs in order to buy market share and drive out competitors. The assumption is that the future payoff from market dominance will more than offset the costs of acquiring it. The value of

new business, however, is likely to be very sensitive to the precise relationship between prices and costs. This is true particularly in the early stages of the learning curve, when the absolute levels of prices, costs, and margins are relatively high and the profit consequences are therefore greater for any given volume. Especially in high-tech industries such as electronics, where the lifetime of technologies is short, the long-term value of the market share bought by overly aggressive learning-curve strategies can be less than the profit eliminated in the early stages by pricing too close to costs.

The framework for SCA proposed in this article is far from complete. Its treatment of product/delivery attributes and capability gaps (notably organizational strength) is impressionistic rather than detailed. It leaves other aspects of the topic (for example, the sustainability of competitive advantage at the corporate level) unexplored.

But a major concern of the business unit strategist is to determine whether the enterprise (or a competitor's) possesses or is in a position to capture an SCA, and, if so, to examine its strategic implications. The conditions for SCA and the implications of SCA for strategy that have been proposed provide an initial framework for these tasks.

### QUESTIONS

1. *What is a sustainable competitive advantage? What conditions must be met for such a strategy to be strategically meaningful?*

2. *By what methods can a firm achieve a sustainable competitive advantage? Which methods are preferable? Why? How does this relate to the notion of "capability gaps"?*

3. *Why doesn't having a sustainable competitive advantage guarantee that a firm will have a successful business strategy?*

4. *How should a firm compete with a competitor that enjoys a sustainable competitive advantage? Is the situation hopeless? Explain your answer.*

*5. *Explain how the concept of a sustainable competitive advantage relates to the concept of a "strategic window" (Reading 6).*

---

*Question relates concepts in this and other readings.

## □ 8

# Information power: How companies are using new technologies to gain a competitive edge

*Catherine L. Harris*

*Computers are becoming extremely important in modern business. Not only is the number of computers in use growing dramatically, but even more importantly, a change in "mind-set" is taking place. Firms are perceiving information technology as a new way to achieve a competitive advantage in the marketplace and thus are seeking innovative ways to use computers to improve their production and marketing efforts. This article explains and illustrates how computers—together with telecommunications and video technology—are now being used to perform marketing and other business functions in creative new ways. As you read the article, note especially how information technology is changing the way that companies relate to their customers and suppliers.*

For all the talk about the Information Age, most computers are still just workhorses—churning out payrolls, reports, numerical analyses. But slowly, stealthily, companies are turning their machines into a lot more.

No longer handmaidens to the back office, office automation and data processing are fast becoming indispensable allies in marketing, customer service, product development, human resource management, strategic planning, and many other jobs. "The diffusion of technology is changing the way we do business and the way companies relate to customers and suppliers," says James I. Cash Jr., a Harvard business school professor. "This is no longer a technological phenomenon but a social one."

### FRESH MIND-SET

In part, the change simply reflects the proliferation of computers. But there's more to it than that. Information technologies are reaching a critical mass. Business is beginning to reconfigure things from the ground up—this time with the computer in mind. The result: entirely different approaches to existing markets and whole new product lines that didn't seem a logical extension of the business before. Retailer J. C. Penney now processes credit card transactions for Shell Oil and Gulf Refining & Marketing as a way to leverage its investment in its information network. Who would have foreseen such relationships 10 years ago?

At the same time, computers, telecommunications, and video technology are merging into something bigger and better than the individual components. What is a telecommunications system these days without a computer? As the technologies become more entwined, the potentials of each suddenly multiply. And as they become part of everyday life, more people are perceiving new ways to use them. What becomes essential is a fresh mind-set, a new way of perceiving the role of information technology in business.

The ability to use computers and telecommunications creatively to collect, make sense of, and distribute information is already spelling the difference between success and mediocrity in indus-

Source: Reprinted from the October 14, 1985, issue of *Business Week* by special permission, © 1985 by McGraw-Hill, Inc. At the time of writing, Catherine L. Harris was on the staff of *Business Week*.

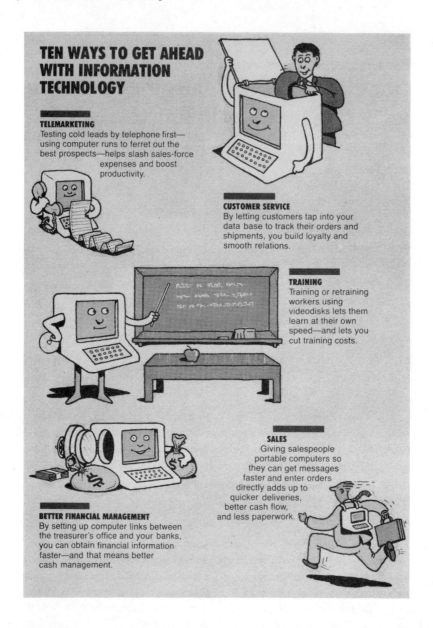

## TEN WAYS TO GET AHEAD WITH INFORMATION TECHNOLOGY

**TELEMARKETING**
Testing cold leads by telephone first—using computer runs to ferret out the best prospects—helps slash sales-force expenses and boost productivity.

**CUSTOMER SERVICE**
By letting customers tap into your data base to track their orders and shipments, you build loyalty and smooth relations.

**TRAINING**
Training or retraining workers using videodisks lets them learn at their own speed—and lets you cut training costs.

**SALES**
Giving salespeople portable computers so they can get messages faster and enter orders directly adds up to quicker deliveries, better cash flow, and less paperwork.

**BETTER FINANCIAL MANAGEMENT**
By setting up computer links between the treasurer's office and your banks, you can obtain financial information faster—and that means better cash management.

tries ranging from banking to bicycle making, at companies as large as General Motors Corp. and as small as automobile body shops. "The difference between now and five years ago is that then technology had limited function. You weren't betting your company on it," says William H. Gruber, president of Research & Planning Inc., a Cambridge (Mass.) consulting firm. "Now you are."

How so? Consider three classic cases, mythologized in Harvard business school case studies and preached with evangelical fervor by a growing cadre of information management experts:

**Merrill Lynch & Co.** used computers to create one of its most successful new products ever: the Cash Management Account. By combining information on a customer's checking, savings, credit card, and securities accounts into one computerized monthly statement and automatically "sweeping" idle funds into interest-bearing money market funds, Merrill Lynch has lured billions of dollars of assets from other places since it introduced CMA in 1978. It now manages $85 billion. And though rivals eventually concocted similar offerings, it still has almost 70 percent of the market.

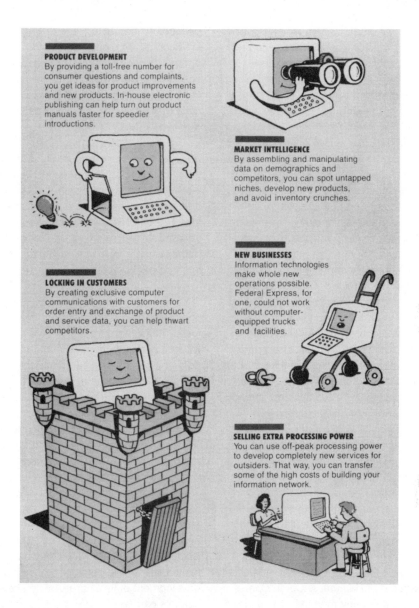

**PRODUCT DEVELOPMENT**
By providing a toll-free number for consumer questions and complaints, you get ideas for product improvements and new products. In-house electronic publishing can help turn out product manuals faster for speedier introductions.

**MARKET INTELLIGENCE**
By assembling and manipulating data on demographics and competitors, you can spot untapped niches, develop new products, and avoid inventory crunches.

**LOCKING IN CUSTOMERS**
By creating exclusive computer communications with customers for order entry and exchange of product and service data, you can help thwart competitors.

**NEW BUSINESSES**
Information technologies make whole new operations possible. Federal Express, for one, could not work without computer-equipped trucks and facilities.

**SELLING EXTRA PROCESSING POWER**
You can use off-peak processing power to develop completely new services for outsiders. That way, you can transfer some of the high costs of building your information network.

**American Hospital Supply Corp.,** which distributes products from 8,500 manufacturers to more than 100,000 health-care providers, saw its market share soar in the 1970s after it set up computer links to its customers and suppliers. Hospitals could enter orders themselves via AHS terminals. The technology let the company cut inventories, improve customer service, and get better terms from suppliers for higher volumes. Even more important, it often locked out rival distributors that didn't have direct pipelines to hospitals. Now, AHS, which agreed to be acquired by Baxter Travenol Laboratories Inc. in July, stays ahead of competitors by analyzing the industry data it collects to spot order trends and customer needs more quickly.

**American Airlines Inc.** has used computer and communications technology to build an entirely new business with sky-high profit margins. American provides its Sabre reservation system, which lists the flight schedules of every major airline in the world, to 48 percent of the approximately 24,000 automated travel agents in the U.S. They pay American $1.75 for every reservation made via Sabre for other carriers. American's parent, AMR Corp., which earned $400 million pretax last year on $5.3 billion in revenues, expects Sabre alone to earn it $170 million before taxes this year on $338 million in revenues. "We are now in the data processing as well as the airline business," says President Robert L. Crandall, a data processing expert who conceived Sabre a decade ago, when he was American's marketing chief.

Such success stories have sent companies in every industry scrambling to find ways to harness the power of information technology—from computers and telephones to communications satellites and videodisks.

As the use of information technology escalates, every industry will be affected, and businesses that stay out of the fray will suffer. But upstaging a rival today is no guarantee of superiority tomorrow. Often competitors respond in kind, bringing the situation back to parity. The aggressor must keep innovating to maintain its edge. Five months after American started installing Sabre, United Airlines began delivering its Apollo system, and now Eastern, Delta, and TWA have systems, too.

Often the biggest beneficiary of such competitive thrusts is the customer, who gets a cheaper air fare, faster service, or a new product. When banks began offering computer linkups between themselves and corporate treasurers in the early 1980s, companies were able to determine earlier how much cash was in their accounts—and thus to manage it better. "Bankers used to live by the '3-5-3 rule': Borrow at 3 percent, lend at 5 percent, play golf at 3 P.M.," says consultant Michael Hammer, president of Hammer & Co. in Cambridge, Mass. "But not any more. Now treasurers are managing much more actively, and I think one of the reasons behind many banks' problems is they don't have a lot of the float from corporate accounts."

## HUNGRY FOR MORE

Although most companies may not have thought of information as a competitive weapon, for years they have been putting in place the infrastructure needed to make it one. In the past decade, according to Harry F. Bunn, senior vice-president at PA Consulting Services Inc., a management consultant in Princeton, N.J., corporate spending on information processing gear has gone up an average of 16 percent a year, and raw computer power for crunching data faster has increased 18-fold.

But using technology to gain a competitive edge has gotten its biggest boost from the personal computer. Until the early 1980s, computers were the preserve of distant data processing managers who spoke a different language than managers. Data processing shops had months or years of backlogged requests for programming, so management rarely took advantage of data locked in corporate computers.

Now, though, managers can manipulate data themselves on personal computers, and they are hungry for more and better information. The most forward-thinking companies have come up with ways to give it to them. The information can come from sources as diverse as portable computers for salespeople in the field, external data bases that provide intelligence on competitors and markets, and inventory management systems. General Electric Co. found that by creating a toll-free hotline for customer complaints and questions, it could generate a wealth of information that helped it improve old products and develop new ones.

Most companies still have a long way to go, though. "There are a lot of personal computers and word processors out there, but most of them are not hooked up," notes Joan C. Trude of Booz, Allen & Hamilton Inc. "Most companies have exploited little of the potential." A look at American's development of its Sabre system shows how difficult this can be.

American started designing Sabre when United Airlines Inc. announced plans for its own reservation system for travel agents, who then made about half of all airline bookings. "Bob Crandall said we had to have a competitive tool—we couldn't allow United to dominate," says Max Hopper, who designed Sabre. The reason: Travel agencies are the distribution system for the industry's commodity—seats.

United's system was just for its own routes. "They thought that would be enough, that it would give agents 70 percent of what they needed,"

# Making data processing pay for itself

Most data processing managers don't think like business strategists. And most executives don't really understand what technology can do. That's a big problem for companies trying to use technology to gain a competitive edge. People are often on different wavelengths.

Security Pacific National Bank thinks it has a solution: Spin off data processing into a separate division, and make it support itself. That way, data processing people will have to think in business terms. If they don't come up with competitive ideas that sell, they'll be out of business.

That's the idea behind Security Pacific Automation Co., a new unit of the bank. The subsidiary will bid on internal bank projects, though bank departments are free to hire competing outfits instead. The unit will also sell its services outside the company, mostly to small and medium-sized banks. That way Security Pacific can spread the cost of its data processing facilities. DuWayne J. Peterson, chairman of the new division, is optimistic about demand for its services. "In banking," he says, "you can't survive without technology—it's becoming a competitive weapon."

So far, the move is dramatically reducing rapid increases in the bank's data processing expenditures. This year's budget of some $250 million represents only a 4 percent rise from last year vs. annual increases of 28 percent for the two previous years.

And the division is already coming up with new services. It is putting terminals into car dealerships to link them with Security Pacific Credit Corp. That way, dealers can run credit checks and close deals faster and consumers can calculate loan payments.

Security Pacific's strategy is not without risks. Other banks have had little success selling data processing, and the division will break even this year at best. But Security Pacific expects some profits by next year, and it is looking for the subsidiary to contribute up to 5 percent of overall corporate earnings in 10 years.

Hopper says. "We made the decision to provide all airlines' schedules. We wanted agents to use the system all the time." By creating total dependence on its system, American gained market share. It listed its own flights first, and many travel agents never went further. "We saw it as a marketing tool from day one," says Hopper, who is now in charge of information systems at Bank of America. "It took United a year or more to catch up."

Eventually, Sabre and Apollo proved to be such powerful competitive tools that other airlines cried foul. Now, under government pressure, the two big carriers have eliminated the bias of listing their own flights first. But they are making up the difference by charging for bookings on other carriers. And Sabre is now also a marketing pipeline. Travel agents can use it to get visas and book hotels. American gets a cut on all the services the agents sell.

It's no surprise that management experts would try to capture the secrets of information strategy in a formula. In his new book, *Competitive Advantage,* Harvard business school professor Michael E. Porter discusses his "value chain" analysis. "The firm is a collection of activities: You have to tear it apart into discrete activities, determine what it costs to do each activity, and what makes it unique," he says. "Information technology can affect how every activity is and can be performed."

# Computing the cost of pounding out a dent

Body-shop estimates almost always leave people feeling queasy. Customers, fearful of being ripped off, worry that knocking out a little dent in a fender will put a big dent in their wallets. Shop owners fret about cost overruns.

Akzo Coatings, the paint division of the $4.6 billion Dutch chemical, paint, and pharmaceuticals company, Akzo, figured that if it could help solve this problem for its body-shop customers, it could strengthen customer loyalty and boost sales in the bargain.

So along with a sister subsidiary, Akzo Systems, Akzo Coatings set out in 1980 to create a way for repair shops to get instant access to spare-parts listings, new repair procedures, and labor-hour guidelines for some 2,000 car models—all through a personal computer. By last January it had perfected the system, which costs $10,000 to $110,000 depending on the size of the body shop. Employees punch in a description of the car and the parts and repair work it needs, and the system spits out a parts-and-labor calculation. Soon, it will tell body shops everything they need to know about paint—particularly Akzo paint.

Akzo figures it has "a two-year lead over the competition," says Egbert Steenhuis, who heads Akzo Systems' product-development and sales in the Netherlands and West Germany. In the Netherlands, Akzo has sold 90 percent of the 75 computer systems bought by body shops this year.

All this means not just better marketing for Akzo Coatings but new revenues for Akzo Systems, as well. "In Germany alone, we expect a 50 percent growth rate in [body shop] sales annually over the next three years and something similar for profits," says Steenhuis. "I think that we've set a kind of standard that's going to permanently change the market." For now, at least, Akzo is the biggest beneficiary of that change.

## 'NEGLECTED FORCE'

Others feel Porter's approach is simplistic. "I would only spend 20 percent of my time on [the value chain]," says Richard L. Nolan, chairman of Nolan, Norton, & Co., a Lexington (Mass.) consultant. "I'd spend the other 80 percent creating the culture to make it happen." He says employees must be computer-literate and management must have learned how to apply information technology. "The reason technology can be such a potent force and is frequently a neglected one is that it often takes a number of years to build the technical infrastructure and skills base with which to compete," asserts Research & Planning's Gruber.

With or without a formula, companies are finding they have to be more creative to make information technology part of their business strategies. Irwin J. Sitkin, vice-president for corporate administration at Aetna Life & Casualty Co., now views his company as "one great big information processing business." The game, he says, "has really become 'Get the right information to the right guy at the right time to make the right decision to beat the other guys out in the marketplace.' " Aetna now gives customers access to its Aecclaims system, which processes group insurance claims. Now the client can do some analysis of his own—on the effectiveness of his own cost containment efforts, for instance—using Aetna's computer files.

Sometimes, whole new enterprises grow out of systems put in place just to provide information. Citibank, which offers financial services and data, has teamed up with McGraw-Hill Inc., which collects data on commodities, to create a 24-hour commodity trading venture called Global Electronic Markets Co. Now, traders can not only get information instantly but also make deals and transfer money in minutes. (McGraw-Hill also publishes *Business Week*.)

Being creative doesn't necessarily mean being first. In the New York City retail banking market, Chemical Bank was the first to put in automatic teller machines in 1969. Its goal was simply to automate the teller's job. But it didn't seem to work, and Chemical pulled back. Citibank, on the other hand, saw an entirely different opportunity. It thought that the primary value of ATMs lay in customer service and marketing. It did a lot of research on customer responses to technology and created much "friendlier" machines. By blanketing the city with them in the late 1970s, it more than doubled its checking and deposit balances and almost tripled its market share, from 5 percent to about 13 percent today.

To spot such opportunities, executives don't necessarily have to know how the technology works. But they do need to understand how to deploy it. Just as no general would leave tactical planning to his quartermaster, executives cannot expect their data processing lieutenants to wage this battle. "The technically sound people are often not creative [in business strategy]," notes Peter Keen, a former Massachusetts Institute of Technology professor who now consults on how to use information technology.

The data processing manager who can talk management's language and explain how to launch a preemptive attack in the marketplace is an invaluable asset. "Companies are competing on a national basis to find this rare commodity," says Herbert Halbrecht, president of Halbrecht Associates Inc., a Stamford (Conn.) executive

---

## Keeping the guests knocking at Red Lion's door

When a computer flagged persistently high vacancy rates recently at four vacation-resort inns in Arizona, Washington State, and Oregon, the Red Lion Inns chain of 52 hotels took quick action. The company sent a computer message to all its hotels and to American Airlines' Sabre reservations network offering seasonal discounts of as much as 50 percent at the four hotels. The result: fewer vacancies.

Red Lion uses a minicomputer at its Vancouver (Wash.) headquarters as a kind of inventory-control system to make sure its 11,000 rooms in eight Western states are filled. It seems to be working. The chain has a 70 percent-plus occupancy rate—two or three percentage points above the national average. That's not bad, given that the depressed lumber industry in the Pacific Northwest is dragging down local economies.

Phones in the lobbies of all Red Lion hotels are linked to its system, enabling guests to make reservations. And a 200-member marketing staff uses the computer in its promotional efforts. "This gives us much more flexibility with rate structures," says Michael McLeod, executive vice-president for operations at the closely held company, which says it had revenues of $250 million in 1984. Red Lion claims to be an industry leader in setting discount rates for tour brokers and travel wholesalers and in offering a "guaranteed rate" for frequent travelers from top corporate accounts, who are assured a room at a stated price for six months.

The next step? Automatic flagging of low occupancy in certain types of rooms for quicker discounting. "It won't necessarily give us new business, but it will help us stay abreast of the competition," says McLeod. The hotel chain must be doing something right. It claims a repeat business of 85 percent, about twice the industry average.

search firm specializing in finding technical executives. "Salaries have been escalating very rapidly."

At $1 billion-plus companies where information technology is "the engine driving the company"— at major insurance companies and banks, for example—annual salary packages for information managers often hit $150,000 to $250,000, almost twice what they were five years ago, Halbrecht says. One company with revenues in the $60 million range offered a salary package of $100,000 to $120,000 for a job whose last occupant, "a real techie," made $70,000 with a minor bonus, he reports.

As information technology becomes a strategic tool rather than simply a support function, data processing managers' roles—and jobs—will have to change, too. "They will have to delight in solving the business problem, not the crossword puzzle that was programming," notes John F. Rockart, a professor at MIT's Sloan School of Management. William R. Synnott, senior vice-president in charge of information systems at Bank of Boston Corp., wonders how many data processing people will make the transition. "A lot won't," he says. "They have come through the technical ranks and have had little management exposure."

## 'BELIEVERS'

Synnott says his own role has already changed "quite dramatically." He has become progressively more involved in strategic planning and marketing and now spends an allotted time each month showing senior management how to use information technology. "The people in management have become believers," he says.

The companies that use information technology best are forging just this kind of partnership between their executives and their technical people. "Just as executives have always had to cope with operations, strategy, financial planning, and people, now they are going to have to deal with information technology as well," says MIT's Rockart.

One executive who spearheaded a technological revolution at his company is Robert F. McDermott, president of the San Antonio-based insurer USAA, formerly the United Services Automobile Assn. When McDermott arrived in 1969 and found boxes of paper spilling into the hall-

ways, he vowed to create a "paperless environment" at the company, which then handled most of its promotions and collections by mail, processed by hand.

Early on, USAA entered names, addresses, and other policy information into computer terminals and cross-referenced them to give service representatives easy access to the data. Other innovations followed. Now the National Insurance Consumer Organization in Alexandria, Va., recommends USAA's Universal Life Policy to consumers largely because automation lets the company do sales and service over the telephone, eliminating agents that boost premiums. Consumers Union, the nonprofit publisher of *Consumer Reports,* ranks USAA at or near the top in customer satisfaction with automobile and homeowner claims handling.

Clearly, more businesses are starting to think hard about how to use information technology strategically. Many analysts have blamed the computer industry slump on buyers' hesitancy to make large-scale purchases until they understand better how the equipment can make them more effective, not just more efficient. Now, companies may be getting ready to buy. "Two years ago clients were hiring us for needs assessments and diagnostics. Now they want strategic planning," says Randy J. Goldfield, president of Omni Group Ltd., a New York market research and office automation consulting firm. "Now it's, 'Let's move ahead, let's implement.'"

These companies may be willing to spend more now than ever, suggests Harvey L. Poppel, a partner at Broadview Associates, a Fort Lee (N.J.) financial consulting firm. "Technology is starting to influence the revenue stream, not just the cost side, and people are becoming less cost sensitive," he says.

## RISKY SAVING

But to get into the game, many businesses are going to have to change the way they justify technology expenditures. "The costs are certain, the benefits are not," notes consultant Hammer. Adds Theodore J. Freiser, president of John Diebold & Associates, a New York management consultant: "You have to be willing to make the investment

## Smoothing out a metal-grinding operation

Richard B. Kennedy used to sell International Business Machines Corp. computers. Now he's in charge of a Norton Co. division that makes grinding wheels for finishing metal surfaces. Seem incongruous? Not to him. "In my business, information technology is going to let me get better quality, better service, and a better cost position," he says.

Kennedy is only one of several technologically sophisticated managers that the 100-year-old Worcester (Mass.) company has put in line jobs to find ways to make its abrasives, engineering materials, petroleum, and mining businesses more competitive. His aim is to strengthen Norton by giving its distributors "the highest service levels in the industry."

To do that, he has set up an information network called the Norton Connection and given distributors terminals so they can enter orders electronically and get details in seconds on the status of orders, pricing, and catalog items. When a customer calls, the distributor can promise a delivery date over the phone, a process that used to take days. This makes it "easier to do business with me and harder to leave," Kennedy says.

It also lets Norton run its plants better and respond to critical orders faster. Norton can now keep closer track of its inventory. And over time, Kennedy plans to tie the Norton Connection link into a larger in-house system, which will take orders, compare them with backlogs and then adjust factory operating schedules to hold down costs.

"Competitors will probably catch up over time," Kennedy says. "But getting the system in first and enhancing it are important. It's a very expensive network, hard for others to reproduce. And it takes a long time to put together. Not everyone is willing to invest the money to do it. That's a competitive advantage for us."

---

without having a correspondingly measurable return. There's no measure we can construct that can isolate the contribution of information and not be also attributable to some other factors. It's subjective."

The key is to stay flexible. "If you're going to use information as a competitive weapon, you don't know what the environment is going to be like in three to five years," Freiser says. But it may be riskier not to spend the money. "If you wait until others make the technology an industry standard and then you do it," he warns, "you are left without the benefits but with all the costs."

The long-term implications of this information technology arms race scare some observers. Michael E. Treacy, an assistant professor at MIT's Sloan School, worries that "the whole thing is being oversold." He fears many industries may

cripple themselves. He cites the effects of computerized reservation systems on airlines: "One or two companies have gotten an advantage, but they have decreased the wealth of the whole industry. With all the information they now have access to, customers have a relatively better bargaining position" and prices have been eroding. Airline stocks, even American's, have performed poorly relative to other investments, Treacy says. The stock price of American's parent, AMR Corp., has risen only 10 percent since yearend 1983, to $40.

Treacy concedes, though, that other airlines have done worse. And that's the rub. Just as Star Wars-style programs are likely to proceed even though they may escalate the chances of nuclear war, business is so competitive that companies are likely to do anything to gain an edge, even though in some cases their industries may be the ultimate victims. And competitors have got to be willing to follow. So businesses must gird themselves for the information technology revolution. The ones who understand how to use the new tools will be the survivors.

## QUESTIONS

1. *Summarize some of the innovative ways that information technology is being used to perform marketing and other business functions more effectively.*

2. *Explain how improved information technology influences or changes decision making within a firm.*

3. *What is the biggest obstacle to applying information technology in new and creative ways within an organization? Explain your answer.*

4. *Suggest a couple of examples, other than those mentioned in the article, of how improved information technology might serve as a competitive weapon for marketers.*

*5. *Would Coyne consider the kinds of competitive advantages discussed in this article to be strategically significant and sustainable (Reading 7)? Why or why not?*

---

*Question relates concepts in this and other readings.

---

## ☐ 9

# The impact of consumer trends on corporate strategy

*Sandra D. Kresch*

---

*Previous readings have emphasized how environmental changes can influence business success or failure. In this article, Kresch identifies four major trends that she believes will "reshape the U.S. marketplace of the 1980s" and have significant impacts on corporate strategy planning. She then uses General Mills as an illustration of a company that has successfully monitored and responded to consumer trends. This provides a good introduction to Reading 10, which also focuses on General Mills and illustrates that the monitoring of consumer trends is a never-ending process.*

---

Over the past few decades, the American corporate community operated in an environment of rapid growth, changing technology, and aggressive expansion into world markets. Throughout this period, productivity increased consistently, resulting in an ever-climbing GNP. With this rising tide of economic progress, the material and social rewards available to the American consumer appeared to be unlimited.

Today, this view of the world—and America's industrial role within it—seems startlingly naive and nostalgic. Declining economic growth coupled with increased global competition and a host of

Source: Reprinted by permission from the *Journal of Business Strategy,* Winter 1983, pp. 58–63. Copyright © 1983, Warren, Gorham & Lamont, Inc., 210 South Street, Boston, Massachusetts. All rights reserved. At the time of writing, Sandra D. Kresch was vice president of Booz, Allen & Hamilton, Inc., a management consulting firm.

other forces has sent shock waves through the business community and the consumer environment. As we move into the 1980s, top management finally is coming to grips with the unique demands of a low-growth, inflationary economy, increased competition, an unstable political/economic environment, the high cost of capital, and falling productivity.

Beyond these concerns, there is an important, though often neglected, overlay of consumer issues that will dramatically affect corporate performance and profitability in the 1980s. So far-reaching is their impact that we believe top management must factor consumer analysis into its planning process along with traditional economic analysis if its strategic business decisions are to be implemented successfully. If top management fails to do so, it runs the risk of being at the wrong place at the wrong time with the wrong products, as recent events in the troubled automotive industry graphically demonstrate.

Without doubt, consumer needs and preferences have always been considered in the planning of consumer packaged-goods firms. Typically, however, they have been researched and acted upon at the micro level—in the areas of new product positioning, for instance, or marketing strategy. Today, by contrast, consumer goods firms are seeing the need to understand, anticipate, and capitalize on a changing consumer environment and developing trends as critical components of their strategic planning and implementation. In the 1980s, the need to link technology, competitive positioning, and customer needs will be equally critical for industrial companies.

Why the greater emphasis on a discipline traditionally viewed as "soft" and peripheral? Mainly because consumer trends now surfacing will impinge upon all facets of corporate strategic planning—from new product development, technology management, and the restructuring of corporate portfolios to productivity, management style, internal operating structure, and executive compensation. The heightened importance of consumer issues raises a number of questions for management:

What are the pivotal consumer/customer trends shaping the new marketing environment of the 1980s?

How can top management use consumer analysis as a strategic tool?

What kinds of business decisions will result from an increased emphasis on consumer trend analysis?

With these questions providing the background, the discussion that follows focuses primarily on the experience of one consumer packaged-goods firm—General Mills—and the way in which it has consistently used sophisticated consumer trends analysis in planning, implementing, and, when necessary, redirecting its corporate strategy.

## THE NEW MARKETING ENVIRONMENT

Four major trends have converged to radically reshape the U.S. marketplace in the 1980s.

### Demographic shifts

Over the past 20 years, a vast body of statistical research about changing U.S. demographics has been developed, yet there is little evidence that this—or the changing population that it profiles—is being integrated into corporate planning.

As we look to the 1980s, demographic analysis points to the emergence of three dominant population segments:

A record number of aging adults, more active and affluent than ever before.

A huge mid-to-late 30s segment at the family formation stage.

An incipient, but modified, baby boom resulting from delays in marriage and child-bearing.

The fastest growing population group will be in the 25-to-44-year-old range, the life stage that focuses on establishing new homes and raising families, providing, as in the past, a market for a broad range of products.

However, this family formation group differs from its predecessors in many respects. Its members, for example, are increasingly more affluent, as two-income families become the norm, higher education levels are achieved, and marriage and children are postponed. Recent analysis suggests that people in this category spend 36 percent more than any other segment on durables. Spending on indulgences during the single years has become a way of life—and young consumers will continue to create a profitable market for products—though the product mix appealing to them is likely to be quite different from that of a generation ago. By 1985, this group will control more than half the nation's wealth.

### Economic instability

Inflation and economic flux have caused sweeping changes in consumer buying patterns by eroding confidence and altering attitudes toward purchasing. As consumers perceive that more money is buying them less, more and more people are beginning to fear that the American dream is no longer "for sale." With inflation cutting into higher disposable incomes, consumers are more inclined than ever to adopt the much-publicized "buy now, save later" motto at the expense of future security.

### Rapid social change

The dramatic recent changes in the structure of the nuclear family and the fabric of American society are familiar and indisputable. First marriages are being delayed, the divorce rate has increased by 96 percent in the last 10 years, and the "single head of household" is now a recognized economic and political entity. An unprecedented 42 million women are now in the work force; through the 1990s, experts predict that they will continue to swell the labor ranks at the rate of 1 million per year. The impact on the corporation, and on virtually every basic service and product—from housing to convenience foods—has been unparalleled.

### Value shifts

Such rapid social upheaval has had its price. Today, consumers no longer believe that technological change, economic growth, and hard work guarantee prosperity—or even a moderately comfortable lifestyle. As the social activists of the 1960s and 1970s move into the traditional family formation stage, some of their behavior patterns appear to reflect or conform to those of previous generations, but the attitudes underlying that behavior are very different.

The 1980s are emerging as a decade in which consumers are preoccupied with maintaining their own economic and emotional stability and with finding personal, not social, fulfillment in an environment that is perceived to be increasingly hostile and uncomfortable.

Receding interest in issues related to social causes has created a new definition of survival: personal comfort and economic security. This has resulted in greater emphasis on successful interpersonal relations, the gratification achieved through leisure time, and social involvement focused largely on the individual. "Quality of life," a rallying principle of the past few decades, has been linked to, or transformed into, a new concept: "quality time." Increasingly, in all forums—from the workplace to the family—emphasis is shifting from the drive to acquire more and "bigger" objects to the search for ways to use limited personal resources—time and money among them—most productively.

As a corollary, there is strong evidence of a continuing decline in the view of work as an expression of identity. With notable exceptions, there appears to be a weaker commitment to the work environment and ethic, more questioning of corporate values and procedures, more job turnover and "burnout," and more demand for employers to assume social as well as economic functions, from child care to retirement counseling.

All the trends capsulized here have and will continue to affect the corporate bottom line through impact on:

Types of consumer products developed.
Product positioning and marketing.
Business segmentation to optimize profitability.
Corporate portfolio structure.
Implementation strategies, from new product introductions to organization design and policy.

General Mills' recent expansion into a broad range of businesses offers a prime example of the effective use of consumer trend analysis as a strategic planning tool. Over a 10- to-15-year period, the company undertook a dramatic diversification program built around the concept of a family of complementary, consumer-oriented businesses and based on its in-depth experience in servicing the customers of its core food business.

## GENERAL MILLS: MATCHING CORPORATE STRATEGY TO CONSUMER DEMANDS

During its 50-year history, General Mills had evolved from a flour milling company into a classic consumer packaged-goods firm. In the 1950s, the company launched its first diversification effort, moving into a series of businesses—home appliances, precision instruments, electronics, and others—all unrelated to consumer foods. These were divested in the early 1960s when they proved unsuccessful in achieving desired growth and profitability goals because they failed to exploit General Mills' major assets: marketing savvy and consumer goods expertise.

A second diversification program—this one playing to General Mills' strengths—was launched in 1966. Analyzing its approach, a four-step planning strategy emerges:

**Step 1: Analysis of existing corporate portfolio and short-term market outlook.** As General Mills reviewed its core food business in the late 1960s, it was clear that the food processing industry was maturing and profits were being squeezed by price controls, inflation, and a recessionary economy and that expansion of its food distribution outlets had peaked. In addition, the company's core businesses were fending off antitrust litigation and consumer campaigns against advertising to children. Growing interest in nutrition and "health" foods also threatened sales in General Mills' flour, cake mix, and frosting categories.

At the same time, demographic data suggested that population growth had slowed and that the number of children—primary consumers of cereals and other core products—was declining. The move of women into the work force indicated a growing demand for convenience foods and other labor-saving products.

**Step 2: Analysis of General Mills' corporate strengths.** Examined from the consumer perspective, General Mills had a number of formidable assets:

Strong, well-known brand names that cut across consumer and market segments.
A tradition of monitoring consumer attitudes and needs through a sophisticated and well-controlled market research function.

National distribution channels and a strong marketing organization.

**Step 3: Analysis of long-term consumer trends and their potential impact.** General Mills identified a variety of long-term consumer shifts that would affect its core operating businesses:

Increased emphasis on "family formation."
A greater proportion of primary market consumers shifting attention from the home to careers.
Changes in spending patterns, including increased financial pressures due to inflation, making discretionary purchasing more difficult, and the need to save time through more costly convenience products.
Increased concern about the quality of food, diet, physical fitness, and "naturalness."
Shifts in food-consumption patterns to increased away-from-home eating and staggered meals in response to more active lifestyles, signaling a decline in the total food dollars spent in the grocery store.
Greater interest in "investment spending" expressed through the purchase of high-quality durables and a shift of discretionary funds from savings to tangibles.
Increased emphasis on do-it-yourself activities fueled both the drive to economize and increased leisure time.

**Step 4: Matching high-growth market segments to corporate strengths.** Using a consumer analysis as a foundation, General Mills embarked on a strategy of aggressive, highly focused diversification. Between 1967 and 1979, it acquired more than 40 companies at a cost of $335 million and 3.5 million shares (excluding full business acquisitions). The underlying theme of its acquisition strategy: every business entered would be consumer oriented and closely tied to the "family market." The result was acquisition of a carefully selected group of businesses in areas ranging from fashion, jewelry, and travel to restaurants, toys, collectibles, and crafts.

Evidence of the strategy's overall success lies in the fact that 33 percent of General Mills' 1980 sales came from products and services introduced in the last five years, representing a dollar volume of about $1.4 billion. Overall, 45 percent of its growth in the same period stems from new products and services developed internally and focused largely on serving changing consumer needs.

Growth in sales has been significantly higher in the new businesses than in the traditional food market: not only have the nonfood operations increased as a proportion of the total business, but all the new units have grown at a substantially faster rate. While consumer foods represented 73 percent of sales and 81 percent of total operating profits in 1971, by 1980 these figures had fallen to 53 percent of sales and 53 percent of profits.

Analysis of several new General Mills businesses illustrates a key reason for this profit picture—the successful interaction between strategic planning and consumer trend analysis.

## Fashion

With the acquisition in 1969 of David Crystal and its prestige sportswear line, Izod/LaCoste, General Mills entered the fashion field—an area in which consumers spend substantial discretionary income. While relatively small when acquired, Izod/LaCoste has become the mainstay of the Crystal business and a major success story. Capitalizing on increased consumer interest in physical fitness, General Mills built Izod's alligator into a highly profitable symbol of quality and broadened its product line to a full range of leisure wear.

Anticipating a trend toward widespread branding in the fashion field, General Mills expanded Izod dramatically through leverage provided to retailers by the use of a consumer pull strategy far more typical of selling cake mix than of the apparel market. The result: a highly profitable business that continues to account for much of the David Crystal Division's growth.

By contrast, other General Mills fashion acquisitions have been less successful in adapting to new consumer demands. The mainstream of the David Crystal line—"dressy" sportswear geared to suburban activities—has proven to be out of tune with apparel market trends. The same is true of Kimberly Knitwear, which suffered from declining consumer interest in knit fabrics, a growing preference for natural textiles, and the changing wardrobe needs of career women.

## Restaurant operations

Foreseeing the trend toward increased away-from-home eating in the 1970s, General Mills began to acquire a variety of restaurant operations. Choosing not to compete in the fast-food market already dominated by McDonald's, the company focused instead on family style, relatively inexpensive restaurants with specific themes. Red Lobster Inns specialized in seafood, York Steak House in mid-price-range steak, and Castle Gallardo in Mexican food. In 1980, General Mills also began development of Good Earth restaurants, specializing in natural foods. Each of these acquisitions has been developed into larger businesses under General Mills' direction and represents an effort to segment away-from-home eating in a way that enables General Mills to achieve high penetration in a well-defined niche: the middle-price family restaurant market.

## Specialty retailing

In developing its Specialty Retailing Group, General Mills used consumer trend analysis to identify new distribution channels for conventional consumer products—chiefly mail-order marketing.

The acquisition of The Talbots, for instance, brought General Mills into the fashion retailing market, while also generating substantial mail-order volume. Built on a reputation for high quality, traditional styles, and durability, The Talbots fashion line proved to be highly compatible with working women's demand for classic, easy-to-care-for "investment" clothing. Initially, General Mills used mail-order marketing to cultivate a strong customer base with a geographic reach beyond The Talbots' original New England locale. Once a strong mail-order operation was established, customer loyalty was easily transferred to additional retail outlets.

Eddie Bauer, another retail acquisition, specializes in high-quality, down-insulated products and outdoor gear. Again, as in the case of The Talbots, a mail-order distribution structure brought Eddie Bauer into the homes of consumers who never would have been exposed to the company through retail outlets and rapidly expanded the business.

In addition, the use of advanced telecommunications and computer technology has streamlined mail-order fulfillment, providing better service to consumers at lower cost. This has an added benefit for General Mills: not only has it tapped into consumer trends related to shipping behavior, it has also positioned itself effectively to move forward into an era of expanded in-home shopping via computer.

## Core convenience foods

General Mills' core business, convenience, food products, was also affected by shifts in its strategy.

References to physical fitness and diet consciousness, for instance, have emerged in product development specifications and advertising. The development of a whole range of Granola-based products, high-fiber cereals, and snack products all reflect consumer interest in "naturalness" and nutrition and offer opportunities for highly sophisticated market segmentation. General Mills has effectively segmented the "nutritional" cereal market in a way that allows it to sustain traditional brands that are highly fortified (meeting the needs of vitamin-conscious consumers), "natural" brands (appealing to a different set of consumers concerned with the negative effects of additives and preservatives), and also reach children (through vitamin-enriched cereals with good taste). At the same time, it has sustained traditional brands like Cheerios and Wheaties through communication strategies that focus on contemporary values.

Similarly, General Mills has entered the high-growth market with Yoplait and the portable food category with Nature Valley Granola Bars—convenience foods that meet consumer demands for "healthy" eat-on-the-run products.

## CONSUMER IMPACT ANALYSIS

As the General Mills experience suggests, sensitive analysis of consumer trends can be a powerful strategic tool for determining how and where to allocate scarce and costly resources. It can help identify corporate strengths, unify corporate objectives, and serve as a frame of reference for the management of technology, new product development, acquisitions, and marketing.

A variation on the concept of environmental impact analysis, consumer trend analysis also pro-

vides an added dimension to traditional strategic planning, which uses financial and other variables as methods for understanding markets and competitors. It also can help pinpoint appropriate timing for new product introductions and determine how new technology can be used most effectively to address consumer needs.

However, two factors appear to deflect management's attention—especially in the United States—from consumer trend analysis: the short-term profit perspective and entrancement with technology.

Much has been written about the impact of short-term objectives on innovation. From the consumer perspective, the key problem is that emerging trends usually result in long-term market opportunities that are difficult to assess precisely in terms of potential or to justify in the face of short-term profit constraint.

At the same time, much of the attention given to technology innovation has focused on potential profits rather than the problems inherent in the process of commercialization. There is a danger—already apparent—that the sheer magnitude of the new technology and applications available will overshadow the need to link product development to consumer needs and benefits. As a result, industrial manufacturers have persisted in introducing technological innovations without regard to their benefits—and have then been baffled when genuinely innovative products based on these technologies have not generated markets as large as expected.

In the consumer appliance industry, for example, manufacturers have electrified household items ranging from crepe pans to vegetable peelers, generating a steady new stream of faddish new products with short-term profit potential rather than sustaining market value. In the process, they have missed early entry into new long-term markets—notably food processors and microwave ovens—which keyed into consumers' changing convenience food needs.

Both consumer and industrial businesses have also failed to pinpoint new buying patterns. In many segments, the demand for middle-price-range products is declining, as economic pressures and value perceptions force buyers into either "investment purchasing"—buying high-quality, high-value products with a long life—or the purchase of low-cost, minimum-feature models if a product is perceived to be disposable, easily replaced, or likely to be made obsolete by changing technology.

In some cases, American companies are finally acknowledging these shifts and redirecting their strategies. Increasingly, they are beginning to understand the need to marry careful market planning with technological innovation at profitable levels.

In many cases, industrial companies have been very successful at providing customer input into their planning and product development. As an example, in the early days of Hewlett-Packard, the "next bench" approach to product development proved very successful. New product ideas came from customers and/or scientists in the HP laboratories; new products were developed using emerging electronics technologies, but always in response to well-defined objectives based largely on customer needs.

In most industrial markets where this close interaction is not typical, the same sort of monitoring of customer trends must become an important component of strategic planning to offset slow growth and increasing competition.

The home entertainment/information industry provides a very timely example of an area in which balancing technological innovation and real consumer value will be paramount. In many cases, strategists in the burgeoning industry are leaping off into the 21st century in terms of technology without effectively analyzing consumer trends and benefits in their market planning. Optimistic projections on markets for personal computers, home electronic information systems, and other ventures are widespread, resulting in huge investments by major corporations in an industry that will have to grow substantially in order to support profitable businesses.

Yet, to date, there is limited evidence of consumer behavior and buying patterns suggesting that the population at large will accept the new products, services, and technologies being developed with anywhere near the rapidity projected. In fact, research indicates that conventional wisdom about the adoption of innovative technology may not be applicable to the consumer environment of the 1980s, driven as it is by rising costs, de-

creased discretionary income, and smaller families.

Whatever the long-term economic outlook, unfounded and poorly conceived consumer strategies could dramatically affect the size and profitability of the markets for electronic innovations in the next decade.

## BUILDING CONSUMER TREND ANALYSIS INTO CORPORATE STRATEGY

Even in the companies with the most sophisticated consumer research capabilities, the data developed often are used only in tactical decisions on very narrowly defined projects—often by lower or middle management. To be successful, however, consumer trend analysis must be integrated into planning at the top level of management. Guidelines for effective integration include:

Integrating a consumer impact component into market/competitive analysis in the formal strategic planning process.

Focusing top-management attention on consumer/customer trends through periodic updates.

Adding consumer/customer market-oriented professionals to strategic planning project teams.

Providing continuing access to data on consumer/customer trends through a strong market research program.

Focusing consumer/customer trend analysis on specific business objectives to avoid ethereal, largely useless data with no strategic relevance.

Integrating consumer trends into strategic planning can provide an entirely new dimension to traditional product/market segmentation. To ensure optimal results:

Segment markets based on consumer variables, as well as traditional factors such as product line, price, and distribution channels.

Do not limit consumer segmentation to demographic characteristics. Increasingly, attitudes related to specific product benefits are more important in identifying market potential and changes.

Integrate consumer/customer needs and feedback on existing products into the product
development processes.

Consider consumer franchise and brand presence as corporate resources equal in value
to physical assets, distribution reach, and
technology.

Carefully assess trade-offs between technology
and consumer benefits. The availability of
new technology applications, unless linked to
concrete consumer benefits, can provide a
springboard not for success but for costly
failure.

Look for convergence of market forces; in combination, dramatic social changes, pricing
shifts, and technological advances can point
to untapped or underexploited markets.

When building consumer trend analysis into the
planning process, analyze internal corporate
structure to ensure that it supports this process. Often, adding the consumer perspective to planning is difficult for managers used
to making strategic decisions based solely
on financial or economic criteria.

"The customer is always right" used to be a
phrase reserved for salespeople at retail counters.
Today, business is finding that it has a new meaning, as consumer attitudes help shape the marketplace. Effectively used, consumer trend analysis
can be a valuable strategic tool in pinpointing
growth markets, identifying new product niches,
and developing new technologies. Increasingly in
the 1980s, both consumer-oriented and industrial
companies will find that it is far more profitable to
actively exploit that tool than to have to defend
against its use by competitors.

## QUESTIONS

1. *Explain your reaction to the four trends
   Kresch has identified. Are they as important
   as she suggests? Are there others that you
   feel should be included?*

2. *Pick another company, and discuss how that
   company should react to these four trends.*

*3. *How to you think Levitt (Reading 5) would
   react to this article? Explain.*

*4. *What sustainable competitive advantages, if
   any, does General Mills have in each of the
   following product-markets: fashion, restaurant
   operations, specialty retailing, convenience
   food products? (See Reading 7.)*

---

*Question relates concepts in this and other readings.

□ 10

# How changing consumer trends forced General Mills to reexamine its marketing opportunities

*Reading 9 described how General Mills successfully diversified into fashion goods, restau-
rant operations, and specialty retailing by monitoring and responding to changing consumer
trends. But as the following two articles illustrate, consumer trend analysis is a never-ending
process—not a one-time effort. Perhaps "blinded" by its success, General Mills apparently
neglected to keep doing some of the things that made it successful in the first place. Now,
like so many other firms, it is getting "back to basics."*

## ☐ 10–A

# When business got so good it got dangerous

*Bill Saporito*

The master marketers at General Mills have kept Cheerios, Gold Medal flour, and Betty Crocker cake mixes on grocery lists for decades. In recent years the Minneapolis company has acquired other businesses, like Izod Ltd., the alligator-brand shirtmaker, and Red Lobster restaurants, in the belief that the Mills' marketing magic would make these businesses soar far beyond the plodding growth rates typical of food companies. In a sense, the strategy worked too well. The phenomenal pace of Izod, whose sales nearly doubled from 1979 to 1982, and the boiling growth of the Red Lobster chain, whose revenues did double over the same period, disguised some serious marketing problems and persuaded management to put off dealing with others.

Though small compared with General Mills' $2.8-billion food business, Izod and Red Lobster together accounted for about 20 percent of General Mills $5.6 billion in revenues and a slightly higher percentage of profits last fiscal year, which ended in May. This year Izod is headed for a 10 percent decline in sales to about $360 million, and profits will be down about 30 percent. Red Lobster

will be up about 10 percent from its 1983 sales of $715 million, but most of that is from new units. Earnings are off about 10 percent. For the first half of fiscal 1984 General Mills' total sales and profits were unchanged from the same period last year. Its stock recently traded at about $47 a share, $10 below the 52-week high.

General Mills' chairman, Bruce Atwater, 52, is phlegmatic about his problem pets. "We've had trouble in virtually every part of General Mills at one time or another," he says, "so we don't panic when we see one of these things."

Or two. Or even three. In fact General Mills is having problems in a third, much smaller subsidiary this year, the video game division of Parker Brothers toy company. This business, which produces cartridges of arcade favorites like Frogger and Q-Bert for use in Atari, Mattel, and Texas Instruments home video machines, also fell on hard times precisely because its management—like

most in the industry—assumed the good times would roll on. In 1982, its first year in the video business, Parker Brothers racked up earnings of $20 million on sales of $74 million. With such an auspicious start, the game company geared up to produce $225 million of cartridges in fiscal 1983. Then the home video industry fell apart, hardware makers closed up shop, and game companies flooded the market, driving prices down. Instead of selling $225 million, Parker Brothers had to settle for revenues of $117 million and took a loss. Parker Brothers isn't likely to get carried away with its own success again soon. James Fifield, 41, executive vice president of the General Mills toy group, doesn't expect the video game business to make a dime until 1986.

Success came only a bit more slowly to Izod. For years the company, acquired in 1969, turned out high-quality if dull sportswear that was standard garb in the Ivy League. But when the preppy look emerged as the first fashion craze of the 1980s, the Izod cotton tennis shirt—first marketed in 1933 by tennis player René Lacoste, nicknamed "le Crocodile"—became a uniform. The alligator shirt (never buttoned) is the "sport shirt of choice," said the *Official Preppy Handbook,* a tongue-in-cheek manual of the style.

Jane Evans, 39, executive vice president of General Mills' fashion group, admits to being overwhelmed by Izod's sudden popularity. "I think it's important to remember that fashion came to Izod. It was not because of anything we did as far as changing the shirt," she says. "All of a sudden we were reclassified as being a fashion line. We didn't understand the implications of that."

Izod's most pressing problem was making enough of the classic shirt—"2058" in the trade— to fill orders. Meanwhile the rest of the animal kingdom was stirring. Rivals were putting foxes, tigers, horses, and other wildlife on shirt fronts that had been the alligator's exclusive habitat.

More serious than me-too competition was Izod's failure to capitalize on the shirt's popularity and update its sportswear lines. Izod never strayed far from primary prep colors—navy, maroon, and green—even as designers like Calvin Klein and Ralph Lauren were moving into pastels, stripes, and other variations of the basic shirt. The design houses were better at selling consumers at total "look" of shirts, pants, sweaters, and acces-

sories. In offering retailers complete lines, and thus the chance for multiple sales, the designers were able to muscle Izod out of prime space on the selling floor.

During Izod's 1982 boom year, 20 percent of all knit shirts were bought by teenage girls—who change styles as fast as most people change underwear. A year later the young ladies were sporting ripped sweat shirts, pink leotards, and miniskirts à la *Flashdance.* Evans maintains Izod has no interest in chasing the juniors. She says flatly, "It's a huge business, it's a dangerous business, and it's not one we'll ever go after."

One business Izod has chased and captured is children's wear. By churning out what salespeople affectionately call "Grandma bait"—cute little outfits made even cuter by the alligator emblem— Izod has created a business out of whole cloth. The kid stuff, having gone from 0 to 36 percent of sales since the 70s, is now Izod's largest business.

Izod is readying a new offensive in the rag wars. General Mills brought in a new president and beefed up the company's design staff—one person used to do the entire men's line. Izod has added two new seasonal men's lines and a premium tennis line positioned against Fila and Sergio Tacchini but priced lower than those $70-a-shirt brands.

The new crew has put forward a radical concept: sell fashion, not alligators. Just two years ago the alligator appliqué appeared on 95 percent of Izod garments. Now the registered reptile is gone from about 15 percent of the clothes and is popping up in strange places—on shirt-tails, collars, or cuffs. A select group of cotton shirts is being featured sans gator. "That's why a lot of people are buying them," reports a salesman at Macy's in Manhattan. That's fine with Izod executives, who want the public to think of Izod as a good label rather than a faddish logo.

The revamped Izod, promises Evans, will concentrate on retailers who buy a broad range of clothing rather than just shirts. Though Izod has tried in the past to distribute its goods selectively, plenty of its merchandise ended up in the off-price market, selling at a deep discount. Dealing with fewer retailers gives selected ones the exclusivity they crave; selling them a broader line gives Izod back the visibility and floor space it lost.

Red Lobster, which also has new products, a new image, and a new advertising agency (Backer & Spielvogel of Miller Lite fame), is going through its second major overhaul in just five years. The financial results of the first one were so impressive management took two years to discover that they were obscuring important changes in the market.

Red Lobster was a three-store shrimp when General Mills acquired it in 1970. Back then the chain was little more than a well-run fried fish and hush puppies operation typical of the Southeast. As it expanded, and as other fish-and-chippers got into the swim, management turned Red Lobster into a mid-priced seafood dinner house. Higher costs, linked largely to rising fuel bills for fishing boats and truck transportation, forced Red Lobster to upgrade its image again in the mid-70s. "We were serving them the same fish as in 1973," says Bill Hattaway, 40, Red Lobster's president, "but at three times the price." The company carpeted the floors, restyled the interior décor, and began adding a few fresh fish dishes to its primarily frozen offerings.

The strategy seemed to work well enough: Red Lobster reached its earnings peak in 1981. But carpets or not, the diners were beginning to squirm. Being forced to wait in a holding room and then hurried through the meal was not their idea of fun. "Our research indicated that our customers wanted a more casual dining experience," explains Joe Lee, 43, executive vice president of General Mills' restaurant group. "And they didn't want to wait on line with nothing to do." Customers said they preferred some sociability along with the sea fare, an atmosphere conducive to drinks, appetizers, and finger food to share instead of Red Lobster's massive platters—fried Atlantic seaboard plus a choice of bread, side dish, and potato. Restaurateurs call this talk-and-eat behavior "grazing." Red Lobster was also running headlong into the granola generation: while seafood was just the ticket, Lobster's image as purveyor of frozen-then-fried fish needed some freshness and polyunsaturating.

The research was telling Lee one thing, Red Lobster's books said something else. "With 370 restaurants, you don't want to do the *wrong* thing," says Lee. "Doing so well—and in the first year of a recession—hid the believability of the research."

Lee and Hattaway became believers the next year when earnings floundered, and began testing ideas to answer their customers' wants. When they finished, they had an entirely new restaurant: the prototype opened in January in Kissimmee, Florida, 12 miles east of Disney World.

The new joint is a grazer's delight. Instead of cooling their heels in a waiting room, diners can now park themselves at a seafood bar, where oysters, raw or cooked, calamari, shrimp, clams, and a variety of other appetizers are served up with a beer or two. Patrons can dawdle over daiquiris, watch the action at a glass-enclosed grill, where fresh seafood is broiled over a mesquite-wood fire, or even gaze out the new picture window. Old Red Lobsters are deliberately windowless so that diners won't take up time vying for a table near the window.

Customers aren't rushed in the dining room either. That's quite a change from the old Red Lobster where robot-like servers ("Hi my name is Kathy and I'll be your waitress tonight") were instructed to try to get an entire order, drinks to dessert, five minutes after patrons had settled in. To keep customers from lingering, the check was deposited with the last course, to be paid on the way out. The help is now being retrained to be themselves and let the diners pace the meal.

The company expects to make a couple of extra clams up front on appetizers and booze. It also lowered dinner prices to get more customers. The menu is being expanded 40 percent to include such items as seafood salads and pastas. Six or eight fresh fish entrées are available, twice as many as in the past.

Red Lobster is planning to overhaul all 370 units for at least $200,000 each. Lee says these outlays can be covered if the chain gets just 6 percent more customers. At the Kissimmee prototype, traffic is up over 10 percent.

Given his problems, Chairman Atwater's cool continues to amaze. "We don't get too hung up on what's in trouble," he says, "but we do pay attention to what we're doing about it." General Mills has lots of experience trying new ideas, failing at some, and making big businesses out of others. It's used to riding fickle industries: fashion, toys, restaurants. And, since its plodding food businesses provide a huge safety net, no failure is fatal. All that makes for equanimity.

## □ 10–B

# It's back to the kitchen for General Mills

*Mary J. Pitzer*

*Judith H. Dobrzynski*

Like other food companies disillusioned with diversification, General Mills Inc. has decided that the best place to prospect for profits is the kitchen after all. On Jan. 28, the maker of Betty Crocker cake mixes, Wheaties cereal, Gold Medal flour, and Gorton's seafoods put two of its three non-food businesses up for sale: apparel-maker Izod and its other fashion operations, and Parker Bros. and Kenner Products, its toy businesses.

Wall Street practically cheered the news. The Minneapolis company's stock jumped 5⅜ points, to 55¼, the day after the announcement. It's no wonder: In the fiscal year ending May 27, 1984, General Mills' food earnings were up—but trouble in apparel, toys, and the Red Lobster restaurant chain put an end to the company's 22-year streak of earnings increases. All told, profits were off 4.8 percent, to $233.4 million, on sales up 1 percent, to $5.6 billion. In the first six months of the current year earnings skidded another 29 percent, on sales up 1.6 percent, compared with the same period in 1983.

When General Mills makes the sales, it will have divested about a quarter of its business. But it will be able at last to attend to areas that it knows best and, more important, that can more easily deliver the increases in earnings to which it has become accustomed. By 1990, the company plans to invest $1.5 billion expanding its three core businesses—consumer foods, restaurants, and specialty retailing, which includes Eddie Bauer, Talbots, and Wallpapers To Go.

Part of the cash is going toward repositioning Red Lobster: The chain is adding lighter, lower-priced items to the menus, installing oyster bars and mesquite grills, and redecorating the restaurants in a brighter, more casual style. In foods, the

company is bringing out several line extensions, such as a fruit-on-the-bottom yogurt for its Yoplait products and more fruit snacks to complement its Fruit Roll-Ups line.

### ON THE SHELF

Outsiders say that General Mills never really understood the nature of its fashion and toy businesses, where this year's best-seller can easily sit on the shelf next year. When it failed to update its line of Izod alligator-clad shirts—once *de rigueur* for preppies—their precipitous sales decline totally shocked a management cadre more attuned to the stodgy food industry. In toys, Kenner's Strawberry Shortcake doll line faded shortly after the bottom fell out of the video game business, one of Parker's big lines. There were no replacements for either product. "The company manages its businesses with concern for financial regimen and control," says John C. Bierbusse, an analyst at Duff & Phelps Inc. "That could have hindered growth opportunities."

Some outsiders credit General Mills for recognizing its inability to turn around the businesses. "One thing the management group prides itself on is that they don't let the problem areas run for long," says L. Craig Carver of A. G. Edwards & Sons in St. Louis. But others wonder whether the company can sell the two troubled units. "I think they will have a tough time selling the toy business for a good price, because two companies

Source: Reprinted from the February 11, 1985, issue of *Business Week* by special permission, © 1985 by McGraw-Hill, Inc. At the time of writing, Mary J. Pitzer and Judith H. Dobrzynski were on the staff of *Business Week*.

[Mattel Inc. and Hasbro Bradley Inc.] dominate the general toy business," says Henry Orenstein, a toy industry consultant. Hasbro says it isn't interested. But Mattel, which lacks a board game business, might be. Izod, too, might go slowly. In any case, the businesses may have to be sold at below their estimated $850 million book value.

Even so, once the businesses are divested, the payoff could come swiftly. "Because of the change in the mix of businesses, [General Mills'] return on assets should improve dramatically," says Alan S. Greditor, who follows General Mills for Drexel Burnham Lambert Inc. He estimates that the company's return on assets on an operating basis will rise from 14 percent in 1984 to 23 percent by 1987. General Mills, in other words, may soon be cooking again.

*Editors' note:* On November 1, 1985, General Mills implemented a spinoff of its troubled toy and fashion businesses. Two new separate companies were formed: Kenner Parker Toys Inc. and Crystal Brands Inc., the latter consisting of General Mills' former Izod/LaCoste, Ship 'n Shore apparel, and Monet jewelry units. For additional details, see "Can the General Mills Babies Make It on Their Own?", *Business Week,* November 18, 1985, pp. 46–47.

## QUESTIONS

1. *Why did General Mills experience so many problems in its fashion, restaurant, and toy businesses after getting off to such a strong start?*

2. *What do you think of the new approach General Mills is taking with Red Lobster? Do you think its current strategy will be successful? Why or why not?*

*3. *Was there ever really a "strategic window" open for General Mills in the fashion and toy businesses (Readings 6 and 9)? If not, why not? If so, why did the window suddenly close?*

*4. *When it first entered the fashion, restaurant, and toy businesses (Reading 9), did General Mills really possess any sustainable competitive advantages (Reading 7)? If so, what were these advantages—and how did its competitors close or eliminate their "capability gaps"?*

*5. *Do you think that Levitt would accuse General Mills of suffering from "marketing myopia" (Reading 5)? Explain your answer.*

---

*Question relates concepts in this and other readings.

# □ 11

# Benefit segmentation: A decision-oriented research tool

## *Russell I. Haley*

*There are different ways to segment a market. While most of the approaches can be valuable, few get at the basic reason a person spends money to buy a product or service—that is, the benefits a person expects to receive from the purchase. In this article, Haley discusses an approach called "benefit segmentation" which focuses specifically on this topic. The article clearly illustrates that benefits are different from demographics and psychographics. It also shows that benefits do not necessarily relate directly to the physical characteristics or performance of a product.*

Market segmentation has been steadily moving toward center stage as a topic of discussion in marketing and research circles. Hardly a conference passes without at least one session devoted to it. Moreover, in March [1968] the American Management Association held a three-day conference entirely concerned with various aspects of the segmentation problem.

According to Wendell Smith, "Segmentation is based upon developments on the demand side of the market and represents a rational and more precise adjustment of product and marketing effort to consumer or user requirements."[1] The idea that all markets can be profitably segmented has now received almost as widespread acceptance as the marketing concept itself. However, problems remain. In the extreme, a marketer can divide up his market in as many ways as he can describe his prospects. If he wishes, he can define a left-handed segment, or a blue-eyed segment, or a German-speaking segment. Consequently, current discussion revolves largely around which of the virtually limitless alternatives is likely to be most productive.

## SEGMENTATION METHODS

Several varieties of market segmentation have been popular in the recent past. At least three kinds have achieved some degree of prominence. Historically, perhaps the first type to exist was geographic segmentation. Small manufacturers who wished to limit their investments, or whose distribution channels were not large enough to cover the entire country, segmented the U.S. market, in effect, by selling their products only in certain areas.

However, as more and more brands become national, the second major system of segmentation—demographic segmentation—became popular. Under this philosophy targets were defined as younger people, men, or families with children. Unfortunately, a number of recent studies have shown that demographic variables such as age, sex, income, occupation, and race are, in general, poor predictors of behavior and, consequently,

---

[1]Wendell R. Smith, "Product Differentiation and Market Segmentation as Alternative Product Strategies," *Journal of Marketing* 21 (July 1956), pp. 3–8.

Source: Reprinted with permission from the *Journal of Marketing,* published by the American Marketing Association, July 1968, pp. 30–35. At the time of writing, Russell Haley was vice president and corporate research director of D'Arcy Advertising in New York City.

less than optimum bases for segmentation strategies.[2]

More recently, a third type of segmentation has come into increasing favor—volume segmentation. The so-called heavy-half theory, popularized by Dik Twedt of the Oscar Mayer Company,[3] points out that in most product categories one half of the consumers account for around 80 percent of the consumption. If this is true, the argument goes, shouldn't knowledgeable marketers concentrate their efforts on these high-volume consumers? Certainly they are the most *valuable* consumers.

The trouble with this line of reasoning is that not all heavy consumers are usually available to the same brand—because they are not all seeking the same kinds of benefits from a product. For example, heavy coffee drinkers consist of two types of consumers—those who drink chain store brands and those who drink premium brands. The chain store customers feel that all coffees are basically alike, and because they drink so much coffee, they feel it is sensible to buy a relatively inexpensive brand. The premium brand buyers, on the other hand, feel that the few added pennies which coffees like Yuban, Martinson's, Chock Full O'Nuts, and Savarin cost are more than justified by their fuller taste. Obviously, these two groups of people, although they are both members of the heavy-half segment, are not equally good prospects for any one brand, nor can they be expected to respond to the same advertising claims.

These three systems of segmentation have been used because they provide helpful guidance in the use of certain marketing tools. For example, geographic segmentation, because it describes the market in a discrete way, provides definite direction in media purchases. Spot TV, spot radio, and newspapers can be bought for the geographic segment selected for concentrated effort. Similarly, demographic segmentation allows media to

be bought more efficiently since demographic data on readers, viewers, and listeners are readily available for most media vehicles. Also, in some product categories demographic variables are extremely helpful in differentiating users from nonusers, although they are typically less helpful in distinguishing between the users of various brands. The heavy-half philosophy is especially effective in directing dollars toward the most important parts of the market.

However, each of these three systems of segmentation is handicapped by an underlying disadvantage inherent in its nature. All are based on an ex post facto analysis of the kinds of people who make up various segments of a market. They rely on *descriptive* factors rather than causal factors. For this reason they are not efficient predictors of future buying behavior, and it is future buying behavior that is of central interest to marketers.

## BENEFIT SEGMENTATION

An approach to market segmentation whereby it is possible to identify market segments by causal factors rather than descriptive factors might be called "benefit segmentation." The belief underlying this segmentation strategy is that the benefits which people are seeking in consuming a given product are the basic reasons for the existence of true market segments. Experience with this approach has shown that benefits sought by consumers determine their behavior much more accurately than do demographic characteristics or volume of consumption.

This does not mean that the kinds of data gathered in more traditional types of segmentation are not useful. Once people have been classified into segments in accordance with the benefits they are seeking, each segment is contrasted with all of the other segments in terms of its demography, its volume of consumption, its brand perceptions, its media habits, its personality and lifestyle, and so forth. In this way, a reasonably deep understanding of the people who make up each segment can be obtained. And by capitalizing on this understanding, it is possible to reach them, to talk to them in their own terms, and to present a product in the most favorable light possible.

The benefit segmentation approach is not new. It has been employed by a number of America's

[2]Ronald E. Frank, "Correlates of Buying Behavior for Grocery Products," *Journal of Marketing* 31 (October 1967), pp. 48–53; Ronald E. Frank, William Massy, and Harper W. Boyd, Jr., "Correlates of Grocery Product Consumption Rates," *Journal of Marketing Research* 4 (May 1967), pp. 184–90; and Clark Wilson, "Homemaker Living Patterns and Marketplace Behavior—A Psychometric Approach," in *New Ideas for Successful Marketing: Proceedings 1966 World Congress*, ed. John S. Wright and Jac L. Goldstucker (Chicago: American Marketing Association, 1966), pp. 305–31.

[3]Dik Warren Twedt, "Some Practical Applications of the 'Heavy Half' Theory," Advertising Research Foundation 10th Annual Conference, New York City, October 1964.

largest corporations since it was introduced in 1961.[4] However, case histories have been notably absent from the literature because most studies have been contracted for privately, and have been treated confidentially.

The benefit segmentation approach is based upon being able to measure consumer value systems in detail, together with what the consumer thinks about various brands in the product category of interest. While this concept seems simple enough, operationally it is very complex. There is no simple straightforward way of handling the volumes of data that have to be generated. Computers and sophisticated multivariate attitude measurement techniques are a necessity.

Several alternative statistical approaches can be employed, among them the so-called Q technique of factor analysis, multidimensional scaling, and other distance measures.[5] All of these methods relate the ratings of each respondent to those of every other respondent and then seek clusters of individuals with similar rating patterns. If the items rated are potential consumer benefits, the clusters that emerge will be groups of people who attach similar degrees of importance to the various benefits. Whatever the statistical approach selected, the end result of the analysis is likely to be between three and seven consumer segments, each representing a potentially productive focal point for marketing efforts.

Each segment is identified by the benefits it is seeking. However, it is the *total configuration* of the benefits sought which differentiates one segment from another, rather than the fact that one segment is seeking one particular benefit and another a quite different benefit. Individual benefits are likely to have appeal for several segments. In fact, the research that has been done thus far suggests that most people would like as many benefits as possible. However, the *relative* importance they attach to individual benefits can differ importantly and, accordingly can be used as an effective lever in segmenting markets.

Of course, it is possible to determine benefit segments intuitively as well as with computers and sophisticated research methods. The kinds of

brilliant insights which produced the Mustang and the first 100-millimeter cigarette have a good chance of succeeding whenever marketers are able to tap an existing benefit segment.

However, intuition can be very expensive when it is mistaken. Marketing history is replete with examples of products which someone felt could not miss. Over the long term, systematic benefit segmentation research is likely to have a higher proportion of successes.

But is benefit segmentation practical? And is it truly operational? The answer to both of these questions is yes. In effect, the crux of the problem of choosing the best segmentation system is to determine which has the greatest number of practical marketing implications. An example should show that benefit segmentation has a much wider range of implications than alternative forms of segmentation.

## AN EXAMPLE OF BENEFIT SEGMENTATION

While the material presented here is purely illustrative to protect the competitive edge of companies who have invested in studies of this kind, it is based on actual segmentation studies. Consequently, it is quite typical of the kinds of things which are normally learned in the course of a benefit segmentation study.

The toothpaste market has been chosen as an example because it is one with which everyone is familiar. Let us assume that a benefit segmentation study has been done and four major segments have been identified—one particularly concerned with decay prevention, one with brightness of teeth, one with the flavor and appearance of the product, and one with price. A relatively large amount of supplementary information has also been gathered (Table 1) about the people in each of these segments.

The decay prevention segment, it has been found, contains a disproportionately large number of families with children. They are seriously concerned about the possibility of cavities and show a definite preference for fluoride toothpaste. This is reinforced by their personalities. They tend to be a little hypochondriacal, and in their lifestyles they are less socially oriented than some of the other groups. This segment has been named The Worriers.

---

[4]Russell I. Haley, "Experimental Research on Attitudes toward Shampoos," unpublished paper, February 1961.

[5]Ronald E. Frank and Paul E. Green, "Numerical Taxonomy in Marketing Analysis: A Review Article," *Journal of Marketing Research* 5 (February 1968), pp. 83–98.

**Table 1 ☐ Toothpaste market segment description**

| Segment name | The Sensory Segment | The Sociables | The Worriers | The Independent Segment |
|---|---|---|---|---|
| Principal benefit sought | Flavor, product appearance | Brightness of teeth | Decay prevention | Price |
| Demographic strengths | Children | Teens, young people | Large families | Men |
| Special behavioral characteristics | Users of spearmint-flavored toothpaste | Smokers | Heavy users | Heavy users |
| Brands dispropor-tionately favored | Colgate, Stripe | Macleans, Plus White, Ultra Brite | Crest | Brands on sale |
| Personality characteristics | High self-involvement | High sociability | High hypo-chondriasis | High autonomy |
| Lifestyle characteristics | Hedonistic | Active | Conservative | Value oriented |

The second segment, comprised of people who show concern for the brightness of their teeth, is quite different. It includes a relatively large group of young marrieds. They smoke more than average. This is where the swingers are. They are strongly social, and their lifestyle patterns are very active. This is probably the group to which toothpastes such as Macleans or Plus White or Ultra Brite would appeal. This segment has been named The Sociables.

In the third segment, the one which is particularly concerned with the flavor and appearance of the product, a large portion of the brand deciders are children. Their use of spearmint toothpaste is well above average. Stripe has done relatively well in this segment. They are more ego-centered than other segments, and their lifestyle is outgoing but not to the extent of the swingers. They will be called The Sensory Segment.

The fourth segment, the price-oriented segment, shows a predominance of men. It tends to be above average in terms of toothpaste usage. People in this segment see very few meaningful differences between brands. They switch more frequently than people in other segments and tend to buy a brand on sale. In terms of personality, they are cognitive and they are independent. They like to think for themselves and make brand choices on the basis of their judgment. They will be called The Independent Segment.

## MARKETING IMPLICATIONS OF BENEFIT SEGMENTATION STUDIES

Both copy directions and media choices will show sharp differences depending upon which of these segments is chosen as the target—The Worriers, The Sociables, The Sensory Segment, or The Independent Segment. For example, the tonality of the copy will be light if The Sociable Segment or The Sensory Segment is to be addressed. It will be more serious if the copy is aimed at The Worriers. And if The Independent Segment is selected, it will probably be desirable to use rational, two-sided arguments. Of course, to talk to this group at all it will be necessary to have either a price edge or some kind of demonstrable product superiority.

The depth-of-sell reflected by the copy will also vary, depending upon the segment which is of interest. It will be fairly intensive for The Worrier Segment and for The Independent Segment, but much more superficial and mood oriented for The Sociable and Sensory segments.

Likewise, the setting will vary. It will focus on the product for The Sensory Group, on socially oriented situations for The Sociable Group, and perhaps on demonstration or on competitive comparisons for The Independent Group.

Media environments will also be tailored to the segments chosen as targets. Those with serious environments will be used for The Worrier and Independent segments, and those with youthful, modern, and active environments for The Sociable and Sensory groups. For example, it might be logical to use a larger proportion of television for The Sociable and Sensory groups, while The Worriers and Independents might have heavier print schedules.

The depth-of-sell needed will also be reflected in the media choices. For The Worrier and Rational segments longer commercials—perhaps 60-second commercials—would be indicated, while for the other two groups shorter commercials and higher frequency would be desirable.

Of course, in media selection the facts that have been gathered about the demographic characteristics of the segment chosen as the target would also be taken into consideration.

The information in Table 1 also has packaging implications. For example, it might be appropriate to have colorful packages for The Sensory Segment, perhaps aqua (to indicate fluoride) for The Worrier Group, and gleaming white for The Sociable Segment because of their interest in bright white teeth.

It should be readily apparent that the kinds of information normally obtained in the course of a benefit segmentation study have a wide range of marketing implications. Sometimes they are useful in suggesting physical changes in a product. For example, one manufacturer discovered that his product was well suited to the needs of his chosen target with a single exception in the area of flavor. He was able to make a relatively inexpensive modification in his product and thereby strengthen his market position.

The new product implications of benefit segmentation studies are equally apparent. Once a marketer understands the kinds of segments that exist in his market, he is often able to see new product opportunities or particularly effective ways of positioning the products emerging from his research and development operation.

Similarly, benefit segmentation information has been found helpful in providing direction in the choice of compatible point-of-purchase materials and in the selection of the kinds of sales promotions which are most likely to be effective for any given market target.

## GENERALIZATIONS FROM BENEFIT SEGMENTATION STUDIES

A number of generalizations are possible on the basis of the major benefit segmentation studies which have been conducted thus far. For example, the following general rules of thumb have become apparent:

It is easier to take advantage of market segments that already exist than to attempt to create new ones. Some time ago the strategy of product differentiation was heavily emphasized in marketing textbooks. Under this philosophy it was believed that a manufacturer was more or less able to create new market segments at will by making his product somewhat different from those of his competitors. Now it is generally recognized that fewer costly errors will be made if money is first invested in consumer research aimed at determining the present contours of the market. Once this knowledge is available, it is usually most efficient to tailor marketing strategies to existing consumer-need patterns.

No brand can expect to appeal to all consumers. The very act of attracting one segment may automatically alienate others. A corollary to this principle is that any marketer who wishes to cover a market fully must offer consumers more than a single brand. The flood of new brands which have recently appeared on the market is concrete recognition of this principle.

A company's brands can sometimes cannibalize each other but need not necessarily do so. It depends on whether or not they are positioned against the same segment of the market. Ivory Snow sharply reduced Ivory Flakes' share of market, and the Ford Falcon cut deeply into the sales of the standard-size Ford because, in each case, the products were competing in the same segments. Later on, for the same companies, the Mustang was successfully introduced with comparatively little damage to Ford and the success of Crest did not have a disproportionately adverse effect on Gleem's market position because, in these cases, the segments to which the products appealed were different.

New and old products alike should be designed to fit *exactly* the needs of some segment of the market. In other words, they should be aimed at people seeking a specific combination of benefits. It is a marketing truism that you sell people one at a time—that you have to get *someone* to buy your product before you get *anyone* to buy it. A substantial group of people must be interested in your specific set of benefits before you can make progress in a market. Yet, many products attempt to aim at two or more segments simultaneously. As a result, they are not able to maximize their appeal to any segment of the market, and they run the risk of ending up with a dangerously fuzzy brand image.

Marketers who adopt a benefit segmentation strategy have a distinct competitive edge. If a benefit segment can be located which is seeking exactly the kinds of satisfactions that one marketer's brand can offer better than any other brand, the marketer can almost certainly dominate the purchases of that segment. Furthermore, if his competitors are looking at the market in terms of traditional types of segments, they may not even be aware of the existence of the benefit segment which he has chosen as his market target. If they are ignorant in this sense, they will be at a loss to explain the success of his brand. And it naturally follows that if they do not understand the reasons for his success, the kinds of people buying his brand, and the benefits they are obtaining from it, his competitors will find it very difficult to successfully attack the marketer's position.

An understanding of the benefit segments which exist within a market can be used to advantage when competitors introduce new products. Once the way in which consumers are positioning the new product has been determined, the likelihood that it will make major inroads into segments of interest can be assessed, and a decision can be made on whether or not counter-actions of any kind are required. If the new product appears to be assuming an ambiguous position, no money need be invested in defensive measures. However, if it appears that the new product is ideally suited to the needs of an important segment of the market, the manufacturer in question can introduce a new competitive product of his own, modify the physical properties of existing brands, change his advertising strategy, or take whatever steps appear appropriate.

## TYPES OF SEGMENTS UNCOVERED THROUGH BENEFIT SEGMENTATION STUDIES

It is difficult to generalize about the types of segments which are apt to be discovered in the course of a benefit segmentation study. To a large extent, the segments which have been found have been unique to the product categories being analyzed. However, a few types of segments have appeared in two or more private studies. Among them are the following:

> *The Status Seeker.* A group which is very much concerned with the prestige of the brands purchased.
> *The Swinger.* A group which tries to be modern and up to date in all of its activities. Brand choices reflect this orientation.
> *The Conservative.* A group which prefers to stick to large successful companies and popular brands.
> *The Rational Man.* A group which looks for benefits such as economy, value, durability, etc.
> *The Inner-Directed Man.* A group which is especially concerned with self-concept. Members consider themselves to have a sense of humor, to be independent and/or honest.
> *The Hedonist.* A group which is concerned primarily with sensory benefits.

Some of these segments appear among the customers of almost all products and services. However, there is no guarantee that a majority of them or, for that matter, any of them exist in any given product category. Finding out whether they do and, if so, what should be done about them is the purpose of benefit segmentation research.

## CONCLUSION

The benefit segmentation approach is of particular interest because it never fails to provide fresh insight into markets. As was indicated in the toothpaste example cited earlier, the marketing implications of this analytic research tool are limited only by the imagination of the person using the information a segmentation study provides. In effect, when segmentation studies are conducted, a number of smaller markets emerge instead of one large one. Moreover, each of these smaller markets can be subjected to the same kinds of thorough analyses to which total markets have been subjected in the past. The only difference—a crucial one—is that the total market was a heterogeneous conglomeration of subgroups. The so-called average consumer existed only in the minds of some marketing people. When benefit segmentation is used, a number of relatively homogeneous segments are uncovered. And, because they are homogeneous, descriptions of them in terms of averages are much more appropriate and meaningful as marketing guides.

## QUESTIONS

1. What is the difference between a descriptive dimension and a causal dimension? Which should prove a better tie to future purchases? Should we ever use the other type for segmenting markets.

2. Take a particular consumer goods market—the ice cream market, for example—and develop a table like Table 1 for this market. (Use your own judgment—do not conduct a survey.)

3. Suggest what a good marketing mix might look like for each of the segments you listed in your answer to Question 2.

*4. Does benefit segmentation have any relevance for nonprofit organizations (Reading 4)? Explain.

*Question relates concepts in this and other readings.

## □ 12

# Car makers use "image" map as tool to position products

*John Koten*

Today, business firms devote a lot of their time and attention to "product positioning"—trying to determine how their products relate to competitive products in the minds of their potential customers. While there are numerous ways to approach product positioning, perceptual image maps (often called product space maps) have become very popular because they provide business executives with a visual picture of their product-markets. The following article illustrates and discusses how the automobile industry is applying image maps to help position their present and future products.

Exasperated by the growing similarity of cars on the road, a former Detroit auto executive recently remarked that if all of today's models were lined up end to end, even the top officers of the Big Three car makers would have a hard time telling them apart at a respectable distance.

The comment addresses an increasing challenge for automotive stylists and marketers. As fuel-efficiency requirements have narrowed design and performance characteristics for cars, the auto companies have had to turn to more subtle ways of drawing distinctions between different models. An example of how that is done is the "brand image" map shown below.

The map, created by the marketing department at Chrysler Corp., shows how car makers try to calculate differences between their products these days. "With size less a dominant factor, it's no longer that easy to know what any single product represents in the minds of consumers," says R. N. Harper, Jr., manager of product marketing plans and research at the No. 3 car maker.

Marketing maps have been in use for some time at consumer-goods companies that sell near-generic items like cigarettes and dog food. But only recently have they become a valuable tool for "positioning" automobiles.

According to Mr. Harper, Chrysler draws up a series of such maps about three times a year, using responses to customer surveys. The surveys ask owners of different makes to rank their autos on a scale of 1 to 10 for such qualities as "youthfulness," "luxury," and "practicality." The answers are then worked into a mathematical score for each model and plotted on a graph that shows broad criteria for evaluating customer appeal.

The illustration below uses the technique to measure the images of the major divisions of U.S. auto makers, plus a few import companies. Using it, Chrysler would conclude, for instance, that the position of its Plymouth division in the lower left-hand quadrant means that cars carrying the Plymouth name generally have a practical, though somewhat stodgy, image. The Chrysler name-plate, by contrast, is perceived as more luxurious—though not nearly as luxurious as its principal competitors—Cadillac and Lincoln.

The map has other strategic significance, as well. By plotting on the map strong areas of customer demand, an auto maker can calculate whether its cars are on target. It can also tell from the concentration of dots representing competing models how much opposition it is likely to get in a specific territory on the map. Presumably, cars higher up on the graph should also fetch a higher price than models ranked toward the bottom, where the stress is on economy and practicality.

After viewing the results for its divisions, Chrysler concluded that Plymouth, Dodge, and Chrysler all needed to present a more youthful image. It also decided that Plymouth and Dodge needed to move up sharply on the luxury scale.

Similarly, General Motors Corp. might find after looking at the map that its Chevrolet division, traditionally for entry-level buyers, ought to move down in practicality and more to the right in youthfulness. Another problem for GM on the map: the close proximity of its Buick and Oldsmobile divisions, almost on top of each other in the upper left-hand quadrant. That would suggest the two divisions are waging a marketing war more against each other than the competition.

Chrysler also uses its marketing map to plot individual models—both those it sells currently and those it plans for the future. By trying to move a model into an unoccupied space on the map through changes in styling, price, or advertising, the company believes it can better hope to carve out a distinctive niche in the market.

**Perceptual map—brand images**

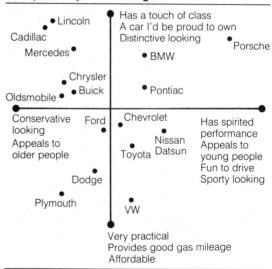

Source: Chrysler Corp.

"The real advantage of the map," says Mr. Harper, "is that it looks at cars from a consumer perspective while also retaining some sort of tangible product orientation." He says, for example, that his bosses were delighted when, on a recent map, Chrysler's forthcoming Lancer and Commander models showed up on the map next to the Honda Accord. (The two new Chrysler compacts are due out this fall.) "That told us that consumers think of our two new cars exactly the way we hoped they would," says Mr. Harper. "It was tangible evidence of where the car would compete in the market. And frankly, that can be hard to get these days."

## QUESTIONS

1. Summarize the various ways that the information in a perceptual image map can be applied by a marketing manager.

2. Why do the auto companies use consumer surveys to develop the image maps? Wouldn't it be faster, easier, and more accurate to have their own product engineers rate the different cars to determine their relative positions?

3. Suppose you were a General Motors marketing executive. Would you be concerned about the close proximity of Buick and Oldsmobile? If so, what would your strategic options be?

4. Choose a different product-market—such as amateur cameras. Then, using your own judgment about the various products available in that product-market, develop a hypothetical image map.

*5. Examine the image map shown in the article. Are all the important product attributes that people consider when buying a car shown on the map? How does this relate to Haley's concept of "benefit segmentation" (Reading 11)?

*Question relates concepts in this and other readings.

---

# □ 13

---

# The new demographics and market fragmentation

*Valarie A. Zeithaml*

---

*The demographics of the American market are changing dramatically. Various demographic trends—such as more women working outside the home, more dual-income families, an older population, and more single-person households—are fragmenting traditional mass markets into numerous smaller-sized market segments. As this article explains, this market fragmentation is increasing the number and variety of market offerings demanded by the marketplace—creating increased pressure on manufacturers and marketing middlemen to change their marketing strategy planning. Although the article focuses on grocery products, the trends discussed clearly have similar implications for many other industries.*

---

Eight years ago, in July 1977, demographic and lifestyle changes in American females were the subjects of a special issue of the *Journal of Marketing*. Demographic changes revealed recently by the 1980 census far exceed changes predicted in that issue. For example, working females were estimated to number 43.7 million by 1990 (Lazer and Smallwood 1977). In 1980, 45.6 million women were working outside the home. Other demographic changes, including the growth of single-parent households (now numbering 4 million, up 100 percent from 1970), nonfamily

Source: Reprinted with permission from the *Journal of Marketing*, published by the American Marketing Association, Summer 1985, pp. 64–75. At the time of writing, Valarie A. Zeithaml was associate professor of marketing at Texas A&M University.

households (now accounting for more than 25 percent of total U.S. households), and the elderly (22.4 percent of all households now include persons 65 or older) outdistance past estimates. Social trends, such as longer life spans, later marriage, and frequent divorce, foreshadow greater changes to come. These demographic shifts may require alterations in the way firms view their target markets, for many traditional markets are being replaced by these new groups of consumers.

demographics will lead to a splintering of the mass market for grocery products and for supermarkets. Traditionally, the primary market for most grocery products was the typical American family, consisting of working father, homemaker mother, and two children. Grocery shoppers were viewed as a homogeneous group: the primary household food shopper was the female-housewife-mother whose role expectations included providing healthy meals at an economical price (Geiken 1964, Sharp and Mott 1956, Wolgast 1958). The 1980 census revealed a startling fact: only 7 percent of the 82 million households surveyed fit the description of the typical American family. Only 13 percent of the households contained a working father, nonworking mother, and children. The remaining households consisted of dual-career couples, single individuals, single parents, or nonfamily households.

How might changing household demographics affect supermarket shopping? First, the demographic composition of shoppers will diversify. One example, foreshadowed by McCall (1977) and recently confirmed by research, is an increase in the number and proportion of males shopping for food. Single and divorced men, as well as married men sharing the food shopping tasks, assumed sole or joint responsibility for approximately 40 percent of shopping trips observed in a field study of supermarkets (Zeithaml 1982). A full 30 percent of these trips were conducted by males shopping alone (28 percent or with a male friend (2 percent). In addition to males, other demographic groups—working females, the elderly, and singles—frequent supermarkets in larger numbers than in the past.

A second pivotal change involves the psychographic profiles of the new demographic segments. While the female-housewife-mother's

psychographic profile was relatively well-defined, the profiles of the new demographic groups are as yet unspecified. To what extent do these new groups engage in traditional supermarket shopping behaviors such as clipping coupons, budgeting, searching the newspapers for special prices, and composing shopping lists? Are the new groups economy-conscious, or does convenience predominate? When most men, single individuals, single parents, or working women assume food shopping responsibilities, they do so in addition to working outside the home. How do these multiple roles affect the time available to plan and execute supermarket shopping? How do these new supermarket shoppers view grocery shopping?

The study reported here was designed to profile the attitudes and behaviors of the new demographic groups with respect to supermarket shopping. The research focuses on the relationship of five demographic factors—sex, female working status, age, income, and marital status—to a wide range of variables associated with preparation for and execution of supermarket shopping. The study's implications extend both to manufacturers and retailers of grocery products. Discussion centers on the ways that changing demographics and family roles may affect firms and how marketers may adapt to these changes.

## THEORETICAL BACKGROUND

Role theory provides one explanation for the division of labor in the social institution of the family (Sarbin and Allen 1968). Traditional roles, such as housewife-mother and husband-father, functioned to circumscribe the responsibilities and behavior of family members. According to the expectations of his role, the husband-father worked outside the home, aided in child rearing, and did much of the yard work (Reilly 1982). According to the expectations of her role, the housewife-mother stayed home, raised children, kept house, prepared meals, and planned and shopped for food. Although individual differences existed in the enactment of the roles, the basic structure of the traditional family was clearly defined, and these housewife-mother, husband-father roles accurately depicted the majority of American families prior to the 1960s.

When the family unit itself changes, the roles of its members are likely to be altered. In a household consisting of a single adult, for example, one individual must execute all tasks and activities formerly divided between husband and wife. Sex roles are merged, with women performing tasks traditionally assigned to men and vice versa (Blood 1963, Green and Cunningham 1975). The individual—male or female—must work outside the home, raise the children (if any are present), keep house, prepare meals, and shop for food.

In a household where both adults work outside the home, role definitions may also be merged (McCall 1977). Research evidence supports changes in sex or gender role norms resulting from women entering the work force (Mason, Oppenheim, and Czajka 1976; Parelius 1975; Scanzoni 1975, 1978). As a consequence, family responsibilities may be reallocated, with husbands performing domestic tasks traditionally associated with the wife (Lazar and Smallwood 1977, McCall 1977).

In many of the households representing the new demographics (e.g., households consisting of singles or couples with dual careers), individuals may be expected to perform multiple roles. The result of performing multiple roles may be role conflict, the presence of conflicting or inconsistent

expectations. Role overload is one form of role conflict that occurs when the volume of behavior demanded by an individual's role exceeds available time and energy (Reilly 1982). Evidence indicates that working women may be especially prone to this form of conflict (Rapoport and Rapoport 1969, Strober and Weinberg 1980).

## RELATIONSHIPS BETWEEN DEMOGRAPHIC CHARACTERISTICS AND SUPERMARKET SHOPPING

This paper assumes that the changing demographic composition of the population will result in alterations in food purchasing and supermarket shopping behaviors. Role theory helps explain these food purchasing changes, for expectations of members are vastly different in these newer households. Table 1 summarizes the hypothesized relationships between demographic variables and supermarket shopping behaviors. While these relationships are complex, and covariation among the variables is expected, the general rationale for the predicted relationships is presented first by individual demographic variables. Following the development of individual variables, their interrelationships will be discussed.

**Table 1 ☐ Hypothesized relationships between demographic variables and supermarket shopping variables**

| Supermarket shopping variable | Sex<br>F = Female<br>M = Male | Female working status<br>WW = Working women<br>NWW = Nonworking women | Age<br>O = Old<br>Y = Young | Income<br>L = Low<br>H = High | Marital status<br>M = Married<br>S = Single |
|---|---|---|---|---|---|
| **Shopping time and frequency** | | | | | |
| Shopping time in minutes | F > M | NWW > WW | O > Y | L > H | M > S |
| Number of weekly trips | F > M | NWW > WW | Y > O | L > H | S > M |
| **Supermarket expenditures** | | | | | |
| Amount spent per trip | F > M | WW > NWW | O > Y | H > L | M > S |
| Weekly grocery expenditures | M > F | WW > NWW | Y < M > O | H > L | M > S |
| **Reported supermarket behaviors** | | | | | |
| Extent of planning | F > M | NWW > WW | O > Y | L > H | M > S |
| Extent of information usage | F > M | NWW > WW | O > Y | L > H | M > S |
| Extent of economizing | F > M | NWW > WW | O > Y | L > H | M > S |
| **Attitudes toward grocery shopping**<br>Agreement with the following items: | | | | | |
| Shopping is fun. | F > M | NWW > WW | O > Y | L > H | M > S |
| Shopping takes too much time. | M > F | WW > NWW | Y > O | H > L | S > M |
| Shopping is important. | F > M | NWW > WW | O > Y | L > H | M > S |

## Sex: Male responses to role conflict

The male-as-breadwinner self-perception may conflict with male-as-housekeeper responsibilities. Men may perceive household duties, such as being "good shoppers," to be less central to their roles. Furthermore, males are less accustomed to performing the behaviors associated with shopping (e.g., clipping and redeeming coupons). As a consequence, they may not allocate time and effort to the tasks and may be less efficient when they try to do so. They may, for example, spend less time in the grocery store and less money per trip, partly because they engage in less planning (e.g., preparing shopping lists, reading newspaper advertising) than females. They may also avoid shopping (make fewer shopping trips) and may spend more money per week (because they are less concerned with the efficiency of their shopping). These and other predicted relationships are shown in Table 1.

## Female working status: Role overload

Females who combine work outside the home with household responsibilities are likely to experience greater time constraints than nonworking women (Allen and Schaninger 1980, Douglas 1976b, McCall 1977, Reilly 1982, Strober and Weinberg 1980). When faced with multiple roles and numerous demands from these roles, the working woman must spend less time performing some tasks. Evidence from past research suggests that working wives spend less time in the supermarket (Hacklander 1978), make fewer shopping trips (Anderson 1972, Douglas 1976b, McCall 1977), and spend fewer hours per day on housework (Reynolds, Crask, and Wells 1977; Robinson and Converse 1972; Stafford and Duncan 1977; Walker and Woods 1976) than their nonworking counterparts.

Douglas (1976b) and McCall (1977) emphasize that appropriate behavior in performing the role of homemaker may be altered in working females. Working women may not expect themselves to be as efficient in supermarket shopping as nonworking women and, indeed, may not need to be as efficient because family income is increased as a result of their employment. As a consequence, price may be a less important consideration than other factors, such as convenience and time savings (Lazer and Smallwood 1977, McCall 1977).

Research evidence documents that working wives are less likely to report checking prices and using price-off coupons (Strober and Weinberg 1980).

Predicted relationships between female working status and supermarket shopping (Table 1) are based on the premise that role overload in working females results in less time and effort devoted to supermarket shopping.

## Age: Established roles

Role theory also leads to a prediction of differences in shopping behavior and attitudes based on age. The older the shopper, the more likely he/she grew up in a traditional household and developed the role expectations of the husband-father and housewife-mother. In contrast, the younger the shopper, the more likely he/she was raised in a modern household which emphasized different role expectations.

Past research has provided support for the hypothesized relationships shown in Table 1. In general, evidence indicates that the older the shopper, the more likely he/she would plan and economize (Mason and Bearden 1978), leading to more time and money spent on a single trip (Miklos 1982), fewer trips (Martin 1975, Miklos 1982), greater use of information (Bernhardt and Kinnear 1975, Clancy 1975, Mason and Bearden 1979), and more positive attitudes toward supermarket shopping (Mason and Bearden 1978, Miklos 1982).

Past research has documented relationships between age and household spending and shopping behavior (e.g., Buss and Schaninger 1983, Green and Cunningham 1975).

## Marital status: Multiple roles for the singles

Single individuals must perform all tasks and activities usually divided between a husband and wife. When the single individual has children, he/she must perform the husband-father and housewife-mother roles simultaneously—working outside the home as well as performing household duties. In that situation, role overload may be experienced, leading to diminished time and energy to devote to household responsibilities and shopping.

When the single individual has no children, the housewife-mother role may be irrelevant, leading

to low expectations regarding cooking and supermarket shopping. Either way, single people are
hypothesized to plan and economize less, to
spend less time and money in the supermarket,
and to possess less positive attitudes toward supermarket shopping than married individuals.

## Income: Less need and diminished role expectations

Individuals with higher incomes may be less inclined to be economical shoppers, partly because
they have less need to conserve money than
those with lower incomes (Speh 1977). Too, research has indicated that as income increases,
the demand for leisure time increases. Activities
associated with food shopping may be viewed as
unnecessarily time-consuming and may be de-
emphasized as income increases (Sharir 1974).

Role theory may also partially explain the effect
of income on supermarket shopping. The higher
the income, the lower the need to perform the
"good shopper" role. Hypothesized relationships,
based both on role theory and on past research
(e.g., Buss and Schaninger 1983, Cox and Rich
1964, Green and Cunningham 1975) are presented in Table 1.

## Interrelationships among variables

For clarity, predictions based on role theory were
developed above by individual demographic variable. The hypothesized relationships, however, are
not expected to be as simple or independent as developed. The demographic variables are highly correlated (e.g., younger respondents are more likely
to be single than middle-aged respondents, dual-
career respondents are likely to have higher family
incomes than single respondents). Consequently,
the effects of each demographic variable are likely
to be moderated by other demographic variables.
The effects of working status, for example, will vary
with sex, marital status, and age.

Predictions could be offered about the specific
combination of variables that would most influence
each dependent variable. To extend the reasoning
presented in Table 3, single young men with no
children and high incomes would be expected to
do the least planning, economizing, and budgeting. Because of the complexity of these interrelationships and the large number of hypotheses

required to specify them, individual hypotheses
will not be developed but can be inferred from the
table.

## METHODOLOGY

### Sample

A combination of judgment and probability
sampling was used to select the respondents for
this study. Supermarkets were chosen using judgment samples; within those supermarkets, respondents were selected randomly to obtain
representative samples of shoppers frequenting
the stores.

**Selection of stores.** To obtain geographic
representation, four cities were selected, one each
from the East, Southeast, Midwest, and Pacific
Coast. Each city was a major metropolitan area
with enough supermarkets to match characteristics with all other cities. Within each city, three supermarkets were selected, using the following
criteria: (1) area of at least 25,000 square feet,
and annual sales volume of at least $5 million; (2)
mixture of urban and suburban stores; and (3)
mixture of scanner-equipped and nonscanner-
equipped stores.

**Selection of subjects within stores.** During
the hours of the study (Thursday 2 to 9 P.M.; Fri-
day 9 A.M. to 9 P.M.; and Saturday 9 A.M. to 3 P.M.),
interviewers systematically selected shoppers to
complete questionnaires. Interviewers began sampling on the hour, continued for one half hour,
then resumed sampling on the next hour.

Interviewers were stationed near the checkout
stands in a position where the entrances to the
store were visible. At the designated sampling
times (on the hour on Thursdays and Fridays and
on the half hour on Saturdays), interviewers identified every eighth shopper or shopping group entering the stores. The interviewers noted
identifying characteristics of the shopper or group
(shopping cart number where available; otherwise,
a physical description) and recorded the starting
time of the shopping trip. Later, when the selected
shopper began checking out, his/her ending time
was recorded. Following checkout, the amount of
purchase was recorded. The selected shopper
was then approached and asked to complete the
questionnaire. If the customer refused, he/she

was asked to take the questionnaire home and mail it back in a stamped, self-addressed envelope.

**Response rate.** To help control for nonresponse, a two-stage system of collecting information was used. First, subjects were asked to complete the questionnaires in the store. Of the 1,416 customers approached, 841 or 59.4 percent complied with the interviewers' requests and provided data in the supermarket. Second, all selected customers who did not fill out the questionnaire in the store were asked to complete it at home and return it. Through this second stage, an additional 135 or 9.5 percent of the original respondents approached returned their questionnaires, making the combined response rate 68.9 percent. Incomplete answers on the demographic questions eliminated 103 of the questionnaires, making the effective response rate equal to 61.7 percent.

Problems involving nonresponse bias were anticipated in this field study. Because working women with less time to shop for groceries may be less amenable to filling in questionnaires, they could have been underrepresented in the sample. Because of this potential problem, checks were made on the sampling procedures to detect nonresponse bias. All customers approached in the stores, even those who did not respond, were asked whether they worked. Interviewers also recorded the sex of the respondent. Through this procedure, a comparison of respondents with nonrespondents was possible on these two pivotal demographic characteristics. No significant differences were found between respondents and nonrespondents based on sex ($\chi^2 = 1.84$, p > .40) or on working status ($\chi^2 = .056$, p > .97).

To determine the overall representativeness of the sample, characteristics of respondents were compared to 1980 U.S. Census figures on age, income, household size, education, and marital status. Demographic characteristics of the sample were comparable to those of the U.S. population except on the dimension of income. The median age of the sample was 37.4 years; the median age of the U.S. population (after eliminating people under 17 and over 75) was 38.6 years. The median reported income of the sample was $27,500; the median household income of the U.S. population was $17,500 in 1979. While the

difference appears quite large, it may be partially explained by nonresponse to the income question (especially by respondents from inner-city stores), by inflation (1982 figures used for the sample and 1979 for the population), and by the possibility that some respondents overreported income. The mean household size in the sample was 2.83; the mean household size in the U.S. in 1980 was 2.75. The median school years completed by respondents in the sample were 12.5, comparable to the median of 11.5 for persons 25 and older in the population. Chi-square analysis for differences between the sample and population in terms of marital status yielded no significance ($\chi^2 = 2.56$, p > .10).

### Measures

Descriptions and measures of all dependent variables are presented in Table 2.

### RESULTS

Role theory provided the foundation for hypotheses concerning supermarket shopping behavior and attitudes of the demographic segments. In general, the hypotheses predicted that supermarket shopping would be less important to several demographic segments (e.g., males, working females, young shoppers) than to the traditional female-housewife-mother segment. A number of specific differences in attitudes and behavior were revealed.

Analysis of variance and covariance were used to examine the differences among demographic groups of shoppers on all dependent variables. Demographic variables incorporated into the models run on all respondents included those expected to affect supermarket shopping based on role theory: sex, age, marital status, and income. To control for differences due to household size and education, these variables were entered as covariates (each was measured on an interval scale). ANOVA results are shown in Table 3. Significant differences in means of supermarket shopping variables by demographic variable are shown in Table 4.

To determine the effect of female working status on the supermarket shopping variables, all

**Table 2 ☐ Descriptions and measures of supermarket variables**

| | Variable | Description |
|---|---|---|
| Shopping time and frequency | Shopping time in minutes | Total number of minutes from store entry to checkout[a] |
| | Number of supermarkets visited weekly | Number of different supermarkets visited weekly |
| | Number of weekly shopping trips | Weekly frequency of supermarket shopping trips |
| Supermarket expenditures | Amount spent | Total purchase amount on observed trip[a] |
| | Dollars spent/minute | Calculated by dividing amount spent by shopping time in minutes[a] |
| | Weekly grocery expenditures | Estimate of respondents' weekly grocery expenditures |
| Reported supermarket behaviors | Extent of planning | Scale formed by summing three items dealing with preparation of shopping lists, budgeting, and planning lists around newspaper advertising (adapted from Guiltinan and Monroe 1978). Coefficient alpha = .85. |
| | Extent of information usage | Scale formed by summing three items dealing with use of nutritional labeling, product freshness dates, and newspaper advertising (adapted from Guiltinan and Monroe 1978). Coefficient alpha = .88. |
| | Extent of economizing | Scale formed by summing four items dealing with shopping for store specials, using unit prices, redeeming coupons, and checking grocery prices (adapted from Guiltinan and Monroe 1978). Coefficient alpha = .75. |
| Attitudes toward grocery shopping | "Shopping is fun." "Grocery shopping takes too much time." "Grocery shopping is important." | Seven-point scales ranging from 1 (strongly agree) to 7 (strongly disagree); scales were adapted from Guiltinan and Monroe 1978. |

[a]These variables were measured or documented by the interviewers. All other variables were reported by the respondents.

**Table 3 ☐ ANOVA results for the effects of demographic variables on supermarket shopping variables (all respondents: n = 976)**

| | F statistics | | | | | | |
|---|---|---|---|---|---|---|---|
| Variable | Sex | Age | Income | Marital status | Education | Household size | Significant interactions |
| Shopping time (minutes) | 9.93[b] | 3.36[b] | 4.46[a] | < 1 | 1.03 | 7.17[b] | |
| Number of supermarkets visited weekly | < 1 | 3.03[c] | 3.05[b] | 2.91 | < 1 | 2.47 | |
| Number of weekly shopping trips | 5.54[b] | 3.53[b] | 1.10 | 1.1 | 2.26 | 8.88[b] | |
| Extent of planning | 20.54[a] | 5.06[a] | 3.30[b] | 21.38[a] | 6.49[c] | 7.93[b] | S × A × I[c] |
| Extent of information usage | 40.21[a] | 10.66[a] | < 1 | 23.24[a] | < 1 | 2.30 | A × MS[b] |
| Extent of economizing | 24.78[a] | 11.25[a] | 2.08 | 16.67[a] | 1.03 | 6.00[c] | |
| Amount spent | < 1 | < 1 | 8.17[a] | 2.01 | < 1 | 23.55[a] | |
| Dollars spent/minute | < 1 | 2.46[c] | 1.49 | 3.08 | < 1 | 5.33[c] | A × MS[c] |
| Weekly grocery expenditures | 1.10 | 5.14[a] | 11.68[a] | 7.27[b] | 4.98[c] | 444.51[a] | I × A[c], I × MS[c] |
| "Shopping is fun." | 2.27 | 3.09[b] | 8.10[a] | 2.6 | 9.96[b] | 1.08 | A × I[b] |
| "Shopping takes too much time." | < 1 | 3.52[b] | 1.98 | < 1 | 5.41[b] | < 1 | S × A[c] |
| "Shopping is an important task." | 17.40[a] | 5.77[a] | < 1 | 10.58[a] | 7.39[b] | < 1 | S × I[c] |

[a]p ≤ .0001.
[b]p ≤ .01.
[c]p ≤ .05.

**Table 4 □ Significant differences in means of supermarket shopping variables by demographic variables**

| Variable | Sex | | Marital status | | Age | | | | | Income | | | | | | All Respondents |
|---|---|---|---|---|---|---|---|---|---|---|---|---|---|---|---|---|
| | Males | Females | Single | Married | 18–24 | 25–39 | 40–49 | 50–64 | 65+ | Under $7,500 | $7,500–14,999 | $15,000–24,999 | $25,000–34,999 | $35,000–44,999 | $45,000+ | |
| Time spent shopping (minutes) | 18.02 | 22.19 | | | 18.96[a] | 20.30[a,b] | 23.41[b,c] | 22.17[c] | 23.71[c] | 18.02[a] | 18.56[a] | 19.23[a] | 20.40[a] | 24.54[b] | 25.60[b] | 21.28 |
| Number of supermarkets visited weekly | | | | | 1.76[a] | 1.84[a] | 2.04[b] | 1.97[a,b] | 2.08[b] | 1.91[a] | 1.83[a,b] | 1.90[a] | 1.96[c] | 1.90[a] | 1.80[b] | 1.91 |
| Number of weekly shopping trips | 2.48 | 2.28 | | | 2.09[a] | 2.23[a] | 2.66[c] | 2.33[a,b] | 2.51[b,c] | | | | | | | 2.33 |
| Extent of planning[1] | 9.21 | 11.31 | 9.61 | 11.46 | 10.83[a] | 10.45[a] | 10.38[a] | 11.74[b] | 12.23[b] | 11.36[a] | 11.57[a] | 10.39[b] | 11.11[a,b] | 11.42[a] | 9.78[b,c] | 10.87 |
| Extent of information usage[2] | 11.03 | 13.23 | 11.59 | 13.32 | 11.52[a] | 12.41[a,b] | 12.67[b] | 14.82[c] | 14.46[c] | | | | | | | 12.77 |
| Extent of economizing[3] | 14.39 | 17.28 | 14.95 | 17.49 | 15.27[a] | 16.12[a] | 16.02[a] | 18.08[b] | 19.92[b] | | | | | | | 16.68 |
| Amount of purchase | | | | | | | | | | $15.82[a] | $19.43[a,b] | $24.68[b,c] | 27.80[c] | $33.69[d] | $38.56[e] | $28.05 |
| Dollars spent/minute | | | | | $1.75[a] | $1.43[a,b] | $1.57[a,b] | $1.29[b,c] | $.94[c] | | | | | | | $1.42 |
| Weekly expenditures on groceries | | | | | $54.53[a] | $72.46[b] | $91.43[c] | $65.41[b] | $50.42[a] | $44.06[a] | $52.40[a] | $61.27[b] | $74.11[c] | $76.65[c] | $91.78[d] | $70.05 |
| "Shopping is fun."[4] | | | | | 4.87[a] | 5.34[b] | 5.73[b] | 4.99[a] | 4.23[c] | 3.65[a] | 4.61[b] | 5.15[c] | 5.22[c] | 5.44[c,d] | 5.89[d] | 5.18 |
| "Shopping takes too much time."[4] | | | | | 3.98[a,b,c] | 3.84[b,c] | 3.58[c] | 4.53[a] | 4.37[a,b] | | | | | | | 3.99 |
| "Shopping is an important task." | 3.58 | 2.80 | 3.32 | 2.80 | 3.43[a] | 3.11[a] | 3.03[a] | 2.58[b] | 2.21[b] | | | | | | | 2.96 |
| n | 189 | 684 | 278 | 595 | 119 | 367 | 138 | 157 | 92 | 57 | 137 | 181 | 210 | 139 | 149 | 873 |

[1]Scale formed by adding the scores of three individual items dealing with planning. Scores on this variable range from 0 to 18, with 0 indicating the lowest amount of planning and 18 indicating the highest amount of planning.

[2]Scale formed by adding the scores of three individual items dealing with the usage of information (e.g., freshness dates). Scores on the variable range from 0 to 18, with 0 indicating the lowest usage of information and 18 indicating the highest usage of information.

[3]Scale formed by adding the scores of four individual items dealing with economizing. Scores on this variable range from 0 to 24, with 0 indicating the lowest usage of information and 24 indicating the highest usage of information.

[4]Scores range from 1 (strongly agree) to 7 (strongly disagree).

[a,b,c]Means with same superscript are not significantly different. Means with different superscripts are significantly different.

models were also run using female respondents only. The ANOVA models shown in Tables 5 and 6 include all demographic variables incorporated in the full models (Tables 3 and 4) plus female working status. The typology used by Yankelovich (1972–1977) and Bartos (1978) was used to classify women into one of four working status groups: *Stay at home, Plan to work, Just a job,* and *Career.*[1]

## Sex

Compared to females, males reported that supermarket shopping was a less important task. As hypothesized, males spent less time on their observed shopping trips: 18.02 minutes, compared to 22.19 by females.

As predicted by role theory, males planned less, used supermarket information less, and economized less than females. On a scale including planning items, such as use of shopping lists, budgeting, and newspaper advertising, males scored 9.21 on average, while females scored 11.31 on average (F = 20.54, p < .0001). Males also reported lower usage of supermarket shopping information, such as unit pricing, product freshness dates, and nutritional labeling (F = 40.21, p < .001). Finally, males revealed a lower emphasis on economy than females by their lower reported shopping for store specials, redemption of coupons, and checking of grocery prices (F = 24.78, p < .0001).

Compared to females, males made more shopping trips per week (2.48, compared to 2.28 by females). While this finding is the opposite of what was expected, it may be explained by the lower level of planning found among males: males may

need to make more frequent trips to pick up last-minute or forgotten items.

No significant differences were found between males and females on the amount of purchase, weekly grocery expenditures, dollars spent per minute, or on two attitudinal variables ("shopping is fun" and "shopping takes too much time").

## Female working status

Female working status showed a significant effect on many of the supermarket shopping variables. Significant differences emerged in number of supermarkets visited weekly, amount of purchase, extent of planning, extent of information usage, and extent of economizing. Differences also occurred in two of the three attitudinal variables: "shopping is fun" and "shopping is an important task."

On most of the shopping variables, working women responded as predicted by role theory. Career women planned less and disagreed more on the subject that shopping is fun than any of the other three female working status groups. Working women also spent significantly more on the observed shopping trip than any other group. Both groups of working women (*Just a job* and *Career*) used information less and economized less than the *Stay at home* and *Plan to work* females. Finally, both groups of working women disagreed significantly more than the nonworking groups that shopping is an important task.

On average, the *Plan to work* female visited more supermarkets per week than any other group. She also used supermarket information and economized significantly more than the average female in the two working groups. She planned more than the career women, but did not differ significantly on this item from the *Stay at home* or *Just a job* female. She spent less on her shopping trip than the *Career* women but more than the *Stay at home* or *Just a job* women. Along with the *Stay at home* women, she felt that shopping was an important task to a greater extent than the working women.

The most striking differences among women occurred between the *Stay at home* and *Career* groups of females. The *Plan to work* group of women appeared to possess attitudes and to demonstrate behaviors that were more consistent

[1]The core concept of female working status has been operationalized in several ways. The simple working/nonworking wife dichotomy has been employed in a number of studies (Anderson 1972, Douglas 1976a, 1976b, Strober 1977, Strober and Weinberg 1980) but has been criticized as too simplistic (Bartos 1978). Schaninger and Allen (1981) developed a three-way classification (nonworking wife, low occupational status wife, and high occupational status wife) comparable to Rapoport and Rapoport's typology (1969, 1971a, 1971b, 1978)—nonworking wife, dual-career family, and dual-income family. Finally, industry studies have reported improved segmentation ability using a four-way scheme which includes *Stay at home, Plan to work, Just a job,* and *Career* women (Bartos 1978, Yankelovich 1972–1977). The four-way scheme was used here to provide the most comprehensive typology of the working status options and to permit analysis of all women in the sample, rather than just married women (as is the case with two- and three-way schemes).

**Table 5 ☐ ANOVA results for the effects on female working status and other demographics on supermarket variables (female respondents only: n = 698)**

| | F statistics | | | | | | |
|---|---|---|---|---|---|---|---|
| Variable | Working status | Age | Income | Marital status | Education | Household size | Significant interactions |
| Shopping time (minutes) | 1.23 | 2.41 | 4.41[a] | < 1 | < 1 | 4.67[c] | |
| Number of supermarkets visited weekly | 3.31[c] | 3.28[c] | 3.40[b] | < 1 | < 1 | 1.90 | |
| Number of weekly shopping trips | 1.92 | 3.14[c] | 1.11 | 3.75 | 10.33[a] | 13.42[a] | A × MS[c] |
| Extent of planning | 6.81[a] | 1.96 | 2.65[c] | 12.18[a] | 1.16 | 1.09 | |
| Extent of information usage | 7.06[a] | 5.02[b] | < 1 | 8.41[a] | 2.57 | < 1 | WS × A |
| Extent of economizing | 7.93[a] | 3.83[b] | 1.04 | 7.08[b] | < 1 | 2.67 | |
| Amount spent | 3.13[a] | < 1 | 8.62[a] | < 1 | < 1 | 25.30[a] | |
| Dollars spent/minute | 1.00 | 1.99 | 1.54 | < 1 | < 1 | 3.73[c] | HH × MS |
| Weekly grocery expenditures | 3.59[b] | 5.08[b] | 8.71[a] | 2.13 | 7.07[b] | 361.02[a] | A × MS[b] |
| "Shopping is fun." | 5.77[a] | 1.22 | 8.28[a] | < 1 | 6.22[c] | 2.45 | |
| "Shopping takes too much time." | 1.49 | < 1 | 2.08 | < 1 | < 1 | < 1 | |
| "Shopping is an important task." | 5.29[a] | 2.39 | 1.26 | 5.51[c] | 1.88 | < 1 | |

[a] $p \leq .001$.
[b] $p \leq .01$.
[c] $p \leq .05$.

**Table 6 ☐ Means of supermarket shopping variables by demographic variables (female respondents only)**

| | Female working status | | | | All women |
|---|---|---|---|---|---|
| Variable | Stay at home | Plan to work | Just a job | Career | |
| Time spent shopping (minutes) | | | | | 22.19 |
| Number of supermarkets visited weekly | 1.95[a] | 2.20[b] | 1.86[a] | 1.79[a] | 1.91 |
| Number of weekly shopping trips | | | | | 2.28 |
| Extent of planning[1] | 12.13[a] | 12.26[a,b] | 11.19[b] | 9.67[c] | 11.31 |
| Extent of information usage[2] | 13.80[a,b] | 14.52[a] | 12.85[b,c] | 12.50[c] | 13.23 |
| Extent of economizing[3] | 18.33[a] | 19.44[a] | 16.63[b] | 15.57[b] | 17.28 |
| Amount of purchase | $28.11[a] | $31.51[b] | $26.04[a] | $34.31[c] | $28.71 |
| Dollars spent/minute | | | | | $1.44 |
| Weekly expenditures on groceries | | | | | $72.89 |
| "Shopping is fun."[4] | 4.09[a] | 4.82[a] | 5.32[b] | 5.96[c] | 4.96 |
| "Shopping takes too much time."[4] | | | | | 4.05 |
| "Shopping is an important task." | 2.42[a] | 2.36[a] | 3.01[b] | 3.20[b] | 2.80 |
| n | 235 | 65 | 269 | 115 | 684 |

[1]Scale formed by adding the scores of three individual items dealing with planning. Scores on this variable range from 0 to 18, with 0 indicating the lowest amount of planning and 18 indicating the highest amount of planning.
[2]Scale formed by adding the scores of three individual items dealing with the usage of information (e.g., nutritional labeling, freshness dates). Scores on the variable range from 0 to 18, with 0 indicating the lowest usage of information, and 18 indicating the highest usage of information.
[3]Scale formed by adding the scores of four individual items dealing with economizing. Scores on this variable range from 0 to 24, with 0 indicating the lowest usage of information, and 24 indicating the highest usage of information.
[4]Scores range from 1 (strongly agree) to 7 (strongly disagree).
[a,b,c]Means with same superscript are not significantly different. Means with different superscripts are significantly different.

with the *Stay at home* women than with the working women. These findings are congruent with predictions based on role theory.

**Age**

Significant age differences were found in all shopping variables except dollars spent per minute. In the majority of cases, differences occurred in the direction predicted by role theory. As age increased, shopping time, number of supermarkets visited weekly, and number of weekly shopping trips all increased. The predicted relationships regarding number of weekly shopping trips was opposite to that expected: as age increased, the frequency of trips increased. One possible explanation is that older shoppers have more discretionary time than younger respondents, and, as a result, spend more time per trip *and* make more frequent trips.

In general, older shoppers planned more for shopping than younger shoppers. The two older groups showed significantly higher scores on this variable than the younger groups. Older shoppers also tended to use information more and to economize more than younger shoppers.

Weekly expenditures on groceries showed a nonmonotonic relationship with age: the youngest and oldest groups of shoppers spent much less per week than the age groups in the middle ($54.43 for 18–24, $50.42 for 65 +, and $91.43 for 40–49). The younger shoppers spent much more per minute than the elderly group ($1.75 per minute in the 18–24 group, compared to $.94 per minute in the 65 + group).

A direct relationship existed between the importance of shopping and age—the younger the shopper, the less important he/she felt shopping to be. The relationships between age and perception of shopping as fun was nonmonotonic: the oldest and youngest groups agreed more than the middle age groups that shopping is fun.

### Marital status

Marital status showed a significant effect on only four of the supermarket shopping variables: extent of planning, extent of economizing, extent of information usage, and importance of shopping. As predicted by role theory, married respondents considered shopping to be more important than did single respondents. Married respondents— whether male or female—planned, economized, and used information significantly more than single shoppers.

### Income

Income affected the time spent shopping, number of supermarkets visited weekly, extent of planning, amount of purchase, weekly expenditures on groceries, and one of the attitudinal variables, "shopping is fun."

Several intriguing results emerged for the income variables. First, while income was related to time spent shopping (as predicted), shoppers with higher income spent more time than those with lower income (direction opposite that predicted). A possible explanation for this finding is that high-income respondents shop less frequently (confirmed by results) and spend more per trip (also confirmed by results). Second, high-income shoppers did not view supermarket shopping as less important and did not differ in the amount of economizing or information use. High-income respondents, however, did plan significantly less than low-income shoppers.

### Interactions

Interactions among the demographic variables were significant in many of the ANOVA models (see Tables 3 and 5). These significant interactions indicate that the effects of the individual demographic variable are often qualified by other demographic variables.

In the models run on all respondents, a three-way interaction (sex × age × income) was found for the extent of planning. Young males with high incomes planned less than any other combination of levels of the three demographic variables; elderly females in the $7,500–14,999 income group planned more than any other group. Two-way interactions were significant for extent of information usage (married females used the greatest amount of information), dollars spent per minute (married women in the 40–49 age group spent more per minute), weekly grocery expenditures (respondents with the highest income in the 40–49 age group spent more per week than any other combination of income and age levels; married women in the highest income group spent more than any other combination of marital status and income levels), and for all three of the attitude dependent variables.

In the models run only on females, significant two-way interactions were found for number of weekly shopping trips (married women 65 + years old made the highest number), extent of information usage (stay-at-home females in the 50–64 age group used information most), dollars spent per minute (married women with the largest households spent most), and weekly grocery expenditures (married women in the 40–49 age group spent most).

## IMPLICATIONS

Based on traditional role definitions in the family, many food retailers and manufacturers continue to key their product developments and promotions to the female-housewife-mother, as she is thought to be the purchaser, the decider, and the planner for the household's food. Census figures strongly indicate that the family unit is changing, shrinking the number of typical female-housewife-mothers in the U.S. population. With 40.1 percent of all U.S. households consisting of single, divorced, or widowed individuals (12 percent of that group with children), and with 45.6 million working women in the population, marketers and retailers of grocery products may want to reexamine their target markets. As McCall (1977) commented:

> They may well find that the crystallized assumptions they have held as blessed for several centuries are as antiquated as the product they are producing, the method used to distribute it, or the appeal they apply to their promotion to sell it. (p. 64)

The opportunities for marketers to adapt to changes brought about by demographic shifts and resulting role redefinitions have been suggested by researchers and practitioners (Bartos 1978, Green and Cunningham 1975). This study suggests a number of emerging segments that may be relevant to both manufacturers and retailers.

### The male customer

The number of men shopping for food is substantial, yet few retailers and manufacturers have acknowledged or addressed this segment. This study indicates that males do not respond as well as females to conventional promotion (newspaper advertising, coupons, price promotions). How can grocery manufacturers and retailers appeal to this segment? Coupons in male-oriented media and advertising messages targeted to males may not work the way they do in female segments because males do not view shopping, planning, and economizing the same way that females view them. Conventional strategies may unnecessarily cut into profits if males are fundamentally not concerned with saving money at the supermarket. Therefore, redesigned packages with masculine appeal and point-of-purchase displays oriented to males may be more appropriate because they fit the male's shopping style. Ways to reach and motivate males to purchase products remain to be researched.

### The working female customer

Working women exemplify what has been called the "time-buying customer" (Berry 1979). Working females reveal a need to conserve time in preparing for and executing supermarket shopping. What strategies can grocery retailers and manufacturers implement to better serve the segment? Methods that reduce time in the store (uncluttered aisles, scanning equipment, extra express lanes, extra checkers during the after-work rush) and increase convenience (extended hours, fully stocked shelves, carryout service, phone in/drive through) may be more critical to this segment than a supermarket's price level and specials. Point-of-purchase displays targeted directly to this segment (featuring quick and easy meals, nutritious snacks, items for brown bag lunches) may be useful to this group. Special delicatessens offering full dinners that may be purchased for consumption at home may also be perceived as a valuable service for the working woman.

### Buying-for-one customer (Berry 1980)

The market for products aimed at single individuals is large, growing, and underserved. Census projections place the percentage of single households in 1990 at 50 percent, yet to date few grocery marketers have introduced products addressing the special needs of this segment. A notable exception is frozen foods, the assortment and sale of which have grown dramatically. Lean Cuisine, a line of low-calorie frozen dinners by Stouffer's, showed a phenomenal market share increase of 13 percent (from 33 percent to 46 percent) and reported sales of more than $120,000 in 1983. While not originally targeted to singles (Stouffer's aimed ads at women and general consumers), Lean Cuisine filled a need for quality and convenience in the singles market. Opportunities exist for other products and services that capitalize on the convenience needs of this segment.

## The senior customer

The elderly customer will increase in importance to manufacturers and retailers in future years because of the aging of the population. In addition to diet and health needs, the elderly have special needs in supermarkets. The profile of this group is very different from younger shoppers. The elderly view shopping as important and exhibit behaviors that reflect a strong traditional orientation. Conventional promotions seem to influence this segment more than any other segment. For this reason, manufacturers and retailers may want to be certain, when adapting to the needs of younger and busier customers, that they do not ignore the service and tradition that will serve the elderly segment.

The splintering of the mass market for grocery products presents challenges and opportunities to retailers and marketers. As U.S. demographics change, purchasing patterns for grocery products also change. The number of U.S. households fitting the traditional mold is shrinking, and marketers need to prepare for the changing marketplace by developing products and services aimed at the emerging segments.

## REFERENCES

Allen, Chris T., and Charles M. Schaninger (1980), "Dual Career, Dual Income, and Non-Work Wife Families: Perspectives and Research Directions," in *1980 Educators' Conference Proceedings,* R. P. Bagozzi et al., eds., Chicago: American Marketing, 93–96.

Anderson, Beverlee (1972), "Working vs. Non-working Women: A Comparison of Shopping Behavior," *Proceedings of the AMA Fall Conference,* Chicago: American Marketing.

Bartos, Rena (1978), "What Every Marketer Should Know about Women," *Harvard Business Review,* 56 (May–June), 73–85.

Bernhardt, K., and T. Kinnear (1975), "Profiling the Senior Citizen Market," in *Advances in Consumer Research,* 3, B. B. Anderson, ed., Chicago: Association for Consumer Research.

Berry, Leonard L. (1979), "The Time-Buying Consumer," *Journal of Retailing,* 55 (Winter), 58–59.

——— (1980), "The New Consumer," in *Competitive Structures in Retail Market, The Department Store Perspective,* Ronald W. Stampfl and Elizabeth Hirschman, eds., Chicago: American Marketing, 1–12.

Blood, Robert O. (1963), *New Roles for Men and Women,* New York: Association Press.

Buss, W. C., and Charles M. Schaninger (1983), "The Influence of Sex Roles on Family Decision Processes and Outcomes," *Advances in Consumer Research,* 10.

Clancy, K. (1975), "Preliminary Observations on Media Use and Food Habits of the Elderly," *The Gerontologist,* 15 (December), 529–532.

Cox, Donald F., and Stuart U. Rich (1964), "Perceived Risk and Consumer Decision Making—The Case of Telephone Shopping," *Journal of Marketing Research,* 1 (November), 32–39.

Douglas, Susan P. (1976a), "Cross-National Comparisons and Consumer Stereotypes: A Case Study of Working and Nonworking Wives in the U.S. and France," *Journal of Consumer Research,* 3 (June), 12–20.

——— (1976b), "Working Wife vs. Non-Working Wife Families: A Basis for Segmenting Grocery Markets?," *Advances in Consumer Research,* 3, 191–198.

Geiken, K. (1964), "Expectations Concerning Husband-Wife Influence in Consumer Purchase Decisions," *Journal of Marriage and the Family,* 25 (August), 349–352.

Green, Robert T., and Isabella C. M. Cunningham (1975), "Feminine Role Perceptions and Family Purchasing Decisions," *Journal of Marketing Research,* 12 (August), 325–332.

Guiltinan, Joseph P., and Kent B. Monroe (1978), "Identifying and Analyzing Consumer Shopping Strategies," working paper no. 122, Virginia Polytechnic Institute and State University.

Hacklander, Effie H. (1978), "Do Working Wives Shop Differently for Food?," *National Food Review,* 2 (April), 14–22.

Lazer, William, and John E. Smallwood (1977), "The Changing Demographics of Women," *Journal of Marketing,* 41 (July), 14–22.

Martin, Claude R. (1975), "A Transgenerational Comparison: The Elderly Fashion Consumer," *Proceedings,* Association for Consumer Research, 453–456.

Mason, J. Barry, and William O. Bearden (1978), "Profiling the Shopping Behavior of Elderly Consumers," *The Gerontologist,* 18 (October), 455 ff.

—— (1979), "Satisfaction/Dissatisfaction with Food Shopping among Elderly Consumers," *The Journal of Consumer Affairs,* 13 (Winter), 362.

Mason, Karen, John Oppenheim, and Sara Arber Czajka (1976), "Change in U.S. Women's Sex-Role Attitudes, 1964–1975," *American Sociological Review,* 41 (August), 573–596.

McCall, Suzanne H. (1977), "Meet the 'Workwife'," *Journal of Marketing,* 41 (July), 55–65.

Miklos, Pam (1982), *The Supermarket Shopper Experience of the Older Consumer,* Washington, D.C.: Food Marketing Institute.

Parelius, Ann P. (1975), "Emerging Sex Role Attitudes, Expectations, and Strains among College Women," *Journal of Marriage and Family,* 37 (February), 146–154.

Rapoport, Rhona, and Robert Rapoport (1969), "The Dual Career Family: A Variant Pattern and Social Change," *Human Relations,* 22 (February), 3–30.

—— (1971a), *Dual Career Families,* Harmondsworth, England: Penguin.

—— (1971b), "Further Considerations of the Dual-Career Family," *Human Relations,* 24 (December), 519–533.

—— (1978), *Working Couples,* New York: Harper.

Reilly, Michael (1982), "Working Wives and Convenience Consumption," *Journal of Consumer Research,* 8 (March), 407–418.

Reynolds, Fred D., Melvin R. Crask, and William D. Wells (1977), "The Modern Feminine Life Style," *Journal of Marketing,* 41 (July), 55–65.

Robinson, John, and Philip Converse (1972), "Social Changes as Reflected in the Use of Time," in *The Human Meaning of Social Change,* Angus Campbell and Philip Converse, eds., New York: Russell Sage.

Sarbin, Theodore R., and Vernon Allen (1968), "Role Theory," in *The Handbook of Social Psychology,* George Lindzey and Elliot Aronson, eds., Reading, Mass.: Addison-Wesley, 488–567.

Scanzoni, John (1975), *Sex Roles, Life-Styles, and Childbearing: Changing Patterns in Marriage and Family,* New York: Free Press.

—— (1978), *Gender Roles and Family Change: A Panel Study,* Lexington, Mass.: Lexington.

Schaninger, Charles M., and Chris T. Allen (1981), "Wife's Occupational Status as a Consumer Behavior Construct," *Journal of Consumer Research,* 8 (September), 189–196.

Sharir, Samuel (1974), "Brand Loyalty and the Household's Cost of Time," *Journal of Business,* 47 (January), 53–55.

Sharp, Harry, and Paul Mott (1956), "Consumer Decision in the Metropolitan Family," *Journal of Marketing,* 21 (October), 149–156.

Speh, Thomas W. (1977), "A Summary of Doctoral Research Relating to Retailing," *Journal of Retailing,* 53 (Spring), 73–82.

Stafford, Frank, and Greg Duncan (1977), "The Use of Time and Technology by Households in the United States," working paper, Department of Economics, University of Michigan.

Strober, Myra H. (1977), "Working Wives and Major Family Expenditures," *Journal of Consumer Research,* 4 (December), 141–147.

—— and Charles B. Weinberg (1980), "Strategies Used by Working and Non-working Wives to Reduce Time Pressures," *Journal of Consumer Research,* 6 (March), 338–348.

Walker, Katherine E., and Margaret E. Woods (1976), *Time Use: A Measure of Household Production of Family Goods and Services,* Washington, D.C.: Center for the Family, American Home Economics Association.

Wolgast, Elizabeth H. (1958), "Do Husbands or Wives Make the Purchasing Decisions?," *Journal of Marketing,* 23 (October), 151–158.

Yankelovich, S. (1972–1977), *Yankelovich Monitor,* New York.

Zeithaml, Valarie A. (1982), *Supermarket Shoppers' Profile,* Washington, D.C.: Food Marketing Institute.

## QUESTIONS

1. *Briefly summarize the major demographic changes that are taking place among the U.S. population, as identified in the article. Are there other demographic variables which you feel have changed and should be included in the discussion?*

2. *What impact, if any, do you think these demographic changes will have on marketing's "four Ps"—product, place, promotion, and price? For manufacturers? For marketing middlemen?*

3. *Will the increased number of market segments (fragments) increase or decrease the efficiency of the U.S. macro-marketing system? Why?*

*4. With increased market fragmentation, will it be easier or harder for firms to achieve a

sustainable competitive advantage? (Reading 7) Why?

---

*Question relates concepts in this and other readings.

---

□ **14**

---

# Last year it was yuppies—this year it's their parents

*Paul B. Brown*

---

*Although America's fascination with youth may be starting to ebb, the "Yuppies" are still the primary target market for many organizations. However, as the following article points out, a lot of marketers are starting to discover another, perhaps even more lucrative target market—older consumers. In total, the over-50 group have more money to spend—and less of their money is committed to buying "necessities." Thus, they may be ideal targets for highly profitable luxury products.*

---

For years, Joe Smith felt left out. As president of Oxtoby-Smith Inc., a New York research firm, he has plenty of discretionary income. Yet few advertisers seemed to court him. Whenever Smith turned on the TV or opened a magazine, he found lots of ads—but few of them were pitched to him. How come? Smith is over 50.

Now marketers are paying plenty of attention to Smith and his contemporaries. His Long Island mailbox is brimming with catalogs from Neiman-Marcus and brochures describing time-share condominiums. "There are fewer pitches assuming I am feeble and lame," says the 59-year-old Smith. "The world has discovered I did not fall off a cliff when I turned 50. I am a desirable consumer."

Indeed he is. Today older is definitely in. Consider these recent developments:

- Sears, Roebuck & Co., the nation's largest retailer, is wooing customers over 50 with discounts up to 25 percent on everything from eyeglasses to lawnmowers. Started just two years ago, the Mature Outlook Club has already attracted 400,000 dues-paying members.
- Airlines such as American and United are rushing to offer discounts to older passengers. These recently introduced promotions could become as widespread as frequent-flyer bonus programs.
- Southwestern Bell Corp. is publishing a series of telephone directories aimed at senior citizens. Revenue from the Silver Pages is exceeding projections.

These efforts go well beyond the 10 percent discounts local drugstores traditionally offer older customers. They represent a fundamental shift by marketing executives, who now recognize that a consumer's preferences can still be influenced at 49 or even 65—and the potential gains can be enormous. "Just as baby boomers and yuppies were hot last year, this year it is the 49-plus market and seniors," says Peter S. Kim, a vice-president at J. Walter Thompson USA.

The decline of traditional marketing strategies explains much of this new direction. "With the growing diversity in consumer lifestyles, mass-marketing is less efficient," says Jeffrey Prupis, a

---

Source: Reprinted from the March 10, 1986, issue of *Business Week* by special permission, © 1986 by McGraw-Hill, Inc. At the time of writing, Paul B. Brown was on the staff of *Business Week*.

vice-president at Yankelovich, Skelly & White Inc., a New York research firm. "Advertisers are becoming more selective. Everyone is looking for areas of disproportionate affluence."

And that's where older Americans top the charts. People over 50 make up about 25 percent of the population but have nearly 50 percent of the nation's disposable income. They buy $800 billion worth of goods and services each year, according to a study by the Conference Board, an independent research group. More important, they are the fastest-growing age segment. In the next 15 years, the number of adults will grow by 14 percent, but the number of people over 50 will increase by 23 percent. By the year 2000, 76 million Americans will be 50 or older.

Now consider spending patterns. For the over-50 crowd, child-rearing costs are often over and done with. Homes either are paid for or have old, low-cost mortgages. Baby boomers are burdened with major expenses their parents have already met. Says Prupis: "Older people have put off benefiting themselves for the sake of the children. Now they are saying things like, 'Let's buy the VCR, because we don't have to pay Johnny's dentist bill.' "

**Older Americans lead in spending power**

| Age | Discretionary income |
|---|---|
| Under 35 | $2,628 |
| 35–50 | 2,904 |
| 50–55 | 3,685 |
| 55–60 | 4,494 |
| 60–65 | 4,571 |
| 65 and over | 5,219 |
| U.S. average | 3,444 |

Data: The Conference Board.

## PAYING DUES

Still, reaching this group is tricky. Typically, older people have established brand preferences. What's more, their spending tends to be concentrated in specific areas. "Seniors already own all the household goods they need and make replacements only as necessary," says Terrence L. Foran, Touche Ross & Co.'s national director of retail consulting. "They have their wardrobes and are not overly fashion-conscious."

That's why clever marketing is needed. One innovative effort is Sears' Mature Outlook Club, created to attract customers over 50. For a $7.50 annual fee, members receive benefits tailored to their needs. Older people, for example, purchase more than one third of all garden tools. So club members have a standing 20 percent discount on any garden tool they buy at Sears. Similarly, they get lower rates on auto insurance through Sears' Allstate unit. This approach supplements Sears' conventional advertising. "The focus there is on younger customers," says William B. Strauss, Mature Outlook's executive director. "We are targeting an older audience. These people have money and the time to consider what you offer them."

Although Sears is the first major retailer to target older customers, both Strauss and Kurt Barnard, publisher of *Barnard's Retail Marketing Report,* an industry newsletter, predict the idea will catch on. "You are starting to see ads and catalogs that show older people," says Barnard. "The infatuation with the very young is fading, for the simple reason there are fewer of them."

## 'LOVE TO TRAVEL'

The trend extends beyond retailers. People over 50 account for a disproportionately large amount of vacation travel and by some estimates spend 30 percent more than their younger counterparts when they go. To attract them, many lodging chains now offer discounts. Travel agencies, too, have stepped up their efforts. Boston-based Grand Circle Travel, which targets customers over 50 by direct mail, will send out 7 million catalogs this year, nearly triple last year's mailing. Says Chairman Alan E. Lewis: "These people love to travel, and they have the money."

Airlines have gotten the message and have begun offering discount programs for seniors. Michael W. Gunn, senior vice-president for passenger marketing at American Airlines Inc., says the recent decision to offer a 10 percent discount to people over 65 represents "a significant opportunity" to get a bigger share of the growing seniors' market and to encourage more older people to fly. Gunn says those 65 and over now account for nearly 7 percent of American's customers.

The same types of studies that prompted American to enter the market also lured Southwestern Bell. While independent directory companies had previously targeted groups such as Christians or gays, there had never been a widespread effort to reach seniors, says Al C. Parsons, president of Southwestern Bell Publications. By June 1984, Southwestern Bell had a prototype in St. Louis, where the company is based. Success there led to the creation of a 1,000-person sales force that will sell advertising in directories for 91 cities by year-end. "We think we've got a win-win-win situation," Parsons says. "Seniors win because our ads offer them discounts. Companies placing the ads win because they attract more business. And we win by getting more advertising."

## BENCHES AND RESTROOMS

Parsons says Southwestern is spending "many millions" to produce its directories, and he is pleased with the initial results. "We are in our second year in Kansas City, and we were expecting a 20 percent increase in revenues," he says. "We actually achieved 41 percent, even with a 5 percent to 6 percent increase in rates."

This sudden focus on people over 49 has some marketers bemused. "We have been selling to the older customer for years," says Mark C. Hollis, president of Publix Super Markets Inc., the large Florida chain. To make shopping easier, Publix places benches in front of its stores, has restrooms, and teaches employees how to make things easier for the elderly. Checkout clerks, for example, give customers two light bags instead of a single heavy one. Says Hollis: "When they are most of your population, you take care of them."

While Publix' attitude may become widespread, there is no guarantee the attempts to lure older people will pay off. With a market this large, generalizations can be tricky. And if companies go overboard in attracting people over 49, they may see a backlash. Young women won't be eager to shop in a store perceived as being for old ladies.

## OVERDRAWN IMAGE

Older Americans, too, can react negatively to an overdrawn age image. The median age is now 31, and studies show that as the population ages, Americans keep pushing back the point at which they are willing to be called old. Most people from 60 to 75, for example, now identify themselves as "middle-aged." Moreover, vanity doesn't decrease with age. People 60-plus commonly say they feel 10 to 15 years younger. For marketers, that means a 65-year-old man may more readily identify with *Miami Vice* star Don Johnson than with George Burns.

It will be years before marketers know if their increased emphasis on older people will pay off. For the time being, though, it seems that many of them believe Linda Evans is right. In the opening line of a current Clairol commercial, the middle-aged *Dynasty* star says: "Let's face it, 40 isn't fatal."

## QUESTIONS

1.  *What has caused the increased attention marketers are now paying to older consumers?*

2.  *What aspects of its marketing mix may have to be changed if a company tries to market its goods or services to the over-50 and senior citizen markets?*

*3.  *Relate the discussion in this article to Zeithaml's discussion about market fragmentation (Reading 13). What are the implications for corporate strategy planning?*

*4.  *How do you think Haley (Reading 11) would respond to this article? Is targeting older consumers consistent with his concept of benefit segmentation?*

*5.  *What implications does this article have for nonprofit organizations (Reading 4)?*

---

*Question relates concepts in this and other readings.

## □ 15

# Psychographic glitter and gold

## *Bickley Townsend*

*Many theories, models, and research approaches have been developed to help marketers understand and predict consumer buying behavior. One very popular approach that has been widely applied in marketing is called "psychographic" or "lifestyle" analysis. Using real-world examples, the following article defines psychographics and describes how two major psychographic research programs operate. The author then assesses the effectiveness of psychographic research and presents some valuable guidelines for using psychographics.*

Anheuser-Busch decided to develop a new kind of beer, one that would capitalize on the shift in consumer values toward natural products and healthy lifestyles. Given Americans' interest in diet, health, and nutrition, what could be more logical than a beer called Natural Light? But Natural Light bombed. So did Real cigarettes, positioned on a similar premise: that there are smokers who are seeking a natural, unadulterated cigarette. Anheuser-Busch eventually came up with a winner, Bud Light, but only after relinquishing the brand name and the positioning that assumed naturalness was meaningful to beer drinkers.

Psychographic segmentation promises a lot, but doesn't always deliver. Anheuser-Busch and the makers of Real cigarettes found out the hard way the danger in taking lifestyle research too far or too literally. "In both instances, the lifestyle assumptions were wrong," says Tony Adams, marketing director of Campbell Soup Company. "Attitudinal segments that may have worked in other product categories could not translate to beer and cigarettes."

But General Foods made psychographic analysis work for Sanka, which suffered from a staid, older image; after all, wasn't it only elderly people who needed decaffeinated coffee? Yet the same trend that set Anheuser-Busch off in the wrong direction—consumers' growing health-consciousness—gave General Foods the opening

it needed to shift Sanka's positioning. The new campaign targeted active achievers of all ages, picturing them in pursuit of adventurous lifestyles—such as running the rapids in a kayak—with the tag line that Sanka "Lets you be your best"—a classic achiever appeal.

### DISSECTING PSYCHOGRAPHICS

Psychographics describes "the entire constellation of a person's attitudes, beliefs, opinions, hopes, fears, prejudices, needs, desires, and aspirations that, taken together, govern how one behaves," and that in turn, "finds holistic expression in a lifestyle."[1] The idea is to go beyond standard demographics to learn your best customers' dreams, hopes, fears, and beliefs. By grouping people into homogeneous segments based on their lifestyles, many marketers believe they have a new tool for understanding the consumer and increasing their bottom-line results.

"It's not to say that demographics don't matter. Of course they do," says Gene Cooper, manager

Source: Reprinted with permission from *American Demographics*, November 1985, pp. 22–29. At the time of writing, Bickley Townsend was an associate editor of *American Demographics*.

[1] Arnold Mitchell, *The Nine American Lifestyles* (New York: Macmillan, 1983), p. vii.

of primary research at ABC News and Sports. "But it is psychological motivation which is the driving force behind behavior."

Interest in psychographics has been on the rise since marketers first began to see the mass defection of the baby-boom generation from expected patterns of behavior and consumption, as the children of Buick-driving Republicans registered Democratic and bought Volkswagens. Even pizza caught on big, according to some observers, because it was the perfect protest food: not only did parents not like it at first, but eating it violated one of the basic rules the boomers had grown up with—never eat with your fingers.

## MONITORING LIFESTYLES

The tools of mass marketing could not capture these dramatically shifting values and attitudes; new research programs emerged in response. The first major syndicated study of changing American values, called Monitor, was developed by Yankelovich, Skelly & White (YSW). Since 1971, Monitor has been charting social values with an annual survey of 2,500 people. Currently, Monitor tracks 52 trends, with names like Novelty and Change, Anti-Bigness, Blurring of the Sexes, and Defocus on Youth. Shifts in these trends are measured through a series of fixed attitude-scale questions. YSW complements the general trend information with examples of how the trends are being expressed, to help marketers link them to their own business concerns. A manifestation of the "Anti-Bigness" trend, for example, is the rise of unbranded pharmaceuticals and supermarket store brands.

YSW has also clustered the trends into six values segments in two major groups. In the vanguard in the 1980s are "Successful Adapters," who include New Autonomous, Gamesmen, and Scramblers; on the "Traditional Values" end are Traditionals, American Dreamers, and Aimless.

Monitor has 120 sponsors who pay about $25,000 the first year (and less thereafter) for the service, which includes some individual consultation. Because Monitor tracks attitudes at the national level, it can serve as a window on the world—a means of learning what's going on in the minds of American consumers. More specifically,

it can help businesses see how values and behavior are changing and link these changes to company products and services. On the basis of Monitor's forecasts of increasing affluence, one sponsor began emphasizing upscale personal-care products long before the sales pattern was evident, according to Florence Skelly, president of YSW. Another sponsor bought a wine company on the basis of forecasts of the growth of wine consumption.[2]

## THE VALUE OF VALS

In its Monitor program, YSW adds and deletes trends over time and its lifestyle clusters are derived primarily from real-world survey data rather than from psychological theory, in contrast with the other major lifestyle classification system, VALS. An acronym for Values and Lifestyles, VALS grew out of research at SRI International, a not-for-profit research firm in Menlo Park, California. Although it did not become a separate program until 1978, and it fielded its first national survey only in 1980, VALS has quickly captured the national marketing imagination. It has grown into a $2 million program with more than 150 members, who pay a minimum of $5,000 to gain access to the research and consulting service, and up to $40,000 if they want to use the databases and the VALS questionnaire.

The VALS typology is based on theories of psychological development, particularly Abraham Maslow's hierarchy of human needs, so the nine VALS lifestyle categories are seen as more or less stable over time. Between the two extremes—the Need Driven categories (Survivor and Sustainer) at the bottom of the developmental ladder, and the elite Integrateds at the pinnacle—people are classified into either Outer-Directed (Emulators, Belongers, Achievers) or Inner-Directed (I-Am-Me, Experiential, Societally Conscious) lifestyle segments. Belongers are the largest segment of the population—family-oriented traditionalists representing one-third of all adults. But Achievers (22 percent) and Societally Conscious (12 percent) have captured more marketing attention: both are

---

[2]Florence R. Skelly, "Using Social Trend Data to Shape Marketing Policy: Some Do's and a Don't," *Journal of Consumer Marketing* 1, no. 1, Summer 1983, p. 15.

affluent, growing segments compared to Belongers, who have moderate incomes and are a stable or declining group.[3]

The original VALS questionnaire was 85 pages long. SRI has since reduced it to a 30-item short form, which it claims yields the same results. Twenty-two of the questions probe attitudes and values with agree-disagree statements on a six-point scale; two items ask about social class and political beliefs; and six questions are demographic. The shorter questionnaire makes it easy for other surveys to incorporate VALS typing.

The 22 attitude questions in the VALS system ask about religious and political beliefs, women's roles, social pluralism, and other values. Is what you do at work more important to you than the money you earn? Then you are likely to be an inner-directed type. Do you get a raw deal out of life? You could be a Survivor. Do you like to be outrageous? I-Am-Me's do. Do you believe that the federal government should encourage prayers in the public schools, and that women should take care of their homes and leave running the country up to men? Those are Belonger traits. Inner-directed segments such as Societally Conscious and Experientials tend to have more liberal social values, supporting legalization of marijuana, federal funding of abortion, and expanded roles for women.

Since 1982, the VALS questionnaire has been administered as part of the annual surveys of both Simmons Market Research Bureau and Mediamark Research, Inc. (MRI), each of which has a national sample of 20,000 respondents. Through a joint agreement with National Family Opinion, a consumer diary panel, VALS is linked with an even larger, 80,000-household database. Several private data companies also VALS-type their geo-demographic databases.[4] In addition, marketers can hold focus groups with specific VALS types,

thanks to an SRI joint venture with the Holtzman Group, a New Jersey market research firm that has developed a computerized respondent bank called Data Base Focus Group.

Avon Products is one satisfied VALS customer. Like many companies, Avon uses product benefits as its principal way to segment the market. But, says marketing director John Gregg, "Psychographics has proven to be wonderfully useful." Avon's direct-selling business depends on its cadre of door-to-door representatives. VALS typing revealed that Avon representatives are decidedly skewed toward Belongers. This insight has raised strategic questions since Avon would like to target potential customers among different VALS segments. VALS has also helped the company recruit, motivate, and communicate with its sales representatives.

"VALS makes it possible to personalize marketing and to understand the target we're trying to reach better than any other piece of research," says Jerry Hamilton, senior vice president and director of marketing research at Ketchum Advertising in San Francisco. "Sure, it may oversimplify. No matter what classification system you use, you're distorting everybody's individuality. But the alternative is to tailor advertising to 80 million individual households. We're no longer the only cobbler in the community who knows everyone and what kind of shoes they want."

We've moved away from the world of individual contact with the customer, but VALS restores some of that personalization, according to Hamilton. For example, knowing that young, college-educated professionals are 60 percent Societally Conscious (compared to 12 percent of the adult population) and 30 percent Achievers explodes the myth that young professionals are interested only in selfish pursuits and materialistic success.

Hamilton credits the insights derived from VALS for much of the success of Ketchum's advertising campaign for Mauna Loa Macadamia Nuts, which have seen a 20 percent increase in sales in the past two years. The agency identified Achievers and Societally Conscious as its two major targets. The challenge was to find an approach that would succeed with these groups, who are demographically similar but attitudinally different. Ketchum used as a spokesperson John Hillerman, the snobbish sidekick on "Magnum

---

[3]For more on the VALS typology, see Bickley Townsend, "Nine Lives," *American Demographics,* December 1983.

[4]Cluster analysis is often described as lifestyle analysis, but this is a misconception reinforced by cluster names like Porch Swings & Apple Pie, Blue Blood Estates, and Tough Times.

The four cluster systems (CACI's ACORN, Claritas' PRIZM, Donnelley Marketing's ClusterPlus, and National Decision System's VISION) are based not on attitudes or values, but on demographic data. They can complement psychographics by helping to locate the target segments "on the ground," while psychographics tell you how to shape the message.

P.I.," a television program popular with both Achievers and Societally Conscious viewers. Hamilton says the Hillerman character appealed to Achievers because of his "upscaleness," and at the same time to the inner-directed Societally Conscious because of the tongue-in-cheek quality of his snobbery. The basic theme of the Hillerman commercials was also designed for dual appeal: "Mauna Loa Macadamia Nuts Are Almost Too Good to Share."

## DO-IT-YOURSELF PSYCHOGRAPHICS

Researchers who want information on values and lifestyles have two choices. They can buy Monitor or VALS, or they can develop their own psychographic segmentation system. Sometimes the choice is determined by cost or convenience. How appropriate an "off-the-shelf" system may be, compared with a tailored segmentation study, also affects the choice.

When ABC wanted to segment the television-viewing audience, it considered using VALS, but rejected it as not applicable enough to its needs. Moreover, says ABC's Cooper, "We believe that many of the VALS groups are demographically driven." So ABC developed its own system for classifying viewers into clusters relevant to television viewing. ABC interviewed a national probability sample of 1,000 respondents by telephone, using an 81-item questionnaire designed to measure self-esteem, opinion leadership, need for group inclusion, cosmopolitanism, and other psychological attributes. Cooper emphasizes that, "First, we did not use demographics to form the groups. Second, we did not use any television viewing or program-preference items in the cluster instrument. Our approach was to use fundamental psychological attributes which we felt would be far more stable and more powerful than transient items related to television."

A factor analysis resulted in eight cluster groups in three broad categories: a "mainstream middle-America" group, a group that is out of the mainstream in various ways, and a "counter-mainstream" group. Individual clusters were given names like Organized Participants, Family Oriented, Liberal Cosmopolitan, and Rigid and Resistant.

Are the clusters merely proxies for such standard demographics as age, sex, income, and education? Cooper insists they are not. Consider the Family Orienteds and the Rigid and Resistants—two groups that are demographically similar. Both skew toward older people and women with average education and household incomes. But there are significant psychographic differences between them, especially since the Family Orienteds are from the "mainstream" branch of the cluster tree, while the Rigids are from the out-of-the-mainstream segment. "The more important differences, at least to ABC, are in television viewing," says Cooper. "The Family group watches a great deal of family-type situation comedies, while the Rigids watch these shows only in average amounts. The Rigids, on the other hand, are heavy viewers of action-adventure shows, unlike the Family group. Families watch information programs in average amounts; Rigids watch information shows below average."

ABC's original 81-item questionnaire was eventually winnowed down to 31 questions that make it possible to add to all of ABC's primary research, without losing much predictive power. ABC continues to expand the role of psychographics in its research efforts—for program diagnostics, scheduling, and promotion, and in examining potential markets for new technologies such as pay-cable services.

## PROMISE OR PERFORMANCE

Has the performance of psychographic segmentation met its promise? It depends on who you talk to. Some researchers question the methodology. "VALS is the Reader's Digest of marketing research," says Edward Spar, president of Market Statistics. "With these predigested, prepackaged systems, someone else gives you the answers, and as a statistician, that makes me a little nervous. They won't tell you the factor loadings or rotations or the explained variance."

John Mather, senior vice president and director of marketing research in Ketchum Advertising's Pittsburgh office, doesn't have any problem with VALS' proprietary secrets. "That's the little black box—it's how they keep us. I know from my own graduate work that a discriminant-function model takes a lot of time to build and refine to be sure it's valid and reliable." Adds Francois Christen, a VALS manager, "The proof is in the pudding—whether VALS predicts how people will differ in terms of product consumption and use. Clearly, it does."

Other critics question how useful psychographic research is, arguing that too often it tells you what you already know. "One of the most frustrating aftermaths of any research is a result that is so obvious everyone is thinking 'So what's new?' " says Tony Adams of Campbell Soup.

Think about a bag lady living in a low-rent hotel room, Adams asks, "Do we need a battery of lifestyle questions to label this consumer as a light user of Gucci shoes, Jordache jeans, Chivas Regal, and Godiva chocolates?" It doesn't help, he adds, when researchers attempt to dress up the obvious: "Men and women who like to cook become Culinary Artisans; people involved in church and community become the Societally Conscious." Why not use plain English instead of jargon, asks Adams.

Psychographic researchers acknowledge that most people don't fit a pure type. In the VALS system, all respondents are assigned a score not only for their primary lifestyle type, but also for each of the other VALS types, based on how closely their questionnaire responses conform to the profile of each type. The VALS researchers have gone further by specifying important subgroups within lifestyle segments. For example, if your customers are primarily Achievers, they might be Achiever/Belongers, Achiever/Societally Conscious, or Super Achievers. Although each group scores highest in the Achiever segment, there are important differences. While Achiever/Belongers are relatively conservative, older, female, and less well-educated, Achiever/Societally Conscious people are more apt to be younger professionals, socially liberal, and able to say "I've got all I need; now I'm ready to start contributing to causes and getting involved in the community," as Ketchum Advertising's John Mather explains it. Super Achievers, by contrast, are "win at all costs" workaholics, totally committed to success in their fields, the most male, most managerial, most affluent, and most Republican of any Achiever subgroup.

Where your customers cluster among these Achiever subgroups may make a difference in how you pitch your product. Such cross-classification is an attempt to increase the subtlety of the VALS typology, although, says Mather, "a lot of us are still trying to become better users of the primary groupings."

## THE PSYCHOGRAPHIC PAYOFF

Like any tool, psychographic research can be tremendously valuable in skilled hands, but it can also be misused. Some guidelines can help ensure that it's effective.

### Use psychographics as one technique among many

Since market segmentation was introduced in the 1950s, it has produced a bewildering array of segmentation modes, including geographic, demographic, behavioral, and attitudinal. Psychographics is the newest kid on the block, the latest and arguably the flashiest technique in a field notable for bells and whistles. Is it the answer to marketing segmentation? Even Arnold Mitchell, the father of VALS himself, says it is not. Is it a useful addition to the tool kit? With qualifications, many marketers say it is.

"Don't put all your eggs in the lifestyle basket," advises marketing manager Diane Hillyard of Campbell Soup. Other forms of segmentation are also important, including demographics, beliefs, and benefits. Lifestyle research is not only not an end in itself—it's not an end at all, but one piece of information that adds dimension to the picture of the consumer.

In particular, don't expect that you can substitute psychographics for demographics. Psychographic insights often build on demographics, and many marketers believe that psychographics are demographically driven.

"Demographics do influence our system—no question about it," says Brooke Warrick, marketing director of VALS. "Belongers are older; I Am Me's are younger; Achievers have more money. But demographics are insufficient," he says. "Survivors and Sustainers, for example, are similar in their income levels; what distinguishes them is their level of hope. Same with Achievers and Societally Conscious: it is their inner- or outer-directedness that differentiates them, far more than their age or income."

## Know how you will use psychographics

Be sure your expectations are realistic. Using psychographic segments as marketing targets is a temptation that Florence Skelly of Yankelovich, Skelly & White has identified as seductive, but misguided. Explains Skelly, "Social-values clusters are an important tool in understanding specific segments; they are not the segments themselves." When the Monitor identified a group called the Aimless as an emerging social values cluster, "We feared that despite our cautions, some would take the Aimless as a target segment rather than as a description of the social structure of the country," says Skelly. "This could open the door to soap geared for the Aimless, an Aimless car, and so forth, an outcome we really worried about."[5]

"Lay out your objectives for the research and make sure you're clear on what you want to get out of it," advises Diane Hillyard. "Then predict how the study might be used. If no one knows what they'd do or how they could use the results, don't do the study!"

## Let the buyer beware

The old adage is applicable to anyone seeking to develop or acquire a psychographic segmentation system. Whatever the system, keep asking questions until you get satisfactory answers about how it is designed, tested, and validated. Ideally, you should validate the system yourself against your own data, including customer databases and survey information. The test is whether it works for a particular product, and whether it predicts differences in behavior among consumers.

In the VALS classification scheme, an individual's primary and secondary scores may be quite close. For example, someone might be classified primarily as an Achiever, with a score of .7403 (indicating 74.03 percent of possible Achiever points scored on the VALS questionnaire). But the same person's secondary type might be Societally Conscious, with a score as high as .6576. Do such

scores suggest an Integrated personality type? Or do they indicate substantial overlap between types often characterized as opposites? Before developing elaborate applications based on a typology such as VALS, researchers should understand the nature and extent of overlap, and be sure they are working with distinct segments.

## Never stop monitoring the marketplace

No matter how confident you are in a psychographic segmentation system, keep monitoring its appropriateness over time and across product categories, because values and lifestyles are constantly changing. As people move from one lifestyle to another, they shift in their attitudes, beliefs, and consumption patterns. I-Am-Me's grow up to be Experientials or Societally Conscious, while successful Emulators become Achievers. Roles change in different situations as well as at different points in the life cycle. You may be an Achiever in the office, Societally Conscious in the supermarket, a Belonger at the PTA meeting, and an Emulator in the computer store.

"The world changes, and no matter how well a segmentation study may have been done at one time, and no matter how accurate the picture of the market may have been, a study allows no more than an informed guess as to how people are likely to respond to any marketing actions you may decide to take," says Russell Haley, professor of marketing at the University of New Hampshire and an expert on marketing segmentation. "Then, too, there are your competitors. The marketing actions that they take can have almost as much influence on your sales, share, and profits as your own actions."[6]

## GOLD IN THE GLITTER

There's gold in the psychographic glitter, but it's not a get-rich-quick proposition. You still have to mine it, and that takes staying attuned to changes in the consumer marketplace. America is moving into the "decade of the real thing," accord-

[5]*Journal of Consumer Research,* Summer 1983, p. 17.

[6]Russel I. Haley, "Benefit Segments: Backwards and Forwards," *Journal of Advertising Research* 24, no. 1 (February/March 1984), p. 25.

ing to VALS' Arnold Mitchell, celebrating light food and drink, natural products and processes, having a "love affair with the lemon," as Ann Clurman, director of YSW's Monitor, has quipped. These are useful insights into lifestyle trends—but they didn't work for Real Cigarettes or Natural Light beer.

"It's important to remember," cautions Ketchum's John Mather, "that lifestyle analysis is not a panacea, it's not the magic crystal ball we've all been looking for in our file cabinets. But used well, psychographics can give us that critical bit of insight we need for added leverage in the marketplace."

## QUESTIONS

1. What exactly are "psychographics"? How do psychographics differ from demographics?

2. Compare and contrast Monitor and VALS as two alternate psychographic research approaches. Which of the two would you choose if you were a marketing manager? Why?

3. How well does psychographic segmentation perform in actual practice? Does it work equally well in all product-markets?

4. Summarize Townsend's four guidelines for working with psychographics.

*5. Compare and contrast psychographic segmentation with benefit segmentation (Reading 11). Which do you think is a better approach and why? Can the two approaches be used together?

---

*Question relates concepts in this and other readings.

---

☐ **16**

# Industrial market segmentation

*Yoram Wind*

*Richard Cardozo*

---

*The previous several readings focused on segmenting consumer markets. Wind and Cardozo discuss segmentation of* industrial *markets, presenting examples of current practice. An "ideal" industrial market segmentation model is proposed—based on consumer market segmentation methods—and current practices are evaluated against this model. The discussion also illustrates some of the differences in industrial marketing.*

---

The concept of market segmentation is a logical outgrowth of the marketing concept and economic theory, and is at least conceptually as applicable in industrial marketing as it is for the marketing of consumer goods. Daniel Yankelovich (1964) showed examples of the usefulness of segmentation in industrial markets. Knowledge of the size and heterogeneity of market segments may be essential to organizing for effective industrial marketing (Ames, 1971).

Source: Reprinted with permission from *Industrial Marketing Management,* no. 3 (1974), pp. 127–133. Copyright © 1974 by Elsevier Science Publishing Co., Inc. At the time of writing, Yoram Wind was professor of marketing at the Wharton School, the University of Pennsylvania, and Richard Cardozo was director of the Center for Experimental Studies in Business at the University of Minnesota.

Recent tests and articles on industrial marketing (Alexander et al., 1967; Rowe and Alexander, 1968; Wilson, 1968; and Dodge, 1970) include, however, no more than brief mention of market segmentation, and only cursory attention to the nature and behavior of the industrial buying decision-making units. Given our initial statement that the concept of segmentation is conceptually a relevant (and even a crucial) ingredient in the design of industrial marketing strategies, the neglect of market segmentation in the industrial marketing literature can be explained if industrial firms do not follow a strategy of market segmentation or, alternatively, if the introductory statement is wrong.

Our research indicates that industrial marketers by no means use market segmentation strategies as widely or effectively as they might. Segmentation appears to be largely an after-the-fact explanation of why a marketing program did or did not work rather than a carefully thought-out foundation for marketing programs. Yet two examples which will be described make it clear that market segmentation can indeed be a profitable strategy for industrial marketers.

## THE CONCEPT AND IMPORTANCE OF MARKET SEGMENTATION[1]

A market segment is simply a group of present or potential customers with some common characteristic which is relevant in explaining (and predicting) their response to a supplier's marketing stimuli. For example, a market segment may consist of all firms whose annual purchases of steel exceed $5 million but are less than $10 million. Buyers of noise-muffling equipment may be divided between those whose applications will be visible, in which appearance is important, and those in whose applications appearance is inconsequential. Buyers of many products may usefully be segmented into two groups: repeat buyers and first-time buyers, which differ with respect to the communications strategy which a prospective supplier might employ (Robinson and Faris, 1967).

As a marketing strategy, market segmentation involves first identifying particular segments and then developing differentiated marketing programs

for each of those segments. These programs may differ with respect to product design, communication or distribution channels used, and advertising and selling messages. To be useful to marketers, segments must be sufficiently large (and profitable) to make such tailoring of marketing programs worthwhile. Segments must also be accessible through specific communication and distribution channels. This accessibility may be, however, either via the media and distribution outlets reaching the segment (controlled strategy), via the message design (self-selection strategy), or in the most desirable case via both the media and message strategies (Frank et al., 1972). Sometimes identification may be very difficult or economically unfeasible, in which case the industrial marketer faces essentially one undifferentiated set of buyers. At the other extreme, each individual customer might conceivably constitute a segment. Unless the customers were few in number and each economically significant, the marketer would face an array of virtually unmanageable variety. The art of employing market segmentation, then, involves appropriate grouping of individual customers into a manageable and efficient (in a cost-benefit sense) number of market segments, for each of which a different marketing strategy is feasible and likely profitable.

Conceptually, the choice of segmentation as a marketing strategy for industrial goods and services is predicated on the same assumptions and criteria as segmentation for consumer goods. The only differences, therefore, between consumer and industrial market segmentation involve the specific bases used for segmentation.

### An "ideal" segmentation model

Because some of these bases differ, we propose that industrial markets be segmented in two stages. The first stage involves formation of macrosegments, based on characteristics of the buying organization and the buying situation. The second stage involves dividing those macrosegments into microsegments, based on characteristics of decision-making units (DMUs). A flowchart which outlines this approach appears in Exhibit 1.

This hierarchical approach enables an initial screening of organizations and selection of those macrosegments which, on the basis of organizational characteristics, provide potentially attractive

---

[1]Portions of this section are drawn from Frank et al., 1972.

**Exhibit 1 ☐ An approach to segmentation of organizational markets**

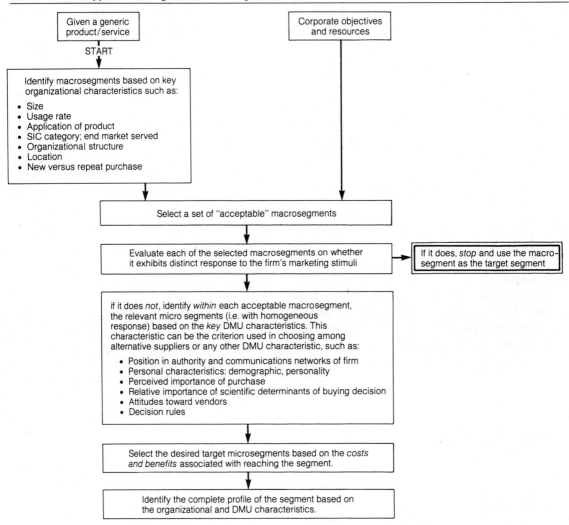

market opportunities. Organizations which may have no use for the given product or service can be eliminated. Starting with the grouping of organizations into homogeneous macrosegments also provides a reduction in the total research effort and cost. Instead of examining detailed buying patterns and attempting to identify the characteristics of the decision-making units in each organization individually, such analysis is limited only to those macrosegments which passed the initial screening. Furthermore, since most of the data for the initial screening can be drawn from available secondary sources (e.g., company files) and the screening procedure can be largely programmed,

the research phase is relatively cheap and can be standardized as part of the firm's marketing information system.

In this first stage, a marketer may use a variety of bases, singly or in combination, to form macrosegments. Size of buying firm and rate of use of the particular product for which the marketer is planning can provide an estimate of potential sales.

Once the marketer has formed a set of acceptable macrosegments, he may divide each of them into microsegments, or small groups of firms, on the bases of similarities and differences among DMUs within each macrosegment. Information for this second stage of segmentation will come primarily from the sales force, based on salesmen's analyses of situations in particular firms, or from specially designed market segmentation studies.

DMUs may differ with respect to the composition and position within a firm and with respect to their decision-making behavior. Composition of the DMU may affect its position in the authority and communications networks of a firm. A DMU composed of relative newcomers to a buying firm, no one of which occupies a top or second-level position in his department, is likely to have little power to press its recommendations on others and may not be fully integrated into the "informal organization," which may frequently be the network necessary to obtain acceptance of new concepts, products, or procedures. Clearly, such a DMU presents a more difficult task for a marketer with a novel offering than one composed of senior established corporate officials who have close contacts throughout the organization.

DMUs may differ with respect to the importance they attach to the purchase of a particular item; the relative weight they attach to such purchase variables as price, quality, and service; their atttitudes toward particular types of vendors; and the specific rules they employ to seek out and evaluate alternative offerings. DMUs which consider a specific product important, require prompt delivery and perhaps technical assistance, wish to deal with well-known vendors, and seek a bid first from a supplier with which they have dealt previously constitute a microsegment of considerable promise to a highly visible supplier with ability to meet delivery and service requirements who has done business with firms in this microsegment. Such a supplier would have distinct advantage over a competitor who sought to enter this microsegment with a low-service, low-price product.

The output from this segmentation model should include (1) a key dependent variable on which firms can be assigned to segments, i.e., the *bases* for segmentation; and (2) a set of independent variables which allow a marketer to predict where along the key dependent variable a particular group of potential customers may lie as well as provide greater insight into the key characteristics of the segment, i.e., the *descriptors* of the segment. For example, a key dependent variable might be "criteria used to evaluate alternative

suppliers." In one situation, a marketer found that "prompt periodic delivery of lots with less than 5 percent defects" was the paramount consideration used by some firms in choosing among suppliers for a particular component part. That same component was purchased by other firms almost entirely on a "lowest cost per thousand units" basis. After some investigation, the marketer discovered that three independent variables differentiated these two types of buyers, or segments: (1) size of firm, measured in number of employees; (2) SIC category; and (3) the type of individual most influential in the buying decision. Customers who insisted on adherence to delivery and quality standards were typically large firms in three SIC codes. Within these firms the most powerful member of the DMU was a quality control man or a purchasing agent with engineering training. In contrast, customers who bought on price were typically smaller firms, in half a dozen SIC codes, only one of which overlapped that of the first type of customer. Principal buying influences in these firms included purchasing agents without technical backgounds and production management personnel.

Selection of appropriate dependent variables should be based on the particular marketing problem the manager wishes to solve. In the preceding example, the problem was to reach new customers with a product which they had previously not purchased in appreciable quantities from any vendor. As users' requirements increased, they solicited numerous bids and began to set standards for reviewing those bids. Consequently, knowledge of those standards became the variable of key importance to the marketer. In another situation, knowledge of buyers' "switching rules" was of central importance. The marketer had lost a few previously loyal customers to competitors and wished to know why. The key dependent variable of interest to him was "buyers' sensitivity to changes in competitors' offerings." He discovered that some buyers would switch for a price reduction of less than 5 percent, while others were reluctant to change suppliers until the price differential on this particular product exceeded 20 percent.

The art of market segmentation involves choosing the appropriate bases for segmenting industrial markets. The bases mentioned here have appeared in the marketing literature (Cardozo, 1968; Feldman and Cardozo, 1969; Frank et al., 1972) and are presented as illustrative but by no means exhaustive of the bases which could be used. Because a marketer may choose key segmentation variables from an array of several dozen (or more), research to identify the most appropriate of those variables may be well worthwhile. Furthermore, because customers' needs and competitors' activities are constantly changing, a marketer must review his segmentation strategy periodically.

After identifying appropriate target segments, the marketer must analyze the profitability of differentiating his marketing program to reach multiple target segments. A first approximation of this cost-benefit analysis may often be made before detailed segmentation analysis is begun.

Relevant costs typically include those associated with product modification, selling, and advertising. Although costs of making initial modifications of a particular product may be modest, the marketer will incur costs in carrying an additional product or line in inventory and may incur hidden costs through confusion or misunderstanding on the part of salesmen and distributors. During the last several years many firms have proliferated their product lines to reach customers with highly individualized requirements. Today, many of those same firms look at product deletion (and not only new product introduction) as a source for increased profitability, hence eliminating the highly specialized and unprofitable offshoots of their principal products.

Sometimes an especially intensive selling effort may be required to reach a particular market segment. If this effort transfers salesmen from their routine calls, there will likely be a cost in terms of sales delayed or lost entirely. If headquarters personnel, in addition to field sales staff, are involved, the costs may be much greater. Because these costs typically involve no internal budget transfers and only modest out-of-pocket expenditures, marketing managers frequently overlook them.

The costs of advertising to reach a particular market segment ordinarily include preparation of separate copy and perhaps illustrations, as well as media costs. Because both types of charges may be highly visible, many firms underutilize dif-

ferentiated advertising as a tool in a marketing segmentation strategy.

## The payoff from segmentation

Two examples illustrate the potential payoff from following a marketing segmentation strategy. The first example describes a situation in which a fairly simple, single-stage segmentation strategy yielded substantial profits. The second example describes a case in which the second stage of segmentation contributed to a substantial increase in profit.

**Single-stage segmentation.** A marketer of spray painting and finishing equipment who had a new system to offer divided his markets into macrosegments on the bases of SIC category, size of buying firm, and location. The marketer developed two distinct strategies: one for large firms in a particular SIC category, all of which were located within four states; another for smaller firms located both in those and in other states. The SIC categories of firms in the second segment overlapped, but were not identical with, those in the first segment. The marketer had observed that decision-making practices for capital equipment differed between the two segments. The large firms were receptive to cost-saving innovations in equipment, tested new equipment extensively, and willingly switched to new equipment which had proved its value in operating tests and benefit-cost analyses. Firms in the second segment were notably resistant to change and historically had adopted new capital equipment innovations only after large firms—like those in the first segment—had done so.

Accordingly, the marketer concentrated his efforts on the first segment. Field salesmen, supported by headquarters staff, diverted their activities from smaller firms to concentrate almost exclusively on the larger ones. The marketer provided equipment for testing and set up and helped to supervise test lines in plants of the largest manufacturers. Later, as this effort became successful, the field sales force reapplied its efforts to smaller firms, without, however, entirely discontinuing contact with the larger ones. These selling efforts to the smaller, more dispersd firms were supported with an advertising campaign which described installations in selected large firms and included endorsements by executives in these firms, but did not include provisions for extensive testing.

Results of this segmentation strategy included penetration of both segments, which had previously been dominated entirely by competitors. Company executives attributed their success to a good product and to following this segmentation strategy, citing instances in which other cost-effective innovations had not been accepted in these markets.

**Two-stage segmentation.** In the preceding example, single-stage segmentation sufficed, because decision-making behavior was correlated closely and positively with size, SIC category, and location. In the following example, decision-making behavior appeared not to be related to size of firm. Consequently, two-stage segmentation was necessary.

A small manufacturer of high-quality metal components had traditionally segmented the geographically concentrated market which it served on the bases of SIC category and size of buying firm. The company concentrated its sales and sales support activities more on some SIC categories than on others and followed a form of "key account" planning, which led to emphasis on customers with large potential volumes. Because sales potentials were frequently not attained, company officials and salesmen attempted to differentiate those customers which gave the company a high proportion of their business from those which gave the company only a small portion of their business. Results from this analysis indicated that the company enjoyed considerable success among customers who purchased its particular type of product simply by telephoning previous suppliers and placing the order with the first one which could meet product and delivery requirements ("satisficers"). The company fared poorly with customers which solicited bids, reviewed them, and finally chose a supplier for this particular type of product ("optimizers").

These differences in "purchasing strategy," which crossed size and SIC categories, suggested a basis for forming microsegments within each SIC category. The company directed its sales and support efforts primarily at the first segment ("satisficers"), with which it had historically been more successful, and reduced its frequency of calls and

sales support activities toward the second segment ("optimizers"). As a result, the company experienced an increase in profits of more than 20 percent. Company officials attributed the increase almost wholly to the new market segmentation strategy.

These examples support the theoretical arguments for market segmentation strategy. With this initial empirical support for our belief that market segmentation was an economically viable approach for industrial markets, we undertook an exploratory study to determine the extent to which market segmentation was employed by industrial marketers and the various ways in which segmentation was used.

## INDUSTRIAL SEGMENTATION: SOME CURRENT PRACTICES

### Data

To access the extent and nature of industrial market segmentation, we first conducted a series of unstructured interviews with marketing managers of five Philadelphia-based industrial companies. Following these unstructured interviews we conducted structured interviews with marketing managers of 25 companies within the Minneapolis metropolitan area. The reporting units in the final sample included both operating divisions of large, decentralized corporations and independent firms. In sales volume, the size of these reporting units ranged from $3 million to more than $2 billion. More than 25 SIC codes were represented.

The interview schedule included questions about the use of different strategies in selling to different customers, the nature of the differentiated strategy, the bases used to segment one's market, the importance of the various bases for segmentation, and company background data.

### Methodology

The unstructured interviews and open-ended questions of the structured interview were content analyzed. The structured parts of the questionnaire were then subjected to cross-classification and multidimensional scaling analyses. This latter procedure was utilized to illustrate graphically the marketing managers' evaluation of the various bases for segmentation.

## Results

The results of this study indicate that industrial marketers do differentiate their marketing programs among customers. But the differentiation appears less a conscious, explicit strategy of market segmentation and more an explanation or concept applied *after* the fact to explain differences in the success of particular marketing programs. Detailed results are grouped under six research questions.

1. To what extent is segmentation strategy used by industrial firms?

All the firms participating in the study indicated that they do use different strategies in selling to different customers. This overwhelming subscription to a policy of differentiation implies acceptance of—or at least lip service to—the concept of market segmentation. Nevertheless, examination of the specific examples given by the respondents suggests that segmentation is used primarily to describe ex post events and not as an explicit strategy which provides the foundation for the industrial marketing program.

2. What is the nature of a segmentation-based industrial marketing strategy?

Industrial firms which differentiate their marketing offerings, to appeal to and reach different market segments, only rarely try to differentiate all their marketing variables. Nevertheless, more than half of the firms differentiated at least one of their marketing variables. Of the various ways in which a company can vary its marketing strategies to meet the needs of its target markets, elements reported as most important were the product and service mix (72 percent) followed by price (18 percent) and only in a very few cases by promotion (5 percent) and distribution (5 percent).

Most of the respondents modify or adapt their products to meet the requirements of particular customers. Product changes vary considerably and include technical as well as symbolic (e.g., changes from manufacturer to private brand) alterations. Quite frequently a firm's product strat-

egy is supplemented or replaced by service strategy—training, maintenance, warranties, and technical information.

In addition to different products and services most of the firms offered a variety of pricing options to their customers. The reasons for such a policy were primarily volume and specific customer requirements.

The majority of respondents indicated that they emphasize different appeals (product benefits) to different customers. Yet, the examples presented suggest that such differentiation is accomplished "intuitively" by field salesmen, or that differentiation is an after-the-fact explanation of marketing activity rather than a carefully designed strategy aimed at emphasizing for each segment the appropriate product benefits and usage situations. About 80 percent of the firms used a variety of promotional tactics—especially different media (trade magazines, direct mail, newspapers, general magazines, TV, radio, and displays)—to reach their markets. No evidence exists, however, that the media selection or the message design decisions were based on an explicit analysis and understanding of the target market segments and the nature of the decision-making units.

More than two thirds of the firms used different channels of distribution in selling to different customers. The selction of the specific channel was based primarily on the nature of the customer (especially government versus nongovernment clients), the nature of the products (components versus systems), the geographic location of the buyers, and the availability of particular channels.

3. What are the bases used to segment industrial markets?

Organizational "demographics" such as size, SIC category, end use of product, and geographic location were the most frequently used bases for segmentation. End use was generally thought to vary directly with the type of business in which the business firm was engaged.

Other bases used—considerably less frequently—by the responding firms to segment their markets were personal characteristics of the decision-making units, such as the function of the buying unit, and the DMU's degree of source loyalty.

4. How do industrial marketers evaluate various bases of segmentation?

Marketers group bases of segmentation into three clusters, which they evaluate on two different sets of criteria. The three clusters of bases for segmentation are (1) organization characteristics, (2) product characteristics, and (3) DMU characteristics. Organization characteristics include type of industry, size of firm, and geographic location. Product characteristics include usage rates, end use, and product specifications. DMU characteristics include buyers' job title and personality and pattern of source loyalty. The three clusters are displayed in a two-dimensional map in Exhibit 2. There were no clear differences in clusters (or in evaluation) among the different types of firms represented in our sample.

Marketers used two sets of criteria to evluate these clusters. The first set included three criteria: (1) cost of identifying segments and differentiating marketing programs, (2) acceptance of bases of segmenting by marketing personnel, and (3) ease of identifying segments and differentiating marketing programs. Of these three, cost was clearly the most important. The other set included one criterion—appropriateness—which respondents construed as a global evaluation, one which had normative futuristic implications.

The two sets of criteria correspond to the two dimensions in Exhibit 2. The vertical dimension can be viewed as the "difficulty of implementing" set of criteria. Given the grouping of the bases into three clusters, within each cluster the vertical spread of the bases reflects their perceived diffi-

**Exhibit 2 □ Two-dimensional configuration of nine bases of segmentation**

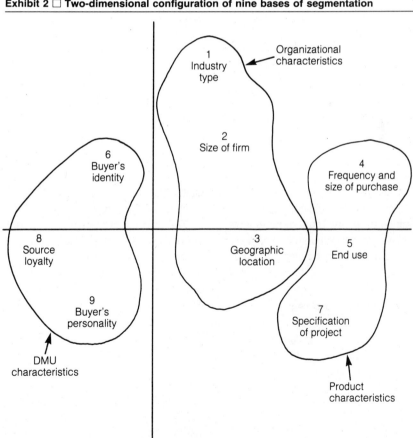

culty of implementing. For example, within the cluster of DMU characteristics the buyer's identity is the easiest to identify, the cheapest, and the most acceptable of the three bases. The buyer's personality, on the other hand, is viewed as the most difficult to identify, most expensive, and least acceptable to marketing management.

The horizontal dimension can be interpreted, consistently with the second set of criteria, as the "appropriateness" dimension, with the DMU characteristics as the most appropriate, followed by organizational characteristics, and the product characteristics perceived as the least appropriate.

The two sets of criteria result, therefore, in quite different evaluations of the three clusters. Marketers evidently now use inexpensive and acceptable means of segmentation, which they consider much less appropriate than what they'd like to use. For examples, DMU characteristics are seen as very appropriate, yet are not currently used as bases of segmentation. Product characteristics, now used in some circumstances, are considered least appropriate as bases for segmentation. Organizational characteristics appear to be used more widely now than may be appropriate. Respondents' evaluations of the two sets of criteria with respect to their appropriateness and frequency of usage are summarized in Exhibit 3.

5.  Which bases for segmentation may be used in the future?

More than 80 percent of the respondents thought that differences of industry type, geographic location, end use of the product, and specification of product (including cost and delivery) would continue to be important determinants of customer requirements and useful bases for segmentation. About 70 percent indicated source or brand loyalty as important factors, while only 62

percent mentioned the size of the firm. Slightly over 50 percent of the respondents thought that the identity of the buyer (e.g., engineer, purchasing agent) and the buyer's personality would be of some importance, while only 42 percent thought that the frequency and size of purchase would have some importance.

6.  What criteria are used to evaluate segmentation-based marketing strategies?

Sales volume (33 percent), profits (23 percent), and market share (11 percent) are the primary criteria used by marketing managers to evaluate their marketing strategies. Growth (10 percent), image (5 percent), length of relationship with customers (5 percent), ability to meet customers' needs (5 percent), and cost (8 percent) were the other criteria used. These measures are not, however, applied separately to each segment. Consequently, marketing segmentation is not employed as a control strategy.

In summary, this study indicates that, while the concept of marketing strategy differentiation is widely accepted among industrial firms, there is little evidence to suggest that firms do follow a conscious segmentation srategy to plan or control their marketing activites. Although marketing managers are aware of the concept of segmentation, they appear not to articulate fully the concept of segmentation or to use the variety of possible bases for segmentation.

## CONCLUSIONS

The concept of marketing segmentation has been one of the major focuses of consumer research since the early 60s. The concept has had a great impact on the thought and practice of

**Exhibit 3 ☐ Evaluation of bases of segmentation**

|  | Bases of segmentation | | |
|---|---|---|---|
| Criteria | Organizational characteristics | Product characteristics | DMU characteristics |
| Set 1<br>Cost<br>Acceptability<br>Ease | Frequently used | Sometimes used | Not used |
| Set 2<br>Appropriateness | Some are appropriate | Least appropriate | Very appropriate |

marketing of consumer goods. These developments have had less impact, however, on industrial marketing management. Results from this study indicate that industrial marketers typically fail to employ market segmentation as a foundation for planning and control of marketing programs. At best, industrial marketers use only single-stage segmentation and by no means employ or even examine some of the other bases of segmentation which might be employed profitably.

Articulation of the concept of market segmentation may by itself provide a basis for more precise marketing planning and for coordination of product development, selling, and sales support activities. A marketer who accepts segmentation as the basis for his marketing strategy will have a basis for conceiving of and estimating potential profits from specific product modifications. Segmenting markets will enable field sales managers to direct their resources more efficiently at particular target firms or groups of firms in their geographic areas. At the same time, sales support materials and activities—including advertising—can be tailored to suit economically viable market segments.

We believe that industrial marketers who do not follow explicit segmentation strategies, planned in advance, either treat all customers alike or treat each customer differently. In the first case, marketers are losing opportunities for profit and laying themselves open to competitive inroads. In the second case, marketers undoubtedly are practicing unprofitable—and uncontrolled—segmentation in many instances. Interestingly, those marketers who permit sales (and sales support) men to treat each customer differently typically believe and state that they treat all customers alike. Those marketers generally lack adequate marketing planning and control techniques, do not provide their sales force adequate support, and typically have not thought about differences among their present and prospective customers.

Research into segmentation, therefore, is an essential precondition for intelligent marketing planning. Such research is feasible and can readily be integrated with other marketing research projects. Once the marketing plan is fully developed, marketing operations may be controlled on a segment-by-segment basis. Such a control mechanism is more precise than most in use today and may be more responsive in a changing environment.

Once segmentation is accepted and articulated as a useful way of looking at markets, marketers can address the discrepancy, revealed in this study, between bases of segmentation which are considered appropriate, but too costly to implement, and those which are inexpensive but not always appropriate. One way to deal with this problem is to identify new, less costly bases of segmentation, perhaps by identifying particular types of behavior and their correlates. Another way is to develop advertising (media and message) and sales management plans, for example, which fit appropriate segments in particular markets. As a marketer gains experience in devising such policies, costs of differentiating marketing programs should decrease.

## REFERENCES

Alexander, Ralph S.; James S. Cross; and Richard M. Hill. *Industrial Marketing.* Homewood, Ill.: Richard D. Irwin, 1967.

Ames, Charles B. "Dilemma of Product/Market Management." *Harvard Business Review* 49 (March–April 1971), pp. 66–74.

Cardozo, Richard N. "Segmenting the Industrial Market." In *Marketing and the New Science of Planning,* ed. R. L. King, Chicago: American Marketing Association, 1968.

Dodge, Robert H. (1970). *Industrial Marketing.* New York: McGraw-Hill.

Feldman, Wallace, and Richard N. Cardozo. "The 'Industrial' Revolution and Models of Buyer Behavior." *Journal of Purchasing* 5, no. 4 (November 1969).

Frank, Ronald E.; William F. Masy; and Yoram Wind. *Market Segmentation.* Englewood Cliffs, N.J.: Prentice-Hall, 1972.

Robinson, Patrick J., and Charles W. Faris. *Industrial Buying and Creative Marketing.* Boston: Allyn & Bacon, 1967.

Rowe, David, and Ivan Alexander. *Selling Industrial Products.* London: Hutchinson & Co., 1968.

Webster, Frederick E., Jr., and Yoram Wind. *Organizational Buying Behavior.* Englewood Cliffs, N.J.: Prentice-Hall, 1972.

Wilson, Aubrey, ed. *The Marketing of Industrial Products.* London: Hutchinson & Co., 1965.

Yankelovich, Daniel. "New Criteria for Market Segmentation." *Harvard Business Review* 42 (March–April, 1964), pp. 83–90.

## QUESTIONS

1. Briefly discuss the authors' "ideal" segmentation model. What is meant by a "two-stage model," and why does their "ideal" model have two stages?

2. Identify the "suggested but unused bases of segmentation" and the "used but not necessarily appropriate bases"? Why is "what ought to be used" different from "what is used"?

3. Why do you think segmentation in industrial markets is less developed than segmentation in consumer markets?

*4. Has marketing become "the new priority" for industrial marketers as much as for consumer marketers (Reading 1)? Why or why not?

---

*Question relates concepts in this and other readings.

---

☐ **17**

# New product strategy: How the pros do it

## *John R. Rockwell*
## *Marc C. Particelli*

---

*New products are a vital source of sales and profit growth for individual companies, as well as a critical economic stimulus for a nation's economy. But new products are also a major source of risk, and unsuccessful new products can have disastrous effects on a firm's profits and ROI. The consulting firm of Booz, Allen & Hamilton has spent many years researching new product strategies to determine why some firms are much more successful at introducing new products than others. This article summarizes their latest findings.*

---

The mythical Sisyphus was condemned to push a large boulder up a mountain, only to find himself at the bottom again after almost reaching the summit. New products managers have faced a similar frustration over the past 25 years.

Although the sophistication and effectiveness of bringing new products to market successfully have improved during the past 25 years, the benefits derived from them have been diluted by a variety of changes in the new products environment: new, global competition; slow-growth markets; sophisticated segmentation; escalating costs; constrained resources.

Improvement in the new products management process has only helped us stay even in performance. On average we have seen no appreciable change in new product success rates during the past 25 years. Like Sisyphus, new product managers are still at the bottom of the mountain striving for the summit. Only the boulder seems to be getting larger and the mountain steeper.

Source: Reprinted with permission from *Industrial Marketing*, May 1982, pp. 49–60. At the time of writing, John R. Rockwell and Marc C. Particelli were senior vice president and vice president, respectively, of Booz, Allen & Hamilton, New York.

Responding to that concern, Booz, Allen & Hamilton conducted a year-long survey of more than 700 U.S. manufacturers in new product management, covering more than 13,000 new product introductions. Exhibit 1 illustrates the types of products introduced.

**Exhibit 1 □ New product definitions**∗

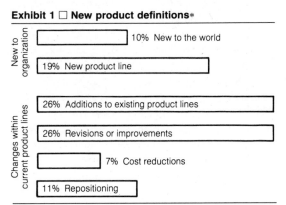

New to organization

- 10%  New to the world
- 19%  New product line

Changes within current product lines

- 26%  Additions to existing product lines
- 26%  Revisions or improvements
- 7%  Cost reductions
- 11%  Repositioning

*Percentage of sample (13,311 new products) indicated.
Source: Booz, Allen & Hamilton, Inc.

Sixty percent of respondents represented industrial goods companies in the information processing, instruments and controls, industrial machinery, chemicals, power-generating equipment, OEM components, and textile industries; 40 percent represented consumer goods companies, divided equally between durables and nondurables.

Our 1981 survey indicates that, on average, our improvement just kept our performance on par. The success rate remains at two out of three commercialized products. However:

It now takes only seven concepts to yield one successful product.

Improvement in mortality has come from changes in new products management and organization.

Those changes have altered how we spend money on new products. More is directed toward homework and less toward testing and commercialization.

That shift in spending has resulted in less of the new products dollar being spent on failures.

## WINNERS AND LOSERS

Clearly, averages are misleading. And beating the average is the name of the game. In the

1960s there were a lot of average players in the new product game. Few companies were above average—not many were below. The vast majority of companies performed adequately and achieved adequate results.

But by the 1970s, the new product game started to polarize. A growing number of "best practices" companies emerged. The number of "average" companies decreased, and the number of companies performing below average increased.

As we enter the decade of the 1980s, it is becoming clear that, even with increasing sophistication, success in new products management will be increasingly difficult. In the future, if the trend continues—and we believe it will—the new products game will have only winners and losers.

New products management will only get more difficult as shifts in the external environment continue to change the requirements for success. But those pressures also create additional product development opportunities.

Our study suggests that those opportunities will bear fruit only in proficient new products organizations. Even those companies with the effective approaches of today are not assured of success tomorrow.

Companies without "best practices" and improvement will not even be in the game.

*The losers* of tomorrow will have characteristics common to many companies performing well today. They will:

Know market characteristics.
Define new products strategy as a planning focus.
Set flexible performance criteria.
Refine their investments in the new products process.
Experiment with organizational structures.
Identify opportunistic advantages.
Accumulate experience.
Manage innovation.
Measure success by volume improvements.

*The winners* of tomorrow will be companies that realize success is a journey, not a moment in time. They will continue to improve. Committed to change, they will:

Address the specific needs of market segments.

Use strategy as a management prerequisite.

Manage with stringent criteria.

Reorder investments, focusing more on homework.

Customize structures based on strategic roles of new products.

Build sustainable advantages in economics and marketplace value.

Exploit cumulative experience from each new product introduction.

Institutionalize entrepreneurship through incentives for risk taking.

Reward the new products manager for return rather than volume.

## THE PROCESS

How well-prepared U.S. companies are to select, develop, and successfully bring new products to the marketplace in the 1980s is suggested by the major survey findings:

*Most companies use a formal new product process, usually beginning with identifying the new product strategy* (Exhibit 2).

Companies that have successfully launched new products—a success being a product which met or exceeded its objectives—are more likely to have had a formal new product process in place for a longer period of time. They are also more likely to have a strategic plan, and be committed to growing through internally developed new products.

The new product strategy links corporate objectives to the new product effort and provides direction for the new product process. The step identifies the strategic roles to be played by new products—roles that depend on the type of product itself and the industry. It also helps set the formal financial criteria to be used in measuring new product performance and in screening and evaluating new product ideas.

Change has altered the mortality curve for new product ideas dramatically.

**Exhibit 2 ☐ Seven stages of the new product process**

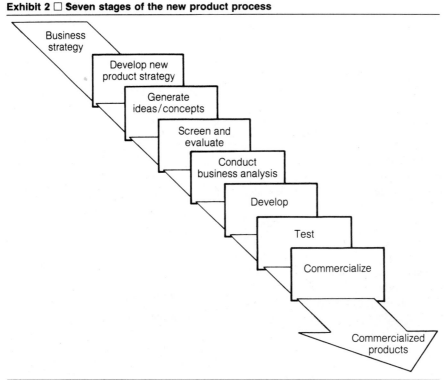

Source: Booz, Allen & Hamilton, Inc.

Our 1968 survey of new product practices found that it took 58 new product ideas or concepts to generate one successful new product. Today, greater understanding of the importance of the marketplace has reduced concept mortality to an average of seven ideas per successful new product, as indicated in Exhibit 3. The change has affected all industries. Packaged-goods companies need 16 concepts per one success; consumer durable companies need 5; industrial goods companies need 7.

*More management attention and more financial resources are devoted to the early steps in the new product process than was the case a decade ago.*

In 1968, roughly one half of all new product expenditures were made during the commercialization stage (Exhibit 4). Today, commercialization accounts for only one fourth of all new product expenditures. Conversely, the portion of expenditures in the early steps—idea/concept generation, screening and evaluation, and business analysis—more than doubled during the same period, from 10 percent in 1968 to 21 percent in 1981.

We are not suggesting, however, that the fundamentals of success in new products management have changed. The factors contributing to success remain much the same as in the past. Products must meet market needs. True innovation often requires identification of as yet unarticulated market needs. Products must be based on technological superiority, and they need support from top management.

Interestingly, comparing product development in the United States and Japan, a major difference is the extent to which the Japanese invest in up-front analysis—defining new products prior to extensive investment. While Americans have improved in that area of new products management, the Japanese are still ahead.

*The percentage of total new product expenditures allocated to products that are ultimately successful has increased.*

As Exhibit 4 illustrates, that percentage grew from 30 percent in 1968 to 54 percent today. The probable causes are the reduction in the number of ideas considered and the increase in resource allocations to early process steps.

*New products managers define specific new product roles.*

Some roles are clearly market driven. Others are internally driven. In many cases, those roles fill multiple needs, as indicated in Exhibit 5, where

**Exhibit 3 □ Mortality of new product ideas (by stage of evolution)**

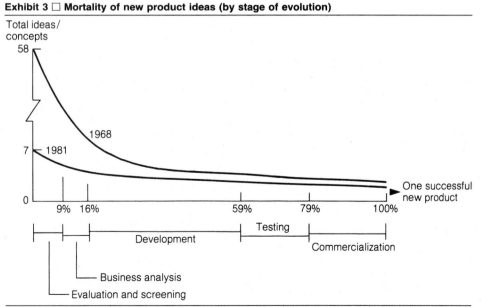

Source: Booz, Allen & Hamilton, Inc.

**Exhibit 4 ☐ Distribution and effectiveness of total new product expenditures, 1968 versus 1981**

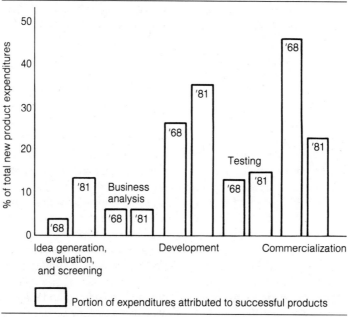

Source: Booz, Allen & Hamilton, Inc.

**Exhibit 5 ☐ Strategic roles for successful new products**

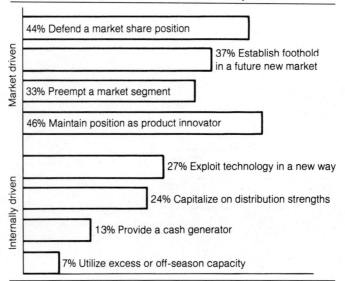

Source: Booz, Allen & Hamilton, Inc.

the percentages based on responses to our survey add up to far more than 100 percent.

*Today, companies have some kind of financial measurement system for detailed new product analysis.*

Of all the firms sampled, 65 percent formally measure new product performance, most using multiple performance criteria.

Their measurement "kits" include such approaches as calculating internal rates of return and present value in addition to the criteria of sales volume, contribution to profit, and length of payback period.

Companies often vary their measurement approach based on the roles expected of their new products efforts. For example, entering a new market with a new-to-the-world product presents high risks and requires a higher expected performance to compensate for those risks. But companies recognize the probable inaccuracy of forecasts. They apply financial criteria as disciplines to thinking rather than impediments to risk taking.

*The more successful companies have pursued a consistent, disciplined new products effort for an extended period of time.*

Another focus of our 1981 study was the value of experience and consistency. We found that experience yields a 71 percent cost curve. That is, after a company has introduced one new product, the cost of introducing the second new product will be 71 percent of the first.

A doubling of the number to four introductions reduces the cost again by 29 percent. At each doubling of the number of new products introduced, the cost of the most recent introduction declines at a 71 percent rate (see Exhibit 6; on a logarithmic scale, the cost curve is a straight line).

An organization can achieve a competitive advantage from experience. For example, if Company A and Company B both introduce two new products and are equally effective in managing them, both will experience the same cost per introduction. If, however, Company B continues to devote resources and attention to new products, moving ahead of Company A in experience, Company B will achieve a sizable and sustainable new product introduction cost advantage.

Experience also improves effectiveness and increase the rate of success. We believe that cost

decline and the benefits of experience require continuity in the new products process. Fits and starts diminish an organization's ability to achieve cost declines and effectiveness improvements.

*Almost half the companies surveyed use more than one type of organization structure to guide new product programs.*

More than three fourths of those companies tie their choice of structure to specific requirements of the products introduced. Some organization schemes can be described as freestanding: a separate team reports to a general manager. Others can be described as functionally based: a team housed within a functional department and relies on part-time support from other departments if required. Exhibit 7 indicates our findings on the distribution of the different types of organizations.

Successful companies tend to use more than one organizational concept, mixing and matching not only the approach but the types of skills and the leadership elements of the team.

## THREE APPROACHES

*Companies use three basic organizational approaches and relate them and their organizational elements to the requirements for differing new product types* (Exhibit 8).

The first is the *entrepreneurial* approach, typically used for developing new-to-the-world products. The structure requires an interdisciplinary venture team and a manager with the ability to integrate diverse functional skills. It operates as an autonomous new products group, usually reporting to a general manager. Success requires the involvement of, and a strong commitment from, top management.

Typically, the process, the measurement structure, and the requirements for formal business planning are less rigid than in other approaches. Usually, an incentive system promotes risk taking by rewarding handsomely for success.

The second is the *collegial* approach, typically used to enter new businesses or add substantially different products to existing lines.

It requires strong senior management support and participation in decision making, a commitment to risk taking, and a formal new products process to guide the effort and ensure discipline.

**Exhibit 6 ☐ Competitive advantage from experience**

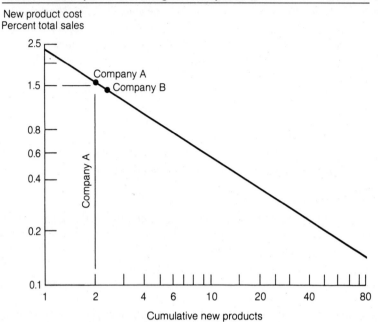

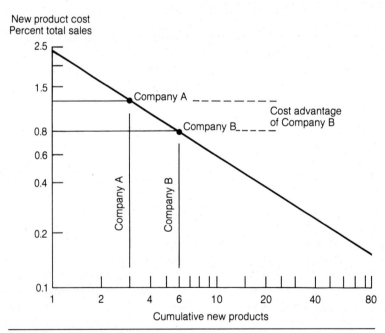

Source: Booz, Allen & Hamilton, Inc.

**Exhibit 7 □ New product organizations**

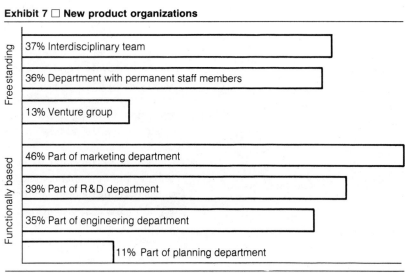

Source: Booz, Allen & Hamilton, Inc.

**Exhibit 8 □ New product organization approaches (best product guidelines)**

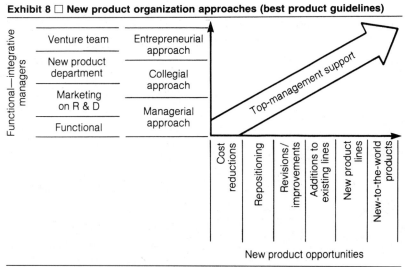

Source: Booz, Allen & Hamilton, Inc.

It also requires a clear commitment to provide whatever is necessary for success and for expediting decisions.

The third is the *managerial* approach. This is the standard process used for existing business management. It involves strong planning and heavy emphasis on functional leadership to drive new products in manufacturing, distribution, marketing, or the like.

It tends to be a rigid new products process involving many levels of management, quick promotion of successful new product managers, limited risk incentives, and rigorous application of financial criteria.

The more successful companies match all those elements to specific new products opportunities. The organizational approach and extent of top-management support vary, based on the specific needs of each new products opportunity. As the newness of the product increases, the entrepreneurial, integrative focus of the team increases, along with the involvement and support of top management, as illustrated in Exhibit 8.

*The success rate of commercialized new products has not improved on average during the last two decades.*

In the period from 1963 to 1968, 67 percent of all new products introduced were successful; they met company-specific financial and strategic criteria. From 1976 to 1981, a 65 percent rate of success was achieved.

More companies are using a more sophisticated new product process, thereby reducing the number of new ideas needed to generate a successful product and increasing the portion of total resources spent on market "winners." And more companies are fitting the organization structures used to their product-specific requirements.

Yet, there has been virtually no change in the rate of successful introductions.

New product managers therefore face the challenge of improving new product performance to meet their greater new product objectives (Exhibit 9).

**Exhibit 9 ☐ Top-management expectations for coming five years (improvement over past five years, 5 percent margin rate)**

| |
|---|
| 30% Number commercialized |

| |
|---|
| 30% Percent of total sales |

| |
|---|
| 35% Percent of total profit |

5% Margin rate

Source: Booz, Allen & Hamilton, Inc.

To that end, and based on our findings from the survey and our in-depth interviews with new product executives, Booz, Allen concludes that the companies most likely to succeed in the develop-

ment and introduction of new products in the 1980s will be those which:

Make the long-term commitment needed to support innovation and new product development.

Implement an approach tailored to the company and driven by corporate objectives and strategies, with a well-defined new product strategy at its core.

Capitalize on accumulated experience to achieve and maintain competitive advantage.

Establish an environment—a management style, organizational structure, and degree of top-management support—conducive to achieving company-specific new product and corporate objectives.

## QUESTIONS

1.  *Does this article support the frequently quoted statistic that "80 percent of all new products fail"?*

2.  *How was the term* new product *defined in the study discussed in this article? How might this affect the results?*

3.  *Name the seven steps of the "new product process." Explain—in terms of time and dollars—how firms have changed their approach to implementing the new product process during the past decade or so.*

4.  *What is the "mortality curve" of new product ideas? What happened to this curve in recent years?*

5.  *Describe the three basic organizational approaches for new product development. Which approach tends to be the most effective—and which requires the most top-management support? Explain.*

*6.  *Where and how would "brand franchise extensions" fit into the new product process described in this article? (See Reading 18.)*

---

*Question relates concepts in this and other readings.

## □ 18

# Brand franchise extension: New product benefits from existing brand names

*Edward M. Tauber*

*A well-recognized and accepted brand name is one of the most valuable assets a firm can possess. In this article, Tauber explains how a firm can use existing brand names to help define the nature of its business, to identify new product opportunities, and to reduce the risk and cost of new product introductions. As you read the article, try to think of successful and unsuccessful "brand franchise extensions" that you have observed in the marketplace.*

Some of the most successful companies in the United States have begun to offer new products which capitalize on the firm's most valuable assets: well-known trademarks on brand names. Items such as General Foods' Jello Pudding Pops, Chesebrough-Pond's Vaseline Intensive Care Bath Beads, Bic Disposable Lighters, Woolite Rug Cleaner, Sunkist Orange Soda, and Clairol Hair Blow Dryer are extensions of a previously known brand name employed by the parent company to enter a new category.

This "new type" of business opportunity is being pursued by an increasing number of firms, though the franchise extension approach to new product development is still in its infancy. As a result, very little has been written about its merits and pitfalls or how to pursue it in a systematic fashion.

The purpose of this article is to distinguish how brand franchise extensions differ from other opportunities, outline their benefits and drawbacks, specify some conditions under which they are and are not appropriate, and overview a procedure for identifying and evaluating alternative extensions for a given brand. An important by-product of this effort offers management a strategic look at alternative ways of defining what business they are in.

## FRANCHISE EXTENSIONS

Differentiation of franchise extension from other new product forms is best understood by viewing opportunities from the standpoint of the parent firm. In Exhibit 1, four types of opportunities are characterized according to whether they are in a product category new to the company (brand) and whether the brand name used is new or already familiar to the consumer.

When a new entry employs a new brand name and the product or service is in a category new to the company, this is a traditional *new product*. If the item employs a new brand but is introduced into a category where the firm already has a market position, it is called a *flanker brand*. Ralston Purina's entry of Butchers Blend Dry Dog Food is a flanker to their Dog Chow line. *Line extensions* represent new sizes, flavors, and the like where items use an existing brand name in a firm's present category. Ragu's Italian Cooking Sauce is an extension of their line of other bottled spaghetti sauces.

Source: Reprinted by *Business Horizons,* March–April 1981, pp. 36–41. Copyright © 1981 by the Foundation for the School of Business at Indiana University. Reprinted by permission. At the time of writing, Edward M. Tauber was professor and chairman of marketing at the University of Southern California.

**Exhibit 1 ☐ New opportunities from the company's viewpoint**

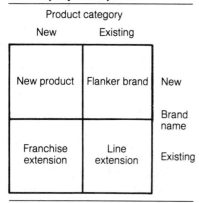

In contrast to these three, *franchise extensions* take a brand name familiar to the consumer and apply it to products that are in a category new to the parent firm. In effect, franchise extension is one method for a company to enter a new business through the leverage of its most valuable asset—the consumer awareness, goodwill, and impressions conveyed by its brand name.

## OPPORTUNITIES FOR GROWTH

Probably the most difficult challenge facing the large corporation today is how to achieve significant sales and earnings growth at acceptable risk within the no/slow growth environment of the American economy. As a result of a variety of factors, new product development is undergoing a dynamic transition, especially among heavy new product marketers such as package goods firms. This transition is reflected in a number of trends that have significantly affected new product development during the 70s and will continue to affect opportunities in the 80s.

The number of new items introduced has dramatically declined. The number introduced in the supermarket in 1979 was half the level monitored in 1972, according to the A. C. Nielsen Company.[1] Further confirmation of this trend is the year-to-year decline in new products in 1978 and 1979, according to the *New Product News.*[2]

A comparative study of the success rate of package goods introduced in 1971 versus 1977 uncovered a sizable decrease. A. C. Nielsen found 47 percent of new products introduced in 1971 were successful, while only 36 percent of those introduced in 1977 met the same criteria.[3]

Compounding the problem for the future is the lower commitment to new product R&D. McGraw-Hill's annual survey of planned R&D expenditures revealed an average 2 percent of sales in 1979, one third lower than the mid-60s peak. Companies are expected to allocate only 35 percent of these monies to new product development.[4]

Some of the contributing factors that have led to the deceleration of new product activity and the increased risk include increasing cost (technology, production, media, promotion), stable volume for supermarket and other consumer items, declining to stable GNP (and therefore disposable real income), inflation pressures due to energy and other resources, and increasing competition both here and abroad from foreign products.

With continuing supply pressures and demand stagnation, I see four major opportunities for the individual firm:

Market expansion through new distribution channels or untapped areas, especially abroad.

Acquisition and merger—a continuing trend.

Line extensions and flanker brands—a defensive tactic to tie up shelf space and "share of mind."

Franchise extensions—leveraging existing brands into new categories.

## DEFINING THE BUSINESS

The process of exploring franchise extensions represents a reasoned approach for selecting what new categories a company might enter. Inherent in this process is the identification of alternative definitions of what business we are in.

Theodore Levitt highlighted this basic strategic question in his now-classic paper, "Marketing Myopia," written almost 20 years ago. He challenged management to think broadly about what was or

[1]"New Product Success Ratios," *Nielsen Researcher,* A. C. Nielsen Company, Chicago, Illinois, 1979.

[2]*New Product News,* Dancer Fitzgerald Sample, Inc., New York, December 1979.

[3]*Nielsen Researcher,* 1979.

[4]*R&D Planned Expenditures* (New York: McGraw-Hill, 1979).

could be their domain, pointing out that the failure of the railroads was due to not recognizing they were in the transportation business. The result was missed opportunities and stiffer competition from other transportation carriers. What Levitt did not do was to provide guidelines or research techniques to aid management in determining how to define their business and what product or service categories to include.

Levitt's example suggests that railroads should have defined their business in terms of all competition that would supply similar transportation service. This is only one way of redefinition. For example, Exhibit 2 reveals some alternative business extensions. Bic has defined its business, not by competition in pens, but instead by a product attribute—disposability. Clairol defined its business by items that offer a head care benefit. Sunkist has limited its extensions to products which have an orange flavor association. Thus, there are many creative ways for any firm to define its territory. A systematic approach to aid management in this task will be presented later. It is important to note here that investigating franchise extensions will likely result in offering new ways of looking at one's business.

**Exhibit 2 □ What business are we in?**

| Railroads | or | Transportation |
|---|---|---|
| Jello pudding | or | Snacks and desserts |
| Clairol shampoo | or | Head care |
| Bic pens | or | Disposables |
| Sunkist oranges | or | Orange-flavored foods and beverages |

It is particularly interesting to note that Bic's decision to define its business as inexpensive consumer disposables led it to razors and lighters. Its initial success with disposable pens could have led it into stationery supplies or office equipment, natural additions given its channel of distribution. Leveraging its production capability of plastic disposables rather than its distribution channel was a critical strategic decision.

## BENEFITS OF FRANCHISE EXTENSIONS

Extending a franchise offers a number of benefits which traditional new product development does not. The major one is that extension capitalizes on the company's most valuable assets—its brand names. Thus, the company moves into a new category from a position of strength—the immediate consumer awareness and impressions communicated by the brand.

A further benefit is that investment outlays typically necessary to establish a new brand—a significant expense—are minimized. An important related payoff is that introduction of a franchise extension can increase sales for the parent brand. The advertising and heightened awareness of the new entry can have a synergistic effect on the original product. This corporate or umbrella effect can create important advertising efficiencies.

Finally, there *may* be reduced risk of failure of the new item when the brand name already strongly conveys benefits desired in the new category.

## APPROPRIATENESS

Each contemplated case of extending a franchise is unique and requires custom analysis. Nevertheless, there are certain conditions which I believe are necessary for a franchise extension to be successful. The parent brand should provide leverage in the new category. There must be a rub-off of perceived superior know-how, effectiveness, or appropriate imagery. Most highly advertised brands are known. They provide significant leverage in a new category. Thus, there should be a benefit of the parent brand that is the same benefit offered and desired in the new franchise extension. For example, Sunkist Orange Soda "promises" the same orange taste as obtained from Sunkist oranges.

Consumers should perceive the new item to be consistent with the parent brand name. Most consumers would probably accept Planters Peanut Butter Candy as a logical extension of the franchise.

Finally, it is critical that the company enter the new category with comparable or superior production/distribution/merchandising and advertising capability. A number of successful franchise extensions have occurred without any technological breakthroughs or product improvements. However, competitive parity is necessary. One case in point is Coleman's successful extension from the camp stove and lantern business to the camping equipment business, offering tents, sleeping bags, and so on.

Franchise extension is not without risk. In fact, its major strength—capitalizing on a previously established brand name—also reflects its No. 1 risk: potential dilution of the brand franchise in the long run.

There are a numer of conditions that can contribute to franchise deterioration. What might appear to be a "natural" extension short term should be pursued with caution as most deleterious effects to a franchise occur gradually over time. Brands like General Electric, Betty Crocker, Quaker, and Gillette have been extended profusely. While they have not stopped being households words, the strong associations they once had with specific products (television, cake mix, oatmeal, and razors) and their related qualities have been diluted.

For this reason franchise extension always carries greater risk when a brand name is used almost synonymously with a specific product. The great lengths to which manufacturers go to protect their trademarks from being judged legally generic testifies to the market value such brands possess. The only thing worse than competitors breaking this brand-product link in the consumer's mind is companies doing it to themselves. A Tab is a sugar-free cola. Now, the Coca-Cola Company offers Tab in a variety of flavors. Other examples of brands that are not legally generic but are often used synonymously with the category are: Kleenex = facial tissues; Perrier = naturally carbonated bottled water; Coke = cola; Scotch Tape = transparent tape; Tampax = feminine hygiene tampon; Band-Aid = adhesive bandages.

Another risky condition when extending a franchise occurs when the new item could create confusion or a negative image for the parent brand.

Finally, sometimes the new item's failure could seriously affect the parent brand. Some years ago, Carnation Company announced its intent to introduce a contraceptive dog food, Lady Friskie, knowing that if this medicated product generated any adverse publicity, even in an isolated test market, sales of the parent brand (Friskies) could be impaired. Later, they tried naming the test product Extra Care. It was never introduced to the market.

## SEARCH AND EVALUATION

Implicit in Levitt's concept of how to define one's business is the notion that it should go be-

yond product description (such as railroads) to benefits, attributes, meanings, and associations. Franchise extension search is based on the question "What's in a name?"

The franchise extension search is a two-stage consumer research method employing bright, articulate people who have the ability to think abstractly. No attempt is made to locate an average or a "representative" group. During the first half of the ideation session, consumers generate meanings and associations surrounding the brand name. In Stage 2, the consumers are asked to identify product or service categories that are related to each association.

Exhibit 3 is a condensed version of the output from a franchise extension search for Vaseline Intensive Care. The brand leads to alternative definitions of the business (moisturizer, medicinal, body care, etc.), and each definition has a list of related product categories. Each chain represents a potential franchise extension. For example, one option is to define the business as offering lotions and introduce products such as Vaseline Intensive Care Sunburn Cream or Vaseline Intensive Care Baby Lotion.

Deciding on the appropriateness of a franchise extension entails using these three criteria which are related to consumer perception:

The consumer perceives the new item to be consistent with the parent brand.

**Exhibit 3 ☐ Franchise extension search**

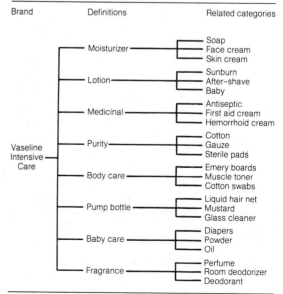

**Exhibit 4 □ Franchise extension search**

Vaseline Intensive Care Lotion

Sunburn cream

Hemorrhoid treatment

Deodorant

Perceived
similar benefits

• Strong to heal injured skin
• Reduces irritation and swelling. Petroleum jelly base.
• For delicate skin

The parent brand provides leverage in the new category which the existing competitors do not have.

A benefit associated with the parent brand is the same one offered and desired from the new franchise extension.

These criteria—perceptual fit, competitive leverage, and benefit transfer—are used when quantitative study is conducted where respondents are asked how likely they would be to expect alternative products such as soap or baby oil from a brand name such as Vaseline Intensive Care (perceptual fit). For each product which is likely, they are asked to list any brands they believe the new item would compete with. Then, they report in what ways, if any, the new product might be better than the competitors and in what ways it might not be as good (competitive leverage). In the final step, each participant thinks of any benefit or advantage the parent product has (Vaseline Intensive Care Lotion) that could be associated with each new item (benefit transfer). See Exhibit 4.

Too often, new product programs are undertaken without sufficient guidance from top mangement. A key source of direction is a tightly written definition of what business the firm wishes to pursue. This initial step is easy to ignore or assume since the products or services the companies offer tend to become the definition of the business— pens, shampoo, jeans, etc. The strategic task of defining a business by prodcut attributes, consumer benefits, or other more abstract associations broadens horizons while at the same time delineates the areas the firm will pursue.

A second key to successful new product activity is management's recognition of what assets it has which are leverageable, such as resource purchasing power, technology, processing capability, and distribution channels. Well-known brand names are for many firms among the most leverageable assets they own.

The process proposed here begins with the brand name, generates alternative definitions of the business through meanings and associations to the brand, and seeks related product categories. These categories become candidates for consideration of a franchise extension. Business judgment and economic factors must be applied to eliminate categories that are of no interest to the firm. Consumer research can be used to evaluate the fit of the brand name to the category, and any competitive leverage that would exist.

## QUESTIONS

1. What is "brand franchise extension," and how does it differ from what the author calls "new products," "flanker brands," and "line extensions"?

2. What are the benefits of brand franchise extension to the firm?

3. When would brand franchise extension be appropriate—and when would it not be appropriate? Why?

4. Name two successful and two unsuccessful attempts at brand franchise extension (not already mentioned in the article).

*5. How does the topic of brand franchise extension relate to Levitt's ideas about "marketing myopia" (Reading 5)?

---

*Question relates concepts in this and other readings.

## ☐ 19

# The rise and fall of "new Coke"

*In the spring of 1985, the Coca-Cola Company shocked the soft drink world—and many of its customers—by changing the secret formula used for making Coca-Cola. Company officials staunchly defended their decision to change the world's most successful soft drink, citing research which showed that the new formula was strongly preferred by cola drinkers. However, there was so much negative customer reaction that Coke was forced to reintroduce the old formula as "Coca-Cola Classic"—giving customers a choice between the old Coke and the new Coke. Some considered Coke's actions a brilliant competitive strategy—but many others believed that Coke had committed a spectacular blunder.*

*The following series of articles describes and comments on Coke's marketing decision making over about a one-year period, starting with the introduction of "new Coke." As you trace the history and progress of new Coke, try to decide for yourself: Did Coke plan and implement a brilliant marketing strategy—or commit a spectacular blunder?*

## ☐ 19–A

# Is Coke fixing a cola that isn't broken?

### *Scott Scredon*

First it was code-named Zeus. As the project developed, it was renamed Tampa, then Eton, and, finally, Kansas. It isn't the latest military project, but in the $22 billion domestic soft-drink business, it's a bombshell. On April 23, Coca-Cola Co. announced it had changed 7X—the secret formula used for making Coke.

Coke's decision to tinker with the world's most successful soft drink sent the industry and its observers into a tizzy, searching for hidden motives. But there don't seem to be any. While conducting research four years ago to find a suitable formula for what would become diet Coke, company chemists stumbled on a syrup that produced a drink that tasted "smoother" than regular Coke. They held taste tests with 191,000 consumers and found that a clear majority liked the new product better. The hard choice was whether to implement the new formula or put it back on the laboratory shelf. "I wish the story could be sexier," says Roberto C. Goizueta, Coke's 53-year-old, Cuban-born chief executive. "But it is not."

### HEALTH TONIC?

Unveiling the new soft drink now—the product will be available in time to celebrate the company's 99th birthday on May 8—Goizueta appears to have two goals in mind. First, the reformulated Coke will be used to try to revive slumping sales in Coke's 154 foreign markets. The company is

Source: Reprinted from the May 6, 1985, issue of *Business Week* by special permission, © 1985 by McGraw-Hill, Inc. At the time of writing, Scott Scredon was on the staff of *Business Week*.

now strengthening its foreign distribution system, and an improved product could only help boost sales. Overseas operations accounted for more than half of the company's $1.1 billion operating earnings last year and 62 percent of its soft-drink volume. But foreign business has been growing slowly the past few years. "They want volume growth above 8 percent," says Emanuel Goldman, a soft-drink analyst at Montgomery Securities. "This is one of the vehicles for that growth."

On the second front, the new product will be used to regain some of the U.S. market share lost to a newly invigorated Pepsi (BW—March 4). While Coke's total soft-drink sales have exploded recently because of the extremely successful introduction of diet Coke, regular Coke has lost nearly a 4 percent share in supermarkets since 1981, according to Jesse Meyers, editor of *Beverage Digest,* an industry newsletter. Meanwhile, Pepsi-Cola USA's aggressive advertising campaign, featuring rock singer Michael Jackson, helped boost regular Pepsi's market share by 1.5 percent in 1984, to 18.8 percent, compared with Coke's 21.7 percent.

But marketing the new Coca-Cola presents potential problems. While the company says 55 percent of consumers chose the new product in all 25 test markets, that means 45 percent like Coke the way it is. Despite these results, Goizueta insists the tests clearly indicate that introducing the new formula is the right decision. "This is our surest move ever," he says. "The consumer made it."

**TAKE THE DAY OFF**

However, Pepsi has already fired the first volley in an attempt to put Coke on the defensive. On the day Coke announced its new product, Pepsi ran national advertisements claiming the reformulation was an admission that Coke's old product was inferior. To celebrate its self-proclaimed victory, Pepsi gave employees a day off. "We look upon this as a real opportunity," say Roger A. Enrico, Pepsi-Cola USA's president. "We won't let it go by."

Wall Street also questioned Coke's decision. While the company's stock climbed 1⅝ in anticipation of the announcement, it fell by 2¾ points in the two days after the product was unveiled.

The decision to change Coke's taste caps a four-year effort by Goizueta to strengthen the company's business by trading on its powerful trademark. The former research chemist, who has no marketing experience, has already scored the industry's biggest success in decades with diet Coke. Diet Coke is now the leading diet soft drink. And with 6.2 percent of the domestic take-home market, it is the industry's third-most-popular drink.

**NO. 1 CONCERN**

Now, Goizueta wants the company to grow by adding new products outside the traditional cola and lemon-lime segments. It is testing Cherry Coke, to take on Dr Pepper, and this summer will introduce Minute Maid orange soda—which contains 10 percent juice. The soft-drink maker is also considering a reformulated Fresca containing citrus juice to compete with bottled waters such as Perrier. Goizueta hopes these products will eventually boost Coke's total U.S. market share to 40 percent from the current 37 percent.

The No. 1 concern for years ahead, however, will be the performance of the flagship brand. Coke will pull out all the stops to market the product aggressively, including a new set of high-energy television ads and new commercials featuring comedian Bill Cosby. The challenge for one of the nation's premier marketing companies is to sell a new, improved version of something many thought was just fine the way it was.

☐ **19–B**

# Coke's man on the spot: The changes Goizueta is making outweigh one spectacular blunder

*Scott Scredon*

*Marc Frons*

Roberto C. Goizueta had never known the taste of failure. Although he fled Cuba immediately after Castro took power, leaving behind a life of prosperity and security, his business career had been marked by one stunning success after another. But ever since the Coca-Cola Co. chief executive scrapped the formula of his company's 99-year-old flagship brand in favor of new Coke in April, he had been under siege: Rivals credited him with the marketing blunder of the decade. Longtime Coke drinkers—and even some bottlers—angrily demanded that he bring back the old Coke. On July 11, he did.

It was an odd turn for the man who awakened Coke from its antebellum torpor. In little over four years, Goizueta (pronounced Goy-SWEAT-a) transformed the Atlanta soft-drink maker into a $7.4 billion diversified giant. His moves have always defied Coke tradition: He replaced weak bottlers, bought Columbia Pictures Industries Inc., and introduced diet Coke. The moves have also paid off: Profit margins have widened by 20 percent, and the price of Coke's stock, down sharply in the pre-Goizueta decade, has doubled since he took over in 1981.

Goizueta has been a bold agent of change in a once-stodgy corporation. Highly organized and meticulous, he has done nothing less than remake Coke's culture. "Roberto sets high standards for himself and expects everyone else to reach that level," says Sam Ayoub, the company's former chief financial officer. Goizueta has orchestrated several brilliant decisions. Perhaps equally important, he has ended almost three years of corporate infighting that had drained Coke of its energy. He replaced almost a dozen executives who were not pulling their weight to "let people know it was not business as usual." And he instituted an open-door management policy that encouraged innovation and the free exchange of new ideas.

Despite his successes, Goizueta was haunted by a problem: the steady decline of Coke's market share against Pepsi-Cola. The rival cola has been outselling Coke in U.S. food stores since 1977. And Coke had been unable to refute the "Pepsi Challenge," which convinced Americans that Pepsi tasted better than The Real Thing. Says Goizueta: "We tried everything—more marketing, more spending. The only thing we had not tried was claiming product superiority."

Goizueta was flabbergasted by the outcry over the elimination of the original Coke. But the company's surprise may have been due to its cast of characters—several international executives who have a firm hand on Coke's global operations, but were out of touch with the symbolic meaning of their own product. "If we still had some of these Southern good ol' boys running this company instead of this international crew, maybe this never would have happened," says one Southern bottler. "They missed the mystique of Coca-Cola, if they ever knew it at all."

## ERRATIC MEMORY

In retrospect, Goizueta's decision to alter the formula seems almost inevitable. He emerged as CEO following one of the worst periods in the company's history. Although Coke's former auto-

Source: Reprinted from the July 29, 1985, issue of *Business Week* by special permission. © 1985 by McGraw-Hill, Inc. At the time of writing, Scott Scredon and Marc Frons were on the staff of *Business Week*.

## Goizueta's big moves

| | |
|---|---|
| March 1981 | Goizueta becomes chairman and CEO; begins replacing weak bottlers |
| November 1981 | Sells Aqua-Chem Inc., steam boiler maker, for $95 million |
| January 1982 | Buys Columbia Pictures Industries Inc. for $700 million in cash and stock |
| February 1982 | Introduces "Coke is it!" ad campaign |
| July 1982 | Introduces diet Coke |
| September 1982 | Buys Ronco Enterprises Inc., pasta maker, for $10 million (sold 1984 for $20 million) |
| November 1982 | Columbia puts up $65 million to launch Tri-Star Pictures with CBS and HBO. |
| May 1983 | Introduces Caffeine Free Coca-Cola, Tab, and diet Coke |
| November 1983 | Sells Wine Spectrum, and its Taylor brand, for $230 million |
| April 1985 | Introduces new Coke and Cherry Coke |
| June 1985 | Buys Embassy Communications and Tandem Productions, TV producers, in a $400 million deal |
| July 1985 | Reverses earlier decision and brings back old Coke as Coca-Cola Classic |

cratic boss, J. Paul Austin, had overseen more than a decade of robust growth, the last 2½ years of his tenure as chief executive were marked by corporate infighting and confusion. Austin was suffering the early effects of Alzheimer's disease. His memory became erratic. "He would tell managers to do something one day, then ask them why they were doing such a stupid thing the next," says a former Coke executive. Austin would even wander into the wrong office and order the person sitting behind the desk to leave.

Austin may have been aware that he was becoming ill. In 1980 he made Goizueta and six other executives vice-chairmen. The seven men, known inside Coke as "The Vice Squad" or "The Seven Dwarfs," battled it out for the top spot. Austin favored an operations man, Ian Wilson, to become the next CEO. He even held a dinner for Wilson and his wife at a posh Atlanta restaurant to celebrate his coming appointment.

But Austin was overruled by Robert W. Woodruff, Coke's legendary chairman, whose name in Atlanta is almost as ubiquitous as the company trademark. Woodruff ran Coke from 1923 to 1955, and even after his retirement from day-to-day operations, he exerted a patriarchal influence on

company affairs. It was Woodruff who not only made the soft drink a part of Americana but also introduced Coke throughout the world. And it was Woodruff who took a liking to an intense young executive named Roberto Goizueta.

Woodruff asked Goizueta to lunch nearly every day in one of Coke's private dining rooms and often invited Goizueta to the Woodruff "plantation" in south Georgia, where the old man liked to hunt quail. "Woodruff believed in Roberto's efficiency and his demand for quality," says Ayoub. "Unlike Paul, who was very guarded, Roberto would share every detail of the business with Woodruff." Until Woodruff died on March 7 at age 95, Goizueta visited his mentor about twice a week.

### PROUDEST MOMENT

Goizueta hardly fit the profile of the traditional Coke executive—a Southerner, preferably from Georgia. The son of a wealthy Havana sugar plantation owner, Goizueta came to the United States at 16 to enter Cheshire Academy, an exclusive Connecticut preparatory school. Goizueta spoke virtually no English when he arrived, but by using a dictionary and "watching the same movies over and over," he quickly learned the language. That same year he was the class valedictorian. "It was the proudest moment of my life," he says.

He graduated from Yale University in 1955 with a degree in chemical engineering and returned to Cuba. He decided not to help manage his father's plantation—an unconventional step at the time. "It's very Latin to want to own your own business," says Goizueta. "But I've always felt more comfortable as part of a bigger scene." Instead, he answered an ad in a Spanish-language newspaper to work in Coke's Cuban research labs.

He might have remained there had it not been for an old classmate in Cuba: Fidel Castro. In 1959, Goizueta, his wife, and their three children fled just a month after Castro seized power and expropriated Coke's Cuban business. Goizueta arrived in the United States with $20. "Everyone expected to go back to Cuba," he recalls. "In the Miami airport, I kept records of where all our equipment was for the time when we returned. But eventually we realized there was no place to go back to."

## CORPORATE POLITICIAN

He resettled in Miami and commuted to the Bahamas, where he oversaw Coke's chemical research facilities. Although he acquired a reputation as an unimaginative and cautious researcher, he became known as a brilliant administrator. "He was not innovative in the labs at all," says one former top executive. "But he was an astute corporate politician, a clean-desk guy, a stickler for minute detail. He knew where every grain of sand was in the office."

Goizueta came to company headquarters in 1965, among the first of a new breed of Coke executive. Instead of choosing managers from old-line Georgia families, Woodruff and Austin were increasingly looking to Coke's rapidly expanding foreign operations for the company's future leaders. During the 1960s and 1970s, Austin brought several young managers to Atlanta who later formed Coke's executive core: the Egyptian-born Ayoub; German Claus M. Halle, now in charge of international operations in 155 countries; and Argentinian Brian G. Dyson, now the head of Coca-

Cola USA. President Donald R. Keough, who hails from Iowa, jokes that he is the company's "token American."

Goizueta has continued that international spirit, but he has transformed Woodruff's empire into his own. As recently as 1981 there was only one Coke, and in Woodruff's day there was only one container—the 6½-oz. glass bottle. (Today only one tenth of 1 percent of all Coke is sold in that bottle.) In what was considered heresy at the time, Goizueta used the sacrosanct company trademark on diet Coke. In less than three years, it became the third-largest-selling soft drink in the United States. Encouraged by that success, Goizueta has attached the Coca-Cola name to five other soft drinks and has even let it grace a line of clothing.

## 'FIRE HIM!'

He has changed Coke in more subtle ways. Woodruff, a conservative financial man, abhorred debt. He paid off all his company's loans just in time for the Great Depression, a cautious fiscal strategy that probably saved Coke from going under. And Woodruff retained his aversion to debt. When he learned that one former chief financial officer wanted to borrow $100 million at 9.75 percent to finance a new building, Woodruff replied: "Fire him! Coke doesn't borrow money!" When Goizueta took over, less than 2 percent of Coke's capital was in long-term debt. Since then, Goizueta has increased that to 18 percent and used it to restructure Coke's bottling operations and invest in Columbia's new movies. He has said he is unafraid to increase the company's debt burden should the right acquisition come along.

Perhaps Goizueta's most significant changes have come in management style: He has created an atmosphere that allows new ideas to flourish. Having come to power after the Austin era, Goizueta is particularly sensitive to the destructive potential of dissension among his top executives. While Goizueta is clearly in charge, he insists that he and his three top officers—Keough, Chief Financial Officer M. Douglas Ivester, and Ira C. Herbert, marketing director—agree before any key corporate decision is made. In fact, Goizueta once vetoed a major acquisition because one member of the team disapproved.

# Will Coke have the last laugh?

When Coca-Cola Co. executives first announced the return of old Coke, competitors were overjoyed. After all, the mighty Atlanta marketing machine had bogged down. They reasoned that Coke would suffer from consumer confusion, diluted promotional efforts, and a lack of space on retailers' shelves.

Coke, of course, may still end up taking a beating because of its hastily concocted change in strategy. But the longer its soft-drink competitors think about the company's desperation move, the more worried they become.

That's because Coca-Cola has suddenly shifted the battleground on its rivals. By bringing back old Coke—and naming it Coca-Cola Classic—the soft-drink giant has bullied the competition into a much more difficult fight. Instead of selling against "new" Coke, which was intended to hurt Pepsi but has met with seemingly universal indifference, competitors must now battle a chastened Coca-Cola that will concentrate on its traditional strengths: selling sodas and winning shelf space.

Meeting Coke on that battleground will not be easy. It commands a $100 million budget to promote the two Cokes, enough to drown out messages from all competitors except free-spending PepsiCo Inc. And Coke's well-financed bottlers are poised to boost local advertising and slash prices to gain market share. "Adding another [Coke-produced] cola makes it even more difficult for Royal Crown, Seven-Up, and Dr Pepper to go on living," notes Michael Norkus, vice-president at Boston Consulting Group. Agrees Emanuel Goldman, a partner at San Francisco's Montgomery Securities: "Coke has backed into a very powerful strategic position."

That may not be evident at first. Most retailers say they will make room for the old Coke by reducing the shelf space they give other Coke products. But space is determined by what sells best, not who makes it. So while old Coke might outperform new Coke—or vice versa—as long as both outsell other soft drinks, they'll get all the room they need. That space will come from shrinking the displays of other, weaker brands. Says Sidney Applebaum, president of Minneapolis-based Rainbow Foods: "We'll watch the oddball brands to see if some of them can be eliminated."

To avoid being cut back, companies such as Seven-Up, Dr Pepper, and Royal Crown have little choice but to join in the spending free-for-all. "It's going to be increasingly difficult to play table-stakes poker," predicts Edward W. Frantel, chief executive of third-ranked Seven-Up Co.

Even more ominous for the small soft-drink marketers is the ongoing push by Coke and Pepsi to expand their empires far beyond colas. A Pepsi bottler who also distributes 7Up might, for example, replace 7Up with Pepsi's new lemon-lime drink called Slice. "For the last 10 years, secondary brands have lived off the distribution systems of their major competitors," says George E. Thompson, beverage analyst at Prudential-Bache Securities Inc.

Indeed, Coca-Cola's current national rollout of Cherry Coke could be particularly bad news for Dr Pepper Co. Although Coke says it hasn't targeted the Dallas-based company's flagship soda, Cherry Coke's similar taste and its major ad budget make it a much more formidable challenger than Coke's existing Mr Pibb. Lemon-lime king Seven-Up must worry not only aobut Slice but also about Coke's increased spending to promote Sprite. And R. J. Reynolds Industries Inc.'s Sunkist Orange brand could be in trouble if Coca-Cola takes its Minute Maid orange soda national later this year. "Coke has the most developed distribution system [in the industry], and they're using all the tools at hand to dominate, or almost monopolize, the business," fumes Seven-Up's Frantel.

### UNDERDOG IMAGE

Frantel is worried about the industry trend toward cooperative marketing agreements between bottlers and supermarkets. Under such agreements, a retailer features only one brand of soft drink in his ads for a specified period of time in exchange for a cash fee and discounts on the featured brand. Coke and Pepsi "are trying to eliminate competition," says James W. Harralson, executive vice-president of Royal Crown Cos.

RC won't go down without a fight. Amid the confusion over new Coke, it launched a new national advertising campaign. And within the past year it began a national accounts program to sell to large supermarket chains, named a marketing manager to push RC on military bases, and started a vending machine financing program for bottlers. Vows Harralson: "These cats are not going to put me out of business, and I do not plan to be a No. 3 cola forever."

RC used to rely on pioneering new products—including the first diet and caffeine-free colas—to stay one step ahead of its larger rivals. But its size and weaker bottling network allowed the industry giants to harvest the fruit of those innovations. So now RC is positioning itself as an underdog fighting giants and is using humor to get its message across. One new commercial shows a Russian politician promoting both Coke and Pepsi as the official state drinks. Then a band of peasants is seen secretly enoying gulps of RC Cola in a Siberian hideaway until KGB-like agents interrupt the festivities.

Still, neither RC's Russian dissidents nor Seven-Up's revived "uncola" campaign can change the rules of combat. Coke and Pepsi have the deepest pockets and the most clout in a $23 billion business that is dominated increasingly by advertising and promotions. Smaller soft-drink makers can cheer Coke's recent stumble, but they cannot expect it to fall. They must still fight to stave off Coke and Pepsi, which seem destined to grow at their expense.

Yet Goizueta is a demanding boss with little tolerance for mistakes. He does not hesitate to sack an executive who is performing poorly. "Personal relations have nothing to do with business for him," says on insider. "He'll love you today and hate you tomorrow." Says Goizueta: "It irks me when somebody hasn't done his homework."

Goizueta always seems to have done his own. He is up every morning at 5:30, using the time to read the morning papers and write letters or speeches. When he arrives at headquarters in a chauffeur-driven Lincoln a few hours later, he sometimes questions his top officers about the day's news. He forbids high-level managers to take vacations in the summer, the prime soft-drink season. In fact, he sees little need for vacations at all. Some 20-year executives, who are entitled to five weeks, often take only a few days. Goizueta has taken one week a year throughout his career, although his wife persuaded him to take two weeks this year.

### QUOTING GRANDPA

Whoever deals with him comes away impressed with Goizueta's intensity and intellect. "His mind is like a piece of crystal," says former Coke Marketing Vice-President J. Wayne Jones, now executive vice-president for marketing at

Stroh Brewery Co. in Detroit. "He sees through issues and gets right to the heart of the matter." He
also has a philosophical bent. "He uses a lot of
Cuban aphorisms; you'll find him quoting his
grandfather a lot," says Francis T. Vincent Jr.,
chairman of Columbia. And Goizueta says he simply enjoys mental gymnastics—"[when] you can
think through a problem so hard you can develop
a sweat."

True to his engineering roots, Goizueta is ob-
sessed with detail. He checks the box-office results daily to determine how well Columbia's
movies are doing, monitors Coke's stock price
several times a day, and out of sheer curiosity
gets involved with virtually every aspect of the
business. "He wants perfection," says Ayoub. "On
weekends, he would take home drafts of the
speeches of his top executives and make corrections." As chief financial officer, Ayoub managed
Coke's huge basket of foreign currencies. "We
used to make little bets on foreign exchange," he
recalls. "He used to walk into my office and bet

me a dollar on what's going to happen to the
sterling."

## WEIGHT LOSS

Goizueta's attention to detail is most striking in
his impeccable appearance. He is trim, having not
gained any weight in the past eight years. Friends
describe him as a man of passion and discipline.
"He'll search all around his office for a piece of
chocolate," says one acquaintance. "But when he
finds one, he'll only take a nibble." Goizueta also
is conscious of the appearances of others. He
often speaks to managers about sloppily dressed
or overweight employees—and even wants to
send one obese vice-president to a weight-loss
clinic.

Coke's chairman is a different man outside the
office. He enjoys playing golf with his wife, reading, lying in the sun at Sea Island off the Georgia
coast, and attending Atlanta Symphony Orchestra

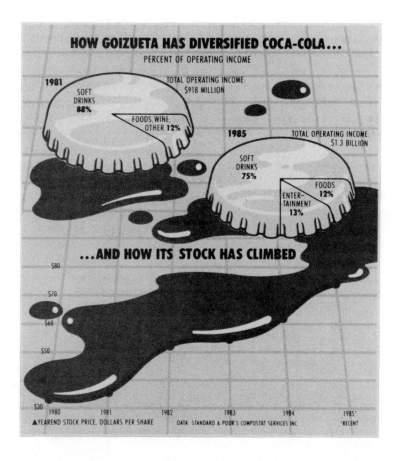

**HOW GOIZUETA HAS DIVERSIFIED COCA-COLA...**
PERCENT OF OPERATING INCOME

**1981**
SOFT DRINKS **88%**
TOTAL OPERATING INCOME: $918 MILLION
FOODS, WINE, OTHER **12%**

**1985**
TOTAL OPERATING INCOME: $1.3 BILLION
SOFT DRINKS **75%**
FOODS **12%**
ENTER-TAINMENT **13%**

**...AND HOW ITS STOCK HAS CLIMBED**

$80
$70
$60
$50
$30

1980    1981    1982    1983    1984    1985*
▲YEAREND STOCK PRICE, DOLLARS PER SHARE    DATA: STANDARD & POOR'S COMPUSTAT SERVICES INC    *RECENT

concerts. And in a social setting, such as a cocktail party, Goizueta is an engaging conversationalist who wants to know what makes his counterpart tick. "He's the kind of fellow you enjoy talking to," says Georgia Senator Sam Nunn, who talks with Goizueta periodically. "There's no stiffness, no big ego."

While he may seem distant on first meeting, he quickly warms up and can in a short time become fast friends with those he likes and respects, such as Herbert A. Allen, the former Columbia chairman who now sits on Coke's board. "Everybody used to say there was no way Herbert would go to Atlanta for a meeting. Herbert himself said he wouldn't do it for more than a year," says Vincent. "But well before the year was up, he said: 'I really like this guy.' Now he goes down there all the time."

Even though Goizueta is wealthy—he earned roughly $1.5 million in salary and bonuses last year—he has always tended to live modestly. He occupies the same house he bought when he came to Atlanta 20 years ago, one with a market value of roughly $150,000. But Goizueta is not averse to living well. "Your priorities change as you get older," he says. "Who knows—someday I may want a big house." But friends say his experience in Cuba, where the revolution swept away his family's wealth, taught him there were more important things than material possessions.

He returns to that experience often in his life. "It gives you a kind of inner fortitude," he says. And it has helped him put the recent series of events in perspective. "A friend of mine called the other day and said: 'You've gone through situations 10 times worse than new Coke,' " says Goizueta.

In the weeks after his decision to eliminate old Coke, even Goizueta's friends assumed he was feeling the sharp sting of public embarrassment. "He must be in tremendous pain," says one former Coke executive. "This is eating him up."

Goizueta would no more admit to failure than he would to drinking Pepsi. But he and other top Coke executives were staggered by the public response over their decision to scrap the original Coke. "We knew some people were going to be unhappy, but we could never have predicted the depth of their unhappiness," says Goizueta. "Just as I could not have predicted the emotional dis-

ruption that resulted from my leaving Cuba—you cannot quantify emotion."

In the past, Goizueta has ditched other strategies that haven't panned out. Coke bought Ronco Enterprises Inc. in 1982 in an attempt to launch a national pasta business. But two years later, Goizueta sold the business after he decided Ronco was not meeting his financial goals. In 1983 he sold Wine Spectrum and its Taylor brand name.

## TIME WILL TELL

To many, the decision to bring back the old Coke demonstrates Goizueta's pragmatism. Two sugar colas—three, including new Cherry Coke—are better than one, he says. While Coke has 18 percent of the take-home market, the company believes its three sugar brands can account for 26 percent within a short period. "Time will tell, but I'm willing to take bets on this one," he says.

There may still be trouble in Coke's executive offices if the new strategy fizzles. Someone, insiders say, will pay the price—no matter how well he has performed until now. "If this doesn't work, the people responsible for the new [Coke] decision will be fired," says one former executive. "Whoever is to blame, Roberto will cut his throat slowly."

Tension in the executive suite was high during this first big crisis. And some feel the free-spending marketers may be getting Goizueta's ear more often since the feisty Ayoub retired last December. Keough has historically supported Brian Dyson at almost every turn in the past—and it was Dyson's group that recommended new Coke. While Ivester, 38, is considered a top-notch finance man, his recent promotion and youth make it difficult for him to fight in the trenches with well-established executives. Some insiders worry that Goizueta is surrounded by yes-men who are too timid to challenge what appear to be prevailing attitudes.

Whether the multi-cola strategy succeeds, however, may be largely out of Coke's control. Several retailers say they will not give the company's cola brands any more shelf space. With roughly one third of Coca-Cola's U.S. sales coming from fast-food outlets such as McDonald's, restaurant owners will also play a significant role in determining which Coke sells best. If Mc-Donald's, which serves roughly 500 million people every month, decides to put Coca-Cola Classic in its spigots rather than new Coke, the company faces serious problems convincing consumers new Coke is for them.

## JUST AS GLAD

The biggest decision of all may be whether to market new Coke overseas. Because the company gets more than half its earnings from international sales, some officials say the new product was conceived with the idea of increasing consumption outside the United States. Bringing out new Coke was "a global decision from the beginning," says Claus Halle.

Goizueta says the international rollout will begin soon, but some foreign bottlers fear a repeat of the U.S. experience and simply don't want new Coke. Some European bottlers say they would rather stay with the original formula. Others are just as glad as American bottlers that the old Coke has been retained. "People keep asking our delivery personnel: 'Why a new formula?' " says Peter Buřfent, a bottler in Bonn. "They say the old Coke is good as is, and I'm happy the old Coke is going to remain."

If Goizueta has to deal with an international backlash, his worries have only just begun. But he remains confident of his company's strategy. "Having known in April what I know today, I definitely would have introduced the new Coke," he says. "Then I could have said I planned the whole thing." And his experience with new Coke has not curbed his desire to take risks. "An old boss once told me I was too much a man of action," says Goizueta. "But I like to quote the poet Antonio Machado, who said: 'Paths are made by walking.' " He will know soon enough whether he has taken the right path.

---

## ☐ 19–C

# Coke's brand-loyalty lesson

*Anne B. Fisher*

Marketers battling to keep competitors from grabbing off customers complain that there just doesn't seem to be as much brand loyalty around as there used to be. Yet when Coca-Cola Co. dared to tamper with a 99-year-old formula to bring out a "new" Coke, outraged U.S. consumers quickly forced the red-faced company to bring back the old brand. Coke's abrupt about-face, front-paged and prime-timed, raises questions about brand loyalty that every marketer has to ponder: how companies get it, how they keep it, and which products inspire such fierce loyalty that they're best left old and unimproved.

Brand loyalty—that certain something that makes a consumer keep buying over and over again—is an elusive quality. It begins with the customer's preference for a product on the basis of objective reasons—the drink is sweeter, the paper towel more absorbent. The brand name is the customer's guarantee that he will get what he expects. But when a branded product has been around a long time and is heavily advertised, it can pick up emotional freight: it can become a part of a person's self-image or summon fond memories of days gone by.

The sense of emotional attachment was palpable among consumers who for years had agreed with Coca-Cola that "Coke Is It." They wanted the Real Thing they had grown up with and in some cases grown old with. They inundated Coca-Cola's Atlanta headquarters with protests ("Dear Chief Dodo: What ignoramus decided to change the formula of Coke?"). In Seattle strident loyalists calling themselves Old Coke Drinkers of America laid plans to file a class action suit against Coca-Cola. They searched out shop owners, vending-machine owners, and others willing to claim that the company's formula change had cost them business. When June sales didn't pick up as the company had expected, bottlers too demanded old Coke's return—fast.

Coke thought it had moved cautiously in deciding to retire the old formula. The company spent about $4 million to taste-test the new soda pop on nearly 200,000 consumers. The tests took many forms. Some were blind tests without the emotion-laden brand name attached to them. Others posed such questions as, What if this were a new Coke taste? But Coca-Cola never disclosed that the product it was testing would replace the old favorite entirely.

So while it learned that more people like the new, sweeter formula than the old, it failed to gauge how people would react once they learned that old Coke was being replaced. Dennis Rosen, who teaches marketing at Indiana University's Graduate School of Business, thinks Coca-Cola unwittingly ran afoul of too many fond memories. "Taste tests," he says, "don't take into account the emotional tie-in with the old brand, which is all wrapped up with people's childhoods. Now that consumers are drinking out of cans labeled *new* Coke, naturally there is an emotional backlash."

When the new Coke hit the shelves in the U.S. in April, consumers felt that the company had broken the first promise of branding: that what you get today will be what you got yesterday. "All of the time and money and skill poured into consumer research on the new Coca-Cola could not measure or reveal the deep and abiding emotional attachment to original Coca-Cola," says Donald R. Keough, Coke's president and chief operating officer. He adds, "Some critic will say Coca-Cola made a marketing mistake. Some cynic will say that we planned the whole thing [for the publicity

value]. The truth is we are not that dumb and we are not that smart."

Many marketing experts are sympathetic with Coke's giant misstep. "All research on brand loyalty is flawed," says John O'Toole, chairman of the Chicago-based advertising agency Foote Cone & Belding, "because you can't get at people's private motivations. In any kind of interview or questionnaire, they want to seem sensible and prudent. They aren't going to tell you how they *feel.*" In Coca-Cola's case, consumers' feelings were not only unfathomable but fickle too. The company's research after the new formula hit supermarket shelves showed a curious turnaround. Before May 30, 53 percent of shoppers said they liked the new Coke, the rest said they didn't. In June the vote began to change, with more than half of all the people surveyed saying they didn't care for the new Coke. Says a Coke spokesman: "We had taken away more than the product Coca-Cola. We had taken away a little part of them and their past. They said, 'You had no right to do that. Bring it back.' " By the time the company decided it had erred in changing the formula, only 30 percent of the 900 consumers surveyed every week answered that they liked the new Coke.

With the old formula reintroduced as Coca-Cola Classic, complete with old-fashioned script logo, shoppers will now find six kinds of Coke on U.S. supermarket shelves—new, classic, caffeine-free, diet, diet caffeine-free, and cherry. (One more variety, the New York *Daily News* noted, and Coca-Cola "will have seven up.") Soft-drink experts believe that the welter of Cokes will give the company a tough time keeping a clear identity in shoppers' minds. Some Coke executives are said to share that fear, though Chief Executive Roberto C. Goizueta called the lineup a "megabrand" and a marketing plus.

He may be right. Other products come in a variety of forms with no evident consumer befuddlement; Marlboro comes to mind, with its king-size and longs and low-tar lights in boxes and soft packs. Goizueta believes his megabrand gives the company an edge in supermarkets, where he who grabs the most shelf space wins. Wall Street seemed to share his confidence: in the week that the reintroduction of old Coke was announced, Coke's stock price jumped $5.50, closing at $73.75 a share.

A Coke loyalist and co-founder of Old Coke Drinkers of America, Frank Olson, 41, says: "They took a great American tradition and turned it into just another soda pop." His Seattle group threatened to sue Coca-Cola if it didn't bring old Coke back.

Some consumers are quite capable of a kind of purchasing polygamy: they can be, and often are, faithful to more than one brand at a time. The phenomenon, known as brand-cluster loyalty, has long been common in the soft drink aisle, and Coke in all its multiple guises is in the same brand cluster with Pepsi and all its variations. "In lots of stores, Coke and Pepsi are on special during alternate weeks," says Allen Rosenshine, president of the ad agency BBDO International. "So a lot of people switch back and forth regularly—even though they buy only Coke and Pepsi, and wouldn't buy any other colas." Pepsi executives, who have been crowing over Coke's embarrassment—Pepsi-Cola USA President Roger Enrico calls the new Coke "the Edsel of the 1980s"— might pause to consider that Coca-Cola now has more entries in that cola cluster.

For companies intent on changing a product without stirring up the natives, brand-loyalty pundits offer some advice. First, some products are safer to change than others. Brand loyalties seem to be most intense with products that are ingested or close to the skin; a study by the Ogilvy & Mather ad agency found that men care more about the brand name on their underwear than on their ties. The more closely a brand is bound to a person's image of himself, the more likely he will be to resist any change in it. This might be called the "I use this, this is me" principle, and it applies to things like cigarettes, perfurme, and beer, all personal items that their users associate with particular ideas about status or even personality. It's not for nothing that Marlboro is the U.S. market leader in the high-loyalty cigarette category: the macho image of the Marlboro Man speaks volumes about how certain smokers see themselves.

Another high-loyalty market leader is Budweiser. "Anheuser-Busch would drop dead before they'd put 'new and improved' on that product," says Charlotte Beers, chief executive of the Chicago ad agency Tatham-Laird & Kudner. "Tradi-

tion is a big part of its appeal." Having the biggest market share, as Marlboro and Bud do, is helpful in establishing brand loyalty, simply because many people are most comfortable buying something that a lot of other people buy. But less ubiquitous products still attract ferocious loyalty. Asks Beers, "Can you imagine a new and improved Chanel No. 5?"

In their quest to make sense of the emotional side of brand loyalty, some marketers have devised quasi-scientific systems for measuring it. One of these is a model, in the form of a grid, that Foote Cone & Belding uses to pinpoint how emotionally involved a customer is likely to be with a given purchase. The higher the level of involvement, the stronger the brand loyalty—and the more hazardous it is to trumpet a big change in the product. At one end of the scale are products like hair coloring, where involvement is high partly because of the element of risk: you'd best get it right the first time, or buy lots of hats. According to John O'Toole of Foote Cone & Belding, consumers' loyalty to Clairol, a Foote Cone client, is "amazingly high."

At the other extreme, in this model, are products like cat litter, paper towels, and clothes pins, which are designed to get boring tasks done as inexpensively as possible. With these humdrum products, most consumers switch back and forth between brands with abandon, picking up whatever's on sale—although some will pay for quality when they come across a brand that they believe does the job better than any other. In any research designed to measure loyalty, cautions Morgan Hunter, vice chairman of Marketing Corp. of America, A Westport, Connecticut, marketing firm, it is important not to confuse a stated preference with what consumers actually do when they're in the store. They may not actually buy the brand they say they prefer if it costs too much more.

Marketers agree that food products, especially those that have been around a long time, are

# Who can be loyal to a trash bag?

When generic products were coming on strong a few years ago, J. Walter Thompson, the New York-based ad agency, gauged consumers' loyalty to brands in 80 product categories. It found that the leader in market share was not necessarily the brand-loyalty leader. At that time, Bayer aspirin was the market share leader among headache remedies, but Tylenol had the most loyal following.

Thompson measured the degree of loyalty by asking people whether they'd switch for a 50 percent discount. Cigarette smokers most often said no, making them the most brand-loyal of consumers (see table). Film is the only one of the top five products that the user doesn't put in his mouth—so why such loyalty? According to Edith Gilson, Thompson's senior vice president of research, 35-mm film is used by photography buffs, who are not your average snapshooter: "It's for long-lasting, emotionally valued pictures, taken by someone who has invested a lot of money in his camera." Plenty of shoppers will try a different cola for 50 percent off, and most consumers think one plastic garbage bag or facial tissue is much like another.

| High-loyalty products | Medium-loyalty products | Low-loyalty products |
|---|---|---|
| Cigarettes | Cola drinks | Paper towels |
| Laxatives | Margarine | Crackers |
| Cold remedies | Shampoo | Scouring powder |
| 35-mm film | Hand lotion | Plastic trash bags |
| Toothpaste | Furniture polish | Facial tissues |

*Brand names matter more in some products than in others, researchers find.*

among the riskiest to "improve," as Coca-Cola has discovered the hard way. "You can make small improvements, but watch out," says Charlotte Beers. "Velveeta cheese, for example, has a distinct taste, but more than that, it is a part of childhood for a lot of people—the way it stirs and mixes and melts. It would be very risky to change any of that." If you must alter a product that reminds consumers of their salad days, brand-loyalty experts say, change it without a lot of hoopla.

Whether Coca-Cola could have gotten away with changing quietly is unknown. It might have succeeded had the change been less noticeable, as it was in Canada. Coke there was already sweeter than the U.S. version. When new Coke was introduced in Canada, shipments of concentrate reportedly jumped 42 percent in the first seven weeks over the year-earlier period. A Coke spokesman also notes that Canadians have less emotional attachment to Coke. Much of Coca-Cola's U.S. advertising has been steeped in Americana.

Over the past few years, marketers have worried that generic and other bargain products were making brand loyalty a thing of the past among increasingly savvy and recession-weary consumers. An annual study by the ad agency Needham Harper & Steers asks 4,000 heads of households, half of them men and half women, whether they agree with the statement: "I try to stick to well-known brand names." The percentage who answer "yes" has dropped from 77 percent in 1975 to 61 percent this year. Coke's debacle has shown decisively that, for some products at least, consumers would still rather fight than switch.

□ **19–D**

# Two Cokes really are better than one—for now

*Scott Scredon*

The early returns indicate that the two-Coke strategy is working. During the first two weeks in August, Coca-Cola Co.'s sugared-cola sales—now including new Coke and Coca-Cola Classic—were substantially higher than last year when only one version of the soft drink was available. The decisions that led to having two Cokes on the grocer's shelf "have been clumsily handled, but luckily, I think it's all going to work out," says Ferdinand M. Bellingrath, president of Coke's U.S. independent bottlers' association.

For the two-week period, Coke's sugared-cola sales were up 15 percent, but a small part of that gain must be attributed to the introduction of Cherry Coke. The company, which refused to discuss market share, does not break out its cola sales by product. But extensive interviews with retailers and bottlers indicate that instead of cannibalizing each other's sales, the two plain colas together have gained a bigger audience than they would have had separately.

## 'SENSATIONAL'

Since popular demand persuaded Coca-Cola Co. to bring back old Coke on July 24, sales of Coca-Cola Classic, as expected, have been strongest in Coke's heartland—the South and Southwest. "It's a sensational item," says a spokesman for Randall's Food Markets Inc., a 31-store chain in Houston. The comment echoes the feeling of bottlers and retailers from North Carolina through Texas. That's good news for Coke, since sagging Southern sales were a major reason it resurrected the old formula. Bottlers up North, where Classic is not yet widely available, say new Coke is doing fine.

But despite the initial success of its two-cola strategy, Coke must still solve a host of marketing problems. The company spent four years and millions of dollars testing new Coke and is determined to make the drink its dominant brand. To do so, Coca-Cola is leaning on its bottlers to make new Coke their lead product. But some bottlers are resisting the pressure, arguing that pulling the original formula off the shelves in the first place was a mistake caused by the company's attempt to dictate to customers. "If we try to force one over the other, this will lead to consumer resistance," says bottler Bellingrath.

There are also signs at Coke's Atlanta headquarters that the company isn't quite sure how to market the two colas. Sources say that Coke officials have fought over whether the two soft drinks should be mentioned in the same commercial and whether new Coke should be touted at Coke Classic's expense. This confusion shows Coke still has not put together a strong sales strategy. "There's no question they are all on edge," the source says.

## BIRTHDAY PARTY

Adding to their concern are the fast-food chains, most of which are set up to carry only one sugared cola. Many of them have not decided which Coke to carry. Since fountain sales make up roughly one third of Coke's American sales, the chains must carry new Coke if it is to become the flagship brand. The nation's third-largest chain, Kentucky Fried Chicken, has already defected, saying it will serve Classic in its 1,150 company-owned restaurants. McDonald's Corp., Coke's biggest fountain account, has not yet de-

Source: Reprinted from the September 9, 1985, issue of *Business Week* by special permission, © 1985 by McGraw-Hill, Inc. At the time of writing, Scott Scredon was on the staff of *Business Week*.

cided which brand to carry. A decision to carry Classic would be a devastating blow to the strategy of making new Coke No. 1.

Coke's biggest worry, of course, is that archrival PepsiCo Inc. will, in coming months, persuade both retailers and fast-food chains to carry more Pepsi at the expense of either Coke. Sometime after Labor Day, Pepsi is expected to make an aggressive push. One likely strategy: Pepsi will play up its new position as the No. 1 cola. At the end of last year, Coke's cola had 21.7 percent of the market and Pepsi-Cola had 18.8 percent. Even if the two-Coke strategy increases Coca-

Cola's total market share, both new Coke and Classic individually are expected to own less of the market than Pepsi's single brand.

It will be months before a clear picture of sugared-cola sales emerges. Whether Coke can claim victory should be known by the time the company celebrates its 100th birthday in May. Coke has already reserved thousands of hotel rooms in Atlanta to house guests from around the globe who will atttend the gala event. The question now is whether Coke will have a reason to celebrate.

---

## ☐ 19–E

# Brian Dyson takes the new Coke challenge

## *Scott Scredon*

After training for just three weeks last year, Brian G. Dyson, 50, entered his first triathlon. Dyson, who heads Coca-Cola Co.'s U.S. operations, swam 1 km, ran 10km, and bicycled 30 km in 2 hours and 31 minutes, finishing ahead of many competitors half his age.

Dyson and Coca-Cola didn't fare so well a year ago when they tried to outdistance Pepsi-Cola with a sweeter-formula Coke to appeal to young soda drinkers. Coke managed to avert a total marketing disaster by quickly bringing back its old formula, now called Coca-Cola Classic. But new Coke remains a loser. It holds only about 2.6 percent of soft-drink sales in U.S. food stores—down from a peak of 15.5 percent—and big food chains such as McDonald's Corp. and Kentucky Fried Chicken Corp. recently dumped it in favor of Classic.

A lot of folks in the soft-drink industry say new Coke has no place in the company's winning lineup that includes Classic Coke, Tab, and Sprite. But Dyson isn't giving up.

One reason to forge ahead, certainly, is to restore some of Coca-Cola's lost pride. But Dyson sees business advantages, too. He says new Coke beats Pepsi in blind taste tests. "We are after the switchers, the folks who aren't brand loyal," he says.

### 'OUT-PEPSI PEPSI'

Dyson is talking mostly about consumers age 12 to 24, and he is now attacking that market. Until recently, ads didn't differentiate between new Coke and Classic. Now new Coke has its own campaign built around the theme "Catch the Wave." It is designed to break Pepsi's hold on teenagers, who drink more cola than anybody.

Source: Reprinted from the May 26, 1986, issue of *Business Week* by special permission. © 1986 by McGraw-Hill, Inc. At the time of writing, Scott Scredon was on the staff of *Business Week*.

To win over this image-conscious audience, new Coke's advertising must "make Pepsi passé," says Arnold J. Blum, group creative director at McCann-Erickson Inc., a Coke ad agency. That's no easy task. Pepsi ads currently feature teen idols such as actor Michael J. Fox and special effects—such as a spaceship that beams aboard a Pepsi vending machine—worthy of a Steven Spielberg movie. And Pepsi isn't slowing down. It just spent $10 million to reenlist singer Michael Jackson to do new commercials.

To "out-Pepsi Pepsi," as Coke officials describe their new strategy, the company has turned to a hot British star called Max Headroom. Max is an actor who, thanks to a four-hour makeup job, appears to have a face made out of plastic. After his act is recorded on videotape, the tape is run through a computer, giving him a synthesized voice that sometimes stutters and is often out of sync with his lips.

A cult figure in Britain who is starting to catch the attention of U.S. youth, Headroom symbolizes the "daring" image Dyson wants for new Coke. He is convinced that the new ads—which also feature rock star Whitney Houston and such special effects as pouring a soda horizontally—will help new Coke become yet another successful product. Already, Dyson has made winners out of cherry Coke and diet Coke. These new brands helped the company capture an additional 2 percent of the $25 billion U.S. soft-drink market last year, despite new Coke's problems.

It's too early to tell if the ads, introduced in February, are boosting sales. Industry sources say Dyson may have to use other tactics such as discounting to turn around new Coke. And time is short. "If the brand keeps sliding, its loser image could affect the other Coca-Cola brands," says Martin Romm, a vice-president at First Boston Corp.

Dyson was instrumental in new Coke's introduction, and he seems determined to remove the blemish from an otherwise spotless record. Born to wealthy Argentinian cattle-ranchers, he joined Coke in 1959 as a plant manager in Venezuela and quickly moved up the ranks in several South American posts. Since he became president of U.S. operations in 1979, total sales have climbed 50 percent, to $2.1 billion. Market share has in-creased from 35.7 percent to 38.6 percent. Pepsi's market share during that time has gone from 25.4 percent. to 27.4 percent. "Dyson's given Pepsi a hard time. He's done a good job," says Sam Ayoub, who retired as Coke's chief financial officer at the end of 1984.

## COKE IS IT

Indeed, Dyson may have done his job too well. Because Classic, cherry, and diet Coke sell so well, bottlers may see little reason to divert their resources to save new Coke. The pressures will be even greater as they try to integrate Dr Pepper, which Coke plans to buy for $470 million. The deal is awaiting approval by the Federal Trade Commission.

In successfully building up Coke's U.S. operations, Dyson has earned a reputation for being strictly business. Associates say he is uncomfortable making small talk, and his devotion to the company is legendary. He refuses to eat in any restaurant or stay in a hotel that doesn't sell Coke products, says his friend Michael J. Kami, who runs a small consulting firm.

Dyson's turnaround plan for new Coke carries big risks. Not only will the company spend tens of millions on promotion, it may also confuse consumers and anger bottlers. But Dyson seeks out opportunities to show his mettle. After completing his first competition, he wrote in *Triathlon Magazine*: "The supreme challenge is to surpass your own expectations." Trying to save new Coke is just the kind of challenge Dyson seems to thrive on.

## QUESTIONS

1. *What do you think? Did Coke plan and implement a brilliant marketing strategy—or did it commit a spectacular marketing blunder? Explain.*

2. *What do you think caused the negative consumer reaction to the reformulation of Coke? Why didn't Coke's market research predict this?*

3. Some people believe that brand loyalty is declining in the United States. Does the new
Coke example support or conflict with this
viewpoint? Explain.

4. Does having two Cokes—new and Classic—
provide the Coca-Cola company with a competitive advantage or a competitive disadvantage? Why? What would you do if you were
Brian Dyson?

*5. After decades of marketing essentially one
product—Coca-Cola—the company now has
numerous products under the "Coke"
brand—including diet and regular, caffeine-
free diet and regular, Coca-Cola Classic, and

Cherry Coke. Is this a successful example of
brand franchise extension (Reading 18)? Is
Coke still an individual brand name, or has it
become a family brand? What is the difference? Strategically, does it make any difference whether Coke is an individual or a
family brand? Why or why not?

*6. Looking at the recent history of the Coca-
Cola Company, do you think that Coke's
management has been guilty of "marketing
myopia" (Reading 5)? If so, how?

---

*Question relates concepts in this and other readings.

---

☐ **20**

# Ten distribution myths

## Michael M. Pearson

---

*Channels of distribution may be the least understood—and most ignored—element of a
firm's marketing mix. Many people have strong misconceptions about distribution channels—particularly the common belief that costs and prices could be reduced greatly by simply "eliminating the middleman." This article explores the "conventional wisdom" about
distribution channels and suggests that it is a collection of myths rather than facts.*

---

Decisions about distribution often rely on a set
of assumptions which can perhaps best be described in terms of Galbraith's concept of "conventional wisdom."[1] The determining criterion for
such "wisdom" is not its quantifiable validity but
rather the degree of its acceptability within a community. Reavis Cox and Thomas Schutte implicitly
recognize this as a characteristic common among
managers with regard to distribution; managers
often operate according to a set of assumptions
about a distribution system without ever question-

ing the validity of those assumptions.[2] Such assumptions or myths abound in the "conventional
wisdom" of distribution management, and while
the 10 myths discussed in this paper are neither
exhaustive nor exclusive, they do seem to be
among the most commonly held.

Source: Reprinted from *Business Horizons.* May-June 1981,
pp. 17–23. Copyright © 1981 by the Foundation for the School of
Business at Indiana University. Reprinted by permission. At the
time of writing, Michael M. Pearson was assistant professor of
marketing at Bowling Green State University.

[2]Reavis Cox and Thomas F. Schutte, "A Look at Channel
Management," in *Marketing Involvement in Society and the
Economy,* ed. Phillip R. McDonald (Chicago: American Marketing
Association, 1969), pp. 99–105.

[1]John Kenneth Galbraith, *The Affluent Society* (Boston:
Houghton Mifflin, 1958), p. 646.

1. A channel of distribution is the movement of a product from the manufacturer to the ultimate consumer.

The first assumption to be considered is that distribution deals only with the movement of a physical product. Distribution, however, also poses problems of utility. No product is ever purchased solely as a physical entity; rather, it is always sold with some service or "value added"[3] attached. Even the shady-looking character who stops you at a street corner and pulls up his sleeve to offer you a dozen wristwatches, gives you some service along with the watch—immediate delivery and a limited selection at a super price. (Admittedly the return privilege is questionable.) More common value-added characteristics include refunds for product failure, transportation of goods, postpurchase servicing, availability of volume discounts, range of product line, and so on. Therefore, given the inevitability of value-added characteristics, a distribution system must be set up to handle not only the product per se but also all the service and utility which attaches to that product.

There has been considerable refinement of the concept of distribution. Originally the concept was formulated in terms of the product moving through a channel, much as water runs through a canal (Level I). The recognition that title to the product also moves through a channel was an intermediate stage (Level II) in the concept, which by now has evolved to a more complex formulation of a series of related transferences through different institutions involving not only the physical possession of the product but also ordering, ownership, financing, risking, promotion, and payment (Level III).[4]

Unfortunately, it is nonetheless still all too common for managers to visualize distribution in terms of the simple canal analogy. Distribution is often diagramed as shown in Exhibit 1. Such representations do not take into account many important dimensions of distribution, including, for example, advertising and financing. Is there an advertising agency participating in a promotional effort, or is a

**Exhibit 1 □**

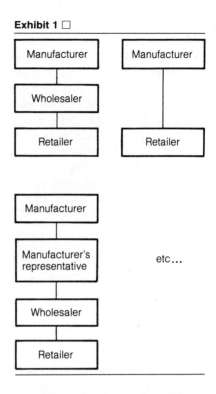

bank, through the use of a bank credit card, a component of the financial transaction?

Consider the prescription drug industry. Drug firms sell the drugs either to wholesalers or directly to the pharmacists. For the sake of simplicity, eliminate the wholesaler and assume a direct manufacturer-to-retailer channel. The retailer fills prescriptions and delivers the goods to the consumer. We therefore have an overgeneralized channel that looks like this:

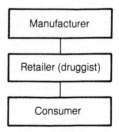

But this simplified graphic does not address the important question of who determines what is sold. The answer does not lie with the manufacturer, the retailer, or the consumer, but with the physician, who prescribes the drug for the consumer. The pharmacist has no choice about what goes into the prescription. In most states, the

[3]Theodore N. Beckman, "The Value Added Concept as Applied to Marketing and Its Implications," in *Frontiers in Marketing Thought,* ed. Stewart H. Rewold (Bloomington: Indiana University, Bureau of Business Research, 1955).

[4]R. S. Vaile, E. T. Grether, and R. Cox, *Marketing in the American Economy* (New York: Ronald Press, 1952), p. 113

pharmacist must supply a brand-name drug if that is what the physician specifies.

Therefore, if the manufacturer is marketing a new drug, the key to success is the physician's acceptance. Promotion is aimed at the physician, who is a major factor in deciding what moves through the channel, even though the doctor neither physically handles the good nor is involved in actually transferring title. The traditional line and box chart in the previous figure is an example of Level I thinking which does not adequately represent the complex workings of this distribution system.

2. A channel's structure is determined by the characteristics of its products.

Large, bulky items or those of high unit value tend to have short channels with few middlemen. Small items and those of low per unit price tend to have long distribution channels with many middlemen. Ideas such as these can be found in most standard marketing textbooks, and while as rules of thumb they might be useful, their implications need to be challenged. Instead of the implied cause-effect relationship, there is instead a correlation effect.

You have undoubtedly been exposed at one time or another to the classification of consumer goods into shopping, convenience, and specialty categories.[5] One can describe the characteristics of each of these product classifications, but the key difference lies not in the goods themselves but in the time and effort put forth into the shopping task *by the consumer*. A shopper is willing to put very little time and effort into the purchase of a convenience product but much time and effort into buying a shopping good. Consumers will go out of their way to purchase specialty goods. The primacy of the consumer in these distinctions can be demonstrated in considering the purchase of an automobile. While one person might consider the car a shopping good, another may think of it as a convenience good, while still another may consider it a specialty good.

There is probably no greater hindrance to efficient decision making in distribution than focusing exclusively on the product. The truly important questions revolve around the consumer:

[5]Melvin T. Copeland, *Principles of Merchandising* (Chicago: A. W. Shaw, 1924).

Who is buying the product?
What is it that the customer is actually buying?
Where does the customer wish to buy?
When is the buying decision made?
How is the buying decision made?
Why does the customer buy?

Once the behavior of the consumer is understood, the retailer's behavior is analyzed using the same questions, and the process leads to an understanding of the entire distribution process. In short, distribution management starts with the consumer and works its way to the manufacturer. In fact, the frequently suggested (but seldom implemented) idea of placing the consumer at the top, rather than at the bottom, of the traditional distribution channel may be the best general guide to distribution management (see Exhibit 2).

3. A distribution channel is managed by the manufacturer.

If this statement is true, someone had better tell Sears, K mart, and J. C. Penney, as well as a great many other retail and wholesale institutions. They too are managing the channel, making such crucial decisions as what to buy, whether or not to manufacture their own products, which institutions to employ, and so on.

Manufacturers are no different, however, in their assumption of control. Certainly they are the ones who plan and manage distribution. Should exclusive, selective, or intensive distribution be used? Should we distribute through our own salespeople or reps? Should we own our own warehouses? Should we own our own retailers?

**Exhibit 2** ☐

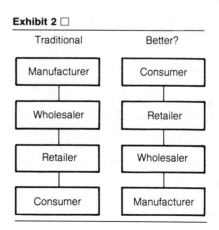

| Traditional | Better? |
|---|---|
| Manufacturer | Consumer |
| Wholesaler | Retailer |
| Retailer | Wholesaler |
| Consumer | Manufacturer |

The institution which runs the distribution channel is often referred to as the channel captain (sometimes the channel commander). Choices which the channel captain must make depend upon environmental conditions, such as competitors' actions, governmental and legal regulations, and the state of the economy. The channel captain's job is further complicated insofar as the retailer is also "managing" the channel. Thus it cannot be simply assumed that the manufacturer manages the channel. While this may certainly be the case in some channels, in other channels the retailer or another institution may manage the channel. Much of the present consumer activism can be viewed as the consumer "institution" trying to manage the channel. In addition, distribution channels sometimes become "managed" by trade associations, by regulatory agencies, or by governmental pressures. No one institution manages the channel by itself.

4.  A firm should strive to maximize cooperation within its distribution channel.

There is much to be said for the advice to manufacturers to "work with your customers" and the advice to retailers to "work with your suppliers." The problem is that this advice is all too often taken to extremes. The ideal is to *promote,* not to *maximize,* cooperation. For example, a salesman for a manufacturer might work long and hard gaining complete satisfaction from a key account. If, however, the demands of the customer become excessive, they could greatly damage the distribution system's overall efficiency.

Cooperation is only one aspect of the distribution process. Conflict is also necessary to make a system more efficient and cost effective. Competition to provide distributive services can lead to reduced costs. As Bruce Mallen explains, "All members have a common interest in selling the product; only in the division of total channel profits are they in conflict."[6] Both conflict and cooperation are necessary and beneficial. The process is not as simple as just maximizing cooperation.

5.  The primary function of a warehouse is storage.

The primary function of a warehouse is movement! Movement satisfies the fundamentally different objectives of manufacturers and consumers. Manufacturers want efficient, continuous production ("I'll give them any color they want as long as it's black"). Consumers, however, have an insatiable appetite for variety. Each would like a special color, design, or package.

Because the objectives of these two groups are at odds, a distribution center develops to satisfy the needs of both the manufacturer and the consumer. Trucks carrying the manufacturers' straight production runs pull into one side of the warehouse to unload. The warehouse has maximized its efficiency if the bulk is broken and directly loaded on trucks going to the retailer.

In a utopia, the warehouser would use his computer to match incoming orders with the varied needs of retailers. The goods would never stop but would be moved by conveyor from one truck to another. Actually such practice is becoming more the accepted operating procedure than the exception.

6.  A firm sells to or buys from another firm.

Does a manufacturer simply sell its product to a merchant middleman, deliver it, and then say, "Thank god, that's a load off my back; now I can relax"? No, his job has just begun. The manufacturer wants to do everything possible for the wholesaler so the inventory will turn over and the product will be reordered. The distribution burden of the manufacturer may extend to the retailer (in the form of cooperative advertising, point-of-purchase displays, demonstrations, or calls by missionary salespeople) and to consumers (in the form of product warranties, instructions, information, "cents-off" coupons, and national advertising). The manufacturer does not sell *to* a wholesaler but *through* a wholesaler.

Armstrong Cork Company markets all their floor products through independent distributors. The job of Armstrong's sales representatives is not just to sell the product to the distributor but to work with the distributor to market the products to retailers and consumers. The Armstrong sales reps work to gain business from key account retailers, set up displays, work up distributor and retail promotions, and use any other means to market through the distributor.

[6]Bruce Mallen, "Conflict and Cooperation in Marketing Channels," in *Reflections on Progress in Marketing,* ed. L. George Smith (Chicago: American Marketing Association, 1964), p. 79.

The perspective is the same for retailers. The retail buyer has a loyalty, not to the source he or she buys from, but rather to the consumer who is being served. If, for example, buyers find an outlet which sells brand-name jeans at a reduced price, they will quickly switch retailers. The goal of the retail buyer is to purchase the best possible merchandise for the consumer *through* (not from) a particular firm or institution.

7. Eliminating the middlemen will reduce distribution costs.

This is probably the most commonly held distribution myth. Take the time to read the letters to the editor in your newspaper, listen to radio talk shows, or read the unsolicited comments on consumer surveys. Naive as it may seem to some, it is a widely held belief that costs could be reduced by eliminating the middlemen in a distribution system.

Middlemen will be around as long as they perform certain functions better than anyone else. If a large grocery chain could gain by owning its own farms, growing its own lettuce, storing, shipping, and warehousing through its own resources, the chain would certainly take advantage of the opportunity. BankAmericard and Master Charge made great inroads into the field of retail credit because they performed this distribution function bettter than could a great many retailers.

The assumption that reducing the number of middlemen will decrease costs is widespread. In reality, it is possible that increasing middlemen might reduce costs even more. The important thing to remember is that distribution functions are being performed by someone. Even in a manufacturer-to-consumer channel, one party or the other is taking care of physically distributing, transferring title, ordering, risk, and so on. The real question is how well these functions are being performed.

8. Administered channels are more efficient than nonadministered channels.

There is a certain amount of debate as to what exactly constitutes an administered channel. While there may be many ways to define it, here it is referred to as a distribution system controlled and directed by one member institution, whether

through ownership, contract (for example, franchising), or force.

It is not possible to assert yet that administered channels are more efficient; opinions are mixed. Until a verdict is in, the question can be addressed in a general fashion simply by understanding the distribution process. Think again in terms of functions. An institution can administer a distribution system to act in the way the "commander" desires. There are many ways of doing this, such as rationing supply or withholding service. Whatever the strategy pursued, it must answer two questions: (1) Is it efficient, and (2) does it benefit one institution or the whole distribution system? Naturally, if the manufacturer forces a product that the consumer does not want through a distribution system and forces commitment by all institutions to inventory, promotion, and planning, the result might well be that the consumer does not buy the product and the whole channel suffers. If the product and strategy are good, the whole channel might benefit. Other decisons could similarly lead to a suboptimization for the entire channel. The manufacturer may force a retailer to carry excessive inventory stocks to prevent stockout. Such a strategy might be beneficial to the manufacturer but might be so inefficient for the retailer that the total cost of the system would increase. Again, it is how well the function is performed that determines efficiency.

It is this shifting of functions that is one of the truly dynamic aspects of distribution—the strategies of large versus small, small versus large, or large versus large. How does an institution gain control? How is control resisted? Such decisions make up the backbone of practical distribution systems. While the problems of categorizing such strategies are clouded by legalities and ethics, the practical worth of such categorizations is considerable.

It is not the intention here to settle the question of whether administered channels are more or less efficient. The purpose is to point out that it is the conventional wisdom that administered channels are more efficient. While this *may* be true, it cannot just be assumed.

9. A profitable channel is an efficient channel.

Does the fact that a firm or distribution system makes a large profit make it an efficient firm or system? Not necessarily—a firm's profitability and distribution efficiency cannot be directly related. A firm may be amazingly efficient from a distribution standpoint but might not be profitable due to its competitive environment. Profit can be obtained as a result of an innovation or risk. It cannot simply be assumed that the profit is a result of the efficiency of distribution.

The task of measuring distribution efficiency is immense. One method of measuring efficiency is to compare the firm's actual efficiency against a standard or potential; the problem is to determine what that standard or potential might be. One could also measure efficiency by comparing one firm or channel with competing firms or channels. The problem here is that products differ, assortments differ, and the amount of service given at one store is more than at another.

Although measuring efficiency is always difficult, there are three key decisions which can help the process. First, decide on the target market and measure efficiency based upon how well that target market is being served. Not only will this help to better pinpoint the direction of the channel; it will allow measurement of a tangible number of end users rather than a vague and undefined target group.

Second, set service-level objectives and measure efficiency within these objectives. What service level the distribution system is to deliver is a major policy decision. Therefore, these service-level objectives should have some stability. They should determine distribution strategy rather than distribution strategy determining objectives. If a retailer cuts expenses in an attempt to increase profits, has he changed the service level of his store? If a manufacturer offers a product with delivery in the first year and without delivery in the second year, has he operated under the same service level? These firms have allowed their service-level objectives to change in response to strategy. The question should be asked: "What strategy can we use to distribute our product, given our service-level objectives?" Now efficiency comparisons can be made.

Third, make those comparisons with a standard of efficiency which you set rather than using an industry average or the standard of a competitor. Each firm offers different service levels and aims

at different target markets. Therefore, an efficiency standard (however it is determined) which is derived individually is more likely to be appropriate than an industry one which may not even be applicable in any particular case.

10. Planning distribution strategy is the responsibility of the distribution manager.

All too often, marketing decisions have to be fitted into an existing structure created by the distribution channel. Some distribution channels often have incorporated within them a heavy fixed cost which makes them extremely difficult to change. The automobile industry is a prime example, with its fixed system of suppliers, manufacturers, distributors, and transportation institutions all geared for one method of distribution. It would be extremely difficult for a new distribution channel, competing on a full-cost basis, to dislodge the existing channel competing on a marginal cost basis. Many other firms distribute their products through a system within which many of the decisions have, for all practical purposes, already been made because of long-established business mores. It may, for example, be impossible for a firm to get a better cash or quantity discount from a supplier because one such discount might create havoc with the long-established distribution practices of the entire system.

In addition, the extreme interrelationships existing within distribution systems make it necessary to make decisions not just for your firm but, in effect, for other firms as well. If your firm commits itself to producing and selling a large quantity of product to a consumer, you are committing your supplier as well. It may be necessary to assist this supplier financially to assure continuing supply.

In spite of, or because of, the importance of distribution, I have never seen a "channel manager" and have very seldom seen a "distribution manager" (in anything outside a purely physical distribution sense). Distribution decisions are so major and so all-encompassing that they have profound affects on all other areas within the firm—personnel, finance, production, promotion, and so on. The decison, say, for a manufacturer to open his own retail outlets has so many implications that it can only be decided at the highest decision-making levels of the firm. The distribution manager is therefore relegated to the level of tactician.

## AND THE MORAL?

The recognition that these myths do exist is in itself an accomplishment because recognizing their existence can help us to better share distribution knowledge and communicate our distribution policies to those guided by the "conventional wisdom" of distribution. The following rules should provide some direction for better communication of distribution knowledge and better management of distribution systems.

**Forget about "channels."** Don't forget the concept of a channel, but stop using the term. Describing a distribution system as a channel—a canal through which water flows—is just too simplistic for what it represents. "Channel" connotes movement of a physical product, a homogeneous product, a single flow and direction, and a prescribed, nonvarying path.

Instead, start referring to your "distribution system." Distribution is a system. Distribution interacts internally not just with the marketing functions but with all the management functions as well. Externally, distribution interacts, reacts, adapts, and innovates within a system of changing consumer trends, competiton, regulation, and economic conditions.

**Include the consumer in your distribution system.** The consumer is the most important institution in your distribution system. Not only does the consumer through his or her wants and needs determine the structure and character of your distribution system, but this consumer can perform any and all of the distribution functions—physical distribution, financing, ordering and payment, risk bearing, and so on. The consumer must be considered in planning distribution, in the distribution itself, and in evaluating the distribution. Not doing so reinforces the incorrect assumption that the consumer has a passive role.

**Do not think of distribution management in the same way as you think of functional management in other business areas.** You can't hire a young college graduate to manage your distribution unless you want to start him or her out as a vice president. You can't put one of your employees in charge of your whole distribution system unless you want to put him or her on your board. Distribution decisions are not just marketing decisions; they require an expertise in production, finance, personnel, control, and every other functional area of the firm. Distribution is certainly managed, but it is managed strategically from the highest managerial levels. To treat it as requiring tactical decisions only reduces it to simple physical distribution.

**Don't ignore the illegal and unethical.** A distribution system is not like a model of pure competition. It does not exist sheltered from reality by assumptions. Pressures of size, shortages, time, opportunities, greed, and power do exist. It would be unrealistic to ignore that some people or firms bend to these pressures with illegal and unethical responses. The study of distribution is a study of institutions and interactions. With the vast number of institutions and interactions that occur in all distribution systems, some will be questionable. I am not advocating illegal and unethical practices. I am simply saying that they are part of distribution's environment and must be recognized.

**Understanding distribution requires a macro rather than a micro perspective.** After all, who is in a position to oversee all of the flows in a distribution system? Even if one person does handle all these decision areas, is he or she in a position to comprehend the same decision-making inputs of other institutions within the same distribution system?

To understand distribution, one must take a step back and observe all the interrelated institutions. Such a recommendation may be counter to the trends prevalent in all areas of business education today, but I don't think it should be. A person must understand macro distribution and distribution myths *before* a micro perspective can be achieved.

## QUESTIONS

1. *Using your own words, explain why each of the "10 distribution myths" is a myth.*

2. *Give three examples of channels with observable conflicts—as well as cooperation—among the channel members. Explain the na-*

ture of the conflicts. Indicate whether these conflicts are necessary and desirable—or counterproductive.

3. Choose a product that is typically distributed through middlemen and explain why "eliminating the middlemen" would not necessarily lower distribution costs and prices.

4. Should marketing students consider becoming "distribution managers" after graduation? Why or why not?

*5. Does "benefit segmentation" (Reading 11) have any relevance for planning distribution strategies? Explain your answer.

---

*Question relates concepts in this and other readings.

# ☐ 21

# GE posts a sentry to give customers better service

*Thayer C. Taylor*

---

*A high-quality product offered at a fair price still might not sell if potential customers cannot be sure they will receive the product when and where they need it. For some customers—especially industrial buyers—accurate, on-time delivery is often more important than price. The following article about the General Electric Supply Company illustrates how some companies are using computers and automated ordering systems to help improve customer service, reduce both selling and buying costs, and increase sales.*

---

Automatic placement of orders, with customer terminals talking to its own computer, helps General Electric Supply Co. (GESCO) boost the productivity both of its salespeople and the purchasing managers they call on. As a result, GESCO's salespeople spend less time writing up orders and more tackling critical customer problems. Buyers save on ordering and inventory costs, and GESCO profits from sharper insights into customer buying patterns.

A wholly-owned General Electric subsidiary, the Bridgeport, CT-based company sells electrical supplies and equipment to a customer base of 50,000 industrial contractors, utilities, and commercial organizations. Economic Information Systems, New York City, a data-base company that tracks industrial firms, puts GESCO's sales at $876 million. The latest count by *Electrical Whole-*

*saling* magazine ranks GESCO third in the industry, with 2,709 employees, behind front-runner Graybar Electric and second-place Westinghouse Electric Supply Co.

GESCO is first in the industry, however, in positioning itself at the leading edge of the computer age that is transforming relationships between distributors and their customers. At the heart of GESCO's thrust is the computer-based Sentry contracting program that embraces four basic elements:

• A catalogue of all items the company stocks for customers at prenegotiated prices;

---

Source: *Sales & Marketing Management* magazine, December 6, 1982, pp. 46–50. Reproduced by permission. At the time of writing, Thayer C. Taylor was senior editor/management sciences for *Sales & Marketing Management*.

- Access devices the buyer uses to get orders into GESCO's computer;
- Order processing at GESCO's 160 local warehouses;
- Reporting and invoicing procedures.

In brief, Sentry chops down the paper work of placing orders, guarantees the customer that the items he uses repetitively will be in stock and delivered to him on time, and gives both GESCO and the customer analytical reports on all transactions.

Customers point to a variety of Sentry-produced savings. Harold Emerling, manager of electrical equipment and mill supply purchases at Allegheny Ludlum Steel, Pittsburgh, estimates he has "saved about 25 percent in inventory costs by having GE carry the stocks." At Signode Corp., Chicago, John Curtis, buyer of stocking equipment and strapping, figures that, by placing an order via CRT (cathode ray tube) terminal instead of writing it up, a transaction "that used to cost around $50 now costs less than $10." Distributor Elmer Stump, president of his own Baltimore firm, says his "buyers spend less than half the time they do when ordering merchandise from other sources because, with Sentry, they avoid the hassle of calling around to find out who has what they need, how much it will cost, and how long it will take to get it."

Elimination of back orders has produced a significant savings for Avco Corp.'s Avco Lycoming Div., Stratford, Connecticut, reports Henry McKinney, a facilities operation buyer. "Sentry is very cost-effective for us," he says, "because the knowledge that specified quantities of your needs will be held by GESCO cuts down on the need to back-order and shifts the inventory-carrying burden from us to them. Also, reducing back orders means savings in the elimination of double transactions, double receiving, and double billing."

What makes Sentry special, says Andrew J. Walsh, general manager of GESCO's marketing programs department, "is that it focuses on boosting productivity at both the selling and buying levels. For every salesperson in there pitching, there's a buyer who is listening. You hear a lot about the high cost of selling but nothing about the high cost of listening. We're tackling the twin problems of high-cost selling and high-cost buy-

ing. Just as we want our salespeople to be more productive, so do our customers want their purchasing people to be more productive. One way to accomplish both goals is to let the computer handle the loads of paper work that go into the taking and placing of orders."

Adds Jack C. Chapman, manager of systems contracting with national responsibility for the Sentry program: "Freed of the routine of writing up orders, buyers can devote more time to important things such as large capital expenditures or major contracts."

The foundation of the Sentry program is a systems contract whereby GESCO is committed to stock, for a specified time, agreed-upon quantities of repetitively purchased items—mostly MRO (material replenishment orders) and OEM (original equipment manufacturer) products—at prenegotiated prices. Although it might seem that such a guarantee would increase his own warehouse costs, Walsh points out that "in today's environment, buyers will do business with the company that has what they want when they need it, especially in industrial marketing where their responsibility involves keeping a factory running. Also, because we have a much bigger user base for these products than any customer does, we can spread the costs more efficiently. Finally, because we now have a better feel of what customers will need, we do a better planning job and cut back on those items where there is little demand."

Sentry's working document is the catalogue, which lists all items, normal order quantity, prenegotiated price, and a variety of computer codes, including that of the National Association of Electrical Distributors, which is used by manufacturers and distributors in the electrical wholesaling industry.

When the buyer is ready to order, he can use any of a variety of computer-access devices, ranging from a simple transaction telephone to a CRT terminal with attached printer. After the buyer identifies himself, the computer asks a series of questions, such as bill-to and ship-to addresses, customer and order reference, desired shipping mode, and date. The buyer then itemizes his order, after which, if he has a video screen or printer, the computer flashes the order's total value. The buyer can also use Sentry to order noncatalogue items, but he won't receive immediate notification of availability.

When GESCO receives the order, its computer automatically generates a purchase order, order acknowledgment, and shipping ticket. The ordered materials are picked from stock and loaded for same- or next-day delivery.

If the ordered quantity is not available from the local warehouse (because the buyer has over-ordered in the past or for other reasons), a second computer system, XPD (Expedite), enters the picture. XPD is an in-house inventory control system, linking all GESCO warehouses in an on-line network. To complete the order, XPD speedily scans all GESCO sites to locate the missing quantity, picks the warehouse nearest the customer, and sets in motion procedures that will get the items to the customer.

## SOME PAPER IS LOVED

Together, Sentry and XPD have led to dramatic service improvements. Walsh claims his order fill rate has climbed from 80 percent in pre-Sentry days to 95 percent today. The rise has been even more striking at Raymark Formed Products Co., Milford, Connecticut, where purchasing manager George Avery says "on-time deliveries have gone from around 50 percent to 95 percent. Before they had Sentry, GESCO was one of our worst suppliers. In fact, we used to flip a coin as to who would have to call them when we had a problem. Since they've gone on Sentry, we've had no problems, and now they're one of our best suppliers."

Ironically, while Walsh and Chapman enthuse over Sentry's elimination of paper work they extol the four monthly reports the system produces for customers at no charge. Two, in particular, are cited by Chapman for the insights they reveal on customer buying patterns.

The first report details what was ordered by individual customer location, such as warehouse or plant department, and includes items, quantities, prices, and number of times orders were placed. "This report," Chapman avers, "is very helpful to a contractor who has several projects going on at the same time. When a project at a particular job site is completed, he can compare the actual usage of materials with what he wanted us to hold in stock, thus getting an idea of how good his estimating procedures are."

The second report summarizes all orders for the year-to-date period and compares them with the year-ago period. Raymark's George Avery thinks this report, with its monthly breakdown, "will enable us to do a better forecasting job next year as to what and how much we'll need at a particular time."

## SALESPEOPLE READ THEM

GESCO's 206 outside salespeople also study the reports keenly, looking for pointers on how they can enhance their customer service. Noncatalogue items ordered on the Sentry system, marked by asterisks in the reports, are followed up with suggestions that they be added to the catalogue. If the customer's order pattern deviates markedly from the estimated usage pattern, the salesperson tries to find out the reasons for it.

Customers, too, get helpful assists from the reports on how to improve their purchasing effectiveness, Walsh claims. "If the buyer sees he has two or three people in different locations ordering the same item," the general manager says, "he can consolidate them to qualify for higher price breaks."

Avco Lycoming's McKinney notes that "we've been able to improve our own inventory control system and management of storage areas because of the information produced by the reports. The data on individual commodities, which are a horrendous task if you try to assemble them manually, are especially valuable because of the insights we gain as to what our high- and low-usage items are."

## CONTROLLING INVENTORY

The reports also sharpen GESCO's inventory planning. "We used to have general reports on customer usage," Chapman observes, "but nothing as detailed as what we get now. Because we have a clearer picture of monthly usage patterns, we're in a better position to have the right items and quantities in stock at the right time."

Just over 200 customers are on the Sentry system. "Not everyone is a prospect," Walsh concedes. "We're still in the learning period as far as

```
ESCO REPORT NO 10SC35-1          SYSTEMS CONTRACTING - DETAIL COST CENTER LISTING 04/01/82                    PAGE
DD CE RGN 70 HSE 275
                                              THE MORELAND CO.
                                           PERIOD ENDING 03/31/82
 E MORELAND CO. - PLANT 1

   COST                                         NAED      COMMODITY              AVERAGE        STND    EXTENDED   NO TIMES
  CENTER     PART NUMBER / DESCRIPTION         NUMBER       CODE    QUANTITY    UNIT PRICE  U/M  PKGE      PRICE   PURCHASE
  ******     *************************         ******    *********  ********    **********  ***  ****    ********  ********
   4075      040X300        MAGNET WIRE      0074-00156    2010        86         188.54     C            162.14      1
   4075      065X340        MAGNET WIRE      0074-00172    4102       170         178.97     C            304.25      1
   4075      102 DC         MAGNET WIRE      0074-00315    4102       138         201.19     C            277.64      1
   4075      138A1091 P1    BELL             0030-00252    2010         2          20.19     E             41.58      2
   4075      138A1091 P5    BELL             0030-00257    2030         1          20.90     E             20.90      1
   4075      14404318 P24   LAMP             3168-27004    2035        48          55.77     C             27.33      1
```

Reports on orders by buyer site help GESCO customers coordinate orders more efficiently.

who are the likeliest candidates. Certainly, the fellow who buys only $5,000 a year is not a prospect, but the fellow who buys $100,000 should be on the system. Probably the average prospect is someone who buys around $4,000 to $5,000 a month."

"The trick," the general manager continues, "is to get a good fix on the prospect's long-term potential. He might do a minimal amount of business the first year or two he is on the system, but may have a potential for a substantial amount further down the road."

For systems-contracting manager Chapman, two attractive candidates are national accounts with several locations and the large single location. One type of prospect he's eyeing is the industrial plant with a sizable stock room for electrical supplies. "With our commitment to stock what the customer needs at a preset price," he says, "Sentry can ideally serve as the plant's stockroom."

Winning customers over to Sentry follows a well-defined sales plan. Once a sales rep and his manager decide on a likely candidate, they send a profile of the prospect to Chapman. Included is information on the customer type, what he buys, estimate of purchases of repetitive items, purchasing methods, and kinds of access devices (if any) he has. Chapman, for his part, weighs the program modifications that must be made to accommodate the prospects and the incremental business Sentry will generate.

## NO MORE SAMPLE CASE

Where Sentry is in place, the salesperson's time is used much differently. "Instead of lugging

a sample case around and spending time writing up orders," Walsh says, "the field sales rep can give a lot more attention to the new products buyers always want to hear about. Also, he is doing much more problem-solving for customers, such as demonstrating how our new energy-saving motors can save them money."

While the sales force talks up Sentry, Walsh looks forward to the system's next milestone: computer-to-computer communications. He has experiments going on with four customers whereby their computers send orders directly into his computer, thus reducing even further the time their buyers must spend placing orders. In these trials, the customer's computer is programmed with maximum and minimum inventory levels for each item. Once a minimum inventory level is reached, the customer's computer automatically transmits a replenishment order to GESCO's machine.

"The nice part about this is that many customers already have this information programmed in their computers as guidance for their purchasing people," Walsh notes. "The tricky part is building a link between their software and ours." He feels the next three to five years will see rapid development in this area.

The pace may be faster than Walsh suspects, based on the successful test the grocery industry staged earlier this year when six manufacturers, five distributors, and two brokers had their computers pass requisition orders among one another. Dr. Richard C. Norris, senior consultant in operations research at Arthur D. Little, Cambridge, Massachusetts, who designed the electronic data interchange (EDI) standards used in the test, says the results were promising enough to suggest that "once appropriate standards are developed, the same structure can be used for such consumer products as health and beauty aids, hardware, or general merchandise, and for such industrial products as chemicals and steel."

He also sees an even broader computerized network emerging, one that links vendor, distributor, and transportation carrier. He says that recent communications and message standards developed by the industry's Transportation Data Coordinating Committee point to the possibility of uniformly formatted orders, invoices, and bills of lading moving freely through networks that link the three types of firms.

Thus automated, electronic shuffling is replacing paper shuffling, giving the field salesperson more time for what he does best: creative selling.

## QUESTIONS

1. *What exactly is Sentry? What does it deal with—inventories, shipments of products, or what? How does it work?*

2. *What are some of the major benefits that have resulted from the Sentry system—both for GESCO and for its customers? Why are these important benefits?*

3. *Why would a company like GE spend a great deal of money to help their customers save money?*

*4. *Does Sentry provide GESCO with a sustainable competitive advantage (Reading 7)? Why or why not?*

---
*Question relates concepts in this and other readings.

---

## ☐ 22

# At-home shopping: Will consumers let their computers do the walking?

*George P. Moschis*

*Jac L. Goldstucker*

*Thomas J. Stanley*

---

*Some observers have hailed at-home or electronic shopping as a major breakthrough in distribution and forecast its rapid growth in the United States. However, while some tests of electronic shopping have met with some success, overall consumer acceptance of the idea to date has been far less than overwhelming. The following article explains the characteristics of at-home shopping, analyzes the results of research completed to date, and discusses the future of this innovative distribution approach.*

---

Recent technological developments in information-related industries are affecting consumer habits and needs and the demand for products and services purchased at home. Consumers are responding favorably to such technological innovations as personal computers that are likely to affect consumer acceptance of at-home shopping.

An estimated 100 projects, many of which include at-home shopping, are being planned, im-

Source: Reprinted from *Business Horizons*, March-April 1985, pp. 22–29. Copyright © 1985 by the Foundation for the School of Business at Indiana University. Reprinted by permission. At the time of writing, George P. Moschis was professor of marketing and Jac L. Goldstucker and Thomas J. Stanley were both associate professors of marketing at Georgia State University.

plemented, or commercialized.[1] Specific experiments with shop-at-home services have produced results positive enough to encourage sponsors to continue expanding their operations.

If at-home shopping becomes a significant part of consumer life style, both in the United States and abroad, the impact on marketing strategy and on other aspects of economic activity will be considerable.

This article (1) *provides a brief overview of the technological developments* in the area of at-home shopping; (2) *identifies patterns of consumer responses* within the context of diffusion theory; and (3) *speculates on the rate at which consumers will adopt the innovation and the effect that the adoption may have* on the management of the marketing mix.

*At-home shopping is defined as an innovation enabling consumers to purchase goods and/or services by means of an electronic device.* That may be a television screen and key pad or a home computer. Characteristics are that:

- The customer can see the merchandise being offered, identify the seller, and receive product/service information.
- The customer can place an order by using the key pad or the home computer.
- Payment can be made by an acceptable credit card, EFT, or an ID number.
- Delivery can be handled by a private firm's own delivery system (for example, Sears), by U.S. mail, or by a private firm's delivery (for example, UPS).

## RESULTS OF MAJOR SURVEYS AND FIELD EXPERIMENTS

Studies have shown positive consumer reactions to specific videotex* services, including at-home shopping, in terms of knowledge, interest, preference, or intentions to use them. A survey of 200 households (100 randomly selected respondents and 100 bank employees, participants of the field experiment Channel 2000) found home banking, public information, and video catalog services to be most useful, in that order. When survey participants were asked if they would be willing to pay $3 a month for each service, catalog shopping was ranked fifth. Potential purchasers of home-information services tend to be young, better educated, and relatively affluent. They are innovators in other related areas such as electronic equipment and cable TV and are heavy users of catalog shopping, automated teller machines (ATMs), and credit cards.

Similar results were obtained from a survey by Reymer and Gersin Associates, Inc., in a national sample of more than 6,000 households.[2] Respondents were asked to indicate intentions to use various home-information services. At-home banking was selected as the most desirable service by 57 percent of the respondents. Shop-at-home and shopping guides were indicated as desirable by 50 percent. However, in the Reymer and Gersin study, no price tag was put on the services.

*CSP International* asked consumers to indicate the amount they would pay monthly for assorted transactional services.[3] On the basis of the price consumers were willing to pay, shop-at-home services were the most desirable.

Booz, Allen & Hamilton asked consumers about catalog shopping, news, home banking, energy and security information, investment and home management, entertainment and reservation services, personal calendars, and electronic and other types of games. The results revealed that more than 50 percent of the respondents intend to buy such home-information services and are willing to pay about $20 a month. Contrary to folklore that the market is upscale, the greatest demand for home-information services was found among middle-income families ($20,000 to $40,000 household income) with children.

The *Viewtron* project was one of the first videotex shopping trials designed to assess consumer reaction to a wide variety of shopping services.

---

[1]James B. Moore, "Videotex Is Part of Larger Game Called Networking," *American Banker*, October 19, 1982, p. 25.

*Videotex* refers to home-information systems with two-way information flows. The user can receive and transmit data. This two-way interactive information system is also referred to as "viewdata." Videotex systems differ from *teletext* systems, which provide only one-way service, with the information flowing from the service vendor to the user.

[2]"Use of Technology Triggers Change in Hospitality Industry's Marketing Efforts," *Marketing News*, November 26, 1982, Sec. 2, p. 18.

[3]"Home Videotex Can Be Made to Pay . . . But It Could Take Seven Years," *Post-News*, July 1982, pp. 1–2.

Consumers could use the computer to place an order, with billing handled through credit cards. Results of the experiment suggest that consumers may use electronic shopping instead of other forms of direct marketing such as catalogs. Consumers ordered an average of $62 worth of merchandise during the nine-month trial period.

On the other hand, several studies, including several field experiments, show low consumer acceptance of shop-at-home services. Blackwell and Offutt's study used participants of the Qube system, currently operational in Columbus, Ohio.[4] Their analysis of "users" versus "nonusers" found low interest in electronic shopping such as catalog-type shopping by television. They found the highest interest in information and entertainment services; the least interest is in electronic shopping such as catalog-type shopping by television. The study also revealed that videotex users tend to be older, with larger families, having more children at home. They have more color TV sets at home, and they are heavy TV viewers.

A study by Benton and Bowles found only 10 percent of a consumer panel to be interested in shopping at home; about 23 percent were interested in at-home banking.[5]

In a telephone survey, Sundel, Nevils and Alston, using a systematic probability sample of 400 respondents, asked subjects how likely they were to use teleshopping.[6] Thirty-nine percent of the sample indicated that they were likely to adopt the new concept of shopping. Compared to their non-adopter counterparts, the potential adopters were younger, more time- and convenience-oriented shoppers, less interested in comparison shopping, more experienced with nonstore marketing, with a greater need for planned shopping trips.

In a recently concluded pilot study by *The Times-Mirror Co.* in southern California, the 350 members of the participating households were able to pay their bills, check snow conditions at local ski resorts, and order advertised items from 35 local retailers. Although news, home banking and shopping, education, and electronic mail were rated among the most "essential" services, games were ranked highest. Specifically, programs rated as essentials were games (79 percent), shopping and product information (72 percent), bill-paying at a bank (71 percent), late-breaking news (60 percent), education for children (57 percent), and electronic mail (56 percent). However, these reported preferences were not consistent with actual behavior. For example, only 53 percent of the participating households made one or more purchases during the nine-month trial.

The *Venture One* project was also designed to test consumer acceptance of at-home shopping services. According to this field experiment, consumers are more likely to use electronic shopping for information than for placing orders.

Field experiments in other parts of the world also provide useful information on consumer reaction to electronic shopping. After all, electronic shopping was first developed and initiated in Europe, Canada, and Japan. Activities soon spread to South America, the Middle East, and Australia. Some of the most notable systems around the world include the British Prestel, the French Teletel, the German Bildschirmtext, and the Canadian Telidon.

*Prestel* is considered to be the most successful system in the world.[7] Introduced in 1979, Prestel was the world's first public videotex service. Thus far it has captured less than 23,000 users. Prestel's growth has been slow; its operations are expected to break even in the 1984–85 fiscal year. Among the interactive services offered are electronic shopping and electronic mail.

*Teletel's* trial was completed in the fall of 1982, using 2,500 volunteer households. Informational and transactional services provided by the French system included teleshopping, computer games, reservations, education services, banking, train schedules, entertainment, and electronic mail. Games and entertainment (for example, horoscopes) were the most widely used videotex features. For this reason, several information providers in France have begun to use video-games to draw users to their data bases, even

---

[4]"Consumers Want Information and Entertainment in Videotex Systems," *Marketing News*, October 1, 1982.

[5]"Research on New Video Technologies," *Marketing News*, May 29, 1981, p. 1.

[6]Harvey H. Sundel, Randall C. Nevils, and Herbert L. Alston, "A Profile of the Potential Teleshopper Customer and Products Most Likely Purchased Through a Teleshopper," *1983 Proceedings-Southwestern Marketing Association Conference*, March 1983, p. 167.

[7]Graham Hudson, "Prestel: The Basis of an Evolving Videotex System," *BYTE Publications, Inc.*, July 1983, pp. 61–129.

though games often have little to do with other services offered.

The field trials of the *Bildschirmtext* system have been successful. The 6,000 participants were offered a variety of informational and transactional services, including shopping and home banking. Commercial implementation of the system has begun, with plans to have 150,000 users by 1984 and a million by the end of 1986.

The *Telidon* system, offering a variety of information and transaction services, is now operational in several areas of Canada.

On the basis of these studies, several general observations can be made:

The results of the various studies are far from conclusive as to consumer acceptance of at-home shopping services, for several reasons:

  Studies, especially field experiments, tested electronic shopping along with a large variety of other services. Consumers appear to respond differently to different mixes of services.

  Measures of consumer acceptance have not been uniform across studies; they ranged from "interest" to "importance," "preference," "intentions," and "actual use."

  Samples in various studies ranged in type (probability, nonprobability), size, and representativeness (self-selection, response rate).

  Different research designs used in the various studies are likely to have produced different results because of biases, limitations, and advantages inherent in the type of design used.

Consumers are likely to accept a cluster of services rather than individual services. Transactional services alone do not seem to generate enough interest; they must be supplemented with information and entertainment services.

Not all videotex services are likely to diffuse at the same rate. Information-related services such as entertainment are likely to be adopted more quickly than transactional services such as at-home shopping.

The rate of adoption of videotex services in general and electronic shopping in particular is uncertain; it is likely to be affected by a host of variables.

## ENVIRONMENTAL FACTORS LIKELY TO IMPINGE UPON CONSUMER ACCEPTANCE OF AT-HOME SHOPPING

Innovations with high perceived *relative advantage, compatibility* with existing values and behavior, *low complexity*, and *high trialability and observability* normally have accelerated diffusion rates. Speed, convenience, and lower cost may enhance the *relative advantage* of shop-at-home services. However, these services must be *compatible* with the life styles, experiences, and buying habits of consumers. The requirements for operating these systems (for example, learning to operate a computer) may enhance their *perceived complexity*. Because some systems may require home terminals for accessing their services, the *trialability* of these at-home shopping services may be hampered when the home computer is not available. Finally, at-home shopping services are not immediately *observable*. Thus, despite evidence of initial acceptance, a variety of factors, many of which are constantly changing, are likely to affect the rate at which electronic shopping diffuses.

### Technological factors

The most common videotex media for delivering information are the telephone and cable. The main drawback of the telephone is its narrow "band width," or information-carrying capacity. Telephones are built to carry voice conversations, not to transmit a lot of information at a rate fast enough to reproduce good quality graphic displays. Using the telephone as a videotex medium keeps the phone busy, thereby preventing its use for other calls. However, AT&T has recently announced its "presentation protocol" for encoding signals carrying graphics.

In contrast to the telephone system, which has nearly total penetration of U.S. households, only about 40 percent of all households are wired for cable TV. Moreover, only a tiny fraction (24 of 4,250) of current cable systems are interactive.[8] Because cable systems serve households in spe-

---
[8]Bill Orr, "Home Banking Prospects: A Status Report on Explosive Growth," *ABA Banking Journal*, October 1981.

cific areas, home terminals cannot be switched easily to other data bases outside the local area, severely limiting the variety of data bases available to the in-home user of a videotex system delivered by cable.

Of the three major alternative delivery systems that can be used to support electronic shopping—telephone, cable TV, and satellite—the telephone network is expected to emerge as the dominant medium. Ninety-five percent of households have telephone service. This penetration far exceeds even the most optimistic projections for cable, an eventual 45 percent of all TV households. Furthermore, the high cost of installing two-way cables could limit cable penetration. Interactive home-information systems are also possible via satellite, but the cost at this time is prohibitive.

The much-heralded growth of videotex systems for delivering information over home-computer terminals has been hobbled by two big problems: the high cost of the terminals and the limited usefulness of the data and services offered. In order to have mass appeal, the present price of the terminal will probably have to be reduced by half.[9] The system will have to carry a wide range of retail shopping information and news and offer subscribers the ability to execute a wide variety of transactions in their homes.

### Legislation

One way to determine how electronic shopping fits into the intricate framework of laws and regulations is to identify the components of videotex systems. The consumer uses a device (telephone, terminal, and/or television set) owned or leased by him/her to transmit and receive, via regulated lines (AT&T or cable), information to and from various institutions or service vendors.

AT&T services the vast majority of telephones in the country. Its subsidiary, Western Electric, which is the largest manufacturer of telecommunications equipment, is currently developing terminals for use in the home; together with AT&T it owns the R&D facilities of Bell Telephone Laboratories. Because AT&T is currently experimenting with the marketing of videotex services, critics argue that there is serious potential for anticompetitive behavior such as cross-subsidization of services and discrimination against competitors who must use AT&T's network in order to compete. Thus the expansion in communication technology, along with its control by major companies, is accelerating while legislation regulating the industry is lagging.

The creation of joint ventures for tapping videotex-related opportunities is likely to create a new set of issues for public policymakers. For example, a wide variety of personal data (programmed purchases, buying preferences, and so forth) will be gathered and processed by more than one enterprise, increasing the risk that consumers may suffer a loss of privacy because such information will be much more accessible. Consumer concerns about such potential threats to their privacy may result in the creation of formal industry-wide privacy protection procedures. These procedures are likely to set the stage for regulation.

### Consumer attitudes

Consumer acceptance might be another roadblock to electronic shopping diffusion. Consumers will be asked to make substantial changes in the way they live. They also might need to become better educated in order to use these innovations. For example, AT&T's studies show that, as consumers become more educated, their need for more specialized and personalized information expands as does their acceptance of automated delivery systems.

Consumer acceptance of these technological innovations will require changes in existing habits and developments of new ones, what Riesman and Roseborough call "resocialization" into a different consumer role.[10] For younger people, the learning of these new patterns of interaction with the marketplace may not be difficult; schools already are teaching children skills related to the use of the new technology. While most adults have developed a passive pattern of interacting

[9]Roy A. Sutherland, "Home Banking Electronic Money Invades the Living Room," *The Futurist*, April 1982, pp. 13–17.

[10]D. Riesman and H. Roseborough, "Carriers and Consumer Behavior," in L. Clark, ed., *Life Cycle and Consumer Behavior* (New York: New York University Press, 1955).

with television, children look at the video screen as a display format that they can actively manipulate. Children interact with television and video screens by playing videogames and using microcomputers in the school and at home. By the time today's children reach adulthood, they may find the use of video output information quite natural.

Growing familiarity with video technology will prepare adults for two-way communications with service vendors. Millions of adults use computer-connected video display terminals in their jobs. The videogame explosion has made consumers familiar with the idea of a computerized console that plugs into a television set. In order to shop at home, the consumer has only to add a keyboard with which to enter instructions.

### Economic demand

Broad trends, such as the increase in two- and three-wage-earner households, escalating fuel costs, rising labor costs, the increasing number of elderly consumers, and declining data-processing costs, are likely to affect demand for electronic shopping and to change consumer needs in the marketplace. Consumer households will have less disposable time and less inclination to travel to perform routine transactions; therefore, services providing convenience will have broader appeal. The constant growth of mail order sales attests to this appeal. At the same time, the costs for delivery of technology-based services compare favorably to services based on more labor-intensive operations.

### Competition

The evolving technology of the booming videotex systems industry presents new and challenging opportunities for businesses ranging from computer companies to banks to cable television providers. Because any videotex system comprises several parts—a terminal at home, a data base that provides information, and a communication network—these opportunities require a high level of cooperation among the businesses that may join together to capitalize on them. Consequently, the marketing of home-information systems on a large scale is likely to involve a high level of synergism among data-base vendors, distributors of equipment, and other vendors.[11] Competition in the future is likely to occur between integrated systems consisting of companies in many different types of industries. Thus, marketers need to be planning the development of new product and services that could be offered through home-information systems, and working with vendors of other information services and home-information components.

## EFFECT OF AT-HOME SHOPPING ON THE MARKETING MIX: SOME SPECULATIONS

Will at-home shopping by electronic equipment catch on to the extent that it will alter retailers' strategies or customers' buying behavior? Eminent retail practitioners disagree. A recent newspaper article quotes Stanley Marcus, chairman emeritus of Neiman-Marcus, as saying: "The most important challenge will be electronic retailing, I think; it's one of the biggest challenges to happen since the development of the supermarket." In the same article Marvin Traub, head of Bloomingdale's, says: "I'm not one of those people who feels strongly about shopping at home by computers."[12]

This uncertainty notwithstanding, each element in the marketing mix is likely to be affected in some manner and to some degree by at-home shopping.

### Price

Under conditions of perfect competition, sellers are price takers rather than price makers. Such competition assumes that consumers have perfect knowledge about the product, including the conditions under which it is offered for sale. It has been argued that, through product and firm differentiation, prices for the same brand of product or for products of similar quality often vary significantly among competing retailers under the existing structure.

Through electronic shopping, consumers will be in a position to acquire more knowledge about

---

[11] George P. Moschis and Mardi Strand, *Home Information Systems: Criteria for Partner Selection* (Atlanta: Payment Systems, Inc., 1982).

[12] "Electronic Retailing Views," *The Atlanta Journal*, June 3, 1983, p. 5.

alternative offerings, knowledge concerning price, brand, retail outlet, and services. Armed with this knowledge, consumers may demand explanations of price differences, especially if the brands are identical or perceived to be close substitutes.

If prices among similar brands do differ, the retailers will have to justify the price differentials, perhaps on the basis of the nonprice variables of the mix, such as credit, return-goods policy, delivery costs, and the like. If retailers cannot justify the price differential between their brand and the same brand being offered at a lower price by competitive retailers, then prices may be driven down to a more nearly "perfectly competitive" level. As a result, retailers may earn little or no more than normal profits. Thus, a drop in prices, brought about by increased consumer knowledge, may well result in losses for the less efficient retailers.

## Product

Whether consumers can shop at home by computer depends upon the type of product. Certain services, such as car repairs, cannot be purchased and delivered by computer. On the other hand, the purchase of tickets—to concerts and sporting events from airlines—lends itself well to this at-home use of electronic equipment.

Products that represent high economic and social risk are less likely to be sold successfully by electronic retailing than those which have the opposite characteristics, as attested to by findings on catalog-shopping behavior.[13] On the other hand, such items as men's, women's and children's apparel could be demonstrated on the TV screen to much greater advantage than they can be pictured in a mail-order catalog. This may also be true of household appliances, hardware items, lawn and garden supplies, household paper goods, and linens and towels.

## Product/service mix

Judging from the results of early experiments in the United States and other countries, consumers are likelier to accept a cluster of home-in-

formation services than any single offering. Electronic shopping will have to be integrated with other, more glamorous information services. Financial institutions are likely to be involved in the development of videotex services. Banking services have increased from 40 percent of all videotex projects announced or started by 1982 to more than 80 percent of all projects announced or started in 1982 and 1983. The number of financial institutions participating in home-information systems projects increased from two in 1980 to more than 80 by 1982.[14] Financial institutions involved in home banking are large and offer ATM services. The banking survey reveals that:

- Banking and shopping alone do not generate enough customer appeal to support a videotex system;
- Interactive services must be integrated with other passive programming (such as games, movies); and
- Nonbank organizations participating in videotex experiments are able to provide financial services in direct competition with banks.

Thus, marketers need to develop new products and services that could be offered through home-information systems and to work with vendors of other information services and home-information components.

The diffusion of videotex services may not be uniform; noninteractive services are likely to be accepted first, followed by other interactive, more complex services. This pattern may be due partly to the individual's familiarity and experience and partly to cultural resistance. In households where the principal user had previous computer experience, home computers were used for more complex applications (such as financial management) than was the case in households without experience.[15] This pattern presents a challenge for strategy development to cross-sell various services.

Designers of videotex services will have to keep in mind the dynamic aspects of product/service diffusion as well as the changing market. Furthermore, not all market segments are

[13]Pradeep Korkaongar, "Consumer Preferences for Catalog Showrooms and Discount Stores: The Moderating Role of Product Risk," *Journal of Retailing*, Fall 1983, pp. 76–88.

[14]"Home Banking Task Force Study," *Thruput: The ABA Operations Automation News Report*, January 1983, p. 1.

[15]Venkatesh Alladi and Nicholas Vitalari, "Household and Technology: The Case of Home Computers," paper presented at the Conference on the Changing Household, Cambridge, Mass: Marketing Science Institute, February 1983.

likely to have the same need or use for the variety of home information services. Market segmentation studies can identify the specific needs of the target markets and develop appropriate service mixes for serving such needs. Life-styles—the way that people spend their time and money— may be better predictors of preference for various types of service than demographics. Some surveys suggest, for example, that shopping at home may have greater appeal to "purchase planners" than to those sensitive to time use.

A wealth of information about the electronic household's life style can be collected and stored by service vendors. Such in-depth profiles of family habits offer potential for preprogrammed or automatic purchases, as well as for the market testing of new products or services.

**Distribution**

The evolving technology is likely to affect the manner in which a company goes about distributing its products and services. There is limited information on the effectiveness and efficiency of various marketing methods for high technology products. Personal computers are currently marketed through various channels of distribution, such as direct selling, mail-order, discount, specialty, and department stores.

The outlook for electronic shopping as a distribution channel appears to be uncertain. Comp-U-Card of America, Inc., the leading electronic home shopping firm, expects teleshopping to grow much faster than traditional retailing. Similarly, *Management Horizon* estimated recently that 20 percent of U.S. retail sales by 1990 will be *electronic* devices. Booz, Allen & Hamilton's recent study projects $50 billion in electronic retail sales by 1995, while estimates by AT&T executives run as high as 30 percent of the general merchandise moving off the shelves by the year 2010.

On the other hand, sponsors of videotex shopping trials are much more conservative in their estimates. The results of Venture One indicate that people used videotex shopping more for information than for placing orders—the equivalent of looking through a catalog or wandering through a mall. Further, this medium was a demand fulfiller rather than a demand creator.

Nevertheless, these results do not preclude the possibility that electronic shopping may emerge,

not as a dominant means of consumer interaction with the marketplace, but as an alternate or supplementary channel. For example, consumers may use electronic shopping instead of other forms of direct marketing such as catalogs.

The emergence of electronic shopping has certain implications for marketers. First, *electronic shopping implies home delivery of a physical product*. This requires order taking and purchase programming, both by the seller and the customer, timely delivery at "convenient" hours, especially for high-value merchandise, and reliable parcel delivery service. Second, *teleshopping is likely to affect other methods of direct marketing* and perhaps have adverse effects on their efficiency, increasing the cost of marketing. Methods and procedures must be established for handling transactions, programming purchases, documentation, handling complaints and returned merchandise. The situation here may be analogous to Automated Teller Machines, which did not decrease the cost of financial transactions as expected but increased it. The number of financial transactions increased due to ATM availability, serving as a supplemental outlet (primarily as a substitute for supermarket check-cashing) and not as a substitute for bank services.[16]

Regardless of the advances in teleshopping, neither the shopping center nor the grocery store is likely to be eliminated. Shopping to many people is a form of recreational activity, an opportunity for social interaction. Videotex poses a threat to social interaction because it preempts interpersonal communication. The marketplaces reinforce selective perceptions of the world, whereas an electronic marketplace may present a monolithic view of life.[17] At-home shopping for perishable products would be difficult; stores selling products requiring trial, demonstration, and fitting are apt to survive. It is likely, however, that the marketplace will change considerably. For example, the mix of stores where items are ordered routinely may be developed in a way that facilitates picking up the items. Stores that provide/require a sensory experience might be "clustered" to facilitate shopping. On the other hand, discount stores and other large magnate stores could disappear.

[16]Thomas J. Stanley, George P. Moschis and Murphy A. Sewall, *Profiling the Affluent Home Terminal-Prone Consumer*, Atlanta: Payment Systems, Inc. Strategic Paper Number 6, 1981.

[17]"Electronic Marketplace," *The New York Times*, June 20, 1982.

Electronic shopping represents convenience in that consumers can shop when they wish without leaving home or work. On the other hand, the convenience of shopping at home may be more than offset by the lack of social involvement which some segments of consumers gain from in-store shopping. Lower and middle classes tend to use shopping as a social activity. Research has shown that a great deal of shopping mall activity fills a social need. In fact, some suggest that shopping malls have taken the place of the bygone "corner drug store."

Upper classes find outlets other than shopping to satisfy their need for social involvement. Therefore, one might speculate that the upper classes may account for most at-home sales, the lower and middle classes representing a much smaller share.

For several retailers, the cost savings of videotex could be considerable. For example, the West German bank, Verbraucherbank, found that, while videotex may not be cheaper to operate in terms of non-staff costs, it increases consumer handling capacity. The bank has been able to assign workers to other more productive and profitable activities, and it has offered reduced rates for banking at home.

### Advertising

Electronic shopping services are also likely to affect the advertising industry and the ways marketers reach consumers. First, some advertising must be directed at service users to inform them of the kinds of information and services available. Second, advertisers are likely to find videotex an irresistible medium. Consumer interaction with home information services preempts other forms of communication and mass media use. The result is likely to be higher cost of advertising through traditional mass media. Other media such as cable channels are already driving up the cost of CPM, forcing advertisers to seek a more direct link to consumer.[18]

Advertisers will have to interact with data base companies and other nontraditional outlets where information is likely to be compiled and processed. For example, product displays and dem-

onstration may be taped at the retailer's establishment rather than at the studio and the information disseminated through a variety of channels and vendors reaching a more specialized audience. Videotex-like services already reach visitors in their hotel rooms.

Consumer acceptance of at-home shopping services appears to be affected by a host of factors. First, environmental factors, including technology, legislation, economic trends, and consumer life styles, are likely to impinge upon the rate and magnitude of consumer acceptance of at-home shopping services. Second, consumer characteristics and learning processes are likely to affect acceptance of teleshopping services. Finally, many types of at-home shopping services are likely to be accepted more readily and by a larger number of consumers than other services. Consumer adoption of at-home services is likely to affect all the elements of the firm's marketing mix and present new growth opportunities.

### QUESTIONS

1. *What exactly is at-home shopping? Give some examples.*

2. *Various research studies have been conducted to measure consumer acceptance of different forms of at-home shopping. Summarize the results of these studies. What do they indicate about consumer acceptance of at-home shopping?*

3. *Explain how environmental and technological variables may affect the rate of consumer acceptance for electronic shopping services such as videotex.*

4. *To what degree and how do you think the introduction and growth of at-home shopping services will affect the marketing mixes of manufacturers, wholesalers, and retailers?*

*5. *How well do you think at-home shopping services would be accepted by consumers in a socialist country such as Romania? (Reading 3) Explain your answer.*

---

[18]Benjamin M. Compaine, "The Future Belongs to: 1. Print, 2. Videotex (Choose One)," *Adweek*, April 4, 1983, p. NR36.

---

*Question relates concepts in this and other readings.

☐ **23**

# Strategic management issues for the retailing of services

*J. Patrick Kelly*

*William R. George*

*Services account for about two thirds of the U.S. gross national product and provide about 7 out of every 10 Americans with jobs. This article focuses on services that are offered to consumers, and illustrates the differences between the retailing of services and the retailing of tangible goods. The authors stress that these differences could cause serious problems for firms that attempt to sell services in the same way they sell goods. The problem areas are identified, and a strategic framework is presented to increase the likelihood of success in the retailing of services.*

Retailing has been synonymous with the selling of tangible products to household consumers. One does not typically think of merchandising programs for selling intangibles as part of the strategy of most major retailers. Yet, the addition of services to the retail offering may provide the greatest growth potential during the coming decade.

Services as a portion of personal consumption expenditures have increased from 39.3 percent in 1950 to 46.3 percent in 1979 (see Table 1). More important may be the stability of service expenditures in comparison with durables and nondurables in periods of economic downturn, such as 1973 through 1975. Additionally, some experts predict that, by 1990, services will account for 50 percent of the total sales of general merchandise retailers (*Chain Store Age*, 1975). In 1981 financial services offered by Sears, Roebuck accounted for $8.8 billion in revenue, while the merchandising efforts reached $16.9 billion. These financial services consisted of insurance, money market funds, stock brokerage, credit operations, and real estate brokerage activities (*Business Week*, 1981). The $8.8 billion does not include the more traditional services offered by Sears.

For the most part, traditional retailing organizations have overlooked the potential opportunities which exist in the retailing of services. All the while, these stores have experienced increasing levels of merchandise competition from discounters and specialty stores as well as declining profit levels. If these retailers do not consider the optional merchandising programs for the retailing of services, their share of consumer expenditures and profit levels will continue to diminish.

One of the greatest competitive advantages for stores like Sears will come through the development of differentiated service retailing which cannot be easily duplicated by smaller retailers and discounters. This advantage exists because of the favorable image customers have for the quality of goods and services currently being offered by these regional full-line department and national chain stores.

Source: Reprinted with permission from the *Journal of Retailing*, Summer 1982, pp. 26–43. At the time of writing, J. Patrick Kelly was professor of retail management at Brigham Young University and William R. George was associate professor of marketing at Rutgers University.

The authors express appreciation to the Skaggs Institute of Retail Management of Brigham Young University for its funding of this study.

**Table 1 □ Personal consumption expenditures per capita (in constant 1972 dollars)**

| | 1950 | | 1955 | | 1960 | | 1965 | | 1970 | | 1971 | | 1972 | |
|---|---|---|---|---|---|---|---|---|---|---|---|---|---|---|
| | $ | % | $ | % | $ | % | $ | % | $ | % | $ | % | $ | % |
| Total per capita | 2,229 | 100.0 | 2,391 | 100.0 | 2,508 | 100.0 | 2,873 | 100.0 | 3,265 | 100.0 | 3,342 | 100.0 | 3,510 | 100.0 |
| Durable goods | 286 | 12.8 | 316 | 13.2 | 291 | 11.6 | 378 | 13.2 | 434 | 13.3 | 474 | 14.2 | 533 | 15.2 |
| Nondurable goods | 1,067 | 47.9 | 1,122 | 46.9 | 1,153 | 46.0 | 1,256 | 43.7 | 1,380 | 42.3 | 1,388 | 41.5 | 1,433 | 40.8 |
| Services | 876 | 39.3 | 953 | 39.9 | 1,064 | 42.4 | 1,239 | 43.1 | 1,451 | 44.4 | 1,479 | 44.3 | 1,544 | 44.0 |

| | 1973 | | 1974 | | 1975 | | 1976 | | 1977 | | 1978 | | 1979 | |
|---|---|---|---|---|---|---|---|---|---|---|---|---|---|---|
| | $ | % | $ | % | $ | % | $ | % | $ | % | $ | % | $ | % |
| Total per capita | 3,648 | 100.0 | 3,590 | 100.0 | 3,627 | 100.0 | 3,807 | 100.0 | 3,955 | 100.0 | 4,080 | 100.0 | 4,194 | 100.0 |
| Durable goods | 579 | 15.9 | 531 | 14.8 | 528 | 14.6 | 585 | 15.4 | 635 | 16.1 | 662 | 16.2 | 667 | 15.9 |
| Nondurable goods | 1,470 | 40.3 | 1,434 | 39.9 | 1,436 | 39.6 | 1,488 | 39.1 | 1,524 | 38.5 | 1,554 | 38.1 | 1,584 | 37.8 |
| Services | 1,599 | 43.8 | 1,625 | 45.3 | 1,663 | 45.8 | 1,734 | 45.5 | 1,796 | 45.4 | 1,864 | 45.7 | 1,943 | 46.3 |

Sources: *Statistical Abstract of the United States, 1976,* table 634, "Per Capita Income and Product," p. 396; and *Statistical Abstract, 1980,* table 729, "Per Capita Income and Product," p. 440.

In discussing service offerings with department store executives, the authors find that these executives usually restrict their thinking to services accompanying tangible goods. These services may be considered as "tangible dominant" since they are connected with the sale of a physical good (Shostack, 1977). Unfortunately, many executives have not recognized the differences in the selling of "intangible dominant" services which are sold apart from any good. Thus, many retailers recognize only two types of products when, in fact, they could be offering three types.

Exhibit 1 illustrates the types of products offered by retailers and classifies them on a "free or paid for" basis. For another taxonomy of retailer involvement in services, see Berry (1981). Tangible goods and services accompanying goods sold are the two types of products on which general merchandise retailers have concentrated. However, it is the third product type, intangible dominant services, that will provide one of the growth opportunities for the leading retailers in the 1980s. Sears has clearly recognized this trend with its new direction into the retailing of financial services (*Business Week*, 1981).

These services, identified in Exhibit 1, may be further classified on the basis of whether they involve the individual or are performed on goods owned by the individual. Examples abound for each of these components in this model of types of products offered by retailers. This article focuses, however, only on those services that provide revenue-producing opportunities—that is, services that are paid for that involve the individual or that are performed on goods owned by the individual. The sales support services (alterations,

warranty repair, engraving, etc.) are included as services only when they are sold directly to customers without the need for the product being serviced to have been purchased within the store.

**THE CHALLENGE OF RETAILING SERVICES**

The fact that differences do exist in the retailing of services as compared with the retailing of goods is well documented. Consumer perceptions differ concerning the buying of services as compared with goods (Guseman, 1977; Johnson, 1969; Lewis, 1976). Different management approaches are required for service operations as compared with tangible goods operations (Chase, 1978; Thomas, 1978; Upah, 1980). Thus the retail executive must understand how new variables, both external and internal, have to be managed in order to succeed in this challenging type of retailing. Since customers behave differently when in the marketplace for services, the merchandising program for the retailing of services requires different strategies than does a merchandising program for tangible goods.

Merchandise managers, department managers, buyers, and others who have backgrounds in the traditional retailing of tangible products may not be able to transfer their experience and skills directly to the merchandising of services because of significant differences between the consumer buying process for goods and services and the managerial procedures required. The purposes of this article are to illustrate how services retailing and goods retailing differ on a number of managerial dimensions and to provide a strategic framework

**Exhibit 1 ☐ Goods and services—classifications with examples**

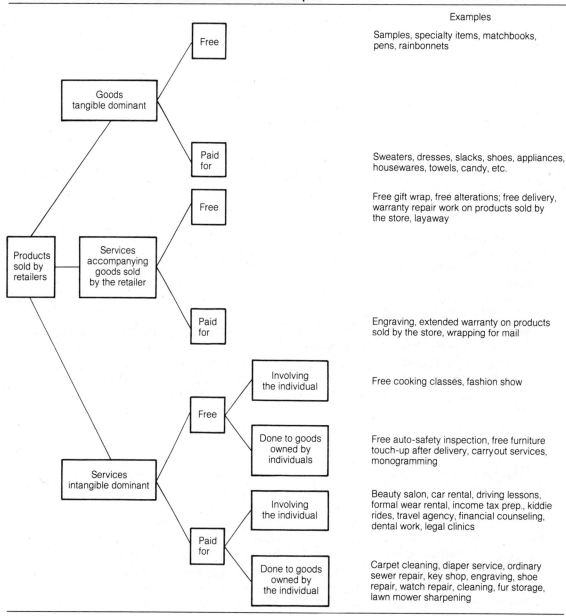

| | Examples |
|---|---|
| Free | Samples, specialty items, matchbooks, pens, rainbonnets |
| Paid for | Sweaters, dresses, slacks, shoes, appliances, housewares, towels, candy, etc. |
| Free | Free gift wrap, free alterations; free delivery, warranty repair work on products sold by the store, layaway |
| Paid for | Engraving, extended warranty on products sold by the store, wrapping for mail |
| Involving the individual | Free cooking classes, fashion show |
| Done to goods owned by individuals | Free auto-safety inspection, free furniture touch-up after delivery, carryout services, monogramming |
| Involving the individual | Beauty salon, car rental, driving lessons, formal wear rental, income tax prep., kiddie rides, travel agency, financial counseling, dental work, legal clinics |
| Done to goods owned by the individual | Carpet cleaning, diaper service, ordinary sewer repair, key shop, engraving, shoe repair, watch repair, cleaning, fur storage, lawn mower sharpening |

for the changes necessary to achieve a successful transition into services retailing.

**Retailing patterns**

Although retailers offering services have the option of using owned, leased, or contracted departments, most regional department stores and national chain stores currently operate their services offerings through leased departments.

Typical of the leasing approach is Sears, Roebuck & Co. It has long recognized the value of offering its customers a wide range of services, including beauty care, carpet and home cleaning, diaper service, driving lessons, income tax preparation, shoe repair, watch repair, key shop, and engraving. Sears has chosen to lease the majority of these departments to outside concessions rather than to own and operate them internally. On the other hand, a less common approach is that followed by Marshall Field's, which also recognizes the value of selling intangibles but operates most of its services as owned rather than leased departments. These services include alterations, carpet and rug cleaning, carpet repair, clock repair, china repair, drapery workroom, fur storage, handbag and luggage repair, and radio and TV services.

Other examples include J. C. Penney's insurance operations and Dayton's ownership of its travel, optical, fur storage, and computerized entertainment ticket services. Because Dayton's has developed the expertise in offering travel services, it acts as the lessee in Diamond's and Hudson's, two sister divisions of the Dayton-Hudson Corporation.

Although some retailers are large enough to successfully manage the service merchandising with internally owned operations, other retailers desiring to offer services may feel an inadequate background in service retailing. This inadequacy provides an opportunity for service firms to act as wholesalers of "packaged" services. A number of services could be offered to retailers by these service firms and, in turn, offered to the retailer's customers. For example, an external organization could develop and provide services such as those of a chiropractor, podiatrist, lawyer, or dentist, as well as appliance repair, home improvement, security systems, insurance, etc. This arrangement solves the problem for the retailer for fragmented services which have diverse management requirements, allows for more efficiency in distribution of services, and eliminates licensing requirements by the retailer for many professional services because these would be met by the wholesale service firm offering the packaged services.

Even though opportunities exist for the wholesale packaging of services, it is our contention that many retailers will shift leased service departments to owned service operations. They will do so as they begin to understand the implications of a greater percentage of consumer expenditures on services.

## MERCHANDISING OPERATIONS FOR SERVICES

Traditional retail management and merchandising tools in many cases cannot be directly applied to the retailing of services. Managers of potential service functions will therefore need to develop new ways of thinking about service offerings. This section reviews a number of the operational areas where differences exist.

### Measuring performance

The offering of driving lessons using automobiles with dual steering systems or in-house dry cleaning can be a fairly expensive, capital-intensive service, while the offering of legal advice or family counseling may require only a comfortable room with functional furniture. Montgomery Ward has a legal clinic which consists of a telephone line to a law office, therefore requiring almost no investment to offer its legal clinic. These differences in capital requirements suggest that a return-on-investment (ROI) approach as a measure of efficiency in offering a service may not be the most appropriate one. Because many of the services will be performed outside the store (lawn care, sewer repair, etc.), the use of sales per square foot may also be an inappropriate measurement. The object of obtaining a certain share of the market may be an appropriate one, yet it is difficult to obtain accurate measurements.

Because service departments do not have inventories of tangible goods, the traditional measures of performance or managerial efficiency, such as turnover, markdown control, open-to-buy limits, and the usual gross margin contributions are not applicable.

The greatest expense in a service area is usually the direct labor costs. Therefore, the best measure of performance seems to be the establishment of each service as its own profit center with the gauge of worth being the level of profit generated after labor costs. Yet, for those services which are required to support the sale of goods, such as appliance warranty work or clothing alterations, the same levels of profit may not be comparable with those of intangible dominant service departments. For example, the alterations function may be responsible for generating $15,000 in income from customers requesting alteration work while earning $5,000 gross profit (sales less labor costs), or a 33.3 percent profit level on that income. But the same alterations area may do $30,000 in transfer sales for the men's department, which are charged to the alterations function at cost without a gross profit margin. Therefore, the alterations function can be measured either on a profit return of 33.3 percent or 11.1 percent (5,000 divided by 45,000). Therefore, a combined measure would be historically inconsistent as the mix of customer-requested and department-requested alterations changed over time.

Choosing between offering two or more different services may require an analysis based upon comparisons of services which are support for merchandise departments or nonsales support services. Those services that are offered as intangible dominant services (income tax preparation, legal clinics) must be compared with other similar services.

Some of the cost accounting problems of services have been discussed by Dearden (1978) and will not be expanded upon here. It is sufficient to say that the accounting and cost controls for the service areas are different enough from goods retailing to receive proper separate attention. Services do not move through the warehouse, loading docks, pricing rooms, or other preparation facilities. The objectives established for services areas should be different from those for the goods areas. As top management evaluates the performance of those responsible for service areas, recognition must be given to these differences.

### Store organization

The management of most goods retailing follows a pattern of a division merchandise manager (DMM) being responsible for a wide range of goods categories. The buyers report to the DMM and have responsibilities for narrower categories of goods. These responsibilities consist of buying and vendor contact, pricing, display, promotion, etc.

Some retailers tend to group the service areas under the supervision of those responsible for closely related goods areas. For example, the buyer of menswear may be responsible for the alterations department. Other retailers that have recognized the differences in overall management of goods and services retailing, such as Marshall Field's, have removed the services areas from the control of the goods managers and have established an organization with management responsibilities exclusively over the service areas. This

position is called "division manager—workrooms." This separate management and supervision for services is also suggested by Woll (1975) and others (e.g., *Retailweek*, 1980).

Another organizational difference between goods retailing and services retailing exists in the personnel functions. Those employees involved in service areas have skill requirements that often make it more difficult to obtain these individuals than those experienced only in goods areas. A clock repairer, licensed plumber, lawyer, or driving instructor seldom is a "walk-in" candidate for employment. Many sales positions can be filled from walk-in applicants, and most of the buyer and assistant buyer positions can be filled from progression by junior executives. But special efforts may be required in locating and evaluating those skilled in providing services. In the past, in order to be able to offer certain services, Marshall Field's has helped some Europeans with special skills to immigrate to this country.

Because it is more difficult to replace those employed in service areas, an effort should be made to minimize employee turnover rates. Therefore, a need exists to provide frequent employee evaluations, measures of job satisfaction, and salary increases for those involved with the offering of services. A clerk may be replaced with another willing to work for the minimum wage, but those with expertise in the service areas are harder to obtain and therefore may typically receive higher wages than those in goods areas at similar organizational levels.

Typically, few of those with technical skills who perform a service move up into the management of that service or to the supervision of a wider range of services. Instead, those trained in managerial skills become the supervisors of the craftworkers physically performing the service. The drapery workroom supervisor may have an MBA degree but know little about drapery manufacturing or installation before being exposed to the actual process. Service departments should be managed by managers, not by the craftworkers.

### Service production

Services are not purchased from a supplier and stored on a shelf until ordered by the customer. Instead, they are manufactured or produced after they are requested by the customer. This in itself sets service retailing apart from goods retailing and places the retailer in the channel as the manufacturer as well as the retailer of the service being sold.

The placement of the retailer as the producer of the service carries with it all the problems associated wih the manufacture of goods—research and development, scheduling, raw materials acquisition, quality control, and service consistency throughout various branch store operations.

The improvement or upgrading of services must be done by the retailer. Constant monitoring of competition and decisions on improving aspects of the service, as well as research into the satisfaction customers are experiencing with their purchases, are part of service management.

Scheduling of services retailing presents a dual problem. If the service is performed on a good owned by the customer (diaper service, china repair, silver polishing, etc.), the production process can be scheduled in an orderly flow of first in, first out. The craftworker focuses on one item and, when finished with it, moves to the next. The scheduling process is more complicated where the service involves the individual (legal services, beauty care, driving lessons, and the like). With these types of service, production and consumption take place at the same time. A scheduling of customers is required to maximize the production capabilities of the service offering. The driving instructor who has no student must sit idle. Greater attention may then be required in scheduling services, especially those involving the customer. This scheduling problem is further expanded by Sasser (1976).

In the retailing of men's suits, the quality control activity is left to the manufacturer. A retailer may choose one supplier over another because of that manufacturer's attention to quality control. Therefore, inspection of items and the establishment of standards rest mostly with the manufacturer, while in the retailing of services, the involvement with quality control standards rests with the retailer. Customers purchasing a shirt at the main store expect the same quality when they purchase an identical shirt at a branch store. This consistency in quality is assumed with goods retailing. The consistency of quality in service retailing is much more in doubt. The driving instructor

at one store may be very different from an instructor at another store within the same retail chain. The involvement of the craftworker in the production process for custom draperies may also differ within the same retail store. To ensure the consistency of a service, the store must establish procedures and policies which can be implemented throughout each branch store within that chain. Central training may be the best way to accomplish this consistency. It is of course possible that a customer may develop a preference or loyalty to one specific craftperson ("our family tailor for years"), but the development of loyalty to the store with consistency of the production process is a more healthy loyalty to cultivate. In this area, the store may try to develop a strong brand-name recognition for its service.

A faulty product may be covered under the manufacturer's liability, yet the retailer, when becoming the manufacturer, must be aware of the sole liability associated with the service. Other than the liability of faulty raw material (a carpet-cleaning agent which should not be used on a certain fabric), there is no other recourse for the retailer to turn to. Store-liability coverage should be considered, and most likely increased, especially for those services performed on the individual (beauty services, dental treatments, chiropody).

### Pricing

Typically, the greatest cost involved in offering a service is the labor of the individual or craftperson involved in producing the service. Because that cost is known, it makes sense to price the service on some time increment. A one-hour driving lesson can be priced very efficiently on the time dimension. The problem occurs when the time to perform the service varies. The length of time to repair a toaster can vary depending upon the complexity of the repair. Also, two craftworkers repairing the same item will take varying amounts of time.

When the time to complete a task varies, be it repair work or hairstyling, pricing is a problem. The problem occurs, not because the eventual costs of producing the service cannot be determined, but because most customers want to know the price before making a commitment for the service. This problem might be solved by quoting the price in a range (for example, $12.50 to $17) or by providing an estimate after an examination of the task to be completed.

Services placed on sale at a reduced price for a limited time have the same considerations for pricing below or near cost as do goods. The concern for the reduction of service prices should be in the perception of quality offered. Because of the intangibility, customers tend to associate a stronger relationship between prices and quality with services than they are apt to do with goods. Caution is required to prevent the customer's associating lower quality with a service because of its reduced price during a sale period.

**Advertising and personal selling**

How customers view services should be the starting point for the retailer's promotion mix (Berry, 1981). Advertising that is more informative and that places a greater emphasis on the role of image is necessary, since customers believe that purchasing services is riskier and less pleasant than purchasing goods (George and Berry, 1981). Higher skill levels for salespeople are required to overcome the greater uncertainty levels of service buyers. Sales training should emphasize pre- and postsales risk reduction and indoctrinate salespeople to communicate their qualifications and abilities as service "producers." Since service consumers have more trouble recognizing quality and believe that it is less consistent in services, salespeople must continually sell the quality factors of the service. Indeed, personal selling frequently plays the key role in service promotion and requires personnel policies that attract high-caliber salespeople and achieve low turnover rates.

How customers buy services as compared with how they buy goods is a second important point in developing promotion approaches. For service purchases, customers place greater reliance on word-of-mouth communications than on advertising, are more influenced by others, and are more dependent on the opinions of others (Johnson, 1969; Schissel, 1978; Davis, Guiltinan, and Jones, 1979). Therefore, the retailer must take an active role in managing "uncontrollable" communications (George and Berry, 1981). For example, satisfied customers always should be encouraged to con-

vey their compliments outward ("Tell a friend") and to pass along the business cards of the service salespeople. The superior services retailer needs higher-quality, better-trained salespeople to participate actively in comparison selling with their customers, since there are fewer comparisons in service buying and less naming of competitors. In addition, the services retailer must develop and continually communicate explicit evaluative criteria in both advertising and personal selling strategies to offset the fact that consumers are less objective when purchasing services.

What takes place during the service transaction itself is a final consideration in the development of the service promotion mix. As compared with selling goods, there is more personal involvement, more personal contact, and more customer input required (Johnson, 1969; Rathmell, 1974). In fact, the personality of the salesperson and the personal relationship with the customer are more important here. The retailer must select and train salespeople who can be conversant with and naturally interested in people. Highly skilled personnel are required for such customized selling. They must be specifically trained in the selling of intangibles. Selling expenses are likely to be higher for services than for goods. Comparisons of labor expenses between service areas and goods areas are less meaningful. Comparisons are best made with other services instead of between goods and services.

**Sales promotion**

A colorful arrangement of bath towels provides for a display of merchandise requiring little sales effort. The touching of the good or a visual inspection may be the only communication required to convince the customer of the value of a product. The communication process is more complex in the retailing of services. Because services cannot be displayed in a window, on a rack, or stacked neatly on a shelf, the need for in-store signing to communicate the availability of each service is increased. The customer must see a visual presentation of the service to know that the retailer has made it available. The name over a department's graphic display or a descriptive listing of services may be possible. Those selling the goods may also be a source of information about services, especially those closely associated with the goods sold by the retailer.

The creation of an impulse purchase is much easier for a good than for a service. It is one thing to decide to buy a new coat while browsing in a store and quite another to decide to purchase a specific service. In fact, most services are purchased after a need is recognized and a degree of search and evaluation is performed, rather than strictly on an impulse. This again illustrates the importance of personal contact and personal selling.

The increase in the number of working women and the desire to purchase items at home through telephone or mail-order shopping suggest another challenge for service retailers. That is, how can they include services in a catalog of merchandise to reach the in-home shoppers? If services are to be offered through a catalog, they must be described in a convincing manner. The customer must know how to order the service. When the service is sold with the involvement of the customer (cooking lesson, decorating class, or modeling school), the catalog must specify the necessary time and place arrangements. When the service sold is performed upon an item owned by the customer, the proper instructions must be included for the item to be delivered to the store (china repair) or for the store to establish contact at the consumer's home (drapery cleaning, plumbing repair, etc.). If the service is to be performed some distance from the store, the proper charge for mileage must be included.

A retailer's catalog may contain a separate section for the intangible dominant services and those associated with products sold by the retailer. Describing all the services together in one section may produce a greater impact than scattering their descriptions throughout a catalog.

Additional promotional support for a retailer's services may be obtained through stuffers included with credit card invoices, or special ads on television or in newspapers specifically to promote the services available and to explain how a customer may use them.

## Complaints

Most retailers have developed the philosophy of business that is based on the premise "If not satisfied, return the item for a refund." That policy is easy to implement in goods retailing, but because of the production and consumption of a service, the return of that service is difficult, if not impossible. One cannot return a two-hour driving lesson, an hour of dental work, or lawn fertilizing. Instead, if the customer is dissatisfied, an alternative, untraditional method must be established to handle the situation.

Even the handling of the complaint must be accomplished in a different and often more delicate manner. The customer is much more likely to feel a physical or psychological involvement with the service if it has been performed on that customer. A haircut which is too short is much more disturbing than an alarm clock which, after being repaired, stills runs a little fast. Refunds, guarantees, complaint handling, and returns should be handled by someone close to the service, knowledgeable about the service, and fully aware of the difference between services performed upon individuals and the goods owned by individuals.

## Controls

Where those responsible for goods must be concerned about shrinkage, markdowns, or the seasonality of goods, those responsible for services must express concern for a completely different set of controls. These controls deal with maintaining a level of efficiency and productivity of those employees in the service areas. Because the service is made up of the labor of the craftspeople, the retailer must be sure that each craftworker is not using the store to develop an outside or moonlighting business. The craftworker will often have the opportunity to suggest to the customer that the service can be performed "at my home" or "at my other office" for less money. This low price is the incentive for the customer to bypass the retailer and deal directly with the craftperson. Of course, the retailer does not want to expend the effort and resources to have the business taken away by the employee. This problem is especially prevalent with low-capital-intensive services which require minimal equipment and maximum human skills.

## EXECUTIVE SUMMARY

The retailing of services provides an excellent area of sales growth potential for most traditional

**Table 2 ☐ Implications for service retailing in seven managerial areas**

| Services as compared with goods | Managerial changes needed for services retailing |
|---|---|
| **a. Measuring performance** | |
| Capital expenditures vary widely for different services | Return on net worth may not be the most important measurement of the value of a service to the retailer |
| Little or no inventories are required to offer services | Turnover, markdown controls, and other goods-related controls are not appropriate |
| Higher labor costs | Profit after labor costs replaces the gross margin of goods retailing |
| Some services support the sale of goods | Sales-supporting services should be evaluated differently from revenue-producing services |
| Cost accounting is more important | Job-specific records will be required to assess the profitability of each sale |
| **b. Store organization** | |
| More specialized supervision | Separate management for service areas will be required |
| More specific search for service employees | Nontraditional sources for identification of employees must be used |
| Lower employee turnover | Frequent salary and performance reviews must be carried out |
| Higher pay for skilled craftspeople than for merchandising personnel | Pay levels will need to be adjusted upward over periods of longevity for service employees |
| **c. Service production** | |
| More involvement in manufacture of the service | Production skills will need to be obtained by supervisors |
| More emphasis on quality control | Supervisors must be able to assess the quality of a service performed for a customer |
| More need to monitor consumer satisfaction | Need for research with prior customers to measure their satisfaction with the service |
| More need to refine scheduling of employees | Maximizing the service employees' time requires matching consumer purchasing to ability to produce the service |
| Quality must be consistent among all outlets | Standards for consistency of the service must be established and continually evaluated; central training may be required for craftworkers in multiple-branch operations |
| **d. Pricing** | |
| Services vary in costs; therefore, pricing is more difficult | Prices may be quoted within a range instead of an exact figure before the purchase |
| More difficulty in price competition or promotion based upon price | Services should be promoted on the basis of criteria other than price |
| **e. Sales promotion** | |
| Value is more difficult for consumers to determine | Consumers need to be convinced of value through personal selling |
| Difficult to display within store | In-store signing or a service center is required to notify customers of services availability |
| Visual presentation is more important | Photographs of before-and-after may be possible with some services; testimonials may be possible with other services |
| Cross-selling with goods is important | A quota or bonus for goods salespersons who suggest services will lead to increased service selling |
| More difficult to advertise in catalogs | Conditions for the sale and away-from-the-store performance must be specified |
| **f. Complaints** | |
| More difficult to return a service | Policies must be established on adjusting the service purchased with a dissatisfied customer |
| A customer is more sensitive about services involving the person | Specific guarantees and policies about adjustments must be established; new types of insurance must be added to cover liabilities |
| **g. Controls** | |
| Greater opportunity to steal customers | Employee assurance of loyalty must be established; protection of store loyalty must be obtained |

goods retailers. Services can be considered as two types: first, those which accompany goods sold by retailers (such as watch repair or drapery installation), and second, those which are sold separately from a good (such as car rental, financial services, dental work, or legal services). This second type offers most retailers the greatest area for growth.

This article illustrates a number of potential management problems associated with the retailing of services, stemming from differences between services retailing and goods retailing. Retailers should be aware of these differences in order to be able to maximize their potential for success in services retailing. These differences and their managerial implications are summarized in Table 2.

The problems outlined should not discourage retailers from pursuing this growth area—rather, the objective is to convince the reader that services are an important part of the future of many retailers, particularly if market share for all consumer expenditures is to be maintained or increased. To make a successful transition from a goods-retailing orientation to one which includes both goods and services, management must adapt the organization to accept services retailing. If the adaptation is successful, the retailer can expect a rewarding future.

## REFERENCES

Berry, Leonard L. "Perspectives on the Retailing of Services." In *Theory in Retailing: Traditional and Non-Traditional Sources*, eds. Ronald W. Stampfl and Elizabeth C. Hirschman. Chicago: American Marketing Association, 1981, pp. 9–20.

Chase, Richard B. "Where Does the Customer Fit in a Service Organization?" *Harvard Business Review*, November–December 1978, pp. 137–42.

"Customer Services: The New Way to Exploit Profits." *Chain Store Age General Merchandise*, September 1975, pp. 124–32.

Davis, Duane L.; Joseph P. Guiltinan; and Wesley H. Jones. "Service Characteristics, Consumer Search, and the Classification of Retail Services." *Journal of Retailing*, Fall 1979, pp. 20–22.

Dearden, John. "Cost Accounting Comes to Service Industries." *Harvard Business Review*, September–October 1978, pp. 132–40.

George, William R., and Leonard L. Berry. "Guidelines for the Advertising of Services." *Business Horizons*, July–August 1981, pp. 52–56.

Guseman, Dennis S. "The Perception of Risk in Consumer Services—A Comparison with Consumer Products." DBA dissertation, University of Colorado, 1977.

Johnson, Eugene M. "Are Goods and Services Different? An Exercise in Marketing Theory." Ph.D. dissertation, Washington University, 1969.

Lewis, William. "An Empirical Investigation of the Conceptual Relationship between Services and Products in Terms of Perceived Risk." Ph.D. dissertation, University of Cincinnati, 1976.

"The New Sears: Unable to Grow in Retailing, It Turns to Financial Services." *Business Week*, November 16, 1981, pp. 140–46.

"Packaging Department Store Services." *Retailweek*, November 1, 1980, pp. 36, 38.

Rathmell, John. *Marketing in the Service Sector*. Cambridge, Mass.: Winthrop, 1974.

Sasser, Earl W. "Match Supply and Demand in Service Industries." *Harvard Business Review*, November–December 1976, pp. 133–40.

Schissel, Martin. "The Marketing of Services: Observations and Opportunities." In *Proceedings of the Southern Marketing Association Conference*, 1978, p. 471.

Shostack, Lynn G. "Breaking Free from Product Marketing." *Journal of Marketing*, April 1977, pp. 73–80.

Thomas, Dan R. E. "Strategy Is Different in Service Businesses." *Harvard Business Review*, July–August 1978, pp. 158–65.

Upah, Gregory D. "Mass Marketing in Service Retailing: A Review and Synthesis of Major Methods." *Journal of Retailing*. Fall 1980, pp. 59–76.

Woll, Milton. "Merchandising Services—Planning for the Next Decade." *Stores*, May 1975, pp. 35–36.

## QUESTIONS

1. *Explain the difference between "tangible dominant" services and "intangible dominant" services. Give examples of each.*

2. *Why are many retail services offered through leased departments in stores that emphasize the retailing of tangible goods? Is this likely to remain true in the future? Why or why not?*

3. *Explain why traditional retail management and merchandising tools often cannot be directly*

applied to the retailing of services in the following operational areas:

a. Measuring performance.
b. Store organization.
c. Service production.
d. Pricing.
e. Advertising and personal selling.
f. Sales promotion.
g. Customer complaints.
h. Controls.

4. Will the continued growth of services almost eliminate manufacturing in the American economy eventually? Why or why not?

---

☐ **24**

# How to sell by listening

*Jeremy Main*

---

*Show me an extroverted, fast-talking, joke-telling, back-slapping individual and I'll show you a "born salesperson"—right? Maybe not! As the following article suggests, good listeners might make more effective salespeople than smooth talkers. Moreover, one does not have to be born with such skills—they can be taught through sales training programs such as those described in the article. As you read the article, think about your own personality traits—and what kind of sales training program would benefit you the most.*

---

Get off the stage, Willy Loman. A smile and a shoeshine won't do it any longer. The fast-talking, yarn-spinning, hard-drinking peddler belongs to the past. Today's sales training teaches the salesperson to be a good listener and questioner, sensitive to the needs of others, knowledgeable about his products, more an adviser than a hustler. The pressure to fill order books hasn't let up. But the salesman shouldn't try to sell the client something he really doesn't need—and certainly not lots on Underwater Acres. He is a thoroughly good sort.

At least that's the high road to selling taught by the three major purveyors of sales training to American business. *Fortune* recently sampled short sales courses offered by the three: Xerox Learning Systems of Stamford, Connecticut, part of Xerox Corp.; Wilson Learning Corp. of Eden Prairie, Minnesota, a subsidiary of publisher John Wiley & Sons; and Forum Corp. of Boston, a $16-million-a-year company that specializes in management and sales training.

Somewhat to our surprise, we weren't taught any tricks of the trade, such as how to get by the dragon guarding your client's office. Instead all three courses stressed a high-principled style of selling that favors a close, trusting, long-term relationship over the quick sell. The approach works best for sales representatives who deal with customers on a continuing basis rather than in one-shot visits or phone calls. Richard D. Songey, an instructor for Forum, explains that "the philosophy is to serve the customer as a consultant, not as a peddler."

The experts in selling clearly know how to sell themselves, and clients like the message. Business is booming, with annual revenues from the sales courses climbing 30 percent or more in recent years. Most big corporations use the courses. Indeed, Xerox Learning alone counts among its clients 80 percent of the Fortune 500 industrial corporations. Wilson Learning taught sales techniques to 92,000 people in 1984, mostly salespersons, supervisors, and trainees. Xerox taught 75,000, and Forum, the newest of the three firms, 30,000. Du Pont uses all three companies to train its salespeople. AT&T is Wilson's biggest client.

The need to sell better has become urgent for several reasons. For example, deregulation made many companies more sales conscious, especially the banks and phone companies, which have to convert passive order takers into aggressive sellers. The average cost of an industrial sales call, as estimated by McGraw-Hill Research, has climbed to $205, so employers want every call to count.

The courses are lively two- or three-day affairs—considered the maximum time a salesman can be pulled out of his territory. No fear of flunking haunts the student. Everybody passes. The reading comes not in heavy tomes but in breezy pamphlets with a lot of empty space on the pages. Students can't lapse into the usual classroom stupor of school and college: at any moment they may be called on to act in an improvised sales skit or analyze the mistakes in video shows produced for the courses. A well-polished instructor keeps the class on its toes by orchestrating an entertaining mixture of video material, lectures, reading, quizzes, and role playing—with no segment dragging on too long. The thought of the cost may also keep the student awake, even though the employer usually pays. For the public seminars sampled by *Fortune,* Xerox charges $800 a head, Forum $570, and Wilson $540. The cost comes way down to $200 or $300 when corporations send students in platoons.

The selling style the courses try to teach is perhaps best defined by what it isn't. The bad salesman, says Curtis R. Berrien, senior vice president for Forum's western division, has "an inability to listen, to care, to get off his agenda and onto the customer's agenda, to be patient. He's pushy, talks all the time, goes in with preconceived notions, shoots down objections, drops a client after he makes the sale. He talks technical characteristics of the product rather than its bene-

fits for the customer. He doesn't know which accounts to call on, how to set priorities, how to follow a strategy." All three companies would pretty well agree that the good salesman is the opposite of these things. They each developed their concept of good salesmanship by sending researchers out with salesmen on calls and noting what worked and what didn't.

But the firms differ in what they teach. Wilson favors a behavioral approach, showing salesmen how to deal with customers' differing personalities. Xerox and Forum concentrate on the steps in the sales call from hello to closing.

Xerox puts on the slickest show. The latest version of its basic selling course, Professional Selling Skills, is presented partly on video-disks, which produce higher-quality graphics and color than do videotapes. The videodisks also allow "interactivity," as the training boffins call it, meaning that the show is not tied to a fixed script but reacts in different ways, depending on the students' answers. For example, the video system can conduct a quiz, with the sound and visual effects of a TV game show, including a fanfare for correct answers.

Will Boston, 29, a former Allstate and Johnson & Johnson salesman, runs the Xerox course I took recently in New York. Though he has given the course almost every week for a year, he retains his sharpness and humor. The class included a typical mix, from a brand-new college graduate to a stockbroker with years of experience. (A New York brokerage firm that Xerox won't identify has put all its partners through the course.)

In 2½ days Boston laid out for us in clear and simple form the basic steps in a sales call. Again and again he told the class that the question is the salesman's chief tool. "When in doubt, probe," he says. You probe to uncover a sales opportunity and then probe further to convert that opportunity into a need for your product. A fictional case, based on several used in Xerox's classrooms, illustrates the various ways the probing should proceed. For example, if you are selling a pen that writes in the water and upside down, you might ask, "Do your employees ever have to write under unusual conditions?" If the client replies that his West Coast people do a lot of their work in hot tubs and some of their best ideas get washed away, you have uncovered an opportunity. Don't bore the prospect with a description of technical features such as the vacuum-driven, supercalibrated, titanium ball point. Rather, talk about the benefits: how well the pen works underwater. You get the prospect to acknowledge the need ("Well, maybe it would be useful to read those notes") and then reinforce with a more pointed probe: "Don't these people lying in their hot tubs try to write upside down sometimes?"

Xerox teaches students how to deal with three kinds of obstacles: skepticism, objections, and indifference, of which indifference is hardest to overcome. When you encounter an indifferent prospect, you have to keep probing to discover an unrecognized need. For instance, if the prospect says the underwater pen has no advantage because his West Coast agents can wait until they dry off to take notes, you might ask, "Do they ever forget what they wanted to write by the time they dry off?" To counter skepticism, offer proof: "Here's an affidavit from the Scooba Dooba Club that they signed with our pen 100 feet underwater." Don't argue with a client; acknowledge his objection and move on to something positive.

All the while, the salesman should be watching for a buy signal—some phrase that indicates the client is ready to sign ("Well, I guess these pens might be pretty useful") or even a gesture or facial expression. The alert salesman moves instantly into the close.

All this seemed straightforward enough until Boston asked students to start play-acting the roles of customer and salesman, using all his techniques in the proper sequence. He was gracious enough not to characterize my efforts as a disaster. However, he did admonish me once, saying, "You're telling, not selling." In other words, instead of getting to know the customer's needs I was just spieling. Later, in my enthusiasm to sell some chemical that I knew nothing about, I was caught in an outright lie about where the product was made, which finished that sales call.

Forum's basic course, Face-to-Face Selling Skills, came on the market a year ago and was an instant success. Revenues from the course amounted to $1 million in the first four months. The Forum terminology is a little different, but the message is basically the same as Xerox's: put yourself in the client's shoes, ask questions, listen

to the answers, and satisfy the customer's concerns. Whereas Xerox stresses a fast move to close as soon as a prospect starts nibbling, Forum teaches a slower approach—wait until you have talked out all the questions with the client before asking for his signature.

Forum instructors talk about the importance of the "high gain" question—the question that gets the client to open up with revealing information about his needs. Unfortunately Forum can't define a high-gain question except in terms of the answer. So the salesman doesn't know if he has asked a high-gain question until he hears the answer. Forum likes to refer to the style it teaches as "consultative selling." In other words, you are trying to help this dear old client, who is practically a member of the family, rather than just pushing iron.

Wilson Learning calls its approach "counselor selling." Founder Larry Wilson developed his ideas after thinking about his own success three decades ago as a life insurance salesman. While he was still in his 20s, his exploits made him a life member of the Million Dollar Round Table, a group of agents who in those days had to sell at least $1 million of life insurance in a year. Life members had to hit the target three years running or four out of five years. Wilson, co-author of the recent best-seller *The One Minute Sales Person,* founded his company 20 years ago to teach what he had learned. He remains chairman, although he sold the company to John Wiley & Sons in 1982.

Social Styles Sales Strategies, the Wilson course I sampled in Scottsdale, Arizona, was taught by Ann Swink Roza, 45, a vivacious former public relations counselor. She began by explaining how Wilson divided people into four behavior types: "analytical," "driver," "amiable," and "expressive." Everybody, she says, has a dominant and a secondary type. Before the course starts, Wilson surveys each student's business colleagues and customers for their opinions of him and feeds the results to a computer. I was classed an analytical type with an expressive secondary strain. Acting on the finding, the Wilson computer printed out a series of horoscopelike comments about me. I was told, for example: "You may want to *temporarily* modify your behavior to limit tension and help others to feel more comfortable with you."

The point of this amateur psychologizing is to know how to deal with the sales prospect. For instance, if the prospect's big hello and vivid clothing tell you he is primarily an expressive type, you will never make a sale unless you take the time to establish a warm personal relationship. When you finally start talking business, don't bore him with too many details. He has a short attention span. If the customer is chiefly analytical, on the other hand, he doesn't expect friendship but does want a lot of facts and reasoning. For two days Roza drilled us in recognizing character types—which proved relatively easy—and then had us practice in some brief skits how to approach the different types. She gave her own dramatic simulations, ranging from an oily amiable to a shouting, finger-pointing driver.

People who take these courses almost invariably say they are great, but objective proof that they improve sales performance is hard to come by. To make a thorough before-and-after analysis of the courses' benefits would cost more than the training itself, so most corporations just take a rough reading on the results. David N. White, director of sales training for Honeywell's information systems division, says, "We don't quantify results. We can't afford it. I measure effectiveness by usage. If what's learned in the course is used, then it is successful." By that reasonable standard, most companies appear well satisfied.

A few have gone a little deeper. Commerce Clearing House Inc., a prosperous publisher of tax information, has found a big improvement in the performance of salespeople who take the Xerox course compared with those who don't. The difference varies from division to division. In one the Xerox-trained salesmen increased their billings by 33.7 percent on average while the others improved by only 2.5 percent. In another division the figures were 14.6 percent and 2.5 percent.

The most common complaint about the courses is that they are too general and don't apply to the specific needs of the client. To meet this criticism, all three companies will tailor their courses, at a price. They will also deliver the courses in a variety of ways to suit the client—for example, by training the client's employees to become instructors and deliver the courses under license.

Adaptability to the client's needs has become a major consideration in selecting the training companies. David White surveyed the field of sales training for Honeywell and rejected Wilson and Xerox because they couldn't customize their courses enough to suit him. He finally chose a smaller company, Spectrum Training Corp. of Salem, Massachusetts, because it was willing to make major revisions, and later added Forum. Gillette Co. also chose Forum after surveying a dozen training companies because Forum was willing to rewrite its course page by page. Gillette is an enthusiastic convert to sales training. Twenty years ago at the razor blade company, says Lewis F. Schoonover, director of sales training development, "you loaded up your car and headed down the road. That was your training." Gillette started in-house sales courses in 1965 and added outside firms in the 1970s.

On one point everyone seems to agree: if there is no follow-up after the course, then the lessons will soon be forgotten. John J. Franco, president of Xerox Learning, notes a big increase in follow-up coaching and reviews in the past few years. Many companies send managers out with salesmen to observe their performance, or send questionnaires to customers. The training companies provide follow-up tapes or booklets to be used from time to time. Wilson and Forum furnish half-day or one-day refresher sessions. Without such reminders, says White, a salesman will lose 90 percent of what he learns within a year.

## Questions

1. *Compare and contrast the characteristics of "good" and "bad" salespeople, as discussed in the article.*

2. *Compare and contrast the emphasis and approach of the three sales training programs described in the article. Which training program would you prefer to go through if you were hired for a sales position right after college? Why?*

3. *Should all salespeople be taught the sales approach stressed in this article? Would the Xerox, Wilson, and Forum training programs be appropriate for all salespeople? Why or why not?*

4. *Think of the best salesperson that you have ever met. Was that person a good listener or a fast talker? Explain the buying situation.*

☐ **25**

# National account managers to the rescue

*Arthur J. Bragg*

*Salespeople have traditionally been assigned to a specific geographic territory and been viewed as "territory managers." Now, to better serve large and important accounts—many of which have centralized their purchasing decisions—many salespeople are being assigned to specific accounts. These "national account managers" are expected to serve their accounts whenever and wherever the account needs them—regardless of geographic location. This article explains this trend in personal selling—discussing the benefits of national account marketing, as well as some of the special problems it creates.*

For anyone keeping up with the "ins" and "outs" in national account marketing—selling your most important customers by giving responsibility for each to managers who handle all of your diverse product lines—here's the latest scorecard:

**Outs.** Long a believer in a corporate national account program, Union Carbide now mostly prefers to let its eight operating divisions each sell their products on their own. Behind the change, it's said, is a loss of zeal for national account marketing by top management and its acceptance of the argument that national account managers cannot match the divisional salespeople's knowledge, product by product. Also out: National Steel.

**Ins.** A true believer, IBM moved even closer to the national account approach as a result of its January reorganization. Also, Air Products & Chemicals, Federal Express, and Shade Information Systems now have a national account program. Likely new candidates in the computer field are Wang Laboratories, Prime Computer, and Teradyne.

**Ifs.** Monsanto management would dearly like to have a program but so far has been unable to solve the problems of setting one up. It's still trying.

Clearly, the "ins" have it. Indeed, many are convinced that national account marketing is to be the trend of the 1980s. The reasons they cite include the growing number of corporate mergers and acquisitions, resulting in an "economic concentration" that means fewer customers and more of them firm believers in centralized purchasing functions. Another reason cited is that many selling companies, like their customers, are growing more complex, with broader product lines that could profit from a national account approach; a case in point is American Bell, AT&T's new subsidiary that sells to many industries.

Also fueling the trend is the anxiety of top management that the revenue from prime customers must be protected, especially now. William R. Lindstrom, vice president for national accounts at Purex, recently told *Progressive Grocer*, "With our company's success so closely linked with that of our prime customers, it was in our own interest to find new ways to be of help to them. We pioneered cost-justified backhaul privileges, prepayment or billback options on performance allowances, and other benefits. The national account marketing function must be just that—a planned program with full accountability and not just a trade relations effort."

Perhaps the most compelling reason of all for the growth in national account marketing is that it fosters joint planning by supplier and customer, a

Source: *Sales & Marketing Management* magazine August 16, 1982, pp. 30–34. Reproduced by permission. At the time of writing, Arthur Bragg was senior editor of *Sales & Marketing Management*.

point not lost on purchasing executives who recall the horrors of the 1972–74 shortages crunch. It was then that many centralized purchasing offices—and a host of national account programs too—were created as companies took steps to prevent the worst elements of that crisis ever happening to them again.

## PURCHASING LIKES THEM

A survey of purchasing executives by the National Account Marketing Association (NAMA), New York City, shows that their zeal for national account marketing is as strong as ever. The survey, which drew more than half its responses from $1 billion-and-over corporations, concludes that "the rapid pace of change requires that customers and suppliers both be equipped to turn on a dime."

Best estimates put the number of national account managers at between 12,000 and 15,000, although most sell only a single product line rather than their company's total product offerings. Says Dr. Rowland T. Moriarty, Harvard Business School, who with Dr. Benson P. Shapiro, also at Harvard, has just completed a massive study of the subject, "National account marketing will be a phenomenal topic in the 1980s."

American Hospital Supply Corporation's (AHSC) Terry Mulligan also expects the 1980s to be a boom period for national account marketing, particularly at AHSC. "In some of our divisions, 40 percent of sales are with corporate clients. It is our greatest growing segment," he says. It is no accident that the marketing structure of the Evanston, Illinois (1981 sales: $3 billion), company is geared specifically toward selling national or corporate accounts. One of the major trends in the hospital field over the past decade has been the consolidation of hospitals into chains, or multiple systems, making national accounts increasingly important.

That, says Mulligan, who is AHSC's vice president of corporate sales, puts the company in the catbird seat. As both manufacturer and distributor of medical and surgical supplies, AHSC's 22 divisions equip hospitals with the gamut of provisions they need, from laboratory and surgical supplies to bedpans, paper, and food services. In the competitive medical supply business, peppered with small, specialized vendors, AHSC's national scope is matched only by Richmond, Virginia-based Wittaker General Medical.

In each of AHSC's highly autonomous divisions, there is a director of national accounts, who in most cases has vice presidential status, making him equal in rank to the division's sales and marketing chiefs. Each coordinates his sales through Mulligan, who, as AHSC's overall corporate sales executive, is responsible for maintaining close contact with every major client's senior management.

AHSC's corporate marketing structure also features a close-knit relationship internally. "Actually, the customer heads the organizational chart," Mulligan says with just a hint of exaggeration. The field representative, who services national accounts on a day-to-day basis, has authority to speak for the company, and he is given training on handling corporate accounts. "It is vital to have the field salesperson in the loop, or you will emasculate him," Mulligan says. AHSC also emphasizes an involvement in corporate accounts by its top management, starting with Chairman Karl Bays. "The large customer knows him and can call him on the phone about a problem," Mulligan says.

A key advantage in all this is that AHSC is able to be consistent both in pricing and in the service it offers to hospital chains in far-flung locations. "We load all pricing in at one point," says Mulligan, "and we can make sure customers are all serviced as stipulated in the contract. This puts us way ahead."

Because it is keyed to those accounts that promise the greatest sales volume and profitability, AHSC's program meets the primary characteristic of successful national account marketing. It also has two other essentials: (1) It has both the support and the active involvement of top management, and (2) it is headed by a sales executive who has status within his company. To succeed, says NAMA executive director Ernest C. Biglow, Jr., a "national account manager must get the resource commitment he needs." Harvard's Shapiro and Moriarty agree that unless the top sales executive has power within his company, even starting up a program will be well-nigh impossible. Biglow notes that the top national account executives at both Dow Chemical, whose program dates back to 1964, and Shell Oil have easy access to their chief executive officers.

Most programs will need a "godfather," usually someone who recognizes that national account marketing will solve a problem vexing the company's traditional sales operation. In their study, being published in installments by Marketing Science Institute, Cambridge, Massachusetts, Shapiro and Moriarty also note that many such programs start with house accounts, handled exclusively by management executives with a historical relationship with these customers, that sooner or later become too valuable or too complex for such an approach. This was the case at Olin Corporation's Chemical Group in the mid-1970s. By the late 1970s, its national account department was born, and soon it was handling 42 accounts representing 50 percent of total dollar sales. Shapiro and Moriarty also report that invariably a national account program starts off "timidly." One should not be undertaken, they add, if the selling process is relatively simple or the product line loaded with many customized items. Also, be prepared to spend an average of one to three years to cultivate each new national account.

## UNION'S MAN IN PITTSBURGH

Also convinced that national account marketing is the wave of the future is Raymond D. Jolicoeur, general manager of national accounts at the 76 Division of Union Oil Company of California, which sells oil, wax, bulk lube, jet fuel, and other petroleum items. His reasoning: "More large companies are centralizing their purchasing decisions because of the computer information they have and the higher costs of the product they buy. You will find more selling companies going the same route."

Union launched its program in 1965 for such clients as railroads, airlines, heavy industrial companies, and the military. Jolicoeur, who reports to Robert E. Robbins, vice president of national marketing, oversees the program from his headquarters in Schaumburg, Illinois. A major benefit it pays, he says, is that it slashes the number of sales calls his division must make to sell its products to customers that need them in many different locations. He cites one of his national

accounts, U.S. Steel, in Pittsburgh, as a prime example. "We couldn't have salesmen from 10 or 15 areas all contacting its headquarters. So we have one man who calls on Pittsburgh for the account for all of our people. Buying companies prefer to have one man call on them rather than several," he says.

Signode Corporation, Glenview, Illinois, which claims to be the world's largest maker of steel and plastic strapping systems, entrusts its 250 biggest customers to its national account department. The three managers assigned to it (there are also an office manager and two administrative assistants) concentrate on the top 100, worth 50 percent of the company's $700 million volume last year, and with the others where necessary. That is one of the heaviest account loads to turn up in *Sales & Marketing Management's* research. To help them turn the trick, says one of the national account managers, John T. Truty, the department relies on a strong communications program started last year. It stresses how national account marketing works at Signode and, as often as possible, why it pays to be a Signode national account.

Now at the printers is the fourth issue of *Focus*, a slick six-page quarterly that runs in-house written features about Signode products or services relevant to the national account customers. "It keeps our name in the customer's mind and helps build confidence in us," Truty explains. "We're the leader in the industry but certainly not the cheapest."

*Focus* also highlights three services that Signode offers exclusively to national accounts:

An annual report on contributions details particular customers' cost savings which Signode products or advice made possible; it also shows how much time the sales force spent on that customer.

A customer application development review offers technical cost-cutting advice to customers. The source: Signode engineers who visit each of the customers' locations looking for ways to cut costs in areas where Signode products are or could be used. As a result, Truty says, "We know more about their organizations than they do."

A visitation program. Although it will not pick up the tab, Signode asks its top customers to inspect its facilities.

## SPOTTING THE TREND

Truty notes that by having had his national account department in place by the mid-1970s, when many of Signode's customers also made the shift to centralized purchasing, the company saved some accounts in the short term. With its traditional strength at the plant level, it could have been caught without needed contacts at customers' headquarters, he says, adding, "We could have been in trouble."

Top management's growing acceptance of the theory that 20 percent of customers account for 80 percent of sales is prompting a surge also in that other kind of national account manager—the one who sells only a single product line to accounts that represent the best sales possibilities. At Sears, Roebuck's Automotive Division, that means major auto fleets, a business the retailer didn't have until it set up a national account program. The national account roster there now includes such companies as Xerox, Hertz, Avis, and Gelco; all use Sears' auto centers or truck tire centers from coast to coast for most routine maintenance needs and for Sears' tires and batteries, all at "national account discounted prices" of up to 35 percent off. George Nelson, who heads Sears' 12-person national account office in Chicago, insists that "it's an easy sell because it means better pricing and cost control for the customer."

Two companies now trying national account selling for the first time are Zenith Data Systems, Glenville, Illinois, and Mansfield Sanitary, Perrysville, Ohio, a division of Interpace Corporation. Zenith's experiment—only one national account manager, Ronald T. Simkins, has been named so far—is aimed at finding "national and multinational corporations" for its desk-top computer units, says national sales manager John Frank, whose 24 regional distributors "will be included in whatever formula we decide upon" in the attempt to tap the major accounts.

## NEW MARKET PENETRATION

Mansfield Sanitary had always concentrated on plumbing and hardware wholesalers; it is now developing a national account program whose targets are national hardware cooperatives and buying groups and, especially, the nation's biggest retailers, notes marketing vice president Mark Haddock. To help Tony Purcell, Mansfield's just-named national account manager, win such accounts, the company is at work on product innovations and four-color packaging that eschews an "industrial" look.

In addition to selling and servicing the accounts, Purcell acts as an adviser to them, offering Mansfield's experience and in-depth product analysis to help determine which merchandise will sell in their stores. "The manufacturer has a responsibility to give guidance to an account and not simply sell the whole catalog," Haddock says.

Since beginning its program, Mansfield has increased its sales to national hardware co-ops, such as Ace and Cotter, and is penetrating hardware buying groups. Progress among the retailers includes products now in test marketing programs at K mart and product presentations to Sears, Roebuck.

Mansfield's program for selling to buying groups is seldom used in the industry, Haddock claims. Describing it as "classic" push-pull marketing, he says Purcell pushes by selling such products as a do-it-yourself toilet repair valve to the groups' merchandise managers, while Mansfield's regional sales representatives use incentive or awards to motivate the hardware wholesalers' sales forces, creating pull.

Companies whose national account managers coordinate the total selling effort of their companies rather than handling a single product line, such as those just described, naturally are prone to special problems. For instance, a national account program may tend to dilute technical and product knowledge, especially when the accounts are handled without much field sales force participation. Also, it may tend to create a "priority conflict"—commodity versus performance volume versus long-term goals.

J. Paul Ekberg, director of marketing services at Tenneco Chemicals, identifies the most common source of conflict, however. "A program that relegates regular salespeople to messenger or water boy roles will be resisted," he says, sometimes to the point of causing the program to fall apart altogether. Trouble can have its source higher up in the chain of command, notes Harvard's Moriarty. "When a national account goes out of a division, the division sales manager goes bananas." Often adding to the turmoil is the aura

# How national account managers are paid

A study for *Sales & Marketing Management* by Sibson & Co., a Princeton-based management consulting firm, shows that there is a considerable difference in the compensation paid to national account managers in consumer durable goods companies (which, in the study, included some light and heavy industrial goods companies) versus that paid to those at nondurable consumer goods concerns. Reason: The greater sophistication required in durable goods selling. The study also shows that there is only a gradual increase in compensation as company revenues increase—suggesting that the amount of sales handled by national account managers tends to remain fairly constant irrespective of total company sales. Apparently, companies add more national account managers instead of increasing the account load of veteran ones. Sibson's specialist for sales and marketing compensation, Matt Savage Walton III, estimates that the top compensation paid national account managers ranges as high as $85,000–$90,000 in companies with sales above $1 billion.

**1982 base salary levels**

Company revenues

| | |
|---|---|
| $1 million | $36,500 |
| $10 million | $40,800 |
| $100 million | $45,500 |
| $500 million | $49,000 |
| $1 billion | $50,500 |

that surrounds many national account salespeople, whether deliberately induced or an accident, which NAMA's Biglow colorfully describes as the "Green Beret syndrome."

The solution? "A number of large corporations assign responsibility jointly between the national account executive and the regional office that has order responsibility," says Tenneco Chemicals' Ekberg. At Union Oil's 76 Division, Raymond Jolicoeur avoids "personality problems" by giving field salespeople "all the credit for the sale." His advice for others is "sell them [field salespeople] on what it is you can do to help them get their job done." Some programs call for splitting commissions with the local field salespeople. But, comments Sibson & Co.'s Matt Walton, who

specializes in sales and marketing compensation (see the Exhibit on pages 192–93): "That can be messy."

## THE PROBLEM OF COSTS

Although its rewards can be considerable—the dollars handled are often "phenomenal," one source declares—having a national account program is costly. Industry sources say that National Steel, Pittsburgh, the sixth-biggest steel producer, recently quit its program partly due to its cost. A company spokesman insists that its major accounts have not been affected, however. Amoco Oil Company, Chicago, just turned over responsi-

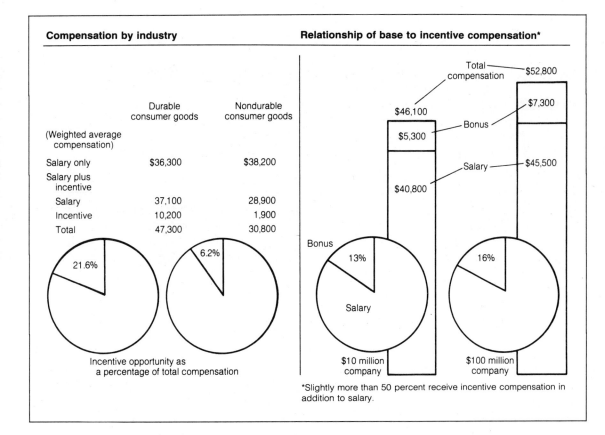

**Compensation by industry**

| (Weighted average compensation) | Durable consumer goods | Nondurable consumer goods |
|---|---|---|
| Salary only | $36,300 | $38,200 |
| Salary plus incentive | | |
| Salary | 37,100 | 28,900 |
| Incentive | 10,200 | 1,900 |
| Total | 47,300 | 30,800 |

21.6%

6.2%

Incentive opportunity as a percentage of total compensation

**Relationship of base to incentive compensation\***

Total compensation $52,800

$46,100

$7,300
Bonus

$5,300

Salary $45,500

$40,800

Bonus

13%

16%

Salary

$10 million company

$100 million company

\*Slightly more than 50 percent receive incentive compensation in addition to salary.

bility for its major trucking customers to local salespeople to cut down its national account people's travel expenses.

Indeed, the cost of setting up programs now is credited with keeping some companies from experimenting with them. "There are very few discretionary dollars out there right now," says V. B. Chamberlain III, former industrial marketing manager at Stanley Works, New Britain, Connecticut, now a national account consultant. But he, and others, are convinced, because national account programs, at the least, permit marketers to defend themselves against what their customers may do or, more important, put them a step ahead of the times, that once the economy soars, such programs will too.

## QUESTIONS

1. *What exactly is a "national account manager," and what are his or her typical responsibilities?*

2. *Why is national account management a growing trend?*

3. *What are the advantages of national account managers for the buyer? For the seller?*

4. *What special personal selling problems are likely to arise when a firm uses national account managers? How can such problems be avoided or minimized?*

5. *Under what circumstances would you advise a firm not to use national account managers? Explain your answer.*

\*6. *Would the selling approach and training programs discussed in Reading 24 be appropriate for national account managers? Why or why not?*

---

\*Question relates concepts in this and other readings.

## ☐ 26

# Behind the scenes at an American Express commercial

## *Mark N. Vamos*

*For more than 10 years, American Express ran its familiar "Do you know me?" TV commercials aimed at successful, older businessmen. Then they decided to switch to a new "Interesting Lives" approach aimed at younger professional women and men. The new approach worked for women—but not for men. The following article describes American Express' latest attempt to reach the young male market. It provides a vivid description of all the marketing research, creative planning, production detail, testing, and sponsor-ad agency negotiations that go into the making of a 30-second television commercial.*

The marketing executives from American Express Co. are unhappy. After months of research, pre-preproduction meetings, preproduction meetings, casting sessions, budget audits, and other preparations for this moment, they arrive on location for the filming of their new television commercial—only to find the leading man wearing the wrong jacket.

In a big national ad campaign, little things like this count. "We believe that advertising is important enough that you want to get it right," says Diane Shaib, vice-president for consumer marketing at American Express. For this commercial, getting it right is especially urgent: Both the client and its agency, Ogilvy & Mather, have a lot riding on the outcome. American Express is eager to get more men in their 20s and 30s to sign for its plastic charge card. Ogilvy needs to come up with a successful commercial after the failure of a recent string of American Express ads that the client pulled off the air. Both nervously await reaction to the 30-second ad, which cost about $100,000 and is now hitting the national airwaves.

### WARDROBE CHAOS

Just days before the filming, the American Express marketers discuss the wardrobe with the agency. What will look more universal, they wonder—a blue blazer or a corduroy jacket? They are still pondering the question and leaning toward the blazer when they walk onto the set and find the actor wearing a dark corduroy jacket. Some of the scenes have already been shot, and the budget clock is ticking. Amid the controlled chaos of a commercial shoot, exasperation is rising behind polite smiles, urgent confabulations are held in corners, and higher authorities are summoned.

For more than 10 years, American Express has been running its "Do you know me?" commercials, aimed at its traditional market: successful, older businessmen. Three years ago, however, AmEx decided to pursue the large number of younger women entering the work force and launched its "Interesting Lives" series. The first commercial, its "New Card" spot, showed a young woman taking her husband out to dinner to celebrate the arrival of her card, and it scored big. Women applied in droves. By last year, they held 27 percent of all AmEx green cards, up from 10 percent in the 1970s. The spot won awards and lavish praise for showing a strong, successful woman.

Source: Reprinted from the May 20, 1985, issue of *Business Week* by special permission, © 1985 by McGraw-Hill, Inc. At the time of writing, Mark N. Vamos was on the staff of *Business Week*.

While that reaction startled American Express, subsequent audience research surprised the company even more. Instead of offending young men by showing a woman taking a man out to dinner, the commercial actually attracted them. "We're talking about three years ago—and markets outside of New York," says Shaib. "That's a bit shocking."

That's also when the trouble started. The company and its agency decided to extend the "Interesting Lives" campaign to attract young men by intention rather than by accident—in effect, to turn it into an all-purpose yuppie campaign. "The mission is to tweak their awareness of the card's appropriateness for them," says Shaib. Over the next three years, the company shot six new ads, but the only things they seemed to tweak were noses. One by one, as audience reaction arrived, AmEx pulled the ads. Two were so troublesome that they never even made it past the test-marketing stage. One showed a woman paying for dinner on a first date, the other a husband accompanying his wife on her business trip. Audience reactions included words such as "abrasive" and "castrating"—not exactly the message American Express wanted to convey. "It's very difficult these days to do ads with men and women as equals," sighs Kathleen O'Shaughnessy, a manager of marketing research at AmEx.

Early this year, the client and the agency agreed to try again, and Ogilvy wrote five new commercials. This time, however, AmEx decided to test the spots in rough form before any were produced, something it had not done before. Each ad was translated into color sketches that were transferred onto slides. Actors recorded the accompanying dialogue. With the roughs in hand, AmEx and Ogilvy headed into the field.

**ONE-WAY MIRROR**

At 8 o'clock one evening in late February, nine men and a moderator sit around a gray conference table in midtown Manhattan. They are the targets of the campaign—young men who are eligible for an American Express card but haven't applied. Each will receive $50 for participating in this focus group, the last of 11 such sessions held nationwide. Observing them from a darkened room behind a one-way mirror are 11 staffers from AmEx and Ogilvy, including account managers, researchers, and copywriters. Surprisingly, in a commercial aimed at men, all the observers are women.

Eugene Shore, a psychologist and president of Business Information Analysis Corp., a Pennsylvania research firm, shows the five rough commercials. He asks the focus group for comments and suggestions after each. Some win raves, others are panned. After one rough is shown, someone says, "If I saw this on TV, I'd just say, 'Boy, this is another one of those dumb commercials that make no sense.' "

Working with comments like these, the marketers have already narrowed the choice to two or three strong candidates, one of which is known as "Young Lawyer." It opens with father and son seated at a restaurant table. The dialogue concerns the son's career and how disappointed the father was when he didn't join the family law firm. But now that the son is "Mr. District Attorney," the father is proud of him. The son objects, saying he's only "an assistant to an assistant." He places his American Express card on the tray that the waiter puts on the table with the check. The father laughs, saying: "The pay must be getting better over at City Hall."

The lights come up, and Shore asks for reactions. "I feel this is pointed at the business community, because you have to be successful to have this card," says Stephen, an accountant. Tim, who works for a menswear designer, disagrees: "He says he's an assistant to an assistant. So maybe I can qualify." The women behind the mirror smile at this response. The line is a crucial one. To attract new cardholders, the commercial must convey accessibility—but not too much. The American Express card is prestige plastic. The ad can't make it seem as easy to get as MasterCard or Visa, which AmEx staffers contemptuously refer to as "shoppers' cards." As O'Shaughnessy, the market researcher, later puts it, "It's very difficult to communicate eligibility and at the same time maintain prestige. We're sort of talking out of both sides of our mouth."

**'TOO NORTHEAST'**

Over the next few weeks, Ogilvy staffers begin scouting locations for "Young Lawyer." They also hunt for a director with a flair for filming realistic dialogue. "This ad lives and dies on being able to cast two people who have believable rapport," says Ann Curry Marcato, the Ogilvy vice-president responsible for producing the spot. And, Shore warns at the session, the father and son risk "coming across as WASP, bank-club, Harvard."

It is late March when the account-management team from Ogilvy and two executives from American Express hold a preproduction meeting to go over the casting, wardrobe, location, and production schedule. That's when the problem of the corduroy jacket first surfaces. "The feedback we've been getting from the research is that the Midwest and West Coast don't respond because they read it as too Northeast," says K. Shelly Porges, director of special markets at AmEx. "Can we do something more cross-country?" Ogilvy's Marcato replies that the agency is aware of the problem, and the discussion moves to other topics.

Ed Bianchi, Marcato's choice for director, who once shot a Dr Pepper extravaganza set on a giant pinball machine, outlines his notion of how the commercial should unfold. He plans to open with a wide shot, showing diners and waiters, and then cut to a close-up of the father and son. "We pick them out through the crowd so you really have the feeling of eavesdropping on them," he says.

Porges objects to opening with a wide shot crowded with 14 extras. "What makes this an interesting life, anyway? The quality of the relationship. What will a long shot add to that?" she asks. Paul Pracilio, a vice-president and associate creative director at Ogilvy, replies: "We have 30 seconds to reach out of that tube and grab someone by the necktie. By cutting in to see them, it's a damn sight more exciting piece of film."

## HAPPY MEDIUM

The discussion moves to the waiter who will bring the check. Since the ad must make the card seem upscale but still accessible, the waiter can't look as if he works at too ritzy a restaurant. "It must be above Brew Burger but below the 21 Club," says Porges. Director Bianchi suggests that the waiter appear early in the commercial, as the son is saying he's only an assistant to an assistant district attorney. "The action of the waiter

bringing the check is a subtle hint of what this commercial is going to be about," he says. Porges objects again. "Because of the 'assistant to an assistant' line, the focus groups said, 'Gee, maybe I could get this card,' " she says. "Getting that part garbled would be disastrous to us."

Three days later, the film crew has converted Jerry's Restaurant in Manhattan into a madhouse. The sidewalk is a jumble of cables, reflecting panels, and tripods. In the dining room, 25 crew members mill about, carrying equipment and shouting. The father-and-son team sits at a table, repeating their lines. The entire commercial will be reshot from several angles, Bianchi explains, to give the editor the option of cutting from one perspective to another.

Representatives from Ogilvy and AmEx are at the back of the room, watching and making suggestions. Still more staffers are in another room, watching a video monitor. Director Bianchi calls for take after take. Frequently, a telephone rings or a bus rumbles past on 23rd Street, ruining the shot. For most of the takes, Bianchi sits next to the camera, his face pressed against the lens so he can see what it is seeing, and grins at the actors.

After 43 takes involving dialogue—and dozens more without sound—Bianchi is satisfied. But suddenly, he insists on one more close-up of the son pulling the charge card from his wallet. The executives from Ogilvy and American Express are crowded around a video monitor, staring intently as the image of the wallet fills the screen. The son's hand reaches over, pulls out the card, and pauses. It's a Visa card. Everyone laughs and goes home.

## TENSE TRYOUT

A week later, the preliminary version of the commercial is ready. A dozen client and agency people sit in red bucket chairs in an eighth-floor screening room at Ogilvy & Mather's New York office. Tension is in the air—not least because, after all the discussion of wide shots and extras, those scenes wound up on the cutting-room floor. "We were thrilled to find so much of the personality of the son and father coming through," Marcato explains as she introduces the commercial. "We thought that it would be strongest to stay up tight."

The commercial is run several times. The ad seems a bit choppy, jumping from close-ups of the son to the father to the check to the wallet and, finally, to the card. The Ogilvy team waits for a reaction.

"I think you've captured them just as I always envisioned them," says Shaib, the AmEx marketing vice-president. "But because of the number of cuts back and forth, I never feel like I'm intimate with them." She also points out that, with all the close-ups, the commercial never shows the father and son together. After some discussion, the Ogilvy representatives agree to reedit the commercial to include the wide shot that American Express had initially argued against.

AmEx executives say they are pleased with the final version, which includes the wide shot. All the research was worthwhile, they say, because it helped them avoid some pitfalls, such as making the father too stern or the son too wimpy. The father's line about his son's pay getting better, for example, was ultimately given to the son because some viewers saw it as a subtle put-down. Now, the marketers say, the father is distinguished but warm, and the son is the kind of likable but independent character with whom the target market can identify.

The ad, which first appeared on May 6, will run for six to eight weeks, after which American Express will assess its impact. The company thinks it has a winner, but there's one little thing that still bothers it a bit: The son is wearing a corduroy jacket.

## QUESTIONS

1. Why did the "Interesting Lives" approach work for young women but not for young men? Should American Express and its ad agency have anticipated this negative reaction from male audiences?

2. Discuss the relationship between marketing research and creative planning (i.e., copywriting, casting, filming, etc.) in the making of a TV commercial. Which is more important?

3. Do you think the "Young Lawyer" commercial will be successful in accomplishing American Express' objectives? Why or why not?

4. Do you think television is the best medium for reaching young males? Would American Express be better off using direct mail, magazines, or some other medium? Explain.

☐ **27**

# How advertising can position a brand

*Robert E. Smith*

*Robert F. Lusch*

*This reading illustrates how advertising accomplishes one of its key functions—creating a psychological position for a brand. Smith and Lusch first distinguish between "product position"— the objective (physical) attributes of a brand relative to competition—and "position"— a product's subjective attitudes relative to competition. Advertising—according to Smith and Lusch—can be used to develop or change the position of a brand. Using an example, the authors demonstrate how this can be accomplished.*

*Positioning* is a term that has enjoyed widespread use in recent years. However, there appears to be considerable confusion as to its exact meaning (Holmes, 1973). Further complicating matters is the present lack of a sound methodological procedure for measuring the success or failure of a positioning or repositioning campaign of a product.

In light of these fundamental problems, this article has two closely related goals. First, in the hope of reducing the ambiguity surrounding this term, we will explicitly define two different types of positions that a product occupies. Second, we will present a practical methodology that can be used to evaluate the effects of an advertising campaign whose stated goal is to reposition a product.

## POSITIONING DEFINED

A product is a bundle of objective and subjective attributes. Objective attributes of an automobile would include power steering, automatic transmission, engine size, color, and price. Subjective attributes are intangible and would include styling, luxury, prestige of ownership, etc. Clearly, marketing is involved with both the objective (product) features and the subjective (consumer perceptions) features. Indeed, for several years

marketers and advertisers have used a term to describe the relative merit of a product's objective attributes. As Trout and Ries (1972a) explain: "Positioning has its roots in the packaged goods field where the concept was called 'Product Positioning.' It literally meant the product's form, package size, and price as compared to competition." Thus, for some time the term *product position* has been used to refer to the objective characteristics of a product vis-à-vis all competing brands.

In 1969, a new type of positioning was delineated in a series of articles by Trout and, later, Ries. Trout and Ries's use of the term *position* differed markedly from the term *product position* in that the newer term dealt with the consumer's perceptions or images of the product (i.e., the brand's subjective features). In this first joint effort, Trout and Ries (1972a) indicated the potency of the position of a product: "For today we are entering an era that recognizes both the importance of the product and the company image, but more than anything else, stresses the need to create a 'position' in the prospect's mind."

Source: Reprinted with permission from the *Journal of Advertising Research*, February 1976, pp. 222–27. Copyright © 1976 by the Advertising Research Foundation. At the time of writing, Robert E. Smith was former director of media and research at the Boelter Company and Robert F. Lusch was assistant professor of business administration at the University of Oklahoma.

There is a fundamental difference, then, between product position and position. *Product position* refers to a brand's objective attributes in relation to other brands. It is a characteristic of the physical product and its functional features. *Position,* on the other hand, refers to a product's subjective attributes in relation to competing products. This perceived image of the brand belongs, not to the product, but rather is the property of the consumers' mental perceptions and, in some instances, could differ widely from a brand's true physical characteristics.

The product position of a gasoline, for instance, will be determined by its octane rating, lead content, additives, miles per gallon, etc. Competing brands are likely to be quite similar with respect to these features. A gasoline's position, however, is determined by subjective attributes or consumers' beliefs about the brand (i.e., their image of that product). Clearly, these perceptions will be influenced by the objective features of the product; but other factors, notably advertising, will play a major role in communicating each brand's image. Thus, oil companies may try to promote their brands on a basis of such subjective characteristics as power ("put a tiger in your tank"), service ("as you travel, ask us"), trust ("you can trust your car to the man who wears the star"), or cleanliness ("a nice place to visit"). By doing so, companies try to convince consumers that although their objective features may be nearly identical, it is their particular mix of subjective attributes that will best satisfy the buyers' needs.

In summary, then, there are two different positions that a product occupies: (1) product position, or a brand's objective characteristics in relation to competing brands; and (2) position, or a brand's subjective characteristics (as perceived by consumers) in relation to competing brands.

## PRODUCT POSITION AND POSITION AS A BASIS OF COMPETITION

Both position and product position are frequently used as a basis of competition in the marketplace. There are a wide variety of product classes, for instance, where firms compete on the basis of a product's objective, physical, or functional attributes. Most shopping goods fall into this category since they generally possess differentiating physical features. Refrigerators, for example, may be self-defrosting, have automatic ice cube makers, offer an ice water dispenser, or even come equipped with tape player built into the unit. In this situation, each brand is likely to possess a "unique selling proposition," that feature which sets it apart from the competition, and firms will not hesitate to play upon this point to their own advantage. Thus, when brands are separated on the basis of product position, objective attributes are crucial to success, and promotion is likely to take the form of Rosser Reeves's USP advertising.

Another common situation is when all or most of the competing brands are nearly identical in objective characteristics. These goods are often referred to as "me-too" products since there is virtually no difference in their product position. Exemplary of this situation are the beer, cigarette, soft drink, and oil industries. In these industries, products, for the most part, simply do not possess a USP and thus must be promoted on another basis. Typically, this other basis is to advertise the brands' subjective attributes—that is, create a favorable image. In these instances, when product positions are inseparable, position becomes an effective basis of competition, and positioning campaigns are often undertaken to expose each brand's favorable subjective features.

Since this paper deals with positioning, we will confine the rest of our discussion to the situation where position rather than product position is the basis of competition.

### Measuring position

*Position,* then, is a relative term. A firm is not interested in how consumers perceive its brand alone but rather where its brand's image stands in relation to competing brand images. Accordingly, if a campaign has the objective of repositioning a brand, the success or failure of the campaign rests on whether there is a change in the position (image) of that brand in the anticipated direction. Thus, to correctly evaluate a repositioning campaign the following steps are necessary:

1. Obtain a measure of the brand's present position.

2. If dissatisfied, initiate a repositioning campaign.
3. Obtain a measure of the brand's position after the campaign.
4. Determine whether the brand's position has significantly changed in the desired direction.

Clearly this is not a trival procedure and has commonly been forsaken in favor of less demanding measures such as sales, profits, brand recognition, etc. Unfortunately, it seems inconsistent to measure the success of a positioning campaign in terms other than a change in consumers' perceptions toward that brand relative to their perceptions of competing brands. Indeed, the firm that judges the effectiveness of a positioning campaign by using changes in sales, profits, etc., is making at least three fundamental errors:

**1. Shortsightedness.** The successful repositioning campaign will alter the product's image relative to other product images. The short-run effect of this might be a reduction in sales since old customers may be quick to discontinue use while potential customers may require a longer time span to adopt the product on a regular basis. Thus, even though the repositioning was accomplished and in the long run sales may increase, the short-run effect could well be a drop in sales. Shortsighted managers may point to this temporary reduction as evidence against the success of the advertising campaign.

**2. Inconsistent logic.** Management has undertaken a repositioning effort because it believes that in the long run there is a more desirable position than its product now occupies. The repositioning campaign is a vehicle to reach this new position. If management's reasoning has been correct, the long-run effect should be a sales increase. However, it is logically inconsistent to use sales to determine whether or not the advertising campaign has actually relocated the brand's position. A drop in sales may not reflect the lack of change in the brand's position but may point out that the achieved position was a poor choice by management. By using sales figures alone, management can only guess at whether an actual change in position has occurred.

**3. Limited perspective.** Because of the initiation of the new positioning campaign, management is likely to infer that any change in sales,

profits, etc., is a result of this lone factor. Actually, however, sales are affected by so many variables that a positive change due to the repositioning effort could be overcome by competitors' actions, a change in economic conditions, changes in the tastes and lifestyles of the consumers, etc. Thus, by using sales, profits, or recognition, management will never know the "true" effect of the positioning campaign.

In light of these difficulties, it appears that a procedure is needed for directly measuring the effects of an advertising campaign on the position of the product.

## ASSESSING THE EFFECTIVENESS OF A POSITIONING CAMPAIGN

For management to correctly gauge the success or failure of a positioning campaign, a procedure is needed whereby consumers' perceptions of competing brands can be compared. Nonmetric multidimensional scaling (MDS), an analytical technique for determining the minimum number of dimensions that account for the interrelationships among a set of brands, can accomplish this. The technical details of nonmetric MDS will not be discussed since they are adequately treated elsewhere (Romney et al., 1972; Shepard et al., 1972; Aaker, 1971).

### L&M

During February 1974, it was announced that Liggett & Myers' L&M brand of cigarettes was "not properly positioned as a brand." It was further stated that "L&M must be repositioned in the full-flavor category" (*Advertising Age,* February 1972). To accomplish this repositioning, Liggett & Myers began by changing L&M's product position. This took the form of a new blend of tobacco and a new cork filter. The mainstay of the repositioning effort, however, was a massive advertising campaign (and a newly designed package). It was also announced that this promotion would take place only in selected West Coast markets. As a result, L&M's new program offered an excellent opportunity to demonstrate how nonmetric MDS could be used as a methodology for evaluating the effectiveness of a repositioning campaign.

## Research design

The first step was to formulate an appropriate research design. A better-after quasi-experimental design with a control group provided the needed measurements (Exhibit 1).

**Exhibit 1 ☐**

| | Experimental group— Tucson | Control group— Madison |
|---|---|---|
| "Before" measurement of 16 brands (February 1974) | Yes | Yes |
| Treatment variable (L&M re-positioning campaign) | Yes | No |
| "After" measurement of 16 brands (April 1974) | Yes | Yes |

## Sampling

In selecting a sample for the control and experimental groups, it was essential that (1) the sample be selected in some random manner and (2) the universe selected from be the target market. Since the major purpose in this paper is to present a methodology and not to make inferences, it was not necessary that these conditions be met. Instead, two convenience samples were selected. The control group was undergraduate students at the University of Wisconsin at Madison. The experimental group consisted of undergraduate students at the University of Arizona at Tucson. The students were stratified into smokers and non-smokers. Results reported on in this paper are for smokers only.

## Methodology

**1. Obtain a measure of the brand's present position.** This is the first step for executives who feel that their brand may occupy an undesirable position. For L&M and 15 other brands, "before" measurements were obtained from student smokers in Tucson, Arizona (experimental group), and Madison, Wisconsin (control group). Perceptions data were gathered by asking respondents to group together those brands of cigarettes that they felt were similar to one another. From their responses, a similarity matrix was developed that shows for each possible pair of brands the pro-

portion of times that respondents put those two brands in the same group. The similarity matrix is thus an average representation of how the group surveyed perceived the 16 cigarette brands. For the "before" measurements there were two similarity matrices, one for the control group and another for the experimental group. These similarity matrices were then input into an MDS computer algorithm (for this study, Guttman-Lingoes Small Space Analysis, 1973, was used), and plots of how the brands compare with one another along with their coordinate points were produced.

One of the questions posed in multidimensional scaling is: What is the appropriate number of dimensions to work with? Since there were 16 brands, to exactly account for all the differences among these cigarettes, 15-dimension space would be needed. Generally, however, obtaining the coordinate points for 16 brands in 15-dimension space is of little help in visualizing how brands relate to one another. Accordingly, the MDS algorithm begins with a one-dimensional representation of the data. The number of dimensions is then systematically increased up to a maximum number which is specified by the user. The question to be answered now is: At what number of dimensions are the major differences among brands still represented? To this end, Kruskal (1964) suggests the use of a statistic he calls "stress." The behavior of stress in our example suggested that a two-dimensional representation results in a good fit of the data.

**Table 1 ☐ Stress values for multidimensional scaling plots**

| Group | Dimensions | Stress |
|---|---|---|
| Smoker control "before" | 1 | .14600 |
| | 2 | .05705 |
| | 3 | .02850 |
| | 4 | .01568 |
| Smoker control "after" | 1 | .28364 |
| | 2 | .04656 |
| | 3 | .02172 |
| | 4 | .01094 |
| Smoker experimental "before" | 1 | .21521 |
| | 2 | .06583 |
| | 3 | .03899 |
| | 4 | .02209 |
| Smoker experimental "after" | 1 | .17289 |
| | 2 | .05891 |
| | 3 | .03908 |
| | 4 | .02317 |

Exhibit 2 tends to confirm, for student smokers in Madison, Liggett & Myers' appraisal of their L&M brand—it is not within the full-flavor group of Marlboro and Winston. Lines have been drawn around the brands of cigarettes that appear to cluster together. It will be noticed that L&M, Benson & Hedges, and Viceroy are grouped together. Marlboro, Winston, and Old Gold form another group. Camel, Pall Mall, Chesterfield, and Lucky Strike form a third group. Vantage and True form a group by themselves. Tareyton, Lark, Parliament, and Kent form a fifth group.

Exhibit 3 also tends to confirm, for student smokers in Tucson, Liggett & Myers' suspicion

**Exhibit 2 □ Control group—before**

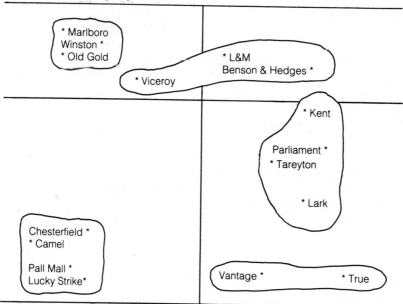

**Exhibit 3 □ Experimental group—before**

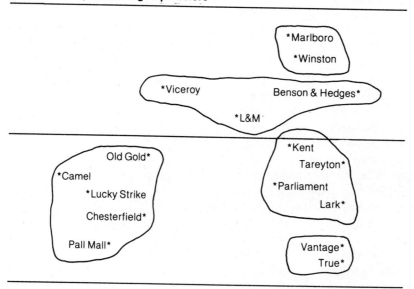

that their L&M brand is not within the full-flavor group. The brands have been visually clustered into five groups. The first group is composed of L&M, Benson & Hedges, and Viceroy. Marlboro and Winston form a second group. A third group is composed of Old Gold, Camel, Pall Mall, Chesterfield, and Lucky Strike. Vantage and True form a group by themselves. Last of all, Tareyton, Lark, Parliament, and Kent form a group.

Visually, the multidimensional scaling plots look quite similar for both the control and experimental groups. In an experimental design of the type proposed earlier (Exhibit 1), it would be ideal if the control and experimental groups had similar perceptions preceding the experimental treatment. Exhibit 4 shows a composite picture of both the experimental and control groups before perceptions of the 16 cigarette brands. Visually, the two groups display a surprising consistency in their views of the 16 brands. However, in order to obtain a quantitative measure of the similarity between the control group and the experimental group, before perceptions, a correlation coefficient

among all possible 120 interpoint distances between the 16 brands was computed. The correlation was .849, showing that the control and experimental groups were quite similar in their perceptions of the 16 brands of cigarettes. It, therefore, seems justified that the Madison students will serve as a good control for the Tucson students.

**2. Initiate a repositioning campaign.** If the present position of a brand is unsatisfactory, as evaluated in step 1, management should take actions to improve the position of its product. Quite often, the first step in this direction will be a change in the product position. For L&M, this took the form of a new cork filter and new tobacco blend. The major tool for accomplishing this change in position, however, will be a repositioning advertising campaign. Trout and Ries (1972a, 1972b, 1972c) have suggested a detailed strategy for effectively repositioning a brand.

For L&M, the repositioning advertising campaign took the form of a series of print ads in which a "rugged, powerfully-built shirtless man

**Exhibit 4 ☐ Composite—before**

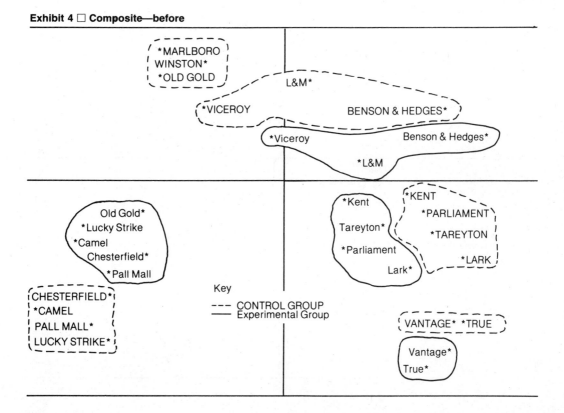

[was] seen clearing an area and building a cabin in the wilderness" (*Advertising Age,* February 1974). Apparently, with a campaign closely resembling that of Marlboro's, Liggett & Myers felt it could effectively reposition its brand into the full-flavor category.

**3. Obtain a measure of the brand's position after the campaign.** This measure is relatively easily obtained by administering the same questionnaire to the same respondents after the campaign has started. But how long should a company wait for this "after" measurement to be taken? The length of this interval will depend on the product, campaign, market, and competition as well as other factors. Management must determine the amount of time it will allow to pass between measures. For L&M's campaign, six weeks elapsed between measurements. This may not be enough time for a print campaign to generate its total effect; however, our purpose is not to draw inferences but to present a methodology.

Exhibit 5 presents the MDS plot for the control group (Madison) six weeks after the campaign be-

gan. Once again, the 16 brands have been visually clustered into groups. The resulting five groups are identical to those obtained for the Madison students six weeks earlier (Exhibit 2).

Exhibit 6 presents the MDS plot for the experimental group (Tucson) six weeks after the campaign began. Again, the brands have been visually clustered into five groups. These groups are almost the same as those of six weeks earlier (Exhibit 3) except that Kent no longer clusters together with Tareyton, Parliament, and Lark but instead now clusters with Viceroy, L&M, and Benson & Hedges.

**4. Determine whether the brand's position has significantly changed in the desired directions.** There are two issues in this, the final step: (1) Has the change in position been in the desired direction? (2) Has the change in position been significant?

The question of direction is not difficult to answer. Using the coordinate points provided by the MDS program and the Euclidean distance formula, all of the 120 distances (for 16 objects) be-

**Exhibit 5** ☐ **Control group—after**

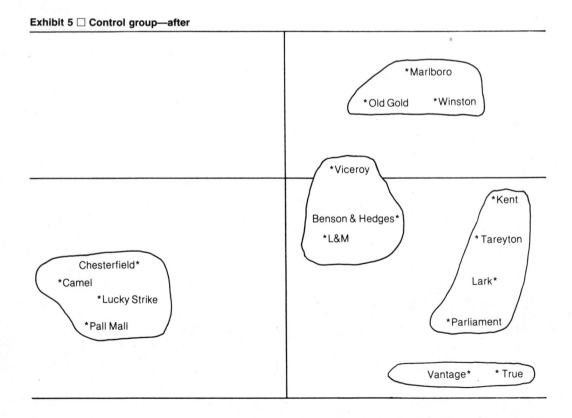

tween brands can be computed. This has been done for the experimental group's "before" and "after" measurements. Then, to see how much and in which direction a particular brand has moved in relation to another brand, simply subtract the two distances. For example, the "before" distance between L&M and Marlboro in the experimental group was 62.48 units. The "after" distance for the experimental group between L&M and Marlboro was 61.80 units. Thus, L&M moved .68 units closer to Marlboro during the six-week time period. Similarly, L&M moved 7.51 units away from Winston during the test period (see Exhibit 7).

To determine whether this movement was significant is a more complex process. What is needed is some criterion against which we can gauge the significance of any movement between a pair of brands. If the experimental design (Exhibit 1) has been carried out correctly, no "causal factors" should have been introduced in the control group. Accordingly, we should expect any movement between brands in the control group to

occur strictly by chance. Thus, by simply summing these random movements along with the associated percentages, we can devise a simple but effective criterion against which to judge movements in the experimental group. A table of the cumulative frequency distribution of random movements that occurred in the control group over a six-week period would show, for example, that 95 percent of the random movements between brands were greater than .8749 units, 70 percent were greater than 9.9167 units, 50 percent were greater than 23.3149 units, and 10 percent were greater than 43.1890 units.

If a 10 percent level of significance is selected, then a change of 43.1890 units must occur before we can accept the hypothesis that a significant movement between brands has occurred. The movement between L&M and Marlboro was .68 units. Obviously, this does not meet our criterion of significance, and we conclude that L&M did not move significantly in relation to Marlboro during the six-week period for the student smokers in our sample.

**Exhibit 6 ☐ Experimental group—after**

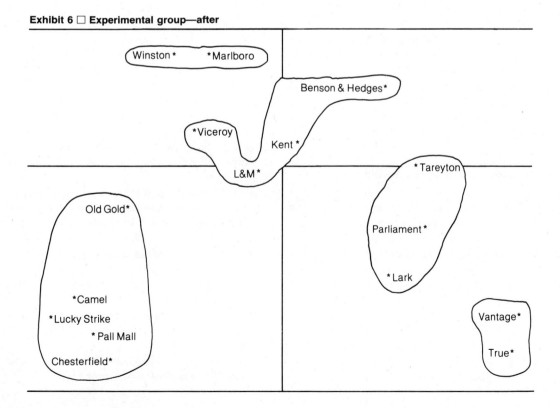

**Exhibit 7** ☐

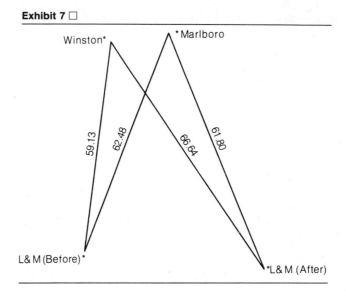

Winston*　　　　　　*Marlboro

59.13　62.48　66.64　61.80

L&M (Before)*　　　　　　　　*L&M (After)

## CONCLUSION

The concept and definition of position have been discussed here. Either position or product position can be the basis of competition for a product depending on situational conditions in the industry. When product position is the competitive basis, USP advertising is the typical form of promotion. When firms compete on the basis of position, positioning advertising campaigns are called for.

In the evaluation of a positioning campaign we have suggested the following procedure:

1. Using nonmetric multidimensional scaling, obtain a measure of the brand's present position.
2. If dissatisfied, initiate a repositioning campaign.
3. Obtain a measure of the brand's position after the campaign, again using nonmetric MDS.
4. Calculate the direction of any position change using the MDS coordinate points and the Euclidean distance formula. Determine the significance of any change by comparing movements in the experimental group to random movements in the control group.

With such a methodology, management can correctly gauge the success or failure of a repositioning campaign.

## REFERENCES

Aaker, David A., ed. *Multivariate Analysis in Marketing: Theory and Application.* Belmont, Calif.: Wadsworth, 1971.

Holmes, John H. "Profitable Product Positioning." *MSU Business Topics,* Spring 1973, pp. 27–32.

Kruskal, J. B. "Multidimensional Scaling by Optimizing Goodness of Fit to a Nonmetric Hypothesis." *Psychometrika* 29 (1964a), pp. 1–27.

―――. "Multidimensional Scaling: A Numerical Method." *Psychometrika* 29 (1964b), pp. 115–29.

Lingoes, J. C. "An IBM 7090 Program for Guttman-Lingoes Smallest Space Analysis—1." *Behavioral Science* 10 (1965), pp. 183–84.

O'Connor, John J. "L&M Brand Being Relaunched into Wider, Full-Flavor Arena." *Advertising Age,* February 11, 1974.

Romney, Kimball A.; Roger N. Shepard; and Sara Beth Nerlove, eds. *Multidimensional Scaling Theory and Applications in the Behavioral Sciences.* Vol. 2. New York: Seminar Press, 1972.

Shepard, Roger N.; A. Miball Romney; and Sara Beth Nerlove, eds. *Multidimensional Scaling Theory and Applications in the Behavioral Sciences.* Vol. 1. New York: Seminar Press, 1972.

Trout, Jack, "Positioning Is a Game People Play in Today's Me-Too Marketplace." *Industrial Marketing,* June 1969.

―――. "Positioning Revisited: Why Didn't GE and RCA Listen?" *Industrial Marketing,* November 1971.

Trout, Jack, and Al Ries. "The Positioning Era Cometh." *Advertising Age,* April 24, 1972a, pp. 35–38.

———. "Positioning Cuts through Chaos in Marketplace." *Advertising Age,* May 1, 1972b, pp. 51–53.

———. "How to Position Your Product." *Advertising Age,* May 8, 1972c.

## QUESTIONS

1. Explain, compare, and contrast the meanings of "product position" and "position". What are their importance in marketing?

2. Explain what techniques were used when Liggett and Myers decided that it wanted to change the position of its L&M brand of cigarettes.

3. Did L&M feel its positioning campaign was successful? How did it judge effectiveness? What are some of the fundamental errors that can occur when a firm tries to judge the effectiveness of a positioning campaign by measures other than MDS?

*4. Does positioning apply to the retailing of services (Reading 23)? Use fast-food chains or banks to illustrate your answer.

5. Is it socially desirable, from a macro-marketing viewpoint, to position a product through promotion rather than by making actual charges in the product itself?

*Question relates concepts in this and other readings.

---

☐ **28**

# High-tech shocks in ad research

*Felix Kessler*

*Reading 8 discussed how firms are using new information technologies to improve their marketing efforts. Following up on that theme, this article describes how marketing researchers are using supermarket scanners, split-cable television systems, and other electronic devices to target TV commercials at specific "scanner panel" households to obtain more accurate measurements of advertising effectiveness and test market results. This ability to track buyers from TV set to checkout counter is providing advertising executives and product managers with invaluable new insights into consumer buying behavior—and challenging conventional thinking about advertising expenditures.*

Sophisticated new techniques of market research are yielding fascinating and sometimes startling facts about how consumers behave and how advertising works—or doesn't. The new methods, introduced a few years ago, have begun to prove their value in an era when familiar brands are dying, new brands are flopping, and all brands are having a tougher time getting on cramped su-

permarket shelves. On this market research frontier, some of Madison Avenue's most venerable verities are being disproved. Most surprising find-

Source: Reprinted with permission from *Fortune*, July 7, 1986, pp. 58–62. Copyright © 1986 Time Inc. All rights reserved. No part of this article may be reproduced in any form without permission from the publisher. At the time of writing, Felix Kessler was a staff reporter for *Fortune*.

ing so far: Trying to goose sales by a big increase in a product's TV ad budget often doesn't pay.

The buzzword for what this research produces is single-source data. The ungainly name is meant to tell you that the research tracks the behavior of individual households from the TV set to the checkout counter. Chicago-based Information Resources Inc. pioneered the technology (*Fortune,* July 25, 1983) and monitors more than 3,000 households in each of eight small-town markets, from Pittsfield, Massachusetts, to Visalia, California. In the sample households, microcomputers record when the television set is on and which station it is tuned to, sending this information by telephone line to a central data-collection office. Sometimes IRI sends out special test commercials over cable channels. At the supermarket checkout, a member of a sample household presents an identification card. The checker records the purchases by scanner, and the data are sent to IRI. "You put all that information together," says Gerald Eskin, vice chairman of IRI, "and you have more insights into people's buying patterns than ever before." IRI's revenues have nearly tripled to $75 million over the past four years.

A. C. Nielsen Co., a unit of Dun & Bradstreet, grabbed a piece of this fast-growing market last July when it began testing a similar operation involving 3,500 households in Sioux Falls, South Dakota, and the same number in Springfield, Missouri. Nielsen can send test commercials over the air, so members of the sample need not be cable subscribers. More competition comes from ScanAmerica, a 200-home pilot project launched last November in Denver. ScanAmerica is a joint venture of Control Data's Arbitron Ratings Co., which measures TV viewing, and Selling Areas-Marketing Inc., or SAMI, a subsidiary of Time Inc., publisher of *Fortune.* Unlike the other two services, ScanAmerica does not send test commercials to homes of sample viewers. Instead it simply monitors sample households' viewing and consumption patterns and plans to sell the data. ScanAmerica participants record purchases at home by passing a penlike wand over goods bearing bar codes. The information is transmitted daily through a device attached to participants' televisions.

The single-source services are reshaping advertising. Graham Phillips, chairman of Ogilvy &

Mather U.S., frankly acknowledges that "we've changed major campaigns and spending levels for several of our clients" after single-source tests. A while back, for example, such tests suggested the agency shift ads for Campbell Soup's Swanson frozen dinners from a serious to a light approach; Campbell marketing executives subsequently clocked a 14 percent rise in sales of Swanson dinners.

Major advertisers like Procter & Gamble, General Foods, General Mills, Campbell, and Quaker Oats say they have gathered a valuable crop of previously inaccessible market data through the services. By correlating test panelists' TV habits and grocery purchases, for instance, Campbell discovered an extraordinary appetite gap between viewers of two daytime serials: "Search for Tomorrow" fans buy 27 percent more spaghetti sauce than average, but 22 percent less V-8 vegetable juice; devotees of "All My Children" feel so-so about spaghetti sauce—but purchase 46 percent more V-8 than the viewer norm. Why the divergence in tastes? "We've been looking for an explanation, trying to unlock this thing," says George Mahrlig, Campbell's director of media services, "but it's still a big mystery." Mahrlig says Campbell has pitched the virtues of Prego spaghetti sauce on "Search" and those of V-8 on "Children" and will probably do so again, a low-risk, high-gain strategy aimed at maximizing sales among the likeliest customers.

Marketers also say scanning lets them take chances on long-shot new products that might not rate an expensive trial. A regional market test could cost $2 million, for example, versus a tenth of that for a test through a scanning service. Quaker Oats recently tested an advertising campaign "for a business where we weren't really very hopeful," says John Blair, vice president for marketing research. "Maybe in 1 case in 10 do you move the needle—and that's what happened here, in a big way." For competitive reasons Blair declines to identify the product, but he says the scanning test's "strong sales response" has persuaded Quaker Oats to take the product national soon.

The scanning services' speed and cheapness pay off in other ways. After only an eight-week trial last winter, Quaker Oats decided on a national launch of Oh!s, a new dry cereal. "Electronic scanners helped us to decide to move ahead much sooner than usual," says Blair, "and in a highly aggressive manner." The services are just as valuable when they point out duds. A negative but accurate verdict that kills a product quickly is preferable to a long, expensive, and perhaps inconclusive regional trial of a product that will fail. "Scanner data give you an earlier read on new products," says D. J. Jefferson, market research manager at Kitchens of Sara Lee. "You get the data store by store and week by week."

In addition to other tasks, clients use scanning services to test so-called advertising weight, meaning spending levels. About half the time the results have been shocking. According to the tests, even doubling TV spending from, say, $5 million to $10 million a year may not pay. Says a somewhat rueful Campbell Soup Co. market manager: "It doesn't move the needle."

Advertisers may test a $10-million ad campaign with one panel and a $5-million campaign with another. Such tests typically take a year. "If it turns out that the people who received the $5-million campaign bought the same amount as the $10-million group, that raises the possibility that a reduction in spending might be in order," says Randall Smith, president of IRI's database division. Richardson-Vicks decided against a stepped-up media schedule for Olay Beauty Cleanser, says Jurgen Fey, director of marketing research in the personal care products division, after IRI tests in Pittsfield and Marion, Indiana, "made clear this would not increase consumer offtake leading to a payout." Translation: The extra ads wouldn't pay for themselves.

Most marketers find the scanning data persuasive. Unless an ad campaign is changed or a product repositioned, notes a market research executive, "increased advertising is usually not sales effective, and that runs counter to the intuitive judgment of an awful lot of people." After supervising more than 450 ad tests, IRI executives say that usually an ad campaign's copy and focus matter more than the number of times a spot runs on TV.

This notion is understandably spooky to people who work in advertising agencies, which generally get paid a percentage of what their clients spend. "It's frightening," admits Ronald Kaatz, director of

media concepts at J. Walter Thompson U.S.A., "but brands double their ad budgets in most of these tests, and nothing happens to sales. That says there have to be a lot of other variables out there."

Agency executives, protecting their own interests, point out some valid considerations. Slashing an ad budget solely on the basis of a relatively brief panel test may be a risky strategy. Brand loyalty built over the years might not be eroded by a one-year drop in advertising. But the brand's long-term franchise with customers could suffer from a sustained advertising decline, they say.

In addition, even carefully constructed market tests can be flawed. The scanning services don't know if viewers are actually watching a television set when it is on, or whether a commercial break will send them to the bathroom. Test participants, who are paid volunteers, might also skew the numbers: They may react in atypical ways simply because they know they are sending a message to advertisers. "The most serious problem with this kind of data is it presumes you can track a commercial on a cash register," says Dave Vadehra, president of Video Storyboard Tests, an advertising research firm. "It takes years to change buying patterns." Only for new products is the single-source process "a pretty viable concept," says Vadehra. Since the product had not existed, initial purchases can be directly linked to advertising.

Other advertising executives note that single-source testing has not been perfected. Tests in small-town markets cannot predict nationwide results, they say. And single-source tests, for all they tell, do not answer the all-important question of *why* people are motivated to buy a product. "Certain TV programs appear to be the best vehicles for selling your products," says Laurence R. Stoddard, an advertising consultant. One of those programs may work fine, but "then you try it again and find it doesn't sell anymore." Other commercials, coupons, and price cuts are constantly roiling the market scene, he explains. Against that background, even ad experts often find it hard to tell why any ad succeeds or fails.

Some advertising executives on the creative side say scanner testing could lead to more distinctive commercials. "One way to break through the commercial clutter today is to have a commercial that's better than the next guy's," says Malcolm MacDougall, president of the Hill Holliday Connors Cosmopoulos ad agency's New York office. Scanner tests should ferret out the winners from the losers faster than more subjective methods, such as interviewing a "focus group" of consumers. "Sales numbers are the only way to judge advertising," says MacDougall.

Where high-tech testing is headed still is not clear. The three main single-source contenders all have drawbacks. While the IRI system monitors network viewing, it can only test commercials over cable systems. This gives IRI's sample a slightly upscale tilt, according to Nielsen, whose system is the only one that can cut into the signals of regular over-the-air stations with test commercials. Nielsen's critics note the system is operating in but two markets and registers only viewing habits of entire households, not individual members. In contrast, ScanAmerica uses "people meters" that keep tabs on each viewer—but only if the viewers remember to push buttons on hand-held devices that register their presence before the tube. ScanAmerica's wand lets participants keep track of all bar-coded products they buy, not just supermarket purchases, but panelists might forget to use it.

Market researchers cheerfully concede their brave new world is still in transition. Laurence N. Gold, a marketing vice president at Nielsen, says national television viewership data in the future may not be measured through the current method of written diaries or people meters. Years from now, says Gold, sensors in homes will automatically detect and report who is watching TV—and perhaps even transmit physiological reactions of viewers to programs they're watching.

Such fanciful projections are far removed from the limited but valuable lessons being learned from the current technology. "It has helped us run our marketing operation more efficiently," says Rudolph Struse, General Mills' director of corporate marketing research. He cautions, however, that he has not yet gleaned any general principles of what makes effective advertising. Other marketers agree. Case by case, they can find out whether campaigns have a reasonable chance to succeed. But none claims to have uncovered the key to what makes people buy. "The one thing we have learned is, there is no magic formula that works on everything," says Ogilvy & Mather's Graham Phillips. Adds John Blair of Quaker Oats: "All we can do is bring as much science as possible to what really is an art."

## QUESTIONS

1. What is "single-source data" and why does it represent a significant breakthrough in marketing research?

2. What are the advantages and disadvantages of conducting a "scanner test"?

3. Compare and contrast the scanner services offered by IRI, A. C. Nielsen, and ScanAmerica. How do they differ? Which would you select if you were a marketing manager and why?

4. Measuring advertising effectiveness has long been a major problem in marketing. Many have considered it almost impossible to do. Have scanner services solved this problem? Explain your answer.

5. Why do people allow the scanner services to monitor and record their TV viewing habits and their supermarket purchases? Isn't this an invasion of privacy? Doesn't this give advertisers more power to control our purchases?

## □ 29

# Are sales promotion expenditures getting out of hand?

*While most consumers are well aware of the extent to which they are constantly being bombarded by advertising, many would no doubt be quite surprised to learn that consumer goods firms actually spend twice as much on sales promotion than they do on advertising. These sales promotion efforts include "consumer promotion"—such as coupons, rebates, sweepstakes, and premiums—and "trade promotion"—the various discounts and allowances that manufacturers offer middlemen as an incentive to push their products.*

*Sales promotion expenditures have grown rapidly during the past decade, sharply cutting into advertising budgets. As the following two articles suggest, however, many believe that such expenditures have gotten out of control—destroying brand loyalty, reducing profits, and undermining the future of many branded products. But manufacturers may be afraid to stop playing a game that has become very popular among both middlemen and consumers.*

## □ 29–A

# The costly coupon craze

*Felix Kessler*

Marketers of consumer products are rewriting the rules of their game. They still spend billions on advertising in hopes of building long-term consumer loyalty for their brands. But increasingly they are weakening that strategy by cutting prices in the short run, offering customers sweepstakes, coupons, premiums ("send in three box tops . . ."), and other incentives. Says Richard Vincent, an executive at the Donnelley Marketing promotion firm of Stamford, Connecticut: "Something is taking place—a groundswell, a trend—in the way companies are selling products."

Those incentives, ranging from coupons that slice 20 cents off a cheese package to $500-and-up rebates on new cars, are known in marketing circles as consumer promotion. It has been around forever. So has trade promotion, offering similar incentives to distributors or retailers. But never have marketers spent as much on promotion as they will this year, nor have they favored it so heavily at the expense of advertising.

Promotion made a lot of sense in the late 70s and early 80s when manufacturers would mark prices up high to stay ahead of inflation, then offer incentives as needed to keep sales perking. But lately, instead of abating with inflation, promotion is accelerating. While no one compiles precise figures on promotion, Joel D. Weiner, an executive vice president for marketing at Kraft Inc., says,

Source: Reprinted with permission from *Fortune*, June 9, 1986, pp. 83–84. Copyright © 1986 Time Inc. All rights reserved. No part of this article may be reproduced in any form without permission from the publisher. At the time of writing, Felix Kessler was a staff reporter for *Fortune*.

"Expenditures for consumer and trade promotions will clearly exceed spending on media advertising and could be above $200 billion." Robert J. Coen, senior vice president and director of forecasting at the McCann-Erickson advertising agency, estimates ad spending in the United States will total $102 billion this year.

One reason marketers are leaning more on promotion is that they are having a harder time coming up with products different from those of competitors. Markets are already overcrowded with brands and varieties. Without a difference to tout in ads, companies have to rely more on price and other come-ons to entice consumers. Promotions also help ensure that retailers give the favored products precious shelf space. Since the manufacturers swallow the price cuts, retailers have nothing to lose and plenty to gain: promotions can boost sales and profits by bringing in more customers.

Industry analysts blame marketers for short-changing the future more than they used to. With pay and bonuses increasingly geared to short-term performance, managers in charge of brands are more likely to "drop a coupon" to energize sales immediately than to invest in advertising aimed at building a brand's image over years. Thomas M. Hamilton, director of sales promotion services at the William Esty Co. advertising agency, acknowledges that promotion produces faster results than advertising: "There's a great temptation for quick sales fixes through promotions. It's a lot easier to offer the consumer an immediate price savings than to differentiate your product from a competitor's."

Marketers of packaged goods are in the trend's forefront. Donnelley Marketing, a Dun & Bradstreet subsidiary, found in a recent survey that these companies spend almost twice as much on promotion as on advertising. Such leading packaged goods producers as Kraft and Nabisco Brands' Del Monte division do not dispute the findings. Says Kraft's Joel Weiner: "We proceed on the premise that one third of all expenditures is for media, which means two thirds is for consumer and trade promotion."

Donnelley notes that the proportion of total marketing expenditures that companies allocate for consumer promotion has risen sharply over the past eight years, climbing in almost direct opposi-

tion to a decline in the proportion spent on advertising (see chart). While Donnelley does not report the dollar value of the expenditures, a computation based partly on Donnelley's survey pegs promotional spending on nondurables at around $43 billion last year, compared with roughly $23 billion for advertising.

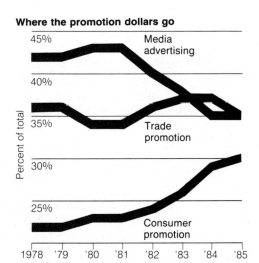

**Where the promotion dollars go**

Coupons, the most popular consumer promotion, have carried the burden of the boom, experiencing "absolutely remarkable, explosive growth," according to Vincent of Donnelley. Packaged goods producers issued 180 billion coupons last year, with a face value of about $50 billion. A. C. Nielsen, another Dun & Bradstreet subsidiary, says consumers redeemed 6.5 billion of these, saving more than $2 billion on their shopping bills.

The promotion trend is taking dollars away from ad media across the board. Industry experts think promotion grew perhaps 8 percent or 9 percent after adjustment for inflation last year, while U.S. ad spending grew only 4.7 percent, the smallest real increase in three years. The weakness is emphasized by comparing last year with 1984, when the Olympics, the personal computer boom, and political campaigns boosted spending. But that does not account for all the suffering of the TV networks and national magazines.

In their first decline in years, network revenues fell 2.5 percent, to $8.3 billion, last year. J. Walter Reed, a senior vice president and media director at the Foote Cone & Belding advertising agency, notes that promotion continues to siphon media dollars and concludes, "Early data suggest 1986 won't be a strong year for the networks." Advertising pages in national magazines fell 3.3 percent last year, though higher ad rates nudged revenues up 4.5 percent to $4.9 billion. Sellers have been relying more on cable TV, local stations, special-interest magazines—and promotion.

Many marketing executives see dangers in the rise of promotion, even as they contribute to it. "Promotion is a double-edged sword," says Hamilton of William Esty. "It is an extremely effective sales tool, but used to excess it can erode your franchise. Price promotion can turn people into shoppers who buy you when you're 'on deal,' then buy the competition when they're on deal." Peter J. Spengler, vice president for advertising services at Bristol-Myers, adds: "There isn't a company around that wouldn't prefer spending less on promotion and more on advertising."

As promotion escalates, it draws competitors into profit-punishing fights—and multiplies the value of strong brands that do not need it. No one seems to doubt that promotion will continue to mushroom, but the most profitable marketers in coming years could be those best at avoiding it.

---

## ☐ 29–B

# The no-win game of price promotion

*Monci Jo Williams*

In many ways trade promotion is the netherworld of marketing. Scott Paper was one of several companies that refused to discuss the practice with *Fortune*. "Allowances," said a Scott spokesman, "are the kind of proprietary thing that should be left unpublished." Quaker Oats also quaked at the idea of talking; it cited "the sensitivity of the manufacturer-distributor relationship." In public, manufacturers and retailers agree that trade discounts have grown too large, are offered too frequently, and should be pruned. But in private, retailers accuse manufacturers of trying to reduce promotions and improve profits at their expense. Manufacturers counter that retailers have used the deals to fatten profits while passing little of the discount on to consumers and demanding ever-bigger deals. Few manufacturers seem willing to admit that they are mired in a swamp of their own making.

Though the $8-billion-a-year figure is a reasonable estimate, it is not precise. Manufacturers don't have to disclose the amounts spent on trade promotion and direct-to-consumer promotions like coupons and samples. Steven Kingsbury, vice president of Majers Corporation in Omaha, which helps manufacturers monitor trade promotion programs, estimates that 10 years ago 20 percent to 30 percent of grocery sales carried discounts to the trade averaging 6 percent to 8 percent of manufacturers' list price. Today roughly 60 percent of all manufacturers' sales are accompanied by a trade deal averaging about 12 percent.

Manufacturers often specify the kind of special treatment they would like in return for these discounts. They might want the retailer to pass along some of the discount to consumers, feature the product in newspaper ads, display the product prominently in the store—or a combination of these things. The manufacturers' sales forces, aided by outside firms like Majers, check up on whether retailers are following through on the promotion. But if they aren't, most manufacturers don't do much about it.

Coffee, tuna, soft drinks, paper products, cake mixes, margarine, salad dressings, cooking oil,

Source: Reprinted with permission from *Fortune*, July 11, 1983, pp. 92–102. Copyright © 1983 Time Inc. All rights reserved. No part of this article may be reproduced in any form without permission from the publisher. At the time of writing, Monci Jo Williams was a staff reporter for *Fortune*.

deodorants, and shampoos are all promoted heavily and frequently. In these categories and others, the weaklings of the grocery shelf—products with the smallest market shares—usually get the heaviest promotion. Because marginal brands lack the "pull" of consumer demand, manufacturers figure they need extra "push" from the retailer. Procter & Gamble, whose products most often hold the top spots in their categories, spends less on trade allowances per sales dollar than, say, Lever Brothers, whose products often have smaller market shares. The allowance compensates the retailer for making room on the shelf for a product lacking powerful consumer appeal.

Trade promotion can also be a potent weapon in the guerrilla wars fought when a new product is introduced. A company may offer a 20 percent discount to encourage the retailer to make space on the shelf for an unproven newcomer. The established competitor, who stands to lose shelf space and market share, may then retaliate with a much bigger discount. In 1973, just before Colgate-Palmolive introduced Peak, a toothpaste with baking soda, P&G offered allowances to get retailers to stock up with Crest. Taking advantage of Crest's special price, consumers stocked up too. That's one reason you've probably never heard of Peak. It came out, sat on the shelf, and in the words of a former P&G sales manager, "just died." Colgate still struggles along with Peak; its share of the U.S. toothpaste market is 0.1 percent.

The escalation of deals comes as the balance of bargaining power between manufacturers and retailers has been shifting. The retailer used to serve as a relatively passive conduit for the manufacturer's goods. But the retail grocery business has been consolidating, and the big retailers and wholesalers have gained buying clout. Since the mid-70s grocers have slowed the rate at which they've been adding space while expanding the number of products they carry. Vitamins, shampoos, greeting cards, panty hose, and dozens of other goods now encroach on the turf groceries once had to themselves. With the advent of checkout scanners and computers that supply information on how quickly products are turning over, retailers are increasingly aware of what makes money and what doesn't. They can demand discounts on marginal goods or throw them off the shelf. The relative scarcity of shelf space

has, in a sense, put the retailer in the real estate business; manufacturers have little choice but to bid for territory to display their wares.

Especially fierce is competition among soft-drink marketers for in-store displays. A typical supermarket has about 50 of these at the ends of aisles and elsewhere. A single display in the front of a store can increase a product's sales sixfold. It's not unusual for buyers to entertain bids for these displays. On more than one occasion, a buyer from one of the largest U.S. chains has called Pepsi after receiving word of Coke's latest discount. His message: "You have a half hour to get back to us with yours."

Promoting soft drinks has one thing to be said for it: the discounts increase total consumption. With most products, discounts mainly shift consumption from one time period to another or from one brand to another. But when consumers who buy soft drinks, cookies, and snacks "on deal" get the stuff into the pantry, it becomes subject to impulse munching and guzzling, and the shopper soon heads back for more.

Worry about price controls in the mid-70s greatly increased the depth and breadth of deals. Manufacturers kept list prices high to protect themselves in case of a federal price freeze and used discounts to remain competitive. After fear of price controls passed, however, the discounts remained. In recent years manufacturers have been trying to signal each other—through speeches at conventions and comments in the trade press—that trade deals have been getting out of hand. But most have been unwilling to cut back for fear that the competition won't follow. They also dread retaliation from retailers. Discussions about how to reduce trade allowances are peppered with "what ifs": What if the retailer reduces my shelf space, throws out my product, or prices the competition a few cents under me? Says the division manager for a major packaged-goods company, "Everyone has been afraid to make the first move, to sustain even a short-term volume loss."

Thomas W. Wilson, Jr., who heads the consumer goods marketing group of McKinsey & Co., management consultants, believes the growth in trade discounts is self-destructive. Wilson is widely respected in the food industry as the man most responsible for developing the Uniform Product Code, the ubiquitous little bars on packaged goods that checkout scanners read. He blames deals for increasing manufacturers' marketing costs and abetting the shift in consumer preference from nationally branded products to house brands and generics.

The consumer franchise for branded products has indeed been breaking down. A recent study by the ad agency Needham Harper & Steers found that the percentage of people who try to stick with well-known brands dropped from 77 percent to 59 percent in eight years. Manufacturers say that the proliferation of trade promotions has helped persuade the consumer to ignore brand and "cherry pick" products sold at deal prices. If that's true, manufacturers have plenty of reason to worry. In effect, they're undermining the billions they spend on brand-name advertising with the billions they spend on trade promotion.

Wilson has been spreading the word to manufacturers that now is the time to cut back promotions and reinvest in the consumer franchise. Some retailers and wholesalers view him as an agent of the opposition, a hired gun for manufacturers who want to bring the discounts down. Wilson denies that accusation, saying he serves as a consultant to both retailers and manufacturers (though he won't identify specific clients) and that his public statements represent his own, not a client's, point of view. Whatever the case, the vehemence that creeps into his voice when he discussed the evils of trade promotion does indicate deep conviction.

Wilson has been trying to put across the idea that the escalation of discounts has been costly not just for manufacturers but for retailers and consumers as well. That's because retailers and wholesalers engage in what's known as forward buying. To take advantage of trade deals, they buy more than they need for normal inventory and draw down that stock instead of rebuying at list price. Many retailers buy enough in one deal to carry them over to the next—"bridge buying," as it's called. Experts estimate that on average wholesalers and retailers "forward buy" about one quarter of their inventory. As a result, says Wilson, as little as 30 percent of the manufacturer's trade promotion dollar gets passed on to the consumer. Much of the rest goes to pay interest and warehouse costs for the excess inventory. That adds costs to the distribution system. "The retailer is taking on excess inventory and storage costs he wouldn't normally have," Wilson says, "and the

manufacturer is faced with uneven demand on production and distribution."

Although the manufacturers blame the retailers for insisting on trade deals, they have come to rely on trade promotions for short-term volume gains in an industry that's growing only about 1 percent a year. Wilson, who also blames the retailers, concedes that manufacturers have tended "to throw money at the problem, to buy growth with dollars rather than gain it by building the consumer franchise." Brand managers now use trade promotions routinely, not just to introduce new products or defend against the competition, but to meet their quarterly and yearly sales and market share goals. They reason that profits on the extra sales stimulated by a promotion will offset the cost of the discounts. But all too often that doesn't happen, and they wind up sacrificing profits to meet market share and volume goals.

The manufacturer's sales force adds to the pressure for price promotions at the end of the year. John A. Quelch, assistant professor at Harvard Business School, points out that salesmen have goals to meet too. "In many companies," he says, "the salespeople have become the best representatives of the retailers' interests." Neither the sales force nor the brand manager, who is likely to be transferred in a couple of years, may have the long-term welfare of the brand at heart. Because retailers load up on deal merchandise during a promotion, the manufacturers may simply mortage future sales to meet short-term goals. As long as they keep their sights trained on short-term targets, Quelch says, "the brand manager and sales force lack a clear incentive to reduce the level of trade promotion activity."

The focus on short-term goals goes all the way up the line. Not long ago a consultant completed a study on trade promotions for a divisional vice president of sales at a major packaged-goods manufacturer. "It was four weeks before the end of the last quarter," says the consultant. "He wanted to find out if he could make his numbers by upping the deals. The point of the study was to find out how much product the trade could absorb. It's not exactly consonant with your image of a well-managed company."

Companies might be less tempted to use trade promotion if they knew what it cost them. Mc-Cormick & Co., the $720-million-a-year spice manufacturer, was dazzled by the illusion that pro-

# Secrets behind the specials

Ever wonder what goes on behind the scenes when your local supermarket runs a special on canned tuna? Here's what happened at a New York City supermarket, whose May 15 flier is shown below. The price specials reflect the discounts (called allowances) that the manufacturer gave the retailer to push the product. The retailer usually pays $1.15 for a can of Bumble Bee white tuna; the allowance brought his net cost to 96 cents. In this instance he marked it up only three cents. But the markup can be deceiving. The retailer cuts prices for only a week or two on most products, though he usually gets the allowances for six to eight weeks. For the remaining weeks the price goes back up. The tuna was recently selling at this store for $1.39, the spaghetti sauce for $1.05, and the instant coffee for $4.79.

**BUMBLE BEE white tuna**

| | |
|---|---|
| List price per 48-can case: | **$55.43** |
| Allowance: | **$9.50** |
| Net cost per can: | **96 cents** |

**RAGÚ spaghetti sauce**

| | |
|---|---|
| List price per 12-jar case: | **$9.50** |
| Allowance: | **96 cents** |
| Net cost per jar: | **71 cents** |

**MAXWELL HOUSE instant coffee**

| | |
|---|---|
| List price per 18-jar case: | **$83.72** |
| Allowance: | **$13.50** |
| Net cost per jar: | **$3.90** |

motions would eventually pay for themselves. Managers in McCormick's grocery products division began offering promotional allowances to meet their profit goals. They soon found that the promotions didn't generate the profits they were supposed to, so they deferred the costs to later quarters. After nearly five years of this the SEC moved in. "As the level of those expenses increased," McCormick said in a document filed with the commission, "the grocery products division planned further deferrals, always with the hope

that it would have an extraordinary quarter in which it could absorb the expenses." When the SEC filed a complaint last year alleging improper accounting practices, McCormick settled (without admitting or denying the charges) and restated 19 quarters of earnings by some $4 million.

Since the late 70s P&G, Kraft, R. T. French, Texize, and others have been setting up planning and analysis systems that weigh the incremental sales and profits from trade promotions against the costs. But few manufacturers use such a system companywide, and the industry as a whole has a long way to go.

One reason promotions fail to pay off is that manufacturers have trouble targeting them geographically. Retailers and wholesalers can sabotage a manufacturer's efforts by buying merchandise on deal in one market and reselling it where the manufacturer is trying to get full price. They may sell to another chain or wholesaler—"diverting," the trade calls it. Or in the case of companies doing business in several markets, they may transfer the product from one branch to another—a form of diverting called transshipping. People in the business guess that both forms of diverting add up to over $1 billion worth of coffee, tuna fish, health and beauty aids, and other products being shipped around the country each year.

The diverter is a shadowy figure. Just who diverts is a matter of fascination in the industry, but retailers, wholesalers, and manufacturers are reluctant to name names. In the mid-70s, General Foods test-marketed new packaging for Maxwell House coffee with tighter-fitting plastic resealable lids that were supposed to keep the coffee fresher. The lids could be identified by a blue ring around the rim. The coffee was introduced with a fat promotional discount in Syracuse, New York. Before long the blue-ringers were turning up in Los Angeles; Portland, Oregon; and Jacksonville, Florida. In a Federal Trade Commission case touching on the matter, General Foods testified that companies transshipping coffee around the East and Midwest ranged in size from a $120-million-a-year Brattleboro, Vermont, wholesaler to Grand Union, the nation's eighth-largest supermarket chain, with annual sales of $4.1 billion.

Manufacturers have been trying to persuade distributors that selling deal merchandise to diverters or buying it from them is unethical and possibly illegal, since distributors are prohibited by the Robinson-Patman Act from accepting promotional allowances if they don't run the promotions. Perhaps surprisingly, some buyers seem more troubled about the ethics than the legality. Alfred Walsh, director of purchasing for Affiliated Food Stores in Little Rock, Arkansas, explains: "We have a relationship with a salesman. We see him once a week; he knows us. I don't like buying the product he sells from some salesman in New Jersey I never saw." William Deskins, who buys for a

family-owned chain in North Tazewell, Virginia, agrees but feels forced to buy diverted merchandise when it comes his way. "If the guy across the street gets a product from a diverter," he says, "and he sells it cheaper than I can, I'd be stupid not to buy from a diverter too."

In the past year or so, P&G and Coca-Cola have taken tentative steps to cut trade discounts on a few products. In the hope of offering consumers more stable prices, and thus lowering the incentive to shop around, the companies reduced both deal rates and list prices. Coke made the move with Hi-C fruit drinks and Minute Maid instant and frozen lemonade, P&G with Bounty paper towels, Charmin and White Cloud bathroom tissues, and Duncan Hines cake mixes. Despite widespread belief that the moves would hurt market share, the products have held their own. Still, the movement has hardly swept the industry.

Looking at the inefficiency of trade promotion, many manufacturers think that putting price cuts directly into the hands of consumers makes more sense. They have been turning increasingly to cents-off coupons distributed by mail, in newspapers and magazines, and packed with the products themselves. Over the past several years coupons have enjoyed phenomenal growth; a record 120 billion were circulated by manufacturers last year, over 1,400 for every American household. But coupons only compound the problems manufacturers have created for themselves with trade promotion: they encourage brand switching and reinforce the consumer's inclination to shop not for brand but for price.

The recent history of trade promotion illustrates the dangers of adopting short-term tactics that collide with long-term goals. A company can't keep hawking its wares at cut rates and expect consumers and retailers to come back later and pay full price. The marketing addiction to price promotion looks like a habit that's almost impossible to kick. Manufacturers seem destined to shuttle back and forth among various short-term volume-building tools, all the while putting the value of their brands in greater jeopardy.

### QUESTIONS

1. *Why have expenditures for sales promotion grown so rapidly during the past decade? Do*

firms believe that sales promotion is more important than advertising?

2. Compare and contrast the nature and purpose of "consumer promotion" and "trade promotion."

3. If many retailers don't follow through on trade promotion allowances—that is, if they don't promote the manufacturers' products as promised—why don't the manufacturers simply stop offering these retailers the promotion allowances?

4. Does the effectiveness of consumer and trade promotion depend on the stage of the product life cycle? If so, how?

5. Why do companies continue to make heavy use of sales promotion if such expenditures actually destroy brand loyalty and undermine the future of branded products?

---

## ☐ 30

# Competition and product management: Can the product life cycle help?

*Sak Onkvisit*

*John J. Shaw*

---

*Although the product life cycle concept has been widely praised as a strategy planning tool, several writers have attacked the concept as being difficult to operationalize and very prone to misapplication. The following article concedes that the PLC needs further research and refinement but nevertheless insists that the PLC has important implications for marketing strategy planning. Suggesting that the PLC is driven by changes in competition and consumer demand, the article presents five different competitive strategies that firms can apply as their products pass through the various stages of the PLC.*

---

It is a misconception to think that the concept of product life cycle ignores competition. What *is* the role of product life cycle in the competitive setting? What competitive strategies can business firms employ to gain a differential advantage within the competitive environment?

**COMPETITION AND THE PRODUCT LIFE CYCLE**

Product life cycle (PLC), a concept that marketing can call its own, is so popular that its classical curve can be found in virtually all marketing texts covering marketing principles and marketing management. Its popularity can be attributed in part to the fact that it "can be the key to successful and profitable product management" and that "it permits management to make adjustments in strategy and tactics which bear directly on product policy."[1]

Source: Reprinted from *Business Horizons*, July–August 1986, pp. 51–62. Copyright © 1986 by the Foundation for the School of Business at Indiana University. Reprinted by permission. At the time of writing, Sak Onkvisit was associate professor of business at San Jose State University and John J. Shaw was associate professor of marketing at Providence College.

[1]John E. Smallwood, "The Product Life Cycle: A Key to Strategic Marketing Planning," *MSU Business Topics* 21 (Winter 1973), p. 30.

It is foolish to ignore a particular stage in the life cycle of a product; it is folly to fail to adjust the marketing mix accordingly.

Recently, the PLC concept has come under attack because some researchers say that the concept ignores "the competitive setting of the product, the relevant profit considerations, and the fact that product sales are a function of the marketing effort of the firm and other environmental forces."[2] PLC is usually thought to be an independent variable that influences the marketing mix. But some scholars believe that it functions in exactly the opposite direction and that it is a dependent variable whose behavior depends on the marketing mix.[3] According to this charge, a product that has been doing poorly for a few years may be assumed to be in the declining stage of its life cycle and is thus condemned to death, resulting in a self-fulfilling prophecy.

But these criticisms are somewhat unfair. It does not matter to a significant degree whether PLC is an independent variable, and it may be impossible to make such a determination. What is important is that PLC and the marketing mix are closely associated. A change in one will profoundly affect the other, regardless of whether PLC is a cause or an effect.

Equally unfounded is the charge that PLC ignores competition. The main reason for studying PLC is that each stage of the PLC actually represents a new and different kind of competitive environment. Because competition dictates both the length and direction of the PLC curve, competitive changes are at the heart of the PLC analysis. It is these changes that necessitate the changes in the marketing mix if a firm is to gain or maintain its differential advantage.

To overemphasize the marketing effort without paying attention to the competitive changes during a product's life cycle can be costly. It is doubtful that a brilliant and expensive marketing campaign can bring back to life an obsolete product such as a slide rule.

When Texas Instruments (TI) priced its Speak and Spell educational product too low in the introductory stage when there was a lack of competition, it was unable to keep up with the demand. Its second mistake was to increase the price significantly when the product entered the growth stage and was facing stiff competition.

Atari likewise failed to understand the competitive implications offered by PLC. Long after its video-game products had moved into the growth stage and were facing numerous newcomers, the company conducted business like a monopolist in the introductory stage. Had Atari and TI acknowledged the proper PLC stages, such costly mistakes in all likelihood could have been avoided.

How can managerial actions mitigate competitive effects as a product moves through its life cycle? In addition to examining competitive and managerial implications, this article will also explore the problems related to the validation and clarification of the concept.

## THEORETICAL FOUNDATIONS OF PLC

Often overlooked are the causes of the changes that occur with a product through its life cycle. Two major causes underlie the variations of product behavior during the life cycle:

1. The instability of demand, and
2. The instability of supply (that is, competitive position).

Two important theories contribute to an understanding of these two kinds of instability:

1. The diffusion process of innovations theory, and
2. The theory of monopolistic competition.

**Diffusion theory.** Diffusion theory seeks to explain the process by which consumers adopt new products and services over time.[4] Because both the PLC concept and the diffusion process are concerned with changes over time, the PLC curve and the cumulative diffusion curve appear quite similar except for one essential difference. The PLC curve is based on *absolute sales levels over time,* whereas the diffusion process de-

[2]Yoram Wind and Henry Claycamp, "Planning Product Line Strategy: A Matrix Approach," *Journal of Marketing* 49 (January 1976), p. 8.

[3]See, for example, William Lazer and James D. Culley, *Marketing Management: Foundations and Practices* (Boston: Houghton Mifflin, 1983), p. 465; and Nariman Dhalla and Sonia Uyspeh, "Forget the Product Life Cycle Concept," *Harvard Business Review* 54 (January–February 1976), pp. 102–12.

[4]See Everett M. Rogers, *Diffusion of Innovations* (Glencoe, Ill.: The Free Press, 1971).

scribes the *cumulative percentage of potential adopters.* Corresponding to the four stages of the PLC concept are the five adopter categories of innovators, early adopters, early and late majorities, and laggards (see Figure 1).

**Theory of monopolistic competition.** Chamberlin's theory of monopolistic competition, by contrast, elaborates on the behavior of firms during a product's life cycle.[5] Monopolistic competition involves a market structure in which many firms sell products that are close, but not perfect, substitutes for each other.

In the *introductory stage,* the number of competitors is minimal. Businessmen deliberately avoid being pioneers due to the high risks and costs involved.[6] While the situation seems to approximate monopoly, one essential element of monopoly is missing. There is free entry into the market—entry barriers are lacking—for any firm that chooses to enter the industry.

Not surprisingly, the number of firms peaks in the *growth stage,* when the product prospers. Everyone wants a slice of the pie. Although pure competition may appear to be at work, this appearance may be deceptive. Instead of being strictly homogeneous, the product can be differentiated.

During the *maturity stage,* the number of competitors is usually stable. Very few firms enter or leave the industry. Weak companies have been weeded out, and new firms find it risky and costly to break into the market because the market already has been divided among survivors. The stability and number of firms tend to resemble somewhat the market structure of oligopoly.

Toward the end of the *decline stage,* a few specialized firms choose to remain in the market. The declining market is financially unattractive for large firms and for many other firms as well. In this regard, much like the diffusion theory, which explains why consumers get in and out of the market, the theory of monopolistic competition explains the variation in the number of firms in the market during the different stages of the PLC.

## RESEARCH PROBLEMS WITH PLC: WHAT AREAS NEED INVESTIGATING?

Social scientists employ a number of criteria to evaluate a given theory. As a theory, PLC satisfies many of these criteria, which include well-formedness, linguistic exactness, stability, empirical interpretability, and falsifiability. One problem with the PLC concept in its present form is that the theory can be both refuted and confirmed at the same time. It can be refuted because some products have been found to contradict the PLC model. But it can be confirmed because many products have followed sales patterns that are consistent with the described phenomenon. Obviously, no theory can be relevant for all products. More work must be done to determine products applicable to PLC and circumstances that influence products to behave in the manner described in PLC.

Given its enormous popularity and application, it is surprising that empirical studies of PLC are so few. One of these few studies found that the time span from rapid growth to maturity is more than 40 years for many industrial products.[7] But the duration of the life cycle for most product types is becoming shorter because of the increasing pace of technological innovations and the rapid rate of new product introduction.[8]

In terms of shape and direction, 17 percent of the product classes and 20 percent of the product brands of 140 product categories in the food, health, and personal care industries were found to follow the sales pattern described by PLC.[9] A more recent study found PLC curves for more than 80 percent of the products investigated.[10] However, unlike the classical bell curve, there are sharp changes from stage to stage, and the turning points are not clearly identifiable.

As a matter of fact, the classical bell curve is only one of the 12 common variations thus far identified.[11] Furthermore, there are peaks and val-

[5]Edward H. Chamberlin, *The Theory of Monopolistic Competition* (Cambridge: Harvard University Press, 1933).

[6]See Steven P. Schnaars, "When Entering Growth Markets, Are Pioneers Better Than Poachers?" *Business Horizons* 29 (March–April 1986), pp. 27–36. The "used apple" approach is used to study the successes and failures of pioneers, early entrants, and late entrants.

[7]Hans B. Thorelli and Stephen C. Burnett, "The Nature of Product Life Cycles for Industrial Goods," *Journal of Marketing* 45 (Fall 1981), pp. 97–108.

[8]William Qualls, Richard W. Olshavsky, and Ronald E. Michaels, "Shortening of the PLC—An Empirical Test," *Journal of Marketing* 45 (Fall 1981), pp. 76–80.

[9]Rolando Polli and Victor J. Cook, "Validity of the Product Life Cycle," *Journal of Business* 40 (October 1969), pp. 385–400.

[10]"Grocery Products Exhibit Different Life Cycle Curve," *Marketing News,* August 6, 1982, p. 6.

[11]David R. Rink and John E. Swan, "Product Life Cycle Research: A Literature Review," *Journal of Business Research* 7 (September 1979), pp 219–42.

**Figure 1 □ Theoretical foundations of PLC**

| Diffusion process (unstable demand: consumer behavior) | PLC stage (unstable sales) | Monopolistic competition (unstable competition: corporate behavior) |
|---|---|---|
| Innovators | →Introduction | ← Monopoly |
| Early adopters | → Growth | ← Monopolistic competition |
| Early majority/late majority | → Maturity | ← Monopolistic competition/ oligopoly |
| Laggards | → Decline | ← Not applicable |

leys in each PLC stage, indicating that competitive and environmental changes are occurring in the marketplace.

More studies are definitely needed to validate the concept. Toward this end, several research problems must be investigated.

### Ambiguity

PLC is a basic, broad generalization that offers an explanation about the circumstances found within its four stages. It does not specify the conditions when and where it is applicable.

The product life concept also fails to specify whether the product in question falls within a product class, a product form, or a brand, and the degree of market applicability in these three cases. There is thus a question of whether all three product levels are supposed to behave in the same way over the stages of the PLC or whether the PLC is supposed to represent one of the three product levels.

In theory, *product class* is the most general and thus the most stable level. *Product brand,* on the other hand, is the most specific and is subject to the greatest variation in PLC applicability. *Product form* is between product class and product brand and therefore falls somewhere in between in terms of stability of market application. It would be useful if the PLC phenomenon could be more specific in indicating the changing conditions found at each product level and providing particular market applications within each of the three product levels rather than implying that the general explanations are valid for all three product levels.

It is impossible to claim that PLC is applicable for all products. The concept must become more specific, therefore, with regard to the products where it is applicable. Does the PLC framework work better with a technical product, an expensive product, a significantly improved product, or a to-

tally new product? Do fads and fashions conform to the phenomenon described? By treating these questions explicitly, the theory can be made more precise and useful for practitioners.

### Measurement

Related to the problem of product ambiguity is the problem of measurement. The PLC hypothesis does not state whether the cycle of a product should be measured in terms of the sales volume (unit or dollar), the number of adopters, the number of firms, or a combination of these factors. Perhaps these measurements can be used together for the purpose of cross-validation.

The issue must also be clarified to determine how much and how long sales must change (increase or decrease) before the product is considered to be in a certain stage (for example, growth or decline). For the sales figures to be meaningful, they should be adjusted for inflation and for economic conditions such as recession.

At some time in the future it may be possible to operationalize the four stages and specify more clearly the conditions under which product measurement takes place. Until some of the conditions for measuring product movement through the PLC are defined more precisely, there always will be a question of what is being measured when providing an analysis of the product life cycle.

### Explanation and prediction

A good theory should be able to explain and predict the phenomenon in question. Insofar as explanation is concerned, the PLC theory is able to describe the phenomenon of sales behavior remarkably well. It goes beyond the merely descriptive aspect by explaining *why* and *how* this sales process changes over time. Undoubtedly, this part of the theory has contributed some richness to the understanding of the competitive nature of the market.

The predictive power of the PLC concept is, however, subject to question. Can the PLC forecast product performance? The issue is not whether prediction can be made but rather with what degree of accuracy. A high degree of accuracy of prediction is unlikely because the dynamic nature of competition makes it difficult to anticipate future consumer response correctly.

The PLC concept shows that a new product will mature and then inevitably enter a decline period. However, the life-cycle stages across product classes show great variation in length. These variations make it difficult to predict when one stage ends and the next one begins, not to mention the difficulty of determining the current stage of the product.

Furthermore, any prediction must take into account exogenous variables such as technology and economic conditions. Many analyses often overlook these variables, which can and do influence the product's movement through its life cycle. For instance, television is again a growth industry. People are encouraged to buy TV sets to use with other technologically new products (videocassette recorders, videodisc players, videogames, TV cameras, satellite antennas, home computers, cable TV, and so on).

## COMPETITIVE STRATEGIES AND THEIR IMPLICATIONS

Theory is a means to an end—not an end in itself. Ultimately, the value of a particular theory must depend on its ability to provide clues and insights for marketers to improve the efficacy of their actions. The PLC theory offers several important implications for product, distribution, pricing, and promotion strategies, all of which can be implemented.

Because competitive characteristics will vary from stage to stage, it is critical to identify and understand the stages that a product passes through as it survives the market. A failure to make timely adjustments in marketing mix variables can result in premature death for the product. It is impractical to believe that a universal solution can be offered for all types of products. But it is possible to provide a framework of general strategies for modifying the four Ps of marketing to make them consistent with the particular stage of a product. What are some of these strategies, and what are their competitive implications?

Five separate strategies will be outlined (see Figure 2):

1. **Fish Where the Fish Are,** an *imitation* strategy;

**Figure 2 ☐ The search for a strategic advantage**

*Pioneer:*
Get first crack at the market.
Obtain patent.
Create legal hurdles for others.
Match/surpass imitators' product features.
Dominate/saturate the market with more of own brands.
Be offensive (give trade discount, samples, coupons, and so forth).
Promote own product system as the industry's standard.

*Imitator:*
Avoid being first.
Let a pioneer open up a new market.
Learn from the pioneer's mistakes.
Be a fast imitator.
Offer an improved product version for differentiation.
If not fast or different, offer a lower price.

*Expansion:*
Promote more frequent usage.
Promote more varied usage.
Attract new users.
Make a new product from the same technical base.

*Transition:*
Look for product replacements.
Use today's stars as cash cows.
Avoid milking cash cows too dry.

*Future:*
Observe new technologies, even in unrelated fields.
Understand the implications of the S-curve.
As the S-curve approaches its technology limit, plan for an orderly switch to a new technology.
Avoid switching too quickly.
Consider cost and timing for switching.

2. **Protect Your Own Turf,** a *defensive* strategy;
3. **It Can Get Better, Not Older,** an *expansion* strategy;
4. **Milking a Cash Cow,** a *transition* strategy; and
5. **Tracing New Technologies,** a strategy for the *future.*

## PROPOSITION 1: FISH WHERE THE FISH ARE—AN IMITATION STRATEGY

Within many product areas, the chances for product failure are much greater than for product success. The performance and success record of most new product introductions is far from being impressive. Nowhere are these statements truer than in the cigarette industry.

Since 1971 more than a hundred brands have been introduced within this industry; most of them (for example, Mermaid, Zack, Tramp, Twist, Dawn, Decade, Real, Fact) promptly disappeared from the scene. In this industry an important question should be, Is it wise to be a pioneer? A better strategy within this industry might be to deliberately *avoid* being the pioneer.

Given the generally poor record of survival for new products, along with the huge investment associated with their introduction, there is a great risk in being a pioneer. As a result, some firms deliberately avoid being first in the market. They prefer to have others gamble first. Then, if the first brand is successful, they move into the same market as the second or third entrant. This market-entry strategy is often referred to as the "used apple" approach.[12]

The strategy has been successfully used by Hiram Walker, whose motto is "Fish Where the Fish Are." The company allows other firms to enter and test new markets and then moves in quickly when the demand is solidly in place.[13]

If this strategy is chosen, an imitator must be either fast or unique in order to survive:

> If competitors are different and coexist, then each must have a distinct advantage over the other. Such an advantage can only exist

if differences in the competitor's characteristics match differences in the environment that give those characteristics their relative value.[14]

According to the "used apple" theory, the imitator cannot afford to wait too long to get into the market because the tenth bite of the apple is not so juicy nor so large as the second or third bite. This explanation implies that one cannot be just another imitator with a "me-too" product but, instead, must be a *good* imitator as well as being a *fast* one.

Philip Morris has perfected this strategy. The company has chosen not to be an innovator, and it never pioneers new product brands in any cigarette category.[15] Capitalizing on the successes and failures of its competitors, Philip Morris rushes into the market with its own brand as soon as it is evident that its pioneering rival is going to be successful in a new segment. Philip Morris used this strategy to match R. J. Reynolds' market success by quickly introducing the Saratoga brand in the 120s category.

When Reynolds created the low-tar cigarette segment with its Vantage and Now brands, Philip Morris wasted no time introducing Merit, its own brand. Exactly as the "used apple" tactic implies, other late entrants—such as L&M's Decade and Brown & Williamson's Fact—failed. By the time other brands tried to enter, Vantage and Merit already had swallowed up the market. The low-tar category, which was nonexistent in 1975, accounted for 61 percent of market in 1982.[16]

What if an imitator is not fast enough? If a marketer is late, the situation is not necessarily hopeless. The market strategy in this case should be to offer a unique product so that some kind of product differentiation is achieved.

This market strategy can be illustrated by examining home permanents. For many years, this market has been controlled substantially by Procter & Gamble's Lilt and Gillette's Toni. Chesebrough-Pond was able to break into the market, however, and capture a surprising 27 percent market share by introducing an odorless

[12]See Theodore Levitt, "Exploit the Product Life Cycle," *Harvard Business Review* 43 (November–December 1965), pp. 81–94.

[13]"Hiram Walker: A Move into Rum Fills a Major Product Gap," *Business Week,* April 24, 1978, pp. 92–93.

[14]Bruce D. Henderson, "The Anatomy of Competition," *Journal of Marketing* 47 (Spring 1983), p. 8.

[15]See "Philip Morris: The Hot Hands in Cigarettes," *Business Week,* December 6, 1976, pp. 60–64.

[16]"Why the Cigarette Makers Are So Nervous," *Business Week,* December 20, 1982, pp. 55–56.

product named Rave that produced a "soft" permanent.[17]

By the same token, Brown & Williamson, which had failed earlier with Fact cigarettes, finally broke into the low-tar segment with a winner. Its Barclay had a unique filter. In terms of initial sales, Barclay is now considered to be the most successful cigarette ever introduced.

If the imitator is neither fast nor unique, a penalty must be paid in the form of lower price. But this penalty can be transformed into a differential advantage. By offering its own versions at drastically lower prices, Helene Curtis takes advantage of the heavy promotional costs its competitors pay to push new shampoo products. Not surprisingly, its Suave shampoo is tops in terms of volume (ounces).

## PROPOSITION 2: PROTECT YOUR OWN TURF—A DEFENSIVE STRATEGY

It is disheartening to see others take advantage of the fruits of one's labor. A pioneer, therefore, should consider in advance how to product itself if it becomes successful with a new idea or product.

That this kind of planning can be critical is shown by Royal Crown's experiences in pioneering the two new segments of diet and decaffeinated colas. Because of its small size, the company was unable to protect its own turf. Before long, its Diet Rite and R.C. 100 were outmuscled by Tab and Pepsi Free, respectively. This phenomenon is similar to the Principle of Mutual Exclusion:

> All competitors who persist and survive have a unique advantage over all others. If they did not, then others would crowd them out.[18]

What strategies can the pioneer firm adopt to turn back these challenges? As a start, patents should be obtained whenever possible. Adopting this tactic can prevent or at least slow down the competition. Atari, for example, was successful in proving that the K. C. Munchkin game infringed

upon its copyright of the popular Pac-Man. It also sued some of its former employees for founding Activision, which then sold video cartridges designed to be used with the Atari machines. Merrill Lynch likewise obtained a patent for its popular CMA (Cash Management Account). Its lawsuits have slowed down other brokerage firms.

To frustrate imitators, the pioneer can match or surpass the product features of its competitors. To counterattack Clorox's Twice as Fresh, which could stand or be waved like a wand, Airwick introduced its own Airwand. After VisiCalc lost its 100 percent monopoly to nearly 40 copycats who offered more power or lower prices, VisiCorp fought back. Its VisiOn saved learning and execution time because its "mouse" controlled the movement of an arrow on the screen. The master of this match-or-surpass strategy is IBM. It continuously shortens the life cycle of its products by ceaseless innovations. Any imitation strategy adopted by competitors is very risky because the imitated versions become rapidly obsolete.

Another defensive strategy is merely to do what competitors are planning to do. In other words, the pioneer assumes the imitator role as well. Thus, the innovator can saturate the new market with more of its own brands, making it too crowded for anybody else to enter. Procter & Gamble employs this strategy with its many brands within the same product category. It simply leaves no retail shelf space for potential competitors. R. J. Reynolds tried to strengthen its dominance in the low-tar cigarette market by introducing additional brands such as Now, Camel Lights, and the ill-fated Real.

The best defensive strategy may be an offensive strategy, as perfected by Chesebrough-Pond. When its Vaseline Intensive Care lotion was challenged by Procter & Gamble's Wondra and Nabisco's Rose Milk, Chesebrough-Pond retaliated aggressively by providing two-for-one offers and other incentives for retailers. The result was that neither Wondra nor Rose Milk captured more than 10 percent of the market.

Hunt Foods suffered a similar fate when it developed the spicier Prima Salsa sauces to challenge Chesebrough's Ragu spaghetti sauce. Chesebrough was quick to turn back the competition by introducing nationwide its Extra Thick and Zesty spaghetti sauce. As a result, Hunt never captured more than 9 percent of the market. This

---

[17]"Chesebrough: Finding Strong Brands to Revitalize Mature Markets," *Business Week*, November 10, 1980, pp. 73–76.

[18]Henderson (note 14): 8.

share has declined to 5.4 percent, representing a loss of $8 million in sales. Campbell has had no better luck with its Prego brand sauces because Chesebrough once again retaliated. Through coupons and special truckload allowances, it practically gave away its Ragu brand.[19]

With a relatively high-technology product, it is critical for the pioneering firm to get its product system to become the industry's standard. This is true even when it means giving a helping hand to competitors through licensing its product knowledge. Incompatible, competing systems confuse consumers and slow down adoption (as with the four-channel sound system and, more recently, with videotex). If the pioneer's product design becomes the industry standard, it can recoup its investment while enjoying the substantial advantages of economies of scale and experience.

Sony made a costly mistake by trying to go it alone with its Betamax video system. It lost most of the market share to Victor Co., which was more liberal in licensing its VHS system. Having learned their lesson, Sony and Philips have agreed to standardize their laser optical readers and compact discs in order to preempt other product formats, thus putting pressure on competitors to give up their competing systems.

## PROPOSITION 3: IT CAN GET BETTER, NOT OLDER—AN EXPANSION STRATEGY

PLC suggests that a product is most profitable when it is growing and that it becomes less profitable when it is declining. This finding suggests that the marketer should attempt to set his strategies to keep sales growing instead of letting sales decline. The product does not have to decline; it can become better and not obviously older. Many older persons stay attractive as they age when they take care of themselves instead of letting themselves go into a decline. Similarly, products should be updated to stay attractive.

Zenith always has updated its TV sets with new features. Recently it has added such features as ready-for-cable channels and the space phone to its current line. Tide, Procter & Gamble's best selling laundry detergent, has maintained its number one position by being updated nearly twenty times.

As Figure 3 shows, there are at least four strategies designed to keep products growing.[20]

Figure 3 □ **Strategies to keep sales growing**

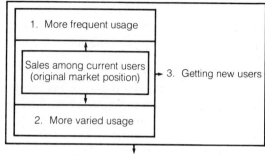

4. New product for a new market

**1. Promote more frequent usage among current users.** This tactic is the simplest because it involves getting users who are quite familiar with the product to use it more frequently. Sanka tries to convince people that, if they drink Sanka at home, they should ask for it when they are dining out. A-1 steak sauce does exactly the same thing. Its commercials show people insisting on the product in restaurants. The aim, of course, is to stimulate sales to restaurants as well as to increase consumer demand.

**2. Promote more varied usage among current users.** This strategy, like the first one, involves current users. The distinction is that, while the "frequent usage" technique is concerned with using the product in its present form to meet one single purpose, the "varied usage" strategy encourages consumers to use the product differently for different purposes under different situations.

Q-Tips does not promote its product to clean the ears because this purpose is well understood by users. What the company does is to show people using Q-Tips to remove fingernail polish and eye makeup.

It is possible to combine the "frequent usage" and "varied usage" strategies. Arm & Hammer has been successful in repositioning its baking soda as a product that can get rid of unpleasant odors in addition to its conventional use. Advertisements encourage users to change the baking soda in their refrigerators more frequently.

**3. Find new users.** Marketers can go only so far in encouraging their current users. Sooner or later, this segment is exhausted, and new users

---

[19]"Chesebrough: Finding Strong Brands" (note 17), pp. 73–76.

[20]As suggested by Levitt (note 12), p. 89.

must be found to support sales. Many people object to using Listerine because of its taste. As a result, Warner Lambert introduced Listermint as well as a cinnamon version of Listerine. Its aim was to attract new users and to retaliate against its chief rival, Scope, which had introduced a similar product. Listerine's latest campaign is to attract customers by showing them that the product can help in removing plaque.

**4. Make a new product based on the basic materials.** While the first three strategies involve virtually no change in the existing product, the fourth recommendation creates a new product for a new market. Campbell, for example, has introduced its Prego spaghetti sauce as an extension of its Franco-American line. Texas Instruments' highly successful product, Speak and Spell, is an extension of the technical knowledge it derived from producing other educational products. TI has introduced another new product called Magic Wand Speaking Reader, which is a further refinement and extension of Speak and Spell.

A company should not abandon its mature products just because they have been around for awhile. The length of time a product has been in the market is irrelevant. Many products appear to remain in the maturity stage forever without slipping over into the decline stage. Liquors and automobiles are prime examples. As a matter of fact, for many companies their major assets may be their mature, proven products.

As long as mature products are not replaced by new technologies within the near future, the company should try to make these products work even harder. The firm can pump new life into its existing products by using product refinements and large doses of advertising. Chesebrough-Pond makes a practice of buying companies in mature or declining markets and then transforming them into fast-growing organizations.[21] The results have been such outstanding products as Pond's Cold Cream, Ragu sauce, Health-Tex children's wear, Adolph's meat tenderizer, Bass, Vaseline, Q-Tips, Cutex nail products, and Prince Matchabelli fragrances.

Good marketers will distinguish between products that are indeed old and declining and those where the decline may be caused by negligence,

which perhaps can be remedied by proper support and better positioning in the marketplace.

## PROPOSITION 4: MILKING A CASH COW—A TRANSITION STRATEGY

Where products are indeed mature, the marketer must look for replacements for today's "stars." "Milking a cash cow" means using the resources generated by mature products to support the needs of new and growing products.

Pillsbury's basic products are flour, cake mixes, and refrigerated biscuits, all of which are in flat markets characterized by strong competition among the rivals. Pillsbury's profitable refrigerated dough is thus used as a "cash cow" to feed the company's Burger King division.

This strategy must be used carefully, however. In many cases the company's image and reputation are strongly associated with its mature products. It is risky to divert resources too quickly from these mature products to the uncertain future of new products that the company may want to introduce into the market. A. B. Dick used to "milk" its mature offset business for the fast-growing automated office system. But after a 5 percent decline in market share of the offset business, it finally stopped using reprographics as a "cash cow."[22]

Using "cash cows" to buy time is only a short-run strategy. Thus, this course of action should supplement and not replace human judgment. In the end, marketers must make their own decisions.

An Wang illustrates foresight and highly developed entrepreneurial instincts. The business world was surprised in the early 1970s when he abandoned programmable calculators, his main business. But he foresaw that mass marketers such as Texas Instruments would dominate the calculator market with mass-produced, low-cost models. Wang sought instead the high-growth market niches in word processors and small business computers. One reason why Wang Labs has outpaced such competitors as IBM over the past decade is this identification of a new market and withdrawal from a profitable one.[23]

[21]"Chesebrough: Finding Strong Brands" (note 17), p. 73.

[22]"A. B. Dick Cranks Up Its Offset Business," *Business Week*, October 18, 1982, pp. 126, 131.

[23]"Wang Labs' Run for a Second Billion," *Business Week*, May 17, 1982, pp. 100–4.

## PROPOSITION 5: TRACKING NEW TECHNOLOGIES—A STRATEGY FOR THE FUTURE

The advance of technology eventually affects every person and every product. A bank that ignores electronic banking may not be around at some date in the future. Paper companies and newspaper executives should be aware that, with new electronic technologies, paper is not the only means of storing, displaying, and retrieving information.

Executives in many industries often assume that a technological change in one industry will not affect their industry and that their products will last forever. Some resist technological change because they want to play it safe with the existing technology or because they underestimate or misunderstand technology's potential.

Technological improvement in any field is eventually limited by the laws of nature and the S-curve which implies that some switching is needed when existing products become mature. Note the similarity of the S-curve in Figure 4 to the PLC curve. RCA, for example, fell prey to very strong technological resistance by holding on too long to its success with vacuum-tube devices. Even after the introduction of transistors and solid-state technology, it insisted on designing more sophisticated tubes.

**Figure 4 □ S-curve and technological limits**

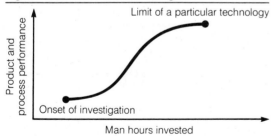

Source: Adapted from Richard N. Foster, "A Call for Vision in Managing Technology," *Business Week*, May 24, 1982, p. 26.

When is it time to switch to a new technology rather than continue with an existing technology? Ten key indicators show when an existing technology (its S-curve) is approaching its limits:[24]

___

[24]See Richard N. Foster, "A Call for Vision in Managing Technology," *Business Week*, May 24, 1982, pp. 24–33.

1. Top managers intuitively sense that R&D productivity is declining.
2. R&D deadlines are missed because improvement is becoming more difficult.
3. The trend is toward process rather than product improvements. Typically, as limits are approached, process improvements are easier to attain.
4. A loss of R&D creativity is perceived.
5. There is disharmony among the R&D staff.
6. No improvement comes, even after R&D leaders or staff are replaced.
7. Profits come from increasingly narrow market segments.
8. Market share is lost—particularly to a smaller competitor—in a specialized market niche.
9. Despite spending substantially more or less than competitors over a period of years, there is little difference in returns.
10. Smaller competitors are taking radical approaches that "probably won't work." If they do work, larger competitors may suddenly become small ones.

Despite the technical implications, marketers should not switch too quickly, especially when their products are still profitable and when switching incurs enormous expenses. Most Japanese makers of videocassette-recorders want to delay the next generation of machines using 1/4-inch tapes. Because the industry anticipates enormous retooling expenses, they do not want to make the booming 1/2-inch tape market obsolete at a time when they are reaping large profits. This is the reason that banks, in spite of huge losses caused by bank-card fraud, are reluctant to use the so-called "smart" cards. Even though they are technically superior to conventional cards, they are expensive and not very durable. Thus, both cost and timing must be taken into account.

The scarcity of PLC research may be due to the ambiguity of the concept, which makes measurement difficult. In its present form, PLC provides broad generalizations—so broad as to make the validation of the concept almost impossible. The problem arises not so much from ignoring competition but rather from failing to make explicit the varying competitive characteristics. It is inappropriate to say that competition affects the length and direction of the PLC. Such a statement is so broad that it makes any confirmation or refutation difficult. The concept must be more specific with regard to the variables (competitive actions, technology, taste change, and so forth) that will affect the PLC curve. The relationships should be made more explicit.

Whether the PLC is a dependent variable or an independent one is a subject of much debate. Actually, it does not matter whether the PLC is a causal factor or an effect. That controversy serves only as a distraction from the real issue:

> The most important fact is that both the PLC and marketing mix variables are highly interrelated. It is impractical and unnecessary to separate a cause from an effect in this case. PLC stages require some adjustment in marketing strategy which in turn controls those life cycle stages themselves.[25]

General Electric has gone so far as to define its products as "grow," "defend," and "harvest." These products are matched by managers of different skills, managers who are classified as "growers," "caretakers," and "undertakers."[26]

In spite of its shortcomings, PLC provides a basis for product analysis. But the concept should not be taken on blind faith and used as a substitute for logical judgment. As Hofer explains, propositions cannot be used this way "because there always are factors unique to each situation that will have an important bearing on the success of the strategy which is chosen." But if the strategy violates some propositions, "it still may be valid, as there are always exceptions to any rule."[27]

In any case, PLC is a valuable tool that suggests a proper course of action to lessen the impact of competitive changes. In the search for a differential advantage, it provides normative implications for decision making.

## QUESTIONS

1.  Why has the product life-cycle concept come under recent attack, and why do Onkvisit and Shaw consider such criticism unfair? Do you agree with them?

2.  Explain the underlying theoretical foundations of the PLC.

3.  Summarize those aspects of the PLC that need to be further researched and refined.

4.  Explain the five strategies outlined in the article. Indicate when and during which stage of the PLC each would be appropriate.

5.  What is an S-curve and how does it relate to the PLC? How can marketers tell whether they are approaching the limits of an S-curve—and what does this imply about their strategic options?

*6.  Where and how does a brand extension strategy (Reading 18) fit into the strategic framework of the PLC?

*7.  How does Levitt's concept of "marketing myopia" (Reading 5) relate to managing a firm's competitive strategy as products move through their product life cycles?

---

[25]Sak Onkvisit and John J. Shaw, "An Examination of the International Product Life Cycle and Its Application within Marketing," *Columbia Journal of World Business* 18 (Fall 1983), pp. 73–79.

[26]"Wanted: A Manager to Fit Each Strategy," *Business Week*, February 25, 1980, pp. 166–73.

[27]Charles W. Hofer, "Toward a Contingency Theory of Business Strategy," *Academy of Management Journal* 18 (December 1975), pp. 807.

*Question relates concepts in this and other readings.

## □ 31

# Competition versus customer satisfaction—which is the key to marketing success

*Visit the business section of your local bookstore and you may come away thinking that West Point was built to train marketing managers rather than military generals! Books about consumerism and the marketing concept have suddenly been bumped off the shelves by a flood of books about "marketing warfare" and "competitive strategy." Instead of satisfying human needs and wants, marketing managers are now being advised to "attack" their competition with frontal attacks, flanking attacks, encirclement attacks, and guerrilla warfare. When attacked by a competitor, one is advised to choose among the fortified front-line defense, the preemptive defense, the counteroffensive defense, the mobile defense, and perhaps even a strategic retreat!*

*Is the marketing concept obsolete? Is looking for your competitor's weaknesses a better marketing strategy than searching for new and better ways to satisfy customer needs? Should marketing be viewed as "warfare"? The following two articles address these questions from opposing viewpoints. The first article reviews a popular new book about marketing warfare, suggesting that "understanding the competition has become a matter of life or death." The second article examines the successful Japanese "invasion" of U.S. markets and concludes that marketing warfare "is a more short-sighted and less productive strategy" than trying to satisfy customer needs.*

## □ 31–A

# Forget satisfying the consumer—just outfox the other guy

*Paul B. Brown*                                    *Barbara Buell*

*Jo Ellen Davis*                                    *Kenneth Dreyfack*

Bam! Another shot in the new marketing wars.

   Last month's full-page newspaper ads by Sperry Corp., snidely pointing out that IBM's PCjr bombed after just 15 months, are the kind of direct assault on a competitor that's become the norm in markets ranging from bagels to computers. But according to Jack Trout, president of New York's Trout & Ries Advertising, the Sperry

campaign will flop. "It's a disaster, it's doomed," he says.

   Source: Reprinted from the October 7, 1985, issue of *Business Week* by special permission, © 1985 by McGraw-Hill, Inc. At the time of writing, Paul B. Brown, Barbara Buell, Jo Ellen Davis, and Kenneth Dreyfack were all on the staff of *Business Week*.

Why the gloomy assessment? According to Trout, it's O.K. to assault your leading competitor with a hard-hitting campaign. Take the successful Burger King Corp. ads that scoffed at the competitor's "grilled" hamburgers. But the Sperry ads go about it all wrong, he contends. By promoting the high performance of its computers, Sperry is directing its attack squarely at the strength of International Business Machines Corp.—its mighty reputation for quality office computers.

## NEEDS AND WANTS

To Trout, the Sperry campaign is an example of many marketing strategies that do not adequately consider the competition. "Knowing what the customer wants isn't too helpful if a dozen other companies are already serving the customer's wants," says Trout. In a new book called *Marketing Warfare* (published by McGraw-Hill Inc., which also publishes *Business Week*), Trout and his longtime colleague Al Ries tear into traditional customer-oriented marketing. "The true nature of marketing today involves the conflict between corporations, not the satisfying of human needs and wants," they contend. "To be successful, a company must . . . look for weak points in the positions of its competitors and then launch marketing attacks against those weak points."

Paying attention to the competition isn't a revolutionary idea. But a surprising number of companies devise marketing approaches without putting enough emphasis on their competitive position. Two examples, says Trout: Prudential-Bache Securities Inc.'s bid to go against bigger brokerage houses with a "me-too" campaign and American Motors Corp.'s persistent effort to battle Detroit's Big Three and foreign competitors in the passenger sedan market.

Now, however, as many marketers face maturity in their product segments and a slow-growth economy, some are starting to put competitors under the microscope. They're hiring consultants to predict what the opposition will do. And increasingly they're designing products and sales strategies intended to harm their rivals.

Says John H. Costello, senior vice-president for marketing and sales at Pepsi-Cola USA: "Consumers are more demanding. They are shopping around more, so you have to know your competi-

tor and develop products that clearly differentiate your product from theirs."

Ries and Trout call that strategy "flanking"—finding an uncontested market from which to attack your well-entrenched opponent. Pepsi, for example, has done that by creating a new product called Slice, a soda with 10 percent fruit juice. By adding the juice, Pepsi has put Coca-Cola on the defensive. Coke's lemon-lime drink, Sprite, contains no fruit juice.

## SECOND PLACE

Initial reports show the tactic is working. Introduced in April, 1984, Slice is now sold in about 75 percent of the country, and in many markets it is beating out Sprite for second place behind 7UP among lemon-lime drinks. Analysts say Slice has captured about 3 percent to 4 percent of the market where it competes. If that holds nationwide, Slice's annual sales would be about $700 million.

Coca-Cola is testing Minute Maid orange soda, its own soft drink with fruit juice, but Pepsi beat it to the punch. Ries and Trout note that it is always easier to defend a position than to take one, a lesson companies such as GE and RCA learned when they tried to attack IBM in computers in the 1960s and 1970s. Sperry may be making the same mistake with its new frontal attack on Big Blue.

Companies such as Sperry that take on a market leader head-to-head believe they have a better product—and that once consumers try it out, the product will take off. But Ries and Trout argue that a better product is virtually irrelevant if people already have a favorite. "The most wasteful thing you can do in marketing today is to try to change a human mind. Once a mind is made up, it is almost impossible to change."

Instead, the authors say, companies should look for ways to outflank their competition. Or they should find specific markets to defend at all costs—what the authors call "guerrilla warfare." For example, American Motors might compete in the car market by offering just one product line—the Jeep—and concentrating all its resources there.

Competitive-oriented marketing makes sense these days for another reason, says Joseph G. Smith, president of Oxtoby Smith Inc., a New York consumer research and consulting firm. "It is perfectly clear the likelihood for really significant product difference is less than it used to be," Smith points out. "Companies are finding their labs have no magic potion. They don't have unique access to raw material. In more and more categories, you are in a parity ballgame."

## LIFE OR DEATH

Companies even approach their markets the same way, says Thomas V. Bonoma, a professor of marketing at the Harvard business school. "Everyone has the same consultants and the same business school graduates," he says. "It is getting harder and harder to differentiate yourself in the marketplace."

Not everyone agrees with Ries and Trout. "To focus too much on the competition means you're relying on them to do their marketing job right," says Michael S. Swavely, vice-president for marketing at Houston-based Compaq Computer Corp., one of the few thriving computer companies. "We'd rather make our own decisions."

Many marketers, of course, clearly drifted away from astute competitive strategizing in the 1970s, when high inflation and expanding markets covered up a lot of mistakes. Now those days are gone, and wayward marketers are being jolted back. Understanding the competition has become a matter of life or death.

---

## ☐ 31–B

# The collaborative approach to marketing

*Larry J. Rosenberg*

*James H. Van West*

The so-called militaristic approach to marketing, which applies the teachings of the great Western military theorists to today's marketplace, is becoming more popular as companies compete for market share rather than market growth in the 80s. The popularity of these military marketing strategies can be attributed in large degree to the defensive position in which many companies perceive themselves to be as a result of Japanese competitors. Their successful "invasions"—in one American industry after another—have set the stage for limited to full-blown warfare for markets.

Many American firms point to the Japanese victories as evidence that the Japanese are using a "samurai-style" of military strategy. Therefore, American companies are responding to these attacks with a similar warlike approach. We assert not only that calling Japanese strategy militaristic misses the essence of what they are really doing, but also that this emphasis on warfare misdirects limited company resources. The militaristic metaphor fixes attention on short-term, expedient solutions which do not provide long-term satisfaction of identified market needs. By excessively focusing corporate energies on defeating the competition—the "enemy"—we dilute the efforts devoted to defining true market needs.

What, then, is a better way for American marketing to proceed? This question led us to explore the underlying tenets of Japan's approach to successful marketing strategies and their misinterpretation as warfare by many American marketers. In noting the strengths of America's culture, we found the "commitment to collaboration;" from this came what we call *collaborative marketing*. This approach seems to describe what several leading American corporations are doing to revitalize their marketing for the 1980s.

Source: Reprinted from *Business Horizons*, November–December 1984, pp. 29–35. Copyright © 1984 by the Foundation for the School of Business at Indiana University. Reprinted by permission. At the time of writing, Larry J. Rosenberg was associate professor of marketing at the University of Massachusetts at Amherst and James H. Van West was president of Management Support Services, Inc., an international consulting and training firm.

## MARKETING IS LIKE WAR

To American business executives, the military approach to marketing is not just a figure of speech; it affirms that the principles of military thinking are instrumental in planning marketing strategy.[1]

Marketing is viewed as a battlefield, competition as the enemy, and customers as the prize to be won or territory to be occupied. Types of warfare can include offensive, defensive, flanking, and guerrilla strategies. Because of the enormous resources required and the legal restrictions of government antitrust policy, total annihilation of one's competition is not usually the goal. Instead, emphasis centers on limited strategic warfare, attacking to rip away market share points from the competition in order to advance one's own market position.

It is not the system of competition that we fault; it generally serves as a stimulus to keeping marketing on its toes and can yield innovative products. We are criticizing the *excessive* attention to competition that warlike mindset can generate. This preoccupation with winning over competitors can distort the most valid basis of marketing excellence—namely, the long-run pursuit of consumer satisfaction.

The warfare model can be viewed as yet another impediment to practicing the "modern marketing concept"—serving customer needs as the best road to corporate long-term profitability. Since its emergence in the 1950s, deviations from it have been repeatedly pointed out. One of the best known of these indictments is "marketing myopia"—a firm's narrow focus on its existing product or technology preventing it from recognizing new market opportunities.[2] The collaborative approach, then, can be looked at as a way to update the practice of the marketing concept for the intensely competitive 1980s.

### Limitations of the military approach

Whether the military model is presented as a useful planning aid or as an inspirational call to battle, it is our contention that it can be counterproductive. Military thinking does a disservice to marketing in three ways.

**Customers matter most.** Although the customer is the prize, emphasis may be shifted away from superior satisfaction of customer needs and directed toward the competition. The strategy and tactics of warfare are formulated at the expense of innovative approaches to developing deep and lasting relationships with customers.

For example, RCA's SelectaVision videodisc system was engaged in fierce competition with Magnavox's MagnaVision and others for a new market. RCA pointed to its product's cheaper price; its rivals stressed their products' more numerous features. What the competitors missed was that the bulk of the market is more interested in the versatile videocassette recorders and a larger range of software (through cassette rentals and pay-TV cable). Given the consumer indifference and the fast pace of video technology, RCA's recent discontinuation of its videodisc operations is not surprising.

Evidence of more misdirections of the military approach—beating the competition at any cost—is provided by many of the "me-too" products available from competitors in so many industries. These have been geared more to capturing market share than to serving market needs. If the end is serving the customer, getting caught up in the military metaphor can be distracting.

**Long-term gains count.** The military model can mean engaging in constant battles, large and small, to prove oneself as a warrior. The focus too easily becomes short-term gains. It is the quick payoff that matters, and short lead times are favored in developing marketing strategies.

Thus, the risk of entering new markets or of launching boldly innovative technologies may be perceived as too high. The company's preference is to finetune existing markets, to play it safe. Industries that have fallen into this trap include automobiles, steel, and consumer electronics. This short-term bias is increasingly being pointed to as one of the principal weaknesses of American marketing in the face of foreign, especially Japanese, competition.[3]

---

[1]Philip Kotler and Ravi Singh, "Marketing Warfare," *The Journal of Business Strategy,* Winter 1981, pp. 30–41.

[2]Theodore Levitt, "Marketing Myopia," *Harvard Business Review,* September-October 1975, pp. 26–44, 173–81.

[3]Robert H. Hayes and William J. Abernathy, "Managing Our Way to Economic Decline," *Harvard Business Review,* July-August 1980, pp. 67–69.

**Militaristic metaphor distorts.** Because executives tend to solve problems by using analogies, there is the risk that metaphors will limit creative decision making. One potential harm of the military metaphor is taking it too literally. If people believe they are at war, winning at any cost becomes important. Price wars, industrial espionage, and sabotage of competitors become acceptable, even desirable. This way of thinking produces stress for the victor as well as for the vanquished.

These limitations in the military model of marketing seriously undermine this approach as a line of thinking to be pursued in the years ahead. Turning one's business inside out to maintain a state of warfare is not consistent with excellence in marketing.

## Samurai-style marketing

Part of the appeal of the military model of marketing is its similarity in form and spirit to the Japanese style of marketing. The modern Japanese executive is considered to be carrying on the samurai tradition, wielding his two swords in a fight to the death.

Although Japan's approach to marketing is inspired by the practice of "martial arts" by a warrior, it would be a misunderstanding to equate this with a military strategy. The martial arts tradition in Japan has an essence and discipline that differs greatly from the Western military orientation. It is a philosophy of life and heavily imbued with the Eastern spiritual tradition. While it is manifest in strategy and fighting, at its core the martial art is the practice of a craft and a path for living life. Thus, the martial art is related as much with poetry and pottery making as it is with fighting.

The alleged bible of modern Japanese business executives, *A Book of Five Rings,*[4] was written in 1645 by a samurai and master of Kendo, "the way of the sword." After an undefeated career, he wrote out his philosophy and strategy. Since 1645, 120 million copies of this book have been sold in Japan.

Although the book discusses swordsmanship and strategy, underlying these are basic principles of fighting which seem closely related to the Japanese way of marketing. They include the following:

**Dedication.** The commitment to learn the particular craft, to do it better and better.

**Clear thinking.** Not being emotionally attached to any particular tradition or bias, but being open-minded and precise about what is needed, why it is needed, and how it can be done, and never losing sight of the desired outcome.

**Keen sight.** Watching the opponent's every move, paying attention to what he is doing, how he is doing it, and when he seems about to act.

**Timing.** Knowing the moment when the goal can be achieved, and only then taking action.

**Flexibility.** Adjusting to the needs of the current situation and the direction it appears to be going.

Developing business strategies based on these principles not only makes sense, but is also consistent with the attributes of successful American companies.[5] These principles, applied to marketing, demand continuous attention to a dynamic marketplace, an understanding of company resources that will define ways in which to serve that market, and a commitment toward achieving perfection in the service of that market.

This strategy works for Japanese firms because of their discipline and commitment to practicing what they preach. Japanese corporate commitment is related to its sheer persistence, to never losing sight of the desired outcome. For example, even when experiencing huge deficits in the hand-held calculator business, the Japanese company, Omron, refused to die. Instead, it bore heavy losses in order to shift its work force, plant, basic technology, and marketing to electronic cash registers.

Fierce competition and flat sales led American manufacturers of radios to cut investment funds and phase out of this market. In contrast, Japanese producers such as Matsushita (Panasonic) and Sony believed in their radios' value and desired to keep these divisions alive. By investing in new technology and more marketing, they created new generations of radios—most recent among them Sony's Walkman portable radio-cassette player.

[4]Miyamoto Musashi, *A Book of Five Rings* (Woodstock, N.Y.: Overlook Press, 1974).

[5]Thomas J. Peters, "Putting Excellence into Management," *Business Week,* July 21, 1980, pp. 196–205.

Also, this strategy has been central to Japan's success in gaining major market shares in the U.S. In working toward this goal, not only did Japanese companies have to overcome an image of cheap, poor-quality products, but also they had to establish credibility and trust with American buyers. Japan accomplished this remarkable turnaround with long-term commitment to quality and reliability.

This type of practice of marketing is embedded in more than 1,000 years of the Japanese culture. Although we cannot directly imitate the Japanese style, we can learn from its basic tenets. What American marketers must do is find a version of this style that springs from our own unique cultural heritage.

## AS AMERICAN AS COLLABORATION

Some American companies have successfully extracted the essentials of the Japanese management style and modified them to fit the American tradition and work force. When this same process is applied to marketing strategies, a pattern emerges which is not only applicable to American companies, but also reflects what has always been one of America's traditional strengths.

Although America admires and extols the power of individual achievement, it cannot be denied that some type of group or team cooperation has contributed to many successful historical ventures. The settlement of the West during the 19th century required a shared effort on the part of early settlers, with a focus on long-term outcome despite many short-terms failures. The unifying spirit that characterized the World War II years was created by a common long-term goal, and enabled the United States and its allies to prevail in spite of heavy initial losses. The American commitment to putting a man on the moon is still another example. Space-age technology alone would not have succeeded without the superb organization of teams of professionals and a host of cooperating organizations.

This "collaborative ethic" is created by the active cooperation of several parties toward accomplishing some worthwhile mission while maintaining high ideals. It typically harnesses energy and resources over the long term, which encourages innovation and puts the importance of short-term gains into a larger perspective.

## Collaborating in marketing

Collaborative marketing can be defined as: the relationship between a company and its customers that maximizes their long-term mutual benefit. This approach incorporates the most basic concept of marketing—a customer-driven orientation.

In the American culture, the "outcome" of a relationship is generally more important than the cultivation of that "relationship" itself. Thus, partners—be they customers, suppliers, or employees—may be turned over at a rapid rate as long as the desired outcome—be it sales, profits, or return on investment—results. This is not the orientation of much of the world, which holds relationships to be as critical, if not more important, than outcomes. This emphasis on relationships must be cultivated in American marketing.

Most companies use the *selling* approach with their customers. Both buyer and seller try to make the best deal they can. This hit-and-run approach does not count on much customer loyalty.

Even the more recent *consultative* approach to marketing is basically only a more sophisticated version of the selling approach. The seller appears to be a consultant who stays as "objective" as possible and provides solutions to the customer's problems. This approach still keeps both parties at arm's length, however, because they remain relatively uninvolved in each other's affairs, especially over the long term.

*Collaborative* marketing is distinguished by a commitment between marketer and customer to work together over time. Some companies have been keynoting this perspective. Hewlett-Packard positions itself as a "business computer partner" with its corporate customers. Sperry touts its listening training programs for its employees worldwide as its approach to anticipating opportunity and developing technological innovations.

Collaborative marketing is characterized by the mutuality of benefits that is sought over the long run between company and customer. Each party admits its need to have the other in a relationship. Both parties realize they will be better off together than alone. Collaboration can include new product development, shared information sources, pricing arrangements, and distribution details. In the spirit of a joint venture, both parties can overcome each other's shortcomings.

Each party invests in learning the needs, concerns, problems, resources, and limits of the other. To truly know the other's world and to develop a cooperative relationship does not come quickly or easily. But over the long haul, collaboration will maximize the benefits that flow from the relationship.

The orientation of collaborative marketing is in sharp contrast to the competitive orientation of the militaristic model. Marketing warfare assumes a "win-lose" situation. The company must win and therefore the competition must lose. In contrast, the collaborative approach emphasizes a "win-win" situation. Here, the company and the customer cooperate to do the real work of marketing—to combine the needs of each for a rewarding exchange relationship.

Collaborative marketing, therefore, focuses on a mutually worthwhile mission, pursuit of quality and reliability, and the cultivation of a market convinced by past performance of the company's credibility.

## HOW TO DEVELOP COLLABORATIVE MARKETING

Developing a collaborative marketing approach requires the steps outlined below.

### Building credibility

A relationship built on trust must be developed over time. This is not always easy to achieve in the pressured environment of the business world. Between seller and buyer, games are played for the advantage of one at the expense of the other.

To commit oneself to a relationship in the collaborative marketing mode means that each party must be open and honest in its dealings. The company, in particular, must be credible in its communications with its customers. This includes the information it seeks, the products it develops and produces, the price it sets, and the distribution it arranges.

The top executives of large corporations who appear in advertisements are trying to build the credibility of their organizations. Chrysler Corporation's comeback from the edge of bankruptcy is due in some part to the forceful personality of its chairman, Lee Iacocca, making its advertisements more believable.

Honesty is not only the best, but is also the only policy on which to build a sound foundation of credibility. For example, the Diet Center franchise system sticks to the promotional policy of telling a simple, straightforward story without gimmicks or embellishments.

When both marketer and customer are organizations, another concern arises. Since it is not organizations but people who relate to each other, high turnover will make it difficult to develop and maintain trust between individuals. Although former IBM executives are eagerly sought by other firms, for example, IBM's relatively low turnover rate fosters long-term relationships between its personnel and its business customers.

### Making customers part of the business

Too many businesses seem to operate on the assumption that as long as they have enough customers, the loss of individual ones simply does not matter. But eroding levels of brand loyalty and the high cost of courting new customers—due to intense wooing by the competition—has made this an expensive and increasingly unreliable approach to marketing.

The development of a relationship means that the gap between the company and the customer might be bridged. Each must be close enough to the other to nurture the relationship.

Many innovative and successful new products actually come directly from product users rather than product manufacturers. Almost 80 percent of current manufacturing process equipment and scientific instruments were invented and operated by innovative users *before* they were offered commercially by the manufacturing companies.[6]

Before Hewlett-Packard followed Xerox and IBM into the "office of the future" market, it enlisted its customers in the design of a new line.

---

[6]Eric A. von Hippel, "Users as Innovators," *Technology Review,* January 1978, p. 31.

H-P engineers, while making service calls on H-P equipment, asked their customers to evaluate the competitors' equipment and what features they would like to have. These ideas helped shape product development. Soon H-P salespeople were calling on the customers again with a new product that reflected what they wanted. The result is that H-P has one of the most satisfied and loyal customer bases in the industry.

Tinker's leadership in the bearing business is based on its unrivaled product support to customers. Its well-trained sales engineers help design customers' equipment. Its customer contact personnel make frequent visits. Rather than have a customer return a malfunctioning product, Tinker personnel will make an on-site visit to get the equipment working again.

Customers can become involved in the business in several ways. One method is through "customer advisory boards"[7] which involve selected representative customers in the organization's decision making about marketing. Customers would be linked even more closely if they owned shares of stock in the supplier organization.

### Appealing to customers' highest values

The assumption that there will be a high rate of turnover among customers has led to a large marketing apparatus geared to persuading customers that the company can serve their best interests. This is exhibited in marketing research, which probes for some angle—specific, minor, or negative—that influences customer behavior. But these factors can come and go over time. This approach offers the "sizzle" but not a real "steak." That is why Cadillac no longer serves as the standard of luxury cars in the world.

For a company to develop credibility with its customers, it must gear its marketing toward values important to them. Satisfying customers' needs provides a firmer foundation on which to build a marketing relationship than relatively low prices, often an advantage offered by foreign competition. Examples of values important to customers are dependability, employment opportuni-

---

[7]Priscilla A. LaBarbera and Larry J. Rosenberg, "How Marketing Can Better Understand Consumers," *MSU Business Topics*, Winter 1980, pp. 31–32.

ties, safety, improvement of health, quality of life, ecological responsibility, and the fostering of the community.

IBM has its lofty reputation because it offers the best customer service in the computer industry. Gearing the company to keep its customers' machines operating is how it delivers service and reliability. Maytag's washing machines are built solid and simple for a decade of trouble-free operation. This dependability has allowed the firm to charge a 15 percent premium and has kept sales growing even during recessions.

Tinker has achieved considerable customer loyalty by concentrating only on tapered bearings made with the most advanced technology and a dedication to quality control. Ford's advertisements in New England stress that their autos are made by New Englanders.

### Competing mainly with yourself

Developing the relationship with customers in collaborative marketing deserves the greatest amount of energy. Efforts put into fighting games with the competition should be lessened.

However, some attention to sizing up the competition is necessary. It makes good sense to obtain ideas for devising one's own marketing strategy by improving on the good ideas of others. It also can help avoid unpleasant surprises.

But beyond this, the ultimate competition is with oneself. This simply means doing the best job possible—improving on what was done previously, recognizing one's limitations and finding ways to surpass them. In the process, one's special marketing capabilities will be developed; distinctive features such as product quality, fast service, and knowledgeable salespeople can make the critical difference. This pursuit of excellence can yield more than comparative analysis with competitors.

Consider the case of Perdue, the leading brand of chicken in the Northeast. A decade ago, consumers believed that one chicken was very much like another, a prime example of the me-too product. Yet, through skillful advertising that concentrated on establishing the credibility of the company's president, Frank Perdue, differentiation was established. The product became special in the minds of customers because it had a higher percentage of breast meat, something that customers highly desired. Recent TV commercials report that Perdue has been so successful at breeding its chickens for larger breast size that gauges used to measure the chicken breast size are no longer large enough. By competing with itself, Perdue has exceeded its original goal and produced a superior product.

As a company gets closer to its customers, it creates more distance between it and its competitors. The more the firm engages in collaborative marketing, the less serious and constant a threat competitors should become.

Philips Medical Systems had enjoyed a strong position in the medical diagnostic x-ray equipment market through its technical links with its European parent. Its initial strategy in the U.S. was based upon importing European technology, but the company came to realize that long-term success would depend on obtaining an adequate understanding of the nature of user problems to guide the application of technology. This required close collaboration with key customers and leading clinical practitioners in various fields.

These insights contributed to the development of Philips' Digital Vascular Imaging, a major diagnostic x-ray advancement. Philips resisted the temptation to compete with other x-ray equipment manufacturers by introducing product features similar to theirs. Instead, Philips focused on improving those areas where it already had a clinical advantage and competed with itself in order to optimize the return on the customer's investment. Presently, Philips claims more than 85 percent of the specialized x-ray diagnostic market for cardiac medicine.

Will collaborative marketing among American companies and customers be an effective strategy against foreign competitors? Along with continued progress in long-term investment, technological and service innovations, and employee participation in the organization, we contend that it will. This combination can counter even the lower-price advantage of certain foreign vendors. Instead of dropping out because they think they cannot compete with foreign rivals, American firms can cultivate relationships with customers through collaborative marketing. Since many industrial customers are themselves in danger of losing their customers to foreign competitors, they may

be more willing to engage in such a collaborative arrangement.

Where does collaborative marketing leave the militaristic approach? We hold that it puts marketing back on the track of satisfying basic customer needs over the long run. The warfare model should not be allowed to interfere with this overriding purpose of marketing. However, military-like concepts can guide the gathering of marketing information to finetune the allocation of marketing resources.

Successful marketing gets and keeps customers by satisfying their basic needs. Collaborative marketing places this process in the framework of a relationship. Thus, it directs companies to win with customers, rather than win over competitors. That is what marketing has been, is, and will be about.

## QUESTIONS

1. Explain why Trout and Ries believe that "the true nature of marketing today involves the conflict between corporations, not the satisfying of human needs and wants."

*2. Use your own examples to explain and illustrate the difference between a "flanking" strategy and "guerrilla warfare." How do these so-called "warfare" strategies differ from a strategy of market segmentation in the face of increasing market fragmentation? (See Readings 1, 11, and 13.)

3. Do you agree with the notion that firms often plan their marketing strategies without adequately considering their competition?

4. What exactly is "collaborative marketing"? How does it differ from the "selling" or "consultative" approaches?

5. Why do Rosenberg and Van West object to the "military approach" to marketing? What dangers or limitations do they see in this approach?

6. What accounts for the success of Japanese marketing efforts? Do the Japanese stress competitive warfare or customer satisfaction? Is their approach applicable to American companies?

*Question relates concepts in this and other readings.

*7. In your opinion, was the introduction of "new Coke" (Reading 19) an example of marketing warfare—or an attempt to better satisfy customer needs? Why?

8. Which is the key to marketing success—competitive strategy or customer satisfaction? What conclusions have you reached and why?

*Question relates concepts in this and other readings.

---

## ☐ 32

# Pampers revisited: P&G's battle to stay on top

*Reading 2 described how careful marketing strategy planning, combined with thorough and systematic marketing research efforts, led to Procter & Gamble's extremely successful introduction of Pampers disposable diapers. But success attracts competition, and between 1975 and 1985 P&G's share of the disposable-diaper market declined sharply. As the first of the following two articles indicates, similar decreases in market share were also occurring for other leading P&G brands such as Tide and Crest. Had P&G lost its competitive edge? Perhaps, but as the second article points out, P&G has not stopped battling. It has reestablished its domination of the disposable-diaper market—at least for now—and achieved surprising market-share gains in the detergent and toothpaste markets.*

---

## ☐ 32–A

# For P&G's rivals, the new game is to beat the leader, not copy it

## John Koten

Long before most companies ever bothered with such things as consumer research, a former manager at Procter & Gamble Co. remembers heading to work for nine months with one brand of deodorant under his right arm and another under his left.

At the end of each day, he would report to a small office where a reseacher would sniff to see how each product was holding up. "We always said only guinea pigs need apply at that company," the former P&Ger recalls. "P&G tested everything imaginable."

Such stories are typical of Procter & Gamble, whose reputation for thoroughness is just one rea-

Source: Reprinted by permission of *The Wall Street Journal,* May 1, 1985, P. 31. © Dow Jones & Company 1985. ALL RIGHTS RESERVED. At the time of writing, John Koten was a staff reporter for *The Wall Street Journal.*

son many regard it as the nation's premier marketing company. Its long dominance of the household-products industry is another. With its record of creating such well-known products as Tide detergent, Crest toothpaste and Pampers disposable diapers, the Cincinnati giant has often seemed in a different league from its rivals.

Recently, however, Brand X has been striking back. No longer behind in marketing sophistication, P&G's competitors have been waging increasingly tough battles in some of its most critical markets. Colgate may be on the verge of passing Crest. Tide is under pressure from Wisk. And Pampers' market share, which reached 75 percent a decade ago, is now down to less than 33 percent.

### WHAT COMPETITORS?

The competitive onslaught reflects improvements in the opposition more than failure at P&G. Nevertheless, as the company's rivals have become sharper, they also have been finding chinks in P&G's armor. Being called into question are such bedrock marketing practices as brand management, network television advertising, and test marketing.

"The old disciplines haven't been as successful as they were in the past," writes Cliff Angers, a senior vice president at Ogilvy & Mather, in a report on P&G to clients of the New York ad agency. One result: For the first time in more than three decades, P&G expects to report a decline in profit for the fiscal year ending in June.

Although its executives rarely publicly acknowledge even the existence of any rivals, P&G's own actions testify to the heightened competition. In recent years, it has taken such uncharacteristic steps as launching products without test marketing, introducing brands that don't exhibit any quality advantage, and experimenting with image advertising.

P&G officials, however, deny that the company has ever faced weak competition. "None of our competitors have ever been pushovers" says a company spokesman. He adds that one reason P&G seems to be fighting tougher competition these days is that it has gone into new markets and is now battling the likes of Coca-Cola Co. and other savvy marketers.

Nevertheless, while P&G officials say they fully expect to make up lost ground, some marketing experts and competitors believe they are witnessing the end of an era in the packaged goods business. "Procter & Gamble probably will never be as dominant as it was in the past," says Laurel Cutler, vice chairman of Leber Katz Partners, a New York ad agency. Emboldened by his company's inroads against P&G in the diaper market, Darwin Smith, chairman of Kimberly-Clark Co., recently vowed to shareholders that the company would "continue making life miserable for Procter & Gamble."

To an extent, P&G has been a victim of its own success. As companies have put more emphasis on marketing, many have raided P&G's ranks for talent. A directory of P&G alumni lists hundreds of former executives now at such companies as Bristol-Myers Co., PepsiCo. Inc., and Warner-Lambert Co. When P&G re-entered the feminine-hygiene market last year, two of its top three opponents—Johnson & Johnson and Tambrands Inc.—both were headed by past Procter & Gamble executives. The third—Kimberly-Clark—had a P&G alumnus in charge of the division responsible for that business.

But P&G's competitors no longer merely copy its system. Geared to selling blockbuster brands to legions of shoppers with similar tastes, the classic P&G mass-market system worked best when the preferences of its customers were more homogeneous than they are today.

Essentially, that system called for entering a market slowly, studying all the angles, and then launching a clearly superior product with a huge advertising blast. Selling a better brand, in turn, meant that P&G usually could charge a higher price, which helped fuel its extensive research activities and big ad budgets.

But in today's faster-moving and less stable market, the supercautious approach can easily backfire—a fact that P&G executives acknowledge and say they are trying to remedy. Kimberly-Clark, for instance, owes part of its recent success in diapers to beating P&G to nationwide sales of a product with refastenable tabs. The two companies actually had begun testing the product improvement at about the same time. While P&G took time to make sure it had the tabs just right, Kimberly-Clark raced into the market and began capturing sales.

## FEWER LAYERS

Edwin Shutt Jr., president of Tambrands Inc., estimates his company was able to develop and market its highly successful Maxithin panty shields in half the time it would have taken at P&G, where he once worked. "Here you have to only go through a few layers to get something approved," Mr. Shutt says. "At P&G it was more like seven or eight."

By improving their technical skills, the opposition also has been making it increasingly difficult for P&G to stick to its policy of selling only the best-quality products. For years, it has taught its executives that a brand must demonstrate in a blind test that at least 55 of 100 consumers prefer it over the closest competitor. These days, however, achieving noticeable superiority in something like a toothpaste or deodorant is a difficult task. And even when it happens, it often doesn't last. When P&G first developed its new Duncan Hines cookies, for instance, the product reportedly had one of the highest blind-test scores in company history. But by the time the cookies were selling nationwide, Nabisco, Frito-Lay and Keebler all had introduced their own versions, eliminating any taste advantage.

P&G has since sued all three of the competitors in Delaware federal court, alleging they violated its patents. Meanwhile, P&G executives, while agreeing that product quality has improved at its competitors, still maintain their brands are the best.

## HOT-SELLING PUMPS

Scores that measure superiority also have become less meaningful as markets have become more fragmented, with dozens of brands offering different advantages to suit different consumer tastes. In such a market, even a product that was outscored 90 to 10 by the leading brand theoretically could become a best seller if the same 10 percent also stuck with it against other brands.

Moreover, such long-time rivals as Colgate-Palmolive Co. and Lever Brothers Co. often have shown more skill at selling products that have less tangible consumer benefits. Colgate, for instance, has moved within striking distance of P&G's Crest by doing a better job with the new pump dispensers. As a result, industry officials say Colgate's share of the market is now within one half a percentage point of Crest and still gaining.

"Procter sometimes hurts itself by giving the consumer too much credit," says a former executive. If they think something is junk, "they won't touch it even if it becomes the next big seller." P&G officials agree that they tend to ignore products that they consider faddish.

Competitors cite just that sort of rationale as a possible explanation of why P&G avoided making a serious effort in the liquid detergent market, where Lever's Wisk has captured nearly a 40 percent share.

## LOWER-PRICED SNUGGLE

The difficulties of maintaining any product advantage also has undermined P&G's historical strategy of slapping premium prices on its brands. Lever Brothers saw an opening in the fabric-softener market two years ago because of the high prices P&G was charging for its Downy brand. Entering with Snuggle, a brand priced at about 15 percent below the P&G product, Lever was able to quickly capture a share of the business.

For similar reasons, competitors say they have forced P&G away from its practice of spending 60 percent of its marketing dollars on advertising, which is better for building long-term franchises, and 40 percent on promotion, which is better for short-term results. Although P&G won't discuss its ad budget, industry officials say that because of constant day-to-day price battles, the company recently has had to pour more money into promotion, thereby raising its costs.

In recent years, many of P&G's rivals also have been moving away from the brand-management system it has been using since the early 1930s. In its classic form, brand management assigns the responsibility for a brand to one executive, who coordinates all business decisions that affect it. Within certain constraints, his job is to build sales of that product as much as possible, even in competition with other company brands.

But just as politicians often try to broaden their appeal by moving closer to center, brand managers are sometimes tempted to do the same with the product for which they are responsible. In a mass market, that might be good. But in a highly fragmented product category, a company is usually better off if each of its entries aim as its own distinct audience.

### DIFFERENT DIAPERS

"The big problem P&G has had in diapers is that its two products, Luvs and Pampers, are too similar," says a former executive. "You have to wonder if that would have happened if Procter wasn't still sticking to its traditional system."

As P&G's rivals have come closer to matching its strengths, their own strong points have worked even more to their advantage. The most noticeable has been the powerful ties of some companies to the wholesale and retail buyers, an area where P&G has traditionally been weak. Although Procter is now scrambling to catch up, companies like General Foods and Pillsbury enjoy long-standing good will. For years, they have cultivated relationships through such steps as conducting studies to help the trade do its business more efficiently.

As P&G has increasingly been beaten in the marketplace, even companies who were self-proclaimed imitators of its system have been changing their ways. Once an equally deliberate and cautious mass marketer, Campbell Soup Co. a few years ago began breaking out of the P&G mold. Emphasizing a far more entrepreneurial approach, it began fragmenting its market segments and targeting more of its new products at selected groups. Following its new system, the company has been the leading introducer of new products for the last five years.

"There was a time here when you would frequently hear people asking 'Is that what P&G would do?' " says Marty Buchalski, general manager of Campbell's refrigerated-foods division. "These days, though, you don't hear that so much anymore."

---

## □ 32–B

# The king of suds reigns again

*Faye Rice*

The Ogilvy & Mather ad agency used to indoctrinate clients with a presentation called "What P&G Believes About Advertising." As the premier purveyor of consumer products in the United States, Procter & Gamble deserved emulation. Then last year Ogilvy reworked the presentation and renamed it "The Change P&G: The Wounded Lion." The switch made sense. Many of P&G's blockbuster brands had lost market share, new products had fizzled, and earnings had dropped 29 percent in fiscal 1985, the biggest decline in 37 years.

But the wounded lion has come roaring back. In the past 12 months P&G has racked up stunning market share gains in diapers, toothpaste, and detergents, products that account for over half its earnings. The company's share of the diaper market has zoomed 15 percentage points to 61.5 percent, propelled by the success of new Ultra Pampers. P&G's toothpaste share has jumped from 32 percent to 37 percent since the company launched Crest Tartar Control last summer. And in the intensely competitive, slow-growing detergent market, new Liquid Tide has lifted P&G's share from 49.5 percent to 51.5 percent. Says Hercules Segalas, a senior vice president of Drexel Burnham Lambert: "The market share rebound has been nothing short of phenomenal."

Though P&G refuses to discuss its operations, three changes in strategy apparently contributed mightily to the resurgence. First, instead of chasing the competition with lackluster, me-too products, as it had done so unsuccessfully in recent years, P&G returned to its old-time practice of outpacing competitors with superior new goods.

Second, the new products have done so well so fast partly because they carry familiar brand names—Pampers, Crest, and Tide. Using old names on new wares—known as brand extensions—is a hoary practice in consumer goods marketing, but it used to be anathema at P&G. With the exception of the name Ivory, which it has stamped on everything from laundry detergent to shampoo, P&G did not exploit existing brands to give new ones an extra boost.

Finally, the new, improved P&G has won the support of distributors and retailers by catering to their needs and desires, something the haughty old P&G rarely deigned to do (*Fortune,* February 4, 1985). For example, it has designed new package sizes that are cheaper to handle.

Selling top-quality products at premium prices had been P&G's strength for decades. But during the past few years the company brought out a flurry of nondescript, mediocre offerings. "P&G took its eye off the ball of superior performance in the early 1980s," says Cliff Angers, a P&G watcher and senior vice president of Ogilvy & Mather.

The triumph in laundry detergents typifies P&G's return to old ways. Wisk, a Lever Bros. product, has dominated liquid detergents for a generation, and liquids have been taking a growing share of the $3.2-billion-a-year detergent market. P&G tried to topple Wisk with run-of-the-laundry-room liquids called Era and Solo, but couldn't come close. Then it developed a liquid with 12 cleaning agents, twice the norm, and a

molecule that traps dirt in the wash water. P&G christened it Liquid Tide and put it in a bottle colored the same fire-bright orange as the ubiquitous Tide box. After just 18 months on the market, Liquid Tide is washing as many clothes as Wisk in the United States, and the two are locked in a fierce battle for the No. 2 position, after powered Tide, among all detergents.

P&G has scored an even bigger victory in disposable diapers. Kimberly-Clark had been snatching market share from P&G since 1979. Consumers saw Kimberly-Clark's Huggies brand, a premium-priced diaper with nonleaking elasticized legs, as superior to P&G's premium-priced Luvs. Around the same time that the big spenders embraced Huggies, budget watchers abandoned medium-priced Pampers for generic and store brands. P&G's share of the diaper market plunged from a commanding 69 percent in 1978 to 47 percent a year ago. The company's pretax profits from diapers nose-dived from a high of $275 million in 1983 to $25 million last year.

P&G's market share began to rebound last December when it came out with Blue Ribbon Pampers, with a leakproof waistband as well as elasticized legs. Then came Ultra Pampers, which hit the market early this year and are transforming the industry. Ultras are thinner than other disposables, making them easier to tote around, and contain a chemical that turns to a gel when damp, absorbing wetness. the baby's bottom stays dry and less susceptible to diaper rash.

The technology for the super-absorbent diaper was developed in Japan by Unicharm Co. In less than two years the diapers captured half the Japanese market. P&G was the first U.S. company to adopt the unpatented technology and spent a stunning $500 million to redesign its diaper machines and plants. Since Ultras landed on grocery shelves, Kimberly-Clark's market share has slipped seven points, to 28 percent. Kimberly-Clark is scrambling to match Ultras, but security analysts say P&G has at least a year's head start. "What's happened to the great Kimberly-Clark juggernaut?" asks Jack Salzman, an analyst at Goldman Sachs. "Pulling a market share over 30 percent will be a pipe dream from now on."

Toothpaste had been almost as disappointing as diapers for P&G. Back in 1979, P&G led Colgate-

PROCTER & GAMBLE
MARKET SHARES

**61.5%**
1986

Disposable
diapers

**47.0%**
1985

**51.5%**
1986

Heavy-duty
detergents

**49.5%**
1984

**37.0%**
1986

Toothpaste

**32.0%**
1985

SOURCE: DREXEL BURNHAM LAMBERT

Source: Drexel Burnham Lambert. Photos by Leslie Wong.

Palmolive, its nearest rival, by 19 percentage points in market share. But P&G snoozed while Colgate and other competitors came up with gels, pump dispensers, and other innovations. By 1985 P&G's lead over Colgate had shrunk to next to nothing—32 percent to 30.5 percent of the market, respectively.

P&G finally struck back with Crest Tartar Control, the first toothpaste to use the cleansing agent sodium pyrophosphate, which reduces tartar buildup. Sodium pyrophosphate is the biggest improvement in toothpaste since P&G pioneered fluoride 30 years ago. Colgate also holds a patent for pyrophosphate, but it did not move as quickly as P&G. Instead it concentrated on Dentaguard, an anti-plaque toothpaste. Colgate plans to belatedly come out with an anti-tartar brand later this year.

The resurgence in P&G's three basic businesses has not come cheap. Security analysts es-

timate, for example, that it spent $1 billion on advertising to launch the two new versions of Pampers on top of the $500 million for retooling. Competitors grouse that P&G has simply bought market share to recapture prominence in major products and refurbish its reputation. Wall Street analysts agree. The question now is whether P&G can hold what it has regained while cutting back enough on advertising and promotion to give a big kick to profits.

A small kick, at least, appears to be coming. Security analysts estimate that profits for fiscal 1986, which ended June 30, were up about 10 percent. They say that earnings should begin to rise somewhat faster now that P&G has the heavy product-introduction expenses behind it. Salzman of Goldman Sachs estimates that P&G's pretax diaper profits have rebounded to $75 million a year and could double in fiscal 1987. As a group, the analysts figure P&G's earnings will climb 15 percent to 20 percent by fall. But even that would leave fiscal 1987 profits below 1984's.

Competitors aren't likely to let P&G pull many more ad dollars out of the market share wars. Lever has spent as much to defend Wisk's turf as P&G has to launch Liquid Tide, and it seems certain to keep spending. Lever's pockets are deep, and the company is committed to improving its standing in the United States (*Fortune,* May 26). More ad dollars will be needed for P&G to counter Colgate's coming tartar-control entry and Kimberly-Clark's introduction of an improved Huggies. And Weyerhaeuser reportedly plans to jump into diapers for the first time with a premium version priced lower than Ultras.

The aroused lion has ferociously defended its corner of the consumer products jungle. But the tigers have tasted the lion's blood and will undoubtedly try for more.

**QUESTIONS**

1. *After so successfully pioneering the disposable-diaper market, how did P&G let its competitors take away so much of its market share? Did it become complacent, or did its competitors just do a better job of marketing strategy planning?*

*2. Could demographic trends (Readings 1 and 13) and/or the product life cycle (Reading 30) have had something to do with the declining market shares P&G experienced for so many of its leading brands? How about declining brand loyalty? Explain.

*3. What marketing strategies might P&G have employed to protect its turf and prevent market-share losses as its brands moved along the product life cycle? (See Reading 30.) What strategies did it finally use to regain market share?

*4. Was the introduction of Ultra Pampers an illustration of "marketing warfare"—or of a firm focusing its efforts on satisfying customer needs? (See Reading 31.) Why? What's the difference?

*5. Has the introduction of Ultra Pampers provided P&G with a sustainable competitive advantage (Reading 7) in the disposable-diaper market? Why or why not?

*Question relates concepts in this and other readings.

---

□ **33**

---

# Conducting and using a marketing audit

*John F. Grashof*

---

*This article describes how to conduct a marketing audit. This is still an art—requiring much judgment—but an organized approach can be helpful. Grashof presents a checklist of factors to consider and forms which can help organize the evaluation process. Note that many of these factors are discussed in other articles—for example: competition, company capabilities, market segments, and marketing mixes.*

---

Over the past several years, many firms have come to realize the necessity of "keeping tabs on" and evaluating various functions within the firm. These control efforts often take the form of audits. For example, many firms conduct management audits to assess their management structures and the strengths and weaknesses of their managers and other employees. The accounting profession conducts audits of financial records for purposes of internal control as well as for the protection of outside investors and lenders. And, during the last couple of years, increasing attention has been given to the social audit, an evaluation of the firm's degree of social responsibility.

With the increasing recognition of marketing, and particularly marketing strategies, as central to the success of all businesses, more attention has been given to the evaluation of this category of a firm's activities. In response to the need for evaluation, more and more academicians and practitioners are calling for marketing audits.[1] "A marketing audit," suggests Martin Bell, "is a systematic and thorough examination of a company's market position."[2] More formally, Abe Schuchman defines a marketing audit as

---

Source: An original contribution. At the time of writing, John Grashof was associate professor and chairman, Department of Marketing, Temple University.

[1]Philip Kotler, *Marketing Management: Analysis, Planning, and Control,* 2nd ed. (Englewood Cliffs, N.J.: Prentice-Hall, 1972), p. 774.

[2]Martin L. Bell, *Marketing: Concepts and Strategies,* 2nd ed. (Boston: Houghton Mifflin, 1972), p. 428.

a systematic, critical, and impartial review and appraisal of the total marketing operation: of the basic objectives and policies and the assumptions which underlie them as well as the methods, procedures, personnel, and organization employed to implement the policies and achieve the objectives.[3]

## MARKETING AUDITS: WHY, WHEN, WHAT, AND WHO

### Are marketing audits really necessary?

Marketing audits are necessary for a number of important reasons, not the least of which is the complex and continually changing environment of the modern corporation. As the marketplace, the competitive scene, and the economic and political climates change, the firm should study its marketing activities to determine what, if any, changes should be made.[4] The marketing audit can be a viable approach to structuring the evaluation of strategies in a meaningful way. By examining the firm's strategies relative to its competitors and the market, and with respect to internal consistency, the audit can highlight strengths and weaknesses.

Audits are typically evaluations of past behavior and present practices, and marketing audits do perform this function. However, marketing audits can not only reveal present weaknesses but also may identify potential problems and, thus, may play an important role with respect to future planning.[5] Marketing managers are typically more concerned that the goals and directions of their marketing efforts are correct than they are that their past performance has been good.[6] Through a critical evaluation of the objectives of the firm, and the plans and programs designed to meet these objectives, the marketing audit serves a role similar to a pro forma or forecast income statement.

### How often should a marketing audit be conducted?

Most authors suggest that audits be conducted on a periodic basis. The length of time between audits may vary among firms, but audits should be a routine part of the planning process of a firm. Audits, in addition to those normally scheduled, may be conducted as desired by management, but such additional audits should not replace those regularly scheduled.

Schuchman suggests that audits can be profitably conducted in extremely good times and may be absolutely necessary in times of crisis.[7] For example, American bicycle manufacturers were largely unprepared for the sudden upsurge in sales that occurred in the early 1970s. The combined impacts of increased concern for physical fitness and the growing environmental problems led to the rediscovery of the bicycle by many adults. Failure to anticipate the increasing sales trend left the industry saddled with a child-oriented product line and insufficient production facilities. Thus, the door was opened for an influx of foreign imports. Apparently, the U.S. firms had been lulled into complacency by years of steady, profitable sales. Had these firms been conducting periodic marketing audits, it is likely that they would have been better prepared for the rapid increase in sales.

### What is the best way to approach a marketing audit?

There are a variety of approaches to conducting a marketing audit. One decision that must be made is whether to examine generally the whole range of marketing activities or to look at one section in detail. Richard Crisp defines these as the horizontal and vertical audits:

> The *horizontal* audit examines all of the elements that go into the marketing whole, with particular emphasis upon the relative importance of these elements and the "mix" between them. It is often referred to as a "marketing mix" audit. The *vertical* audit singles out certain functional elements of the

---

[3]Abe Schuchman, "The Marketing Audit: Its Nature, Purposes, and Problems," in *Analyzing and Improving Marketing Performance,* report no. 32 (New York: American Management Association, 1959), p. 13.

[4]Ibid., p. 15.

[5]Ibid., pp. 12–14.

[6]Bell, *Marketing,* p. 429.

[7]Schuchman, "Marketing Audit," pp. 15–16.

marketing operation and subjects them to thorough, searching study and evaluation.[8]

Which approach is best for a particular firm at a point in time must be determined by that firm. The choice will depend on a number of factors, including where the firm is experiencing success and where it is having problems. However, in those cases where the firm selects a vertical audit, it must not completely ignore evaluation of the mix aspect of its marketing program.

An alternative view of the components of a marketing audit is presented by Kotler, Gregor, and Rodgers.[9] They identify six components of an audit as follows:

1. *Marketing environment audit.* An evaluation of the uncontrollable variables which surround and impact upon the firm and the marketing institutions and agencies with which the firm interacts, including customers, suppliers, ad agencies, and dealers and distributors.
2. *Marketing strategy audit.* A consideration of the marketing strategies of the firm, given the opportunities available to them, the resources they have available, and the guidance provided by top-management objectives.
3. *Marketing organization audit.* A study of the marketing organization, the structure through which the resources of the firm are applied to achieve its objectives. The audit will consider whether the organization is appropriate, given the objectives, and effective, given the resources of the firm.
4. *Marketing systems audit.* An examination of the nature of the system by which the marketing managers obtain the information they need for decision making, as well as the quantity and quality of information that the system makes available.
5. *Marketing productivity audit.* An attempt to understand, through an examination of accounting data, the costs and revenues associated with specific elements of the firm's activities,

such as customers or products. The objective is to understand which of the firm's activities are contributing to profits and which are not profitable.
6. *Marketing function audits.* A detailed investigation into specific functional activities of the firm's marketing program, such as its distribution system or its sales force. These are conducted at the suggestion of an auditor, with the agreement of management, when specific problems are noted.

The six components listed above are semiautonomous. That is, they can be conducted independently of each other, depending on the specific problems a firm is having or the objectives of the audit. A complete marketing audit of a firm would include all six components.

## Who should conduct the marketing audit?

The selection of an individual or team to be responsible for conducting the marketing audit can obviously have a significant impact on the quality of the completed evaluation. The auditor should be unbiased, experienced, and knowledgeable about the company and industry. Crisp lists six alternative sources of auditors.

1. *Self-audit.* A company can ask the executive who is directly in charge of an activity to appraise its strengths and weaknesses.
2. *"Audit from across."* A company can assign persons in a related activity on the same function level to prepare an audit of the neighboring activity.
3. *"Audit from above."* The audit can be conducted by the executive to whom the manager reports.
4. *Company auditing office.* The company can establish an office with the responsibility for conducting all company marketing audits.
5. *Company task force audit.* The company can appoint a team of company executives with varied backgrounds and experience to conduct the audit.
6. *Outside audit.* The company can hire an outside individual or agency to conduct the marketing audit.[10]

[8]Richard D. Crisp, "Auditing the Functional Elements of a Marketing Operation," in *Analyzing and Improving Marketing Performance,* report no. 32 (New York: American Management Association, 1959), pp. 16–17.

[9]P. Kotler, W. Gregor, and W. Rodgers, "The Marketing Audit Comes of Age," *Sloan Management Review* 18 (Winter 1977), pp. 25–43.

[10]Crisp, "Auditing the Functional Elements," pp. 41–44.

Crisp feels that the sixth alternative, the outside audit, is usually the best choice. The outside agent is able to be more objective since he is not examining his own or a co-worker's performance and since he is not so likely to be subjected to pressure from superiors or co-workers.

## CONDUCTING A MARKETING AUDIT

Conducting a marketing audit and the subsequent strategy evaluation is a three-step process, as outlined in Exhibit 1. Step 1 consists of the accumulation of a great many facts concerning the firm's marketing program. Step 2 is the evaluation of the information gathered in Step 1 with respect to the firm and its competition and the internal consistency of the firm's marketing program. The third and final step is the development of a set of recommendations based on the analysis conducted in Step 2.

**Exhibit 1 □ The marketing audit process**

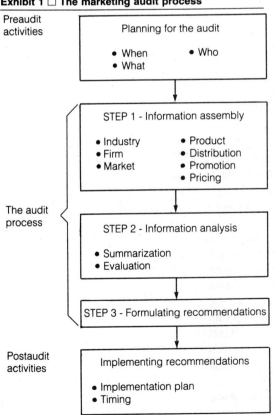

### Step 1: Information assembly

The information assembly step of a marketing audit is the most time-consuming and may be the most frustrating. A detailed examination of a firm's marketing program involves a great deal of data, and a comprehensive listing of the information required for a marketing audit would be lengthy. Seven major areas which affect a firm's marketing program need to be examined. They are:

1. The industry.      5. Distribution.
2. The firm.          6. Promotion.
3. The market.        7. Pricing.
4. The product.

Table 1 outlines these general areas and lists a few of the more important factors to be studied under each.

### Step 2: Analyzing the audit information

Once the information concerning the industry, the firm, and its marketing programs has been gathered, the audit team needs to analyze this information to obtain a more complete picture of the firm's marketing activities. Often, effectiveness of a firm's marketing program hinges not on the individual activities that it undertakes but, rather, on the way in which these activities fit together into a comprehensive marketing mix. As a starting point, a summary judgment should be made concerning the extent to which the firm embraces and follows the dictates of the marketing concept. Following this summary evaluation, other, more specific analyses can be made of particular aspects of the firm's marketing activities.

One analysis that the auditors should carry out is a comparison of the firm with its competitors. Throughout the information-gathering step of the marketing audit, the audit team has been collecting data not only about the subject firm but about the activities of its competitors. This information should now be tied together to develop a comprehensive picture of the marketing program of the firm and the marketing operations of its competitors. These two should then be compared in a side-by-side evaluation.

Table 2 presents a possible format for such an evaluation. Some of the judgments will be difficult,

**Table 1 ☐ Checklist of areas to be examined in a marketing audit**

I. The industry
  A. Characteristics.
    1. Size (in units produced, dollar sales)
    2. Number of firms
    3. Nature of competition
    4. Geographic concentration
    5. Interaction with other industries
    6. Product life cycle
    7. Governmental and societal constraints
  B. Trends
    1. Sales volume and number of firms
    2. Geographic localization
    3. Size of firms
  C. Firm's position
    1. Size relative to industry leaders
    2. Market strength
    3. Leader or follower
II. The firm
  A. History
    1. Growth and expansion
    2. Financial history
    3. Past strengths and weaknesses
  B. Goals and objectives
  C. Current strengths and weaknesses
    1. Market
    2. Managerial
    3. Financial
    4. Technical
    5. Market information mechanisms
III. The market
  A. General structure
    1. Number of customers
    2. Geographic spread and/or grouping
    3. Breadth of product use
    4. Urban versus rural
    5. Demographics of current customers
  B. Firm's approach to market segmentation
    1. Degree to which firm has segmented the market
    2. Degree of specification of target markets
    3. Bases of segmentation used
      a. Socioeconomic and demographic
      b. Psychographic
      c. Geographic
      d. Use patterns
  C. Segments identified by the firm
    1. What are characteristics?
    2. Degree of difference among segments
    3. What segments have been selected by the firm as target markets
  D. Has the firm considered factors which affect the market?
    1. Income effects
    2. Price and quality elasticity
    3. Responsiveness to marketing variables
    4. Fashion cycles
    5. Seasonality
IV. The product
  A. List the company's products

    1. Strengths
    2. Weaknesses
    3. Distinctive features
  B. Competitive position
    1. Price and quality relative to competitors
    2. Market share
    3. Patents or trademarks
  C. Product policy
    1. Written or verbal
    2. Product line width and depth
    3. New product policy
    4. Product deletion policy
V. Distribution
  A. Channels of distribution
    1. Description of channel(s) used
    2. Institutions in each channel
    3. Basis for selection of institutions used
  B. Distribution policy
    1. Extent and depth of market coverage
    2. Role of distribution in marketing mix and marketing plans
  C. Physical distribution
    1. PD organization within firm
    2. Customer service level policy
    3. Inventory
      a. Number of locations of stock
      b. Type of warehouse (i.e., public versus private)
      c. Planned and actual inventory levels
    4. Transportation
      a. Product shipment terms
      b. Mode of transportation used
      c. Type of carrier
        (1) Common
        (2) Contract
        (3) Private
VI. Promotion
  A. Goals of promotional activities
    1. Advertising
    2. Personal selling
    3. Sales promotion
  B. Promotion blend
  C. Advertising
    1. Budget in dollars and percent of sales
    2. Tasks assigned to advertising
    3. Evaluation procedures
  D. Personal selling
    1. Organization of sales force
    2. Sales force management
    3. Tasks assigned to the sales force
VII. Pricing
  A. Goals and role of pricing in the marketing mix
  B. Approach used to set prices
    1. Basis on which prices are set
    2. Flow of pricing decisions within the firm
  C. Prices compared with competitors
  D. Trade discount and allowances
  E. Financing and credit arrangements

Source: Based in part on an outline for a marketing audit developed by B. J. La Londe, James R. Riley Professor Marketing and Logistics, The Ohio State University.

**Table 2 ☐ Suggested format for comparative evaluation of firm and competitors**

| | Description of factor for | | |
| --- | --- | --- | --- |
| Factor* | The firm's approach | Major competitor's approach | Differences |
| 1. *Market* | | | |
|    Has the market been segmented? | (Highly, somewhat, or not segmented) | | |
|    What is segmentation based on? | (Demographics, psychographics, or benefits; specific attributes | | |
|    Size of market served | (Local, regional, or national) | | |
| 2. *Product* | | | |
|    Quality level | (High, medium, or low quality) | | |
|    Width and depth of product line | (Broad, medium, or narrow; deep, moderate, or thin) | | |
|    Is the firm an innovator? | (Typically innovator, typically follower) | | |
|    Brand strength in market | (Brand unrecognized, recognized, preferred, or insisted upon) | | |
|    Market penetration | (Largest, average, or small market share) | | |
|    Goods class of products | (Industrial or consumer goods; subclasses) | | |
| 3. *Distribution* | | | |
|    Direct or indirect distribution? | (Direct or indirect; number of intermediaries) | | |
|    Type of middlemen used | (Handles own distribution or uses others; specific type of middlemen used)(Intensive, selective, or exclusive) | | |
|    Degree of market coverage | (Best in market, average, poorest) | | |
|    Service level | (Once central warehouse or field warehouse system; public or private transportation and/or warehouses) | | |
|    Physical distribution system | | | |
| 4. *Promotion* | | | |
|    Amount of advertising | (Percent of budget; total dollars) | | |
|    Target or promotion | (Consumers for pull strategy or middlemen for push strategy) | | |
|    Type of appeal | (Factual, emotional, humorous) | | |
|    Type of media | (Print, broadcast; local, national) | | |
|    Promotion blend | (Percent advertising versus personal selling) | | |
|    Organization of sales force | (By territory, division, product line; company sales staff or manufacturers' agents) | | |
|    Functions of sales force | (Technical design, customer systems design, nontechnical) | | |
| 5. *Pricing* | | | |
|    Price level | (High, medium, or low price) | | |
|    Terms and/or discounts | (Strict or liberal; better, same, or less than industry) | | |
|    Use of price competition | (Price major competitive weapon, competes on other bases) | | |

*The factors listed are suggestions and are not intended to be exclusive or exhaustive. Further, the descriptors for each of the factors are only suggestive.

but the process of trying to accomplish such an analysis will be beneficial to the auditors and the firm. While a firm need not, indeed probably should not, be doing exactly the same thing as its competitors, such an evaluation does point out where their activities are the same and where they are different. Where they are the same, they should be examined for possible changes that would give the firm an advantage over the competitors. Where they are different, each difference should be evaluated to determine whether it is a strength or a weakness. Such side-by-side evaluation can mean much to a firm in identifying competitive strengths and weaknesses and in developing suggestions for ways to make its marketing programs relatively stronger.

In addition to the comparative analysis of the firm's marketing program and that of its competitors, the market offerings of the firm should be evaluated with respect to each market segment it is attempting to serve. In analyzing the market, each segment was identified along with those factors which cause persons in the segment to buy the firm's product versus the product of a competitor. The degree of congruence between the factors which are important in a segment's purchase decision and the marketing offering of the firm should be evaluated. Further, the trends in specific aspects of the behavior of market segments should be evaluated with respect to proposed changes in the firm's market offerings. Such an evaluation will help to ensure that the firm is adjusting to the changing needs of the market it serves. For example, a marketing audit might have shown the U.S. auto companies the shift in consumers' preferences toward smaller, more economical cars. Had the strength of this trend been identified earlier, the U.S. companies might not have suffered as much as they did from imported car competition.

In evaluating the firm's offerings to the several market segments it serves, the internal consistency of the marketing mix should be given close scrutiny. While a firm's marketing mix is made up of many different aspects, there are strong relationships among these aspects. For example, products which are considered to be convenience goods in the consumer goods classification system should have intensive distribution, whereas products that are in the shopping goods categories may need only selective or perhaps even exclusive distribution. This was relevant for the Elgin Watch Company, a prestigious manufacturer of high-quality men's products. The company suffered irreparable damage when the U.S. Time Company began selling inexpensive Timex watches as convenience goods. A marketing audit could have helped Elgin revise its marketing strategy to compete effectively with Timex. By identifying the shift in goods class of wristwatches for a large segment of the population, an audit might have given Elgin the information necessary to make better decisions.

One approach to such an evaluation is to select several control points or factors which have been identified as being critical to the firm's marketing program. Potential control points include product attributes such as quality and number of special features, distribution considerations such as number and type of retail outlets and service level along the channel, promotional appeals used and media selected, and pricing policies. The performance of the firm with respect to each control point can then be evaluated. Deviations should be noted, and those that are significant will be points about which suggestions for improvement need to be made.[11]

Evaluation of a firm's marketing strategies can be made even more valuable if the control points selected are tied to characteristics of the target markets selected. Table 3 suggests one approach to such an evaluation.

---

[11]Mark E. Stern, *Marketing Planning: A Systems Approach* (New York: McGraw-Hill, 1966), pp. 131–36.

To be used most effectively, an approach such as that suggested by Table 3 requires that the dimensions of the firm's approach and the target market characteristics be similar. With similar dimensions considered in both columns, congruence and discrepancy between the firm's marketing strategy and the characteristics of the target market are easily seen. For example, a firm might select as a target market stereo enthusiasts who want good quality sound and are willing to build kits in order to save money (target market characteristics) but offer only poor quality kits that are extremely difficult to assemble (the firm's marketing approach). Listing these factors on a form such as Table 3 would make the discrepancy more obvious.

### Step 3: Developing recommendations

Once the analysis of the information about the firm's marketing programs has been completed, the audit team should complete its activities by making specific recommendations regarding the firm's marketing program. The recommendations should be based on the strengths and weaknesses of the firm's activities, as identified in Step 2 of Exhibit 1. If the analysis was done well, such recommendations will often be relatively simple to make because discrepancies become quite obvious.

In making recommendations, the audit should be concerned more with how the firm's marketing program can be modified to improve it in the future rather than pointing the finger at poor performance in the past. While management errors should be identified, it should be done from the point of view of not making the same mistakes twice rather than a "witch hunt" to single out poor performers. This approach will establish confidence in managers concerning the value of an audit and the ability of an audit to help them.

### CONCLUSION

A marketing audit is often a time-consuming and perhaps expensive project. However, the benefits which result from such a comprehensive evaluation of a firm's past programs and present

**Table 3 □ One approach to firm vis-à-vis target market strategy evaluation**

| Strategy aspect | Target market characteristics | The firm's approach |
|---|---|---|
| **1. Product** | | |
| Quality level | | (The firm's quality level should match that desired by the target market) |
| Features/options | | (Those of the product should be those desired by the target market) |
| Services offered | | (Such as delivery, installation, and repair) |
| Guarantee | | (Consistent with desires of target market?) |
| Selection offered | | (Consistent with variability within target market?) |
| **2. Distribution** | | |
| Store type | | (Characteristics of retail outlets must be consistent with desires of target market) |
| Market coverage | | (Be consistent with target market's view of product; i.e., intensive if convenience good) |
| Channel structure | | (Provide services desired by target market) |
| **3. Promotion** | | |
| Type of appeal | | (Firm's message must be consistent with what will affect the target market) |
| Media use | | (Must be media that reach target market) |
| Personal sales effort | | (Self-service versus sales aid versus high-pressure salesperson) |
| **4. Price** | | |
| Price level | | (Consistent with target market; also consistent with product quality and promotional appeals) |
| Discount structure | | (Meet needs of target market; i.e., quality discounts if customers buy in quantity) |
| Price as competitive factor | | (Use price if major factor in purchase decision, and vice versa) |

Note: The strategy aspects and characteristic descriptors listed are only examples and are not intended to be exhaustive. The approach is based on the concept of identifying those factors that are determinants of purchase behavior *for the target market selected* and comparing the firm's market offerings to the needs of the target market.

activities often more than justify the time and money invested. Further, the insights gained can be profitably applied to future planning of the firm's marketing activities. The improved future planning that can be accomplished as a result of a marketing audit may be just the edge needed to provide a breakthrough opportunity for the firm.

Marketing audits should be a regular part of the firm's planning process. The audits should be conducted by experienced and knowledgeable people who are in a position to be unbiased in their evaluation of the firm and the industry. The firm may choose to examine either the whole range of its marketing activities at a general level or part of its activities in depth. In either case, the audit should concentrate on the marketing mixes of the firm with respect to the industry in which it operates, its competitors, and, most importantly, the market segment(s) which the firm is attempting to serve.

**QUESTIONS**

1. What is a marketing audit? Why is it needed?

2. List and briefly explain the three steps that are involved in conducting a marketing audit.

3. Try to complete Table 3 for one of the cases in this textbook. Then make the appropriate recommendations.

☐ *34*

# Customizing global marketing

*John A. Quelch*

*Edward J. Hoff*

*Global marketing—offering world-wide markets standardized products made with the best technology at the lowest cost source—is no longer a debated idea. The issue today is not whether to go global, but rather how and to what degree. The following article discusses strategies for implementing global marketing and shows how companies such as Coca-Cola and Nestlé have tackled the job.*

In the best of all possible worlds, marketers would only have to come up with a great product and a convincing marketing program and they would have a worldwide winner. But despite the obvious economies and efficiencies they could gain with a standard product and program, many managers fear that global marketing, as popularly defined, is too extreme to be practical. Because customers and competitive conditions differ across countries or because powerful local managers will not stand for centralized decision making, they argue, global marketing just won't work.

Of course, global marketing has its pitfalls, but it can also yield impressive advantages. Standardizing products can lower operating costs. Even more important, effective coordination can exploit a company's best product and marketing ideas.

Too often, executives view global marketing as an either/or proposition—either full standardization or local control. But when a global approach can fall anywhere on a spectrum from tight worldwide coordination on programming details to loose agreement on a product idea, why the extreme view? In applying the global marketing concept and making it work, flexibility is essential. Managers need to tailor the approach they use to each element of the business system and marketing program. For example, a manufacturer might market the same product under different brand

names in different countries or market the same brands using different product formulas.

The big issue today is not whether to go global but how to tailor the global marketing concept to fit each business and how to make it work. In this article, we'll first provide a framework to help managers think about how they should structure the different areas of the marketing function as the business shifts to a global approach. We will then show how companies we have studied are tackling the implementation challenges of global marketing.

## HOW FAR TO GO

How far a company can move toward global marketing depends a lot on its evolution and traditions. Consider these two examples:

- Although the Coca-Cola Company had conducted some international business before 1940, it gained true global recognition during World War II, as Coke bottling plants followed

Source: Reprinted by permission of the *Harvard Business Review.* "Customizing Global Marketing" by John A. Quelch and Edward J. Hoff (May/June 1986). Copyright © 1986 by the President and Fellows of Harvard College; all rights reserved. At the time of writing, John A. Quelch was associate professor of business administration at the Harvard Business School and Edward J. Hoff was a Ph.D. candidate in business economics at Harvard University.

the march of U.S. troops around the world. Management in Atlanta made all strategic decisions then—and still does now, as Coca-Cola applies global marketing principles, for example, to the worldwide introduction of Diet Coke. The brand name, concentrate formula, positioning, and advertising theme are virtually standard worldwide, but the artificial sweetener and packaging differ across countries. Local managers are responsible for sales and distribution programs, which they run in conjunction with local bottlers.

• The Nestlé approach also has its roots in history. To avoid distribution disruptions caused by wars in Europe, to ease rapid worldwide expansion, and to respond to local consumer needs, Nestlé granted its local managers considerable autonomy from the outset. While the local managers still retain much of that decision-making power today, Nestlé headquarters at Vevey has grown in importance. Nestlé has transferred to its central marketing staff many former local managers who had succeeded in their local Nestlé businesses and who now influence country executives to accept standard new product and marketing ideas. The trend seems to be toward tighter marketing coordination.

To conclude that Coca-Cola is a global marketer and Nestlé is not would be simplistic. In Exhibit 1, we assess program adaptation or standardization levels for each company's business functions, products, marketing mix elements, and countries. Each company has tailored its individual approach. Furthermore, as Exhibit 1 can't show, the situations aren't static. Readers can themselves evaluate their own *current* and *desired* levels of program adaptation or standardization on these four dimensions. The gap between the two levels is the implementation challenge. The size of the gap—and the urgency with which it must be closed—will depend on a company's strategy and financial performance, competitive pressures, technological change, and converging consumer values.

## Four dimensions of global marketing

Now let's look at the issues that arise when executives consider the four dimensions shown in

Exhibit 1 in light of the degree of standardization or adaptation that is appropriate.

**Business functions.** A company's approach to global marketing depends, first, on its overall business strategy. In many multinationals, some functional areas have greater program standardization than others. Headquarters often controls manufacturing, finance, and R&D, while the local managers make the marketing decisions. Marketing is usually one of the last functions to be centrally directed. Partly because product quality and accounting data are easier to measure than marketing effectiveness, standardization can be greater in production and finance.

**Products.** Products that enjoy high scale economies or efficiencies and are not highly culture-bound are easier to market globally than others.

*1. Economies or efficiencies.* Manufacturing and R&D scale economies can result in a price spread between the global and the local product that is too great for even the most culture-bound consumer to resist. In addition, management often has neither the time nor the R&D resources to adapt products to each country. The markets for high-tech products like computers are not only very competitive but also affected by rapid technological change.

Most packaged consumer goods are less susceptible than durable goods like televisions and cars to manufacturing or even R&D economies. Coca-Cola's global policy and Nestlé's interest in tighter marketing coordination are driven largely by a desire to capitalize on the marketing ideas their managers around the world generate rather than by potential scale economies. Nestlé, for example, manufactures its packaged soups in dozens of locally managed plants around the world, with some transference of engineering know-how through a headquarters staff. Products and marketing programs are also locally managed, but new ideas are aggressively transferred, with local managers encouraged—or even prodded—to adapt and use them in their own markets. For Nestlé, global marketing does not so much yield high manufacturing economies as high efficiency in using scarce new ideas.

*2. Cultural grounding.* Consumer products used in the home—like Nestlé's soups and frozen foods—are often more culture-bound than products used outside the home such as automobiles

**Exhibit 1 □ Global marketing planning matrix: How far to go**

| | | Adaptation | | Standardizaton | |
|---|---|---|---|---|---|
| | | Full | Partial | Partial | Full |
| **Business functions** | Research and development | | | Nestlé | Coca-Cola |
| | Finance and accounting | | | Nestlé | Coca-Cola |
| | Manufacturing | | Nestlé | Coca-Cola | |
| | Procurement | Nestlé | | Coca-Cola | |
| | Marketing | | Nestlé | | Coca-Cola |
| **Products** | Low cultural grounding / High economies or efficiencies | | | | Coca-Cola |
| | Low cultural grounding / Low economies or efficiencies | | | | |
| | High cultural grounding / High economies or efficiencies | | Nestlé | | |
| | High cultural grounding / Low economies or efficiencies | | | | |
| **Marketing mix elements** | Product design | | | Nestlé | Coca-Cola |
| | Brand name | | | Nestlé | Coca-Cola |
| | Product positioning | | Nestlé | | Coca-Cola |
| | Packaging | | | Coca-Cola | |
| | Advertising theme | | Nestlé | | Coca-Cola |
| | Pricing | | Nestlé | Coca-Cola | |
| | Advertising copy | Nestlé | | | Coca-Cola |
| | Distribution | Nestlé | Coca-Cola | | |
| | Sales promotion | Nestlé | Coca-Cola | | |
| | Customer service | Nestlé | Coca-Cola | | |
| **Countries** Region 1 | Country A | | | Nestlé | Coca-Cola |
| | Country B | | | Nestlé | Coca-Cola |
| Region 2 | Country C | | Nestlé | | Coca-Cola |
| | Country D | | Nestlé | | Coca-Cola |
| | Country E | Nestlé | | | Coca-Cola |

☐ Nestlé    ■ Coca-Cola

and credit cards, and industrial products are inherently less culture-bound than consumer products. (Products like personal computers, for example, are often marketed on the basis of performance benefits that share a common technical language worldwide.) Experience also suggests that products will be less culture-bound if they are used by young people whose cultural norms are not ingrained, people who travel in different countries, and ego-driven consumers who can be appealed to through myths and fantasies shared across cultures.

Exhibit 1 lists four combinations of the scale economy and cultural grounding variables in order of their susceptibility to global marketing. Managers shouldn't be bound by any matrix, however; they should find creative ways to prepare a product for global marketing. If a manufacturer develops a new version of a seemingly culture-bound product that is based on new capital-intensive technology and generates superior performance benefits, it may well be possible to introduce it on a standard basis worldwide. Procter & Gamble developed Pampers disposable diapers as a global brand in a product category that intuition would say was culture-bound.

**Marketing mix elements.** Few consumer goods companies go so far as to market the same products using the same marketing program worldwide. And those that do, like Lego, the Danish manufacturer of construction toys, often distribute their products through sales companies rather than full-fledged marketing subsidiaries.

For most products, the appropriate degree of standardization varies from one element of the marketing mix to another. Strategic elements like product positioning are more easily standardized than execution-sensitive elements like sales promotion. In addition, when headquarters believes it has identified a superior marketing idea, whether it be a package design, a brand name, or an advertising copy concept, the pressure to standardize increases.

Marketing can usually contribute to scale economies most significantly by creating a standard product design that will sell worldwide, permitting savings through globalized production. In addition, scale economies in marketing programming can be achieved through standard commercial execu-

tions and copy concepts. McCann-Erickson claims to have saved $90 million in production costs over 20 years by producing worldwide Coca-Cola commercials. To ensure that they have enough attention-getting power to overcome their foreign origins, however, marketers often have to make worldwide commercials expensive productions.

To compensate local management for having to accept a standard product and to fit the core product to each local market, some companies allow local managers to adapt those marketing mix elements that aren't subject to significant scale economies. On the other hand, local managers are more likely to accept a standard concept for those elements of the marketing mix that are less important and, ironically, often not susceptible to scale economies. Overall, then, the driving factor in moving toward global marketing should be the efficient worldwide use of good marketing ideas rather than any scale economies from standardization.

In judging how far to go in standardizing elements of the marketing mix, managers must also be mindful of the interactions among them. For example, when a product with the same brand name is sold in different countries, it can be difficult and sometimes impossible to sell them at different prices.

**Countries.** How far a decentralized multinational wishes to pursue global marketing will often vary from one country to another. Naturally, headquarters is likely to become more involved in marketing decisions in countries where performance is poor. But performance aside, small markets depend more on headquarters assistance than large markets. Because a standard marketing program is superior in quality to what local executives, even with the benefit of local market knowledge, could develop themselves, they may welcome it.

Large markets with strong local managements are less willing to accept global programs. Yet these are the markets that often account for most of the company's investment. To secure their acceptance, headquarters should make standard marketing programs reflect the needs of large rather than small markets. Small markets, being more tolerant of deviations from what would be locally appropriate, are less likely to resist a standard program.

As we've seen, Coca-Cola takes the same approach in all markets. Nestlé varies its approach in different countries depending on the strength of its market presence and each country's need for assistance. In completing the Exhibit 1 planning matrix, management may decide that it can sensibly group countries by region or by stage of market development.

## TOO FAR TOO FAST

Once managers have decided how global they want their marketing program to be, they must make the transition. Debates over the size of the gap between present and desired positions and the speed with which it must be closed will often pit the field against headquarters. Such conflict is most likely to arise in companies where the reason for change is not apparent or the country managers have had a lot of autonomy. Casualties can occur on both sides:

• Because Black & Decker dominated the European consumer power tool market, many of the company's European managers could not see that a more centrally directed global marketing approach was needed as a defense against imminent Japanese competition. To make his point, the CEO had to replace several key European executives.
• In 1982, the Parker Pen Company, forced by competition and a weakening financial position to lower costs, more than halved its number of plants and pen styles worldwide. Parker's overseas subsidiary managers accepted these changes but, when pressed to implement standardized advertising and packaging, they dug in their heels. In 1985, Parker ended its much heralded global marketing campaign. Several senior headquarters managers left the company.

If management is not careful, moving too far too fast toward global marketing can trigger painful consequences. First, subsidiary managers who joined the company because of its apparent commitment to local autonomy and to adapting its products to the local environment may become disenchanted. When poorly implemented, global marketing can make the local country manager's job less strategic. Second, disenchantment may reinforce not-invented-here attitudes that lead to game playing. For instance, some local managers may try bargaining with headquarters, trading the speed with which they will accept and implement the standard programs for additional budget assistance. In addition, local managers competing for resources and autonomy may devote too much attention to second-guessing headquarters' "hot buttons." Eventually the good managers may leave, and less competent people who lack the initiative of their predecessors may replace them.

A vicious circle can develop. Feeling compelled to review local performance more closely, headquarters may tighten its controls and reduce resources without adjusting its expectations of local managers. Meanwhile, local managers trying to gain approval of applications for deviations from standard marketing programs are being frustrated. The expanding headquarters bureaucracy and associated overhead costs reduce the speed with which the locals can respond to local opportunities and competitive actions. Slow response time is an especially serious problem with products for which barriers to entry for local competitors are low.

In this kind of system, weak, insecure local managers can become dependent on headquarters for operational assistance. They'll want headquarters to assume the financial risks for new product launches and welcome the prepackaged marketing programs. If performance falls short of headquarters' expectations, the local management can always blame the failure on the quality of operational assistance or on the standard marketing program. The local manager who has clear autonomy and profit-and-loss responsibility cannot hide behind such excuses.

If headquarters or regions assume much of the strategic burden, managers in overseas subsidiaries may think only about short-term sales. This focus will diminish their ability to monitor and communicate to headquarters any changes in local competitors' strategic directions. When their responsibilities shift from strategy to execution, their ideas will become less exciting. If the field has traditionally been as important a source of new product ideas as the central R&D laboratory, the company may find itself short of the grassroots creative thinking and marketing research information that R&D needs. The fruitful dialogue that characterizes a relationship between equal partners will no longer flourish.

## HOW TO GET THERE

When thinking about closing the gap between present and desired positions, most executives of decentralized multinationals want to accommodate their current organizational structures. They rightly view their subsidiaries and the managers who run them as important competitive strengths. They generally do not wish to transform these organizations into mere sales and distribution agencies.

How then in moving toward global marketing can headquarters build rather than jeopardize relationships, stimulate rather than demoralize local managers? The answer is to focus on means as much as ends, to examine the relationship between the home office and the field, and to ask what level of headquarters intervention for each business function, product, marketing mix element, and country is necessary to close the gap in each.

As Exhibit 2 indicates, headquarters can intervene at five points, ranging from informing to directing. The five intervention levels are cumulative; for headquarters to direct, it must also inform, persuade, coordinate, and approve. Exhibit 2 shows the approaches Atlanta and Vevey have taken. Moving from left to right on Exhibit 2, the reader can see that things are done increasingly by fiat rather than patient persuasion, through discipline rather than education. At the far right, local subsidiaries can't choose whether to opt in or out of a marketing program, and headquarters views its country managers as subordinates rather than customers.

When the local managers tightly control marketing efforts, multinational managers face three critical issues. In the sections that follow, we'll take a look at how decentralized multinationals are working to correct the three problems as they move along the spectrum from informing to directing.

**Inconsistent brand identities.** If headquarters gives country managers total control of their product lines, it cannot leverage the opportunities that multinational status gives it. The increasing degree to which consumers in one country are ex-

posed to the company's products in another won't enhance the corporate image or brand development in the consumers' home country.

**Limited product focus.** In the decentralized multinational, the field line manager's ambition is to become a country manager, which means acquiring multiproduct and multifunction experience. Yet as the pace of technological innovation increases and the likelihood of global competition grows, multinationals need worldwide product specialists as well as executives willing to transfer to other countries. Nowhere is the need for headquarters guidance on innovative organizational approaches more evident than in the area of product policy.

**Slow new product launches.** As global competition grows, so does the need for rapid worldwide rollouts of new products. The decentralized multinational that permits country managers to proceed at their own pace on new product introductions may be at a competitive disadvantage in this new environment.

### Word of mouth

The least threatening, loosest, and therefore easiest approach to global marketing is for headquarters to encourage the transfer of information between it and its country managers. Since good ideas are often a company's scarcest resource, headquarters efforts to encourage and reward their generation, dissemination, and application in the field will build both relationships and profits. Here are two examples:

- Nestlé publishes quarterly marketing newsletters that report recent product introductions and programming innovations. In this way, each subsidiary can learn quickly about and assess the ideas of others. (The best newsletters are written as if country organizations were talking to each other rather than as if headquarters were talking down to the field.)
- Johnson Wax holds periodic meetings of all marketing directors at corporate headquarters twice a year to build global esprit de corps and to encourage the sharing of new ideas.

By making the transfer of information easy, a multinational leverages the ideas of its staff and spreads organizational values. Headquarters has

**Exhibit 2 □ Global marketing planning matrix: How to get there**

|  |  | Informing | Persuading | Coordinating | Approving | Directing |
|---|---|---|---|---|---|---|
| **Business functions** | Research and development | | | | | |
| | Finance and accounting | | | | | |
| | Manufacturing | | | | | |
| | Procurement | | | | | |
| | Marketing | | | | | |
| **Products** | Low cultural grounding / High economies or efficiencies | | | | | |
| | Low cultural grounding / Low economies or efficiencies | | | | | |
| | High cultural grounding / High economies or efficiencies | | | | | |
| | High cultural grounding / Low economies or efficiencies | | | | | |
| **Marketing mix elements** | Product design | | | | | |
| | Brand name | | | | | |
| | Product positioning | | | | | |
| | Packaging | | | | | |
| | Advertising theme | | | | | |
| | Pricing | | | | | |
| | Advertising copy | | | | | |
| | Distribution | | | | | |
| | Sales promotion | | | | | |
| | Customer service | | | | | |
| **Countries** Region 1 | Country A | | | | | |
| | Country B | | | | | |
| Region 2 | Country C | | | | | |
| | Country D | | | | | |
| | Country E | | | | | |

☐ Nestle          ■ Coca-Cola

to be careful, however, that the information it's passing on is useful. It may focus on updating local managers about new products, when what they mainly want is information on the most tactical and country-specific elements of the marketing mix. For example, the concentration of the grocery trade is much higher in the United Kingdom and Canada than it is in the United States. In this case, managers in the United States can learn from British and Canadian country managers about how to deal with the pressures for extra merchandising support that result when a few powerful retailers control a large percentage of sales. Likewise, marketers in countries with restrictions on mass media advertising have developed sophisticated point-of-purchase merchandising skills that could be useful to managers in other countries.

By itself, however, information sharing is often insufficient to help local executives meet the competitive challenges of global marketing.

**Friendly persuasion**

Persuasion is a first step managers can take to deal with the three problems we've outlined. Any systematic headquarters effort to influence local managers to apply standardized approaches or introduce new global products while the latter retain their decision-making authority is a persuasion approach.

Unilever and CPC International, for example, employ world-class advertising and marketing research staff at headquarters. Not critics but coaches, these specialists review the subsidiaries' work and try to upgrade the technical skills of local marketing departments. They frequently visit the field to disseminate new concepts, frameworks, and techniques, and to respond to problems that local management raises. (It helps to build trust if headquarters can send out the same staff specialists for several years.)

Often, when the headquarters of a decentralized multinational identifies or develops a new product, it has to persuade the country manager in a so-called prime-mover market to invest in the launch. A successful launch in the prime-mover market will, in turn, persuade other country managers to introduce the product. The prime-mover market is usually selected according to criteria in-

cluding the commitment of local management, the probabilities of success, the credibility with which a success would be regarded by managers in other countries, and its perceived transferability.

Persuasion, however, has its limitations. Two problems recur with the prime-mover approach. First, by adopting a wait-and-see attitude, country managers can easily turn down requests to be prime-mover markets on the grounds of insufficient resources. Since the country managers in the prime-mover markets have to risk their resources to launch the new products, they're likely to tailor the product and marketing programs to their own markets rather than to global markets. Second, if there are more new products waiting to be launched than there are prime-mover markets to launch them, headquarters product specialists are likely to give in to a country manager's demands for local tailoring. But because of the need for readaptation in each case, the tailoring may delay rollouts in other markets and allow competitors to preempt the product. In the end, management may sacrifice long-term worldwide profits to maximize short-term profits in a few countries.

**Marketing to the same drummer**

To overcome the limits of persuasion, many multinationals are coordinating their marketing programs, whereby headquarters has a structured role in both decision making and performance evaluation that is far more influential than person-to-person persuasion. Often using a matrix or team approach, headquarters shares with country managers the responsibility and authority for programming and personnel decisions.

Nestlé locates product directors as well as support groups at headquarters. Together they develop long-term strategies for each product category on a worldwide basis, coordinate worldwide market research, spot new product opportunities, spark the field launch of new products, advise the field on how headquarters will evaluate new product proposals, and spread the word on new products' performance so that other countries will be motivated to launch them. Even though the product directors are staff executives with no line authority, because they have all been successful line managers in the field, they have great credibility and influence.

Country managers who cooperate with a product director can quickly become heroes if they successfully implement a new idea. On the other hand, while a country manager can reject a product director's advice, headquarters will closely monitor his or her performance with an alternative program. In addition, within the product category in which they specialize, the directors have influence on line management appointments in the field. Local managers thus have to be concerned about their relationships with headquarters.

Some companies assign promising local managers to other countries and require would-be local managers to take a tour of duty at headquarters. But such personnel transfer programs may run into barriers. First, many capable local nationals may not be interested in working outside their countries of origin. Second, powerful local managers are often unwilling to give up their best people to other country assignments. Third, immigration regulations and foreign service relocation costs are burdensome. Fourth, if transferees from the field have to take a demotion to work at headquarters, the costs in ill will often exceed any gains in cross-fertilization of ideas. If management can resolve these problems, however, it will find that creating an international career path is one of the most effective ways to develop a global perspective in local managers.

To enable their regional general managers to work alongside the worldwide product directors, several companies have moved them from the field to the head office. More and more companies require regional managers to reach sales and profit targets for each product as well as for each country within their regions. In the field, regional managers often focus on representing the views of individual countries to headquarters, but at headquarters they become more concerned with ensuring that the country managers are correctly implementing corporatewide policies.

Recently, Fiat and Philips N. V., among others, consolidated their worldwide advertising into a single agency. Their objectives are to make each product's advertising more consistent around the world and to make it easier to transfer ideas and information among local agency offices, country organizations, and headquarters. Use of a single agency (especially one that bills all advertising expenditures worldwide) also symbolizes a commit-

ment to global marketing and more centralized control. Multinationals shouldn't, however, use their agencies as Trojan horses for greater standardization. An undercover operation is likely to jeopardize agency-client relations at the country level.

While working to achieve global coordination, some companies are also trying to tighten coordination in particular regions:

- Kodak recently experimented by consolidating 17 worldwide product line managers at corporate headquarters. In addition, the company made marketing directors in some countries responsible for a line of business in a region as well as for sales of all Kodak products in their own countries. Despite these new appointments, country managers still retain profit-and-loss responsibility for their own markets. Whether a matrix approach such as this broadens perspectives rather than increases tension and confusion depends heavily on the corporation's cohesiveness. Such an organizational change can clearly communicate top management's strategic direction, but headquarters needs to do a persuasive selling job to the field if it is to succeed.
- Procter & Gamble has established socalled Euro Brand teams that analyze opportunities for greater product and marketing program standardization. Chaired by the brand manager from a "lead country," each team includes brand managers from other European subsidiaries that market the brand, managers from P&G's European technical center, and one of P&G's three European division managers, each of whom is responsible for a portfolio of brands as well as for a group of countries. Concerns that the larger subsidiaries would dominate the teams and that decision making would either be paralyzed or produce "lowest common denominator" results have proved groundless.

### Stamped & approved

By coordinating programs with the field, headquarters can balance the company's local and global perspectives. Even a decentralized multinational may decide, however, that to protect or exploit some corporate asset, the center of gravity for certain elements of the marketing program should be at headquarters. In such cases, management has two options: it can send clear directives to its local managers or permit them to develop their own programs within specified parameters and subject to headquarters approval. With a properly managed approval process, a multinational can exert effective control without unduly dampening the country manager's decision-making responsibility and creativity.

Procter & Gamble recently developed a new sanitary napkin, and P&G International designated certain countries in different geographic regions as test markets. The product, brand name, positioning, and package design were standardized globally. P&G International did, however, invite local managers to suggest how the global program could be improved and how the nonglobal elements of the marketing program should be adapted in their markets. It approved changes in several markets. Moreover, local managers developed valuable ideas on such programming specifics as sampling and couponing techniques that were used in all other countries, including the United States.

Nestlé views its brand names as a major corporate asset. As a result, it requires all brands sold in all countries to be registered in the home country of Switzerland. While the ostensible reason for this requirement is legal protection, the effect is that any product developed in the field has to be approved by Vevey. The head office has also developed detailed guidelines that suggest rather than mandate how brand names and logos should appear on packaging and in advertising worldwide (with exceptions subject to its approval). Thus the country manager's control over the content of advertising is not compromised, and the company achieves a reasonably consistent presentation of its names and logos worldwide.

### Doing it the headquarters way

Multinationals that direct local managers' marketing programs usually do so out of a sense of urgency. The motive may be to ensure either that a new product is introduced rapidly around the world before the competition can respond or that every manager fully and faithfully exploits a valu-

able marketing idea. Sometimes direction is needed to prove that global marketing can work. Once management makes the point, a more participative approach is feasible.

In 1979, one of Henkel's worldwide marketing directors wanted to extend the successful Sista line of do-it-yourself sealants from Germany to other European countries where the markets were underdeveloped and disorganized as had once been the case in Germany. A European headquarters project team visited the markets and then developed a standard marketing program. The country managers, however, objected. Since the market potential in each country was small, they said, they did not have the time or resources to launch Sista.

The project team countered that by capitalizing on potential scale economies, its pan-European marketing and manufacturing programs would be superior to any programs the subsidiaries could develop by themselves. Furthermore, it maintained, the already developed pan-European program was available off the shelf. The European sales manager, who was a project team member, discovered that the salespeople as well as tradespeople in the target countries were much more enthusiastic about the proposed program than the field marketing managers. So management devised a special lure for the managers. The project team offered to subsidize the first-year advertising and promotion expenditures of countries launching Sista. Six countries agreed. To ensure their commitment now that their financial risk had been reduced, the sales manager invited each accepting country manager to nominate a member to the project team to develop the final program details.

By 1982, the Sista line was sold in 52 countries using a standard marketing program. The Sista launch was especially challenging because it involved the extension of a product and program already developed for a single market. The success of the Sista launch made Henkel's field managers much more receptive to global marketing programs for subsequent new products.

### MOTIVATING THE FIELD

Taking into account the nature of their products and markets, their organizational structures, and

# The universal drink

In the postwar years, as Coca-Cola strove mightily to consolidate its territorial gains, its efforts were received with mixed feelings. When limited production for civilians got under way in the Philippines, armed guards had to be assigned to the trucks carting Coke from bottlers to dealers, to frustrate thirsty outlaws bent on hijacking it. In the Fiji Islands, on the other hand, Coca-Cola itself was outlawed, at the instigation of soft-drink purveyors whose business had been ruined by the Coke imported for the solace of G.I.s during the war. Most of the opposition to the beverage's tidal sweep, however, was centered in Europe, being provoked by the beer and wine interests, or by anti-American political interests, or by a powerful blend of oenology and ideology. Today, brewers in England, Spain, and Sweden are themselves bottling Coke, on the if-you-can't-lick-'em-join-'em principle. . . . In Western Europe, Coca-Cola has had to fight a whole series of battles, varying according to the terrain, not all of which have yet been won, though victory seems to be in sight. Before Coca-Cola got rolling in West Germany, for instance, it had to go to court to halt the nagging operations of something called the Coördination Office for German Beverages, which was churning out defamatory pamphlets with titles like "Coca-Cola, Karl Marx, and the Imbecility of the Masses" and the more succinct "Coca-Cola? No!" In Denmark, lobbyists for the brewers chivied the Parliament into taxing cola-containing beverages so heavily that it would have been economically absurd to try to market Coke there. . . . At last word, the Danes were about to relent, though. But in Belgium the caps on bottles of Coke, including bottles sold at the Brussels Fair, have had to carry, in letters bigger than those used for "Coca-Cola," the forbidding legend *Contient de la cafeine.*

Source: From *The Big Drink* (Randon House). ©1959 by E. J. Kahn, Jr. Originally in The New Yorker.

their cultures and traditions, multinationals have to decide which approach or combination of approaches, from informing to directing, will best answer their strategic objectives. Multinational managers must realize, however, that local managers are likely to resist any precipitate move toward increased headquarters direction. A quick shift could lower their motivation and performance.

Any erosion in marketing decision making associated with global marketing will probably be less upsetting for country managers who have not risen through the line marketing function. For example, John Deere's European headquarters has developed advertising for its European country managers for more than a decade. The country managers have not objected. Most are not marketing specialists and do not see advertising as key to the success of their operations. But for country managers who view control of marketing decision making as central to their operational success, the transition will often be harder. Head-

quarters needs to give the field time to adjust to the new decision-making processes that multi-country brand teams and other new organizational structures require. Yet management must recognize that even with a one- or two-year transition period, some turnover among field personnel is inevitable. As one German headquarters executive commented, "Those managers in the field who can't adapt to a more global approach will have to leave and run local breweries."

Here are five suggestions on how to motivate and retain talented country managers when making the shift to global marketing:

1. Encourage field managers to generate ideas. This is especially important when R&D efforts are centrally directed. Use the best ideas from the field in global marketing programs (and give recognition to the local managers who came up with them). Unilever's South African subsidiary developed Impulse body spray, now a global brand. R. J. Reynolds revitalized Camel as a

global brand after the German subsidiary came up with a successful and transferable positioning and copy strategy.

2. Ensure that the field participates in the development of the marketing strategies and programs for global brands. A bottom-up rather than top-down approach will foster greater commitment and produce superior program execution at the country level. As we've seen, when P&G International introduced its sanitary napkin as a global brand, it permitted local managers to make some adjustments in areas that were not seen as core to the program, such as couponing and sales promotion. More important, it encouraged them to suggest changes in features of the core global program.

3. Maintain a product portfolio that includes, where scale economies permit, local as well as regional and global brands. While Philip Morris's and Seagram's country managers and their local advertising agencies are required to implement standard programs for each company's global brands, the managers retain full responsibility for the marketing programs of their locally distributed brands. Seagram motivates its country managers to stay interested in the global brands by allocating development funds to support local marketing efforts on these brands and by circulating monthly reports that summarize market performance data by brand and country.

4. Allow country managers continued control of their marketing budgets so they can respond to local consumer needs and counter local competition. When British Airways headquarters launched its £13 million global advertising campaign, it left intact the £18 million worth of tactical advertising budgets that country managers used to promote fares, destinations, and tour packages specific to their markets. Because most of the country managers had exhausted their previous year's tactical budgets and were anxious for further advertising support, they were receptive to the global campaign even though it was centrally directed.

5. Emphasize the general management responsibilities of country managers that extend beyond the marketing function. Country managers who have risen through the line marketing function often don't spend enough time on local manufacturing operations, industrial relations, and government affairs. Global marketing programs can free them to focus on and develop their skills in these other areas.

## QUESTIONS

1. *What is the difference between a decentralized multinational firm and a global marketing firm?*

2. *What is the "implementation challenge" in becoming a global marketer? What issues need to be resolved?*

3. *Discuss the four dimensions of global marketing that must be considered in determining the appropriate degree of global standardization. How have Coca-Cola and Nestlé tried to handle these dimensions? Do their approaches differ, and if so, why?*

4. *What are the three critical issues that decentralized multinationals have to overcome to become more global in operation? How is this best accomplished?*

5. *Can a firm go global without losing all the talented managers in each country who don't favor the idea of worldwide decision making and marketing? If so, how?*

☐ **35**

# Top management's concerns about marketing: Issues for the 1980s

*Frederick E. Webster, Jr.*

*How does top management feel about marketing? According to a study reported in this article, top management views marketing as the most important management function—and it expects marketing to become even more important in the future. However, executives are concerned about a number of critical marketing issues that should also be of concern to marketing managers, educators, and students. As you read about these issues, consider what implications they have for your education and career.*

This article reports the findings of a study of top managers' views of the marketing function. The potential value of these findings lies in that they focus attention on a number of issues of concern to top management, helping to define research hypotheses and productive areas of inquiry. Many of these issues have not received the research attention they need and deserve.

It is valuable, from time to time, for marketing academicians to attempt a validity check on their own views of the field as compared with marketing managers who are an important set of beneficiaries, ultimately, of the results of research in marketing (and who frequently provide the financial support needed to conduct the research). How else can academicians be sure that their efforts are meaningful and useful? Are we concerned about and working in areas that management is interested in? It also is helpful to know which issues will be most likely to generate management interest and support in the future.

A recent study by the Marketing Science Institute identified marketing managers' principal areas of concern as: improving marketing productivity, government regulation and marketing practice, effective corporate communications with a variety of constituencies, and integrating marketing and strategic planning with a company-wide marketing orientation (Greyser, 1980). The current research

suggests that top management has a somewhat different view of major issues facing marketing management in the 1980s.

**Purpose of the research**

The research reported here was designed to determine how a sample of chief executive and operating officers in a variety of American corporations viewed the marketing function. It was intended that the interviews should reveal the major issues and concerns that these top managers see facing the marketing function. The purpose was not to gather data that would tell marketing managers how to do their job better or to determine the degree of acceptance of particular analytic and decision-making techniques. Rather, the purpose was to report to marketing managers and scholars that set of issues that is currently foremost in the thinking of top managers as they direct and evaluate the marketing management function. These findings thus have some specific implications for marketing managers as they pre-

Source: Reprinted with permission from the *Journal of Marketing,* published by the American Marketing Association, Summer 1981, pp. 9–16. At the time of writing, Frederick E. Webster, Jr., was associate dean and E. B. Osborn Professor of Marketing, Amos Tuck School of Business Administration, Dartmouth College.

pare for the challenges of the 1980s, and they suggest a number of areas and hypotheses for future research.

## SAMPLE AND INTERVIEWS

Interviews were conducted by the author with chief executive officers, chief operating officers, or other members of top management (with titles such as vice chairman and executive vice president—director) in a total of 21 corporations. Approximately one third of these executives had marketing management backgrounds. While large, multinational firms dominated the sample, a number of smaller, primarily industrial products firms were also included. In addition, nine trustees of the Marketing Science Institute interviewed top management representatives of their own firms and reported the results to the author. These interviews were conducted using the same interview guide used by the author. The total sample, therefore, includes 30 top managers. The companies included in the sample are:

AMCA International Corporation
American Can Corporation
Champion International Corporation
Connecticut Mutual Life Insurance Company
DeLorean Motor Company
Donaldson Company
Eastman Kodak Company
Economics Laboratory
Emery Air Freight Corporation
General Electric Company
General Foods Corporation
General Mills, Inc.
Gillette Company
Gould, Inc.
Graco, Inc.
International Business Machines Corporation
International Paper Company
ITEK Corporation
S. C. Johnson & Son, Inc.
Markem Corporation
Mobile Oil Corporation
Norton Company
Philip Morris, Inc.
Provident National Bank
Quaker Oats Company

Joseph E. Seagram & Sons, Inc.
Sentry Insurance
Toro Company
Union Carbide Corporation
Xerox Corporation

This is clearly a convenience sample. Although there was some attempt to obtain a sample that contained a reasonably broad variety of industries and functional backgrounds among the respondents, the sample is by no means representative in a statistical sense. Likewise, the interpretation of the research results is highly subjective and impressionistic. It is obviously improper to generalize from these findings to all top managers, and it must also be recognized that comments about the rank order of importance of issues discussed are based on the author's interpretation of comments, not on hard quantitative measures of importance. All the same, it is likely that these findings have value as indicators of current concerns and as guides to research questions and hypotheses of some importance, because of the nature of the executives interviewed, not easily accessible to academic researchers, and the companies they represent. More research with executives at this level of the corporate hierarchy was called for by Jerry Wind in a *Journal of Marketing* editorial considering research priorities in marketing for the 1980s (Wind, 1980).

Each interview took from one to three hours. While each was conducted according to a standard interview guide, each also tended to follow its own logic. Themes once established were persistent. The respondents were cordial and open and in all instances seemed truly interested in the research and the research questions. An important motive for participating in this research was an interest in comparing one's thoughts and opinions with others who have similar responsibilities.

These managers do not spend a great deal of time thinking about the marketing function in the abstract; they focus on the problems of their own businesses and see marketing, when asked to think about it, in that light. Thus, they were not talking about marketing as it is studied and taught so much as marketing as it is practiced, intertwined with other business problems and functions. A good portion of these executives had trouble separating marketing from corporate strategy and planning, which would seem to under-score the concern of some authors that marketing scholars in the 1980s need to examine more closely the relationships between marketing and corporate strategy, and to support the observation that academic marketing researchers have been too concerned about tactical decisions rather than truly important strategic issues (Day and Wind, 1980).

## MARKETING COMPETENCE MORE IMPORTANT IN THE FUTURE

Despite the tendency of the research questions to focus on issues and concerns, a large majority of the respondents found the opportunity to ex-press positive opinions and support for the mar-keting function in their businesses. In those firms where marketing is well established and profes-sional marketing competence is longstanding, such as in the large consumer package goods firms, it is clear that marketing is the prime line management function and that marketing compe-tence is the key competitive weapon. In some other large firms, often with a mix of consumer and industrial products and markets, marketing was seen as a critical strategic area that would become more important in the more competitive, slower-growth markets of the 1980s. But, there was also a sense in many of these firms that mar-keting management competence would have to improve. The executives in this second group of companies, having been somewhat critical of their marketing managers' performance in the past, would typically add that the responsibility for mar-keting failures and disappointments had to be shared with top management—i.e., themselves. A third group of top managers, typically those in smaller companies serving industrial markets (al-though not all of the smaller companies are in this set and not all firms in this set are small), saw a lack of marketing orientation as a historical weak-ness of their firms but still stressed that increased marketing competence was a key priority for them for the 1980s.

In summary, there was virtually unanimous agreement, expressed spontaneously in most in-stances, that the marketing management function was a critical strategic function and that it would

become even more so in the 1980s. (Perhaps some of this represents a bias introduced by the respondents' perceptions that the interviewer was identified with the marketing function, but care was taken to avoid leading questions and to mini-mize this potential problem.) Several respondents expressed the opinion that the financial manage-ment orientation that tended to dominate corpo-rate strategy in the 1970s may have created a relatively short-term orientation that left firms in a somewhat weakened position to meet market con-ditions of the 80s. In the words of one respondent, "This led to an overstatement of the financial con-siderations versus what you can accomplish with good marketing." Other writers have recently noted that management's excessive concern for short-term, financial performance has created a competitive weakness for American firms as they enter the more competitive world markets of the 1980s (Hayes and Abernathy, 1980; Mauser, 1980).

## MAJOR ISSUES AND CONCERNS

Although a given individual's major concerns were usually expressed in ways specific to his business, there was a surprising degree of con-sensus in the interviews as to the major issues facing marketing management. These issues will be highlighted and summarized first, next dis-cussed briefly, and then some underlying ques-tions will be defined. The principal issues that were uppermost in the minds of the executives in-terviewed can be summarized, in order of priority, as follows:

Marketing managers are not sufficiently innova-tive and entrepreneurial in their thinking and decision making.

The productivity of marketing expenditures ap-pears to be decreasing as marketing costs, especially for advertising media and field selling, rise.

Marketing managers are generally unsophisti-cated in their understanding of the financial dimensions of marketing decisions and lack a bottom-line orientation. They tend to focus more on sales volume and market share changes than on profit contribution and re-turn on assets.

The product management system, and the marketing competence it brought, are no longer the exclusive properties of the firms that developed the system. For those firms that have used it the longest, the system may have become an inhibitor of innovative thinking.

Marketing people with MBA degrees tend to think alike, to be risk averse, to want to move into general management too quickly, and not to want to pursue careers in sales and sales management.

The acceptance of the marketing concept as a management philosophy is still incomplete, especially in smaller, more technically oriented, and industrial (versus consumer) firms.

Each of these concerns, summarized here and asserted as conclusions supported by admittedly subjective data, has significant implications for marketing managers as well as for marketing teachers/scholars in their roles as educators and researchers.

## Lack of innovative and entrepreneurial thinking

The lack of innovative and entrepreneurial thinking by marketing people was expressed as a major concern by a majority of these respondents and came up in the discussion in several different contexts, including:

Failure to provide proper stimulation and guidance for R&D and product development.

Failure to exploit and develop markets for new products developed by R&D.

Inability to define new methods for promoting products to customers in the face of major increases in the costs of media advertising and personal selling.

A general unwillingness to stick one's neck out and take a necessary risk.

A failure to innovate in distribution and other areas in order to keep up with the changing requirements of industrial customers doing business on a multinational basis.

A tendency for product managers and higher levels of management in the product management organization, all of whom have sim-

ilar education, training, and experience, to approach problems in the same way.

Attempting to meet significant new competition with traditional ways of doing business.

Inability to refine and modify product positioning.

These observations about the lack of innovative and entrepreneurial thinking by marketing people echo a management concern expressed by other authors, that American managers in general have emphasized short-term financial results and developed an institutionalized aversion to risk (Hayes and Abernathy, 1980). If it is indeed true that marketing managers do not often think in an innovative and entrepreneurial fashion, part of the problem must be found in the systems used to direct, evaluate, and control marketing performance. In addition, one must look to the organizational arrangements made to facilitate two-way communication between marketing and research and development. Several of the respondents noted these connections and commented that these were a top-management responsibility. One chief executive observed that the budget planning and review process encouraged marketing managers to stick to the proven path; truly innovative and distinctive marketing approaches have a low probability of surviving the hierarchical budget planning process.

## Marketing productivity

The second major set of issues indentified by these business leaders concerned the declining productivity of marketing expenditures in the face of increased costs of doing business and, as noted above, failure to find innovative, more efficient approaches for communicating with customers. For the large, consumer package goods marketers the issues centered around increased media costs, particularly the costs of broadcast media. For firms in such areas as insurance and business machines, the concern was for the increased costs of fielding a national sales organization, especially in those cases where unit product prices were decreasing significantly. While the use of sophisticated decision models and analytic techniques was not a major concern of these top executives, positive or negative, none of the respondents felt, when asked, that such models and techniques had made significant contributions to the efficiency of marketing expenditures. A few, however, did describe marketing experiments currently under way to assess the productivity of advertising expenditures.

These impressions held by this sample of top managers are not inconsistent with the conclusions of marketing scholars who have looked at the contributions of management science to marketing. Myers, Greyser, and Massy (1979, p. 27) in their report on the American Marketing Association's Commission on the Effectiveness of Research and Development for Marketing Management noted that "a significant amount of marketing research effort, new knowledge development, model-building, and theorizing has had relatively little impact on improving marketing management over the [1955-80] period." It is possible that a major part of the problem is that significant developments of potentially high relevance have simply not been reported in the literature that top management reads, nor has it been adequately communicated to them by their marketing staffs. It may also be significant to note that the most frequently cited work on marketing productivity analysis is still a small textbook published over 15 years ago (Sevin, 1965). (See also Bucklin, 1978, and Heskett, 1965.) There appears to be little or no connection at the moment between marketing productivity analysis and concepts and techniques of management science developed in the last two decades.

**Financial performance**

A third set of issues focused on marketing managers' lack of understanding of the financial dimensions of corporate strategy and management decision making. The major criticism was that marketing managers do not understand basic concepts of financial management and are unable to consider the financial consequences of their decisions. As a result, they are said to concentrate on sales volume and market share objectives rather than such measures of profitability as profit contribution margin, ROI, and return on assets employed by business segment (i.e., product, customer, region, etc.).

There is much more to this concern than these most obvious issues. A central dimension is performance evaluation and the relationship between what marketing managers emphasize in their decision making and how they are evaluated and rewarded. A second dimension concerns how much emphasis should be placed on financial considerations by marketing managers. Some of these executives expressed a concern that marketing people could place too much emphasis on financial dimensions, worrying about things other than how to get orders, build market share, and improve competitive effectiveness, which should be their major concerns. Yet another consideration is the way in which top management has changed the signals as they relate to marketing management. In the words of one respondent, "We used to say to them, 'You get the sales and profit margins, and we'll worry about how to finance them.' Not any more."

Related to this is the fact that some top managements have had difficulty assessing the trade-offs between current, short-term financial performance—sales volume, contribution margin, and cash flow—and future, long-term financial performance—market share and long-range return on investment. As a result, their marketing organizations have been receiving confused, changing, and conflicting signals. Astute top managers do tend to recognize this problem and take a major share of the blame for the less than satisfactory marketing performance that often resulted.

**The product manager system and the MBA**

Concern about the functioning of the product management system of marketing organization is relatively straightforward and is also intertwined with a concern about the nature of MBA-trained managers. The product manager system per se no longer conveys the inherent competitive advantage that it held for those large consumer package goods firms that innovated the concept. Their smaller and newer competitors have copied the system and hired away some of the talent developed by the leaders. As these systems mature, higher levels of management are staffed by persons who have been promoted from lower levels of the product management organization. Thus, several levels of management can have very similar training and experience. These former product managers can tend to continue to dabble in the details of product management to a degree that hinders the effectiveness of management at the lower levels.

According to some of the executives interviewed in the larger consumer package goods firms, product managers used to come from many areas within the firm—sales, manufacturing, engineering, and others—as well as from outside. Today, in contrast, the standard source is the top 20 or 30 MBA programs in leading universities throughout the country. Among the opinions expressed by these top-management representatives about the MBA talent being recruited by their organizations are that MBAs all tend to think alike, to approach problems the same way, to obscure a problem with excessive number-crunching and analysis, to want to move into general management too quickly, to be unwilling to stay in a position long enough to develop competence and learn the details of the business, and to have no interest in sales and sales management careers. These are familiar concerns about MBAs, but that does not make them invalid.

Not only do these concerns about MBA aspirations and performance relate to the performance of the product manager system. They also relate directly to the observation that marketing managers do not like to take risks and are unable to approach problems in an innovative and entrepreneurial fashion.

## Incomplete acceptance of the marketing concept

As noted earlier, there was virtual unanimity among these executives that marketing is the critical management function in their firms from a strategic viewpoint and that it is likely to become even more important in the current decade. In the most sophisticated marketing organizations (i.e., the consumer package goods firms primarily), marketing is the line management function and the marketing concept is the dominant and pervasive management philosophy. In the rest of the companies in the sample, however, there appeared to be an incomplete acceptance of the marketing concept.

In the most obvious situation, the respondent executive could point to an absence of any senior executive with clear responsibility for marketing within the organization. In these instances, there had been a history of strong production-, technical- (engineering or R&D), or sales-oriented thinking dominating the firm. Another symptom of the problem was an absence of any market segmentation strategy. There also were a few cases where the respondent executive felt that marketing weakness was due to a failure by top management to devote the necessary financial and managerial resources to the marketing task.

In the industrial products and services firms especially, and also in some of the consumer products firms, marketing and sales were organizationally distinct, with sales being seen as a line function and marketing as a staff responsibility, often associated with the corporate planning function. The marketing function in these circumstances was said to be responsible for long-range marketing planning and market development, whereas the sales function was responsible for current year sales volume and profit performance through the implementation of marketing plans through specific sales and promotion programs. Not all of these top managers would agree that the separation of marketing and sales within the organization is evidence of incomplete acceptance of the marketing concept.

One senior executive made the important observation that getting the marketing concept understood and accepted is still the biggest challenge faced by any organization, despite the fact that the concept is now more than a quarter-century old. In his extensive experience in the top ranks of both industrial and consumer products firms, he noted that marketing "tends to degenerate into a sales orientation and an exclusive concern for marketing communications." He felt that there was an inevitable tendency in industrial firms for large customers, because of their importance, to bring pressures on the firm that create a very short-term orientation and a concern for specific orders and problems. He also pointed to sheer numbers of sales personnel compared with marketing as another reason why sales tends to dominate marketing. While these particular observations are attributable to a single CEO, they capture a set of issues of concern to a significant portion of this sample.

## SOME IMPLICATIONS AND SUGGESTIONS FOR FUTURE RESEARCH

Although these concerns of top management are interesting for their own sake, and suggest some directions in which the marketing profession might look to find areas for improved management effectiveness, they also point to some underlying basic issues. These issues can be phrased as questions requiring further research and discussion.

**How does management performance evaluation impact on marketing performance?**

There has been only minimal cooperation between organizational behavior and marketing scholars as revealed in the research literature, yet some of the most interesting and important issues of marketing decision making may be those that relate to the human side of enterprise. Criticism of marketing for failure to innovate and take risks is an obvious area where behavioral issues are at the core, not technical issues of marketing science and decision making. Part of the issue here is to explore relationships between various corporate financial goals and marketing performance as they are mediated through formal and informal performance appraisal systems. While recent months have seen some discussion of this issue in the management literature, it is an area that needs a great deal more management attention and academic research. Investigators need to look at relationships between measures of a firm's innovativeness, such as the rate of new product introductions, and how management in that firm is evaluated and rewarded. Marketing scholars need to become familiar with the work of scholars in organizational behavior on such topics as risk taking, organizational structure, and innovativeness, and integrate this into their own investigations of marketing performance and organization effectiveness.

**How serious is the problem of decreasing productivity of marketing expenditures?**

The assertion that marketing productivity has declined needs to be tested by careful analysis of changes in marketing costs and marketing effectiveness. Expenditure patterns need to be documented, adjusted for inflation, and related to changes in market share, sales volume, profit margin, and other measures of performance. A

concern for such macro issues of marketing strategy and marketing performance has largely been left to the economists. Marketers have tended to focus their attention on the nuances of interbrand competition and the battle for market share and have not addressed some of the broader issues defined and outlined in this study.

At the minimum, marketers should be able to sort out the effects of cost inflation per se from the rest of the equation of marketing effectiveness that relates marketing dollar expenditures to marketing performance measures if they are to deal with the charge of declining productivity. It is not likely that most marketing managers can defend themselves adequately against this charge, whether warranted or not, because they probably could not demonstrate any relationship between expenditures on marketing activities and traceable sales and profit results. The real issue here may not be productivity per se but an inability to measure cause-effect relationships between marketing expenditures and results.

**What has happened to the product manager system?**

There are several projects here for ambitious marketing scholars. A first step would be simply to track changes that have occurred in the nature and scope of product manager organizations in those firms that first developed such systems. A second step could be to trace their diffusion to other firms in the consumer packaged-goods area and then beyond that to industrial product firms, providers of financial services, and other types of organizations, looking for adaptations that reflected the new environment of application. A third stage could define problems inherent in the system as perceived by product managers and their superiors in the organization. These descriptive stages could provide the base from which to investigate some more subtle and complex issues such as whether these systems stifle innovation and discourage risk taking. One hypothesis worth testing is that the training programs used by companies to develop product managers (not MBA programs) tend to develop rote approaches to problem analysis and solution. The issues here clearly trace back to issues of performance evaluation.

## What are the barriers to implementation and maintenance of a marketing viewpoint in an organization?

The obvious wisdom of customer orientation, market segmentation, and long-term strategic thinking based on sound market information, which are the hallmarks of the marketing concept, is hardly ever questioned, yet a substantial portion of this sample of some of the nation's top managers report frustration in getting that viewpoint implemented. Students of organizations and human behavior are seldom surprised by the gap between theory and practice, concept and implementation, but the difficulties of implementing the market concept need to be understood in much greater detail. An important dimension to examine here is the central role played by the chief executive officer in promoting a marketing viewpoint, developing a truly integrated marketing organization, and supporting the marketing management team, especially as it competes with strong managers in engineering, R&D, production, sales, and other areas for scarce financial resources.

Some observers would argue that the emergence of strong strategic planning departments has weakened the position of the marketing department in the corporate hierarchy. That issue needs to be examined carefully. The conclusion will probably depend on the extent to which marketing is perceived to be part of, if not completely absorbed by, strategic planning. Another interesting issue here is whether a strong planning function serves as a stimulus or a barrier to innovative thinking. A reasonable hypothesis would be that it is intended to be the former but usually proves to be the latter.

## SUMMARY AND CONCLUSIONS

These chief executives and operating officers believe that marketing is the most important management function in their businesses, and they see it becoming more important in the future. Whether they come from a marketing background or not, they believe that the development and maintenance of an effective marketing organization is a major requirement for success in the economic environment of increased competition and slow growth that will be characteristic of most markets in the 1980s. Having said that, however, these executives are critical of their marketing managers for a failure to think creatively and innovatively and to understand the financial implications of their decisions. They see marketing costs increasing faster than the effectiveness of those expenditures. They worry that the product management system may be becoming obsolete and express frustration with the difficulties of instilling and maintaining a true marketing orientation in their businesses. As CEOs and COOs, they feel a personal responsibility for the quality of their marketing managers and their performance and suspect that they have been guilty of giving conflicting signals to the marketers in their organizations because they, the top executives, have not resolved the complex trade-offs between short-term and long-term measures of financial performance.

Against this background of management concerns, marketing managers and teachers/scholars in the field can assess their own activities, interests, and priorities. There are suggestions here that managers need to become more willing to take risks and more innovative and entrepreneurial in their thinking. Marketing managers need to devote more attention to financial analysis relevant to their decisions, especially relating to measures of return on investment and return on assets employed. This is a question of developing the necessary knowledge of financial management concepts as well as an issue of management attitude and viewpoint.

Those marketing managers who have the benefit of an MBA education may wish, in addition, to examine their own priorities and career plans. Does the career plan allow for adequate time to develop the necessary skills and understanding of the business to progress toward higher levels of marketing and general management? Does it recognize the importance of understanding the customer, the marketplace, competition, and distribution—knowledge that can often best be gained by significant exposure to field sales situations? MBAs must be sensitive to the way they are perceived by other members of the organization and must take steps to change the basis for those perceptions as well as the perceptions themselves.

For marketing academicians, some sobering self-analysis may also be in order. Are we asking the right questions? Marketing is different from finance and production, the other areas of management decision making where operations research and econometrics have been applied so forcefully and effectively. Marketing management is still more art than science and has yielded slowly to attempts to make it more scientific. Marketing data are by their very nature less precise, and cause-and-effect relationships are usually time lagged and hard to pin down. Yet marketers aspire to the same degree of rigor that has characterized the analysis of their colleagues in these other functions. The result may have been a significant sacrifice of relevance (Mauser, 1980).

The issues identified in this research as central in the thinking of top management are, by and large, qualitative, messy issues relating to organization, management direction and control, performance evaluation, goal setting, etc. There is a real need for marketing researchers to refocus their attention on issues such as these, not just increasingly sophisticated issues of research methodology.

## REFERENCES

Bucklin, Louis P. *Productivity in Marketing.* Chicago: American Marketing Association, 1978.

Day, George S., and Yoram Wind. "Strategic Planning and Marketing: Time for a Constructive Partnership." *Journal of Marketing* 44 (Spring 1980), pp. 7–8.

Greyser, Stephen A. "Marketing Issues." *Journal of Marketing* 44 (January 1980), pp. 89–92.

Hayes, Robert H., and William J. Abernathy. "Managing Our Way to Economic Decline." *Harvard Business Review* 58 (July–August 1980), pp. 67–77.

Heskett, J. L., ed. *Productivity in Marketing.* Columbus: College of Commerce and Administration, Ohio State University, 1965.

Mauser, Ferdinand. "Marketing Issues: The Marketing Fraternity's Shortfall." *Journal of Marketing* 44 (Fall 1980), pp. 97–98.

Myers, John G.; Stephen A. Greyser; and William F. Massy. "The Effectiveness of Marketing's 'R&D' for Marketing Management: An Assessment." *Journal of Marketing* 43 (January 1979), pp. 17–29.

Sevin, Chester H. *Marketing Productivity Analysis.* New York: McGraw-Hill, 1965.

Wind, Yoram. "Marketing in the Eighties." *Journal of Marketing* 44 (January 1980), pp. 7–9.

## QUESTIONS

1. Why do top managers consider marketing to be the most important function in their businesses?

2. Using your own words, summarize the major issues and concerns expressed by top management about marketing. Do you think these are valid issues for top management to be concerned about?

3. How responsible is top management for the various marketing problems discussed in this article? Are they just "passing the buck" for their own failures and shortcomings?

# Case 1

# Automated Office

## INTRODUCTION

Automated Office (AO) is a small word processing/typing service located in East Lansing, Michigan. It provides word processing and typing services for a variety of clients—including small businesses, professional organizations (attorneys and CPAs), authors, and students attending Michigan State University. A complete description of AO's scope of services appears in Exhibit 1. Since the company is less than one year old, it has not yet established a production volume large enough to afford sophisticated copying or binding equipment. These services are sold—but produced by other companies at the present time.

### Exhibit 1 □ Scope of professional services

One objective of Automated Office is to provide a full range of professional typing and business services. The scope of our professional services directed toward serving small businesses, governments, professional organizations, authors, and students, is identified below:

**Document Preparation and Revision**
Books
Camera ready copy
Proposals
Reports
Financial and statistical data
Dissertations
Theses
Term papers
Resumés
Business correspondence
Personalized repetitive letters
Mailing lists (customer lists)
Transcription
Envelopes

**Document Storage**
Automated Office stores documents on disk or diskette to facilitate revisions, editing or re-printing of the stored information.

**Document Reproduction**
Reprinted original copy (duplicate printed directly from word processing printer)
High-quality duplication

**Document Binding**
Spiral (coil) binding
Velo (strap) binding (the method used to bind this document)
Hard cover (book) binding

**Proofreading**

This case was prepared by Professor E. Jerome McCarthy of Michigan State University.

Automated Office occupies approximately 500 square feet in the city's small business district near the university campus. The company's inventory of production equipment includes:

Four word processing entry stations.
Three letter-quality word processing printers.
One Selectric typewriter.
Two document binding machines.
Two dictation/transcription units (recorder and transcriber).
One adding machine.

Automated Office operates as a partnership—with two general partners. The general partners do not participate in the day-to-day management. But, they do set operating policy and provide overall direction to the company's full-time manager. Their intent is to determine whether a "franchise-type" business is possible in this product-market area. A complete organization chart for Automated Office is provided in Exhibit 2.

**Exhibit 2 ☐ Organization chart for automated office**

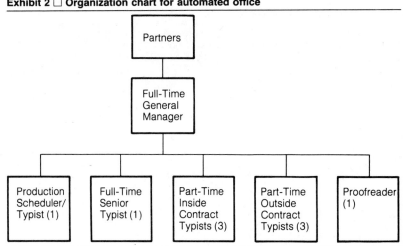

## THE WORD PROCESSING/TYPING MARKET

The market for word processing and typing services is composed of several very different customer types. Quality requirements, location preferences, ability to pay, etc., are considerably different for each customer type.

One requirement that is common to almost all customers is fast turnaround for typed copy. As a result, the potential market is limited to people within a five-mile radius of the office. AO has identified the area that it believes it can adequately service. Within that area, the company has developed information on the size and volume potential for each major customer type. This data is summarized in Exhibit 3. Exhibit 3 also presents various characteristics of each major customer type.

The market potential estimates for customer types are based on some simple volume assumptions. For example, as shown in the table on page 276, it is

**Exhibit 3 ☐ Customer market information summary**

| Type of customer | Number of customers | Annual market potential (pages) | Location require- ment | Pricing | Typing needs | Quality require- ment | Miscellaneous characteristics |
|---|---|---|---|---|---|---|---|
| University students: Undergraduate | 32,000 | 480,000 | Close to campus | Requires low price for 90% of market (10% not price sensitive) | Resumés, term papers | Low–medium | Large volume of small jobs < 20 pages. Generally need finished product next day. Bounced check follow-up sometimes required. |
| Masters level | 4,500 | 270,000 | Close to campus | Low to medium range pricing (25% not price sensitive) | Resumés, term papers, theses, special projects | Medium–high | Usually allow 2–3 day lead-time on jobs. Some large jobs (theses.) |
| Doctoral level | 2,500 | 175,000 | Close to campus | Medium range (30% not price sensitive) | Resumés, dissertations, term papers | High | Prefer going to one place to have dissertation produced. Requires statistical typing. Dissertations are well suited to word processing capabilities. |
| Law firms | 32 | 8,000 | Within 5-mile radius | Willing to pay top prices for high quality | Overload typing volume | High | Usually have their own word processing equipment. Use outside services for overload only. |
| Accounting firms | 40 | 10,000 | Within 5-mile radius | Willing to pay top prices for high quality | Overload typing volume | High | Concerned about confidentiality. Large volume of statistical typing. |
| Small businesses | >2000 | ? | Within 5-mile radius | Medium to high | Brochures, mailing lists, miscellaneous correspondence | Medium | Most do not have in-house word processing capability. Biggest potential is mailing lists which require word processing. |
| Authors | 100 | 30,000 | Within 5-mile radius | Medium | Books, articles | High | Word processing well suited and less expensive than typewriter for revision work. Many authors at university. |
| Others (associations, clubs, churches, politicians, etc.) | ? | ? | Within 5-mile radius | Medium | Mailing lists brochures, business letters | Medium–high | Many needs are well suited to word processing. |

assumed that an average undergraduate university student will need a minimum of 30 typed pages during the year. Of course, many of these pages will be typed by the student—or by a friend of the student at no charge. Therefore, a percentage factor is applied to determine a more realistic customer market size. For non-student customers, estimated market potential includes only service requirements that are "out-sourced" by the customer.

| | Number of customers | Realistic potential | Realistic number of customers | Double-spaced pages required annually per customer | Market potential (pages) |
|---|---|---|---|---|---|
| Students. | | | | | |
| Undergrad | 32,000 | 50% | 16,000 | 30 | 480,000 |
| Masters | 4,500 | 60 | 2,700 | 100 | 270,000 |
| Doctoral | 2,500 | 70 | 1,750 | 100 | 175,000 |
| Accounting firms | 40 | 50 | 20 | 500 | 10,000 |
| Law firms | 32 | 50 | 16 | 500 | 8,000 |
| Authors | 100 | 100 | 100 | 300 | 30,000 |
| | | | | | 973,000 |

Pricing is a key factor in obtaining market share—especially in the student markets. Most undergraduate students, for example, are unwilling to pay more than $1.50 per standard double-spaced page. However, there are some in every customer group who are not price-sensitive (up to $1.80 or so per page). In the premium markets (e.g., professional firms) up to $2 per page is acceptable if a very high level of quality can be delivered.

One difference between customer types is the need for word processing versus typing. For example, mailing lists that must be sorted, added to, changed, edited, etc., require word processing. Using electric typewriters would be inefficient and expensive. Other typing needs (e.g., student term papers) can be efficiently produced using either word processors or typewriters—depending on the amount of revision anticipated. Typing needs which are best served by word processing are noted under miscellaneous characteristics in Exhibit 3.

## COMPETITION

The market for word processing and typing services in East Lansing is extremely competitive. Although only a few word processing service businesses are in the area, several other kinds of typing service providers compete in the local typing market. The manager of Automated Office has identified four basic competitor types.

**Home typists.** The East Lansing area has several typists who work out of their homes. Customers usually must deliver their drafts and pick up their final typed copy at the typist's home. These competitors use professional electric typewriters (like IBM Selectrics) which cost less than $1,000. (The initial dollar investment required for word processing equipment—$6,000 to $10,000—precludes most home typists from using word processors.) The quality of finished product provided by home typists varies considerably—as do the prices they charge. Generally, the price charged by home typists for a standard 8½ × 11-inch double-spaced page ranges from $1.00 to $1.50.

**Traditional typing services.**  Traditional typing services, as defined by AO's manager, are service businesses that operate out of a retail location—but do not use word processing equipment. There are currently only two such businesses in the East Lansing area. The quality provided by these competitors is usually quite good. Prices range from $1.25 to $1.65 per standard 8½ × 11 double-spaced page.

**Word processing services.**  The East Lansing area currently has three other word processing service businesses (similar to Automated Office). These competitors charge between $1.50 and $1.85 for a standard double-spaced page.

Smith, Pierson & Company concentrates on the overflow volume generated by attorneys in the area, although they accept other types of work. In addition to providing word processing services, Smith, Pierson & Company also provides temporary legal secretarial support services.

Word King, Inc., adjacent to the university campus, does a high volume of resumé work for students. They also do a fair volume of business correspondence, letters, and dissertations for graduate students. The production volume of Word King, Inc., however, is limited by having only two word processors and one printer.

A-Plus Typesetting Company provides both word processing and typesetting services. It is located in the business district near the campus and is about the same size as Word King. This competitor has only been in business for about three months. It provides services for both students and businesses. Prices are competitive with the other word processing businesses.

**The guys down the hall.**  AO's general manager describes one group of competitors as "the guys down the hall." This description refers to college student typists who provide typing for other students at either very low prices or for no charge at all! Although these typists often do not provide a level of quality competitive with professional word processing or typing services, they have a substantial share of the student market.

A summary of the characteristics of AO's competitors is provided in Exhibit 4.

### The first six months (January to June, 1983)

Automated Office has just completed six months of operation and the results are not good. The partners expected to be breaking even (at least) by now. Instead, additional partner capital has been required. And if the present method of operation is continued, even larger losses are projected. The results of projecting the first six months to the end of the year (December 31, 1983) are shown in the pro forma (expected) income statement and balance sheet for the year ended December 31, 1983—see Exhibit 5. It is clear that some changes are needed.

The original plan was to cater to the student and faculty market first—to get some sales and develop experience with the word processing machines. Then, AO would go after businesses, professional people, associations, and any other markets which might need *word processing*. This plan seemed to make sense because the university community could provide "immediate" sales, while the other

**Exhibit 4 □ Summary of competitive characteristics**

| Competitors | Pricing (standard double-spaced page) | Location | Type of equipment | Specialization | Miscellaneous |
|---|---|---|---|---|---|
| Home typists | $1.00–1.50 | Local neighborhoods (from 2 blocks to 2 miles from campus) | IBM Selectric or similar typewriter | Anything/everything | |
| Traditional typing services | $1.25–1.65 | Business districts adjacent to university campus | IBM Selectric or similar typewriter | Anything/everything | |
| "Guys down the hall" | $0–1.00 | Dormitories, student apartment complexes | Manual or non-professional electric typewriter | Anything/everything | |
| Smith, Pierson & Company | $1.50–1.85 | Suburban office 2 miles from university campus | 3 word processors | Legal transcripts, other large documents | Provide legal secretarial support services |
| Word King, Inc. | $1.50–1.85 | Retail location adjacent to campus | 2 word processors | Resumés, business letters, dissertations | Located next to a resumé counseling service |
| A-Plus Typesetting | $1.60–1.85 | Retail location adjacent to campus | 1 word processor | Anything/everything | Also provide typesetting service |

**Exhibit 5 □ Expected financial statements**

AUTOMATED OFFICE
Expected Income Statement
For the Year Ended 12-31-83
(if no changes are made)

| | | |
|---|---|---|
| Revenue | | $37,620 |
| Costs: | | |
| Salaries and wages . . . . . . . . . . . . . . . . . . | $48,180 | |
| Office supplies . . . . . . . . . . . . . . . . . . . . . | 2,600 | |
| FICA . . . . . . . . . . . . . . . . . . . . . . . . . . . | 3,228 | |
| FUTA . . . . . . . . . . . . . . . . . . . . . . . . . . . | 1,300 | |
| State unemployment tax . . . . . . . . . . . . . | 482 | |
| Advertising . . . . . . . . . . . . . . . . . . . . . . . | 3,100 | |
| Depreciation . . . . . . . . . . . . . . . . . . . . . . | 4,600 | |
| Utilities . . . . . . . . . . . . . . . . . . . . . . . . . . | 1,800 | |
| Insurance expense . . . . . . . . . . . . . . . . . | 400 | |
| Rent (office) . . . . . . . . . . . . . . . . . . . . . . | 2,700 | |
| Miscellaneous expense . . . . . . . . . . . . . . | 4,140 | |
| Total expenses . . . . . . . . . . . . . . . . . . . . | | 72,530 |
| Net income (loss) . . . . . . . . . . . . . . . . . . . | | ($34,910) |

AUTOMATED OFFICE
Expected Balance Sheet
At 12-31-83
(if no changes are made)
*Assets*

| | |
|---|---|
| Cash . . . . . . . . . . . . . . . . . . . . . . . . . . . . . . . . . . . . . . . | $ 2,100 |
| Accounts receivable . . . . . . . . . . . . . . . . . . . . . . . . . . . | 4,800 |
| Furniture and fixtures | |
| (net of depreciation) . . . . . . . . . . . . . . . . . . . . . . . . | 1,430 |
| Machinery and equipment | |
| (net of depreciation) . . . . . . . . . . . . . . . . . . . . . . . . | 23,000 |
| Security deposits . . . . . . . . . . . . . . . . . . . . . . . . . . . . . | 500 |
| Total assets . . . . . . . . . . . . . . . . . . . . . . . . . . . | $31,330 |

*Liabilities and partners' capital*

| | |
|---|---|
| Accounts payable . . . . . . . . . . . . . . . . . . . . . . . . . . . . . | $ 1,010 |
| Accrued payroll payable . . . . . . . . . . . . . . . . . . . . . . . . | 580 |
| Notes due to partners . . . . . . . . . . . . . . . . . . . . . . . . . . | 20,000 |
| Partners' capital . . . . . . . . . . . . . . . . . . . . . . . . . . . . . . | 9,740 |
| Total liabilities and partners' capital . . . . . . . | $31,330 |

markets would probably be slower to adopt—because it would require a change in behavior (doing work outside and/or in a different way).

The original promotion effort used daily ads in the student paper, notices on university bulletin boards, and letters to Ph.D. candidates (who have to prepare a thesis eventually) and faculty members. Then, over 1,000 brochures were sent to various businesses and professionals. A few follow-up phone calls were made by the general manager, but these were not very fruitful, and she soon became more involved in managing the "flood" of inquiries and student work which began to come in. In fact, all promotion effort, except the daily ad in the student paper, was dropped in favor of "getting the business in and the work out" as "word of mouth" seemed to take over—and repeat student business came, too.

Michigan State University is on the quarter system, so the usual mid-term and final papers flowed almost continuously. And with Ph.D. thesis deadlines and resumé work—which was always "urgent"—AO became a "zoo" at times. Several students might be waiting to leave or pick up work. And others would be waiting for corrections—sometimes standing right behind the machine operator and adding to the confusion. AO had some operators work longer hours and hired (and trained) many part-time people. And a production scheduler was hired to help get the work out. About this time—after three months' operation—the general manager decided that she wanted a regular nine-to-five job and resigned. A new manager was quickly hired, and the previous manager stayed on to smooth the transition. Nevertheless, there was a learning time. Also, much of the learning was about how to manage the "zoo." Business continued to come in from students—all of it "rush." And even the end of spring term didn't reduce the activity very much. Resumés and theses kept coming—as well as a variety of other work. But not much "business and professional" work came in. And there just didn't seem to be time to "sell" this kind of work.

Throughout these first six months, the partners had to put in more capital to keep the business going. This was expected to begin with, but as sales volume increased and AO was "swamped with work," it seemed as though the company should at least break even. The original plan showed that it would, but there had been setbacks—machine breakdowns causing work loss, losing the first manager, slower-than-expected training times for new operators, and higher-than-expected costs for "good" operators. In fact, the production side of the business was more costly and more difficult to manage than the partners expected. This increased costs in the short run. But it may be an asset in the long run, providing "barriers to entry" and unexpectedly high costs to potential competitors for word processing business. In fact, it seems clear that casual users will never capture the value of word processors. The manuals provided with the machines only "get you started." Much "trial and error" and continued use (at least 10 hours per week) seem to be necessary to be proficient.

Now that the first six months have passed and it is obvious that some changes are necessary, the partners and general manager are reviewing the business—to identify problems and refine their strategic plan. The results of their operations review are summarized below.

1. During the first six months, AO earned the equivalent of $1.65 per standard double-spaced page.
2. Most of the revenue during 1983 came from students. A breakdown of where the work originated appears below:

| Type of customer | Type of work | Percent of total revenue |
|---|---|---|
| Undergraduate student | Term papers | 40% |
| Undergraduate student | Resumés | 10 |
| Graduate student | Theses/ dissertations | 25 |
| Authors | Books | 15 |
| Businesses | Mailing lists and business letters | 5 |
| Miscellaneous typing and binding | | 5 |
| | | 100% |

3. Approximately half of the brochures were still on hand.
4. Several production inefficiencies resulted from inexperienced word processing operators. AO's general manager estimates that the typing staff is operating about 15 percent more efficiently now compared to three months ago.
5. Approximately 25 percent of the jobs completed have been for less than 10 typed pages. The general manager feels that jobs of less than 10 typed pages are not profitable—due to the administrative time spent on each job, as well as the time that must be spent at the counter receiving and delivering finished work. Almost all of the small jobs (less than 10 pages) come from undergraduate students.

    An exception to the conclusion about work less than 10 pages is re-sumé work—which is billed at $7 per page and therefore seems to be profitable.
6. AO's original plan called for the general manager to spend about 20 hours a week making personal sales calls to develop work from small businesses and professional firms. However, all the general manager's time was spent on day-to-day operations. As a result, very little "premium-priced" work was gen-erated (only 5 percent of the total revenue came from small business and professional firms).
7. AO's monthly volumes varied significantly because they paralleled student needs for term papers, dissertations, resumes, etc.
8. Growing volume seemed to require the addition of a production scheduler. The production scheduler spent about 75 percent of her time typing and 25 percent scheduling production and training new typing staff.
9. With the addition of a production scheduler, AO's fixed salary costs increased significantly. A schedule of monthly fixed costs is provided in Exhibit 6.

**Exhibit 6 ☐ Schedule of monthly fixed costs**

| | |
|---|---:|
| Salaries and wages including employer taxes and benefits: | |
|     General manager | $1,900 |
|     Production scheduler | 1,355 |
|     Senior typist | 1,250 |
| Equipment maintenance | 75 |
| Advertising | 100 |
| Insurance | 25 |
| Depreciation | 383 |
| Rent | 225 |
| Utilities | 120 |
| Office supplies | 200 |
| Miscellaneous | 100 |
| | 5,733 |

10. An analysis of fixed wages and salaries indicate that the senior typist's contri-bution (to overhead and profit) per month is approximately $470. However, the general manager and the production scheduler together create approxi-mately $1,970 of fixed overhead per month. Therefore, to break even, AO would need four full-time equivalent typists. Since AO only has four word pro-cessing terminals, either a second shift operation must be organized or addi-

tional equipment purchased. The analysis of fixed wages and salaries appears below:

| | Monthly cost | Pages typed | Dollar contribution at $1.65 per typed page |
|---|---|---|---|
| General manager | $1,900 | 0 | $ 0 |
| Production scheduler | 1,355 | 780 | 1,287 |
| Senior typist | 1,250 | 1,040 | 1,716 |

11. If the decision is made to purchase additional equipment, AO must move from its present location (which has only 500 square feet). If such a move is made, rent will increase from $225 to about $400 per month.

**Possible changes**

After reviewing the past efforts, the partners and general manager considered many possible changes, including the following:

1. Pursuing more "business and professional" work, which could increase the gross margin and reduce the break-even point, because it is "premium" work. This could be the job of the general manager (as originally planned), or a sales rep (one is available) could be paid a commission of 10 percent on *new* "non-student" business obtained by her efforts.
2. Adding new equipment and moving to larger office space—to permit a larger production volume. It was decided to delay moving—the rent would rise and each new word processor would cost $6,000–10,000—until the business at least breaks even.
3. Eliminating positions that require fixed salaries—thereby reducing the break-even point. This could include the production scheduler—whose duties would have to be assumed by the general manager—and the senior typist. All production work would be done by contract typists. To simplify the analysis, the general manager estimates that a "senior typist" should be able to produce the equivalent of eight double-spaced pages per hour at a cost of $.75 per page. This allows for interruptions, helping the "junior typists," and personal time. The "junior typists" (after a few weeks of break-in) should be able to produce the equivalent of six double-spaced pages per hour at a cost of $.65 per page.
4. Establishing a minimum charge—to discourage small orders (or make them profitable). The general manager estimates that a $9 minimum charge will do the job and has already made this change. See revised price list in Exhibit 7.
5. Sending out the rest of the brochures—and following up with phone calls—to sell more "premium" work.
6. Raising prices 10 to 20 percent on "student" typing—counting on some students being willing to pay more for word processor quality and/or the convenience, speed, and quality that AO offers.
7. Raising the "business and professional" work prices from $16 to $20 per hour. This will be above the "competitive rate" in the Lansing area. But it will still be below the rates charged in Detroit, Ann Arbor, and Grand Rapids (nearby cities where wage rates are similar). The present rates were set to "meet competition," and the manager has been reluctant to raise them because some customers complain about $16 per hour. One of the partners feels that higher prices may be possible for some kinds of service. ("The local car dealer charges $36 for repair service, and people still keep coming!")

**Exhibit 7** ☐ **Revised price list**

# AUTOMATED OFFICE

### PROFESSIONAL TYPING AND BUSINESS SERVICES
220 Albert, Suite 212 • East Lansing, Michigan 48823
Phone 517-337-0812

---

**Price list (minimum charge = $9)**

**Straight text (per page)**

|  | Typed | | Handwritten | |
|---|---|---|---|---|
|  | Double | Single | Double | Single |
| Pica | $1.50 | $3.00 | $1.75 | $3.50 |
| Elite | 1.75 | 3.50 | 2.00 | 4.00 |
| Legal | 1.90 | 3.80 | 2.20 | 4.40 |
| Footnotes within body | | | | |
| of text: | | | | |
|   Pica | $2.25 | $3.75 | $2.25 | $4.25 |
|   Elite | 2.50 | 4.25 | 2.75 | 4.75 |
|   Legal | 2.65 | 4.55 | 2.95 | 5.15 |
| Footnotes/bibliography | | | | |
| (at end of paper): | | | | |
|   Pica | | $3.25 | | $3.75 |
|   Elite | | 3.75 | | 4.25 |
| Title page | | $ .75 | | $ .75 |
| Blank pages | | .25 | | .25 |
| Standard typing (Selectric) | | | $16/hour | |

**Binding (up to 1 inch)**
| | |
|---|---|
| Coil | $2.50 |
| Velo | 3.50 |
| Hard Cover | 9.00 |

**Copies**
| | |
|---|---|
| Carbon Copy | 4¢ per copy |
| Kodak/Xerox | 10¢ per copy |
| Our Printer | 60¢ per copy |

**Delivery**     50¢ per mile

**Diskette storage fee**     (holds approximately 60 double-spaced pages)
| | |
|---|---|
| 1 year (rent) | $10 |
| Purchase | 20 |

**Editing* (professional)**     $16/hr. ($4 minimum)

**Envelopes**

|  | Yours | Ours |
|---|---|---|
| 1 address | .25 | .35 |
| 2 addresses | | |
| (return and address) | .35 | .40 |

Set-up fee     $12/100

**Labels**
$.15/label (less than 50)
  .12/label (50+)
$10/1000 for hard copy ($5 min.)
Editing†
$.10/label additions and changes
  .05/label deletions
  .025/label to rerun

**Letters‡**
Individual     $2.75/page ($1.75 min./revision)
           .04 each for carbon copy.

| Merge/repetitive | | |
|---|---|---|
| 5–25 | $ .95 | Per unit pricing |
| 26–49 | .85 | includes printing |
| 50–99 | .75 | of letter and en- |
| 100+ | .65 | velope (client sup- |
|  |  | plies stationery). |

**Overtime**     $24/hour

**Proofreading***
(Matching our copy to     Add: $ .75/double-spaced page
yours *only*)             $1.00/single-spaced page

**Resumé**
$ 9/page (our format)
  12/page (custom format)
  16/hr. to help write.
($2 minimum/revision)

Special storage
$15/1-page with 1-year storage
  24/2-page with 1-year storage

**Revisions**     $16/hr. ($4 minimum)

**Statistical**
Charts and/or
tables     $18/hr.

**Transcription**     $14/hr.

*Must be left overnight.
†Must pay $10 storage fee (one year).
‡Add 12 cents per unit if we supply stationery.

# Case 2

# First Care Urgent Care Center

Ms. Ann DeAngelo, RN, is the administrator of the emergency room at Mercy General Hospital. She is also responsible for the operation of First Care—Mercy General's recently acquired urgent care center.[1]

Ann had just received a memo from Dave Farmer, Mercy General's administrator, asking her to prepare a marketing plan for First Care—with special focus on the strategic marketing aspects. DeAngelo knows that she has her work cut out for her—especially since she has had little formal marketing or planning training. And Mr. Farmer wants the plan in six weeks.

Ms. DeAngelo knows of two sources for the information she needs. The hospital recently completed its own planning cycle—including a discussion of the mission of the hospital and the role that First Care was expected to play. The plan is her starting point. And she remembers that a marketing consultant recently completed an analysis of the patient mix of First Care. She made a note to dig the consultant's report out of her files.

## MERCY GENERAL HOSPITAL

Mercy General Hospital is owned by the board of trustees who operate the hospital under a mandate to foster the purpose of the Sisters of Care—to *promote healing services.*[2]

### The mission of Mercy General

The mission of Mercy General is:

To optimize the long-term provision of healing services through balanced increases in quality and quantity of medical services offered, consistent with the resources available, through operation of a medical surgical hospital focusing on sub-specialty services.

This mission requires Mercy General to seek to:

1. Increase the number of patients, especially in high-profit DRGs.[3]
2. Increase the range of services offered.

---

This case was prepared by John F. Grashof, Professor and Chair, Department of Management and Marketing, Kennesaw College. All Rights Reserved.

The materials in this case are not based on any specific hospital or urgent care center. They are, however, representative of "typical" facilities. The case is not an example of either good or poor management practice and is intended for instructional use only.

[1]An urgent care center is a facility that offers medical treatment on short notice, typically with no appointment, to the general public. Such units are not intended to provide emergency treatment for serious cases such as heart attack victims, but rather focus on persons without a primary physician or those whose primary physician is unavailable. They offer extended hours, convenient locations, and reasonable fees.

[2]The Sisters of Care is a Roman Catholic order dedicated to service to humanity in the area of health.

[3]DRGs are diagnostic-related groups, a way of classifying hospital treatments for reimbursement. Medicare pays a set fee for each procedure. The hospital increases its profit by controlling costs and keeping them below the reimbursement amount.

3. Increase the quality of healthcare.
4. Increase available resources and/or productivity.
5. Increase revenues relative to costs.

## Definition of the business

The business of Mercy General Hospital is defined, in part, by the nature of the services that it can and/or may offer. But some limitations were established at the time of Mercy General's move to its current location. As part of a "gentleman's agreement" with Highland Hospital and Children's Health Center, Mercy General agreed not to go into or expand its services in obstetrics, pediatrics, emergency room, or psychiatry. There has been some softening of positions regarding this agreement, but the intent of the agreement still exists. This agreement does not limit Mercy General's ability to offer these services at other locations.

There are other services that Mercy General cannot offer because they are not consistent with the mercy mission of the Sisters of Care. For example, birth control and abortion services are not offered.

Mercy General wants to emphasize sub-specialty services. So it has been focusing on general medical/surgical services for adults, cardio-thoracic and pulmonary services, and cancer treatment for anyone, regardless of sex or age. Mercy General is dedicated to providing the highest quality services in these areas. As part of this aspect of its service, Mercy General Hospital attempts to develop and maintain a "unique position" in the markets it serves—based on quality of care.

On the financial side, Mercy General seeks to operate in the best financial position possible without sacrificing quality of medical care offered or the quality of life of all people associated with the hospital. The board of trustees has established two goals: a 20 percent return on the $50 million equity in the organization and a return of 5 percent of revenues over expenses on the $45 million annual revenue.

While these financial goals are not necessarily required of all operating units, those units external to the hospital facility must directly benefit the hospital facility. The two general benefits sought are: (1) increasing the number of patients and (2) increasing the excess of revenues over costs. If an external unit does not make a substantial contribution in Benefit 1, then it must exceed the hospital profitability goal.

First Care was acquired by Mercy General for a number of reasons—perhaps the most important was to provide a model for "off-campus" activities. In order to serve as a role model, First Care must be well managed, fit into the overall structure with well-defined goals, and perform well against those goals.

Within this context the mission of First Care is defined in the following ways:

**A. Increase the number of patients.** This can be accomplished a number of ways:

1. Direct admission via a physician on staff at Mercy General.
2. Direct referral for services (e.g., tests, lab work) at Mercy General.
3. Referral for out-patient service by a physician on Mercy General's staff—which may eventually lead to an admission.

**B. Support of physicians.** First Care's mission is the support of physicians on Mercy General's staff. This support is mainly through the referral mechanism, although it is possible that additional support—such as coverage during non-office-hour periods—could be established. First Care is *not* intended to compete with Mercy General's staff physicians.

**Figure 1 ☐ First Care FY 1986 budget***

| Item | FY 1986 budget | |
|---|---|---|
| Personnel: | | |
| MDs | $150,000 | |
| RNs and technical | 75,000 | |
| Staff | 67,000 | |
| | | $282,000 |
| Rent | | 63,000 |
| Supplies: | | |
| Medical | | |
| Medical supplies | 7,786 | |
| Instruments | 875 | |
| Minor equipment | 2,400 | |
| Drugs | 11,485 | |
| Lab tests | 3,865 | |
| Needles | 750 | |
| | | 27,161 |
| Surgical | | |
| General supplies | 7,650 | |
| Gloves | 1,000 | |
| Sutures | 3,470 | |
| IV supplies | 1,400 | |
| Equipment | 4,875 | |
| | | 18,395 |
| Orthopedic | | |
| General supplies | 8,450 | |
| X-ray film | 4,760 | |
| | | 13,210 |
| Office | | |
| Office supplies | 3,700 | |
| Electricity | 5,600 | |
| Telephone | 8,400 | |
| Copy equipment | 1,110 | |
| Forms | 4,750 | |
| Contract services | 17,530 | |
| Coffee | 600 | |
| Meetings | 900 | |
| Collections | 1,200 | |
| Water | 875 | |
| Natural gas | 1,700 | |
| Cleaning | 750 | |
| | | 47,115 |
| Total budget | | $450,881 |

*Based on an assumed patient load of 12,000 patients.

**C. Increase net revenues.** First Care is expected to provide revenues in excess of its costs of operations. Thus, First Care would increase the resources of Mercy General and permit expansion of the hospital's services.

## SITUATION ANALYSIS

The following paragraphs outline the current situation facing Mercy General with respect to its First Care Urgent Care Center. Each section deals with a specific aspect of First Care.

## Background

First Care is a free-standing urgent care facility. The business was begun in the summer of 1983 and purchased by Mercy General Hospital in August of 1984.

The facility is located on New Industrial Highway in a suburban area near a city of about 800,000. The area is experiencing rapid growth, especially in small businesses and light industry. The facility is about five miles from Mercy General.

First Care is staffed by contract physicians who have staff privileges at Mercy General Hospital. Additional staff include full- and part-time RNs, clerical workers, and laboratory/x-ray technicians. First Care is managed by the Emergency Room Administrator at Mercy General—Ann DeAngelo, RN.

During its first year of operation, First Care treated 9,475 patients—and patient traffic was increasing. However, First Care was operating below breakeven. For FY (fiscal year) 1985 (April 1, 1984, to March 31, 1985), First Care treated about 11,500 patients and was operating near breakeven. The patient flow during the last few months (January–March, 1985) was sufficient to generate a small profit. Figure 1 presents the FY 1986 budget for First Care as based on projected patient flows.

The number of referrals from First Care to Mercy General Hospital and/or its medical staff has been disappointing. During the first year of First Care's operation, few patients were referred. Referrals increased somewhat following the acquisition of First Care by Mercy General. A study of the records showed that during September, October, and November of 1984, a total of 173 patients were referred to Mercy General Hospital's medical staff. During this period a total of 2,968 patients were treated, making the referral rate 5.8 percent.

## Market share

Market share for First Care is hard to estimate since no study exists regarding the number of physician visits by persons living or working in First Care's market area. However, share can be estimated based on population and the rate of visits (see Figure 2). Estimates of incidence of visiting a physician range from 2.7 visits per person per year to 3.2. Based on these rates, First Care's market share is between 2.4 percent and 2.8 percent in its primary served market.

However, the market share is much higher in the two ZIP Code areas closest to First Care—12 percent to 15 percent in the "home" ZIP Code and 38 percent to 45 percent in the neighboring ZIP Code. In two other ZIP Code areas, First Care has market share in the 5 percent to 9 percent range (see Figure 2).

**Figure 2 □ Analysis of First Care's served market**

| ZIP Code | Percent of visits | Estimated population | Percent males | Percent under age 14 | Percent between 15 and 60 | Percent over age 60 | Estimated market share | Estimated number of businesses[†] |
|---|---|---|---|---|---|---|---|---|
| 971* | 23% | 6,470 | 47% | 11% | 86% | 3% | 15% | 250 |
| 972 | 21 | 2,500 | 46 | 12 | 84 | 4 | 43 | 375 |
| 973 | 8 | 5,742 | 44 | 10 | 88 | 2 | 10 | 1,500 |
| 974 | 7 | 4,869 | 48 | 15 | 78 | 7 | 8 | 1,150 |
| 975 | 7 | 5,986 | 48 | 17 | 73 | 10 | 6 | 800 |
| 976 | 6 | 4,768 | 46 | 18 | 75 | 7 | 5 | 250 |
| 977 | 5 | 5,689 | 49 | 16 | 76 | 8 | 3 | 950 |
| 978 | 4 | 3,564 | 47 | 13 | 81 | 6 | 3 | 700 |
| 979 | 3 | 4,669 | 48 | 17 | 82 | 1 | 2 | 1,050 |
| 980 | 2 | 6,597 | 47 | 18 | 80 | 2 | 2 | 300 |
| Others | 14 | 34,257 | 49 | 16 | 75 | 9 | 1 | 850 |
| Total | 100 | 85,111 | 48 | 17 | 79 | 4 | | 8,175 |

*First Care's "home" ZIP Code.
[†]To determine the market potential, assume an average company size of 15 and an incidence rate of 9.8 visits per 100 employees.

### Competition

Competition for First Care comes from several alternatives including:

1. Private MDs and other urgent care centers.
2. Hospital emergency rooms.

Figure 3 shows the numbers of these alternatives for the ZIP Codes relevant to First Care. Other than in ZIP 980, the number of competitors is not great. As Figure 3 shows, there is only one other provider within First Care's home ZIP Code. Thus First Care should be able to gain significant market share.

**Figure 3 ☐ First Care's competition**

| ZIP Code | MDs, etc. | Hospitals |
|----------|-----------|-----------|
| 971 | 1 | 0 |
| 972 | 12 | 0 |
| 973 | 16 | 1 |
| 974 | 11 | 1 |
| 975 | 6 | 0 |
| 976 | 2 | 1 |
| 977 | 46 | 1 |
| 978 | 10 | 0 |
| 979 | 8 | 0 |
| 980 | 5 | 1 |

Additional competition comes from DOs, chiropractors, medically trained friends, and self-treatment. These latter alternatives may be increasing but are assumed to have little impact.

### Strategic direction

First Care's strategy has been to seek business from all sources—with little focus on specific markets. The previous owner attempted to develop an industrial medicine business but had to drop the idea due to lack of funds. Promotional efforts have been limited to a few mailers and the sign in front of the building.

A major promotion campaign was undertaken in the spring of 1985. This program included openhouses, new signage, a billboard reminding passersby of First Care and its location, and mailers to businesses. It is anticipated that the effort will increase the level of business. It is also expected that the new business will follow the same pattern as the previous business.

### The pattern of current business

A sample of patient records was examined by the marketing consultant—to better understand the current business. Figures 4 and 5 show the distribution of current business according to the type of service performed and payment type.

The largest portion of the business—over 50 percent—comes from medical services, with orthopedic and surgical services each contributing another 11 percent. The average revenue per patient is estimated to be $43.51.

**Figure 4 □ Pattern of business***

| Service | Percent of occurrences | Charges per visit |
|---|---|---|
| Orthopedic | 11.0% | $62.00 |
| Surgical | 11.0 | 59.00 |
| Medical | 50.5 | 40.00 |
| Ophthalmology | 4.6 | 39.00 |
| Gynecological | 3.6 | 65.00 |
| Allergy | 9.2 | 8.00 |
| Lab tests | 7.3 | 22.00 |
| Audio tests | 2.8 | 15.00 |

*Estimates based on sample data.

**Figure 5 □ Payment types***

| Payment type | Number of visits | Average fees | Estimated annual revenue |
|---|---|---|---|
| Workers' comp | 109 | $57.00 | $136,800 |
| Private pay | 436 | 40.13 | 385,320 |
|  | 545 | 43.51 | 522,120 |

*Estimates based on sample data.

Over 38 percent of the workers' compensation patients come from ZIP 971, compared with 23 percent of the total patient flow. This suggests that distance to the facility is a major factor in selection of a source for treatment for workers' compensation patients.

Figure 6 shows the number of times each category of service was used by the patients included in the sample data. Figure 6 also shows the average fee charged. Orthopedic, surgical, and medical patients use most of the services offered by First Care—in about equal proportions. Orthopedic patients use x-ray more frequently than do other types of patients, as would be expected, but about 30 percent of the medical patients also have x-rays taken.

X-rays have the highest average service fees (see Figure 6), followed by professional fees. Of special interest are the fees charged for the services under "Other tests." This category is a "catch-all" for a variety of services, but it is assumed that for medical patients the services are EKGs. This is of special interest to Mercy General because of its strong interest in coronary cases.

### Recent performance

Since Mercy General Hospital acquired First Care, First Care's performance has improved in several areas. First, there has been an increased number of referrals to Mercy General Hospital and to the medical staff. Second, First Care operations have become more efficient. Some of this improvement is due to increased capital available to maintain appropriate stocks of supplies. And recently some money was spent on marketing/promotional efforts that should increase patient flow. First Care has reached breakeven and should now begin to generate profits for Mercy General Hospital.

**Figure 6** ☐ **Number and average amount of fees by Service type**

| Type of serivce | Professional fee | X-ray | Lab | Supply | Pharmacy | Other tests | Patient total |
|---|---|---|---|---|---|---|---|
| Orthopedic | 58 | 35 | 2 | 35 | 20 | 0 | 60 |
| | $29.05 | $37.80 | $19.33 | $17.76 | $9.40 | $0.00 | |
| Surgical | 60 | 8 | 2 | 41 | 30 | 1 | 60 |
| | $32.97 | $28.88 | $31.00 | $19.90 | $10.41 | $15.00 | |
| Medical | 268 | 20 | 120 | 15 | 20 | 7 | 275 |
| | $26.61 | $38.40 | $16.37 | $6.46 | $11.38 | $31 25 | |
| Ophthalmological | 25 | 0 | 0 | 10 | 10 | 0 | 25 |
| | $28.08 | $0.00 | $0.00 | $8.38 | $11.67 | $0.00 | |
| Gynecological | 50 | 0 | 10 | 10 | 0 | 0 | 50 |
| | $32.00 | $0.00 | $47.00 | $5.00 | $0.00 | $0.00 | |
| Allergy | 0 | 0 | 0 | 0 | 25 | 0 | 25 |
| | $0.00 | $0.00 | $0.00 | $0.00 | $7.33 | $0.00 | |
| Lab work | 0 | 0 | 40 | 0 | 0 | 0 | 40 |
| | $0.00 | $0.00 | $17.67 | $0.00 | $0.00 | $0.00 | |
| Audio | 0 | 0 | 0 | 0 | 0 | 10 | 10 |
| | $0.00 | $0.00 | $0.00 | $0.00 | $0.00 | $15.00 | |

## WHAT NEXT?

A couple of weeks have passed since Ann DeAngelo received Mr. Farmer's memo. She has collected a great deal of information from hospital files, her own files, First Care's records, and other sources. She has only four weeks to complete the marketing plan. How should she proceed? What strategies look promising? What should she recommend?

# Case 3

# Midtown YWCA

Ruth Sims, recently appointed executive director of the Midtown YWCA, nervously tapped her fingers on her desk as she thought about tomorrow morning's meeting with her organization's board of directors. The board's chairperson, Susan Winston, had asked Ruth to review the architect's proposed design for the YWCA's new building and to make specific recommendations concerning what kinds of facilities, programs, and services the new YWCA should offer its members. In particular, the board wanted to hear about health and physical fitness programs, as they considered such programs the key to attracting new members.

## THE MIDTOWN YWCA

The Midtown YWCA is located in the Great Lakes area within a metropolitan area whose population numbers close to 250,000. Its 600 members, almost all fe-

This case was prepared by Professors Andrew A. Brogowicz and Lowell E. Crow of Western Michigan University. Names and data have been disguised, and certain aspects of the case have been fictionalized to stimulate analysis and discussion. All rights reserved.

male, range in age from young girls under 10 to elderly women in their 90s. They pay an annual individual membership fee of $15 for adults and $5 for children. This entitles them to attend free mini-lectures on various topics and to use the YWCA's meeting rooms, exercise rooms, indoor track, and locker rooms. The members also receive a discount rate on individually priced educational and fitness-related programs and enjoy guest privileges at YWCAs in other cities.

Among the many social programs the Midtown YWCA offers its members and the general public are a Christian feminists' support group, comprehensive child care for working or student parents, children's recreation programs, post-mastectomy counseling, childbirth preparation classes, and adolescent counseling. The YWCA is especially well-known for its domestic assault and criminal sexual assault crisis intervention programs, offering emergency shelter and supportive services for adult and child assault victims.

Along with a self-programmed exercise and fitness area, the Midtown YWCA offers a broad range of health and fitness programs including aerobics, dance (jazz, tap, ballet, etc.), dancercise during pregnancy, gymnastics, weight control, and yoga. A licensed massologist is available by appointment.

Many of the YWCA's members do not actually participate in these programs but maintain their memberships to support the organization's viewpoints and social programs. As one elderly member stated, "I bought my young grandchild a membership so that she would learn the values of young Christian women just like I did as a child."

## THE PRESENT BUILDING

The Midtown YWCA is housed in a 60-year-old building located near the heart of the city's thriving downtown area. It contains an indoor track and gymnasium, as well as offices and meeting rooms which are also used by various community organizations. The building also contains a once-popular cafeteria and a swimming pool, both of which were closed a few years ago due to high maintenance costs.

The YWCA's aging facility is overcrowded and burdened with high energy and maintenance costs. The exercise and locker facilities are run down, unattractive, and inefficient. Barrier-free facilities for the handicapped are lacking, and more space is needed to shelter the assault victims. Another major problem is the lack of convenient and safe off-the-street parking.

## THE NEW BUILDING

With its present facility having aged to the point that many services have become economically impractical to continue, the YWCA's board of directors has initiated a major fund drive to raise $3 million to build a new building. The new building site, while still in the downtown area, will not be as centrally located as the present building. However, there will be space for a fair amount of off-the-street parking.

While the building plans are still sketchy pending the board of directors' approval of Ruth Sims' forthcoming recommendations, there is general agreement on several points. The new two-story building will contain a modern indoor track and fitness center, a child day care center, meeting rooms, a member lounge, twice as many rooms to shelter assault victims, and several administrative and counseling offices. Space limitations, however, will rule out any indoor or outdoor tennis courts.

Construction is expected to begin soon and take about 18 months to complete. However, several important unresolved issues need to be cleared up first, which is why tomorrow's board meeting has been scheduled.

## UNRESOLVED ISSUES

When Ruth Sims accepted the position of executive director for the Midtown YWCA less than two months ago, she was aware of the plans for a new building. However, she did not realize at the time how much disagreement there was and still is among the 15 directors concerning what the new building should contain and how it should be operated.

Perhaps the major area of conflict among the board revolves around the issue of whether or not the building should contain a swimming pool. Several of the current board members had strongly opposed the closing of the pool and the termination of swimming classes in the present facility, a move that apparently led to numerous membership nonrenewals. They consider it sheer folly to try to operate a successful health and fitness center without an indoor pool.

Other board members, including Mrs. Winston, are vehemently opposed to the idea of a swimming pool, however. They view the construction and maintenance costs associated with a new pool as being prohibitively expensive. According to the architect, the smallest possible regulation-size indoor pool would cost about $800,000 to build, and such a pool would be considerably smaller than those currently available at several area schools and the local YMCA.

Another hotly debated issue concerns the architect's recommendation that a $1/13$-mile rooftop track be built on top of the new building, in addition to the planned indoor track. Several area track coaches and fitness consultants have spoken out in favor of this proposal. However, a number of board members have questioned the need for a rooftop track given the existence of two college and another two public school outdoor tracks within about a five-minute drive from the downtown area. Some directors have voiced a preference for a combined rooftop sundeck and snack-bar area.

Other unresolved issues include a possible increase in membership dues and fees, whether parking should be free or paid, how much and what kind of exercise equipment to provide, and how many frills and amenities to offer (such as saunas, carpeted dressing rooms, towel service, child care for program participants, etc.).

An issue that the board has not raised but that Ruth Sims intends to bring up herself at tomorrow's meeting concerns the YWCA's operating hours. Currently, the YWCA is open weekdays from 7 A.M. to 8 P.M., and from 9 A.M. to 3 P.M. on Saturdays. The facility is closed on Sundays and holidays. Ruth realizes that the YWCA operates on a tight budget, but nonetheless wonders whether or not these operating hours adequately meet the needs of the membership.

One thing all the directors agree on is that the new building's health and fitness center should not only be self-sufficient in terms of revenues and costs, but that it should also serve as a "cash cow"—generating revenues to help defray the costs of the nonprofit organization's various social programs.

## MARKETING RESEARCH SURVEY

Shortly before Ruth Sims became executive director of the Midtown YWCA, her predecessor, Acting Director Jane Garfield, contracted with a local marketing research firm to conduct a mail survey of YWCA members and of nonmembers living in the metropolitan area to help determine what kinds of health and fitness facilities, programs, and services should be offered in the new YWCA building. Questionnaires were mailed to about 450 members (members under 18 years of age were excluded from the mailing list), and 254 completed questionnaires were returned. An additional 1,200 questionnaires were mailed to a systematic (probability) sample of nonmember households in the YWCA's immediate county that was drawn from the Polk City Directory.[1] A total of 365 completed questionnaires were received from the nonmember households.

In designing the survey, the research firm decided that it might be misleading to compare member data with nonmember data because so many of the nonmember households would probably have little interest in joining the YWCA. Therefore, they used a "buying intention scale" to sort out those nonmember survey respondents who would have a "high likelihood" of joining the Midtown YWCA after it moves into its new building. The respondents were asked to check one of the following responses to indicate their likelihood of joining the YWCA—both **with** and **without** an indoor pool. Those nonmembers who checked either one of the first two responses were categorized separately in the data summaries provided to the YWCA officials.

- I'm absolutely certain that I would join.
- It's very likely that I would join.
- There is some chance that I would join.
- It's very unlikely that I would join.
- I'm absolutely certain that I would not join.

## SURVEY FINDINGS

One of the survey findings that disturbed Ruth Sims the most was an indication that some 40 percent of the members surveyed also belong to at least one other health and fitness organization. The other organizations include aerobic dancing and fitness centers, weight control clinics, gymnastics academies, tennis clubs—and, in particular, the local YMCA.

Ruth was amazed to learn that almost 20 percent of the YWCA member households also have memberships at the YMCA. Located about two miles southwest of the YWCA, the YMCA offers two indoor swimming pools, both indoor and outdoor tennis courts, racquetball courts, and a large junior high school outdoor

---

[1]There are an estimated 60,000 to 65,000 nonmember households in the YWCA's immediate county, excluding student and retiree households.

**Table 1 ☐ Demographic profiles for member and nonmember respondents with a high likelihood of joining YWCA without and with swimming pool**

| | YWCA members (n = 254) | Nonmembers | |
|---|---|---|---|
| Item | | Join/no pool* (n = 40) | Join/with pool† (n = 114) |
| **Sex:** | | | |
| Male | 1.2% | 12.8% | 8.0% |
| Female | 98.8 | 87.2 | 92.0 |
| **Highest level of education:** | | | |
| Some high school | 2.8 | 7.7 | 4.4 |
| High school graduate | 4.4 | 23.1 | 23.9 |
| Some college | 24.2 | 38.5 | 37.2 |
| College graduate | 29.8 | 20.5 | 27.4 |
| Advanced college degree | 38.9 | 10.3 | 7.1 |
| **Work in downtown area:** | | | |
| Yes | 36.9 | 31.4 | 22.1 |
| No | 37.8 | 51.4 | 51.9 |
| Does not apply | 25.3 | 17.1 | 26.0 |
| **Spouse works in downtown area:** | | | |
| Yes | 20.3 | 17.1 | 16.7 |
| No | 43.7 | 45.7 | 50.9 |
| Does not apply | 36.0 | 37.1 | 32.4 |
| **Marital status:** | | | |
| Single | 24.3 | 25.0 | 20.2 |
| Married | 58.6 | 55.0 | 64.0 |
| Divorced/separated | 10.8 | 17.5 | 12.3 |
| Widow/widower | 6.4 | 2.5 | 3.5 |
| **Dependent status:** | | | |
| No children | 39.6 | 38.5 | 31.0 |
| Youngest child less than 6 years old | 12.2 | 33.3 | 30.1 |
| Youngest child 6–13 years old | 6.1 | 10.3 | 17.7 |
| Youngest child 14–18 years old | 11.4 | 2.6 | 10.6 |
| Youngest child 19 years old or over | 30.6 | 15.4 | 10.6 |
| **Age:** | | | |
| Under 18 | 1.2 | 2.5 | 1.8 |
| 18–24 | 4.0 | 15.0 | 12.3 |
| 25–34 | 27.9 | 40.0 | 41.2 |
| 35–49 | 26.3 | 20.0 | 30.7 |
| 50–64 | 27.9 | 15.0 | 11.4 |
| 65 or over | 12.7 | 7.5 | 2.6 |
| **Number of adult wage earners in household:** | | | |
| None | 12.9 | 15.0 | 10.6 |
| One | 36.1 | 37.5 | 41.6 |
| Two | 45.4 | 45.0 | 42.5 |
| Three or more | 5.6 | 2.5 | 5.3 |
| **1985 household income:** | | | |
| Under $10,000 | 5.4 | 10.9 | 11.4 |
| $10,000–$14,999 | 7.6 | 16.7 | 17.3 |
| $15,000–$24,999 | 18.5 | 25.0 | 28.8 |
| $25,000–$49,999 | 47.6 | 45.4 | 39.5 |
| $50,000 and over | 20.9 | 2.0 | 3.0 |
| **Occupation:‡** | | | |
| Homemaker | 19.7 | 28.0‡ | |
| Executive/professional | 37.1 | 25.0 | |
| White-collar | 14.1 | 22.0 | |
| Blue-collar | 5.0 | 12.0 | |
| Educator | 11.8 | 8.0 | |
| Retired | 9.1 | 3.0 | |
| Student | 2.0 | 2.0 | |
| Unemployed | 1.2 | 3.0 | |

*This column shows percentages for nonmember respondents who indicated a high likelihood of joining the YWCA *without* a pool. The maximum range of sampling error for this group is plus or minus 15 percent.
†This column shows percentages for nonmember respondents who indicated a high likelihood of joining the YWCA *with* a pool. The maximum range of sampling error for this group is plus or minus 9 percent.
‡The occupation percentages shown are for all 365 nonmember respondents. The maximum range of sampling error for this group is plus or minus 5 percent.

**Table 2 □ Health and fitness activities of members and nonmembers (percentage of respondents indicating participation in activity)**

| | YWCA members (n = 254) | Nonmembers | | |
|---|---|---|---|---|
| Activity | | All (n = 365) | Join/no pool (n = 40) | Join/pool (n = 114) |
| Aerobics | 27.6% | 25.2% | 35.0% | 33.3% |
| Basketball | 7.9 | 10.7 | 10.0 | 12.3 |
| Biking—outdoor | 35.0 | 46.8 | 42.5 | 57.0 |
| Biking—indoor | 14.2 | 13.7 | 10.0 | 10.5 |
| Bowling | 13.8 | 32.3 | 30.0 | 37.7 |
| Dance—ballet, tap, jazz | 5.9 | 2.5 | 5.0 | 5.3 |
| Dance—ballroom, country, disco | 10.6 | · 9.3 | 17.5 | 11.4 |
| Golf | 25.6 | 31.0 | 25.0 | 29.8 |
| Gymnastics | 3.6 | 3.0 | 2.5 | 6.1 |
| Ice skating | 4.7 | 8.2 | 10.0 | 14.0 |
| Martial arts | 3.5 | 1.9 | 2.5 | 2.6 |
| Racquetball | 9.4 | 14.0 | 15.0 | 18.4 |
| Roller skating | 3.9 | 12.3 | 17.5 | 20.2 |
| Rowing | 1.2 | 4.4 | — | 5.3 |
| Running/jogging | 26.4 | 28.2 | 37.5 | 37.7 |
| Skiing—cross country | 29.1 | 17.3 | 10.0 | 16.7 |
| Skiing—downhill | 9.4 | 8.8 | 2.5 | 12.3 |
| Soccer | 7.5 | 4.1 | 2.5 | 5.3 |
| Softball | 13.8 | 24.4 | 27.5 | 27.2 |
| Swimming | 49.6 | 44.4 | 42.5 | 59.6 |
| Tennis | 19.7 | 18.6 | 22.5 | 18.4 |
| Volleyball | 9.1 | 8.8 | 10.0 | 11.4 |
| Walking | 65.0 | 58.6 | 55.0 | 66.7 |
| Weightlifting | 9.4 | 14.8 | 22.5 | 20.2 |
| Yoga | 16.5 | 2.7 | 7.5 | 4.4 |

**Table 3 □ Preferred YWCA health and fitness center fee structures for members and nonmembers (percent responding)**

| | | Nonmembers | | |
|---|---|---|---|---|
| Alternative fee structures | Members (n = 254) | All (n = 365) | Join/no pool (n = 40) | Join/pool (n = 114) |
| a. Annual flat fee | 14.6% | 12.1% | 12.5% | 14.9% |
| b. Quarterly flat fee | 8.7 | 19.7 | 20.0 | 21.1 |
| c. Nominal ($15–25) annual fee plus pay as you use | 43.7 | 32.9 | 45.0 | 35.1 |
| d. Pay as you use | 24.8 | 25.8 | 17.5 | 22.8 |
| e. No response | 8.3 | 9.6 | 5.0 | 6.2 |

track located right across the street. Although the YMCA's membership rates are considerably higher, it does offer a "family rate"—which the Midtown YWCA does not.

About two thirds of the nonmember households surveyed do not belong to any health and fitness organization. For those that do, the largest percentage (10.1 percent) belong to the YMCA.

The rest of the marketing research firm's survey findings are summarized in tables 1 through 7.

**Table 4 ☐ Median importance scores for various health and fitness facilities and services for members and nonmembers\***

| | | Nonmembers | |
|---|---|---|---|
| Facility/service | YWCA members (n = 254) | Join/no pool (n = 40) | Join/pool (n = 114) |
| Indoor track | 2.443 | 3.667† | 3.086‡ |
| Rooftop track | 1.411 | 2.083 | 1.804 |
| Cushioned floor | 3.524 | 3.389 | 3.583 |
| Hot tubs | 2.186 | 3.731† | 3.574‡ |
| Indoor swimming pool | 3.923 | 3.792 | 4.425 |
| Outdoor swimming pool | 1.563 | 2.083 | 2.800‡ |
| Private showers | 3.615 | 4.526† | 4.533‡ |
| Gymnastics equipment | 2.224 | 3.500† | 3.536‡ |
| Sauna | 2.591 | 4.036† | 3.733‡ |
| Exercise bikes | 2.803 | 3.867† | 3.654‡ |
| Weights and weight machines | 2.267 | 4.000† | 3.750‡ |
| Private dressing booths | 3.130 | 4.000 | 4.000‡ |
| Whirlpool | 3.209 | 3.964† | 4.109‡ |
| Racquetball/paddleball courts | 2.015 | 3.250† | 3.220‡ |
| Carpeted dressing rooms | 1.414 | 2.550† | 2.000‡ |
| Indoor tennis courts | 1.722 | 2.750 | 2.731‡ |
| Outdoor tennis courts | 1.548 | 3.125† | 2.820‡ |
| Steam room | 1.841 | 3.313† | 2.826‡ |
| Sundeck and covered patio | 1.622 | 3.000† | 2.845‡ |
| Free parking | 4.358 | 4.267 | 4.589 |
| Yoga instructions | 2.606 | 1.929† | 1.788‡ |
| Swimming lessons | 2.980 | 3.571 | 4.121‡ |
| Free child care | 1.377 | 2.667† | 2.750‡ |
| Low-cost child care | 1.853 | 3.333 | 3.632‡ |
| Aerobics/aerobic dance classes | 3.156 | 3.667 | 3.817‡ |
| Weight control clinic | 3.113 | 3.900† | 3.844‡ |
| Towel rental | 2.031 | 2.688 | 2.574‡ |
| Self-defense classes | 2.510 | 2.600 | 2.964 |
| Ballroom, disco, or country dance classes | 2.128 | 2.611 | 2.603 |
| Tap, ballet, or jazz dance classes | 2.206 | 2.722 | 2.580 |
| Gymnastics classes | 2.036 | 3.150† | 3.145‡ |
| Low-cost laundry service | 1.236 | 1.583† | 1.435‡ |
| Holistic health classes | 3.052 | 2.714 | 2.744 |
| Supervised exercise activities | 3.458 | 3.450 | 3.783 |
| Individual fitness programs | 3.373 | 4.113† | 4.121 |
| Professional massage staff | 2.702 | 2.786 | 2.800 |

\*Respondents rated each item on a scale of 1 through 5, where a score of 5 = extremely important, 4 = very important, 3 = fairly important, 2 = slightly important, and 1 = not at all important.
†Indicates a statistically significant difference between the median scores for YWCA members and nonmembers who indicated a high likelihood of joining the Y *without* a pool in the new building. There is less than a 5 percent chance that the median scores differ because of sampling error.
‡Indicates a statistically significant difference between the median scores for YWCA members and nonmembers who indicated a high likelihood of joining the Y *with* a pool in the new building. There is less than a 5 percent chance that the median scores differ because of sampling error.

## WHAT TO RECOMMEND

As Ruth Sims studied these tables, she became increasingly apprehensive about tomorrow's meeting with the YWCA board of directors. How would the board react to the results of the marketing research survey? What recommendations should she make, and how would the board respond to her recommendations?

**Table 5** □ **Anticipated daily usage of YWCA health and fitness facilities by members and nonmembers (percentage using the YWCA each day)**

| Day of week | YWCA members (n = 254) | Nonmembers | | |
| | | All (n = 365) | Join/no pool (n = 40) | Join/pool (n = 114) |
| --- | --- | --- | --- | --- |
| Sunday | 26.0% | 32.9%* | 40.0%* | 38.6%* |
| Monday | 58.7 | 46.3* | 55.0 | 57.9 |
| Tuesday | 62.6 | 42.7* | 37.5* | 48.2* |
| Wednesday | 58.7 | 50.1* | 60.0 | 63.2 |
| Thursday | 59.4 | 41.9* | 45.0* | 43.0* |
| Friday | 44.1 | 41.4 | 40.0 | 51.8* |
| Saturday | 35.0 | 42.7* | 57.5* | 53.5* |

*Indicates a statistically significant percentage difference between members and nonmembers. There is less than a 5 percent chance that these percentages differ because of sampling error.

**Table 6** □ **Anticipated *weekday* hourly usage of YWCA health and fitness facilities by members and nonmembers (percent usage)**

| Time of day | YWCA members (n = 254) | Nonmembers | | |
| | | All (n = 365) | Join/no pool (n = 40) | Join/pool (n = 114) |
| --- | --- | --- | --- | --- |
| Early morning (7–9) | 25.6% | 17.8%* | 20.0%* | 24.6% |
| Late morning (9–11) | 28.7 | 30.7 | 30.0 | 31.6 |
| Lunch (11–1) | 25.6 | 12.3* | 5.0* | 17.5* |
| Early afternoon (1–3) | 21.7 | 19.7 | 17.5 | 24.6 |
| Late afternoon (3–6) | 41.3 | 29.9* | 32.5* | 26.3* |
| Evening (6–9) | 45.7 | 50.4* | 60.0* | 53.5* |

*Indicates a statistically significant percentage difference between members and nonmembers. There is less than a 5 percent chance that these percentages differ because of sampling error.

**Table 7** □ **Anticipated *weekend* hourly usage of YWCA health and fitness facilities by members and nonmembers (percent usage)**

| Time of day | YWCA members (n = 254) | Nonmembers | | |
| | | All (n = 365) | Join/no pool (n = 40) | Join/pool (n = 114) |
| --- | --- | --- | --- | --- |
| Early morning (7–9) | 15.0% | 21.4%* | 27.5%* | 25.4%* |
| Late morning (9–11) | 35.4 | 34.8 | 22.5* | 38.6 |
| Lunch (11–1) | 10.2 | 11.2 | 7.5 | 12.3 |
| Early afternoon (1–3) | 27.6 | 32.6* | 37.5* | 36.0* |
| Late afternoon (3–6) | 20.9 | 28.5* | 35.0* | 34.2* |

*Indicates a statistically significant percentage difference between members and nonmembers. There is less than a 5 percent chance that these percentages differ because of sampling error.

# Case 4

# Jamestown Foods Corporation

## INSTANTRICE

After reviewing InstantRice[1] sales data for 1973, Mr. Earl Swarthol, product manager for InstantRice, was concerned when he discovered that sales were continuing to decline (see Exhibit 1). (InstantRice and other "quick" rices contain rice that has been processed and precooked, so that the user need boil the rice for less than five minutes before serving. Regular long-grain rice had to be boiled for 20 or 25 minutes before serving.)

**Exhibit 1** ☐ **InstantRice shipments, 1964–1973 (millions of pounds)**

| Year | 16-oz. package | 8½-oz. package | 24- and 32-oz. packages (combined) | Total |
|------|------|------|------|------|
| 1964 | 14.9 | 2.6 | 1.7 | 19.2 |
| 1965 | 15.0 | 2.4 | 1.9 | 19.3 |
| 1966 | 15.0 | 2.5 | 1.9 | 19.4 |
| 1967 | 14.8 | 2.7 | 1.8 | 19.3 |
| 1968 | 14.6 | 2.7 | 1.9 | 19.2 |
| 1969 | 14.4 | 2.6 | 2.0 | 19.0 |
| 1970 | 14.2 | 2.5 | 2.2 | 18.9 |
| 1971 | 14.0 | 2.1 | 2.5 | 18.6 |
| 1972 | 13.7 | 1.9 | 2.7 | 18.3 |
| 1973 | 13.2 | 1.6 | 3.1 | 17.9 |

Source: Company records.

Sales of InstantRice in 1973 were just under $12.5 million. Sales of the company's regular rice products, which were the responsibility of a senior product manager and his staff, were more than six times that amount. Sales of specialty rices, responsibility for which was divided between two different product managers, were slightly less than $20 million. Responsibility for all Jamestown rice sales lay with a product group manager, to whom Swarthol and his three colleagues reported.

In 1973 Jamestown total sales exceeded a quarter of a billion dollars, 70 percent of which came from within the United States. Sales had recently been growing at an annual rate of 10 to 15 percent. Earnings after taxes had increased slowly to more than 4 percent of sales. In addition to rice, Jamestown marketed a wide variety of specialty foods.

InstantRice was sold through grocery stores, which accounted for more than 90 percent of sales of rice in the United States. Retailers typically priced the popular 16-ounce package at 88 cents and earned a margin of 18 percent on Instant-Rice. Direct manufacturing costs amounted to approximately 72 percent of the revenues received by Jamestown for InstantRice. Sales and sales support costs

---

Certain data in this case have been disguised and are therefore not useful for research purposes. Richard N. Cardozo, *Product Policy: Cases & Concepts,* © 1979, Addison-Wesley, Reading, Massachusetts. Pgs. 61–70 (Jamestown Food Case). Reprinted with permission.

[1]InstantRice was Jamestown's brand of precooked (or "quick") rice.

amounted to 6 percent of sales. Trade and consumer advertising and promotion accounted for about 7 percent. InstantRice contributed 15 percent of its sales to allocated general expenses and profit. Company officials believed that the expense and profit structure of InstantRice was fairly typical of that for many long-established packaged foods.

Approximately half of the total advertising and promotion budget for Instant-Rice was devoted to consumer advertising. Trade promotion accounted for about 30 percent of the budget. The balance was divided about equally between consumer promotion and direct administrative costs.

Consumer advertising for InstantRice was intended to increase consumption among present users by stressing the multiple uses for InstantRice. Although more than one of every three households stocked some brand of precooked rice at one time or another, the typical user employed the product for only one or two different foods. In addition to picturing different uses on the package itself, the company advertised InstantRice in women's magazines.

Consumer advertising expenditures for InstantRice during 1973 amounted to less than 10 percent of total rice advertising (see Exhibit 2). InstantRice advertising was divided between print and television. Advertising for competing precooked rices was concentrated in local newspapers. Regular rice and specialty rice products were advertised primarily on television and to a limited extent in magazines and newspapers.

**Exhibit 2 □ Annual advertising expenditures for major rice product classes for all advertisers ($000)**

| Year | InstantRice | Total precooked rice* | Regular rice | Specialty rices |
|------|-------------|-----------------------|--------------|-----------------|
| 1970 | $635 | $ 682 | $1,987 | $ 970 |
| 1971 | 600 | 1,105 | 2,216 | 2,002 |
| 1972 | 370 | 930 | 1,973 | 3.200 |
| 1973 | 450 | 1,045 | 1,480 | 3,068 |

*Totals include InstantRice.

Source: Company records.

## COMPETITION

Company officials believed that InstantRice competed against several different types of product, including (1) other precooked rices, (2) specialty rices (e.g., Spanish rice and onion rice), and (3) regular long-grain rice. (Shorter-grain rice was important primarily in the South for specific uses.)

Precooked rice accounted for 14 to 18 percent by weight of the 550 to 600 million pounds of rice purchased in grocery stores. Total volume of precooked rice had declined over the past three years. InstantRice accounted for approximately 25 percent of dollar sales of precooked rice and ranked second to the leading brand, which held an estimated 35 to 40 percent share. One other major brand held approximately 15 percent of the market; the remainder was divided among more than five brands. According to company officials, the average retail price of some competing precooked rices generally offered retailers margins which were at least as great in dollars as that of InstantRice.

Specialty rice sales had risen markedly during the past three years, and currently amounted to about twice the volume of precooked rice. Specialty rice mixes

typically included regular long-grain rice together with the dried vegetables and
spices necessary for a particular food. To serve a specialty rice dish, the consumer
ordinarily added liquid to the mix and heated it. (Wild rice, which was classified as
a specialty rice product, could not be duplicated by any precooked rice and had to
be prepared in a manner similar to long-grain rice.) Specialty rices cost 30 to 50
percent more than precooked rice plus the individual ingredients necessary to prepare an equivalent amount of a specialty rice dish. Jamestown personnel believed
that InstantRice, when combined with individual ingredients, produced foods that
were superior to those made from some specialty rice mixes but that other specialty mixes produced dishes that the consumer could seldom match with
InstantRice.

Long-grain rice accounted for more tonnage than any other type of rice, and
the volume of long-grain rice purchased by consumers had remained relatively stable during the past several years. Many consumers preferred the taste and consistency of long-grain rice to precooked rice and/or specialty rice mixes. Regular long-
grain rice was priced substantially below all brands of precooked rice.

The importance of these three sources (precooked, specialty, and regular
rice) varied somewhat among the dishes for which rice was used (see Exhibit 3).
Historical changes in the relative importance of these sources for selected foods
appear in Exhibits 4 through 8. In addition, Mr. Swarthol noted that the popularity

**Exhibit 3** ☐ **Sources of selected rice-based food, 1973 (millions of pounds)**

| | | Sources | | | |
| Foods | InstantRice | All precooked rice* | Regular long-grain rice | Specialty rice (includes wild rice) | Total sources |
|---|---|---|---|---|---|
| Plain rice dishes | 8.6 | 11.1 | 117.9 | 67.4 (chiefly wild rice) | 196.4 |
| Spanish rice | 3.6 | 27.1 | 14.3 | 14.3 | 55.7 |
| Ethnic rice | 1.7 | 7.1 | 3.6 | 15.0 | 25.7 |
| Other flavored rice | 0.4 | 0.7 | 5.3 | 9.3 (includes flavored plain rice and flavored wild rice) | 15.3 |
| Rice pudding | 0.9 | 1.6 | 1.0 | 1.1 | 3.7 |
| Total | 15.2 | 47.6 | 142.1 | 107.1 | 296.8 |

*Includes InstantRice.
Note: Figures in this exhibit represent foods accounting for approximately 85 percent of InstantRice sales
and about half of all sales of rice through retail outlets.

Source: Company records. Estimates based on consumer diary panel data.

**Exhibit 4** ☐ **Sources of plain rice dishes (millions of pounds of precooked rice or equivalent)**

| Year | InstantRice | All other brands of precooked rice | Regular rice | Specialty rice | Total |
|---|---|---|---|---|---|
| 1964 | 8.9 | 2.1 | 217.5 | 14.5 | 243.0 |
| 1965 | 8.8 | 2.1 | 201.6 | 17.0 | 229.5 |
| 1966 | 8.8 | 2.1 | 187.0 | 21.6 | 219.5 |
| 1967 | 8.7 | 2.2 | 175.4 | 28.2 | 214.5 |
| 1968 | 8.7 | 2.2 | 161.1 | 34.0 | 211.0 |
| 1969 | 8.5 | 2.2 | 158.5 | 39.8 | 209.0 |
| 1970 | 8.6 | 2.3 | 147.9 | 46.2 | 205.0 |
| 1971 | 8.6 | 2.4 | 135.3 | 55.7 | 202.0 |
| 1972 | 8.7 | 2.3 | 128.9 | 60.6 | 200.5 |
| 1973 | 8.6 | 2.5 | 117.9 | 67.4 | 196.4 |

Source: Company records.

**Exhibit 5 □ Sources of Spanish rice (millions of pounds of precooked rice or equivalent)**

| Year | InstantRice | All other brands of precooked rice | Regular rice | Specialty rice | Total |
|------|-------------|-----------------------------------|--------------|----------------|-------|
| 1964 | 2.1 | 25.4 | 14.9 | — | 42.4 |
| 1965 | 2.2 | 26.3 | 15.3 | — | 43.8 |
| 1966 | 2.1 | 27.4 | 15.3 | — | 44.8 |
| 1967 | 2.2 | 27.7 | 15.3 | — | 45.2 |
| 1968 | 2.9 | 27.0 | 15.8 | 1.4 | 47.1 |
| 1969 | 3.3 | 26.2 | 15.8 | 3.7 | 49.0 |
| 1970 | 3.5 | 26.0 | 15.5 | 5.1 | 50.1 |
| 1971 | 3.6 | 25.0 | 15.5 | 7.3 | 51.4 |
| 1972 | 3.7 | 23.8 | 15.3 | 10.2 | 53.0 |
| 1973 | 3.6 | 23.5 | 14.3 | 14.3 | 55.7 |

Source: Company records.

**Exhibit 6 □ Sources of rice pudding (millions of pounds of precooked rice or equivalent)**

| Year | InstantRice | All other brands of precooked rice | Regular rice | Specialty rice | Total |
|------|-------------|-----------------------------------|--------------|----------------|-------|
| 1964 | 1.2 | 0.1 | 2.9 | 0.3 | 4.5 |
| 1965 | 1.1 | 0.2 | 2.8 | 0.4 | 4.5 |
| 1966 | 1.0 | 0.3 | 2.6 | 0.5 | 4.4 |
| 1967 | 1.1 | 0.3 | 2.3 | 0.6 | 4.3 |
| 1968 | 1.2 | 0.3 | 2.0 | 0.7 | 4.2 |
| 1969 | 1.3 | 0.2 | 1.8 | 0.8 | 4.1 |
| 1970 | 1.2 | 0.4 | 1.5 | 0.9 | 4.0 |
| 1971 | 1.1 | 0.5 | 1.3 | 1.0 | 3.9 |
| 1972 | 1.0 | 0.6 | 1.2 | 1.0 | 3.8 |
| 1973 | 0.9 | 0.7 | 1.0 | 1.1 | 3.7 |

Source: Company records.

**Exhibit 7 □ Sources of "ethnic" rice dishes (millions of pounds of precooked rice or equivalent)**

| Year | InstantRice | All other brands of precooked rice | Regular rice | Specialty rice | Total |
|------|-------------|-----------------------------------|--------------|----------------|-------|
| 1964 | 1.8 | 5.6 | 6.1 | 4.0 | 17.5 |
| 1965 | 1.8 | 5.6 | 6.0 | 5.1 | 18.5 |
| 1966 | 1.9 | 5.5 | 6.0 | 6.3 | 19.7 |
| 1967 | 1.8 | 5.4 | 5.6 | 8.2 | 21.0 |
| 1968 | 1.8 | 5.5 | 5.2 | 9.7 | 22.2 |
| 1969 | 1.7 | 5.4 | 4.8 | 11.7 | 23.6 |
| 1970 | 1.8 | 5.4 | 4.5 | 12.4 | 24.1 |
| 1971 | 1.7 | 5.5 | 4.0 | 13.4 | 24.6 |
| 1972 | 1.7 | 5.4 | 3.8 | 14.2 | 25.1 |
| 1973 | 1.7 | 5.4 | 3.6 | 15.0 | 25.7 |

Source: Company records.

**Exhibit 8 □ Sources of flavored rice dishes, excluding Spanish rice, "ethnic" rice dishes (millions of pounds of precooked rice or equivalent)**

| Year | InstantRice | All other brands of precooked rice | Regular rice | Specialty rice | Total |
|------|-------------|-----------------------------------|--------------|----------------|-------|
| 1964 | 0.8 | 0.7 | 8.1 | 3.1 | 12.7 |
| 1965 | 0.8 | 0.8 | 7.6 | 3.6 | 12.8 |
| 1966 | 0.8 | 0.7 | 7.4 | 4.1 | 12.9 |
| 1967 | 0.8 | 0.6 | 7.2 | 4.8 | 13.4 |
| 1968 | 0.8 | 0.6 | 6.6 | 6.0 | 14.0 |
| 1969 | 0.7 | 0.7 | 5.8 | 7.3 | 14.5 |
| 1970 | 0.6 | 0.6 | 5.6 | 8.1 | 14.9 |
| 1971 | 0.5 | 0.5 | 5.3 | 8.8 | 15.1 |
| 1972 | 0.4 | 0.4 | 5.3 | 9.1 | 15.2 |
| 1973 | 0.4 | 0.3 | 5.3 | 9.3 | 15.3 |

Source: Company records.

of rice and of particular rice dishes varied considerably among different regions within the United States. Rice purchased through retail stores exceeded 4 pounds per person in the West but amounted to just 2 pounds in the Midwest (see Exhibit 9). Plain rice was most popular in the South; Spanish rice and ethnic rice dishes (e.g., fried rice and certain flavored rices used with Chinese or Indian foods) in the West; and rice pudding in the Midwest (see Exhibit 10).

The competitive position of InstantRice varied both by food and by region. Nationally, InstantRice accounted for more than 75 percent of sales of precooked rice used in selected plain rice dishes but for less than 15 percent of precooked

**Exhibit 9 ☐**

The geographic regions referred to throughout the case and exhibits are defined as shown on the map below. Approximate populations, total rice purchased through retail stores, and per capita consumption are given for each region.

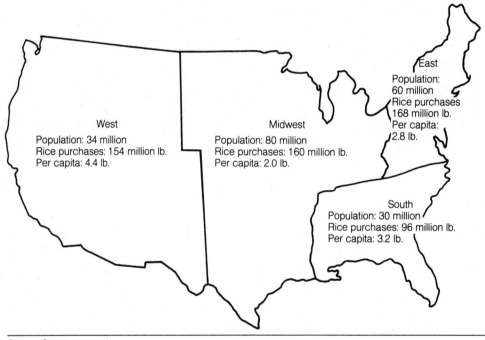

West
Population: 34 million
Rice purchases: 154 million lb.
Per capita: 4.4 lb.

Midwest
Population: 80 million
Rice purchases: 160 million lb.
Per capita: 2.0 lb.

East
Population: 60 million
Rice purchases 168 million lb.
Per capita: 2.8 lb.

South
Population: 30 million
Rice purchases: 96 million lb.
Per capita: 3.2 lb.

Source: Company records.

**Exhibit 10 ☐ Regional index of servings of selected rice foods**

| Food | East | Midwest | South | West | Total United States |
|------|------|---------|-------|------|---------------------|
| Plain rice | 25* | 30 | 300 | 50 | 100 |
| Spanish rice | 80 | 105 | 80 | 125 | 100 |
| Ethnic rice | 85 | 85 | 85 | 145 | 100 |
| Rice pudding | 150 | 200 | 75 | 60 | 100 |

*Average per capita consumption of plain rice in the East was one fourth the national average. These regional index numbers reflect differences among regions and are not meaningful for comparing different foods within a particular region. These numbers do not necessarily reflect total volumes served in each region, because of differences in sizes of regions.

Source: Consumer diary panel.

rice used in Spanish rice (see Exhibit 3). But in the West, according to consumer panel data, use of InstantRice for plain rice dishes was 1.8 times the national average for the brand; for Spanish rice, more than twice the national average for InstantRice. Mr. Swarthol believed that, for all food uses combined, InstantRice enjoyed greater market penetration in the West, and less in the Midwest, than the brand's national market share. He noted that some 35 percent of InstantRice shipments went to the West, 30 percent to the East, 20 percent to the Midwest, and 15 percent to the South.

## CONSUMER PROFILE

Data from a variety of sources indicated to Mr. Swarthol that use of InstantRice was related to family size, age, and income. Relationships between family size and InstantRice consumption appear in Table 1.

Older consumers were somewhat more important to InstantRice than were younger consumers. An index of InstantRice usage by age group appears in Table 2.

A 1970 study of housewives indicated that income and use of precooked rice (all brands combined) were positively correlated (see Table 3).

**Table 1 □ Family size and InstantRice use**

| Family size | Percent of InstantRice sales | Percent of families |
|---|---|---|
| 1 or 2 individuals | 30 | 42 |
| 3 | 22 | 20 |
| 4 or 5 | 34 | 28 |
| 6 or more | 14 | 10 |

Source: Company records.

**Table 2 □ Age of housewife and index**

| Age | Purchase index |
|---|---|
| Under 25 | 67 |
| 25–34 | 96 |
| 35–44 | 108 |
| 45–54 | 106 |
| 55–64 | 106 |
| 65 and over | 104 |
| All age groups combined | 100 |

Source: Company records.

**Table 3 □ Income and purchase of precooked rice**

| Family income level | Purchase index |
|---|---|
| Less than $4,000 | 79 |
| $4,000–$8,000 | 90 |
| $8,000–$12,000 | 105 |
| More than $12,000 | 134 |
| All income level combined | 100 |

Source: Company records.

## ALTERNATIVES

One alternative to remedy declining sales was to develop a slightly different product formulation for the western United States. Some company officials believed that a large market in the West that was currently using regular long-grain rice to make Spanish rice would offer InstantRice an opportunity for a significant increase in sales volume. It appeared that the Spanish rice now being made from

InstantRice did not meet the tastes of Westerners, who preferred rice of a different texture and flavor from that desired in other parts of the country for Spanish rice. Swarthol knew of one study which indicated that Westerners made Spanish rice from scratch (i.e., by preparing from fresh foods the ingredients to be added to regular long-grain rice) as often as they made it with precooked rice; nationally, almost twice as much precooked rice as regular rice was used to make Spanish rice. Specialty Spanish rice mixes, including that made by Jamestown, enjoyed only limited success in the West.

Jamestown food technicians had formulated a precooked rice that appeared to satisfy Westerners' tastes in Spanish rice. This new formulation could be prepared by baking the rice with liquid and other ingredients in Spanish rice, rather than by first boiling the rice and then combining it with other ingredients and baking it in a Spanish rice casserole. If the new formulation were to be served as plain rice, it could, like the present InstantRice, be prepared by boiling.

Taste tests indicated, however, that Westerners preferred the present product to the new formulation for all dishes except Spanish rice and that consumers in other regions preferred the present product over the new formulation for all uses.

If the new formulation were to perform well in consumer use tests, Mr. Swarthol could recommend test-marketing it in selected areas in the West. If test market results warranted, he could recommend introducing the new product throughout that region.

Up to $150,000 in new equipment would be required to produce the new formulation. The new formula would require the use of ingredients which would increase manufacturing costs by about two cents per pound. Some company marketing personnel believed that Jamestown could charge considerably more for the new formulation, but others doubted that InstantRice could increase consumer prices above the present premium level. Swarthol estimated that the amount spent on advertising and promotion in the West would have to be twice the $125,000 now being allocated to that area if the new formulation were to succeed. If the new formula were introduced in the West, the present product formulation would continue to be sold in the rest of the United States. Swarthol had not determined whether the present InstantRice would be withdrawn from the western market once the new formulation was introduced.

Other alternatives were to utilize a specialized advertising strategy in each region, but without a product change, or to reduce expenditures for trade and consumer advertising and promotion. If spending were cut, Mr. Swarthol believed that InstantRice sales would likely continue to decline gradually. He believed that a proposal to increase promotional expenditures would meet considerable skepticism from senior Jamestown executives unless persuasive justification were presented.

Mr. Swarthol knew that in some long-established product categories, such as coffee and ketchup, price reductions and private brands were employed in an attempt to secure sales increases. Although he was not certain whether either or both approaches would be appropriate for InstantRice, he recalled that representatives of major grocery chains had individually approached Jamestown about packaging precooked rice under their own store labels.

Within six months, Mr. Swarthol would have to submit a proposed budget for InstantRice for the coming year. If he were to decide against test-marketing or introducing the new formula in the West, Mr. Swarthol believed he had to recommend some plan which would reverse the decline in InstantRice sales. "There's a lot of pressure on me to produce," he commented. "I'm due for a promotion in a year, and I may not get it unless I can show some positive results with this brand. In fact, corporate [Jamestown's top-management group] has set some almost unbelievably high sales targets for each product management group. My boss [the product group manager] has let it be known that product managers who don't help him meet his quotas may as well start sending out their résumés. It's a 'grow or go' plan."

# Case 5

# Island Shores

In February 1982, Tom Smith, vice president and project manager of Enterprise Developers, Inc., was contemplating marketing alternatives available to the firm and the associated risks inherent in real estate development during such turbulent economic times. As Mr. Smith sat in his St. Petersburg, Florida, office trying to organize his thoughts and the market information at his disposal in some meaningful fashion, he was well aware that should the firm act on his recommendation, tens of millions of dollars would be at stake. Within the firm Smith was known for his good insights and solid judgment. While his previous decisions had successful outcomes, there was no guarantee that he was immune from mistakes and in this business mistakes were costly. Corporate expectations to meet a target return on investment of 18 percent added to the pressure that the selected project be more than marginally successful. The final plan to be submitted to the board of directors would have to include consideration of the designated target market, site selection, and architectural design requirements as well as price and promotional strategy.

## COMPANY BACKGROUND

The history of Enterprise Developers was characterized by risk taking and an unusually high rate of success. The firm was founded by three businessmen from New York who had grown up in one of the worst boroughs in the city. They had banded together in the late 1950s to renovate and refurbish a neighborhood tenement building. After buying the burned-out shell from the city for $1,000 they rebuilt it themselves with sweat equity into a model example of low-income housing worth several hundred thousand dollars. The group invested the profits from the sale of this building into other pieces of real estate. Middle-income housing, apartment

This case was written by Cynthia J. Frey, Assistant Professor of Marketing, Boston College and Maria Sannella as a basis for class discussion rather than to illustrate either effective or ineffective handling of an administrative situation.

buildings, and townhouses followed. With each renovation success the profits were reinvested in more property. The group was always alert to a new opportunity.

Encouraged by a friend and the possibility of more lucrative ventures, the trio moved to Miami in 1969. The next five years were spent developing rental units in the central city area. Close to the major business district, these mid-rise style buildings provided convenient access to the city for office workers. The skills that Enterprise acquired in New York City developing high density, urban living units were equally successful in Miami.

During this time period extensive condominium development was occurring along Florida's east coast, particularly in the Fort Lauderdale area. Two of the primary groups of buyers were retirees desiring low maintenance home ownership in a warm climate, and investment buyers who might spend three or four weeks a year in their unit and rent the remaining weeks to Florida vacationers looking for an alternative to high priced, crowded hotel accommodations. While this was a time of extraordinary growth for east coast condominium building, with units being sold before construction was even started, little of this development was occurring on the west side of the state.

In an attempt to take advantage of the condominium boom in the early 1970s, Enterprise investigated possible sites throughout the Florida peninsula but found most of the areas best suited to resort or retirement communities vastly overpriced or unavailable. One alternative which caught the trio's interest was a so-called spoil spot in Boca Ciega Bay, 350 miles from Miami between St. Petersburg and Clearwater. From dredging operations by the Army Corps of Engineers, a 320-acre island had been formed. Two bridges connected the island with the northernmost portions of the city of St. Petersburg 25 minutes away by car. The island was comprised of coarse bottom sand from the Bay. Vegetation was sparse and uncultivated giving the area a decidedly remote and desolate atmosphere.

The 320-acre island was offered for sale by a prominent insurance company. Although friends and business associates advised against the acquisition of the parcel for the planned high amenity community, Enterprise purchased the site for $18 million. While clarification of zoning ordinances was the first concern for the developers, taming the wilderness to support human creature comforts would be a time-consuming task.

## ST. PETERSBURG AREA

St. Petersburg is known for its mild temperatures and beautiful year-round weather. According to the local paper, the *St. Petersburg Independent,* 361 days of sunshine per year are guaranteed. On days when the sun does not appear by 3 P.M., the newspaper distributes the afternoon edition free of charge. Since 1910, only 30 editions have been given away. The record for consecutive days with sunshine is 546.

St. Petersburg, the fourth largest city in Florida, is located on the southern tip of the Pinellas Peninsula. This point of land takes its name from the Spanish Punta Pinales or Point of the Pine Trees. Tampa Bay is on the east and to the south, the Gulf of Mexico on the west. St. Petersburg Beach, on Long Key, is one of the Holiday Isles, a ribbon of keys separated from the mainland and St. Petersburg by Boca Ciega Bay.

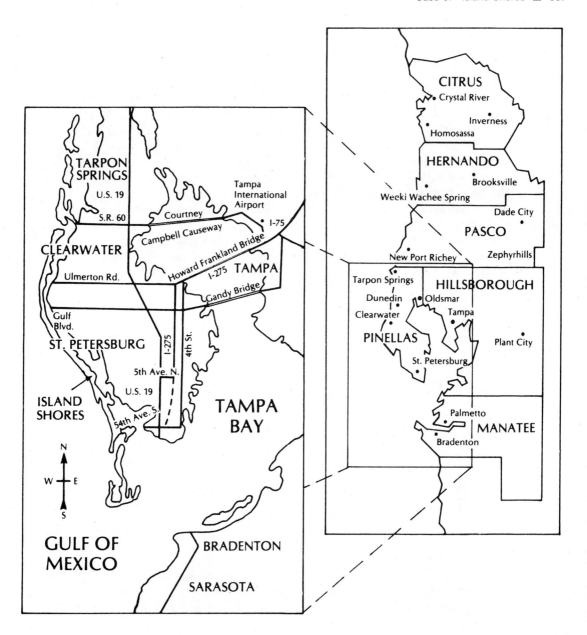

Although the Spanish explorer Narvaez landed on the peninsula in 1528 and marched to Tampa Bay, John C. Williams of Detroit is credited as the city's founder. Williams acquired 1,700 acres of wilderness land in 1876 which later became the nucleus of downtown St. Petersburg. Williams's intention was to establish a resort community to take advantage of the fine weather. However, his remote location had no transportation connection with other Florida population centers. As a result, he agreed to a partnership with Russian exile Piotr Alexeitch Dementieff (a.k.a. Peter Demens) contingent on Demens's completion of a railroad trunk line into the area.

The Orange Belt Line from Lake Monroe near Sanford, Florida, was completed in 1888 when Williams's little community had a population of 30. As the story goes, Williams and Demens flipped a coin to decide who would name the new town. Demens won and elected to name the town St. Petersburg after his birthplace. Williams's resort hotel completed around 1890 was fittingly named The Detroit.

As early as 1885 the American Medical Association praised the climate and healthful surroundings as ideal. With its accessibility improved by the Orange Belt Line, the population had climbed to 300 by 1892 when the town was incorporated. Many of the early settlers were British who had emigrated to the Bahamas and Key West. In an effort to expand the resort reputation of St. Petersburg, the Chamber of Commerce established its first promotional budget of $150 in 1902. In 1907 a special tax was levied on year-round residents to support tourist promotion.

Today, thousands of people arrive daily at the Tampa International Airport which also serves St. Petersburg and Clearwater. Considered one of the most modern and efficient airports in the world, Tampa International has shuttle trains from the main terminal to the gates, an assortment of restaurants and boutiques, and a hotel with a revolving penthouse. Fifteen major air carriers fly into the airport, many with international routes to Central and South America and Europe.

St. Petersburg is also known as the Boating Capital of the United States. With boating activity supported by the Municipal Marina downtown and the St. Petersburg Yacht Club, St. Petersburg is home base to some of the most important sailboat and power boat races in the Gulf. The Swift Hurricane Classic, Isla de Mujeres Race, and the Southern Ocean Racing Conference championships represent the highlights of the season.

Fishing is also a favorite pastime in St. Petersburg where people can be seen lining the bridges fishing late into the night. Golf courses are widely available as are tennis courts.

While St. Petersburg has become a preferred retirement community for many, the city has tried to promote business development in the area to balance the population demographics. Since 1970, construction of new plants and plant expansions has totaled 1,196, and 19,005 new jobs have been created. Changes in population demographics in St. Petersburg and the surrounding counties between 1970 and 1979 are presented in Exhibit 1.

A survey of newcomers to the St. Petersburg area conducted by Suncoast Opinion Surveys in 1980 reveals some further information. This group of newcomers is considered to represent approximately 19 percent of the adult population in Pinellas County. Survey results are presented in Exhibit 2.

## BACKGROUND ON ISLAND SHORES

Management at Enterprise was convinced that careful planning and gradual development would be critical to the success of the Island Shores project given their previous experience. In order to appeal to both retirees and second-home vacationers, Island Shores had to represent a distinct combination of benefits. While many of the Florida condominium complexes were just places to hang one's hat and residents were dependent on the Ft. Lauderdale or Miami communities for things to do and places to go, the location of Island Shores required that many of these entertainment and recreation options be available on the island. Enterprise's plan called for development of the following amenities: angling, beaches, golf, jogging and bicycle paths, open areas, clubhouse and restaurant, sailing, shopping, sunbathing, swimming pools, tennis and racketball courts, and water skiing. In order to attract buyers in the early stages of development at least some of these planned benefits had to be apparent, so the golf course and clubhouse went into construction immediately.

The plan for the island called for high density residential units to be built on the water's edge and a golf course in the center. Since the golf course was considered a major drawing feature, the problems associated with growing grass where none had grown before had to be faced immediately. In 1974 work on the golf course began at the same time as condominium construction. After several false starts and experimentation with many varieties of grass, ground-covers, and shrubs, reasonably well-manicured greens appeared three years later. It became painfully clear that landscaping a "spoil spot" would take perseverance, patience, and a great deal of money. Costs associated with construction of the golf course alone totaled a million dollars.

Michele Perez, an award winning architect from California, was responsible for designing the residential structures in harmony with the island environment. Due to the priority given the 18-hole golf course in the 320-acre parcel and the desire to maximize picturesque views from each condo unit, the residential development plan called for high density construction along the water's edge. The land utilization goal of 14 condominiums per acre was met by Perez's plan for positioning units diagonally to the water rather than lining them up parallel to the beach frontage in traditional fashion. These clusters form miniature neighborhoods while maximizing ocean views. For each cluster a swimming pool and sunbathing deck was constructed which acts as a social gathering spot and provides a recreational area with a relatively large amount of privacy. The large "community pool" concept was considered by Enterprise to be unappealing to many potential residents who were expected to value easy access to the pool's ambience more than its Olympic proportions. Resident parking was designed underneath the buildings to minimize the asphalt perspective so typical of high density living environments.

Four-story and 12-story high-rise units, 2-story townhouses, and freestanding condominium villas were constructed. The units in greatest demand between 1975 and 1980 were villas. Many of them sold before construction was even begun. Two bedroom units in the mid- and high-rise buildings were also very popular. One bedroom high-rise units and townhouses were still available although on a limited basis.

The primary construction materials were stucco and wood which blended with the Spanish architectural influence throughout the St. Petersburg area. As each building was completed, landscaping was carefully undertaken. The landscape architects working for Enterprise were sent to Disney World in Orlando to study plantings. Using similar shrubs which could adapt to conditions at Island Shores, sculptured shrubs and ever-blooming varieties of plants created a garden atmosphere. In 1981 alone, the cost of landscaping approached $1.5 million not counting individual building phases.

In 1975 the condominiums on Island Shores ranged in price from $42,000 to $50,000. The average market value of these units for resale in 1982 is $108,034. Smith's records showed that in December 1981, 70 units had been sold for a total

**Exhibit 1 □ Population and population characteristics change, 1970 to 1979**

| | Metro area | | | Pinellas | | | Pasco | | | Hillsborough | | |
|---|---|---|---|---|---|---|---|---|---|---|---|---|
| | April 1, 1979, population | Percent of total | Percent change since 1970 | April 1, 1979, population | Percent of total | Percent change since 1970 | April 1, 1979, population | Percent of total | Percent change since 1970 | April 1, 1979, population | Percent of total | Percent change since 1970 |
| Total | 1,521,799 | 100.0% | +39.8% | 725,457 | 100.0% | +38.9% | 161,873 | 100.0% | +113.1% | 634,469 | 100.0% | +29.4% |
| 0–14 years | 285,296 | 18.8 | +14.7 | 112,546 | 15.5 | +14.8 | 25,662 | 15.9 | +93.7 | 147,088 | 23.2 | +7.0 |
| 15–24 years | 217,866 | 14.3 | +43.3 | 82,771 | 11.4 | +40.1 | 17,515 | 10.8 | +111.6 | 117,580 | 18.5 | +38.8 |
| 25–44 years | 323,700 | 21.3 | +51.2 | 129,227 | 17.8 | +49.0 | 23,962 | 14.8 | +122.1 | 170,511 | 26.9 | +46.3 |
| 45–64 years | 338,423 | 22.2 | +38.4 | 171,011 | 23.6 | +37.3 | 39,528 | 24.4 | +101.5 | 127,884 | 20.2 | +27.4 |
| 65 and over | 356,514 | 23.4 | +55.6 | 229,902 | 31.7 | +49.4 | 55,206 | 34.1 | +129.8 | 71,406 | 11.2 | +39.5 |
| 18 and over | 1,165,496 | 76.6 | +47.9 | 584,955 | 80.6 | +45.5 | 130,413 | 80.6 | +117.6 | 450,128 | 70.9 | +38.1 |
| Median age | 40.9 years | — | +2.5 years | 49.5 years | — | +1.4 years | 52.0 years | — | −1.4 years | 31.2 years | — | +2.7 years |
| White | 1,385,288 | 91.0% | +42.5% | 671,331 | 92.5% | +40.4% | 157,783 | 97.5% | +119.4% | 556,174 | 87.7% | +31.8% |
| Nonwhite | 136,511 | 9.0 | +17.2 | 54,126 | 7.5 | +22.2 | 4,090 | 2.5 | +1.5 | 78,295 | 12.3 | +14.9 |
| Male | 716,075 | 47.1% | +39.1% | 334,017 | 46.0% | +38.9% | 77,599 | 47.9% | +110.7% | 304,459 | 48.0% | +28.1% |
| Female | 805,724 | 52.9 | +40.4 | 391,440 | 54.0 | +38.8 | 84,274 | 52.1 | +115.4 | 330,010 | 52.0 | +30.6 |

|  | Manatee | | | Citrus | | | Hernando | | |
|---|---|---|---|---|---|---|---|---|---|
|  | April 1, 1979, population | Percent of total | Percent change since 1970 | April 1, 1979, population | Percent of total | Percent change since 1970 | April 1, 1979, population | Percent of total | Percent change since 1970 |
| Total | 141,188 | 100.0% | +45.4% | 42,397 | 100.0% | +120.9% | 38,182 | 100.0% | +124.5% |
| 0–14 years | 23,837 | 16.9 | +27.2 | 7,155 | 16.9 | +85.1 | 7,399 | 19.4 | +73.8 |
| 15–24 years | 15,049 | 10.6 | +37.1 | 3,717 | 8.8 | +81.7 | 4,166 | 10.9 | +93.8 |
| 25–44 years | 24,504 | 17.4 | +58.1 | 6,215 | 14.6 | +113.4 | 7,104 | 18.6 | +120.7 |
| 45–64 years | 33,874 | 24.0 | +50.1 | 11,909 | 28.1 | +121.4 | 10,268 | 26.9 | +161.9 |
| 65 and over | 43,924 | 31.1 | +49.8 | 13,401 | 31.6 | +168.4 | 9,245 | 24.2 | +167.4 |
| 18 and over | 112,346 | 80.0 | +51.3 | 33,869 | 79.9 | +134.5 | 29,253 | 76.6 | +144.9 |
| Median age | 49.2 years | — | +.5 years | 51.9 years | — | +2.8 years | 45.8 years | — | +7.6 years |
| White | 128,068 | 90.7% | +50.1% | 40,622 | 95.8% | +134.3% | 35,833 | 93.8% | +146.1% |
| Nonwhite | 13,120 | 9.3 | +11.5 | 1,775 | 4.2 | 4.4 | 2,349 | 6.2 | – 3.9 |
| Male | 66,700 | 47.2% | +46.7% | 20,397 | 48.1% | +119.9% | 18,833 | 49.3% | +125.7% |
| Female | 74,488 | 52.8 | +44.2 | 22,000 | 51.9 | +121.8 | 19,349 | 50.7 | +123.5 |

Source: University of Florida, Bureau of Economic and Business Research "Age, Race and Sex Components of Florida Population—1979," and 1970 Census. Prepared by Research Department, *St. Petersburg Times* and *Evening Independent*, May 1980.

of $7,562,389. Overall, new sales in 1980 were $32 million and sales in 1981 were $34 million. Prices for units still under construction in the Colony Beach portion of the project as of 1982 are shown here.

|  | Colony Beach (6 story) | |
| --- | --- | --- |
| Model | Size | Price |
| Madrid | 1 bedroom—1½ bath | $70,000–$ 92,900 |
| Sevilla | 2 bedroom—2 bath | $90,900 $125,000 |
| Villa | 2 bedroom—2 bath | $86,900–$107,000 |

|  | Colony Beach (12 story) | |
| --- | --- | --- |
| Model | Size | Price |
| Barcelona | 2 bedroom—2 bath | $133,000–$162,000 |
| Sevilla | 2 bedroom—2 bath | $135,000–$166,000 |
| Villa | 2 bedroom—2 bath | $110,000–$117,000 |

**Exhibit 2** ☐ **Demographic profile of Pinellas residents**

|  | | By length of residency | | |
| --- | --- | --- | --- | --- |
|  | Total Pinellas adults | Newcomers (2 years or less) | Midterm residents (3–10 years) | Long-term residents (over 10 years) |
| Total | 100% | 19% | 35% | 46% |
| Sex |  |  |  |  |
| Male | 45% | 46% | 51% | 40% |
| Female | 55 | 54 | 49 | 60 |
| Age |  |  |  |  |
| 18–24 years | 10% | 25% | 7% | 6% |
| 25–34 years | 17 | 20 | 22 | 13 |
| 35–49 years | 21 | 24 | 18 | 22 |
| 50–64 years | 22 | 19 | 23 | 22 |
| 65–74 years | 18 | 10 | 22 | 18 |
| 75 years and over | 12 | 2 | 8 | 19 |
| Median adult age (years) | 51.4 | 38.1 | 52.0 | 56.1 |
| Where born* |  |  |  |  |
| Pinellas County | 8% | 1% | 1% | 16% |
| Other Florida | 5 | 7 | 4 | 5 |
| Northeast | 32 | 31 | 37 | 29 |
| Midwest | 31 | 35 | 31 | 29 |
| South | 15 | 17 | 14 | 14 |
| West | 3 | 3 | 4 | 2 |
| Outside United States | 6 | 6 | 9 | 5 |
| Education |  |  |  |  |
| Grammar school | 4% | 1% | 4% | 6% |
| Some high school | 11 | 6 | 12 | 12 |
| High school graduate | 34 | 28 | 32 | 37 |
| Technical, business school graduate | 7 | 8 | 8 | 7 |
| Some college | 21 | 24 | 21 | 20 |
| College graduate | 23 | 33 | 23 | 18 |

*Northeast includes Connecticut, Maine, Massachusetts, New Hampshire, New Jersey, New York, Pennsylvania, Rhode Island, and Vermont.
Midwest includes Illinois, Indiana, Iowa, Kansas, Michigan, Minnesota, Missouri, Nebraska, North Dakota, Ohio, South Dakota, and Wisconsin.
South includes Alabama, Arkansas, Delaware, Washington, D.C., Georgia, Kentucky, Louisiana, Maryland, Mississippi, North Carolina, Oklahoma, South Carolina, Tennessee, Texas, Virginia, and West Virginia.
West includes Alaska, Arizona, California, Colorado, Hawaii, Idaho, Montana, Nevada, New Mexico, Oregon, Utah, Washington, and Wyoming.

**Exhibit 2 (*continued*)**

|  | Total Pinellas adults | By length of residency | | |
|---|---|---|---|---|
|  |  | Newcomers (2 years or less) | Midterm residents (3–10 years) | Long-term residents (over 10 years) |
| **Employment status** |  |  |  |  |
| Employed full time | 43% | 56% | 46% | 35% |
| Employed part time | 7 | 5 | 7 | 7 |
| Temporarily out of work | 3 | 6 | 1 | 3 |
| Retired | 32 | 19 | 35 | 34 |
| Housewife | 11 | 11 | 7 | 15 |
| Disabled | 2 | 1 | 3 | 3 |
| Other | 2 | 2 | 1 | 3 |
| **Women** |  |  |  |  |
| Employed outside home | 40% | 49% | 41% | 36% |
| Not employed outside home | 60 | 51 | 59 | 64 |
| **Household income** |  |  |  |  |
| Under $10,000 | 23% | 21% | 18% | 28% |
| $10,000–$15,000 | 18 | 24 | 16 | 17 |
| $15,001–$20,000 | 19 | 12 | 23 | 19 |
| Over $20,000 | 40 | 43 | 43 | 36 |
| Median | $17,400 | $17,100 | $18,500 | $16,300 |
| **Own/rent residence** |  |  |  |  |
| Own, with mortgage | 47% | 37% | 52% | 47% |
| Own, no mortgage | 33 | 19 | 32 | 40 |
| Rent | 19 | 42 | 15 | 13 |
| Other | 1 | 2 | 1 | † |
| **Type of residence** |  |  |  |  |
| Single family | 69% | 53% | 68% | 77% |
| Apartment | 11 | 19 | 10 | 7 |
| Condominium | 9 | 11 | 10 | 7 |
| Mobile home | 9 | 11 | 10 | 7 |
| Other | 2 | 6 | 2 | 2 |
| **Household size** |  |  |  |  |
| 1 person | 21% | 14% | 16% | 26% |
| 2 persons | 41 | 45 | 48 | 35 |
| 3 persons | 13 | 15 | 9 | 14 |
| 4 persons | 15 | 15 | 15 | 16 |
| 5 or more persons | 10 | 11 | 12 | 9 |
| Average | 2.5 | 2.6 | 2.6 | 2.5 |
| **Children present in household** |  |  |  |  |
| No children present | 69% | 68% | 69% | 69% |
| Child(ren) present | 31 | 32 | 31 | 31 |
| **Race** |  |  |  |  |
| White | 96% | 97% | 98% | 94% |
| Nonwhite | 4 | 3 | 2 | 6 |
| **Household income sources** |  |  |  |  |
| Wages/salaries only | 40% | 53% | 39% | 36% |
| Wage/salary and other regular sources‡ | 25 | 21 | 26 | 26 |
| Other regular sources only | 34 | 26 | 34 | 37 |
| No income sources | 1 | — | 1 | 1 |
| **Number of wage earners in household** |  |  |  |  |
| None | 35% | 26% | 35% | 39% |
| One wage earner | 31 | 30 | 33 | 30 |
| Two wage earners | 26 | 36 | 19 | 27 |
| Three wage earners | 6 | 6 | 11 | 2 |
| Base | (501) | (93) | (175) | (233) |
| Four or more | 2% | 2% | 2% | 2% |
| Average | 1.1 | 1.3 | 1.1 | 1.0 |

†Less than one half of 1 percent.
‡Other regular sources—Other than wages and salaries: includes social security, dividends, interest, alimony, child support, disability, pension, welfare, or other benefits.

**Exhibit 2 (concluded)**

| | Total Pinellas adults | By length of residency | | |
|---|---|---|---|---|
| | | Newcomers (2 years or less) | Midterm residents (3–10 years) | Long-term residents (over 10 years) |
| **Residence** | | | | |
| North of Ulmerton Road | 43% | 55% | 44% | 37% |
| South of Ulmerton Road | 57 | 45 | 56 | 63 |
| **Daily newspapers read regularly** | | | | |
| St. Petersburg Times | 83% | 83% | 82% | 84% |
| Evening Independent | 22 | 15 | 18 | 27 |
| Clearwater Sun | 23 | 23 | 28 | 20 |
| Tampa Tribune | 3 | 6 | 4 | 2 |
| Other | 3 | 4 | 2 | 3 |
| None | 4 | 3 | 3 | 5 |
| **Daily newspapers read yesterday** | | | | |
| St. Petersburg Times | 67% | 59% | 68% | 69% |
| Evening Independent | 16 | 11 | 8 | 23 |
| Clearwater Sun | 18 | 18 | 21 | 15 |
| Tampa Tribune | 2 | 3 | 2 | 2 |
| Other | 1 | 1 | — | 2 |
| None | 15 | 21 | 13 | 14 |
| **Sunday newspaper read last Sunday** | | | | |
| St. Petersburg Times | 74% | 72% | 70% | 78% |
| Clearwater Sun | 17 | 16 | 19 | 15 |
| Tampa Tribune | 1 | 2 | 2 | — |
| **Broadcast media** | | | | |
| Watched television yesterday: | | | | |
| 6:00–8:59 A.M. | 8% | 7% | 6% | 8% |
| 9:00–11:59 A.M. | 10 | 7 | 10 | 11 |
| Noon–5:59 P.M. | 34 | 37 | 27 | 35 |
| 6:00–8:59 P.M. | 67 | 66 | 70 | 65 |
| 9:00–10:59 P.M. | 61 | 63 | 63 | 59 |
| 11:00 P.M. or later | 30 | 26 | 30 | 31 |
| Don't know when watched | 1 | — | 2 | 1 |
| Did not watch TV yesterday | 11 | 13 | 8 | 13 |
| Subscriber to cable TV | 11% | 11% | 14% | 9% |
| Not cable TV subscriber | 89 | 89 | 86 | 91 |
| Listened to radio yesterday | 34% | 39% | 38% | 30% |
| 6:00–8:59 A.M. | 28 | 28 | 29 | 26 |
| 9:00–11:59 A.M. | 32 | 27 | 37 | 31 |
| Noon–5:59 P.M. | 15 | 13 | 14 | 16 |
| 6:00–8:59 P.M. | 9 | 2 | 11 | 10 |
| 9:00–10:59 P.M. | 7 | 2 | 10 | 8 |
| 11:00 P.M. or later | 2 | 2 | 1 | 3 |
| Don't know when listened | | | | |
| Did not listen to radio yesterday | 37 | 38 | 34 | 40 |
| **Checking account** | 90% | 92% | 91% | 88% |
| Base | (501) | (93) | (175) | (233) |
| **Savings account** | 89% | 82% | 92% | 90% |
| At bank | 74 | 76 | 77 | 71 |
| At savings and loan | 43 | 34 | 38 | 51 |
| At credit union | 26 | 21 | 30 | 24 |
| **MasterCard or Visa** | 55% | 56 | 59 | 52 |
| MasterCard | 36 | 39 | 41 | 31 |
| Visa | 46 | 48 | 46 | 45 |
| **Other credit cards:** | | | | |
| American Express | 10% | 18% | 13% | 6% |
| Diners Club | 3 | 4 | 4 | 2 |
| Carte Blanche | 2 | 2 | 3 | 2 |
| Passport | 18 | 11 | 22 | 18 |
| Base | (501) | (93) | (175) | (233) |

Prices vary for the models depending on what floor they are on in the building and their relative exposure. Each unit has its own balcony, carpeting, a full set of appliances, and assigned parking. Two bedroom–two bath models had been the most in demand with different square footage and floor plans distinguishing Sevilla, Villa, and Barcelona models. Recent prices at Island Shores for villas had been in the range of $79,000 to $112,000, mid-rise units from $70,000 to $250,000, and high-rise units $95,000 to $166,000. Smith was concerned that as costs escalated the project was being priced out of the reach of most people in the market for vacation homes. While the number of one bedroom units could be increased, in the future they did not appear to be the most desirable. He wondered if square footage in the two bedroom-two bath models could be reduced further or if the target market should be narrowed to primary home buyers rather than including vacation home buyers. This would have implications for the physical design of the units and the required storage space. The Colony Beach area with a planned 1,200 units was not scheduled for completion until 1988. Based on previous experience, it was currently estimated that the 340 units, as yet unsold, would be fully occupied by the end of 1984.

## COMPETITION

Smith knew from friends in the business and his own observations that competitors' sales had declined in recent months. While he felt Island Shores was more desirable than similar high-rise condominium units located on the Intracoastal Waterway or the Mandalay Channel, he had collected pricing information hoping it would help him develop his marketing plan. In general, unit square footage ranges from 950–1,450 and the selling price from $77–$115 per square foot. Exhibit 3 presents data for projects comparable to the units in Colony Beach.

It was clear that the development firms behind the competition were aggressive and unlikely to give market share to Island Shores without a battle. Smith didn't know for sure how they would respond to the recent market downturn, but

**Exhibit 3 □ Competitive prices**

### Marina walk

| Model | Description | Price range | Units building |
|---|---|---|---|
| J | 2 bedroom—2 bath | $125,000–$150,000 | 20 |
| K | 2 bedroom—den—2 bath | $140,000–$165,000 | 20 |
| L | 2 bedroom—2 bath | $112,500–$142,000 | 20 |
| M | 1 bedroom—1½ bath | $ 90,000–$110,000 | 20 |
| NE | 2 bedroom—2 bath | $155,000–$185,000 | 20 |
| NW | 2 bedroom—2 bath | $167,500–$202,500 | 20 |

### Sailfish Key

| Model | Description | Price range | Units building |
|---|---|---|---|
| Sunfish | 1 bedroom—1 bath | $ 97,900–$ 99,900 | 6 |
| Yacht | 1 bedroom—1½ bath | $110,000–$126,400 | 10 |
| Corsair | 2 bedroom—2 bath | $136,500–$149,500 | 12 |
| Brigantine | 2 bedroom—2 bath | $167,000–$175,000 | 6 |
| Galleon | 2 bedroom—2 bath* | $171,000–$179,500 | 10 |
| Frigate | 2 bedroom—2 bath—den | $215,000 | 2 |
| Clipper | 3 bedroom—2½ bath | $270,000 | 2 |

*Corner.

he suspected it would be through strengthened promotional efforts. It was likely that the promotion budget for the Colony Beach community would have to be increased just to keep pace with the competition and maintain the build-out schedule for 1984–85.

## BUYER PROFILES

In 1975 the average age of Island Shores condominium buyers was 58. More recently, the average age had decreased to approximately 52 with many buyers in their late 40s. Smith was unsure how to interpret this trend. During the early stages of development, many retirees and investment buyers came from Illinois, Ohio, and Michigan. As economic conditions in these areas worsened, fewer and fewer newcomers seemed to come from the Midwest. To Smith's surprise, an increasing number of European and South Americans were coming to Island Shores over any number of other condominium areas. It seemed that there were growing numbers of buyers from West Germany, France, Venezuela, Argentina, and Mexico. Each nationality tended to cluster together at Island Shores and to maintain close social ties. Whether this pattern would present problems in the long run for the total community was unclear.

A growing concern voiced by condominium residents was the issue of security. The small groupings of units actually facilitated security since neighbors knew each other's comings and goings and watched out for one another. The problem seemed to be caused by transients. When investment buyers rented their condominiums long distance they could exercise very little control over their tenants. Similarly, management at Island Shores had scant information about renters and no power to intervene unless explicit rules and regulations were being violated. Compared to other condominium developments in the St. Petersburg area the relative crime rate at Island Shores was very low. St. Petersburg itself had little crime compared to other major cities like Miami. Smith began to wonder whether the residents' perceptions of security were more at issue than the occasional burglary. Since one of the objectives of the management was to create an atmosphere of stability in a relaxing environment, any tensions caused by real or imagined security problems would have to be resolved.

Smith wondered if there was some way to encourage more permanent residents and fewer speculative investors to minimize the transient issue. If security personnel were increased it was not clear whether the result would be to alarm or calm the residents and potential buyers. As it had turned out so far, some of the individuals sampling life at Island Shores by renting from absentee owners eventually purchased units on the island although the number of such individuals was small.

## MARKETING DECISIONS

Before Smith could recommend a marketing program he needed to establish the basic target market and whether or not to continue building at Island Shores. Secondary data showed that more people leave New York for the South every year than any other state. If this market was to be reached, however, there would be a lengthy process of registering Enterprise with New York state authorities in order to promote land sales to New York residents. Smith estimated this process would take about a year. Enterprise was already registered in Michigan, Illinois, Indiana, Ohio, and Pennsylvania.

Another possible market was comprised of people already in the St. Petersburg area. Considering the escalation of land values in recent years, many individuals could sell their existing property for twice its purchase price. In this event the extensive amenity package at Island Shores, offering both quality golf and boating, might prove very attractive. Promotional efforts would certainly be reduced in reaching this market segment Smith thought.

The international market seemed to be one of growing importance. If this market was actively pursued, the cost and methods of reaching buyers were difficult to determine. The long-run potential of this market was unclear. Smith became even more unsure as he thought about international currency fluctuations and the recent devaluation of the peso.

Expanding on the plan for development at Island Shores was by far the easiest plan of action to adopt in the short run, but Smith wondered if perhaps a lower amenity package with a golf course but no ocean access might not recapture the Midwest market. He knew of projects such as The Westside near Tampa Airport which concentrated on patio homes, both attached and detached, with prices from $45,000 to $70,000. The patio home concept was relatively new. There was no yard to speak of with the house, just the fenced patio. In some parts of the country they were known as zero-lot homes. They offered single-family housing with very low maintenance which might prove appealing to retirees and young families. Patio homes had gained acceptance as starter homes for young couples, and there seemed to be encouragement to expand the target market.

A parcel of 200 acres just east of Bradenton in Manatee County was available for purchase which might prove suitable. With the lower yield per acre of about 6 units compared to 14 units per acre at Island Shores, Smith felt there would be a potential 350–380 units with the remaining land used for a golf course. While the price of the parcel was open to negotiation, the asking figure was $6 million. Smith had 10 days to pick up a 90-day option on this property. This would mean a commitment of $5,000.

If building was continued immediately at Island Shores, the mix of high-rise, mid-rise, and villas needed to be considered as did the two-bedroom and one-bedroom proportion. If prices were to be reduced, something would have to change. Existing plans called for development of the Ocean Watch portion of the project which was a mid-rise building series with 50 two- and three-bedroom condominium units from $175,000 to $260,000. This was a 1982 estimate, but completion was not scheduled until 1985 when prices would certainly be higher. The current plan called for surface preparation of the area beginning in 1983. If the market became highly price sensitive a potential option was to sell the units under a time-sharing arrangement. Smith knew that existing owners in Colony Beach had voiced objection to such a proposal earlier, but then again, Ocean Watch was a different situation. The target market for this type of vacation home would be a totally new one for Enterprise.

Smith realized that forecasting the demand for seasonal vacation homes versus year-round retirement homes was a critical issue that would strongly influence project location and physical design decisions. Until the best target market was identified, little in the way of price or promotional decisions could be resolved. The person interested in a $200,000 condominium would not likely be the same individual considering a $60,000 patio home.

Since the attributes and amenities of the projects would be very different, the promotional messages would also be very different. Smith was responsible for developing the overall marketing strategy for his projects and would make decisions on promotional strategy as well. A local advertising agency would handle the details of implementation such as art, collateral materials, production, and media buying.

Smith felt strongly that when the real estate market picked up, the Tampa–St. Petersburg area would be among the first to lead the upturn. It was difficult to determine, however, which segments of the market represented the best opportunities for Enterprise. As Smith tried to evaluate the different opportunities facing him, he knew that it was going to be a long weekend. Next Wednesday's board meeting would come all too soon.

# Case 6

# Green Acres Seed Company

Green Acres Seed Company began operations in 1929. Originally, it was a family operation located on the farm of the father and operated by the son. Green Acres' main business was the production and sale of seed corn. In 1935, the opportunity arose to purchase a small seed processing plant in a nearby town. At this time, two other brothers joined the business to form the nucleus of the present organization. In 1956, the partnership was transformed into a corporation.

The years following 1935 were years of rapid growth for Green Acres. In 1936, a modest research program was established and a dealer organization was set up consisting of many farm store accounts. In 1939, Green Acres experienced a serious setback. The industry was changing, and this change was not immediately recognized by the management of Green Acres. Farm stores, the traditional retailing agent for seed corn, were passing out of the picture in favor of farmer dealers. Since Green Acres had not established a farmer-dealer organization, they realized a substantial decline in sales. Work was immediately started on a farmer-dealer organization, and sales picked up again the next year.

In the early 1940s, Green Acres embarked on an expansion program. A new plant was constructed to have an eventual annual capacity of over 300,000 bushels of processed seed. This is the present facility utilized by the firm.

Sales of seed corn in 1971 amounted to $1.78 million for 110,983 bushels of seed (Tables 1 and 2). Of this total, approximately 70 percent were single cross varieties and the remaining 30 percent were double crosses. Although pretax profits had been declining since 1968, management became concerned about this situation only after it learned that profits in 1971 were $13,000 below those of 1970. In attempting to isolate the problem, management observed that all of its costs had been increasing over the period 1967 to 1971. Cost of sales per unit sold had increased from approximately $7 a bushel in 1967 to over $9 a bushel in 1971. This, however, was to be expected because the proportion of single crosses was in-

---

This case was prepared by Professor T. F. Funk of the University of Guelph, Ontario, Canada.

**Table 1**

GREEN ACRES SEED COMPANY
Statement of Income and Expenses
1967–1971
(000)

|  | 1971 | 1970 | 1969 | 1968 | 1967 |
|---|---|---|---|---|---|
| Sales of seed corn . . . . . . . . . . | $1,782 | $1,608 | $1,367 | $1,292 | $1,211 |
| Cost of sales . . . . . . . . . . . . . . | 998 | 833 | 691 | 635 | 618 |
| Gross margin . . . . . . . . . . . . . . | 784 | 775 | 676 | 657 | 593 |
| Expenses: | | | | | |
| Selling expenses . . . . . . . . . . | 509 | 497 | 414 | 308 | 315 |
| Administrative | | | | | |
| expenses . . . . . . . . . . . . . | 195 | 185 | 113 | 162 | 163 |
| Net profit . . . . . . . . . . . . . . . . . | $ 80 | $ 93 | $ 149 | $ 187 | $ 115 |

**Table 2 □ Unit sales of seed corn**

| Year | Single cross (bushels) | Double cross (bushels) | Total sales (bushels) |
|---|---|---|---|
| 1971 | 77,688 | 33,295 | 110,983 |
| 1970 | 62,485 | 41,658 | 104,143 |
| 1969 | 45,808 | 46,372 | 92,180 |
| 1968 | 36,280 | 54,421 | 90,701 |
| 1967 | 26,502 | 61,840 | 88,342 |

creasing and the cost of producing single crosses was known to be considerably higher than that of double crosses.[1]

Administrative costs had also increased since 1967, but the absolute increase had been relatively small. On a bushel basis it had actually declined. Marketing costs, on the other hand, had increased substantially in terms of both absolute dollars and dollars per bushel sold. In 1967, total selling costs were $3.56 a ton compared with $4.59 in 1971. The current financial position of the company is described in Table 3.

On the basis of this analysis, management felt that the real problem it faced was in marketing. It thought that it was simply spending too much money on a marketing program which wasn't effective. To remedy this situation, management felt that a major change was needed. As a result, it immediately began to search for a new marketing manager. In October 1971, Peter Jenkins was hired to direct the company's marketing program.

Jenkins came to Green Acres from Topco, a regional feed manufacturing firm in Illinois, where he had been a sales manager. He had had this position for the past six years. As sales manager for Topco, he had been responsible for supervising the activities of 25 salespeople selling feed directly to farmers. In addition, he had worked closely with the marketing manager in the development of the total feed marketing program. Management at Green Acres was delighted to obtain his

---

[1]Single and double cross varieties are the major classifications of hybrid seed corn. Single cross hybrids result from the combination of two inbred lines or use of closely related inbred lines on one or both sides of the hybrid pedigree. They offer the highest uniformity and yield potential to the farmer but may also have a great deal of performance variability under different environments. Double crosses arise from the combination of four relatively unrelated inbred lines. These have a wider genetic base and therefore are more variable and adaptable to varying environmental conditions.

services and felt that he was just the right person to get their marketing program moving again.

Because Jenkins arrived at Green Acres in October, it was too late to make major changes in the marketing program for 1971–72. The program for 1971–72 had been developed months earlier and was in full swing by October. Jenkins thus decided that the best thing he could do would be to spend his time becoming familiar with the seed industry in general and the situation at Green Acres in particular. Once he had done this, he felt he would be in a position to develop a new marketing approach for Green Acres in 1972–73.

## PRODUCT LINE

Green Acres sold 25 different varieties of seed corn, of which 18 were double crosses and 7 were single crosses (Table 4). The varieties were grouped into three categories—short season, medium season, and full season—depending on their relative maturities. The short season varieties were well adapted and most popular in the northern corn belt, the medium season in the central corn belt, and

**Table 3** ☐

GREEN ACRES SEED COMPANY
Balance Sheet
August 31, 1971

| Assets | | Liabilities and Net Worth | |
|---|---:|---|---:|
| Current assets: | | Current liabilities: | |
| Cash | $ 190,450 | Accounts payable | $ 82,000 |
| Accounts receivable | 372,500 | Obligations due within | |
| Inventories | 155,600 | the year | 380,000 |
| Work in process | 49,700 | Accrued expenses | 52,000 |
| Total current assets | 768,250 | Total current liabilities | 514,000 |
| Investments: | | Long-term liabilities: | |
| Common stock | 185,600 | Mortgages payable | 79,600 |
| Fixed assets: | | Net worth: | |
| Cost | 1,137,500 | Capital stock | 240,000 |
| Less reserve for | | Earned surplus | 585,150 |
| depreciation | 672,600 | Total net worth | 825,150 |
| Total fixed assets | 464,900 | Total liabilities | |
| Total assets | $1,418,750 | and net worth | $1,418,750 |

**Table 4** ☐ **Current product line**

| Short season | | | Medium season | | | Full season | | |
|---|---|---|---|---|---|---|---|---|
| Variety | Type of cross | Days to maturity | Variety | Type of cross | Days to maturity | Variety | Type of cross | Days to maturity |
| 263 | DX | 87 | S33 | SX | 105 | 8535 | DX | 116 |
| 22 | DX | 88 | S35 | SX | 105 | 678 | DX | 116 |
| 31A | DX | 91 | 2570 | DX | 106 | 5907 | DX | 117 |
| S19 | SX | 93 | S30A | SX | 107 | 603 | DX | 117 |
| 201 | DX | 95 | 3340 | DX | 111 | S69 | SX | 117 |
| 2610 | DX | 97 | 593 | DX | 113 | S75 | SX | 118 |
| 224 | DX | 99 | 5900 | DX | 114 | 706 | DX | 119 |
| 233 | DX | 101 | | | | 891 | DX | 121 |
| S27 | SX | 103 | | | | | | |
| 214 | DX | 104 | | | | | | |

the full season in the southern corn belt. However, many farmers would schedule their planting dates in such a manner that they could plant some varieties in each of the three maturity categories.

The product line of Green Acres was similar to that of other seed corn firms. Of the 25 varieties in the product line, only 2 were considered by management as being truly outstanding. These were S27 and 5900. For the past three years, they had shown up extremely well in state yield trials and in commercial applications. Most farmers who had tried them were anxious to use them again.

## PRICING POLICY

The overall pricing policy at Green Acres had been to price double cross varieties at approximately the same level as competitive firms but to price single cross varieties substantially lower than competition. In 1971, the price of double crosses was set at $13.50 a bushel for the medium flat kernel size. This was slightly lower than the average price charged by major competitors (Table 5). Single cross varieties were sold at $19.75 a bushel in 1971. This represented the lowest price for single cross varieties in the industry in 1971.

**Table 5 □ Current industry prices**

| Company | Double cross price | Single cross price |
|---|---|---|
| P.A.G. | $13.80 | $26.00 |
| Pride | 13.70 | 19.80 |
| Jacques | 13.70 | 20.00 |
| Weathermaster | 13.70 | 19.80 |
| Haapala | 13.70 | 20.00 |
| N.K. | 13.75 | 23.50 |
| Trojan | 13.90 | 22.00 |
| Acco | 13.60 | 21.00 |
| United | 13.75 | 25.00 |
| Pioneer | 13.70 | 24.00 |
| Moews | 13.50 | 21.00 |
| DeKalb | 13.90 | 19.80 |
| Pfister | 13.20 | 25.90 |
| Green Acres | 13.50 | 19.75 |
| Lowe | 12.95 | 25.25 |

In 1970, several seed corn firms adopted the practice of grouping varieties for pricing purposes. The idea was to develop a group of outstanding varieties for which demand was high and to sell these at a premium over other varieties. Usually the premium was from $1 to $3 a bushel. Green Acres was aware of this practice but decided not to follow it. It felt that farmers would not buy the higher-price varieties in sufficient volume.

## RESEARCH AND DEVELOPMENT

Research and development is an important function for Green Acres Seed Company. Since 1936, Green Acres had been actively engaged in seed research. Beginning in 1965, Green Acres also began some basic genetic research. Of primary importance in research is the development of new and improved varieties. The policy of Green Acres in this respect is to develop as many new varieties as possible for further testing in the 20 test plots maintained by the company throughout the corn belt.

In addition to its research and testing responsibilites, the research department also has primary responsibility for quality control. This involves checking on the performance of all other departments involved in producing and processing the seed to ensure that quality standards are continually maintained. At the present time, the research department employs four full-time professional plant breeders. The research and development budget is approximately $100,000 a year.

## SALES AREA

In 1971, Green Acres sold seed in 13 states (Table 6). Although seed corn is used to some extent in all 48 contingent states, over 80 percent is used in the 13 states composing Green Acre's marketing area. In total, Green Acres seed accounts for approximately 1.4 percent of the total market in the 13-state area. This varies from a high of nearly 5 percent in Michigan to a low of only 0.2 percent in Missouri. The Missouri market was opened in 1970.

**Table 6 ☐ Sales area**

| | Seeding rate (bushels/acre) | Acres planted— to corn | Industry sales | Company sales | Market share |
|---|---|---|---|---|---|
| Eastern states | 0.19 | 2,018,000 | 383,420 | 4,908 | 1.3 |
| Wisconsin | 0.22 | 2,726,000 | 599,720 | 4,822 | 0.8 |
| Indiana | 0.20 | 5,134,000 | 1,026,800 | 20,513 | 2.0 |
| Missouri | 0.18 | 3,379,000 | 608,220 | 1,522 | 0.2 |
| Ohio | 0.21 | 3,185,000 | 668,850 | 16,822 | 2.5 |
| Michigan | 0.20 | 2,024,000 | 404,800 | 18,987 | 4.7 |
| Iowa | 0.20 | 10,467,000 | 2,093,400 | 11,170 | 0.5 |
| Illinois | 0.20 | 9,993,000 | 1,998,600 | 32,239 | 1.6 |
| Total | 0.20 | 38,926,000 | 7,783,810 | 110,983 | 1.4 |

## MARKETING PROGRAM

The marketing program of Green Acres is similar to that of other seed companies its size. The basic philosophy is to build up a large farmer-dealer organization and push as much seed through these dealers as possible. Thus, the major marketing effort is directed through personal selling. The total marketing expenditures of Green Acres over the period 1967–71 are shown in Table 7.

### Advertising

Green Acres has never relied heavily on advertising. In 1971, total advertising expenditures amounted to only $28,000. Of this total, approximately one half was spent on roadside signs and field markers. The other half was devoted to company literature and advertising in farm magazines. Company literature, for the most part, consisted of a seed catalog describing all of the varieties the company offered for sale and a monthly house organ sent to all the company's dealers. The

**Table 7 □ Marketing expenditures**

|  | 1971 | 1970 | 1969 | 1968 | 1967 |
|---|---|---|---|---|---|
| Advertising |  |  |  |  |  |
| Publications | $ 2,700 | $ 8,600 | $ 10,400 | $ 3,800 | $ 5,400 |
| Signs | 14,800 | 24,800 | 11,400 | 16,300 | 15,500 |
| Literature | 10,500 | 5,500 | 6,300 | 2,600 | 3,200 |
| Total | 28,000 | 38,900 | 28,100 | 22,700 | 24,100 |
| Promotion |  |  |  |  |  |
| Exhibits | 14,100 | 11,100 | 3,900 | 2,700 | 2,900 |
| Premiums | 22,200 | 33,400 | 20,200 | 34,000 | 48,900 |
| Discounts | 172,000 | 126,000 | 91,400 | 76,900 | 70,100 |
| Free seed | 17,000 | 19,800 | 36,000 | — | — |
| Total | 225,300 | 190,300 | 151,500 | 113,600 | 121,900 |
| Salespeople | 245,400 | 258,300 | 221,800 | 162,700 | 161,100 |
| Sales training | 10,500 | 9,400 | 12,600 | 8,900 | 8,500 |
| Total | $509,200 | $496,900 | $414,000 | $307,900 | $315,600 |

expenditure of $2,700 for publications advertising represented the cost of a half-page ad in the July issue of the Indiana and Illinois edition of the *Prairie Farmer* plus other miscellaneous ads in local newspapers.

**Promotion**

Promotional expenditures accounted for approximately 40 percent of Green Acres' marketing expenses in 1971. A total of $14,100 was spent on exhibits at farm shows, county fairs, and so on. An additional $22,200 was spent on various types of sales premiums. These premiums varied from year to year and in 1971 consisted of jackets and caps with the company emblem, ballpoint pens, and electric frying pans. The jackets and caps were given to all dealers selling in excess of 25 bushels of seed corn. The electric frying pans were given to dealers selling 50 or more bushels. It was felt that these frying pans would appeal to the dealers' wives and that they would encourage their husbands to sell more so they could receive one.

The largest promotional expense was discounts. The most significant were quantity discounts, early order discounts, and cash discounts. The quantity discount used by Green Acres was similar to that used by most other seed companies. The quantity schedule is shown in Table 8. In addition to the discounts, the company also had a policy of giving away free seed. In most cases, this seed was used as payment to dealers for erecting and maintaining field signs.

**Personal selling**

The largest marketing expenditure incurred by Green Acres was for salespeople or, as they are called in the seed industry, district sales managers. In 1971, Green Acres employed 15 full-time district sales managers in eight sales regions. In a few cases, these district sales managers would hire part-time assistants to aid in the delivery of seed prior to planting.

Table 9 provides some information on the sales force in 1971. The average age of Green Acres' salespeople was 44 years. Many of the salespeople above the average age were retired farmers who had previously been successful seed corn dealers. A few of the younger salespeople were university-trained agronomists. The number of years with Green Acres varied from a high of 18 to a low of

1, with an average number of 7. The average cost per salesperson, including salary, bonus, and expenses, was $17,891 in 1971, or $2.42 per bushel sold.

The major job of district sales managers was to service their existing dealer organization. This involved several calls each year to ensure that dealers were properly equipped and informed to carry out their selling function. It also involved arranging and conducting dealer meetings in local areas at least once each selling season. Whenever time permitted, district sales managers were instructed to accompany dealers on sales calls. The purpose of this activity was to give the district sales manager the opportunity to observe the sales approach used by the dealer and to make suggestions for improvement. It was also intended to get the dealer started making sales calls. Green Acres management felt that most of its dealers were not aggressive enough.

Another task performed by district sales managers was establishing new dealerships. Because dealer turnover was high (10 to 20 percent each year), it was necessary to get at least this many new dealers each year to avoid losing sales.

**Table 8** ☐ **Quantity discounts**

| Total bushels customer orders | Number of bushels customer pays for |
|---|---|
| 1 through 4 | All |
| 5 through 9 | ½ bushel less than ordered |
| 10 through 18 | 1 bushel less than ordered |
| 19 through 27 | 2 bushels less than ordered |
| 28 through 36 | 3 bushels less than ordered |
| 37 through 45 | 4 bushels less than ordered |
| 46 through 54 | 5 bushels less than ordered |
| 55 through 63 | 6 bushels less than ordered |

**Table 9** ☐ **Sales force data**

| Area/Sales manager | Age | Years with company | Number of dealers | Total sales | Total salary, bonus, and expenses | Salesperson cost per bushel |
|---|---|---|---|---|---|---|
| Eastern states | | | | | | |
| Dietrich | 41 | 4 | 110 | $ 4,908 | $14,878 | $3.03 |
| Wisconsin | | | | | | |
| Thedens | 32 | 5 | 103 | 4,822 | 13,649 | 2,83 |
| Indiana | | | | | | |
| Williams | 43 | 1 | 128 | 9,445 | 20,001 | 2.11 |
| Briggs | 45 | 13 | 160 | 7,604 | 21,378 | 2.81 |
| Findlay | 42 | 16 | 160 | 3,464 | 9,006 | 2.60 |
| Missouri | | | | | | |
| Vanderkamp | 58 | 2 | 85 | 1,522 | 7,245 | 4.76 |
| Ohio | | | | | | |
| Heiserman | 48 | 4 | 135 | 8,294 | 17,946 | 2.16 |
| Hanusik | 36 | 9 | 122 | 8,528 | 21,197 | 2.48 |
| Michigan | | | | | | |
| Smith | 60 | 18 | 250 | 18,987 | 38,406 | 2.02 |
| Iowa | | | | | | |
| Pieper | 33 | 9 | 200 | 8,142 | 19,385 | 2.38 |
| Larson | 25 | 2 | 71 | 3,028 | 11,765 | 3.88 |
| Illinois | | | | | | |
| East | 33 | 9 | 210 | 9,046 | 22,152 | 2.48 |
| Brown | 56 | 2 | 100 | 3,763 | 9,118 | 2.42 |
| Mefford | 58 | 1 | 125 | 3,927 | 15,918 | 4.05 |
| Rieker | 52 | 12 | 250 | 15,503 | 27,684 | 1.78 |
| Average | 44 | 7 | 147 | $ 7,398 | $17,891 | $2.42 |

Although most seed was shipped directly from the main processing plant to the dealers following receipt of farmers' signed orders, a certain amount of each variety was also shipped to area warehouses. The additional seed was intended to meet last-minute orders when it would be impossible to fill these orders from the main warehouse. The area warehouses were operated by the district sales managers, who would attempt to fill these orders from their available inventory. If this were not possible, they would check with other dealers who, because of canceled orders, might have a surplus of the variety needed elsewhere. In addition to handling the paperwork involved in these transfers, the district sales manager would also handle the actual movement of the seed.

Because all dealers handled Green Acres seed on a consignment basis, frequently it was necessary for the district sales managers to pick up unsold seed at the conclusion of the selling season. This seed would be returned to the area warehouses, where it was assembled and returned to the main company warehouse to be rebagged or sold as market corn. All district sales managers at Green Acres were required to account for their activities by filling out daily activity summaries and sending these to the sales manager every week. A summary of the activities of each district manager in 1971 is shown in Table 10.

### Dealer organization

All of the seed sold by Green Acres was sold through the company's dealer organization. Green Acres employed two basic types of dealers—farmer dealers and store dealers. The farmer dealers were farmers who agreed to sell Green

**Table 10 □ Activities of district sales managers**

| Area/Sales manager | Setting up new dealers (weeks) | Servicing old dealers (weeks) | Selling with dealers (weeks) | Direct selling (weeks) | Seed delivery (weeks) | Seed pickup (weeks) | Collection (weeks) |
|---|---|---|---|---|---|---|---|
| Eastern states | | | | | | | |
| Dietrich | 7.5 | 12.5 | 2.5 | 2.5 | 12.5 | 5.0 | 7.5 |
| Wisconsin | | | | | | | |
| Thedens | 6.0 | 24.0 | 4.0 | 4.0 | 5.0 | 5.0 | 2.0 |
| Indiana | | | | | | | |
| Williams | 15.0 | 20.0 | 10.0 | 0.0 | 2.5 | 1.5 | 1.0 |
| Briggs | 2.5 | 25.0 | 5.0 | 7.5 | 7.5 | 1.0 | 1.5 |
| Findlay | 7.5 | 19.5 | 0.5 | 2.5 | 7.5 | 5.0 | 7.5 |
| Missouri | | | | | | | |
| Vanderkamp | 17.5 | 10.0 | 5.0 | 2.5 | 7.5 | 5.0 | 2.5 |
| Ohio | | | | | | | |
| Heiserman | 6.0 | 24.0 | 4.0 | 4.0 | 5.0 | 5.0 | 2.0 |
| Hanusik | 2.5 | 31.5 | 2.5 | 0.5 | 5.0 | 4.0 | 4.0 |
| Michigan | | | | | | | |
| Smith | 5.0 | 20.0 | 1.0 | 1.5 | 10.0 | 2.5 | 10.0 |
| Iowa | | | | | | | |
| Pieper | 5.0 | 35.0 | 1.0 | 1.0 | 4.0 | 2.5 | 1.5 |
| Larson | 6.0 | 24.0 | 4.0 | 4.0 | 5.0 | 5.0 | 2.0 |
| Illinois | | | | | | | |
| East | 3.5 | 27.5 | 2.5 | 5.0 | 7.5 | 1.5 | 2.5 |
| Brown | 12.5 | 17.5 | 2.5 | 2.5 | 7.5 | 5.0 | 2.5 |
| Mefford | 15.0 | 17.5 | 2.5 | 0.0 | 2.5 | 5.0 | 5.0 |
| Rieker | 5.0 | 35.0 | 1.5 | 1.0 | 4.0 | 2.5 | 1.0 |
| Average | 7.7 | 22.9 | 3.2 | 2.6 | 6.2 | 3.7 | 3.5 |

Acres seed to their neighbors. For their efforts, they received a commission based on the number of bushels sold. In 1971, the commission schedule was:

| Type of seed | Number of bushels | Commission |
|---|---|---|
| Double cross | 1 to 99 | $1.50 |
| | 100 to 249 | 2.00 |
| | 250 or more | 2.50 |
| Single cross | 1 to 99 | 2.00 |
| | 100 to 249 | 2.50 |
| | 250 or more | 3.60 |

Store dealers were local farm supply outlets such as feed stores and grain elevators, which operated on the same commission schedule as the farmer dealers. In 1971, Green Acres had 2,029 farmer dealers and 180 store dealers. Their distribution and size are shown in Table 11.

**Table 11 □ Location and size of current dealers**

| Sales territory | Number of farmer dealers | Bushels sold by farmer dealers | Average farmer dealer size (bushels) | Number of store dealers | Bushels sold by store dealers | Average store dealer size (bushels) |
|---|---|---|---|---|---|---|
| Eastern states | 101 | 4,315 | 42.7 | 9 | 593 | 65.8 |
| Wisconsin | 96 | 4,758 | 49.6 | 7 | 64 | 9.1 |
| Indiana | 376 | 18,450 | 49.7 | 72 | 2,063 | 28.6 |
| Missouri | 85 | 1,522 | 17.9 | — | — | — |
| Ohio | 219 | 14,799 | 67.7 | 38 | 2,023 | 53.2 |
| Michigan | 236 | 17,919 | 75.9 | 14 | 1,068 | 76.2 |
| Iowa | 266 | 10,954 | 41.2 | 5 | 211 | 42.2 |
| Illinois | 650 | 31,291 | 48.1 | 35 | 948 | 27.1 |
| Total | 2,029 | 104,008 | 51.2 | 180 | 6,970 | 38.7 |

A breakdown of dealers by size is shown in Table 12. This shows that approximately one half of Green Acres dealers sell less than 25 bushels per year. Management suspects that most of these small dealers do not, in fact, sell seed, but rather become dealers so that they can get the larger discount for their own requirements. This may be true to some extent for the 26–50-bushel dealers also. Probably only 51-bushel-and-greater dealers actually sell to their neighbors and friends.

**Table 12 □ Dealer size distribution, 1965**

| Bushels sold | Number of dealers |
|---|---|
| 0–25 | 1,012 |
| 26–50 | 530 |
| 51–100 | 417 |
| 101–200 | 227 |
| 200 and greater | 60 |
| Total | 2,246 |

In addition to the information in Tables 1 through 12, Jenkins had access to a market research study which had been run on 700 corn farmers (Appendix A). He also found some figures in a university publication showing recent trends in the seed corn industry (Appendix B). After reviewing all the available data, Jenkins began preparing a report to present to the executive committee of the Green Acres Seed Company. Jenkins knew he would be in for some sharp questions from the committee, and he wanted to be sure to cover all elements of the marketing mix in his new program for the 1972–73 year.

## APPENDIX A: RESULTS OF MARKETING RESEARCH SURVEY

**How many acres of corn did you have this past year?**

| Acres | | Number of farmers | Percent |
|---|---|---|---|
| A | 1–59 | 177 | 25.3 |
| B | 60–119 | 249 | 35.6 |
| C | 120–249 | 210 | 30.0 |
| D | 250 or more | 64 | 9.1 |
| | | 700 | 100.0 |

**From how many different companies did you buy seed last year?**

| | A | B | C | D | Total |
|---|---|---|---|---|---|
| No answer | 12.4% | 12.0% | 12.4% | 12.5% | 12.3% |
| One | 28.8 | 16.5 | 11.4 | 18.8 | 18.3 |
| Two | 23.2 | 24.1 | 17.1 | 15.6 | 21.0 |
| Three | 20.9 | 27.3 | 23.3 | 20.3 | 23.9 |
| Four | 10.7 | 12.4 | 18.6 | 14.1 | 14.0 |
| Five | 2.3 | 5.6 | 9.5 | 7.8 | 6.1 |
| Six or more | 1.7 | 2.0 | 7.6 | 10.9 | 4.4 |

**Where did you purchase seed corn last year?**

| | A | B | C | D | Total |
|---|---|---|---|---|---|
| No answer | 0.0% | 0.8% | 0.0% | 0.0% | 0.3% |
| Seed store | 11.3 | 9.2 | 9.0 | 10.9 | 9.9 |
| Farmer dealer | 79.7 | 81.1 | 83.3 | 76.6 | 81.0 |
| Company salesperson | 19.2 | 25.3 | 29.0 | 29.7 | 25.3 |
| Combined order | 0.0 | 2.4 | 2.4 | 6.3 | 2.1 |
| Elevator | 4.5 | 3.6 | 3.3 | 3.1 | 3.7 |
| Co-op | 2.8 | 5.6 | 3.3 | 3.1 | 4.0 |
| I am a dealer | 9.0 | 7.2 | 7.6 | 20.3 | 9.0 |

**When you want more information about seed corn, where do you get this information?**

| | A | B | C | D | Total |
|---|---|---|---|---|---|
| No answer | 5.1% | 5.6% | 6.2% | 7.8% | 5.9% |
| Retail store | 2.8 | 3.2 | 1.9 | 1.6 | 2.6 |
| Farmer dealer | 61.6 | 61.0 | 67.1 | 57.8 | 62.7 |
| Agricultural college | 11.9 | 19.3 | 21.0 | 25.0 | 18.4 |
| Magazine articles | 26.6 | 24.1 | 21.0 | 25.0 | 23.9 |
| Seed corn ads | 16.4 | 18.1 | 12.4 | 15.6 | 15.7 |
| County agent | 6.8 | 11.2 | 17.1 | 14.1 | 12.1 |

Where have you seen the seed corn you planted last year advertised?

|                  | A     | B     | C     | D     | Total |
|------------------|-------|-------|-------|-------|-------|
| No answer        | 5.6%  | 7.6%  | 3.3%  | 9.4%  | 6.0%  |
| Billboards       | 20.3  | 14.5  | 18.6  | 26.6  | 18.3  |
| Field signs      | 61.0  | 63.1  | 70.0  | 75.0  | 65.7  |
| Newspaper ads    | 26.6  | 22.5  | 29.5  | 37.5  | 27.0  |
| Farm magazine ads| 79.7  | 74.3  | 81.4  | 75.0  | 77.9  |
| Radio program    | 27.7  | 30.9  | 33.3  | 28.1  | 30.6  |
| TV commercials   | 14.7  | 15.7  | 16.2  | 4.7   | 14 6  |

How would you rank the following reasons in terms of importance to you in deciding on the seed you planted last fall?

|           | A      | B      | C      | D      | Total  |
|-----------|--------|--------|--------|--------|--------|

**A.  Used this variety before**

|         | A     | B     | C     | D     | Total |
|---------|-------|-------|-------|-------|-------|
| First   | 15.8% | 23.3% | 25.2% | 20.6% | 22.3% |
| Second  | 4.5   | 4.0   | 5.7   | 4.7   | 4.7   |
| Third   | 1.1   | 1.6   | 1.4   | 3.1   | 1.6   |
| Fourth  | 0.6   | 1.6   | 2.4   | 0.0   | 1.4   |
| Fifth   | 0.0   | 0.8   | 0.0   | 0.0   | 0.3   |
| Sixth   | 0.0   | 0.0   | 0.0   | 0.0   | 0.0   |
| Seventh | 0.6   | 0.0   | 0.0   | 0.0   | 0.1   |

**B.  A neighbor used this brand and recommended it to me.**

|         | A     | B     | C     | D     | Total |
|---------|-------|-------|-------|-------|-------|
| First   | 0.6   | 2.8   | 2.4   | 1.6   | 2.0   |
| Second  | 7.3   | 9.6   | 7.6   | 9.4   | 8.4   |
| Third   | 5.1   | 6.4   | 6.7   | 9.4   | 6.4   |
| Fourth  | 1.7   | 3.6   | 3.8   | 1.6   | 3.0   |
| Fifth   | 0.6   | 1.2   | 1.9   | 1.6   | 1.3   |
| Sixth   | 0.6   | 2.0   | 0.0   | 0.0   | 0.9   |
| Seventh | 0.6   | 0.0   | 0.0   | 0.0   | 0.1   |

**C.  A salesperson or dealer called on me and wrote my order.**

|         | A     | B     | C     | D     | Total |
|---------|-------|-------|-------|-------|-------|
| First   | 5.6   | 6.4   | 5.2   | 4.7   | 5.7   |
| Second  | 4.5   | 7.2   | 6.7   | 3.1   | 6.0   |
| Third   | 2.3   | 6.4   | 10.8  | 6.3   | 6.4   |
| Fourth  | 3.4   | 2.8   | 3.8   | 4.7   | 3.4   |
| Fifth   | 0.0   | 1.2   | 1.9   | 0.0   | 1.0   |
| Sixth   | 1.7   | 1.6   | 1.0   | 3.1   | 1.6   |
| Seventh | 0.6   | 0.8   | 0.0   | 0.0   | 0.4   |

**D.  I saw official state yield test results.**

|         | A     | B     | C     | D     | Total |
|---------|-------|-------|-------|-------|-------|
| First   | 1.1   | 2.0   | 3.3   | 3.1   | 2.3   |
| Second  | 3.4   | 4.4   | 6.7   | 10.9  | 5.4   |
| Third   | 3.4   | 3.6   | 5.7   | 4.7   | 4.3   |
| Fourth  | 4.5   | 4.4   | 3.3   | 1.6   | 3.9   |
| Fifth   | 0.0   | 2.0   | 1.9   | 3.1   | 1.6   |
| Sixth   | 1.1   | 0.0   | 1.0   | 3.1   | 0.9   |
| Seventh | 0.0   | 1.2   | 1.0   | 0.0   | 0.7   |

**E.  I saw a field marked by a seed corn company sign.**

|         | A     | B     | C     | D     | Total |
|---------|-------|-------|-------|-------|-------|
| First   | 0.0   | 0.8   | 1.4   | 1.6   | 0.9   |
| Second  | 1.7   | 4.0   | 3.3   | 3.1   | 3.1   |
| Third   | 2.8   | 4.4   | 5.2   | 4.7   | 4.3   |
| Fourth  | 2.3   | 5.2   | 3.3   | 6.3   | 4.0   |
| Fifth   | 3.4   | 0.8   | 1.0   | 1.6   | 1.6   |
| Sixth   | 0.0   | 3.2   | 2.9   | 0.0   | 2.0   |
| Seventh | 0.0   | 1.6   | 0.0   | 0.0   | 0.6   |

**F.  I saw or heard an advertisement.**

|         | A     | B     | C     | D     | Total |
|---------|-------|-------|-------|-------|-------|
| First   | 0.6   | 0.0   | 0.0   | 0.0   | 0.1   |
| Second  | 0.6   | 2.4   | 1.0   | 0.0   | 1.3   |
| Third   | 1.7   | 2.4   | 2.4   | 1.6   | 2.1   |
| Fourth  | 0.6   | 2.4   | 3.8   | 1.6   | 2.3   |
| Fifth   | 1.7   | 2.8   | 2.4   | 1.6   | 2.3   |
| Sixth   | 0.6   | 2.8   | 2.4   | 1.6   | 2.0   |
| Seventh | 1.7   | 2.8   | 1.9   | 3.1   | 2.3   |

## APPENDIX B: TRENDS IN SEED CORN MARKETING

The data in Tables 13 and 14 are taken from a university publication and show the marketing mix allocations and detailed advertising and promotion break-downs. The principal retailing agent of hybrid seed corn is the farmer dealer. In 1970, farmer dealers handled 76 percent of the seed corn sold, and the other channels—store dealers, direct sales, and farm supply centers—accounted for the remainder.

**Table 13 □ Marketing expenditures for seed corn firms**

|  | Small | | | Medium | | | Large | | |
|---|---|---|---|---|---|---|---|---|---|
|  | 1960 | 1965 | 1970 | 1960 | 1965 | 1970 | 1960 | 1965 | 1970 |
| Advertising |  |  |  |  |  |  |  |  |  |
| Dollar |  |  |  |  |  |  |  |  |  |
| expenditure | 9,279 | 13,409 | 21,919 | 57,408 | 87,620 | 100,782 | 295,350 | 349,288 | 429,126 |
| Percent | 11.8 | 9.3 | 10.8 | 26.9 | 22.5 | 21.5 | 40.9 | 30.6 | 27.6 |
| Promotion |  |  |  |  |  |  |  |  |  |
| Dollar |  |  |  |  |  |  |  |  |  |
| expenditure | 3,669 | 7,370 | 9,760 | 41,967 | 71,223 | 75,549 | 174,240 | 198,410 | 354,639 |
| Percent | 4.7 | 5.1 | 4.8 | 19.6 | 18.3 | 16.2 | 24.1 | 17.4 | 22.6 |
| Personal selling |  |  |  |  |  |  |  |  |  |
| Dollar |  |  |  |  |  |  |  |  |  |
| expenditure | 52,010 | 109,899 | 148,576 | 88,640 | 186,253 | 217,695 | 73,952 | 317,534 | 444,847 |
| Percent | 66.4 | 76.1 | 73.4 | 41.5 | 47.8 | 46.5 | 10.3 | 27.8 | 28.4 |
| Research |  |  |  |  |  |  |  |  |  |
| Dollar |  |  |  |  |  |  |  |  |  |
| expenditure | 13,348 | 13,645 | 22,206 | 25,453 | 44,532 | 73,682 | 177,750 | 276,500 | 339,767 |
| Percent | 17.1 | 9.5 | 11.0 | 12.0 | 11.4 | 15.8 | 24.7 | 24.2 | 21.4 |
| Total dollar |  |  |  |  |  |  |  |  |  |
| expenditure | 78,306 | 144,332 | 202,461 | 213,468 | 389,628 | 467,708 | 721,292 | 1,141,732 | 1,568,379 |

**Table 14 □ Advertising and promotional allocations for seed corn firms**

|  | Small | | | Medium | | | Large | | |
|---|---|---|---|---|---|---|---|---|---|
|  | 1960 | 1965 | 1970 | 1960 | 1965 | 1970 | 1960 | 1965 | 1970 |
| Advertising expenditures for seed (as percent of total advertising) |  |  |  |  |  |  |  |  |  |
| Outdoor signs | 33% | 14% | 12% | 28% | 32% | 16% | 22% | 21% | 17% |
| Store displays | — | — | — | 1 | — | — | — | — | — |
| Farm magazines | 25 | 22 | 33 | 26 | 39 | 48 | 29 | 28 | 32 |
| Newspapers | 10 | 5 | 5 | 4 | 2 | 1 | 7 | 7 | 8 |
| Radio and TV | 4 | 40 | 35 | 23 | 15 | 8 | 13 | 14 | 14 |
| Direct mail | 19 | 11 | 12 | 4 | 1 | 10 | 16 | 18 | 17 |
| Other | 9 | 8 | 3 | 14 | 11 | 17 | 13 | 12 | 12 |
|  | 100 | 100 | 100 | 100 | 100 | 100 | 100 | 100 | 100 |
| Promotional expenditures for seed (as percent of total promotion) |  |  |  |  |  |  |  |  |  |
| Fair and farm shows | 5 | 4 | 6 | 6 | 4 | 7 | 7 | 6 | 5 |
| Dealer meetings | 3 | 8 | 14 | 14 | 12 | 16 | 28 | 30 | 19 |
| Company field days | — | 5 | 8 | 3 | 4 | 4 | 2 | 2 | 1 |
| Dealer incentives | 74 | 53 | 45 | 73 | 62 | 63 | 60 | 58 | 37 |
| Customer incentives | 18 | 23 | 23 | 1 | 4 | 3 | 1 | 1 | 35 |
| Other | — | 7 | 4 | 3 | 14 | 7 | 2 | 3 | 3 |
|  | 100 | 100 | 100 | 100 | 100 | 100 | 100 | 100 | 100 |

# Case 7

# New Horizons Travel, Inc.

As her plane for Raleigh took off from Logan Airport on July 5, 1977, Sara Wade thought about events of the last four days. She and her partner, Ellen Wolfe, had made progress in planning the August 1978 start-up of their New Horizons Travel agency. Sara regretted that she had had so little free time just to enjoy Boston's sights. She smiled remembering Ellen's toast, "To independence!" and the accompanying cheers of friends at the Boston Pops Esplanade concert on the Fourth of July. Sara found the idea of independence in the context of starting a new business exhilarating but a bit scary.

Sara's basic optimism about the new venture seemed well founded. After all, Ellen had had four years' experience as a travel agent and was now in charge of a major division of a recognized Boston travel agency. Sara herself was about to enter the second year of the MBA program at the University of North Carolina at Chapel Hill and had had several years' experience at the same agency. Both young women were mobile, energetic, and enthusiastic about travel and starting their own business.

That morning Sara and Ellen had agreed that they were ready to go to potential investors: their fathers, some relatives, and an investor in Winston-Salem who had already approached them. Because their ability to move to their target city was so important to the venture, Sara and Ellen, both single, had given New Horizons Travel priority over any developments in their personal lives that might jeopardize their mobility. Now that they were ready to present their plan to potential investors, this understanding had become even more crucial.

For the rest of the flight, Sara reviewed their business plan as any potential investor might.

## NEW HORIZONS TRAVEL, INC. ELLEN WOLFE AND SARA WADE, FOUNDERS

New Horizons Travel, Inc., is an innovative concept strategically designed to maximize profits and growth in the retail and/or wholesale travel business. The management team is well suited to this endeavor: Ms. Wolfe has four years of practical experience at the retail travel level and is now in a position of authority at the well-known Colonial Travel Agency in Boston; Ms. Wade will have just completed her MBA degree at the University of North Carolina at Chapel Hill and brings to the team experience in sales, advertising, and marketing as well as business expertise. The proposed business plan for a travel agency requires relatively low initial investment and working capital, while affording excellent prospects for long-term growth and profitability. In this report we have attempted to make a real-

This case was prepared by Mary Ellen Templeton and Professor Richard I. Levin of the University of North Carolina at Chapel Hill. Copyright © 1978 by the School of Business Administration, University of North Carolina at Chapel Hill.

istic assessment of the market, its environment, and the product types to develop a comprehensive marketing strategy outlining the growth of one or more retail travel agencies.

## OVERVIEW OF THE TRAVEL SERVICE INDUSTRY

The travel agency acts as an intermediary between the traveling public and transportation companies. It is similar to an independent distributor or retail outlet, selling a standard wholesale travel package to the consumer. The product it sells has the same price and the same characteristics as the product of the agency down the street. To make matters worse, there is no need for the consumer to go through a travel agency to obtain his required travel package. He can simply deal directly with the transportation company.

The travel agency must not only sell the customer on the benefits of its services and conveniences, but it must also convince him that its own unique dispensation of these services deserves his patronage. Differentiation is the key to a successful operation: the agency must market a package of services that is sufficiently distinctive from the service packages of other agencies to win the customer as a loyal client.

## MARKET ANALYSIS

**1. The environment.**   The travel service industry is closely linked to the government-regulated transportation industry. It is thus subject to unforeseeable market fluctuations imposed from such external sources as government regulatory agencies, technological change, economic factors, and changing consumer preferences. The greatest risk the travel agent faces is the fact that he cannot control his end product. He can control only the way he delivers and promotes the product to his customer. The travel agency, in effect, does not sell "travel" but sells the "service" of obtaining travel for the customer. There is a wide variety of substitutable services to compete with the travel agency. Furthermore, a potential customer can simply telephone his order directly to the airline rather than telephoning his travel agency.

**2. Major product types.**   *Wholesale travel* is a package put together by an agency and sold directly to the customer. A major advantage is price control—the wholesaler can set his own prices and markups and at the same time enjoy quantity discounts. He has total control over the travel product. The operation is riskier than retail because the liability rests with the wholesaler (he must guarantee his product to the retailer) and much more capital is required to be at stake.

*Retail travel* sells the packages put together by the wholesaler and is required by law to accept the prices as given. Control over the travel product is practically nonexistent. About 30 percent of all retail agencies sell wholesale tours on a limited basis, usually to give special service and protection to good customers. The motive here is good customer relations, not profitability.

*Corporate business travel* provides the major source of business for the retail agency. It is stable, steady, and does not fluctuate with economic conditions.

*Vacation travel* is often profitable but is extremely volatile and fluctuates with seasonal and economic influences.

*Commission schedules* vary with the different product types:

| | |
|---|---|
| International air fare | 8% |
| Domestic air fare | 7 |
| Hotels and car rentals | 5–10* |
| Tours | 11† |
| Amtrak | 10 |

*These are usually incidentals, part of a package.
†The highest profit item.

The commissions of an agency usually average 7.5 percent because the majority of travel sold is domestic air fare.

**3. Demand analysis.**    Travel agencies usually have three sources of customer demand:

*Walk-ins* respond to an agency's promotion—an advertisement, a newsletter, or often the Yellow Pages.

*Established customers* are the mainstay of the business and are valued for their contact potential.

*Reference customers* are the key to successful growth; they come to an agency because an established customer recommended it. These contacts play a major role in the growth of the agency.

The volume of business coming from these demand sources depends on the location of the agency, how long it has been in operation, the types of business it has built up in the past, and its methods of advertising and promotion.

It is difficult to overemphasize the importance of the "word of mouth" reference: An agency often guards its contacts like cherished jewels. Contacts spur demand growth. Once a customer's loyalty is won, he will refer his friends and acquaintances to the agency, and business increases exponentially.

Contacts are the primary means of entering a market. New agencies have historically used several strategies to obtain the crucial contacts necessary to break into a market:

1. Buying an existing agency that already has contacts.
2. Moving into a town with a dying agency and stealing its contacts.
3. Finding an area with fast-growing businesses and cultivating these new untapped contacts.
4. Hiring employees away from competing agencies and hoping that contacts will follow the employees to the new business.

**4. Identifying the target customer.**    Many types of people travel: families, businesspeople, retired couples, the affluent, students, honeymooners, singles, specialty groups. The successful travel agency must find the customer types that are most likely to contribute to the growth and profitability of the agency.

An agency should use these criteria for selecting the target customer:

a. Potential for developing contacts.
b. Variety of travel products that the customer may want. (A doctor may go on professional group trips and also want a vacation.)
c. Stability of demand volume. (The agency prefers steady corporate business to volatile vacation business.)

New Horizons will focus on two categories of travel customers:

1. *The professional:* Will do steady volume of business travel; has the time and money for a vacation trip; has access to a large pool of potential contacts.
2. *The affluent:* Will do steady business of vacations—even during recessions; have ample time and money for travel; have access to a large pool of potential contacts.

**5. Promotion strategies.** An optimal promotion strategy is designed not only to sell the specific travel product but also to sell the agency's unique brand of service. Promotions are the means of making potential customers aware that the agency is available, helpful, and free of charge. The strategy should be designed to appeal specifically to the more profitable segments.

An aggressive promotion strategy is necessary in inverse proportion to the length of time the agency has been operating and the number of contacts it has. The fledgling agency with no contacts is forced to rely on promotion strategy as the only means of cultivating a clientele.

*Types of promotions* can vary widely. Word of mouth, of course, is the most reliable and successful method and the least expensive. Control of this valuable tool is, unfortunately, out of the agency's hands.

The desirability and effectiveness of promotions are questioned by many agencies. Agencies that do little or no advertising usually have been in business long enough to develop a stable clientele.

The following types of promotions, however, are used successfully by a number of agencies.

a. *Newspaper advertising* is usually limited to the travel section of the newspaper and often promotes a specific tour package.
b. *Yellow Pages advertising* has proved invaluable for many agencies, particularly those just starting out. It is an excellent way to develop cold contacts.
c. *Radio advertising* is sometimes used to promote a special tour package or to promote a contest.
d. *Direct mail promotions* have become more popular in recent years. Newsletters full of lavish descriptions of exotic places are sent to present and potential clients.
e. *Travel parties* are also useful. The agency throws a free "theme" party such as a luau and invites all of its clients. Travel films are usually shown at such events to tickle the customer's travel fantasies.

## MARKET RESEARCH

**1. Evaluating a potential market.** Our market research is focused on the selection of a location for our business. There must be market development potential. The town or community chosen is therefore a crucial factor in the success of the agency. A location will be examined against a set of criteria covering the community, competition, and future customers.

### a. Evaluating the town and community:

Carefully analyze the demographic makeup of the area. Check income, age groups, and professions to find the number of people in the target customer segment.

Evaluate possible sources of travel demand: university, schools, industry. Is there a dominant organization with which to ally?

Evaluate accessibility of travel: near an airport? trains?

Evaluate economic characteristics. Is there a rapidly growing business sector whose business can be captured? Is the town's economy expanding or contracting? The new business growth will be a good indicator of growth potential for our market.

### b. Evaluating the competition:

Does the competition have more business than it can handle?

Are the competing agencies "Mom and Pop" outfits that are being run lackadaisically?

Check the competing agencies' advertising and promotion strategies. Are they in the Yellow Pages?

Are they serving their customers well?

Are their locations convenient?

How effectively have they saturated the market?

How long have they been in existence?

Find out prices, market shares, services offered, size of sales force.

### c. Evaluating potential customers:

Identify traffic patterns within the community, and find a location that will attract walk-in traffic.

Check on specialized travel requirements in the community.

Is the consumer purchasing behavior stable or fluctuating?

What amounts of business can be expected from groups, vacations, businesses? What is the development potential in these areas?

**2. The create versus buy decision.** The market can be entered by creating an agency or buying out an existing one. An existing agency has the advantage of established, developed contacts, but it also locks us into an already established reputation and image and perhaps even a dying situation.

These areas must be examined if we decide to buy into an existing business:

Net worth, income potential, growth potential.

The agency's types of contacts and customers.

Goodwill, physical assets, momentum.

Who are the customers, and why do they come to this agency?

Breakdown of business sources: walk-ins, vacations, tours, business.

Volume linked to previous owner's skills, reputation, contacts?

What is the agency's reputation in the industry and in the community?

Evaluate location of agency for future growth trends.

Determine why the present owner wants to sell.

Evaluate the development potential of the agency as well as the current sales level.

## THE MARKETING PLAN

Our marketing plan will focus on four elements that we have identified as critical to the success of our agency:

a. *Differentiation:* Delivering the service in a way different from that of similar agencies by emphasizing *service* and *convenience.*

b. *Promotion:* Creating the image that the product is better than, or different from, its competitors.

c. *Location:* Establishing the agency in an economically healthy community and in a visible, convenient location.

d. *Service:* Ensuring a knowledgeable, friendly agent at the point of sale.

The marketing strategy is designed to create differentiation through promotion, location, and a carefully developed personal selling strategy and to reach target customers through promotion, contacts, and location. Since the product is a standard one, differentiation is the key. By packaging the product differently with a different image, we can achieve a "brand" identity and compete effectively for the customer's business.

**1. Location.** We will search for an optimum location in the Sun Belt region of the Southeast because that area is growing at a fast rate and its people are becoming increasingly cosmopolitan and well traveled. Within the area we will select a community that affords very good market development potential, preferably near an educational institution or a major business area.

Location within the city or community is crucial. It must be both convenient and visible. A location in a well-populated business area will bring important walk-in traffic from potential high-volume customers, help introduce the new agency to new clients, and establish the agency's reputation as accessible and convenient.

**2. Personal selling strategy.** The personal selling strategy is designed to develop and keep a loyal clientele. Our unique package of the travel service will center on service, knowledge, and friendliness to convince the customer that we are better than our competitors.

Our sales agents will be very knowledgeable in all areas of the travel business. We plan to send them to seminars and agent schools whenever possible to ensure that they are well versed in the complex changing rules and regulations of the industry. The agent with the latest information usually can give the best price on a travel package. Since our product is actually information, we consider it most important to be fast, efficient, and accurate.

At the point of sale, we insist that our agents be pleasant and friendly. We particularly value politeness, patience, and friendliness because these are necessary to win and keep customers. Since we feel that an important part of the product we sell is us, we must always present the most pleasant view to the public and maintain high product quality.

**3. Target customers.**  Our promotion package is designed to develop long-term relationships with target customers: the affluent who regularly travel and business and professional people who will give us steady business volume as well as seasonal vacation business. These people are very useful in developing contacts among their friends, and their demand will not fluctuate widely with changing economic conditions.

**4. Promotion strategy.**  Advertising is very important at first to establish the agency's reputation, image, and name. Our advertising will convey the image of a knowledgeable, efficient, and energetic agency. Its tone will be pleasant, relaxed, in good taste, and not commercial or hard sell. It will be directed to target customers first and the general public second.

The name of our agency, New Horizons, implies adventure, the future, and newness, and it has good advertising value.

The advertising budget will be $200 a month the first year and will gradually decrease over the next four years as we rely more heavily on contacts for new business.

We will use a newsletter to promote travel ideas to our clients and to encourage a sense of service to the clientele, and we will immediately begin to develop a mailing list.

A large Yellow Pages advertisement is a crucial component of our plan to develop new business.

We may use travel parties in years 4 and 5 after we are well established.

**Promotion budget**

| Year | 1 | 2 | 3 | 4 | 5 |
|---|---|---|---|---|---|
| Newspaper | $1,100 | $ 900 | $ 600 | | |
| Radio | 700 | 500 | 100 | | |
| Yellow Pages | 600 | 600 | 600 | $600 | $600 |
| Direct mail | | | 100 | 100 | 100 |
| Travel parties | | | | 100 | 100 |
| Total | $2,400 | $2,000 | $1,400 | $800 | $800 |

**5. Product strategy.**  Our product strategy is designed to promote the high-profit travel items when possible. We will carefully cultivate the business travel to ensure a steady demand level. We will also promote and specialize in group tours for maximum profit and will market ourselves as "the place for groups" by year 2. By year 3, we plan to begin putting together our own group tours and going into the wholesale end of the business. This will happen only after we are satisfactorily established in the retail trade and have a good financial position.

## 6. Sales forecast.

**Year 1**

| Month | Income source | | | Total |
|---|---|---|---|---|
| | Business | Vacation | Groups/tours | |
| 1 | $ 2,500 | $ 1,500 | | $ 4,000 |
| 2 | 3,800 | 2,200 | | 6,000 |
| 3 | 5,700 | 3,300 | | 9,000 |
| 4 | 8,200 | 4,800 | | 13,000 |
| 5 | 11,600 | 5,400 | $ 1,000 | 18,000 |
| 6 | 13,500 | 8,500 | 3,000 | 25,000 |
| 7 | 16,000 | 9,000 | 5,000 | 30,000 |
| 8 | 19,900 | 11,100 | 6,000 | 37,000 |
| 9 | 24,300 | 12,700 | 8,000 | 45,000 |
| 10 | 27,000 | 15,000 | 8,000 | 50,000 |
| 11 | 32,400 | 18,600 | 9,000 | 60,000 |
| 12 | 33,000 | 22,000 | 10,000 | 70,000 |
| Total | $202,900 | $114,100 | $50,000 | $367,000 |

Note: The percentage of income from each product category will change as the agency becomes more established.

**Years 1 and 2**

| Business | 54% | Business | 50% |
|---|---|---|---|
| Vacations | 30 | Vacations | 27 |
| Groups/tours | 16 | Groups/tours | 23 |

Note: Group tours, the highest profit item at 11 percent commission, will contribute an increasing share of gross sales, commissions, and net profit.

**Years 1–5**

| Year | Gross sales | Commission income |
|---|---|---|
| 1 | $ 367,000 | $ 27,525 |
| 2 | 700,000 | 52,500 |
| 3 | 1,500,000 | 112,500 |
| 4 | 2,000,000 | 160,000 |
| 5 | 2,500,000 | 212,500 |

Years 1–3, commissions at average of 7.5 percent of sales.
Year 4, commissions at 8 percent of sales.
Year 5, commissions at 8.5 percent of sales resulting from increased groups/tours at 11 percent commission rate.

## FINANCIAL ISSUES

### 1. Expense schedule.

| | |
|---|---:|
| Start-up costs | |
| Capitalized: | |
|   Leasehold improvements for office ..... | $3,000 |
|   Electricity and phone installation ....... | 300 |
|   Incorporation legal fees .............. | 350 |
|   Licenses ........................... | 400 |
|   Equipment: Typewriters ............. | 600 |
| | 4,650 |

| | | |
|---|---:|---:|
| Other: | | |
|   Printing costs ...................... | $ 200 | |
|   Insurance .......................... | 1,000 | |
|   Introductory advertising ............. | 600 | |
|   Supplies ........................... | 400 | |
| | 2,200 | |
|     Total .......................... | | $6,850 |

| Monthly overhead costs | |
|---|---:|
| Rent ..................... | $ 600 |
| Equipment rental .......... | 175 |
| Salaries ................. | 2,000 |
| Advertising .............. | 200 |
| Utilities .................. | 150 |
| Phone ................... | 120 |
| Legal/CPA ............... | 75 |
| Postage and supplies ..... | 10 |
| Miscellaneous ........... | 65 |
| Interest ................. | 400* |
| | $4,400 |

*On $5,000 note at 8 percent interest.

### 2. Pro forma profit and loss.

| Year | 1 | 2 | 3 | 4 | 5 |
|---|---:|---:|---:|---:|---:|
| Gross sales ............... | $ 367,000 | $700,000 | $1,500,000 | $2,000,000 | $2,500,000 |
| Due to carriers ............. | (339,475) | (647,500) | (1,387,500) | (1,840,000) | (2,287,500) |
| Commission income ........ | 27,525 | 52,500 | 112,500 | 160,000 | 212,500 |
| Operating expenses ........ | (52,800) | (52,800) | (61,000) | (69,000) | (78,800) |
| Net income/loss ........... | (25,275) | (300) | (51,500) | 91,000 | 133,700 |
| Expenses/start-up costs ..... | (2,200) | | | | |
| First-year loss .............. | (27,475) | | | | |
| Tax ...................... | (6,044.5) | (66) | (24,720) | (43,680) | (64,176) |
| Profit/loss after tax ......... | $(21,430.5) | $ (233) | $ 24,720* | $ 47,320 | $ 69,524 |

*Operating losses in the first two years will be carried forward to offset taxes in the third year.

## 3. Balance sheet.

### Beginning of Year 1

#### Assets

| | | |
|---|---:|---:|
| Current assets: | | |
| Cash .................................... | $31,050 | |
| Prepaid insurance ...................... | 1,000 | |
| Prepaid expenses ...................... | 1,200 | |
| Total current assets ............... | | $33,250 |
| Other assets: | | |
| Incorporation and licenses ............. | $   750 | |
| Leasehold improvements ............... | 3,300 | |
| Typewriters ............................ | 600 | |
| Total other assets ................ | | 4,650 |
| Total assets ............................. | | $37,900 |

#### Liabilities and Owners' Equity

| | | |
|---|---:|---:|
| Liabilities: | | |
| Three-year note payable, bank .......... | $ 5,000 | |
| Four-year note payable, grandfather ..... | 5,000 | |
| Total liabilities ................... | | $10,000 |
| Owners' equity: | | |
| Founder Wade ......................... | 9,300 | |
| Founder Wolfe ........................ | 9,300 | |
| Investor Y ............................ | 9,300 | |
| Total owners' equity .............. | | 27,900 |
| Total liabilities and owners' equity ......... | | $37,900 |

## 4. Cash flow: Year 1.

| | Month | | | | | |
|---|---:|---:|---:|---:|---:|---:|
| | 1 | 2 | 3 | 4 | 5 | 6 |
| Sales ..................................... | $ 4,000 | $ 6,000 | $ 9,000 | $13,000 | $18,000 | $25,000 |
| Commissions earned but not received* ..... | 300 | 450 | 675 | 975 | 1,350 | 1,875 |
| Expenses ................................ | 4,400 | 4,400 | 4,400 | 4,400 | 4,400 | 4,400 |
| Over/short ............................... | (4,400) | (4,400) | (4,400) | (4,400) | (4,400) | (4,400) |
| Cumulative credit needed ................. | 11,250† | 15,650 | 20,050 | 24,450 | 28,850 | 33,250 |

| | Month | | | | | |
|---|---:|---:|---:|---:|---:|---:|
| | 7 | 8 | 9 | 10 | 11 | 12 |
| Sales ..................................... | $25,000 | $30,000 | $45,000 | $50,000 | $60,000 | $70,000 |
| Commissions earned ..................... | 2,250 | 2,775 | 3,375 | 3,750 | 4,500 | 5,250 |
| Expenses ................................ | 4,400 | 4,400 | 4,400 | 4,400 | 4,400 | 4,400 |
| Over/short ............................... | (2,150) | (1,625) | (1,025) | (650) | 100 | 850 |
| First six months' commissions ........................... | 5,625 | | | | | |
| Cumulative credit needed ................. | 29,775 | 31,400 | 32,425 | 33,075 | 32,975 | 32,125 |

*The Air Traffic Conference of America withholds commissions earned for the first six months while it examines your financial structure. At the end of this time, if the conference is assured that you are solvent and legitimate, it will license you and send you a check for the commissions earned.
†Cash needed for start-up costs: $6,850.

## RETURN ON INVESTMENT

The long-term growth opportunities of this plan afford the investor a very high return on investment. For an initial investment of only $9,300, the investor obtains a one-third interest in the future earnings and growth of the agency. Using the five-year planning horizon, here is a calculation of the present value of the one-third interest in the agency's earnings, using a 40 percent return rate.

| Year | Agency earnings | One-third interest × | Present value factor at 40 percent |
|------|-----------------|----------------------|------------------------------------|
| 1    |                 |                      |                                    |
| 2    |                 |                      |                                    |
| 3    | $24,700         | $ 8,150 ×            | 0.364 = $ 2,966                    |
| 4    | 43,300          | 14,289 ×             | 0.260 = 3,715                      |
| 5    | 69,500          | 22,900 ×             | 0.186 = 4,259                      |
|      |                 |                      | $10,940                            |

These earnings will be reinvested in the business, of course, instead of being distributed, but the calculations do give a good indication of the growth and profitability potential of the business and what the investor's original investment will be worth in only five years.

## ORGANIZATION

**1. General organization.** *The two founders* have divided responsibilities as follows: Wolfe will be in charge of all product-related matters, employee training, hiring and firing, and operating systems. Wade will be responsible for all financial matters, marketing, advertising, taxes, and general administration. The founders are a talented and cohesive team blending practical experience with technical know-how.

*Employees* will be hired in accordance with the following schedule, depending on the gross sales volume.

*The board of directors* will be composed of major investors and respected, experienced people in the field and in business.

**2. Employee policy.** We consider good people to be one of the secrets of success in the travel service business, and we will pay more to have them.

Our requirements for employees:

1. Experience working in an agency in the town.
2. Contacts in the town and community.
3. Good motivation and willingness to work.
4. Participation in agent training schools when necessary.
5. Willingness to go on agency- or carrier-sponsored trips to develop knowledge of the product.

We estimate that we can get a good person fulfilling these requirements for $700 a month, or $8,400 a year.

Our hiring policy will be on the basis of gross sales with an emphasis on high productivity:

| Gross sales* | Average agency employs | Our agency employs |
| --- | --- | --- |
| $ 500,000 | 4 people | 3 people |
| 700,000 | 6 | 4 |
| 1,000,000 | 7 | 6 |
| 2,000,000 | 11 | 8 |

*This information is form *Travel Weekly*, March 9, 1977, the Harris Survey of Travel Agencies.

Our hiring timetable will be:

Year 1: The two founders and one employee.
Year 2: One additional employee.
Year 3: Two additional employees.
Year 4: One additional employee.
Year 5: As needed.

We will use part-time help to cover peak demand periods.

# Case 8

# Hanover-Bates Chemical Corporation

James Sprague, newly appointed North East district sales manager for the Hanover-Bates Chemical Corporation, leaned back in his chair as the door to his office slammed shut. "Great beginning," he thought. "Three days in my new job, and the district's most experienced sales representative is threatening to quit."

On the previous night, James Sprague, Hank Carver (the district's most experienced sales representative), and John Follet, another senior member of the district sales staff, had met for dinner at Jim's suggestion. During dinner, Jim had mentioned that one of his top priorities would be to conduct a sales and profit analysis of the district's business in order to identify opportunities to improve the district's profit performance. Jim had stated that he was confident that the analysis would indicate opportunities to reallocate district sales efforts in a manner that would increase profits. As Jim had indicated during the conversation, "My experience in analyzing district sales performance data for the national sales manager has convinced me that any district's allocation of sales effort to products and customer categories can be improved." Both Carver and Follet had nodded as Jim discussed his plans.

---

This case was prepared by Professor Robert E. Witt, The University of Texas, Austin. The case is intended to serve as a basis for class discussion rather than to illustrate effective or ineffective management.

Hank Carver was waiting when Jim arrived at the district sales office the next morning. It soon became apparent that Carver was very upset by what he perceived as Jim's criticism of how he and the other district sales representatives were doing their jobs—and more particularly, how they were allocating their time in terms of customers and products. As he concluded his heated comments, Carver had said:

This company has made it darned clear that 34 years of experience don't count for anything . . . and now someone with not much more than two years of selling experience and two years of pushing paper for the national sales manager at corporate headquarters tells me I'm not doing my job. . . . Maybe it's time for me to look for a new job . . . and since Trumbull Chemical [Hanover-Bate's major competitor] is hiring, maybe that's where I should start looking . . . and I'm not the only one who feels this way.

As Jim reflected on the scene that had just occurred, he wondered what he should do. It had been made clear to him when he had been promoted to manager of the North East sales district that one of his top priorities should be improvement of the district's profit performance. As the national sales manager had said, "The North East sales district may rank third in dollar sales, but it's our worst district in terms of profit performance."

Prior to assuming his new position, Jim had assembled the data presented in Exhibits 1 through 6 to assist him in analyzing district sales and profits. The data

**Exhibit 1 ☐ Hanover-Bates Chemical Corporation—summary income statements, 1975–1979**

|  | 1975 | 1976 | 1977 | 1978 | 1979 |
|---|---|---|---|---|---|
| Sales | $19,890,000 | $21,710,000 | $19,060,000 | $21,980,000 | $23,890,000 |
| Production expenses | 11,934,000 | 13,497,000 | 12,198,000 | 13,612,000 | 14,563,000 |
| Gross profit | 7,956,000 | 8,213,000 | 6,862,000 | 8,368,000 | 9,327,000 |
| Administrative expenses | 2,606,000 | 2,887,000 | 2,792,000 | 2,925,000 | 3,106,000 |
| Selling expenses | 2,024,000 | 2,241,000 | 2,134,000 | 2,274,000 | 2,399,000 |
| Pretax profit | 3,326,000 | 3,085,000 | 1,936,000 | 3,169,000 | 3,822,000 |
| Taxes | 1,512,000 | 1,388,000 | 790,000 | 1,426,000 | 1,718,000 |
| Net profit | $ 1,814,000 | $ 1,697,000 | $ 1,146,000 | $ 1,743,000 | $ 2,104,000 |

**Exhibit 2 ☐ District sales quota and gross profit quota performance, 1979**

| District | No. of sales reps | Sales quota | Sales— actual | Gross profit quota* | Gross profit— actual |
|---|---|---|---|---|---|
| 1 | 7 | $ 3,880,000 | $ 3,906,000 | $1,552,000 | $1,589,000 |
| 2 | 6 | 3,750,000 | 3,740,000 | 1,500,000 | 1,529,000 |
| 3 | 6 | 3,650,000 | 3,406,000 | 1,460,000 | 1,239,000 |
| 4 | 6 | 3,370,000 | 3,318,000 | 1,348,000 | 1,295,000 |
| 5 | 5 | 3,300,000 | 3,210,000 | 1,320,000 | 1,186,000 |
| 6 | 5 | 3,130,000 | 3,205,000 | 1,252,000 | 1,179,000 |
| 7 | 5 | 2,720,000 | 3,105,000 | 1,088,000 | 1,310,000 |
|  |  | $23,800,000 | $23,890,000 | $9,520,000 | $9,327,000 |

*District gross profit quotas were developed by the national sales manager in consultation with the district managers and took into account price competition in the respective districts.

had been compiled from records maintained in the national sales manager's office. Although he believed that the data would provide a sound basis for a preliminary analysis of district sales and profit performance, Jim had recognized that additional data would probably have to be collected when he arrived in the North East district (District 3).

**Exhibit 3** □ **District selling expenses, 1979**

| District | Sales reps' salaries* | Sales commission | Sales reps' expenses | District office | District manager's salary | District manager's expenses | Sales support | Total selling expenses |
|---|---|---|---|---|---|---|---|---|
| 1 | $177,100 | $19,426 | $56,280 | $21,150 | $33,500 | $11,460 | $69,500 | $ 388,416 |
| 2 | 143,220 | 18,700 | 50,760 | 21,312 | 34,000 | 12,034 | 71,320 | 351,346 |
| 3 | 157,380 | 17,030 | 54,436 | 22,123 | 35,000† | 12,382 | 70,010 | 368,529 |
| 4 | 150,480 | 16,590 | 49,104 | 22,004 | 32,500 | 11,005 | 66,470 | 348,153 |
| 5 | 125,950 | 16,050 | 42,720 | 21,115 | 33,000 | 11,123 | 76,600 | 326,558 |
| 6 | 124,850 | 16,265 | 41,520 | 20,992 | 33,500 | 11,428 | 67,100 | 315,655 |
| 7 | 114,830 | 17,530 | 44,700 | 22,485 | 31,500 | 11,643 | 58,750 | 300,258 |
| | | | | | | | | $2,398,915 |

*Includes cost of fringe benefit program, which was 10 percent of base salary.
†Salary of Jim Sprague's predecessor.

**Exhibit 4** □ **District contribution to corporate administrative expense and profit, 1979**

| District | Sales | Gross profit | Selling expenses | Contribution to administrative expense and profit |
|---|---|---|---|---|
| 1 | $ 3,906,000 | $1,589,000 | $ 388,416 | $1,200,544 |
| 2 | 3,740,000 | 1,529,000 | 351,346 | 1,177,654 |
| 3 | 3,406,000 | 1,239,000 | 368,529 | 870,471 |
| 4 | 3,318,000 | 1,295,000 | 348,153 | 946,847 |
| 5 | 3,210,000 | 1,186,000 | 326,558 | 859,442 |
| 6 | 3,205,000 | 1,179,000 | 315,376 | 863,624 |
| 7 | 3,105,000 | 1,310,000 | 300,258 | 1,009,742 |
| | $23,890,000 | $9,327,000 | $2,398,636 | $6,928,324 |

**Exhibit 5** □ **North East (District 3) and North Central (District 7) sales and gross profit performance by account category, 1979**

| District | A account | B account | C account | Total |
|---|---|---|---|---|
| Sales by account category | | | | |
| North East | $915,000 | $1,681,000 | $810,000 | $3,406,000 |
| North Central | 751,000 | 1,702,000 | 652,000 | 3,105,000 |
| Gross profit by account category | | | | |
| North East | $356,000 | $623,000 | $260,000 | $1,239,000 |
| North Central | 330,000 | 725,000 | 255,000 | 1,310,000 |

**Exhibit 6** □ **Potential accounts, active accounts, and account call coverage: North East and North Central Districts, 1979**

| District | Potential accounts (A) | (B) | (C) | Active accounts (A) | (B) | (C) | Account coverage (total calls) (A) | (B) | (C) |
|---|---|---|---|---|---|---|---|---|---|
| North East | 90 | 381 | 635 | 53 | 210 | 313 | 1,297 | 3,051 | 2,118 |
| North Central | 60 | 286 | 499 | 42 | 182 | 218 | 1,030 | 2,618 | 1,299 |

In response to the national sales manager's comment about the North East district's poor profit performance, Jim had been particularly interested in how the district had performed on its gross profit quota. He knew that district gross profit quotas were assigned in a manner that took into account variation in price competition. Thus, he felt that poor performance in the gross profit quota area reflected misallocated sales efforts either in terms of customers or the mix of product line items sold. To provide himself with a frame of reference, Jim had also requested data on the North Central sales district (District 7). This district was generally considered to be one of the best, if not the best, in the company. Furthermore, the North Central district sales manager, who was only three years older than Jim, was highly regarded by the national sales manager.

## THE COMPANY AND INDUSTRY

The Hanover-Bates Chemical Corporation was a leading producer of processing chemicals for the chemical plating industry. The company's products were produced in four plants located in Los Angeles, Houston, Chicago, and Newark, New Jersey. The company's production process was, in essence, a mixing operation. Chemicals purchased from a broad range of suppliers were mixed according to a variety of user-based formulas. Company sales in 1979 had reached a new high of $23,890,000, up from $21,980,000 in 1978. Net pretax profit in 1979 had been $3,822,000, up from $3,169,000 in 1978. Hanover-Bates had a strong balance sheet, and the company enjoyed a favorable price-earnings ratio on its stock, which traded on the OTC market.

Although Hanover-Bates did not produce commodity-type chemicals (e.g., sulfuric acid and others), industry customers tended to perceive minimal quality differences among the products produced by Hanover-Bates and its competitors. Given the lack of variation in product quality and the industry-wide practice of limited advertising expenditures, field sales efforts were of major importance in the marketing programs of all firms in the industry.

Hanover-Bates's market consisted of several thousand job shop and captive (i.e., in-house) plating operations. Chemical platers process a wide variety of materials, including industrial fasteners (e.g., screws, rivets, bolts, washers, and others), industrial components (e.g., clamps, casings, couplings, and others), and miscellaneous items (e.g., umbrella frames, eyelets, decorative items, and others). The chemical plating process involves the electrolytic application of metallic coatings such as zinc, cadmium, nickel, brass, and so forth. The degree of required plating precision varies substantially, with some work being primarily decorative, some involving relatively loose standards (e.g., 0.0002 zinc, which means that anything over two ten thousandths of an inch of plate is acceptable), and some involving relatively precise standards (e.g., 0.0003–0.0004 zinc).

Regardless of the degree of plating precision involved, quality control is of critical concern to all chemical platers. Extensive variation in the condition of materials received for plating requires a high level of service from the firms supplying chemicals to platers. This service is normally provided by the sales representatives of the firm(s) supplying the plater with processing chemicals.

Hanover-Bates and the majority of the firms in its industry produced the same line of basic processing chemicals for the chemical plating industry. The line consisted of a trisodium phosphate cleaner (SBX); anesic aldehyde brightening agents for zinc plating (ZBX), cadmium plating (CBX), and nickel plating (NBX); a protective postplating chromate dip (CHX); and a protective burnishing compound (BUX). The company's product line is detailed in the accompanying table.

**Product line data**

| Product | Container size | List price | Gross margin |
|---|---|---|---|
| SBX | 400 lb. drum | $ 80 | $28 |
| ZBX | 50 lb. drum | 76 | 34 |
| CBX | 50 lb. drum | 76 | 34 |
| NBX | 50 lb. drum | 80 | 35 |
| CHX | 100 lb. drum | 220 | 90 |
| BUX | 400 lb. drum | 120 | 44 |

## COMPANY SALES ORGANIZATION

Hanover-Bates's sales organization consisted of 40 sales representatives operating in seven sales districts. Sales representatives' salaries ranged from $14,000 to $24,000, with fringe benefit costs amounting to an additional 10 percent of salary. In addition to their salaries, Hanover-Bates's sales representatives received commissions of one half of 1 percent of their dollar sales volume on all sales up to their sales quotas. The commission on sales in excess of quota was 1 percent.

In 1977, the national sales manager of Hanover-Bates had developed a sales program based on selling the full line of Hanover-Bates products. He believed that if the sales representatives could successfully carry out his program, benefits would accrue to both Hanover-Bates and its customers: (1) sales volume per account would be greater, and selling costs as a percentage of sales would decrease; (2) a Hanover-Bates sales representative could justify spending more time with such an account, thus becoming more knowledgeable about the account's business and better able to provide technical assistance and identify selling opportunities; and (3) full-line sales would strengthen Hanover-Bates's competitive position by reducing the likelihood of account loss to other plating chemical suppliers (a problem that existed in multiple-supplier situations).

The national sales manager's 1977 sales program had also included the following account call frequency guidelines: A accounts (major accounts generating $12,000 or more in yearly sales)—two calls per month; B accounts (medium-sized accounts generating $6,000 to $11,999 in yearly sales)—one all per month; C accounts (small accounts generating less than $6,000 yearly in sales)—one call every two months. The account call frequency guidelines were developed by the national sales manager after discussions with the district managers. The national sales manager had been concerned about the optimum allocation of sales effort to accounts and felt that the guidelines would increase the efficiency of the company's sales force, although not all of the district sales managers agreed with this conclusion.

It was common knowledge in Hanover-Bates's corporate sales office that Jim Sprague's predecessor as North East district sales manager had not been one of the company's better district sales managers. His attitude toward the sales plans and programs of the national sales manager had been one of reluctant compliance rather than acceptance and support. When the national sales manager succeeded in persuading Jim Sprague's predecessor to take early retirement, he had been faced with the lack of an available qualified replacement.

Hank Carver, who most of the sales representatives had assumed would get the district manager job, had been passed over in part because he would be 65 in three years. The national sales manager had not wanted to face the same replacement problem again in three years and had also wanted someone in the position who would be more likely to be responsive to the company's sales plans and policies. The appointment of Jim Sprague as district manager had caused considerable talk, not only in the district but also at corporate headquarters. In fact, the national sales manager had warned Jim that "a lot of people are expecting you to fall on your face. They don't think you have the experience to handle the job, in particular, and to manage and motivate a group of sales representatives most of whom are considerably older and more experienced than you." The national sales manager had concluded by saying, "I think you can handle the job, Jim. I think you can manage those sales reps and improve the district's profit performance, and I'm depending on you to do both."

# Case 9

# Coastal Plastics Company

Mr. Alan Buford, manager of the Coastal Plastics Company, a division of the Arnol Corporation, was considering a directive he had just received from top management of the parent organization. He was told by Arnol management in June 1970 that he was to come up with a specific marketing strategy and plan designed to stop the losses of the division as soon as possible and to provide a base for continued growth in the future.

## COMPANY BACKGROUND

Coastal Plastics, located in the Puget Sound area of the state of Washington, was a plastic pipe extruder serving the Pacific Northwest. The company began operations in the early 1950s, with Buford as one of the original founders. The firm was acquired in 1967 by the Arnol Corporation, a large company in an unrelated field. Sales of the Coastal Plastics Company had grown from $60,000 during its early years to $2 million in 1969, making it the second-largest extruder in the Pacific Northwest. Profits, however, had declined, and the company had operated at a loss for the past year and a half.

The management staff at Coastal Plastics consisted of Mr. Buford, who acted as both general manager and sales manager; Mr. George Timkin, the plant manager; Mr. Alan Britt, the plant engineer; and a plant foreman.

---

This case is produced with the permission of its author, Dr. Stuart U. Rich, professor of marketing and director, Forest Industries Management Center, College of Business Administration, University of Oregon, Eugene, Oregon.

## INDUSTRY BACKGROUND

Thermoplastic pipe was made from four types of plastic resins: polyvinyl chloride (PVC), rubber-modified styrene (styrene), acrylonitrile butadiene styrene (ABS), and polyethylene (poly). The resins differed in chemical and physical characteristics, such as resistance to acids and bases, strength, melting point, and ease of extrusion. These plastic resins were bought from the large national petrochemical suppliers.

Plastic pipe competed with iron, aluminum, and asbestos-cement pipe in the Northwest market. In comparison with the other materials, plastic pipe was considered superior in terms of lower cost, ease of installation and maintenance, and lack of deterioration from environmental influences. Plastic pipe was considered inferior to the other materials in terms of crushability, strength, and melting temperature. Plastic pipe could not be extruded in sizes greater than 10 inches in diameter, and it also had a high degree of thermal expansion that restricted its use in some applications.

A machine called an extruder was used to form plastic pipe by heating the resin to near its melting point, forcing the fluid mass through a die, and then cooling the formed pipe in a water bath. A relatively unsophisticated plant to manufacture plastic pipe could be built for approximately $150,000. In fact, one of the successful competitors in the ABS market in the Northwest, the PJ&J Company, had what was called a "backyard operation" and operated out of a converted garage.

The different resins could all be satisfactorily extruded on the same machine, with the possible exception of PVC, which required a stainless steel die instead of the usual mild steel die. All that was required to change resin type was to change the resin fed into the machine. A die change to make different-size pipe was even simpler. The extruder could be left hot and the pressure relieved so that the die could be changed.

## COASTAL PLASTICS' EXTRUDED PIPE

By 1968, all four thermoplastic resins were being converted by Coastal Plastics into plastic pipe ranging from 1/2 inch to 8 inches in diameter. The final product had pressure ratings from 80 psi to 600 psi. The company's pipe was of standard quality and was comparable to that produced by competing pipe extruders.

In 1969, Coastal Plastics had just completed capital expenditures for new resin-blending and pipe-extrusion equipment that executives described as "the most technically advanced in the industry." By 1970, the company had a plant investment of over $2 million. In view of Coastal's unprofitable operating performance, it was considered doubtful that the Arnol Corporation would agree to additional capital expenditure appropriations for Coastal. Coastal owned and operated four modern pipe-extruding machines as well as three older machines. In spite of the modern production setup, a production problem arose from the firm's inability to maintain adequate control over pipe wall thickness. Pipe production used 7 percent more resin material than was theoretically required to ensure a minimum pipe wall thickness. The plant engineer was in charge of quality control, but due to a substantial workload, he had spent little time on the costly material waste problem.

Since 1965, when corporate management imposed tight limits on finished goods inventories, Coastal Plastics had aimed at minimizing inventories. Rush orders, which frequently could not be filled from inventory, necessitated daily extrusion machine changeovers. A relative cost study conducted in 1970 by the plant engineer showed that Coastal could conceivably hold a much larger finished goods inventory and still not reach the point where costs of holding inventory would exceed machine changeover costs. Coastal Plastics average seven machine changeovers per day, at an average loss to contribution to fixed overhead of $25 per changeover.

## PLASTIC PIPE MARKET SEGMENTS

In July 1970, Coastal Plastics was producing some 200 separate pipe products of varying sizes and resin types to supply 11 market segments. Buford felt that in order to utilize plant capacity to the utmost, Coastal had to reach all of these end-use segments. Coastal's sales volume was highest in water transportation markets for PVC and styrene pipe. The company's total pipe production by resin type (in pounds) for the first six months of 1970 was as follows:

|        |           |
|--------|-----------|
| Poly   | 450,000   |
| PVC    | 3,871,000 |
| ABS    | 769,000   |
| Styrene | 1,032,000 |
| Total  | 6,122,000 |

Arnol Corporation market researchers had concluded that demand for plastic pipe would increase during the next five years in all market segments in the states served by Coastal Plastics, that is, in Oregon, Washington, Idaho, and northern California. A summary analysis of each market segment follows, including 1970 consumption estimates and five-year growth projections for Washington alone and for the four-state region including Washington.

### Agriculture irrigation

In 1970, this segment was the largest-volume plastic pipe market in the Pacific Northwest. Plastic pipe, however, accounted for only 11 percent of all pipe used for agriculture irrigation. Newly developed plastic component systems, particularly plastic component sprinkler irrigation systems, were replacing many open-ditch and metal pipe water transportation systems. Arnol market researchers in describing growth potential for this plastic pipe market, stated that the "pendulum is swinging from metal to plastic pipe as the primary water transportation method." PVC resin pipe was used almost exclusively to supply this segment. Total plastic pipe consumption in Washington in 1970 was 8.25 million pounds. Total for the four-state market area (Washington, Oregon, Idaho, and northern California) was 16.5 million. Estimated growth rate for the next five years for Washington, as well as for the whole region, was 17 percent.

### Private potable water system market

Building codes in 1970 continued to favor copper and aluminium and to exclude plastic pipe from use for home water supply systems. Although public utilities were utilizing PVC plastic pipe for public water systems, plumbing contractors shied away from using polyethylene pipe in private systems. Total plastic pipe consumption for Washington was 145,000 pounds. For the Northwest region, it was 350,000 pounds. No growth was forecast for the next five years.

### Mobile home market

Most ABS plastic pipe sold to this segment was used in plumbing fixtures. Most mobile home manufacturers sought to buy plastic fixtures on a national contract basis. It was a rare occasion when one of these national concerns purchased pipe from a local or regional extruder. Washington plastic pipe consumption was 130,000 pounds; regional consumption was 1.4 million pounds. A 90 percent growth figure was forecast for Washington, and 75 percent for the region.

### Public potable water

Some public water utilities were using PVC plastic pipe for water service lines that connect households to main water distribution lines. Styrene pipe had given way in recent years to the stronger, less brittle, more inert PVC pipe. Washington consumption was slightly over 2 million pounds, and regional consumption over 5 million pounds. A 100 percent growth figure was projected for both the state and the region.

### Industrial market

Plastic pipe applications in processing, material supply, transfer, and waste disposal were severely limited in this segment. According to Mr. Buford, it was due to thermoplastic pipe's sensitivity to steam, sparks, and hot fluids. The most prominent industrial application was in copper mining, with minor applications in pulp and paper manufacturing, food processing, and seawater transfer. Total consumption in Washington was 600,000 pounds; for the region, slightly over 1 million pounds. Growth rate was projected at 45 percent for both the state and the region.

### Turf irrigation market

Turf irrigation included applications such as public and private lawn watering systems. Small-diameter PVC pipe was generally used by this market segment. Consumption in Washington was 3 million pounds; in the region it was 5.9 million. The projected five-year growth rate was 66 percent for Washington and 57 percent for the region.

### Drain waste and vent market

DWV was defined as all plumbing pipe running from and venting sinks, toilets, and drains to the structure drain. ABS pipe accounted for 86 percent to 90 percent of the market, with the remaining amount held by PVC. Plumbing unions had opposed the use of plastic pipe in favor of traditional materials, apparently due to the easy installation of plastic pipe with its resultant labor savings. Yet the unions claimed the traditional steel and iron pipes were superior. Consumption in Washington was slightly over 1 million pounds; regional consumption was 1.75 million. Washington growth was projected at 27 percent; regional growth at 35 percent.

### Conduit

Electric conduit was used primarily to protect and insulate electric power lines and telephone lines, both underground and in the buildings. Competitive materials included the traditional aluminum metals. Major users in this market were large contractors and utilities that bought on a competitive bidding system. Consumption in Washington was 465,000 pounds; regional consumption was 1 million pounds. A 75 percent growth figure was projected for Washington, and 50 percent growth was forecast for the region.

### Sewer and outside drain

This market segment used plastic pipe for connections from house to septic tanks and sewer systems, downspout drainage, water drainage, and septic tank drainage. The primary resins used were styrene and PVC. The major competitive materials were asbestos fibers, cast iron, and vitrified clay; however, they were generally competitive only in the large sizes used in a public sewer system. The FHA had recently approved plastic pipe for rural homes. Washington consumption was 1.4 million pounds, and regional consumption was 2.8 million. A 90 percent growth figure was forecast for Washington, and 78 percent growth was predicted for the region.

### Gas transportation market

Plastic pipe in this segment was used to distribute low-pressure natural gas from major terminals through distribution mains to residences, businesses, and industrial users. Gas companies, which bought the pipe in large lots or on a yearly basis, had tested the plastic pipe and were not entirely pleased with the results. They favored the traditional steel pipe and the new epoxy-coated steel pipe that combined the inherent advantages of both plastic and steel. Washington consumption was 123,000 pounds; regional consumption, 300,000 pounds. The growth projection was marginal.

### Water well service and stock water

Plastic pipe was used in rural areas to bring water from the individual farm wells into the home and to distribute it to outlying farm buildings to water livestock. The primary resins used were PVC and polyethylene. Washington consumption was 400,000 pounds, and regional consumption was 900,000 pounds. Relatively little growth was projected.

The four types of plastic pipe varied in their adaptability to use in the various markets just described. Adaptability depended on the physical attributes of the resin type as well as cost advantages needed for low-grade applications. PVC was the most versatile and was used in all market segments. Poly was suitable for use in all markets except sewer and outside drain, mobile homes, and drain waste and vent. ABS was adaptable for use in 6 of the 11 markets: public potable water, private potable water, turf irrigation, mobile homes, drain waste and vent, and gas transportation. Styrene was used for the most part in sewer and outside drain, drain waste and vent, and conduit markets.

## PROMOTION AND SALES

Coastal Plastics used a limited amount of advertising in promoting its plastic pipe, preferring to rely on personal selling as its main promotional device. In the past, the company had advertised in trade journals and in agriculturally oriented magazines such as *Pacific Farmer*. It also sponsored early-morning farm radio programs on local stations and utilized the usual product information folders and catalogs.

Recently Coastal had used a mailer soliciting inquiries on a "spike sprinkler" coupling for irrigation. The spike sprinkler was a device to position a sprinkler in the field, and it was considered a superior pipe coupling. The company had contracted for exclusive distribution of the coupling to be used with its pipe but did not itself produce the device. Coastal had mailed 1,000 of the product folders and had received 200 inquiries. Mr. Buford was enthusiastic about the response and planned to increase mailer promotion in the future.

The company salesmen were assigned by geographic area, and they called on pipe distributors and large end users in each area. They were responsible for sales of all company products in their respective areas. The three main sales areas were: the Seattle–Puget Sound area, the Portland and eastern Oregon–eastern Washington area, and the southern Oregon–northern California area. Each of these areas was covered by one salesman. In addition, Mr. Buford had a number of working contacts and made visits to major accounts. This was relatively simple because most of the major distributors were located within short distances from the division office.

In addition to the field salesmen, there was one in-house salesman who handled small "drop-in" business, short-notice orders, and customers requiring a quote on an order of pipe. Often a distributor would phone in an order asking for a price quote and delivery at the end user's site the next day. If the company was not capable of meeting a price and delivery schedule, the customer would take his business elsewhere. The company tried its best to provide service on these accounts so that it could maintain plant capacity, even it if meant machine changeovers to produce the order.

Since the salesmen were assigned one to an area, they were responsible for missionary, maintenance, and service selling. They were compensated, according to corporate policy, by straight salary, with no commmissions paid for different product sales. They called on distributors and large end users and were expected to educate distributors on product knowledge and use and to handle field complaints. Often these complaints emanated from a do-it-yourself end user who had not followed the directions for joining pipe sections together correctly. At times, the salesmen tried to stimulate sales by going to the end user and providing tehnical service such as product specification and pipe system design.

## DISTRIBUTION

Coastal sold the majority of its plastic pipe through distributors, with 20 percent of the accounts contributing 75 percent of gross revenue. Only in the case of large end users such as utilities and major contractors did the company try to sell directly. In such cases, the company paid the regular commission to the area distributor only if the distributor managed to learn of the sale and the distributor was of some importance to the company. Marketing terms were 2/10, net 30.

Pipe distributors, who were paid a commission of 5 to 10 percent of sales, performed several major functions: (1) they broke bulk and sold to many retailers in their area; (2) they used the pipe along with many other components in the piping systems that they installed, such as agricultural irrigation systems, plumbing systems, and turf irrigation systems; and (3) they provided financing and inventory service for their customers. Distributors held preparatory inventory in seasonal markets such as agricultural irrigation. In preparation for the seasonal demand, Coastal would deposit "dated" shipments at the distributor's warehouse.

Pipe distributors in most market segments considered price to be the most important factor determining from whom they bought pipe; most distributors agreed that one pipe was as good as another; they considered delivery service to be the next most important factor. They did not feel that technical service offered by the manufacturer was very important in their choice of suppliers. In fact, some distributors were very ambivalent about the usefulness of manufacturers' salesmen. They did not feel that technical service by the manufacturer was very important in the sale of pipe. Some felt that the best thing salesmen could do was stay out of the field. They disliked pipe salesmen "muddying the water" at the end user level and making promises to the end user that the distributor was unable or unwilling to fulfill. Other distributors, however, felt that pipe salesmen could and did help by providing product knowledge to the distributor salesmen. Under no circumstances did any of the distributors favor having pipe salesmen contact the end user.

Distributors generally viewed the price competition within the industry with disfavor. One reason was the lowered profit margin on sales of the pipe. Since distributors usually made a fixed percentage on sales, their income was reduced by lowered prices. Another reason was the concern of the distributor that when he was making a bid on a system including plastic pipe, his competitor might get a more favorable quote on plastic pipe and therefore be able to quote a lower bid. The distributors wanted plastic pipe prices stabilized so that their bids could be based on their own competence and economic situation rather than on the pricing practices of the pipe manufacturers.

Although distributors disliked price competition, they were glad to see that Coastal and other producers had lowered the price to the point where imported pipe was not a major source of market supply. Many were reluctant to handle shipload quantities of imported pipe with its resultant inventory and handling problems. They much preferred a convenient source of supply, which the local producers could provide.

Although some distributors had considered making their own plastic pipe, they did not at the time consider such production attractive. For the time being, they were content to buy pipe from suppliers. Coastal had been a factor in this decision by improving service and by lowering prices.

In view of the continuing poor profit situation of his division, Buford had considered trying to integrate forward and capture the distributor's margin. One of the salesmen had felt that Coastal salesmen could do as good a job selling plastic pipe to end users as the distributors did.

## TRANSPORTATION

Approximately 75 percent of Coastal's annual volume was shipped via common carrier, with the remaining 25 percent being delivered by company-leased trucks or through factory "will call" by customers. Because of competitors' practices, most of Coastal's shipments were either prepaid to Northwest destinations or comparable freight allowances were made from gross sales price when pipe orders were picked up at the plant by customers. Because plastic pipe was so bulky, shipping costs averaged about 15 percent of the selling price. This meant that each competitor had a substantial advantage in selling in his own home market.

## PRICING POLICY

Buford looked over the profit summary report (see Exhibit 1) and wondered whether changes in the present pricing policy might lead to improvements in the profit picture of his division. The present policy of "meeting or beating the price offered by any other supplier" had been initiated in 1968. It was during that year that the Japanese began exporting large quantities of plastic pipe into the Pacific Northwest. Due to lower raw material costs and a suspected dumping policy, they were pricing their products below local suppliers. Even though there were disadvantages in the sales agreements offered by the Japanese (such as order sizes of shipload quantities only), the Japanese were able to capture a significant portion of the market due to their low price.

The effects of the Japanese entry into the Pacific northwest market were immediately felt by Coastal Plastics since the Japanese were marketing PVC—the major resin type produced by Coastal. At that time, Mr. Buford reasoned that the size of the Pacific Northwest market could not accommodate another supplier of plastic pipe. He felt that steps must be taken immediately to drive the Japanese out of the Pacific Northwest.

**Exhibit 1 □ Coastal Plastics Company profit summary report, per pound basis, first six months, 1970**

|  | Poly | PVC | ABS | Styrene |
|---|---|---|---|---|
| Gross sales price ...................... | $0.3625 | $0.2760 | $0.3648 | $0.2762 |
| Less: Discounts, freight, allowances ..... | 0.0710 | 0.0138 | 0.0378 | 0.0377 |
| Net sales price ........................ | 0.2915 | 0.2622 | 0.3270 | 0.2385 |
| Less: Variable cost (raw materials and conversion)* .................... | 0.3050 | 0.2230 | 0.3392 | 0.2110 |
| Direct margin (contribution to fixed cost) .......................... | −0.0135 | 0.0392 | −0.0122 | 0.0275 |
| Less: Fixed cost ...................... | 0.0397 | 0.0375 | 0.0501 | 0.0314 |
| Profit ................................ | −$0.0532 | $0.0017 | −$0.0623 | −$0.0039 |

*For analysis purposes, treat conversion as *changeover costs* only. Other labor costs are included in fixed cost figure.

To achieve this, Coastal adopted its present pricing policy, thus forcing the Japanese to compete on terms other than price, such as speed of delivery, where the Japanese were at a strict disadvantage. Soon after this, other suppliers followed suit. The average price levels gradually eroded from 28 cents per pound down to 26 cents per pound. With the decreased price, the Japanese left the Pacific Northwest market, and Mr. Buford felt that they would not reenter it until the price came back to 28 cents per pound.

In 1969, the Sierra Plastic Pipe plant had burned to the ground. This company had been the major supplier for southern Oregon and northern California. A number of the other suppliers, including Coastal, increased their plant capacity in anticipation of taking over the accounts that they were sure Sierra would lose. To prevent the loss of its accounts, Sierra bought plastic pipe on the open market and was thus able to maintain its customers while its plant was being rebuilt. Because Sierra was able to remain in business and because the growth of the Pacific Northwest market was not up to expectations, a considerable overcapacity on the part of all suppliers soon developed in the Pacific northwest. In 1970, this overcapacity was estimated at 30 to 40 percent, but some suppliers were continuing expansion.

Because of the overcapacity and the desire on the part of executives to maintain market share, Coastal had continued its present pricing policy. It was reasoned by Mr. Buford that a reduction in price would increase market share, which would increase production and narrow the gap between plant capacity and the production level, thus minimizing fixed cost per unit.

In evaluating the present pricing policy, Mr. Buford came to two conclusions. First, the profit picture for his division was most likely quite similar to that of the other regional suppliers. Secondly, while the distributors enjoyed the low price that was resulting from the fierce price competition, they were unhappy with the volatility of the price levels that were also generated.

## COMPETITION

Domestic competition in Coastal's marketing area came from six regional manufacturers and five to eight major national producers. The number of national producers varied because some of them moved in and out of the Northwest market, depending on economic conditions. The regional manufacturers had about 75 percent of the market, while the larger national firms and a few import firms controlled the rest. Three of the regional firms controlled 60 percent of the Northwest market. Sierra Plastics was a leader, although Coastal and Tamarack Pipe closely followed. The three companies produced essentially the same products.

Tamarack Pipe was within 50 miles of Coastal Plastic's plant and was a strong competitor in the Portland, Oregon, market and the Puget Sound market. Due to its location in southern Oregon, Sierra Plastics had a strong competitive position in the southern Oregon–northern California market due to its lower transportation cost in this area compared with Coastal and Tamarack.

Coastal Plastics had tried to differentiate its product in the past but had met with limited success. In an attempt at differentiation, Coastal had changed the color of its PVC pipe from gray to white. Other competitors, especially the nationals, had made some progress in differentiating their products. Babbit Corporation, a national supplier of pipe and piping systems to industry, had added plastic pipe to its product line and advertised in such nationwide periodicals as *Chemical Engi-*

*neering.* Babbit was very strong in the industrial segment of the market. Cable Company had distinguished its pipe by application to sump pump installations and had a virtual monopoly in this specialized application. PJ&J in northern California was the chief supplier of ABS pipe in the Pacific Northwest, primarily by being the lowest marketer. For example, Coastal was able to buy PJ&J pipe and resell it at less cost than Coastal could produce comparable pipe.

In recent months, Coastal salesmen had reported that Tamarack had begun to concentrate more on the agricultural irrigation market, while Sierra was concentrating on being the primary supplier of plastic pipe for conduit. Even though this market was small, it was anticipated to mushroom when the housing market resumed its growth. The large national firms had concentrated on the mobile home industry and appeared to have the greatest number of manufacturers, since contracts are negotiated on a countrywide basis.

The large national manufacturers were either owned by or affiliated with national petrochemical companies. These companies usually adjusted to the prevailing market conditions and were a stabilizing influence in the market.

The competitive conditions which had prevailed in the Northwest had depressed the financial conditions of some of the smaller independent firms, and it was not known how much longer they could continue operations. The larger independent firms, although experiencing losses, were as well financed as Coastal and were still battling for increased market share.

## CONCLUSION

Mr. Buford realized that a number of changes were needed in many parts of his company's marketing program. He saw that some of these changes were interrelated; for example, decisions on pricing strategy might have an important impact on product policy, and vice versa. Certain decisions had to be made very soon if the company's profit position were to be improved, whereas other decisions could be postponed for a while.

Mr. Buford felt that his planning task was made more difficult by the limited size of the management staff in his division. Although the parent corporation provided help in market research and some coaching in general planning procedures, the actual planning and strategy determination were Mr. Buford's responsibility. Because of the need to keep division overhead expenses down to a minimum, Buford knew that no additional management staff could be hired at the present time.

As he walked into his office, pondering what to do first in the way of planning, his phone rang and the in-house salesman asked him to OK a price quote on a drop shipment for the next day. Mr. Buford OK'd the quote and then sat down, muttering, "How can I find time to plan for the months and years ahead when daily operating problems demand so much of my time?"

# Case 10

# Big Sky of Montana, Inc.

## INTRODUCTION

Karen Tracy could feel the pressure on her as she sat at her desk late that April afternoon. Two weeks from today she would be called on to present her recommendations concerning next year's winter season pricing policies for big Sky of Montana, Inc.—room rates for the resort's accommodation facilities as well as decisions in the skiing and food services areas. The presentation would be made to a top-management team from the parent company, Boyne USA, which operated out of Michigan.

"As sales and public relations manager, Karen, your accuracy in decision making is extremely important," her boss had said in his usual tone. "Because we spend most of our time in Michigan, we'll need a well-based and involved opinion."

"It'll be the shortest two weeks of my life," she thought.

## BACKGROUND: BIG SKY AND BOYNE USA

Big Sky of Montana, Inc., was a medium-sized destination resort located in southwestern Montana, 45 miles south of Bozeman and 43 miles north of the west entrance to Yellowstone National Park.[1] Big Sky was conceived in the early 1970s and had begun operation in November 1974.

The 11,000-acre, 2,000-bed resort was separated into two main areas: Meadow and Mountain villages. Meadow Village (elevation 6,300 feet) was located two miles east of the resort's main entrance on U.S. 191 and seven miles from the ski area. Meadow Village had an 800-bed capacity in the form of four condominium complexes (ranging from studios to three-bedroom units) and a 40-room hostel for economy lodging. Additional facilities included an 18-hole golf course, six tennis courts, a restaurant, a post office, a convention center with meeting space for up to 200 people, and a small lodge serving as a pro shop for the golf course in the summer and cross-country skiing in the winter.

Mountain Village (elevation 7,500 feet) was the center of winter activity, located at the base of the ski area. In this complex was the 204-room Huntley Lodge, offering hotel accommodations, three condominium complexes (unit size ranged from studio to three-bedroom), and an 88-room hostel, for a total of 1,200 beds. The Mountain Mall was located here, next to the Huntley Lodge and within a five-minute walk of two of the three condominium complexes in Mountain Village. It housed ticket sales, an equipment rental shop, a skier's cafeteria, two large meet-

This case was prepared by Anne Senausky and Professor James E. Nelson, University of Colorado at Denver. Copyright © 1978 by the Endowment and Research Foundation at Montana State University.

[1]Destination resorts were characterized by on-the-hill lodging and eating facilities, a national market, and national advertising.

ing rooms with a maximum occupancy of 700 persons (regularly used as sack lunch areas for skiers), two offices, a ski school desk, and a ski patrol room, all of which were operated by Boyne. Also in this building were a delicatessen, a drug-store/gift shop, a sporting goods store/rental shop, a restaurant, an outdoor cloth-ing store, a jewelry shop, a T-shirt shop, two bars, and a child day-care center. Each of these independent operations held a lease that was due to expire in one to three years.

The closest airport to Big Sky was located just outside Bozeman. It was served by Northwest Orient and Frontier Airlines with connections to other major airlines out of Denver and Salt Lake City. Greyhound and Amtrak also operated bus and train service into Bozeman. Yellowstone Park Lines provided Big Sky with three buses daily to and from the airport and Bozeman bus station (the cost was $4.40 one-way, $8.40 round trip) as well as an hourly shuttle around the two Big Sky villages. Avis, Hertz, National, and Budget offered rent-a-car service in Boze-man with a drop-off service available at Big Sky.

In July 1976, Boyne USA, a privately owned, Michigan-based operation, pur-chased the Huntley Lodge, Mountain Mall, ski lifts and terrain, golf course, and tennis courts for approximately $8 million. The company subsequently invested an additional $3 million in Big Sky. Boyne also owned and operated four Michigan re-sort ski areas.

Big Sky's top management consisted of a lodge manager (in charge of oper-ations within the Huntley Lodge), a sales and public relations manager (Karen), a food and beverage manager, and an area manager (overseeing operations exter-nal to the Lodge, including the Mall and all recreational facilities). These four posi-tions were occupied by persons trained with the parent company; a fifth manager, the comptroller, had worked for pre-Boyne ownership.

Business figures were reported to the company's home office on a daily ba-sis, and major decisions concerning Big Sky operations were discussed and ap-proved by "Michigan." Boyne's top management visited Big Sky an average of five times annually, and all major decisions, such as pricing and advertising, were ap-proved by the parent for all operations.

## THE SKIING

Big Sky's winter season usually began in late November and continued until the middle of April, with a yearly snowfall of approximately 450 inches. The area had 18 slopes between elevations of 7,500 and 9,900 feet. The terrain breakdown was as follows: 25 percent novice, 55 percent intermediate, and 20 percent ad-vanced. (Although opinions varied, industry guidelines recommended a terrain breakdown of 20 percent, 60 percent, and 20 percent for novice, intermediate, and advanced skiers, respectively.) The longest run was approximately three miles in length; the temperatures (highs) ranged from 15 to 30 degrees Fahrenheit through-out the season.

Lift facilities at Big Sky included two double chair lifts, a triple chair, and a four-passenger gondola. Lift capacity was estimated at 4,000 skiers per day. This figure was considered adequate by the area manager, at least until the 1980–81 season.

Karen felt that the facilities, snow conditions, and grooming compared favor-ably with those of other destination resorts of the Rockies. "In fact, our only real drawback right now," she thought, "is our position in the national market. We need more skiers who are sold on Big Sky. And that is in the making."

## THE CONSUMERS

Karen knew from previous dealings that Big Sky, like most destination areas, attracted three distinct skier segments: local day skiers (living within driving distance and not utilizing lodging in the area); individual destination skiers (living out of state and using accommodations in the Big Sky area); and groups of destination skiers (clubs, professional organization, etc.).

The first category typically comprised Montana residents, with a relatively small number from Wyoming and Idaho. (Distances from selected population centers to Big Sky are presented in Exhibit 1.) A 1973 study of four Montana ski areas, performed by the Advertising Unit of the Montana Department of Highways, characterized Montana skiers as:

1. In their early 20s and males (60 percent).
2. Living within 75 miles of a ski area.
3. From a household with two skiers in it.
4. Averaging $13,000 in household income.

**Exhibit 1**

**Proximity of population centers to Big Sky**

| City | Distance from Big Sky (miles) | Population (U.S. 1970 census) |
|---|---|---|
| Bozeman, Montana | 45 | 18,670 |
| Butte, Montana | 126 | 23,368 |
| Helena, Montana | 144 | 22,730 |
| Billings, Montana | 174 | 61,581 |
| Great Falls, Montana | 225 | 60,091 |
| Missoula, Montana | 243 | 29,497 |
| Pocatello, Idaho | 186 | 40,036 |
| Idaho Falls, Idaho | 148 | 35,776 |

**Approximate distance of selected major U.S. population centers to Big Sky**

| City | Distance to Big Sky* (in air miles) |
|---|---|
| Chicago | 1,275 |
| Minneapolis | 975 |
| Fargo | 750 |
| Salt Lake City | 375 |
| Dallas | 1,500 |
| Houston | 1,725 |
| Los Angeles | 975 |
| San Francisco | 925 |
| New York | 2,025 |
| Atlanta | 1,950 |
| New Orleans | 1,750 |
| Denver | 750 |

*Per passenger air fare could be approximated at 20 cents per mile (round trip, coach rates).

5. Intermediate to advanced in ability.
6. Skiing five hours per ski day, 20 days per season locally.
7. Skiing four days away from local areas.
8. Taking no lessons in the past five years.

Karen was also aware that a significant number of day skiers, particularly on the weekends, were college students.

Destination, or nonresident, skiers were labeled in the same study as typically:

1. At least in their mid-20s and males (55 percent).
2. Living in a household of three or more skiers.
3. Averaging near $19,000 in household income.
4. More intermediate in ability.
5. Spending about six hours per day skiing.
6. Skiing 11–14 days per season, with 3–8 days away from home.
7. Taking ski school lessons.

Through data taken from reservation records, Karen learned that individual destination skiers accounted for half of last year's usage based on skier days.[2] Geographic segments were approximately as follows:

| | |
|---|---|
| Upper Midwest (Minnesota, Michigan, North Dakota) | 30% |
| Florida | 20 |
| California | 17 |
| Washington, Oregon, Montana | 15 |
| Texas, Oklahoma | 8 |
| Other | 10 |

Reservation records indicated that the average length of stay for individual destination skiers was about six or seven days.

It was the individual destination skier who was most likely to buy a lodging/lift package; 30 percent made commitments for these advertised packages when making reservations for 1977–78. Even though there was no discount involved in this manner of buying lift tickets, Karen knew that it was fairly popular because it saved the purchaser a trip to the ticket window every morning. Approximately half of the individual business came through travel agents, who received a 10 percent commision.

The third skier segment, the destination group, accounted for a substantial 20 percent of Big Sky's skier day usage. The larger portion of the group business came through medical and other professional organizations holding meetings at the resort, as this was a way to "combine business with pleasure." These groups were typically comprised of couples and individuals between the ages of 30 and 50. Ski clubs made up the remainder, with a number coming from the southern states of Florida, Texas, and Georgia. During the 1977–78 season, Big Sky drew 30 ski clubs with memberships averaging 55 skiers. The average length of stay for all group destination skiers was about four or five days.

---

[2]A skier day is defined as one skier using the facility for one day of operation.

A portion of these group bookings was made through travel agents, but the majority dealt directly with Karen. The coordinator of the professional meetings or the president of the ski club typically contacted the Big Sky sales office to make initial reservation dates, negotiate prices, and work out the details of the stay.

## THE COMPETITION

In Karen's mind, Big Sky faced two types of competition, that for local day skiers and that for out-of-state (i.e., destination) skiers.

Bridger Bowl was virtually the only area competing for local day skiers. Bridger was a "nonfrills," nonprofit, and smaller ski area located some 16 miles northeast of Bozeman. It received the majority of local skiers, including students at Montana State University, which was located in Bozeman. The area was labeled as having terrain more difficult than that of Big Sky and was thus more appealing to the local expert skiers. However, it also had much longer lift lines than Big Sky and had recently lost some of its weekend business to Big Sky.

Karen had found through experience that most Bridger skiers usually "tried" Big Sky once or twice a season. Season passes for the two areas were mutually honored at the half-day rate for an all-day ticket, and Big Sky occasionally ran newspaper ads offering discounts on lifts to obtain more Bozeman business.

For out-of-state skiers, Big Sky considered its competition to be mainly the destination resorts of Colorado, Utah, and Wyoming. (Selected data on competing resorts are presented in Exhibit 2.) Because Big Sky was smaller and newer than the majority of these areas, Karen reasoned, it was necessary to follow an aggressive strategy aimed at increasing its national market share.

**Exhibit 2** ☐ **Competitors' 1977–1978 package plan rates,* number of lifts, and lift rates**

| | Lodge double (2)† | Two-bedroom condo (4) | Three-bedroom condo (6) | Number of lifts | Daily lift rates |
|---|---|---|---|---|---|
| Aspen, Colorado | $242 | $242 | $220 | 19 | $13 |
| Steamboat, Colorado | 230 | 230 | 198 | 15 | 12 |
| Jackson, Wyoming | 230 | 242 | 210 | 5 | 14 |
| Vail, Colorado | 230 | 242 | 220 | 15 | 14 |
| Snowbird, Utah | 208 | none | none | 6 | 11 |
| Bridger Bowl, Montana | No lodging available at Bridger Bowl | | | 3 | 8 |

*Package plan rates are per person and include seven nights' lodging, six lift tickets (high-season rates).
†Number in parentheses denotes occupancy of unit on which price is based.

## PRESENT POLICIES

### Lift rates

It was common knowledge that there existed some local resentment concerning Big Sky's lift rate policy. Although comparable to rates at Vail or Aspen, an all-day lift ticket was $4 higher than the ticket offered at nearby Bridger Bowl. In an attempt to alleviate this situation, management at Big Sky instituted a $9 "chair pass" for the 1977–78 season, entitling the holder to unlimited use of the three chairs plus two rides per day on the gondola, to be taken between specified time periods. Because the gondola served primarily intermediate terrain, it was reasoned that the chair pass would appeal to the local, more expert skiers. A triple chair serving the bowl area was located at the top of the gondola, and two rides on the gondola would allow those skiers to take ample advantage of the advanced terrain up there. Otherwise, all advanced terrain was served by another chair.

However, if Big Sky was to establish itself as a successful, nationally prominent destination area, Karen felt that the attitudes and opinions of all skiers must be carefully weighed. Throughout the season she had made a special effort to grasp the general feeling toward rates. A $12 ticket, she discovered, was thought to be very reasonable by destination skiers, primarily because Big Sky was predominantly an intermediate area and the average destination skier was of intermediate ability but also because Big Sky was noted for its relative lack of lift lines, giving the skier more actual skiing time for the money. "Perhaps we should keep the price the same," she thought. "We do need more business. Other destination areas are likely to raise their prices, and we should look good in comparison."

Also discussed was the possible abolition of the $9 chair pass. The question in Karen's mind was whether its elimination would severely hurt local business or would sell an all-lift $12 ticket to the skier who had previously bought only a chair pass. The issue was compounded by an unknown number of destination skiers who opted for the cheaper chair pass too.

Season pass pricing was also an issue. Prices for the 1977–78 all-lift season pass had remained the same as last year, but a season chair pass had been introduced which was the counterpart of the daily chair lift pass. Karen did not like the number of season chair passes purchased in relation to the number of all-lift passes and considered recommending the abolition of the season pass as well as an increase in the price of the all-lift pass. "I'm going to have to think this one out carefully," she thought, "because skiing accounted for about 40 percent of our total revenue this past season. I'll have to be able to justify my decision not only to Michigan but also to the Forest Service."

Price changes were not solely at the discretion of Big Sky management. As was the case with most larger western ski areas, the U.S. government owned part of the land on which Big Sky operated. Control of this land was the responsibility of the U.S. Forest Service, which annually approved all lift-pricing policies. For the 1976–77 ski season, Forest Service action kept most lift rate increases to the national inflation rate. For the 1977–78 season, larger price increases were allowed for ski areas which had competing areas nearby; Big Sky was considered to be such an area. No one knew what the Forest Service position would be for the upcoming 1978–79 season.

To help Karen in her decision, an assistant had prepared a summary of lift rates and usage for the past two seasons (Exhibit 3).

**Room rates**

This area of pricing was particularly important because lodging accounted for about one third of the past season's total revenue. It was also difficult because of the variety of accommodations (Exhibit 4) and the difficulty in accurately forecasting next season's demand. For example, the season of 1976–77 had been unique in that a good portion of the Rockies was without snow for the initial months of the

**Exhibit 3 ☐ Lift rates and usage summary**

| Ticket | Consumer cost | Skier days* | Number season passes sold |
|---|---|---|---|
| **1977–78 (136 days' operation)** | | | |
| Adult all-day all-lift | $ 12 | 53,400 | |
| Adult all-day chair | 9 | 20,200 | |
| Adult half-day | 8 | 9,400 | |
| Child all-day all-lift | 8 | 8,500 | |
| Child all-day chair | 5 | 3,700 | |
| Child half-day | 6 | 1,200 | |
| Hotel passes† | 12/day | 23,400 | |
| Complimentary | 0 | 1,100 | |
| Adult all-lift season pass | 220 | 4,300 | 140 |
| Adult chair season pass | 135 | 4,200 | 165 |
| Child all-lift season pass | 130 | 590 | 30 |
| Child chair season pass | 75 | 340 | 15 |
| Employee all-lift season pass | 100 | 3,000 | 91 |
| Employee chair season pass | 35 | 1,100 | 37 |
| **1976–77 (122 days' operation)** | | | |
| Adult all-day | $ 10 | 52,500 | |
| Adult half-day | 6.50 | 9,000 | |
| Child all-day | 6 | 10,400 | |
| Child half-day | 4 | 1,400 | |
| Hotel passes† | 10/day | 30,500 | |
| Complimentary | 0 | 480 | |
| Adult season pass | 220 | 4,200 | 84 |
| Child season pass | 130 | 300 | 15 |
| Employee season pass | 100 | 2,300 | 70 |

*A skier day is defined as one skier using the facility for one day of operation.
†Hotel passes refers to passes included in the lodging/lift packages.

winter, including Christmas. Big Sky was fortunate in receiving as much snow as it had, and consequently many groups and individuals who were originally headed for Vail or Aspen booked in with Big Sky.

Pricing for the 1977–78 season had been made on the premise that there would be a good amount of repeat business. This came true in part but not to the extent that had been hoped. Occupancy experience had also been summarized for the past two seasons to help Karen make her final decision (Exhibit 5).

As was customary in the hospitality industry, January was a slow period and it was necessary to price accordingly. Low-season pricing was extremely important because many groups took advantage of these rates. On top of that, groups were often offered discounts in the neighborhood of 10 percent. Considering this, Karen could not price too high, with the risk of losing individual destination skiers, or too low, such that an unacceptable profit would be made from group business in this period.

**Food service**

Under some discussion was the feasibility of converting all destination skiers to the American plan, under which policy each guest in the Huntley Lodge would be placed on a package to include three meals daily in a Big Sky–controlled facility. There was a feeling both for and against this idea. The parent company had been successfully utilizing this plan for years at its destination areas in northern Michigan. Extending the policy to Big Sky should find similar success.

Karen was not so sure. For one thing, the Michigan resorts were primarily self-contained and alternative eateries were few. For another, the whole idea of ex-

**Exhibit 4 □ Nightly room rates***

| | Low-season range | High-season range | Maximum occupancy |
|---|---|---|---|
| **1977–78** | | | |
| Huntley Lodge | | | |
| Standard | $ 42–62 | $ 50–70 | 4 |
| Loft | 52–92 | 60–100 | 6 |
| Stillwater Condo | | | |
| Studio | 40–60 | 45–65 | 4 |
| One-bedroom | 55–75 | 60–80 | 4 |
| Bedroom with loft | 80–100 | 90–110 | 6 |
| Deer Lodge Condo | | | |
| One-bedroom | 74–84 | 80–90 | 4 |
| Two-bedroom | 93–103 | 100–110 | 6 |
| Three-bedroom | 112–122 | 120–130 | 8 |
| Hill Condo | | | |
| Studio | 30–40 | 35–45 | 4 |
| Studio with loft | 50–70 | 55–75 | 6 |
| **1976–77** | | | |
| Huntley Lodge | | | |
| Standard | $ 32–47 | $ 35–50 | 4 |
| Loft | 47–67 | 50–70 | 6 |
| Stillwater Condo | | | |
| Studio | 39–54 | 37–52 | 4 |
| One-bedroom | 52–62 | 50–60 | 4 |
| Bedroom with loft | 60–80 | 65–85 | 6 |
| Deer Lodge Condo | | | |
| One-bedroom | 51–66 | 55–70 | 4 |
| Two-bedroom | 74–94 | 80–100 | 6 |
| Three-bedroom | 93–123 | 100–130 | 8 |
| Hill Condo | | | |
| Studio | 28–43 | 30–45 | 4 |
| Studio with loft | 42–62 | 45–65 | 6 |

*Rates determined by number of persons in room or condominium unit and do not include lift tickets. Maximums for each rate range apply at maximum occupancy.

**Exhibit 5 □ Lodge-condominium occupancy**

**In room-nights (1977–78)***

| | December (26 days' operation) | January | February | March | April (8 days' operation) |
|---|---|---|---|---|---|
| Huntley Lodge | 1,830 | 2,250 | 3,650 | 4,650 | 438 |
| Condominiums† | 775 | 930 | 1,350 | 100 | 90 |

**In room-nights (1976–77)**

| | December (16 days' operation) | January | February | March | April (16 days' operation) |
|---|---|---|---|---|---|
| Huntley Lodge | 1,700 | 3,080 | 4,525 | 4,300 | 1,525 |
| Condominiums‡ | 600 | 1,000 | 1,600 | 1,650 | 480 |

**In person-nights§**

| December 1977 (1976) | January 1978 (1977) | February 1978 (1977) | March 1978 (1977) | April 1978 (1977) |
|---|---|---|---|---|
| 7,850 (6,775) | 9,200 (13,000) | 13,150 (17,225) | 17,900 (17,500) | 1,450 (4,725) |

*A room-night is defined as one room (or condominium) rented for one night. Lodging experience is based on 124 days of operation for 1977–78, while Exhibit 3 shows the skiing facilities operating 136 days. Both numbers are correct.
†Big Sky had 92 condominiums available during the 1977–78 season.
‡Big Sky had 85 condominiums available during the 1976–77 season.
§A person-night refers to one person using the facility for one night.

tending standardized policies from Michigan to Montana was suspect. As an example, Karen painfully recalled a day in January when Big Sky "tried on" another successful Michigan policy of accepting only cash or check payments for lift tickets. The reactions of credit card–carrying skiers could be described as ranging from annoyed to irate.

If an American plan were proposed for next year, it would probably include both the Huntley Lodge Dining Room and Lookout Cafeteria. Less clear, however, were the prices to be charged. There certainly would have to be consideration for both adults and children and for the two independently operated eating places in the Mountain Mall (see Exhibit 6 for an identification of eating places in the Big Sky area). Beyond these considerations, there was little else other than an expectation of a profit to guide Karen in her analysis.

**Exhibit 6** ☐ **Eating places in the Big Sky area**

| Establishment | Type of service | Meals served | Current prices | Seating | Location |
|---|---|---|---|---|---|
| Lodge Dining Room* | A la carte | Breakfast<br>Lunch<br>Dinner | $  2–5<br>2–5<br>7–15 | 250 | Huntley Lodge |
| Steak House* | Steak/lobster | Dinner only | 6–12 | 150 | Huntley Lodge |
| Fondue Stube* | Fondue | Dinner only | 6–10 | 25 | Huntley Lodge |
| Ore House† | A la carte | Lunch<br>Dinner | 0.80–4<br>5–12 | 150 | Mountain Mall |
| Ernie's Deli† | Deli/restaurant | Breakfast<br>Lunch | 1–3<br>2–5 | 25 | Mountain Mall |
| Lookout Cafeteria* | Cafeteria | Breakfast<br>Lunch<br>Dinner | 1.50–3<br>2–4<br>3–6 | 175 | Mountain Mall |
| Yellow Mule† | A la carte | Breakfast<br>Lunch<br>Dinner | 2–4<br>2–5<br>4–8 | 75 | Meadow Village |
| Buck's T–4† | Road house restaurant/bar | Dinner only | 2–9 | 60 | Gallatin Canyon (two miles south of Big Sky entrance) |
| Karst Ranch† | Road house restaurant/bar | Breakfast<br>Lunch<br>Dinner | 2–4<br>2–5<br>3–8 | 50 | Gallatin Canyon (seven miles north of Big Sky entrance) |
| Corral† | Road house restaurant/bar | Breakfast<br>Lunch<br>Dinner | 2–4<br>2–4<br>3–5 | 30 | Gallatin Canyon (five miles south of Big Sky entrance) |

*Owned and operated by Big Sky of Montana, Inc.
†Independently operated.

### The telephone call

"Profits in the food area might be hard to come by," Karen thought. "Last year it appears we lost money on everything we sold." (See Exhibit 7.) Just then the telephone rang. It was Rick Thompson, her counterpart at Boyne Mountain Lodge in Michigan. "How are your pricing recommendations coming?" he asked. "I'm about done with mine and thought we should compare notes."

"Good idea, Rick—only I'm just getting started out here. Do you have any hot ideas?"

**Exhibit 7 □ Ski season income data (percent)**

|  | Skiing | Lodging | Food and beverage |
|---|---|---|---|
| Revenue | 100.0% | 100.0% | 100.0% |
| Cost of sales: |  |  |  |
|    Merchandise | 0.0 | 0.0 | 30.0 |
|    Labor | 15.0 | 15.9 | 19.7 |
|    Maintenance | 3.1 | 5.2 | 2.4 |
|    Supplies | 1.5 | 4.8 | 5.9 |
|    Miscellaneous | 2.3 | 0.6 | 0.6 |
|      Total cost of sales | 21.9 | 26.5 | 58.6 |
| Operating expenses | 66.2 | 66.4 | 66.7 |
| Net profit (loss) before taxes | 11.9% | 7.0% | (25.2)% |

"Only one," he responded. "I just got off the phone with a guy in Denver. He told me all of the major Colorado areas are upping their lift prices one or two dollars next year."

"Is that right, Rick? Are you sure?"

"Well, you know nobody knows for sure what's going to happen, but I think it's pretty good information. He heard it from his sister-in-law, who works in Vail. I think he said she read it in the local paper or something."

"That doesn't seem like very solid information," said Karen. "Let me know if you hear anything more, will you?"

"Certainly. You know, we really should compare our recommendations before we stick our necks out too far on this pricing thing. Can you call me later in the week?" he asked.

"Sure, I'll talk to you the day after tomorrow; I should be about done by then. Anything else?"

"Nope—gotta run. Talk to you then. Bye."—and he was gone.

"At least I've got some information," Karen thought, "and a new deadline!"